A Pronouncing Dictionary of
English Place-Names

A Pronouncing Dictionary
of English Place-Names
including standard local
and archaic variants

KLAUS FORSTER

ROUTLEDGE & KEGAN PAUL · LONDON, BOSTON AND HENLEY

First published in 1981
by Routledge & Kegan Paul Ltd
39 Store Street, London WC1E 7DD,
9 Park Street, Boston, Mass. 02108, USA, and
Broadway House, Newtown Road, Henley-on-Thames,
Oxon RG9 1EN

Printed in Great Britain by
Redwood Burn Ltd, Trowbridge

Reprinted in 1982

British Library Cataloguing in Publication Data

Forster, Klaus
    A pronouncing dictionary of English place names.
    1. Names, Geographical—England—Pronunciation
    —Dictionaries
    I. Title
    914.1'0014   DA645   80-41300

    ISBN 0-7100-0756-6

Contents

Preface

This dictionary presents a collection of the phonetic forms of about 12,000 different names of English counties, towns, villages, farms, fields, rivers, lakes, mountains, islands, and even street-names of some major English cities (such as Bristol, Leeds, and London).

The material has been taken from printed sources published during the past hundred years or so; they include publications on English place-names, dialects, phonology and local history as well as pronouncing dictionaries. The periodical publications of various local historical and other learned societies proved to be valuable sources.

In contrast to most pronouncing dictionaries, not only the standard pronunciation of a place-name is given; in fact, the aim set by the author was to collect forms of pronunciation which are now either archaic, obsolescent or even obsolete, or are used by the natives of a particular place or by people living in the neighbourhood of that place.

At first the intention was to start at around 1900 in order to restrict the dictionary to forms which have been used in the present century. But later on it was decided to widen the time bracket to a little more than a hundred years, which enabled the author to include the glossaries of the EDS, Hope's glossary of local place-nomenclature and other glossaries published in the second half of the nineteenth century. Yet it should still be possible to say that all pronunciations recorded in the present dictionary have been used within living memory.

This dictionary does not claim to be complete; neither does it contain all the place-names of England nor does it offer both the standard, local and archaic forms of pronunciation for each name listed. Much work remains to be done for the fieldworker in collecting forms of pronunciation which have never been recorded and which are likely to become extinct soon.

Aware that such a project is beyond the means of a single onomastician, the author would welcome any suggestion for the improvement of this dictionary, as well as contributions of additional forms and references to sources which have escaped his attention.

Erlangen   K.F.

Arrangement of the Dictionary

All the place-names are listed in alphabetical order. No difference has been made between names spelt as one word and those spelt as two words (thus, e.g., *Brough, Brougham, Brough Sowerby,* etc. are listed in that order). Place-names prefixed by common nouns (such as Bishop, Church, Market, etc.) and adjectives (such as Great, High, North, etc.) are listed under their principal name, with the prefix only being placed in brackets after the principal name if it is necessary to distinguish between various places, or if there is only one such prefixed place-name (e.g. Bishop's Stortford is listed under *Stortford* (*Bishop's*); Great Malvern and Little Malvern are listed under *Malvern* without the prefixes being added). A phonetic transcription of these prefixes will not be given, unless there is a particular local or dialectal form. In this case the place-name and its pronunciation are listed under the prefixed name and a cross-reference will be found under the principal name.

A county reference will follow each place-name unless the place-name is found in more than three counties (e.g. Copeland/Cu,Nb,We). For convenience the traditional county-names have been used throughout. As to the names of rivers, a county reference is always given, comprising all counties through which the river passes. Groups of county-names set apart by a semi-colon indicate several rivers of that name (e.g. Stour/ Ca,Ess,Sf;Do,Ha,W).

Place-names other than the names of major inhabited places are marked 'f.n.' (for field-name), etc. (see list of abbreviations).

If the spellings of a place-name differ in my sources, alternative spellings are also quoted and cross-references will be given.

After each phonetic form the source from which it has been taken is indicated in an abbreviated form; the full bibliographical data will be found in the bibliography following this introduction. From them the reader will see when a particular form was recorded and whether it is likely still to be in current use. Dictionaries, glossaries and other publications with alphabetical lists of place-names are quoted without page references; in all other instances the numbers following the bibliographical abbreviation refer to the volume (if applicable) and pages (or paragraphs, note, etc., whatever is applicable). Explanatory notes found in the sources are quoted either before the pronunciation or after the reference.

Phonetic Symbols

Great care has been taken in rendering the various phonetic transcriptions used in the sources in the phonetic alphabet of the Inter-
national Phonetic Association (IPA). This proved particularly diffi-
cult in the case of some sources which were inconsistent in the use
of the phonetic symbols explained in their introductions, and in the
case of different interpretations of Standard English vowels (e.g.
the vowel in 'there' is sometimes rendered/ɛ:/, sometimes /ɛə/). In
many other sources, which did not use any approved phonetic alphabet
(IPA, Romic, Glossic, etc.), letters or combinations of letters were
often ambiguous (e.g. ow ≙ [ou] or [au]? u ≙ [u] or [ʌ]?). Hope's
glossary is a notorious example.[1] Again, in other instances th and
s are indiscriminately used both for [ð]/[þ] and [z]/[s] resp. In
some cases it was mere guesswork to find out what sound the author
meant. In these cases the original notation is added in a footnote
and the reader is invited to check this against my rendering.

The phonetic notation used in this dictionary is a modified broad
transcription, i.e. only some major dialectal variants are distin-
guished (e.g. [o:] - [ɔ:], [e:] - [ɛ:]), others have been reduced to
their nearest Standard English equivalent, e.g. [au, ɑu, ʌu] > [au],
[ai, ɑi, ʌi] > [ai], [ou, ɔu, əu] > [ou], [ei, ɛi, əi] > [ei],
[a:, ɑ:] > [ɑ:], etc.

---

1) cf. H.Alexander's remark: "Many of Hope's records are unintelligible
   or ambiguous because of the absence of any obvious phonetic notation" (H.A.(2)34).

The following phonetic symbols are used in this dictionary:

a) short vowels:

i	e.g.	pin
e		pen
æ		pan
a		German Mann
u		put
o		as in November; also a variant of /ɔ/ before r
ɔ		pot
ʌ		but
ə		unstressed vowel of father

b) long vowels:

i:	e.g.	beat
e:		German nehmen
æ:		long variant of /æ/ before voiced and unvoiced consonants
ɛ:		there (monophthong!)
ɑ:		stressed vowel of father
ɔ:		saw
o:		German Sohn
u:		food
ə:		bird

c) diphthongs:

ai	e.g.	my
ɔi		boy
ei		day
au		cow
ou		show

uə	e.g.	poor
iə		fear
ɔə		variant of /ɔ:/ before r
ɛə		Mary

Occasionally other self-explanatory combinations of vowel symbols are used for diphthongs (e.g. oa, eu, etc.).

d) consonants:

p	e.g.	pit	l	e.g.	low	þ	e.g.	thorn
b		bit	r		row	ð		then
t		tea	s		see	j		year
d		day	z		zeal	h		hat
k		key	f		fine	χ		velar fricative
g		go	v		vine			(German ch)
m		man	ʃ		shoe	?		glottal stop
n		no	ʒ		measure	w		win
ŋ		sing	tʃ		church	hw		when
			dʒ		judge			

e) stress:

ˈ   placed before the stressed syllable (if no stress symbol is used, the main stress is on the first syllable)

- ́   The name is stressed on the syllable indicated.

f) other symbols:

For convenience phonetic notations have not been enclosed in square brackets; square brackets, however, have been used for phonetic notations in quotations.

Abbreviations and Symbols

(for bibliographical abbreviations see Bibliography)

Ave.	Avenue	Mx	Middlesex
Bd	Bedfordshire	N	North
Bk	Buckinghamshire	Nb	Northumberland
Brk	Berkshire	Nf	Norfolk
Ca	Cambridgeshire	Np	Northamptonshire
Chs	Cheshire	nr	near
Co	Cornwall	NRY	North Riding of
co.	county		Yorkshire
Ct	Court	Nt	Nottinghamshire
Cu	Cumberland	O	Oxfordshire
D	Devon	occ.	occasionally
Db	Derbyshire	oth.	otherwise
dial.	dialect, dialectal	Pk	Park
	(also used in	p.n.	place-name
	quotations)	Pt	Point
Do	Dorset	pron.	pronounce, pronounced,
Du	Durham		pronunciation (also
E	East		used in quotations)
EDS	English Dialect	Rd	Road
	Society	r.n.	river-name
EPNS	English Place-Name	RP	Received Pronunciation
	Society	Ru	Rutland
ERY	East Riding of	S	South
	Yorkshire	Sa	Shropshire
Ess	Essex	Sf	Suffolk
Fm	Farm	s.n.	street-name; sub nomine
f.n.	field-name	So	Somerset
Gdn	Garden	Sq.	Square
Gl	Gloucestershire	Sr	Surrey
Gn	Green	St	Staffordshire; Street
Gt	Great	StE	Standard English
Ha	Hampshire	Sx	Sussex
Hd	Hundred	Twr	Tower
He	Herefordshire	Upr	Upper
Ho	House	vol.	volume
Hr	Higher	vulg.	vulgar, vulgarly (also
Hrt	Hertfordshire		used in quotations)
Hu	Huntingdonshire	W	West
Is	Island	W,Wilts.	Wiltshire
K	Kent	Wa	Warwickshire
La,Lancs.	Lancashire	We	Westmorland
Ldn	London	Wo	Worcestershire
Le	Leicestershire	WRY	West Riding of
Li,Lincs.	Lincolnshire		Yorkshire
loc.	local, locally (also	Wt	Isle of Wight
	used in quotations)	Yorks.	Yorkshire
Lt	Little	→	see s.n.
Lwr	Lower		
Mt,mt	Mount, mountain	-	sign of repetition

B i b l i o g r a p h y

a. Sources and their abbreviations

AB
Anglia Beiblatt.

Alexander
J.J. Alexander, "South Devon Place-Names", Dev. Ass. 66 (1934), 279-313.

Amph.
J. Amphlett, "Clent Placenames and Fieldnames", Mid.Ant. 1 (1882-3), 162-9.

Anon.(1)
Anon., "Etymologies invited", Wilts.Arch.Mag. 1 (1854), 67.

Anon.(2)
Anon., "Garston" , Wilts.Arch.Mag. 1 (1854), 131.

Ant.Mag.
Antiquarian Magazine and Bibliographer.

Ant.Sunderland
Antiquities of Sunderland and its Vicinity.

Arch.Ael.
Archaeologia Aeliana.

Arch.Hist.Soc.
Chester
Journal of the Architectural, Archaeological and Historic Society for the County and the City of Chester and North Wales.

Archiv
Archiv für das Studium der neueren Sprachen und Literaturen.

Arch.J.
Archaeological Journal.

Arch.Rev.
The Archaeological Review.

Arkell
W.J. Arkell, "Some topographical Names in South Dorset", Do Nat.Hist.Soc. 62 (1940), 39-49.

Ass.Arch.Soc.
Association of Architectural Societies' Reports and Papers.

Atkinson
J.C. Atkinson, "Derivations of Place-Names", Arch. Rev. 1 (1888), 430-34.

Bardsley
Ch.W. Bardsley, A Dictionary of English and Welsh Surnames, London 1901.

Bate
C.S. Bate, "A Contribution towards Determining the Etymology of Dartmoor Names", Dev.Ass. 4 (1870-71), 520-35.

Bau.
H. Baumann, Londinismen. Wörterbuch der Londoner Volkssprache, Berlin 1887, 2nd ed. 1902, 3rd ed. 1913.

BBC
G.M. Miller, BBC Pronouncing Dictionary of British Names, London 1971.

BCE
A.L. James, Broadcast English II: Recommendations to announcers regarding the pronunciation of some English place-names, London 1936 (second ed.).

Bchm.
E.Buchmann, Der Einfluß des Schriftbildes auf die Aussprache im Neuenglischen, Sprachen und Kulturen der germanischen und romanischen Völker, A. Anglistische Reihe xxxv, Breslau 1940 (diss.).

Beds.Rec.Soc.
Publications of the Bedfordshire Historical Record Society.

Benham
Ch.E. Benham, "The Essex Dialect", YDS 3/19 (1917), 13-29.

Berks.Arch.J.
Berkshire Archaeological Journal.

Berks.Bucks.
Oxon.Arch.J.
Berkshire, Buckinghamshire and Oxfordshire Archaeological Journal.

BG
J. Bartholomew, The Survey Gazetteer of the British Isles, Edinburgh 1950 (9th ed.).

B'ham Arch.Soc.
Transactions of the Birmingham Archaeological Society.

B'ham Midl.Inst.
Transactions of the Birmingham and Midland Institute, Archaeological Section.

Bristol Glos.
Arch.Soc.
Transactions of the Bristol and Gloucestershire Archaeological Society.

Brit.Arch.Ass.
Journal of the British Archaeological Association.

Brunner   K. Brunner, "Die Schreibtradition der Dialektschrift-
                   steller von Lancashire", EStn 6o (1925/26), 158-79.
Brushf.   T.N. Brushfield, "Tideswell and Tideslow", DAJ 27
                   (19o5), 59-73.
Burl.   E.W. Burlingame, "Etymologies of Burlingame (Bur-
                   lingham)", MLN 37 (1922), 123-24.
BzN   Beiträge zur Namenforschung.
Camb.Ant.Soc.   Proceedings of the Cambridge Antiquarian Society,
                   Antiquarian Communications.
Camb.arch.eth.
series   Cambridge archaeological and ethnological series.
Chanter   J.F.Chanter, "Devonshire Place-Names, pt I: The
                   Parishes", Dev.Ass. 5o (1918), 5o3-32.
Chis.   G.G. Chisholm, A Pronouncing Dictionary of Geo-
                   graphical Names, London [1912].
Chope   R.P. Chope, "Folk Etymology of Devonshire Place-
                   Names", Dev.Yearb. 25 (1934), 48-53.
Cole   E.M. Cole, "On the Place-Names of Wetwang", Saga
                   Book 4 (19o5), 1o2-6.
CPhon   E.Sivertsen, Cockney Phonology, Oslo Studies in
                   English 8, Oslo 196o.
CPP   W. Matthews, Cockney Past and Present, London 1938.
Crosl.   Ch. Crosland, "The Vowel Sounds and Substitutions of
                   the Halifax Dialect", YDS 1/2 (1899), 49-53.
Cu Ass.Lit.Sc.   Transactions of the Cumberland Association for the
                   Advancement of Literature and Science.
Cu We Ant.Arch.
Soc.   Transactions of the Cumberland and Westmorland
                   Antiquarian and Archaeological Society.
DAd   A. Hargreaves, A Grammar of the Dialect of Adlington
                   Lancs., Anglistische Forschungen, Heidelberg 19o4.
DAJ   Journal of the Derbyshire Archaeological and Natural
                   History Society.
DAl&Hd   A. Easther, A Glossary of the Dialect of Almondbury
                   and Huddersfield, ed. by Th Lees, EDS 39, London
                   1883, repr. Vaduz 1965.
Davies   G.S. Davies, Surrey Local Names, Godalming 1881.
Davis   W.E.Davis-Winstone,"Field Names in the Parish of
                   Feckenham", B'ham Arch.Soc. 46 (1923 for 192o),36-48
Davy   Ch.H.Davy, List of Words, Names and Places, mostly
                   early XVth century spelling, London 19o9.
DBo   J. Sixtus, Der Sprachgebrauch des Dialektschrift-
                   stellers Frank Robinson zu Bowness, Palaestra 116,
                   Berlin 1912.
DCu   A.C. Gibson, The Folk-Speech of Cumberland and Some
                   Districts Adjacent, London-Carlisle 1869.
DCu(i)   R. Ferguson, The Dialect of Cumberland, with a
                   chapter on its place-names, London 1873.
DDd   B. Hedevind, The Dialect of Dentdale in the West
                   Riding of Yorkshire, Acta Universitatis Upsaliensis,
                   Studia Anglistica Upsaliensia 5, Uppsala 1967.
DDo   B. Widen, Studies on the Dorset Dialect, Lund Studie
                   in English 16, Lund 1949.
de Barri   B.de Barri "Is Yours a Derby County Name?", Derby
                   Life 43/1, 1978, 43-4.
DEPN   E.Ekwall, The Concise Oxford Dictionary of English
                   Place-Names, Oxford 1936, 3rd ed. 1947, 4th ed. 1966
                   (unless stated otherwise, quotations are taken from
                   the fourth edition; quotations from the first and
                   third editions are marked DEPN(1) and DEPN(3) resp.)

Derby Life   Derbyshire Life and Countryside.
DEss   Th. Albrecht, _Der Sprachgebrauch des Dialektdichters_
                      Charles E. Benham zu Colchester in Essex, Palaestra
                      111, Berlin 1916.
Dev.Ass.   Reports and Transactions of the Devonshire Associ-
                      ation.
Dev.Yearb.   Devonian Yearbook.
DEY   M.C.F. Morris, _The Vowel Sounds of the East York-_
                      shire Folk-Speech, London 19o1.
DHa   J. Wilson, _The Dialect of the New Forest in Hamp-_
                      shire as Spoken in the Village of Burley, Oxford
                      1914.
DHd   W.E. Haigh, _A New Glossary of the Dialect of the_
                      Huddersfield District, London 1928.
DHe   W.Leeds, _Herefordshire Speech_. The South West Mid-
                      land dialect as spoken in Hereford and its environs,
                      Ross-on-Wye 1972.
DHtl   P. Pearse, _The Dialect of Hartland, Devonshire_, EDS
                      65, London 1891, repr. Vaduz 1965.
DK   W.D.Parish, W.F. Shaw, _A Dictionary of the Kentish_
                      Dialect, EDS 54, London 1887, repr. Vaduz 1965.
DKe   T.O. Hirst, _A Grammar of the Dialect of Kendal, We_,
                      Anglistische Forschungen 16, Heidelberg 19o6.
DLa   H. Bröker, _Zu den Lautverhältnissen der Lancashire_
                      Dialekte, Berlin 193o (diss.).
DLi   J.E.Oxley, _The Lindsey Dialect_, Leeds 194o.
DLo   B.Brilioth, _A Grammar of the Dialect of Lorton_,
                      Cumberland, Uppsala 1913.
DNDu   K.-H. Borgis, _Der Sprachgebrauch in Nord-Durham_ (mit
                      Berücksichtigung von Süd-Durham und Südost-Northumber-
                      land), Palaestra 2o4, Leipzig 1936.
DNf   J.Mardle (alias E.Fowler), _Broad Norfolk_,The Wensum
                      Dialect Series, Norwich 1973, 4th ed. 1976.
DNSo   F.C.Perry, "The Dialect of North Somerset", _YDS_ 4/
                      22 (1921), 17-31
Dobson   E.J.Dobson, _English Pronunciation_, 2 vols, Oxford
                      1957.
Dodgson(2)   J.McN. Dodgson, "Various Forms of Old English -_ing_
                      in English Place-Names", BzN, N.F. 2 (1967),325-96.
Dodgson(3)   J.McN. Dodgson, "Various English Place-Name For-
                      mations Containing Old English -_ing_", BzN, N.F. 3
                      (1968), 141-89.
DOld   K.G. Schilling, _A Grammar of the Dialect of Oldham_
                      (Lancashire), Darmstadt 19o6 (diss.).
Do Nat.Hist.Soc.   Proceedings of the Dorset Natural History and
                      Archaeological Society.
DPe   P.H. Reaney, _A Grammar of the Dialect of Penrith_,
                      Publications of the University of Manchester, English
                      Series 15, Manchester 1927.
DPew   J. Kjederqvist, "The Dialect of Pewsey (Wiltshire)",
                      Phil. Soc. 19o3-19o4, 1-144.
DSChs   Th. Darlington, _The Folk-Speech of South Cheshire_,
                      EDS 53, London 1887, repr. Vaduz 1965.
DSDu   H.Orton, _The Phonology of a South Durham Dialect_,
                      London 1933.
DSEY   A. Müller, _Der heutige Sprachgebrauch im südöstlichen_
                      Yorkshire, Palaestra 2o4, Leipzig 1936.
DSf   H. Kökeritz, _The Phonology of the Suffolk Dialect_,
                      Uppsala Universitets Arsskrift, Uppsala 1932 (diss.).
DSh   J.D. Jones, "Historical Notes on the Sheffield Dia-
                      lect", _YDS_ 2/14 (1913), 36-48.

DSLa	F.E. Taylor, The Folk Speech of South Lancashire, Manchester 19o1.
DSto	W.Klein, Der Dialekt von Stokesley in Yorkshire, Palaestra 124, Berlin 1914.
DSWY	A. Lamprecht, Der Sprachgebrauch im südwestlichen Yorkshire, Palaestra 21o, Leipzig 1937.
DSx	W.D.Parish, A Dictionary of the Sussex Dialect, EDS 6* , London 1875 (=Lewes 1875), repr. Vaduz 1965 (expanded by H. Hall, Chichester 1957, new edition Bexhill 1967).
DUCd	F.H. Marsden, "Notes on the Grammar and Phonology of the Dialect of Upper Calderdale", YDS 4/22 (1921) 14-16.
Duignan(1)	W.H. Duignan, "On Some Midland Place Names", B'ham Midl.Inst. 2o (1894), 45-59.
Duignan(2)	"On Some Shropshire Place-Names", Shrops.Arch.Soc., 2nd series, 6 (1894), 1-18, 9 (1897), 385-4oo, 1o (1898), 1-17.
Duignan(3)	"On Some Midland Etymologies", Mid.Ant. 1 (1882), 131-135, 2 (1883), 121-23 and 168-72.
DWdl	J. Wright, A Grammar of the Dialect of Windhill in the West Riding of Yorkshire, EDS 67, London 1892, repr. Vaduz 1965.
DWSo	F.Th. Elworthy, The Dialect of West Somerset, EDS 7, London 1875, repr. Vaduz 1965.
DWSo (i)	E. Kruisinga, A Grammar of the Dialect of West Somerset, Bonner Beiträge zur Anglistik XVIII, Bonn 19o5.
DWt	W.H. Long, A Dictionary of the Isle of Wight Dialect, and of Provincialims used in the island [..], London 1886.
DYorks	M.C.F. Morris, Yorkshire Folk Talk, London [2]1911 (first ed. 1892).
E&St	Essays and Studies in English and Comparative Literature by Members of the English Association.
East Angl.Mag.	East Anglian Magazine.
East Herts.Arch. Soc.	East Hertfordshire Archaeological Society Transactions.
EAT	Transactions of the Essex Archaeological Society.
ED	G.L. Brook, English Dialects, London 1963.
EDD	J. Wright, English Dialect Dictionary, 6 vols, Oxford 1898-19o5, repr. New York 1963.
EDG	J. Wright, English Dialect Grammar, Oxford 19o5.
EDS	English Dialect Society.
EHS	English Historical Review.
Ekwall	E.Ekwall, "Etymological Notes", SN 1 (1928), 97-1o8.
Ellis	A.J. Ellis, On Early English Pronunciation, part V, London 1889.
Elw.	F.T. Elworthy, F.H. Dickinson, "Selworthy Place-Names", NQ.So Do 1 (189o), 2o3-6.
Eminson(1)	T.B.F. Eminson, " Scothorn and some other Thorn Names of Lindsey", Lincs.NQ. 12 (1913), 182-3.
Eminson(2)	T.B.F. Eminson, "The River Trent", DAJ 39 (1917), 154-73.
EPD	D. Jones, English Pronouncing Dictionary, London 1917 (2nd ed. 1924, 4th ed. 1937, 13th ed. 1967, repr. 1974, 14th ed. 1977; unless stated otherwise, quotations are taken from the 1974 edition; the 14th edition has not yet been published during the compilation of this dictionary).

EPN H.G. Stokes, English Place-Names, London 1948, [2]1949.
EPNS English Place-Name Society (publications of).
ES English Studies.
ESpr. K. Brunner, Die englische Sprache, 2 vols, Tübingen 1960.
EssDD E. Gepp, An Essex Dialect Dictionary, London [2]1923 (first ed. 1920).
EStn Englische Studien.
F.B.S. F.B.S., "Fairlight", Sx NQ. 2 (1928/29), 65.
Fenland NQ. Fenland Notes and Queries.
Ferguson R. Ferguson, "Notes on the Place-Names of Cumberland and Westmorland", Cu Ass.Lit.Sc. 8 (1882-83), 1-15.
FnSDb W. Fraser, Field-Names in South Derbyshire, Ipswich 1947.
Förster M. Förster, "Proben eines Englischen Eigennamen-Wörterbuches", GRM 11 (1923), 86-110.
Fraser(1) W. Fraser, "Some Current Field-Names in the Parish of Repton, Derbyshire", DAJ 64 (1943), 26-48.
Fraser(2) W. Fraser, "Field-Names in the Parish of Findern, Derbyshire", DAJ, 65 (1944-45), 66-82.
F.W.Jones F.W.Jones, "Baldhu", Old Cornw. 2, pt 2 (1931),17-8.
GlossChs R. Holland, A Glossary of Words Used in the County of Chester, EDS 44, 46, 51, London 1886, repr. Vaduz 1965 (in particular pp. 427-433).
GlossChs (i) E.Leigh, A Glossary of Words Used in the Dialect of Cheshire, London-Chester 1877, repr. East Ardsley (Yorks.) 1973 with a new introduction by S.F. Sanderson.
GlossClv J.C. Atkinson, A Glossary of the Cleveland Dialect, London 1868.
GlossCots R.W. Huntley, A Glossary of the Cotswold (Gloucestershire) Dialect, London-Gloucester 1868.
GlossCu W. Dickinson, A Glossary of Words and Phrases Pertaining to the Dialect of Cumberland, EDS 20, 24, London 1878, repr. Vaduz 1965 (this is a revised and enlarged edition of A Glossary of the Words and Phrases of Cumberland, London 1859).
GlossCu(re-arr.) W. Dickinson, A Glossary of the Words and Phrases Pertaining to the Dialect of Cumberland, re-arranged, illustrated and augmented by quotations by E.W. Prevost, London 1899 (in particular p. lxxvii-lxxxix).
GlossCu (Suppl.) E.W. Prevost, Second Supplement to the Glossary of the Dialect of Cumberland, London-Carlisle 1924.
GlossCuWeNLa T. Ellwood, Lakeland and Iceland (being a glossary of words in the dialect of Cumberland, Westmorland and North Lancashire), EDS 77, London 1895, repr. Vaduz 1965.
GlossEA W. Rye, A Glossary of Words Used in East Anglia (founded on that of Forby), EDS 75, London 1895, repr. Vaduz 1965.
GlossEss R.S. Charnock, A Glossary of the Essex Dialect, London 1880.
GlossFu J.P. Morris, A Glossary of the Words and Phrases of Furness (North Lancashire), London 1869.
GlossHa W.H. Cope, A Glossary of Hampshire Words and Phrases, EDS 40, London 1883, repr. Vaduz 1965.
GlossHe F.T. Havergal, Herefordshire Words and Phrases, Colloquial and Archaic, Walsall 1887.
GlossHol F.Ross,R.Stead,Th.Holderness, A Glossary of Words Used in Holderness in the East Riding of Yorkshire, EDS 16, London 1877, repr. Vaduz 1965.

GlossHtn — F.M.T. Palgrave, <u>A List of Words</u> and <u>Phrases</u> in <u>everday Use by the Natives of Hutton-le-Hole in the County of Durham</u>, EDS 74, London 1896, repr.Vaduz 1965.

GlossLe — A.B. Evans, ed. by S. Evans, <u>Leicestershire Words, Phrases, and Proverbs</u>, EDS 31, London 1881, repr. Vaduz 1965.

GlossLi — J.E. Brogden, <u>Provincial</u> Words and Expressions <u>Current in Lincolnshire</u>, London 1866 (in particular pp. 237-241).

GlossM&C — E. Peacock, <u>A Glossary of Words</u> Used <u>in the</u> Wapentakes <u>of Manley</u> and <u>Corringham</u>, Lincolnshire, EDS 15, London 1877, repr. Vaduz 1965.

GlossMY — C.C. Robinson, <u>A Glossary</u> of <u>Words Pertaining to the Dialect of Mid-Yorkshire</u>, EDS 14, London 1876, repr. Vaduz 1965.

GlossO — Mrs Parker, "A Glossary of Words Used in Oxfordshire", EDS 12, London 1876, repr. Vaduz 1965, p. 11o-121.

GlossO(suppl.) — Mrs Parker, "Supplement to Glossary of Words Used in Oxfordshire", <u>EDS</u> 32, London 1881, repr. Vaduz 1965, p. 65-1o2.

GlossR&R — H. Cunliffe, <u>A Glossary of Rochdale-with-Rossendale Words</u> and <u>Phrases</u>, London 1886.

GlossRu — Chr. Wordsworth, <u>Rutland</u> Words, EDS 64, London 1891, repr. Vaduz 1965.

GlossSa — G.F. Jackson, <u>Shropshire Wordbook</u>. A Glossary of Archaic and Provincial Words,etc.,Used in the County, London 1879.

GlossSEWo — J. Salisbury, <u>A Glossary of Words</u> and <u>Phrases</u> Used <u>in South East Worcestershire</u>, EDS 72, London 1893, repr. Vaduz 1965 (in particular pp. 81-82).

GlossSh — S.O. Addy, <u>A Glossary of Words Used in the</u> Neighbour<u>hood of Sheffield</u>, EDS 57, London 1888, repr. Vaduz 1965.

GlossSh(suppl.) — S.O. Addy, <u>A Supplement to the Sheffield Glossary</u>, EDS 62, London 1891, repr. Vaduz 1965.

GlossSt — Ch.H.Poole, <u>An Attempt towards a Glossary of the Archaic and Provincial Words of the County of Stafford</u>, Stratford 188o.

GlossSWLi — R.E.G. Cole, <u>A Glossary of Words Used in South-West Lincolnshire</u>, EDS 52, London 1886, repr. Vaduz 1965.

GlossW — G.E. Dartnell, E.H. Goddard, <u>A Glossary of Words Used in the County of Wiltshire</u>, EDS 69, London 1893, repr. Vaduz 1965.

GlossWa — G.F.Northall, <u>A Warwickshire Wordbook</u>, EDS 79, London 1896, repr. Vaduz 1965.

GlossWby — F.K. Robinson, <u>A Glossary of Words Used in the Neighbourhood of Whitby</u>, EDS 9,13, London 1876, repr. Vaduz 1965.

GlossWCo — M.A.Courtney, "Glossary of Words in Use in Cornwall. West Cornwall", <u>EDS</u> 27, London 188o, repr. Vaduz 1965, pp. ix-xv and pp. 1-65.

GlossWt — H.Smith, C.R. Smith,"A Glossary of Words in Use in the Isle of Wight", <u>EDS</u> 32, London 1881, repr. Vaduz 1965, p. 1-64.

GlossWWo — Mrs Chamberlain, <u>A Glossary of West Worcestershire Words</u>, EDS 36, London 1882, repr. Vaduz 1965.

Goodall — A. Goodall, "The Scandinavian Element in Yorkshire Place-Names", <u>YDS</u> 3/17 (1915), 28-54.

Gordon   C.J. Gordon, "Place and Field Names at Gt Salkeld,
                        Cumberland", Cu We Ant.Arch.Soc. n.s. 25 (1925),
                        114-27.
Greenwich Ant.Soc. Transactions of the Greenwich Antiquarian Society.
Grigson   G.Grigson, E.G.H. Kempson, "Wiltshire Place- and
                        Field-Names III", Wilts.Arch.Mag. 55 (1953-54),
                        7o-74.
GRM   Germanisch-Romanische Monatsschrift.
Grüning   B. Grüning, Schwund und Zusatz von Konsonanten in
                        den neuenglischen Dialekten, Strasbourg 19o4 (diss.).
Guardian   The Guardian, London and Manchester.
H.A.(1)   H.Alexander, "The Particle ING in Place-Names",
                        E&St 2 (1911), 158-182.
H.A.(2)   H. Alexander, "Place Names and Dialect Study", YDS
                        2/13 (1912), 24-46.
Haigh   W.E. Haigh, "A New Glossary of the Dialect of
                        Huddersfield District", YDS 4/27 (1926), 2o-22.
Halifax Ant.Soc.   Transactions of the Halifax Antiquarian Society.
Hancock   F. Hancock, "Local Place-Names in Selworthy Parish",
                        NQ.So Do 1 (1888-89), 193-95.
Hants.Field Cl.   Papers and Proceedings of the Hampshire Field Club
                        (and Archaeological Society).
Hants.NQ.   Hampshire Notes and Queries.
Hav.   F. Haverfield, "The Place-Names of Drumbrugh",
                        Cu We Ant.Arch.Soc. 16 (19oo), 1oo-1o3.
Hedev.   B. Hedevind, "Scandinavian Elements in the Dialect
                        and Place-Names of Dent in the West Riding of York-
                        shire", YDS 1o/57 (1957), 26-35.
Heslop   O. Heslop, "Dialect Notes from Northermost England",
                        YDS 1/5 (19o3), 7-31.
Hewett   S. Hewett, The Peasant Speech of Devon, London [2]1892
                        (first ed. 1892).
Hist.Soc.La Chs   Transactions of the Historic Society of Lancashire
                        and Cheshire.
HL   W. Horn, M. Lehnert, Laut und Leben. Lautgeschichte
                        der neueren Zeit (14oo-195o), 2 vols, Berlin 1954.
Höfer   H. Höfer, "Die moderne Londoner Vulgärsprache, ins-
                        besondere nach dem Punch", NS 4 (1896-97), 89-1o4,
                        15o-168,296-3o4, 363-68,431-42,486-98.
Home Counties Mag. Home Counties Magazine.
Hope   R.C. Hope, A Glossary of Dialectal Placenomencla-
                        ture, 2nd ed. London 1883 (first ed. Scarborough
                        1882), repr. 1968.
Horn   W. Horn, "Vom Einfluß des Schriftbildes auf die Aus-
                        sprache im Englischen", Anglia 64 (194o), 135-51.
Horn(Beiträge)   W.Horn, Beiträge zur Geschichte der englischen
                        Gutturallaute, Berlin 19o1.
HSM   E.Ekwall, A History of Modern English Sounds and
                        Morphology (transl. by A. Ward), Oxford 1975.
Hunt.   G.W.B. Huntingford, "Berkshire Place-Names", Berks.
                        Arch.J. 38 (1934), 1o9-27, 39 (1935), 11-34 and
                        198-9.
Hyde   T. Hyde-Parker, "A Southerner on East Yorkshire
                        Dialect", YDS 5/36 (1935), 37-4o.
IPN   A. Mawer (ed.), Introduction to the Survey of English
                        Place-Names, pt 2: The Chief Elements Used in English
                        Place-Names, Cambridge 1924.
J.D.   J. Davies, "On the Races of Lancashire, as Indicated
                        by the Local Names and the Dialect of the County",

	Phil.Soc. 1855, 21o-284 (in particular pp. 218-25, 257-65 and 281f.).
JEGPh	Journal of English and Germanic Philology.
Jenner(1)	H. Jenner, "Cornish Place-Names", Roy.Inst.Cornw. 18 (191o), 14o-146.
Jenner(2)	H. Jenner, "Some Rough Notes on the Present Pronunciation of Cornish Names", Revue Celtique 24 (19o3), 3oo-3o5.
JEPNS	Journal of the English Place-Name Society.
Jespersen	O. Jespersen, "The Nasal in Nightingale, etc.", EStn 31 (19o2), 239-242.
Jones	D. Jones, An Outline of English Phonetics, 7th ed. Leipzig 1949 (first ed. 1914).
Keef	H.W. Keef, "Place-Names: Framfield", Sx NQ. 2 (1928-29), 51f.
Koeppel	E. Koeppel, Spelling Pronunciations. Bemerkungen über den Einfluß des Schriftbildes auf den Laut im Englischen, Strasbourg 19o1 (diss.).
Kruis.	E. Kruisinga, A Handbook of Present-Day English. Pt 1: English Sounds, Utrecht 1925 (in particular pp. 274-311, which contain a "Select List of Proper Names").
Kuurman	J. Kuurman,"The Study of English Place-Names", Dutch Quarterly Review of Anglo-American Letters 3(1973), 2-1o.
Laws	J.A. Laws, "Local Place Names", East Angl.Mag. 4 (1938-39), 222f.
LCo	M.F. Wakelin, Language and History in Cornwall, Leicester 1975.
Leeds Phil.Soc.	Proceedings of the Leeds Philosophical and Literary Society.
Leics.Arch.Soc.	Transactions of the Leicestershire Archaeological Society.
Le Ru NQ.	Leicestershire and Rutland Notes and Queries.
Leyland	J. Leyland, The Peak of the Derbyshire, 1891.
Lincs.Hist.	The Lincolnshire Historian.
Lincs.Mag.	The Lincolnshire Magazine.
Lincs.NQ.	Lincolnshire Notes and Queries.
Lloyd	R.J. Lloyd, Northern English, Leipzig-Berlin [2]19o8.
March	H.C. March, C.H. Mayo, "Cernel Bridge", NQ.So Do 8 (19o2-3), 24-26.
Mawer(1)	A. Mawer, "Notes on Some Place-Names of Northumberland and County Durham", Arch.Ael. 3rd series 16 (1919), 82-1o2.
Mawer(2)	A. Mawer, "English Place-Names and Their Pronunciation", E&St 17 (1932), 9o-1o5.
Mawer(3)	A. Mawer, "Variant Spellings of Thurleigh", Beds. Rec.Soc. 8 (1924), 174.
Mawer(4)	A.Mawer, "English Place-Names and Their Pronunciation", Discovery 5 (1924), 284f.
Mayo	Ch.H. Mayo, "Local Names, Buckland Newton", NQ.So Do 1 (1888-89), 65-67.
MEG	O. Jespersen, A Modern English Grammar on Historical Principles, vol. I, Heidelberg 19o9.
Meiklejohn	M.J.C. Meiklejohn, "The Place-Names of Northfield District", Home Counties Mag. 8 (19o6), 1o2-11o and 161-17o, with corrections by W.F. Prideaux.

Mid.Ant.	Midland Antiquary.
Miller	S.H. Miller, "Origin of the Name Ely", Fenland NQ. 2 (1892–94), 316–18, with additions by H.R.S. on p. 371.
MLN	Modern Language Notes.
MLR	Modern Language Review.
Moberley	G.H. Moberley, "Local Names near Cirencester", Bristol Glos.Arch.Soc. 2 (1877–78), 118–127.
Morris	M.C.F. Morris, "The Treasures of Dialect, with Illustrations from the Folk-Speech of the Woldsmen", YDS 2/11 (1910), 5–35.
NED	J. Murray et al., A New English Dictionary on Historical Principles, 11 vols, Oxford 1888–1928.
Newbury Field Cl.	Transactions of the Newbury District Field Club.
NoB	Namn och Bygd.
NQ.	Notes and Queries.
NQ.So Do	Notes and Queries for Somerset and Dorset.
NS	Die Neueren Sprachen.
Old Cornw.	Old Cornwall.
ON	J. Bielefeld, Untersuchungen zum zweiten Teil der englischen Ortsnamen, Münster 1926 (diss.).
ONCa	C. Schererz, "Studien zu den Ortsnamen von Cambridge-shire", ZONF 3 (1927), 13–26 and 176–199.
ONwick	H. Cornelius, "Die englischen Ortsnamen auf -wick, -wich", SEP 50 (1913), 352–416 (Festschrift Morsbach).
Pal.Noteb.	Palatine Notebook.
P&RNLi	T.B.F. Eminson, The Place and River Names of the West Riding of Lindsey/Lincolnshire, Lincoln 1934.
Parkinson	M.C. Parkinson about Lancs. pl.ns in Pal.Noteb. 2 (1882), 250 (v. also s.n. Rose, below).
Pezzack	W. Pezzack, "Memories from Mousehole", Old Cornw. 2, pt 3 (1932), 1–5.
Phil.Soc.	Transactions/Proceedings of the Pilological Society.
Picken	W.M.M. Picken, "The Placenames of Morval", Old Cornw. 5 (1951–61), 131–33, 143–49 and 186–97.
PNBdHu	A. Mawer et al., The Place-Names of Bedfordshire and Huntingdonshire, EPNS 3, Cambridge 1926.
PNBk	A. Mawer et al., The Place-Names of Buckinghamshire, EPNS 2, Cambridge 1925.
PNBrk	W.W. Skeat, The Place-Names of Berkshire, Oxford 1911.
PNCa	P.H. Reaney, The Place-Names of Cambridge and the Isle of Ely, EPNS 19, Cambridge 1943.
PNCa (i)	W.W. Skeat, The Place-Names of Cambridgeshire, Cambridge 1901, repr. 1905.
PNChs	J.McN. Dodgson, The Place-Names of Cheshire, 5 vols, EPNS 44-48 and 54-55, Cambridge 1970-83.
PNChs (i)	S. Potter, Cheshire Place-Names, Liverpool 1955 (repr. from Hist.Soc.La Chs 106).
PNCu	A.M. Armstrong et al., The Place-Names of Cumberland, EPNS 20-22, Cambridge 1950-52.
PNCuWe	W.J. Sedgefield, The Place-Names of Cumberland and Westmorland, Publications of the University of Manchester, English series 7, Manchester 1915.
PND	J.E.B. Gover et al., The Place-Names of Devon, 2 vols, EPNS 8-9, Cambridge 1931-32.
PNDb	K. Cameron, The Place-Names of Derbyshire, 3 vols, EPNS 27-29, Cambridge 1959.

PNDb (i) B. Walker, "The Place-Names of Derbyshire", pt I, DAJ 36 (1914), 123-284, pt II, DAJ 37 (1915), 97-244.

PNDo A.D.Mills, The Place-Names of Dorset, EPNS 52-53, Cambridge 1977-80.

PNDo (i) A. Fägersten, The Place-Names of Dorset, Uppsala 1933.

PNDu Ch.E. Jackson, The Place-Names of Durham, London 1916.

PNDVall W.G. Arncott, The Place-Names of the Deben Valley Parishes, Ipswich 1946.

PNE&W J.B.Johnston, The Place-Names of England and Wales, London 1915.

PNERY Th. Holderness, Some Place-Names of the East Riding of Yorkshire, Driffield 1881, 2nd ed. 1899.

PNE'side J.G. Goodchild, "Traditional Names of Places in Edenside", Cu We Ant.Arch.Soc. 6 (1881-82), 50-76.[1]

PNEss P.H. Reaney, The Place-Names of Essex, EPNS 12, Cambridge 1935.

PNGl A.H. Smith, The Place-Names of Gloucestershire, 4 vols, EPNS 38-41, Cambridge 1964-65.

PNGl (i) W.St.C. Baddeley, The Place-Names of Gloucestershire, Gloucester 1913.

PNHe A.T. Bannister, The Place-Names of Herefordshire, Cambridge 1916.

PNHe (i) W.St.C. Baddeley, "Herefordshire Place-Names", Bristol Glos.Arch.Soc. 39 (1916), 87-200.

PNHrt J.E.B. Gover et al., The Place-Names of Hertfordshire, EPNS 15, Cambridge 1938.

PNHu W.W. Skeat, "The Place-Names of Huntingdonshire", Camb.Ant.Soc. 10 (1904), 317-57.

PNing E.Ekwall, English Place-Names in -ing, Lund [2]1962.

PNK F.W. Hardman, The Pronunciation of Kent Place-Names, Southwold 1933.

PNLa E.Ekwall, The Place-Names of Lancashire, Publications of the University of Manchester, English series 11, Manchester 1922.

PNLa (i) J. Sephton, A Handbook of Lancashire Place-Names, Liverpool 1913.

PNLa (ii) H.C. Wyld, T.O. Hirst, The Place-Names of Lancashire, London 1911.

PNLe A.C. Wood, "Leicestershire Place-Names", Phil.Soc. 1917-20, pt I, 57-78.

PNL'pool H. Harrison, The Place-Names of the Liverpool District or the History and Meaning of the Local and River Names of South-West Lancashire and the Wirral, London 1898.

PNMx J.E.B. Gover et al., The Place-Names of Middlesex, EPNS 18, Cambridge 1942.

PNMx (i) J.E.B. Gover, The Place Names of Middlesex, London 1922.

PNNbDu A. Mawer, The Place-Names of Northumberland and Durham, Camb.arch.eth.series 10, Cambridge 1920.

PNND B. Blomé, The Place-Names of North Devonshire, Uppsala 1929 (diss.).

PNNf G. Munford, An Attempt to Ascertain the True Derivation of the Names of Towns and Villages, and of Rivers, and other Great Natural Features of the County of Norfolk, London 1870.

PNNf (i) W. Rye, A List of Norfolk Place Names, Norwich 1923.

1) Reprinted almost at length but differently arranged in Ellis 602-07.

PNNp   J.E.B. Gover et al., The Place-Names of Northampton-
            shire, EPNS 1o, Cambridge 1933.
PNNt   J.E.B. Gover et al., The Place-Names of Nottingham-
            shire, EPNS 17, Cambridge 194o.
PNNt (i)   H. Mutschmann, The Place-Names of Nottinghamshire,
            Camb.arch.eth.series 13, Cambridge 1913.
PNNY   A.H. Smith, "The Place-Names of North Yorkshire",
            YDS 4/27 (1926), 7-19.
PNO   M. Gelling, The Place-Names of Oxfordshire, 2 vols,
            EPNS 23-24, Cambridge 1953-54.
PNO (i)   H. Alexander, The Place-Names of Oxfordshire, Ox-
            ford 1912.
PNSa   E.W. Bowcock, Shropshire Place-Names, Shrewsbury
            1923.
PNSf   W.W. Skeat, The Place-Names of Suffolk, Cambridge
            1913.
PNSr   J.E.B. Gover, The Place-Names of Surrey, EPNS 11,
            Cambridge 1934.
PNSr (i)   D. Hopwood, The Place-Names of the County of Surrey
            Including London in Surrey,Annals of the University
            of Stellenbosch, vol. iv, section B, no. 2, Cape-
            town 1926.
PNSt   W.H. Duignan, Notes on Stafforshire Place Names.
            London 19o2.
PNSWY   A. Goodall, Place-Names of South-West Yorkshire,
            Cambridge 1914.
PNSx   A. Mawer et al., The Place-Names of Sussex, 2 vols,
            EPNS 6-7, Cambridge 1929-3o.
PNSx add.   Additions and corrigenda to PNSx in Sx NQ. 3(193o-31),
            112-16, 151-54, and 2o5-7; also passim in vols. 4-7.
PNSx (i)   R.G. Roberts, The Place-Names of Sussex, Camb.arch.
            eth.series 15, Cambridge 1914.
PNW   J.E.B. Gover et al., The Place-Names of Wiltshire,
            EPNS 16, Cambridge 1939.
PNW (i)   E. Ekblom, The Place-Names of Wiltshire, Uppsala
            1917 (diss.).
PNWa   J.E.B. Gover et al., The Place-Names of Warwick-
            shire, EPNS 13, Cambridge 1936.
PNWa (i)   W.H. Duignan, Warwickshire Place Names, London 1912.
PNWe   A.H. Smith, The Place-Names of Westmorland, 2 vols,
            EPNS 42-43, Cambridge 1967.
PNWo   A. Mawer et al., The Place-Names of Worcestershire,
            EPNS 4, Cambridge 1927.
PNWo (i)   W.H. Duignan, Worcestershire Place Names, London
            19o5.
PNWRY   F.W. Moorman, Place-Names in the West Riding of
            Yorkshire, Publications of the Thoresby Society 18,
            Leeds 191o.
PNW'stow   P.H. Reaney, The Place-Names of Walthamstow,
            Walthamstow Antiquarian Society official publication
            no. 3o, 193o.
PNWt   H. Kökeritz, The Place-Names of the Isle of Wight,
            Nomina Germanica 6, Uppsala 194o.
PNYE   A.H. Smith, The Place-Names of the East Riding of
            Yorkshire, EPNS 14, Cambridge 1937.
PNYN   A.H. Smith, The Place-Names of the North Riding of
            Yorkshire, EPNS 5, Cambridge 1928.
PNYW   A.H. Smith, The Place-Names of the West Riding of
            Yorkshire, 8 vols, EPNS 3o-37, Cambridge 1961-63.

Pogatscher   A. Pogatscher, "Die englische $\bar{æ}$ / $\bar{e}$ - Grenze", _Anglia_ 23 (1901), 3o2-9.

Potter   S. Potter, _Changing English_, London 1969.

Powley   Miss Powley, "A Plea for the Old Names", _Cu We Ant. Arch.Soc._ 4 (1878-79), 19-22, 28o-84, and 6 (1881-82) 272-79

RD   P.H. Reaney, _A Dictionary of British Surnames_, London 1961, second and enlarged ed. 1976.

Reaney (1)   P.H. Reaney, "A Survey of Essex Place-Names", _EAT_ n.s. 16 (1921-23), 251-257.

Reaney (2)   P.H. Reaney, "Gernon, Garland and Garnish", _EAT_ n.s. 17 (1924) 172-78.

Reaney (3)   P.H. Reaney, "Essex Place-Names in -_ing_", _MLR_ 19 (1924), 466-69.

Rec.Bucks.   Records of Buckinghamshire.

RES   Review of English Studies.

RIOno   Revue Internationale d'Onomastique.

RitterLa   O. Ritter, "Über einige Ortsnamen aus Lancashire", _EStn_ 54 (192o), 187-93.

RitterNt   O. Ritter,"Zu den Ortsnamen der Grafschaft Nottingham", _ZAA_ 4 (1956), 448-62.

RN   E. Ekwall, _English River Names_, Oxford 1928, repr. 1968.

RNY   E.V. Gordon, A.H. Smith, "The River Names of Yorkshire", _YDS_ 4/26 (1925), 5-3o.

ROS   P.H. Reaney, _The Origin of English Surnames_, London 1967.

Rose   I. Rose, "Pronunciation of Local Names", _Pal.Noteb._ 3 (1883), 29f. (this article is an answer to M.C. Parkinson's article; see above, s.n. Parkinson).

Roy.Hist.Soc.   Transactions of the Royal Historical Society.

Roy.Inst.Cornw.   Journal of the Royal Institution of Cornwall.

RSp   E.M. Wright, _Rustic Speech and Folk-lore_, London 1914 (2nd ed.).

Saga Book   Saga Book of the Viking Club/Society.

ScandPN   E.M. Cole, _On Scandinavian Place Names in the East Riding of Yorkshire_, York 1879.

Schr.   A. Schröer, _Neuenglisches Aussprachwörterbuch mit besonderer Berücksichtigung der wichtigsten Eigennamen_, Heidelberg 1922 (first ed. 1913).

SEP   Studien zur englischen Philologie.

Shell   J. Hadfield, _The Shell Guide to England_, London 197o

Shore   T.W. Shore, "Traces of the Languages of the Prehistoric and Other Ancient Races of Hampshire Contained in the Place-Names of the County", _Hants. Field Cl._ 3 (1894-97), 233-56.

Shrops.Arch.Soc.   Transactions of the Shropshire Archaeological and Natural History Society.

Simpson   G. Simpson,"Grasmere Field-Names", _Cu We Ant.Arch. Soc._ n.s. 28 (1928), 273-91.

Smith(1)   A.H. Smith, "The Place-Names Jervaulx, Ure, and York", _Anglia_ 48 (1924), 291-96.

Smith(2)   A.H. Smith, "Place-Names of the Ancient Parish of Halifax", _Halifax Ant.Soc._ 1936, 215-33.

SN   Studia Neophilologica.

Som.Arch.Soc.   Proceedings of the Somersetshire Archaeological and Natural History Society.

Southend Ant.Hist. Soc.   Transactions of the Southend-on-Sea and District Antiquarian and Historical Society.

Språk.Säll.   Språkvetenskapliga Sällskapets i Uppsala Förhand-
               lingar.
St.Mod.Språk. Studier i modern Språkvetenskap.
Sx Arch.Soc.   Anon.,"Sussex Archaeological Society", Sx NQ.
               1 (1926–27), 42.
Sx NQ.   Sussex Notes and Queries.
Tanger   G. Tanger, Englisches Namenlexikon, Berlin 1888.
Tengstrand   E. Tengstrand, "Marginal Notes to the Place-Names
               of Dorset", SN 6 (1933–34), 9o–1o3.
Thomp.   D. Thompson, "The Name 'Arbor Low'", DAJ 76 (1956),
               67–7o.
Thorn.   Rev. Thornley, "The Field Names of the Parish of
               Kirkoswald", Cu We Ant.Arch.Soc. 15 (1899), 48–81.
Times   The Times, London.
TLS   The Times Literary Supplement.
Turner (1)   A.G.C. Turner, "Notes on Some Somerset Place-Names",
               Som.Arch.Soc. 95 (195o), 112–24.
Turner (2)   A.G.C. Turner, "A Selection of North Somerset Place
               Names", Som.Arch.Soc. 96 (1951), 152–59.
Ump.   A.S. Umpleby, "The Dialect of Staithes", YDS 5/36
               (1935), 24–36.
Urlau   K. Urlau, Die Sprache des Dialektdichters William
               Barnes (Dorsetshire), Berlin 1921 (diss.).
Walker   B. Walker, "Interchange and Substitution of Second
               Elements in Place-Names", EStn 51 (1917–18), 25–36.
Whiteh.   H. Whitehall, "Scaitliffe: A Place-Name Derivation",
               Essays and Studies in English and Comparative Liter-
               ature by Members of the English Department of the
               University of Michigan 13, Ann Arbor 1935, 73–79.
W.H.Jones   W.H. Jones, "The Names of Places in Wiltshire",
               Wilts.Arch.Mag., 14 (1874), 156–18o, 253–279, and
               15 (1875), 71–98.
Wilde   H.O.Wilde, Der Industriedialekt von Birmingham,
               Studien zur englischen Philologie 94, Halle 1938.
Wilts.Arch.Mag. Wiltshire Archaeological and Natural History Magazine.
WP   I. Taylor, Words and Places, London 1863, 2nd ed.
               1865; ed. with corr. and add. by A.S. Palmer, London
               19lo, repr. 1968.
Wyld   H.C. Wyld, A History of Modern Colloquial English,
               3rd ed. Oxford 1956 (first ed. 192o).
YDS   Transactions of the Yorkshire Dialect Society.
YorksNQ.   Yorkshire Notes and Queries.
ZAA   Zeitschrift für Anglistik und Amerikanistik.
Zachr.(1)   R.E.Zachrisson, "The Suffix *-ingja in Germanic
               Names", Archiv 133 (1915), 348–53.
Zachr.(2)   R.E.Zachrisson, "Marylebone – Tyburn – Holborn",
               MLR 12 (1917), 146–56.
Zachr.(3)   R.E.Zachrisson, "Change of ts to ch, ds to dg and
               other Instances of Inner Soundsubstitution", St.Mod.
               Språk. 8 (1921), 123–34.
Zachr.(4)   R.E.Zachrisson, "English Place-Names in -ing of
               Scandinavian Origin", Språk.Säll. 1922–24, 1o7–3o.
Zachr.(5)   R.E. Zachrisson, "The French Element", IPN, pt 1,
               93–114.
ZONF   Zeitschrift für Ortsnamenforschung.

b. Other works consulted

Alexander, J.J., "The Place-Names of Devon", Dev.Yearb. 31 (1930), 65-70.

Alexander, J.J., "The Place-Names of Torbay", Dev.Ass. 64 (1932), 538-42.

Alexander, J.J., "East and North Devonshire Place-Names", Dev.Ass. 65 (1933), 353-77.

Alexander, J.J., "Devon River Names", Dev.Ass. 67 (1935), 399-419.

Anderson, O.S., The English Hundred-Names, Lund Universitets Årsskrift vols 3o, 35, and 37, Lund 1934-39.

Anon., "Pronunciation of Local Place-Names", Pal.Noteb. 2 (1882),197 [this is not an original list, but a selection taken from Hope].

Anon., "Lincolnshire Names", Lincs.NQ. 6 (19o1), 2o-28,41-45,67-71, 172-5,2o3-6,228-31; 7 (19o4), 4-7,5o-53,71-74,1o6-8.

Anon., "Sussex Place-Names", SxNQ. 1 (1926-27), 248.

Anscombe, A., "English Place-Names", TLS 1921, 26o.

Anscombe, A., "The Name of Funtingdon", SxNQ. 1 (1926-27), 35-36.

Anscombe, A., "The Name of Portslade", SxNQ. 1 (1926-27), 7o-72.

Anscombe, A., "Halnaker or Halfnaked", SxNQ. 1 (1926-27), 1o1-2.

Anscombe, A., "The Name of Mayfield in Sussex", Anglia 52(1928), 76-78

Arkell, W.J., "Further Notes on Topographical Names in South Dorset", Do Nat.Hist.Soc. 63 (1941), 33-4o.

Arkell, W.J., "Place-Names and Topography in the Upper Thames Country: A Regional Survey", Oxoniensia 7 (1942), 1-23.

Arkell, W.J., "Some Topographical Names in Wiltshire", Wilts.Arch.Mag. 49 (194o-42), 221-24.

Arngart, O., "Two Cheshire Place-Names", SN 43 (1971), 43o-34.

Arrowsmith, G.M., Bannard, H.E., "Hurley Place and Field Names", Berks.Bucks.Oxon.Arch.J. 28 (1924), 179-93.

Atkinson, J.C., "Additions to 'A Glossary of the Cleveland Dialect'", EDS 12, London 1876, repr. Vaduz 1965, 1-8.

Atkinson, J.C.,"The Place-Name Somerset", NQ.So Do 1 (189o), 153f. and 257-9.

C.B.,"The Name Somerset", NQ. So Do 1o (19o6-o7), 244f.

J.B.B., "Some Leicestershire Place-Names", Le Ru NQ. 1 (1889-91), 273f

Baddeley, St.C., "Cirencester Place-Names: Lewis Street", Bristol Glos Arch.Soc. 44 (1922), 314-16.

Bannister, J., A Glossary of Cornish Names, London 1871.

Barber, H., "Place Names of Northamptonshire which are Included in the Fenland District", Fenland NQ. 3 (1895-97), 312-15.

Barber, H., "Etymologies of Derbyshire Place-Names", DAJ 19 (1897), 53-79.

Barbier, P., "Dialect", YDS 5/35 (1934), 1o-14.

Barnes, W., A Grammar and Glossary of the Dorset Dialect, Phil.Soc., London-Berlin 1863, 2nd ed. London 1886, repr. St.Peter Port 197o.

Berm,[1] "Bucknall End, Castlebromwich", Mid.Ant. 1 (1882), 89.

Blackie, C., A Dictionary of Place-Names, Giving Their Derivations, London 1887.

Bourke, C.F.J., "Notes of Place-name Endings in Buckinghamshire", Rec. Bucks. 8 (1898-1903), 327-39, with additions by J.P. on pp. 339-41.

Bradley, H., "English Place-Names", E&St 1 (1910), 7-41.

Bradley, H., review of R.E.Zachrisson, A Contribution to the Study of Anglo-Norman Influence on English Place-Names, in: EHS 24 (1919), 766-8.

Brandl, A., Zur Geographie der altenglischen Dialekte, Abhandlung der preußischen Akademie der Wissenschaften, phil.-hist. Klasse, 4, 1915.

Branston, R.V., "The Dialect of Denby Dale", YDS 5/37 (1936), 18-27.

Brentnall, H.C., "Wiltshire Place-Names", Antiquity 15 (1941), 33-44.

Browne, W.R., "On the Distribution of English Place Names", Phil.Soc. 1880-81, 86-98.

Brunner, K., Die Dialektliteratur in Lancashire, Wien 1920.

Cameron, K., "Work on Place-Names in Lincolnshire, a Preliminary Discussion", Lincs.Hist. 2 (3) (1955-56), 1-11.

Cameron, K., English Place-Names, London 1961, [2]1963, [3]1977.

Chance, S.W., Place-Names in Harlow, Harlow Museum Advisory Committee 1968.

Coleman, W.L., "Some Place and Field Names of the Parish of Staveley", DAJ 16 (1894), 190-97.

Collier, W.F., "Devonshire Dialect", Dev.Ass. 25 (1893), 276-85.

Copley, G.J., English Place-Names and Their Origins, Newton Abbot 1968 (2nd ed. 1971).

Copley, G.J., Names and Places, London 1963, repr. 1964.

Couch, Th.Q., "Glossary of Words in Use in Cornwall. East Cornwall", EDS 27, London 1880, repr. Vaduz 1965, 67-109.

Cowling, G.H., The Dialect of Hackness (North-East Yorkshire), Cambridge 1915.

Cox, J.Ch., "Place and Field Names of Derbyshire, which Indicate Vegetable Production", DAJ 3 (1881), 73-89.

Cox, J.Ch., "Place and Field Names of Derbyshire, which Indicate the Fauna", DAJ 4 (1882), 57-75.

Crawford, O.G.S., "Place-Names", Arch.J. 78 (1921), 31-46.

Crawford, O.G.S., "Deadman's Hill, Sandon, Herts.", Antiquity 10 (1936), 96f.

Crawford, O.G.S., "Hertfordshire Place-Names", Antiquity 12 (1938), 432-36.

Crookshank, A.C., "West Hoathley Field Names", Sx NQ. 1 (1926-27), 194f., supplemented by E. Straker on p. 229, and by T.H.W. Buckley on p. 257.

---

1) This is the pen-name of Joseph Hill; his identity is revealed by H.New in "Some Street-Names in Birmingham", B'ham Arch.Soc. 42(1917), p. 62.

Crosland, C., "Some Place-Names in the Parish of Halifax", YDS 1/4 (1902), 3-23.

Cummings, C.L., "The Place-Name of Sunderland [in Durham]", Ant.Sunderland 18 (1918-25), 22f.

Cunnington, B.H., "Devizes Street Names and Their Origin", Wilts.Arch. Mag. 51 (1945-47), 179-83.

Daniel. F., "Place-Name Botteredg", NQ.SoDo 27 (1961), 124.

Darby, St., Place and Field Names, Cookham Parish, Berks., no place, 1899 (for private circulation).

Davies, T.L.O., A Supplementary English Glossary, London 1881.

Davis, F., "The Etymology of Some Derbyshire Place Names", DAJ 2 (1880), 33-71.

Dickinson, W., A Glossary of the Words and Phrases of Cumberland, Whitehaven-London 1859 (see also above, s.n. GlossCu).

Dickinson, W., "Additional Supplement to the Cumberland Glossary", EDS 32, London 1881, repr. Vaduz 1965, 1o5-11o.

Dinsdale, F.T., A Glossary of Provincial Words Used in Teesdale in the County of Durham, London 1849.

Dodgson, J.McN., "The -ing in English Place-Names like Altrincham and Birmingham", BzN, N.F. 2 (1967), 221-245.

Dunlap, A.R., "The Replacement of /ə/ and /i/ in the English Pronunciation of Names", Names 22 (1974), 85-92.

Dyer, S., The Dialect of the West Riding of Yorkshire, Brighouse 1891.

Dyson, B.R., "The Sheffield Cutler and His Dialect", YDS 5/33 (1932), 9-36.

Earle, J., "On Local Names [around Bath]", Bristol Glos.Arch.Soc. 8 (1884), 5o-61.

Earle, J., "The Place-Name Somerset", NQ.SoDo 1 (189o), 174f.

Egar, S., "Place-Names", Fenland NQ. 3 (1895-97), 361f.

Ehrmann, L., Die Norfolker Dialektgruppe, Palaestra 185, Leipzig 1933.

Ejder, B., "Notes on Yorkshire Place-Names", ES 46 (1965), 11o-113.

Ekwall, E., "A Note on i-mutated Primitive English a before l followed by a consonant", AB 29 (1918), 73-76.

Ekwall, E., "A Few Notes on English Etymology and Word-History", AB 29 (1918), 195-2o1.

Ekwall, E., "Notes on the Palatalization of k (c) in English", AB 32 (1921) 155-68.

Ekwall, E., "An Old English Sound-Change and Some English Forest Names", AB 36 (1925), 146-51.

Ekwall, E., "The Name Salcey", AB 37 (1926), 191f.

Ekwall, E., "Etymological Notes", SN 2(1929),28-4o;EStn 64(1929),21y-26.

Ekwall, E., "Early Names of Britain", Antiquity 4 (193o), 149-56.

Ekwall, E., "Some Notes on English Place-Names Containing Names of Heathen Deities", EStn 7o (1935), 55-59.

Ekwall, E., "The Place-Names of the Fylde", in: A Scientific Survey of Blackpool and District, ed. A. Grime, British Association 1936, 41-44.

Ekwall, E., Studies on English Place-Names, Stockholm 1936.

Ekwall, E., "Some English Place-Names Etymologies", SN 1o (1937-38), 1o3-18.

Ekwall, E., "The Place-Name Lingfield", Anglia 63 (1939), 392-7.

Ekwall, E., "Notes on Some Middlesex Place-Names", SN 17 (1944-45), 25-34.

Ekwall, E., Street-Names of the City of London, Oxford 1954.

Ekwall, E.,"A Hundred Name", RES n.s. 8 (1957), 4o8f.

Ekwall, E., Old English wic in Place-Names, Nomina Germanica 13, Lund 1964.

Elworthy, F.T., The West Somerset Wordbook. A Glossary of Dialectal and Archaic Words Used in the West of Somerset and East Devon, EDS 5o, London 1886, repr. Vaduz 1965.

Eminson, T.B.F., "The River Dove", DAJ 42 (192o), 31-45.

Evans, E.D.P., The Meaning of Severn, Ouse, Minster, etc., no place, 1931 (this is a collection of papers entitled "The Severn and other Wye Rivers" and "The Meaning of Minster in Place-Names" read before the Philological Society in 1928 and 1927 resp.).

F., "Nomenclature near the Border Villages of Lancashire and Yorkshire", Ant.Mag. 4 (1883), 169-77.

Fairfax-Blakeborough, J., "A Yorkshire Dialect Survey", YDS 5/29 (1928), 9-23.

Falkner, E.F., "Wiltshire Place- and Field-Names II", Wilts.Arch.Mag. 52 (1947-48), 116.

Farnell, E.N., "Berkshire Place Names", Newbury Field Cl. 8/4 (1946), 29o-3oo.

Field, J., Discovering Place-Names, Tring 1971, [2]1976.

Field, J., English Field-Names. A Dictionary, Newton Abbot 1972.

Field, J., The Place-Names of Greater London, London 198o.

Field, J., Place-Names of Great Britain and Ireland, London 198o.

Flasdieck, H.M., "Studien zur schriftsprachlichen Entwicklung der neuenglischen Velarvokale in Verbindung mit R ", Anglia 56 (1932), 113-264 and 321-42o.

Fleming, L., "Seton, in Pagham", Sx NQ. 11 (1946-47), 3-6.

Forester, A., "Washburn Place Names", Yorks.NQ. 1 (1888), 232.

Fortescue, Rt.Hon.Earl, "Some Devonshire Farm Names", Dev.Ass. 62 (193o), 311-4o.

Fowler, G.H., "The Meeting Place of Manshead Hundred", Beds.Rec.Soc. 8 (1924), 174f.

Fowler, J., "Ruggewell", NQ.SoDo 27 (1961), 184.

Mrs Francis, "South Warwickshire Provincialisms", EDS 12, London 1876, repr. Vaduz 1965, 122-35.

Franzmeyer, F., Studien über den Konsonantismus und Vokalismus der neuenglischen Dialekte, Strasbourg 19o6 (diss.).

Fry, G.S., "Shillingston Field Names from Tithe Return, 21st July, 1838", NQ.SoDo 18 (1926-28), 13o-32.

Fry, G.S., "Shillingston Holdings and Field Names", NQ.SoDo 2o (193o-32) 217f.

Gelling, M., "Some Notes on the Place-Names of Birmingham and the Surrounding District", B'ham Arch.Soc. 72 (1956 for 1954), 14-17

Gelling, M., The Place-Names of Berkshire, 3 vols, EPNS 49-51, Cambridge 1973 ff.

Gevenich. O., Die englische Palatalisierung von k zu č im Lichte der englischen Ortsnamen, Göttingen 1917 (diss.) and Studien zur englischen Philologie 57, Halle 1918 (expanded edition).

Gill, W.W., "Cheshire and Dorset Dialect Words", NQ. 179/5 (1940), 78f.

Gordon, E.V., "Scandinavian Influence in Yorkshire Dialects", YDS 4/24 (1923), 5-22.

Gover, J.E.B., "Cornish Place-Names", Antiquity 2 (1928), 319-27.

Gower, G.L., "Surrey Provincialisms", EDS 12, London 1876, repr. Vaduz 1965, 79-1o9.

Gower, G.L., A Glossary of Surrey Words, EDS 7o, London 1893, repr. Vaduz 1965.

Graves, Ph.P., "Wallop, Guollopum and Catguoloph", Antiquity 12 (1938, 474-76.

Gregory, J.V., "Place-Names of the County of Northumberland, with Reference to the Ancestry of the People", Arch.Ael. n.s. 9 (1882) 57-71.

Gregory, J.V., "Place-Names of the County of Durham", Arch.Ael. n.s. 1o (1885), 173-85.

Grundy, G.B., "The Place-Names of Wiltshire", Wilts.Arch.Mag. 41 (1921), 335-53.

Grundy, G.B., "On Place-Names in General and the Hampshire Place-Names in Particular", Hants.Field Cl. 9 (192o-25), 22-261.

H., F.W.W., "Somerset River Names", NQ.SoDo 3 (1892-93), 273, and 4 (1894-95), 327.

M.S.H., "Notes on Some Sussex Place-Names", Sx NQ. 3 (193o-31), 9of.

W.T.H., "Two Place-Names", Old Cornw. 2/12 (1936), 38.

Haggard, A., Dialect and Local Usages of Herefordshire, London 1972.

Halliwell, J.O., Dictionary of Archaic and Provincial Words, Obsolete Phrases, Proverbs and Ancient Customs from the XIV th Century, London 19o4 (reprint of the 185o edition).

Hamlin, F.R., "Bibliographie sommaire des études de toponymie aux Iles Britanniques", RIOno 14 (1962), 299-31o, and 15 (1963), 293-95.

Hardcastle, C.D., "Washburn Place-Names", Yorks.NQ. 2 (189o), 57-61.

Hardman, F.W., The Danes in Kent. A Survey of Kentish Place-Names of Scandinavian Origin, Walmer 1927.

Hardwicke, G., "Yorkshire Dialect", YDS 4/25 (1924), 5-7.

Harland, J., A Glossary of Words Used in Swaledale, Yorkshire, EDS 3, London 1873, repr. Vaduz 1965.

Harrison, P., "Local Names", Cu Ass.Lit.Sc. 3 (1877-78), 61-75.

Haverfield, F., "The Antiquity of Place-Names", Arch.Hist.Soc.Chester 6/1 (1897), 36-41.

Hearne, F., "Some Field Names and Place Names in the Parishes of Little-hampton, Poling and Angmaring", Sx NQ. 6 (1936-37), 118.

Heilig, O., "Die nordbadischen Ortsnamen", ZONF 7 (1931), 2o8-17.

Henderson, C., "Clodgy", Old Cornw. 2/4 (1932), 37f.

Henderson, C., "Two Names of Streams", Old Cornw. 2/5 (1933), 16f.

Heslop, O., Northumberland Words. A Glossary of Words Used in the County of Northumberland and the Tyneside, EDS 66, 68, 71, London 1892-94, repr. Vaduz 1965.

Hewett, S., Nummits and Crummits. Devonshire Customs, Characteristics and Folk-lore, London 19oo.

Hill, J., The Place-Names of Somerset, Bristol 1914.
(see also above, s.n. Berm)

Hirst, T.O., "Some Features of Interest in the Phonology of the North, Midland and West-Northern Dialects", YDS 2/1o (19o8), 6-16.

Holden, W.H., "A Miscellany of Place Names", DAJ 7o (195o), 21-34.

Horn, W., "Beiträge zur Namenforschung", Archiv 188 (1951), 3-7.

Horsley, J.W., Place-Names in Kent, Maidstone 1921.

Hoskins, W.H., "The Anglian and Scandinavian Settlement of Leicester-shire", Leics.Arch.Soc. 18 (1934-35), 1o9-47.

Houtzager, M.E., Unconscious Sound- and Sense-Assimilations, Amsterdam 1935 (diss.).

Huntingford, G.W.B., "Traces of Ancient Paganism in Berkshire", Berks. Arch.J. 37 (1933), 17-22.

Huntingford, G.W.B., "The Name 'Berkshire'", Berks.Arch.J. 37 (1933), 34-37.

Irvine, W.F., "Place-Names in the Hundred of Wirral", Hist.Soc.La Chs 43-44 (n.s. 7-8) (1893-94), 279-3o4.

Jackson, Ch.E., The Place-Names of Durham, London 1916.

Jackson, K., "Nennius and the 28 Cities of Britain", Antiquity 12 (1938) 44-55.

Jackson, K., "Wallop", Antiquity 13 (1939), 1o5f.

Jago, F.W.P., The Ancient Language and the Dialect of Cornwall with an enlarged Glossary of Cornish Provincial Words, Truro 1882.

Johnstone, P.K., "Kelliwic in Cornwall", Antiquity 19 (1945), 156f.

Jolliffe, J.E.A., "The Old English Term 'Snade'", Antiquity 9 (1935), 22o-22.

Jones, J.P., "Tettenhall Place and Field Names", Mid.Ant. 2 (1883), 83-86.

Jones, J.P., A History of the Parish of Tettenhall, London 1894.

Jones, W.H.R., "On Some Place-Names near Malmesbury, and Their Historic Teachings", Wilts.Arch.Mag. 21 (1884), 61-74.

Karlström, S., "Miscellaneous Notes on the Place-Names of North Devon-shire", SN 2 (1929), 67-69.

Karlström, S., "Kilvington and Some Related English Place-Names", SN 4 (1931-32), 12o-4o.

Karlström, S., "Notes on the Place-Names of Northamptonshire", NoB 22 (1934), 52-87.

Kay, J.T., "Lancashire and Cheshire Place-Names", Pal.Noteb. 3 (1883) 13-17 and 63-67, with a note by J.P.Earwaker on p. 5of.

Kirkby, B., Lakeland Words. A Collection of Dialectal Words and Phrases as Used in Cumberland and Westmorland (with a preface by J. Wright), Oxford 1898, repr. New York-East Ardsley/Yorks. 1975

Kuper, M.E., "Field Name Survivals in the Parish of Daston", Cu We Ant.Arch.Soc. 1o (1889), 253-7o.

Lang, W.D., Arber, M.A., "Names of the West Dorset Cliffs", NQ.So Do 23 (1939-42), 278-81.

Lattey, R.T., "Field-Names of Enstone and Little Tew Parishes, Oxon." Oxoniensia 17-18 (1952-53), 265f., and Oxoniensia 21 (1956), 84

Lawson, R., Upton-on-Severn Words and Phrases, EDS 42, London 1884, repr. Vaduz 1965.

Lewis, J.W., Concise Pronouncing Dictionary of British and American English, London 1972.

Lowsley, B., A Glossary of Berkshire Words and Phrases, EDS 56, Londo 1888, repr. Vaduz 1965.

MacKey, M.S. and M.G., The Pronunciation of 1o,ooo Proper Names, New York 19o3 (2nd ed. 1922, repr. 1931).

Macleod, D., "Heathfield Place-Names", Sx NQ. 1 (1926-27), 4of., 72-7 1o2-1o5.

Malone, K., "Some Linguistic Studies of 1933 and 1934", MLN 5o (1935) 515-535 (about p.ns on pp. 521-24).

Malone, K., "On the Etymology of Lingfield (Surrey)", Anglia 6o (1936 366-68.

Malone, K., "Lingfield Again", Anglia 63 (1939), 65f.

Marble Arch [a pen-name], "Local Place Names", Hants.NQ. 1 (1883), 67-81.

Maskelyne, N.S., "The Place-Name Cricklade", Wilts.Arch.Mag. 3o (1898 95-97.

Matthews, C.M., Place-Names of the English-Speaking World, London 197

Mawer, A., "Scandinavian Influence on the Place-Names of Northumberland and Durham", Saga Book 8 (1913-14), 172-21o.

Mawer, A., "Animal and Personal Names in O.E. Place-Names", MLR 14 (1919), 233-44.

Mawer, A., "Sussex Place-Names", Sx NQ. 1 (1926-27), 259f.

Mawer, A., "The River-Names of Northumberland and Durham", Arch.Ael. 4th series 4 (1929), 175-82.

Mawer, A., "Notes on the Place-Names of Devon", Phil.Soc. 1931-32, 68-72.

Mawer, A., Stenton, F., "The Place-Names of Sussex", RES 8 (1932), 86-88.

Michaelis, H., Jones, D., A Phonetic Dictionary of the English Language, Hannover-Berlin 1913.

Miller, S.H., "Friday Bridge", Fenland NQ. 3 (1895-97), 151-53.

de Montmorency, J.E.G., "Blackheath and Greenwich Place Names", Gree wich Ant.Soc. 1 (19o7), 186-89.

Moor, E., Suffolk Words and Phrases, London 1823, repr. with a new
    introduction by S. Ellis, Newton Abbot 1970.

Moore, S., Meech, S.B., Whitehall, H., "Middle English Dialect Char-
    acteristics and Dialect Boundaries", Essays and Studies in Eng-
    lish and Comparative Literature by members of the English Depart-
    ment of the University of Michigan 13, Ann Arbor 1935, 1-60.

Morris, G.E., "The Place-Names and Settlement of Part of North Derby-
    shire", Leeds Phil.Soc. 6 (1944-47), 137-47.

R.M.N., "Avon and Dowr", Old Cornw. 5 (1951-61), 274f.

R.M.N., "Costislost", Old Cornwall 5 (1951-61), 353.

R.M.N., "Hints for Place-Names Study", Old Cornw. 3 (1937-42), 257-
    60, 396-98,482-85.

Nance, R.M., A Guide to Cornish Place-Names, 3rd ed.[St.Ives 1960]
    (first ed. [Marazion] 1952).

New, H., "Some Street-Names in Birmingham", B'ham Arch.Soc. 42 (1917),
    41-67.

Nodal, J.H., Milner, G., A Glossary of the Lancashire Dialect, EDS
    10,35, London 1875, repr. Vaduz 1965.

Orton, H., "The Dialects of Northumberland", YDS 5/31 (1930), 14-25.

Orton, H., "Dialectal English and the Student", YDS 7/47 (1947),27-38.

Otsuka, T., et al., English Pronouncing Dictionary of Proper Names,
    Tokyo 1969.

F.J.P., "Kelston and Kilton", NQ.SoDo 4 (1894-95), 177.

Page-Turner, F.A., "Toddington Field Names", Beds.Rec.Soc. 2 (1914),
    266f.

Parsons, F.G.,"Some Additional Notes on the Name of 'Risborough'",
    Rec.Bucks. 13 (1934-40), 470-72.

Payling, L.W.H., "Geology and Place-Names in Kesteven", Leeds Studies
    in English and Kindred Languages 4 (1935), 1-13.

Peacock, E., A Glossary of Words Used in the Wapentake of Manley
    and Corringham, Lincolnshire, EDS 58,59, 2nd. ed. London 1889
    (see also above s.n. GlossM&C).

Peacock, R.B., A Glossary of the Dialect of the Hundred of Lonsdale
    North and South of the Sands, in the County of Lancaster, ed. by
    J.C. Atkinson, London 1869.

Pegge, S., "An Alphabet of Kenticisms", EDS 12, London 1876, 9-78
    (reprint of the 1736 edition).

Picton, J.A., "On Place-Names in Norfolk", Brit.Arch.Ass. 36 (1880),
    137-45.

Poole, E.H.L., "Wiltshire Place- and Field-Names I", Wilts.Arch.Mag.
    51 (1945-47), 611f.

Prevost, E.W.,[1]A Supplement to the Glossary of the Dialect of Cumber-
    land, with a Grammar of the Dialect by S.D. Brown, London 1905.

Prideaux, W.F., "The Place-Names of Northwood", Home Counties Mag.
    9 (1907), 155f. (this is a reply to Meiklejohn's article in
    vol. 8 (1906), p. 102 and 161).

1) see also above, s.n. GlossCu etc.

Quiggin, E.C., "Some Celtic River Names", Phil.Soc. 1911-14, 99-1oo.

Reaney, P.H., "The Place-Names of the Rochford Hundred", Southend Ant.Hist.Soc. 2/2 (1932), 1o3-12.

Reaney, P.H., "Lesteneston", EAT 2o (1933), 95f.

Reaney, P.H., "Honywand", EAT 2o (1933), 1o1.

Reaney, P.H., "Dury Falls in Hornchurch", EAT 2o (1933), 279-81.

Reaney, P.H., The Origin of English Place-Names, London 196o, [4]1969.

Rideout, E.H., "Wirral Field Names", Hist.Soc.La Chs 76 (n.s.4o) (1924). 125-46.

Rigge, H.F., "The Name of Cartmel", Cu We Ant.Arch.Soc. 8 (1886), 263-66.

Ritter, O., "Zur englischen $\bar{æ}$ / $\bar{e}$ - Grenze", Anglia 37 (1913), 269-75

Ritter, O., "Zu einigen Ortsnamen aus Oxfordshire", EStn 56 (1922), 292-3oo.

Roberts, R.J., "Bibliography of Writings on English Place- and Personal Names", Onoma 8 (1958-59), pt 3, 1-62.

Robertson, J.D., A Glossary of Dialect and Archaic Words Used in the County of Gloucestershire, ed. by Lord Moreton, EDS 61, London 189o, repr. Vaduz 1965.

Round, J.H., "Norse Place-names in Essex", EAT 16 (1921-23), 169-177.

Round, J.H., "Parsloes, Becontree Heath, Squirrel's Heath and Dene's Hall", EAT 16 (1921-23), 88-94.

Sandred, K.-I., English Place-Names in -stead, Acta Universitatis Uppsaliensis, Uppsala 1963.

Sandred, K.-I., "Beachampstead - a complicated place-name in Huntingdonshire", ES 5o (1969), 495-99.

Schram, K.O., "Place-Names in -sett in the East of England", ZONF 3 (1927), 2oo-211.

Schram, K.O., "Two Norfolk Place-Names", RES 5 (1929), 73-76.

Schram, K.O., "Fenland Place-Names", in: The Early Cultures of North-West Europe (H.M. Chadwick Memorial Studies), ed. by C. Fox and B. Dickins, Cambridge 195o, p. 429-441.

Sedgefield, W.J., "The Place-Name 'Hale', 'Haile', 'Haugh', 'Eale'", MLR 9 (1914), 24of.

Sills, G., "Etymology of Gedney",Fenland NQ. 5 (19o1-o3), 272f. and 314f.

Skeat, W.W., The Place-Names of Hertfordshire, Hertford 19o4.

Skeat, W.W., "Old Place-Names of Hertfordshire", East Herts.Arch.Soc. 3/1 (19o5), 1o7-9.

Skeat, W.W., The Place-Names of Bedfordshire, Cambridge Antiquarian Society Publications, octavo series 42, Cambridge 19o6.

Skeat, W.W., "Place-Names of Hertfordshire", East Herts.Arch.Soc. 4/2 (191o), 179-81.

Smith, A., Dictionary of City of London Street Names, Newton Abbot 197o.

Smith, A.H., "A Note on Yorkshire Place-Names", Phil.Soc. 1935, 74.

Smith, A.H., "Two Notes on Some West Yorkshire Place-Names", in: The Anglo-Saxons. Studies in some Aspects of their History and Culture presented to Bruce Dickins, ed. by P. Clemoes, London 1959, p. 311-315.

Smith, G.E., "Minehead", NQ.So Do 7(1900-01), 258f.

Smithard, W., "Place-Names at or near Derby", DAJ 34 (1912), 139-44.

Stead, R., "The Two Yorkshire Dialects", YDS 1/8 (1906), 5-22.

Stenton, F.M., "Godmundesleah", EHS 20 (1905), 697-79.

Stenton, F.M., The Place-Names of Berkshire, Reading 1911.

Stenton, F.M., "Place-Names of Lincolnshire", Lincs.Mag. 3 (1936), 151-53.

Stenton, F.M., "The Historical Bearing of Place-Names Studies", Roy. Hist.Soc. 21 (1939), 1-19; 22 (1940), 1-22; 23 (1941), 1-24; 24 (1942), 1-24; 25 (1943), 1-14.

Stevenson, W.H., "Notes on the place-name 'Filey'", Transactions of the East Riding Antiquarian Society 14 (1907), 10-12.

Stevenson, W.H., "Derivation of Nursling", Hants.Field Cl. 9 (1920-25), 414-16.

Stone, G., "The Place-Names of the Test Valley", Hants.Field Cl. 18 (1954), 154-6.

Straker, E., "Notes on some Sussex Place-Names", Sx NQ. 3 (1930-31), 89f.

Sutton, E., "North Lincolnshire Words", EDS 32, London 1881, repr. Vaduz 1965, 113-22.

Taylor, R.V., "On the Yorkshire Dialects", YDS 1/1 (1898), 26-33.

Thomson, T.R., The Place-Names of Cricklade, The Cricklade Historical Society, 2nd ed. 1964 (first ed. 1957).

Thorson, P., "Some English Lake-Name Forms", JEGPh 30 (1931), 26-47.

Venables, E., "Place-Names in the Isle of Axholme", Ass.Arch.Soc. 38/1 (1885), 1-12.

Viereck, W., Phonematische Analyse des Dialekts von Gateshead-upon-Tyne/Co. Durham, Hamburg 1966.

Voitl, H., "Schreibung und Aussprache bei englischen Familiennamen als methodisches Problem", Disputationes ad Montium Vocabula aliorum-que Nominum Significationes Pertinentes", 10. Int. Kongreß für Namenforschung, Wien 1969, vol. I, 161-69.

Wainwright, F.T., "Fieldnames", Antiquity 17 (1943), 57-66.

Wainwright, F.T., "Field-Names of Amounderness Hundred", Hist.Soc. La Chs 97 (1945), 181-222.

Wakelin, M.F., English Dialects, London 1972.

Wallenberg, J.K., Kentish Place-Names, Uppsala 1931.

Wallenberg, J.K., Place-Names of Kent, Uppsala 1934.

Warriner, F., "Some South Cumberland Place-Names", Cu We Ant.Arch.Soc. n.s. 26 (1926), 77-102.

Watts, William, "The Place-Names of Leicestershire", Ass.Arch.Soc. 31/1 (1911), 225-42.

Webster's New Collegiate Dictionary, 2nd ed. Springfield 1945 ("A Pro
nouncing Gazetteer containing more than ten thousand names of
places" on pp. 1o54-117o).

Wheeler, G.H., "The Method of Formation of Old English Place-Names in
'hæme', '-sætan', '-tuningas'", MLR 11 (1916), 218f.

Whittaker, M., "East or West, which is Best? The Dialects of Dewsbury
and Holderness Compared", YDS VI/38 (1937), 36-45.

Wicks, A.T., "Cold Harbour", NQ. SoDo 18 (1926), 132-34.

Wiegert, H., "Jim an' Nell" von W.F.Rock. Eine Studie zum Dialekt von
Devonshire, Palaestra 137, Berlin 1921.

Wildman, W.B., "Yetminster", NQ. SoDo 1o (19o6-o7), 11f.

Williams, I., "Lanercost", Cu We Ant.Arch.Soc. n.s. 52 (1952), 67-69.

Williamson, F., "Notes on Walker's Place-Names of Derbyshire", DAJ 49
(1927), 143-198, and DAJ 5o (1928-29), 1-5o.

Williamson, F., "Old Derby Street Names", DAJ 63 (1942), 1-27.

Wilson, J., "The Original Name of Hayes Castle", Cu We Ant.Arch.Soc.
n.s. 16 (1916), 29-39.

Wyld, H.C., The Name 'Liverpool'. Its Origin and History. Liverpool
19o9.

Wyld, H.C., "The Treatment of Old English $\bar{y}$ in the Dialects of the Mid
land, and South Eastern Counties, in Middle English", EStn 47
(1913), 1-58.

Wyld, H.C., "Old English $\bar{y}$ in the Dialects of the South, and South
Western Counties in Middle English", EStn 47 (1913), 145-66.

Zachrisson, R.E., A Contribution to the Study of Anglo-Norman Influence on English Place-Names, Lund Universitets Årsskrift,
Lund 19o9.

Zachrisson, R.E., "The French Definite Article in English Place-
Names", Anglia 34 (1911), 3o8-53.

Zachrisson, R.E., "Some Yorkshire Place-Names, York, Ure, Jervaulx",
MLR 21 (1926), 361-67.

Zachrisson, R.E., "Six Groups of English River-Names", ZONF 2 (1926),
134-47.

Zachrisson, R.E., "Two Anglo-Keltic Place-Names", SN 1 (1928), 1o9-1

Zachrisson, R.E., "River-Names in Suffolk and North Devonshire",
SN 2 (1929), 56-66.

Zachrisson, R.E., "English Place-Name Puzzles", SN 5 (1932-33), 1-69.

Zachrisson, R.E., "The Meaning of English Place-Names in the Light of
the Terminal Theory", SN 6 (1933-34), 25-89.

Zachrisson, R.E., "The Meaning of the Place-Names of Dorset in the
Light of the Terminal Rule", SN 6 (1933-34), 133-63.

Zachrisson, R.E., English Place-Name Puzzles, Uppsala 1935.

Zachrisson, R.E., "English Place-Name Compounds Containing Descriptiv
Nouns in the Genitive", EStn 7o (1935-36), 6o-73.

Zachrisson, R.E., "Studies on the -ing Suffix in Old English Place-
Names with Some Etymological Notes", SN 9 (1936-37), 66-129.

1

A

Abbey/Cu
  æbə GlossCu xvii
Abbey Foregate/Sa (in Shrewsbury)
  æbi fɔrit GlossSa 515
Abbotsford/Nf
  æbətsfəd EPD,Schr.,Kruis.
Abbotsham/D
  æpsəm PND 83
  æbətsəm BBC,BCE
Abbotskerswell/D
  'æbəts'kə:zwəl BBC,BCE
Abbotsley/Hu
  ævəzli, olim
  ɔ:bzli PNBdHu 252
Abbotston/W
  loc. æbəstn PNW(i) 5
Abdon/Sa
  æbdən Schr.
Abenhall/Gl
  'abənɔ:l PNGl III/21o
Aberford/WRY
  abəfəþ PNYW IV/97
Abingdon/Brk
  æbiŋdən EPD,DEPN,Schr.,Chis.
  æbiŋdn Kruis.
Abinger/Sr
  æbindʒə PNSr 259,EPD,BBC,
            DEPN,Schr.,Kruis.,
            Dodgson(2)359 and
            (3)142,Zachr.(1)349
  æbəndʒə PNWa(i)28,PNE&W
Abinger Hammer/Sr
  æbindʒə hæmə BBC,PNE&W
Abington/Ca,Np
  æbintən BBC,ONCa 24
Abram/La
  æbrəm DEPN,BBC,BCE
Abridge/Ess
  'eibridʒ PNEss 6o,DEPN,BBC,
  Abthorpe/Np   BCE
  adþrəp PNNp 89
Aby/Li
  eibi DEPN,BBC,BCE
Acaster Selby/WRY
  'e:kastə PNYW IV/216
  jækistə Hope
Accrington/La
  ækriŋtən EPD,Schr.
Ackholt/K
  eikɔl PNK
Ackingford Bridge/Ess
  ɔ:kənfɔ:d PNEss 53
Acklam/ERY,NRY
  akləm PNYE 147,PNYN 162
Ackroyd/WRY
  ækrɔid, eik- PNSWY 52

Ackton/WRY
  eiktən, æk- PNSWY 52
Acland/D
  æklənd EPD
Acle/Nf
  eikl DEPN,BBC,BCE,DNf 42
  eikli BCE; see also note below
Acol/K
  'eikɔl BBC,PNK
Acol Rd/Ldn
  æk(ə)l EPD
Acomb/Nb
  eikəm EPD,BBC
  jekəm PNNbDu 1
Acomb/NRY
  eikəm EPD,BBC,BCE
  jækəm PNYN 44,ED 61
  jekəm ED 61
Acomb/WRY
  eikəm EPD,BBC,Hope
  jækəm PNYW IV/228,Hope
  e:kəm PNYW IV/228
Acorn Bank/We
  ækərən bæŋk PNE'side 65
Acre/La,Nf
  eikə, ɑ:kə Schr.
Acre/WRY
  eakər DDd 12
Acreland Gn/Ess
  eglən PNEss 484
  aglən; eglənd ("a modern cor-
            ruption") EssDD 158
Acrewalls/Cu
  jækəwɔ:z GlossCu xvii
Acrise/K
  eikri:s BBC,PNK
  eikris BBC
Acton æktən EPD,Schr.
Acton/Chs
  aktən, aktn PNChs 126
  akn DSChs 21
Acton Bridge/Chs
  akn PNChs II/ix,GlossChs
Acton Burnell/Sa
  'æktən bə:'nel BBC
Adamthwaite/We
  ædəmfət PNE'side 67
  ædəmþweit EPD
Adbaston/St
  ædbəstən BBC
Adderstone/Nb
  eðəsən PNNbDu 2
Addingrove/Bk
  ɑ:ngrouv PNBk 126
Addington ædintən EPD,Schr.
Addiscombe/Sr
  olim ædʒkəm PNSr 49
  ædiskəm EPD

1) "The villagers of the present day call the place ACLEY [= ækli ?]
   and OAKLEY [= oukli]" (PNNf).

Addlestone/Sr
  ædlstoun BBC
  ædlstən EPD
Addlethorpe/WRY
  adlþrəp PNYW V/33
Adel/WRY
  adl, aðl PNYW IV/189
  ædl DEPN,EPD,BBC,BCE
Adel-cum-Eccup/WRY
  ædl kəm ekəp BBC
Adelphi/Ldn
  ə'delfi EPD
Adgarley/La
  adgɑ:li PNLa 21o
Adgestone/Wt
  ædʒtn, ædʒəstn PNWt 51
Adisham/K
  ædiʃəm BBC,PNK
  ædsəm PNK,Hope
Adlestrop/Gl
  ædlstrəp PNGl I/211
  ædlstrɔp BBC
Adlington/Chs
  olim adlitn PNChs II/vii,
                GlossCu
  adliŋtən PNChs II/vii
Adstone/Np
  ædsən PNNp 38
Adur/Sx (r.n.)
  eidə BBC
Adversane/Sx
  'ædvəsein BBC
Adwalton/WRY
  'adwɔltən, adətən PNYW III/2o
  æðətən Hope
Adwick-le-Street/WRY
  'ædik lə 'stri:t DEPN,BBC,
                      BCE,Hope
Adwick-upon-Dearne/WRY
  ædik DEPN,ONwick 363
Affpuddle/Do
  ɑ:fpʌdl PNDo(i)166
  ɑ:fpidl PNDo I/288,DDo
Afton/D
  ɑ:tən PND 5o5
Afton/Wt
  æ:ftən PNWt 124
Agar/Ldn
  eigɑ:, eigə EPD
Aglionby/Cu
  ælənbi Hope
Agney/K
  ægni PNK
Aigill Sike/Cu (r.n.)
  aikəl PNCu 3
Aike/ERY
  jak, jak əbak ə(d) arəm
            PNYE 16o

Aiketgate/Cu (also spelt Aiket Gate
  ɛ:kətjət PNCu 2o5
  ɛ:kət jet PNE'side 76
Ailsia/Co
  eiljə BCE
Ailwood/Do
  eilud PNDo I/7,PNDo(i)118
Ainderby Quernhow/NRY
  ɛəndəbi kwɑ:nə PNYN 223
Ainstable/Cu
  enstəbl PNCu 168,PNE'side 74
Ainsworth/La
  einzwə:þ EPD
  einzwəþ EPD,Kruis.
Ainsworth Lane/Chs
  einz- PNChs III/196
Ainthorpe/NRY
  eintrəp, -þrəp GlossClv,s.n.
           Thorp,EDD,s.n.Thorpe
Aira Beck/Cu (r.n.) → Airy Beck
Air(e)y Beck/Cu (r.n.)
  ɛ:rə RN 3
  ɛəri EPD
Aish/D
  æʃ BBC,BCE
Aiskew/NRY
  ɛəskiu PNYN 236
Aislaby/Du
  eizlbi BBC
Aislaby/NRY
  eizlbi EPD ("loc."),BBC,BCE
  eizləbi EPD
in Pickering Lythe Wapentake:
  ɛəzləbi PNYN 77
  hesəlbi Atkinson 432
in Whitby Strand Wapentake:
  ɛəzəlbi PNYN 119
Aisthorpe/Li
  eisþɔ:p BBC,BCE
  eistrəp GlossSWLi
Akeld/Nb
  'eikeld DEPN,BBC,BCE[1]
Akeman Street
  eikmən BBC
Albany/Ldn
  ɔ:lbəni, ɔl-, æl- EPD
Albemarle/Sr
  'ælbimɑ:l EPD,MEG
  'ælbə'mɑ:l EPD,Schr.
  ´ _ _   Chis.,Kruis.
Alberbury/Sa
  ɔ:lbəbəri BBC
Albourne/Sx
  a:bərn PNSx 215
  ɔ:lbɔ:n BBC,Hope
Albright Hussey/Sa
  ɔ(:)lbrait EPD

1) "There seems now to be no trace of the old pron. with loss of
    final d" (PNNbDu 3).

Albrighton/Sa
 ɔ:l'braɪt(ə)n BBC
 'ɔ:braɪtn, 'ɔ(:)l- EPD
Albrighton nr Shrewsbury/Sa
 eɪbətən GlossSa 515
Albrighton nr Shiffnal/Sa
 ɔ:bətn GlossSa 515
Alburgh/Nf
 a:bərə PNNf,DNf 42
Albury/Hrt,Sr
 ɔ:lbəri PNSr 219,BBC,Schr., Bchm.8
 a:bəri, ɔlbəri PNHrt 169
Alcester/Wa
 ɔ:lstə DEPN,EPD,BBC,BCE, Schr.521,Kruis., PNWa 193
 ɔlstə EPD,Schr. 521
 ɔ:stə Hope,GlossSEWo 81
Alchester/O
 ɔ:lstə PNO 241
Alciston/Sx
 a:sən, a:stən PNSx 414
 ɔ:lsistən BBC,BCE
 a:stn DEPN
 ælsistən PNSx(i)2
Alconbury/Hu
 ɔ:kənbri PNBdHu 231
 ɔ:lkənbəri, ɔ:k(ə)nbəri BBC
 ɔ:(l)kənbəri BCE
Alcott/Gl
 ɔ:lkət EPD,Schr.521,Kruis.
 ɔlkət EPD
Alcumlow/Chs
 'alkəmlou, a:kəmlou PNChs II/3o4
Aldborough/Nf
 ɔ:l(d)bərə, ɔl- EPD
 ɔ:ldbərə BBC
 ɔ:lbə Hope
Aldborough/WRY
 ɔ:ldbərə BBC
 ɔ(:)l(d)b(ə)rə, loc.
 ɔ:brə EPD
Aldbourne/W
 olim ɔ:bərn PNW 291,Hope
 ɔ:lbɔ:n BBC
Aldbrough/ERY
 ɔ:bruf, ɔ:lbrə PNYE 59
 ɔ:ldbrə BBC
 ɔ:bræf, ɔlbrə Hope,GlossHol 17
 ɔ:bərə Hope
Aldbrough/NRY
 ɔ:dbrə PNYN 296
 ɔ:ldbrə BBC,BG

Aldburgh/NRY
 ɔ:dbrə PNYN 23o
Aldbury/Hrt
 ɔ:b(ə)ri PNHrt 26
 ɔ(:)ldb(ə)ri EPD
 ɔ:l(d)bəri BBC,BCE
Aldby/Cu
 ɔ:lbi PNCu 186 (for A. in Dacre Hd),PNE'side 74,GlossCu xvii
 ɔlbi PNCu xli (for A. in Dacre Hd)
 ɔ:dbi Hope
Aldchurch/Wo
 ɔ:ltʃə:tʃ Hope
Aldcliff/La
 ɔ:klif PNLa(ii),RitterLa 188
Alde/Sf (r.n.)
 ɔ:ld BBC
Aldeburgh/Sf (= Aldborough)
 ɔ(:)l(d)b(ə)rə EPD
 ɔ:lbərə BBC,BCE,Kruis.
 ɔ:ldbərə BCE
Aldeby/Nf
 ɔ:ldəbi BBC
Aldenham/Hrt
 olim ɔ:dnəm PNHrt 59
 ɔ(:)ldnəm EPD
 ɔ:ld(ə)nəm BBC
 ɔ:ldənəm Kruis.
Alderbury/W
 ɔ:ldəbəri BBC
Alderley/Chs
 olim ɔ:ðərli, ɔ:dərli, now
 ald-, ɔ:ldərli PNChs II/vii
 ɔ:ldəli BBC
Alderley Edge/Chs
 ɔ:ðərli edʒ PNChs II/vii,Gloss Chs (see note 1)
 ɔ:dli PNChs II/vii,GlossChs,Hope
Aldermaston/Brk
 ɔ:ldəmɑ:st(ə)n BBC
Aldersey/Chs
 ɔ:ldərsi PNChs IV/82
Aldersgate/Ldn
 ɔ:ldəzgit, -geit EPD,Schr.,Kruis.
 ɔl- EPD
 ɔ:ldəzget Schr.
 ɔldəzgit CPP (for A.Street[2] under-ground)
Aldershot/Ha,Np
 ɔ:ldəʃɔt EPD,BBC,BCE (for A. in Np),Schr.
 ɔl- EPD
Aldersley/St
 ɔ:ðəli Hope

1) "The latter [is] not often heard now [i.e. in 1886], but [was] frequent forty years since" (GlossChs).
2) This underground station is now called Barbican.

Alderton/Gl
 ɔldətən, ɑ:- PNGl II/49
Alderton/Sf
 ɔlətn PNDVall 54
Alderwasley/Db
 ældəwəz'li: EPD,BBC,BCE
 æləz'li: BBC,BCE
 ænəzli:, æləzli Hope[1]
 æl- DEPN
Aldford/Chs
 ɔ:ldfəd, ɔ:d- PNChs IV/77
Aldgate/Ldn
 ɔ:l(d)git, ɔl-, -geit EPD
 ɔ:ldgit Schr.
 ɔlgit CPP 66
 rarely -get Bchm.57
Aldingbourne/Sx
 ælnbɔ:rn, ældiŋbɔ:n PNSx 62
 ɔ:ldiŋbɔ:n Hope(see note 1)
Aldridge/St
 ɔ(:)ldridʒ EPD
Aldrington/Sx
 ɔ:ldriŋtən Hope[1]
Aldsworth/Gl,Sx
 ɔ(:)ldzwə(:)þ EPD
Aldwark/Db
 ɔ:ldwək BBC
Aldwark/NRY
 ɔ:dwɑ:k PNYN 2o
 ɔ:ldwək BBC,BCE
Aldwick/Sx
 ɔ:ldwik BBC
Aldwinkle/Np
 ɑ:nikəl PNNp 177
Aldworth/Brk
 ɔ:ldwəþ Schr.521
Aldwych/Ldn
 ɔ:ldwitʃ EPD,BBC
 ɔl- EPD
Alethorpe/Nf
 eilþɔ:p BBC,BCE
Alfardisworthy/D
 ɔ:lzəri PND 133,PNND 138
Alfold/Sr
 ɔ:(l)fould PNSr 222
 ælfould, ɑ:fould BBC,BCE
 ɔ:lfould BCE
 ɑ:lfould Hope
Alford/Ha,Li,So
 ɔ:lfəd EPD,BBC (for A.in Li),
 BCE (for A. in Li),
 Schr.,Kruis.
 ɔl- EPD
 æl- Kruis.,MEG 291
 loc. ɑ:l- Schr.

Alfreton/Db
 ɔfətən PNDb 187,Hope[2]
 ɔ(:)lfrit(ə)n EPD,BBC
 ɔ:lfrətən BCE,Hope
Alfrick/Wo
 ɔlfrik, ɑ:frik PNWo 28
Alfriston/Sx
 ɔ:stən, ɑ:fstən, ɑ:səntaun
 PNSx 4
 ɔ:l'frist(ə)n BBC
 ɔ:l'fristən EPD,BCE,Hope
 ɔl'fristən EPD
 ɑ:fstən Hope
 ɔ:sən SxArch.Soc.
Algarkirk/Li
 ɔ:lgəkə:k, ɔ:ldʒə- BBC,BCE
Alkborough/Li
 ɔ:lkbərə BBC
Alkerton/O
 ɔ:lkətən PNO 392
Alkham/K
 ɔ:(l)kəm BBC,BCE,PNK
Alkington/Gl
 ɔ:lkiŋtən BBC
Alkington/Sa
 ɔ:(l)kiŋtən BBC
Alkrington/La
 ɔ:lkriŋtən BBC
All Cannings/W
 kæninz GlossW 214
Allen/Co;Do;Nb (r.n.)
 ælin EPD
Allendale/Nb
 ælindeil EPD
 ælən- EPD,Schr.
Allen Haw/WRY
 ælən ɑ: DDd 12
Allenheads/Nb
 ælinhedz Schr.
Allens/Wt
 ælənz PNWt 286
Allenten/Nb → Alwinton
Aller/D,Do,So
 ælər DDo
 ɔlə, ɔ:lə BBC,BCE (for A. in S
Allerston/NRY
 ɔləstən PNYN 93
Allerton/La,So,WRY
 ælət(ə)n EPD,BBC
 ɔlət(ə)n BBC
 ælətən BCE (for A. in La),
 Schr.
 ɔlətən BCE (for A. in Li),
 Schr. ("locally")

1) Hope's transcriptions are <u>Allersley,Alldingbourne</u> and <u>Alldrington</u>.
2) Hope's transcriptions <u>Offerton</u> and <u>Orlfreton</u> are rendered [ɔfətn]
 and [ɔ:lfritn] in PNDb(i) I/159f.

Allerton Mauleverer/WRY
 ælət(ə)n mɔːl'evərə BBC
Allesley/Wa
 ɔːzli PNWa 152
 ɔːlzli BBC
Allestree/Db
 aləstri PNDb 423
 alistri: BBC
 æləstri: BCE
Allet Common/Co
 ælit BBC
Alleyn Pk (in Dulwich),
Alleyn's School/Ldn
 ælin(z) BBC
Alleyne's Grammar School in
Stevenage/Hrt
 æleinz BBC
Allhallows Fm/D
 ælenz PND 564
Allingham/Sa
 æliŋəm EPD
Allington
 æliŋtən BBC,BCE (for A.
  in K)
Allisland/D
 ɔːlənd PND 1o6
Allostock/Chs
 ɔːlostək PNChs II/ix
 ɔːlɔstək GlossChs
 ɔːlɔstɔk PNChs II/216
Alma/Db
 ælmə EPD
Almeley/He (also spelt Almerley)
 æmli, :m li BBC,BCE
Almer/Do
 ælmə BBC
Almerley/He → Almeley
Almiston/D
 amsən PND 8o
Almodington/Sx
 ɔːlmɔdiŋtən PNSx 85
Almondbury/WRY
 eimbri DEPN,PNYW II/256,
  PNSWY 57,Hope
 ɔːmbri PNYW II/256,Schr.
  ("loc."),PNSWY 57
 oːmbri, eːmbri DHd 78
 aːmbr , ɔːmbrə, oumbi Hope
 aːmbəri Kruis.
 eimbəri, ɔːmbəri EPD,BBC,BCE
 ælmən(d)bəri, aːmən(d)- EPD
 ælməndbəri BBC,BCE
 ɔːməndberi Schr.
 aːmən(d)b(ə)ri Bchm.241

Almonds/WRY
 ɔːməndz, ɔlməndz DDd 15
Almondsbury/Gl
 ɔːmzbəri, aːmənzberi PNGl III/1o5
 aːmən(d)zb(ə)ri EPD
 aːmzbəri BBC
 eimzbəri Hope
Almshoe/Hrt
 olim ɔːlsi PNHrt 13
Aln/Nb (r.n.) (also spelt Alne)
 eil DEPN,RN 5,PNNbDu 4
 jel RN 5,PNNbDu 4
 æln DEPN,BBC,BCE
Alne/Nb (r.n.) (see previous entry)
Alne/NRY
 ɔːn DEPN,EPD,BBC,BCE,PNYN 21
 aːn PNYN 21
 hɔːn Hope
Alne/Wa (Gt and Lt A.)
 ɔːn PNWa 194,EPD,BBC,BCE
 ɔːln BBC,BCE
Alne/Wa (r.n.)
 ɔːn DEPN,RN 8
 æn Schr.
Alnemouth/Nb → Alnmouth
Alney/Gl (an island)
 ɔːlni Schr.
Alnham/Nb
 jeldəm PNNbDu 4
 ælnəm DEPN,BBC,BCE
Alnmouth/Nb
 eilmauþ DEPN,EPD,BBC,BCE,Schr.,
  284,Schr.("loc."),PNE&W,
  Hope
 ælnmauþ EPD,BBC
 ænmauþ, -məþ Schr.
 eilməþ Chis.,Kruis.
 jelməþ PNNbDu 4
Alnwick/Nb
 ænik DEPN,EPD,BBC,BCE,Schr.,
  Chis.,Hope,PNE&W,Kruis.,
  MEG 2o8,Mawer(2)92
 anik PNNbDu 5
 æln(w)ik Mawer(2)92
Alperton/Mx
 olim æpətən PNMx 52
 ælpət(ə)n EPD,BBC
Alphamstone/Ess
 ælf'æmstən PNEss 4o5
Alpheton/Sf
 æl'fiːt(ə)n BBC
 æl'fiːtən BCE
Alpington/Nf
 ælpiŋtən BBC

1) "[The place] is called by the polite Aimbury [= eimbri]; by the gen-
uine Yorkshireman, Aumbury [= ɔːmbri], or, better still, Oambury
[= oum-]" (DAl&Hd).

Alpraham/Chs
  ælprəm   PNChs III/3oo
  ɔːprəm   PNChs III/3oo,Gloss
              Chs
  ɔːpərəm   GlossChs
Alresford
  ɔːlrisfəd EPD,Kruis.
  ælrisfɔːd Schr.
Alresford/Ess
  ɑːlzfəd   PNEss 325,DEPN
  -s-   BBC,BCE
  eils-   BBC
Alresford/Ha
  ɔːlsfəd   DEPN,EPD("loc."),
           BBC,BCE,Schr.
           ("loc."),Kruis.,
           Bchm.,Hope
  ɑːls-   BBC
  ælrisfəd Bchm.9
Alrewas/St
  ɔːlrəs   DEPN,BBC,BCE,Hope
  ɔːlrəwəs BBC
Alsager/Chs
  'ɔːlseidʒər PNChs III/2
  ɔːseidʒə Hope
  ɔːl'seidʒə EPD,BBC
  ɔːl'sædʒə PNE&W
  'ɔːlsədʒə DEPN,EPD,BBC,BCE
  'ɔːlsidʒə EPD
  ɔːdʒər   PNChs III/2 ("older
           local"),GlossChs
  ɔːdʒə   GlossChs(i)xi,H.A.(2)
           45
Alsatia (old name for Whitefriars
    in London)
  æl'seiʃə EPD,BBC
  æl'seiʃjə, -ʃiə EPD
Alscott/D
  ɔːlskət   BCE
  (see also s.n. Alverdiscott)
Alsop/Db
  ɔːlsɔp, ɔl-, -səp EPD
Alston/Cu,D,La
  ɔlstən   EPD
  ɔːlstən EPD,BBC,BCE (for A.
          in Cu)
  ɔːstən   PNCu 171,Hope (for A.
          in Cu)
  ɔlstn   PNLa 145
  ɔːstən   PNE'side 66 (for A.
          in Cu)
Alstone/Gl
  ɔːlstən PNGl II/41
  ælstən   BBC
Alston(e)field/St
  ɔːrsfild Ellis 444
Alswick Hall/Hrt (or -wyck)
  ɔːsik   PNHrt 181
  æsik   BBC

Alt/La (r.n.)
  ɔːlt   BBC
Altarnun/Co
  æltə'nʌn BBC,PNE&W
Altcar/La
  'ɔːltkɑ. BBC
  ækər, ɔːlkə PNLa(ii)
Altham/La
  ɔːlθəm, æltəm, ɔːltəm BBC,BCE
Althorne/Ess
  'ɔːlθɔːn BBC
Althorp/Np
  ɔːltrəp   PNNp 78,EPD,BBC,BCE
  ɔːlθɔːp, ɔl-, ɔltrəp EPD
  ɔlθrəp   EDD,s.n. Thorpe
Althorpe/Li
  ɔːlθɔːp BBC,BCE
  ɔːθrəp   Hope
Altofts/WRY
  ɔːltəfts, ɔltəs BBC
Alton
  ɔːlt(ə)n EPD,BBC
  ɔl-   EPD
  ɔːltən, æltən Schr.
  ɔːltn   Kruis.
Alton/Ha
  ɔːltən   BCE,Hope
Alton Pancras/Do
  ɔːltən   PNDo 193
Altrincham/Chs
  ɔltriŋəm PNChs II/7,EPD
  ɔːltriŋəm EPD,BBC,BCE,PNE&W,
           Hope
  ɔːtridʒəm PNChs II/ix,GlossChs,
           DSLa,MEG 35
  ɔltridʒəm Dodgson(2)226
  ɔːtrintʃəm GlossChs(i)xi
  ɔːtədʒəm PNChs II/ix,GlossChs,
           Hope
  ɔːtrindʒəm Hope
  -indʒ-   Dodgson(2)36o ("former
           ly"),DEPN
  θrutʃəm GlossChs
  θrʌtʃəm Hope (or -u- ?)
Altringham/Sa
  ætʃəm   Hope
  ɔːltriŋəm Chis.
Alum Bay/Wt
  æləm bei PNWt 227
Alvanley/Chs
  ɔːvənli PNChs III/219 ("older
           local"),GlossChs(i)xi
           GlossChs,Hope,H.A.(2)
           45
  alvənli PNChs III/219
  ɔːvnli   Ellis 421
Alvaston/Chs
  alvəstən PNChs III/28
  ælvəstən BBC

Alvaston/Db
  ælvəstən   BBC
  ɔlvəstən   PNDb 425
  ɔ:lvəstən Hope[1]
  ɔ:vəstən Ellis 446
Alvechurch/Wo
  ɔ:lvtʃə:tʃ   BBC,EPD
  ɔ:ltʃə:tʃ   PNWo 332,PNWo(i)4,
            DEPN,Hope,GlossSEWo
            81
  ælvtʃə:tʃ Bchm.8
Alvecote/Wa
  ɔ:kət   PNWa 24
Alvediston/W
  ɔ:lstən PNW 199
Alveley/Sa
  ɑ:vli   PNWo 333
  ævli   BBC
Alverdiscott/D (=Alscott)
  ælvə'diskət BBC ("the more
             usual form"),BCE
  ɔ:lskət PND 112,PNND 49,BBC
          Hope
Alverstoke/Ha
  'ælvəstouk BBC
Alverstone/Wt
  (h)ælvərstn PNWt 51
  ɔ(:)lvəst(ə)n EPD
Alverstone Fm/Wt
  ælvərstn PNWt 235
Alverthorpe/WRY (now called
         Kirkhamgate)
  'ɔ:lvəbɔ:p BBC,BCE
Alverton/Nt
  ɔlvətn   PNNt(i) 1
Alvescot/O[2]
  tɔ:lzkɔt,ælvzkɔt,ælvezkɔt
          PNO 298
  ɔ:lskət DEPN,EPD ("loc."),
          BBC,BCE,PNO(i)38,
          Bchm.8
  ælskət BBC,BCE,PNO(i)38
  ælviskət EPD,Schr.
  ælviskɔt EPD,BBC,Bchm.8
  ælveskɔt BCE
Alveston/Gl,Wa
  ælvistən EPD(for A.in Gl),
          BBC
Alvingham/Li
  'ɔ:lviŋəm BBC,BCE
Alvington/D
  ɔ:lviŋtən PND 288,BBC,BCE
Alvington/Gl
  ælviŋtən BBC,BCE
  ælintən Hope

Alvington Manor/Wt
  ælvntn PNWt 95
Alwalton/Hu
  ælətən PNBdHu 180,Hope
  ɔ:lwɔ:lt(ə)n BBC
Alwin Gallery/Ldn
  ɔ:lwin BBC
Alwinton/Nb (=Allenton)
  'ælwint(ə)n BBC
  aləntən PNNbDu 5
Alwoodley/WRY
  ɔ:dlə PNYW IV/179
  'ɔ:lwudli PNYW IV/179,BBC,BCE
Alwoodley Gate/WRY
  ænli geit Hope
Amberley/Sx
  æməli PNSx 146
  æmbəli Schr.
Ambersham/Sx
  æməʃəm PNSx 97
  æmbəʃəm BBC
Ambleside/We
  æmblsaid EPD,Schr.
  æmlsid PNE'side 69
  amlsəd DBo
Ambresbury/W → Amesbury
Ambrosden/O
  æmɑ:zdən PNO 161,Hope
  'æmbrouzdən BBC

Amen Corner, - House/Ldn
  eimən EPD,BBC
America Cottages, - Wood/Wt
  ə'mɑ:riki PNWt 168
Amersham/Bk
  æməʃəm EPD,BBC
Amesbury/W (=Ambresbury)
  eimzbəri PNW(i) 13,Kruis.
  ei- DEPN
  eimzb(ə)ri EPD
  æmbri (or eimbri?) Hope[3]
Ameshaugh/Cu
  eimshɑ:f PNCu 173
Amos Hill/Wt
  eiməs PNWt 227
Amotherby/NRY
  æməbi, eməbi PNYN 45
  eiməbi Hope
Amounderness/La
  -'--- DEPN
Ampleforth/NRY
  æmplfɔ:b BBC
Ampney Crucis/Gl
  'æm(p)ni 'kru:sis BBC

1) Hope's transcription <u>Orlverstun</u> is rendered [ɔ:lvəstn]in PNDb(i)I/164.
2) Hope's transcription <u>Alscott</u> could be any of the above.
3) His transcription is <u>Ambry</u>.

Ampney St. Peter/Gl
  'æm(p)ni snt 'pi:tə BBC
Ampthill/Bd
  æm(p)t(h)il EPD,Bchm.lo5
  æmthil BBC,Schr.
  æmtəl PNBdHu 67
Ancaster/Li
  æŋkəstə Kruis.
Ancholme/Li (r.n.)
  æŋkhoum EPD
  æŋk- DEPN
Ancoats/La
  'æŋkouts BBC
Andover/Ha
  'ændouvə EPD,BBC
  ændəvə EPD,Schr.,Kruis.
Andoversford/Gl
  'andəvəz'fɔ:rd PNGl I/i68
  ændouvəzfɔ:d BBC
Anerley/K
  ænəli Schr.,PNK
Angarrack/Co
  æŋ'gærək Jenner(2)3oo,3o3
Angerholme/We
  æŋgrəm PNE'side 65
Angersleigh/So
  'eindʒə zli BBC,BCE
  eindʒ- DEPN
Angerton Moss/La
  aŋətn PNLa 221
Anglia
  æŋgliə EPD,Schr.
  æŋgljə EPD
Angmering/Sx
  'æŋməriŋ BBC,BCE
Anick/Nb
  einik PNNbDu 6,BBc,BCE
Anlaby/ERY
  ænləbi BBC,BCE
Annaside Rake/We
  ænəsit rɛ:k PNE'side 69
Annesley/Nt
  ænzli PNNt 112,PNNt(i)2,
             BBC,BCE
  ænizli BBC
  ænəzli BCE
Annesley Woodhouse/Nt
  vulgo wudəs PNNt 112
Annet/Co (an island)
  ænit BBC
Anstey
  ænsti EPD
Ansty/Do
  ɑ:nsti DDo
Ansty/Sx (also spelt Anstye)
  æn'stai PNSx 261,BBC,BCE
Anthorn/Cu
  entərn PNCu 123

Antony/Co
  æntəni BBC
Anwick/Li
  ænik EPD,DEPN
Apes Down/Wt
  eips dæun PNWt 96
Apethorpe/Np
  æpþɔ:p PNNp 198,BBC
  eipþɔ:p BBC
Apperley/Gl,Nb,WRY
  æpəli EPD
Appleby/Le,Li,We
  æplbi EPD,Schr.,PNE'side 68
                  (for A. in We)
  aplbi DKe 6 (for A. in We)
Appledore/D,K
  æpldɔ: EPD,Schr.
  æpldɔə EPD ("rare")
Appledram/Sx (also spelt Apuldram
  æpldrəm PNO(i) 15o,BCE
Appleford/Brk,Wt
  æplfəd EPD,DWt,s.n.rearen
  æplvərd PNWt 14o
Applehaigh/WRY
  æblda: Hope
Appleshaw/Ha
  aplʃɑ: DDo
Applethwaite/Cu
  aplþət PNCu 321
  æplþət PNE'side 66
Appleton
  æplt(ə)n EPD
  eipəltən PNK (for A. in K)
Appletreewick/WRY
  apt(ə)rik PNYW VI/78
  'æpl'tri:wik BBC
  æplwik Hope,ONwick 363
Appuldurcombe Ho/Wt
  'æplikəm, -ku:m, æpl'də:rkəm
                      PNWt 141
  æpldə'ku:m EPD
Apronfull of Stones/WRY (f.n.)
  æprən ful ə stu:ənz GlossSh 29
Apse Manor Fm/Wt
  æps PNWt 168,DWt,s.n. mummy
Apsley/Bd,Hrt,Wa
  æpsli EPD
Apuldram/Sx → Appledram
Arborfield/Brk
  ɑ:bəfi:ld BBC
Arbor Low/Db
  ɑ:tə Leyland 188
  "Arbor or Arbe as it is various
  called" Thomp.68 (quoting fro
  an article by J.Lubbock in The
  Reliquary XX, p.81, who visite
  the place in 1879)

Archenfield/He
  ɑːkənfiːld (for the diocese)
  ɑːtʃənfiːld (for the place)
  dial. ɑːtʃnfiːld   DHe 43
Arcot/Nb
  ɑːˈkɔt   EPD,Schr.
  ˈɑːkət, ˈɑːkɔt   Schr.
Ardale Head/Cu
  ɑːrl hiːd   PNCu 229,PNE'side 74
Ardeley/Hrt
  jɑːdli   PNHrt 151 ("olim"),Hope
Ardeley Wood End/Hrt
  jɑːdli wud iːnd,
  jɑrli wud iːn   Ellis 2ol
Arden/Chs,Wa,NRY
  ɑːdn   EPD
  ɑːdən   Schr.,Kruis.
Ardingley/Sx
  ɑːdiŋˈlai   PNSx 251,Mawer(4)285
          DEPN,BBC,BCE
  ˈɑːdiŋlai   EPD,Hope
  ɑːdiŋli,ˈærdiŋlai   PNSx(i)6
Ardeleigh/Ess
  ɑːdli   EPD
Ardley/O
  ɑːdli   EPD
Ardwick/La
  ɑːdwik   BBC,EPD
Areley Kings/Wo
  ɛːəli   PNWo 29
Arey Force/Cu
  ɛːrə foərs   PNE'side 63
Arfleet Mills/Do
  ˈæfliːt   PNDo I/7
  ɑːfliːt   PNDo(i)118
Argam/ERY
  arəm   PNYE lo8
Arkesden/Ess
  ɑːkizdən , olim ɑːgzdən
             PNEss 516
  ɑːksdən   BBC
Arkholme with Cawood/La
  ɑːkhoum wið keiwud   BBC
  ærəm   DEPN,PNLa(ii),Hope,
          H.A.(2)33 ("locally")
Arlecdon/Cu
  ɑːlkdən, æːrəltən   PNCu 335
  ɑːrəltən   GlossCu xvii
  ɑːləkdən   BBC,BCE
  ɑːltən   Hope
Arlesey/Bd
  ɑːlzi   BBC
Arleston/Db,Sa
  ɑːlstən   BBC,BCE(for A. in Sa)
Arlingham/Gl
  ɑːliŋəm   BBC

Arlington/D,Gl,Sx
  æliŋtən   PNSx 4o8
  ɑːliŋtən   EPD
  ɑːliŋtn   Kruis.
Armathwaite/Cu
  ɑːmwit   Hope
  ɑːrmhwit   PNE'side 7o
Armboth/Cu
  armbə   PNCu 311
  ærmbəþ   PNE'side 64
Armingford/Ca
  ɑːmiŋfəd   ONCa 186
Armitage/St
  ˈɑːmitidʒ   EPD
Armon Ho/Cu
  armənt   PNCuWe 8
Arne/Do
  ɑːn   EPD
Arnold/K,Nt,ERY
  ɑːnəld, vulgo ɑːnəl   PNNt 113
  ɑːn(ə)ld   EPD
Arnos Grove/Mx
  ɑːnouz   PNMx 68
Arpinge/K
  ˈɑːpindʒ   PNK,BBC,BCE,H.A.(i)179
Arram/ERY (two places)
  arəm   PNYE 79, PNYE 19o
Arrathorne/NRY
  arəþɔːn   PNYN 24o
Arreton/Wt
  ærətn   PNWt 6
  ærit(ə)n   BBC
Arrington/Ca
  æriŋtən   ONCa 24 [1]
Arrowe/Chs
  arou   PNChs IV/261
Arthington/WRY
  ɑːðintən   PNYW IV/193
Artlebrook Bridge, - Fm/Chs
  artl-   PNChs III/72
Arun/Sx (r.n.)
  ærən   BBC
  ær(ə)n   EPD
Arundel/Sx
  ɑːndəl   PNSx 136, RD
  ˈærəndl   DEPN,BBC,BCE,Schr.,
          Kruis.
  ɑːndl   Hope,Schr. ("loc.")
  ær(ə)ndl   EPD
  ˈærəndel   Chis.
Asby/We
  azbi   PNWe II/54
Ascot/Brk,O
  æskət   EPD,Schr.,Kruis.,Bchm.64
  æskɔt   Schr.,Bchm.64 ("rarely")

---

1) [ærŋitən] in ONCa 24 is an obvious misprint.

Asenby/NRY
  ɛəzənbi PNYN 182
Asgarby/Li
  æzgəbi BBC,BCE
Ash/K
  eʃ PNK
Ashampstead/Brk
  'æʃəmsted BBC
Ashbourne/Db
  æʃbɔːn, -bɔən,-buən,-bəːn EPD
  aʃbə(r)n Ellis 426
Ashburnham/Sx
  eʃb(ə)rəm PNSx 477
  eʃbrəm PNSx(i)7,Schr.("loc.")
  'æʃbəːnəm EPD,BBC,BCE,Kruis.
  æʃbənəm Schr.
  æʃ'bəːnəm Schr.521
  -ə:- more often heard than -ə-
Ashburton/D Bchm.67
  'æʃbətən PND 462,BCE
  æʃ'bəːtən BBC
  'æʃbəːtn EPD,Kruis.
Ashbury/Brk,D
  æʃbəri EPD
Ashby
  æʃbi EPD,BBC
Ashby nr Bottesford/Li
  æsbi GlossM&C,s.n.Assby
Ashby-de-la-Launde/Li
  'æʃbi də lə 'lɔːnd BBC
  - - lɑ - BCE
Ashby-de-la-Zouch/Le
  æʃbi də lə zuːʃ BBC
  - - lɑ - BCE
  - di lə 'zuːʃ, -zauʃ Schr.
  - de lə 'zautʃ Schr. 521
  æʃbidəlɑːˈzuːʃ EPD
  -delə- EPD
  'æʃbidələ'zuː(t)ʃ Kruis.
Ashby St. Ledgers/Np
  æʃbi snt ledʒəz BBC
Ashby Woulds/Le
  æʃbi wouldz BBC
Ashcombe/D,So
  æʃkəm EPD,Kruis.
Ashcombe Ho/Sx
  æʃ'kuːm PNSx 32o
Ashdon/Ess
  eizn PNEss 5o2
Ashdown/Sx
  æʃdaun EPD
Ashengrove/Wt
  'æʃngrouv PNWt 285
Ashey/Wt
  æʃi PNWt 25
Ashfield
  æʃfiːld EPD

Ashford
  æʃfəd EPD,Schr.
Ashford/Db
  aʃfərt, aʃfəd Ellis 426
Ashford/K
  eʃfəd, æʃfəd PNK
Ashhill/Wt
  æʃil PNWt 216
Ash Ho/WRY (a fm nr Castle Hill)
  æʃəs DHd 5
Ashill/Nf,So
  æʃhil BBC
  æʃəl Hope (for A. in Nf)
Ashington/Nb
  aʃətən DSDu
Ashknowle/Wt
  'æʃnɔːl PNWt 256
Ashley
  æʃli EPD,ONCa 183,PNK
  eʃli PNK
Ashman(h)augh/Nf
  'æʃ'mænə BBC
Ashmansworthy/D
  æʃənʒəri PND
  æʃəndʒəri PNND 31,DHtl 8
Ashmolean Museum/O
  æʃ'mouliən BBC,Schr.
  æʃmɔ'liːən Schr.
Ashmore/Do
  'æʃmɔː EPD,Bchm.69
  'æʃmɔə EPD
Ashop Clough/Db
  æʃəp klʌf BBC
Ashopton/Db
  æʃəptən EPD
Ashorne/Wa
  'æʃhɔːn BBC
Ashover/Db
  aʃə PNDb 19o
  'æʃouvə EPD
  aʃər Ellis 445
Ashow/Wa
  æʃou BBC,BCE
Ashreigny/D (also called Ringash)
  æʃ'reini PND 355,BBC,BCE
Ashton
  æʃt(ə)n EPD
  æʃtən Schr.
Ashton/Chs
  aʃn GlossChs
Ashton/Wo
  eiʃən GlossSEWo 81
Ashton Keynes/W
  æʃtən keinz PNW 4o,BBC,BCE
Ashton-in-Makerfield/La
  æʃtən in meikəfiːld BBC
Ashton-under-Lyne/La
  eiʃin Hope

Ashurst/Ha,K,Sx
  'æʃhə:st BBC
  eʃə:st,æʃə:st PNK
Ashwell
  æʃw(ə)l, -wel EPD
Ashwell (a well in Kirton-in-
  Lindsey/Li)
  eʃwel GlossM&C,s.n.Esh-well
Ashwellthorpe/Nf
  'æʃwəlþɔ:p BBC
Ashworth/La
  'æʃwɑ:þ EPD
  æʃəþ GlossR&R,DSLa
Aske/NRY
  æsk EPD
Askern/WRY (or Askerne)
  'æskə:n BBC
  æskrəm Hope,H.A.(2)45
Askerswell/Do
  æskəzwel BBC
Askham/Nt
  askəm PNNt 44
  æskəm BBC,BCE
Askham/We
  æskəm BBC,PNE'side 65
Askrigg/NRY
  æskrig EPD
Askwith/WRY
  æskit DHd 5
  æskwiþ EPD
Aslackby/Li
  eizlbi BBC,BCE,BG,Hope
Aslacton/Nf
  æsltən Hope
Aslockton/Nt
  ɔlim aslətən PNNt 219
  'æzlɔktn BBC
Asmall/La → Aspinwall
Aspatria/Cu
  spi:atri PNCu 261
  speitr PNCu 261,PNE&W
  speiətri Hope
  spiətri GlossCu xvii
  spi'atri Ellis 562
  æs'peitriə BBC,BCE
Aspenden/Hrt
  æpsdən, ɑ:spidən PNHrt 171
Aspinwall/La (also spelt Asmall)
  'æspinwɔ:l Schr.
  asməl PMLa 124
Aspley Guise/Bd
  ɑ:spli PNBdHu 113
  'æspli 'gaiz BBC
Aspull/La
  æspə PNLa(ii)
Astbury/Chs
  asbəri PNChs II/ix,GlossChs
  æsbəri PNChs II/286
  æs(t)b(ə)ri EPD,Bchm.131

Asterby/Li
  eistəbi DEPN,BBC,BCE
Astey Wood/Bd
  ɑ:sti PNBdHu 44
Astahll Leigh/O
  'æstɔ:l li:, - lei BBC
Astlam/Mx
  æsləm PNMx 17
Astle/Chs
  asl PNChs ("olim"),GlossChs
  astəl PNChs II/vii
  æsl EPD
Astley
  æstli EPD,Schr.,Bchm. 16, 132
Aston æst(ə)n EPD
Aston/Chs
  asn DSChs 21
Aston/Db
  æsn Hope
Aston/Hrt
  vulgo ɑ:sən PNHrt 117
Aston/Sx
  æstən PNSx(i) 61
Aston Clinton/Bk
  ɑ:stən klintən PNBk 142,
                  Mawer(4)285
Aston End/Hrt
  ɑ:səni:nd PNHrt 118
Aston Ingham/He
  'æstən 'iŋəm BBC
Aston juxta Mondrum/Chs
  astn [dʒʌkstə] mɔndrʌm
                PNChs III/128
Aston Rowant/O
  ɑ:stən PNO 1o2
  'æstən 'rouənt BBC
Aston Subedge/Gl
  'astən 'subidʒ PNGl I/232
Astwell/Np
  æstəl PNNp 47
Astwick/Bd
  ɑ:stwik PNBdHu 1oo
Astwick Manor/Hrt
  ɑ:stik PNHrt 126
Astwood/Bk
  æstəd PNBk 3o
Atcham/Sa (also called Attingham)
  ættʃəm Dodgson(2)361
  ætʃəm Hope,PNWa(i)28
Atchen Hill/Wo
  ættʃən Dodgson(2)361
Athelbampstone/Sf
  æþəltən Hope (or -ð- ?)[1]
Athelhampton/Do
  'æþələmtən PNDo(i)17o,
              PNDo I/299
Athelington/Sf
  æliŋtən Hope (or ɔ:1- ?)[1]

1) Hope's transcriptions are Atheltun and Allington resp.

Athelney/So
  æþ(ə)lni   EPD,BBC
  æþəlni   Schr.
Atherfield/Wt
  æðərvil, æðərfild, ɑ:þərfild
                PNWt 217
  æðəvel DWt,s.n. hobnails
Atherington/D
  æðriŋtən PND 357,PNND 57
Atherley/Sa
  ædəli Bardsley,s.n.Adderley
Atherstone/So,Wa
  æþəstoun BBC
Atherton/La
  æðət(ə)n BBC
  æþət(ə)n BBC,EPD
  æðətən,æþətən BCE
  æðətn Kruis.
Attenborough/Nt
  ætnbrə, -bərə, bʌrə EPD
Attercliffe/WRY
  ætəklif EPD
Attingham/Sa → Atcham

Attleborough/Nf,Wa
  ætlbrə,ætlbərə EPD,BBC
  ætlbʌrə EPD
Atwick/ERY
  atik PNYE 79
  ætik PNERY,Hope,ONwick 365
Atworth/W
  vulgo ætfərd PNW 115
Aubourn/Li
  ɔ:bə GlossLi
Auburn/ERY
  ɔ:bən PNYE 87,Schr.,EPD
  ɔ:bə:n EPD,Kruis.
  ɔ:brən PNERY
Auckland (Bishop A.)/Du
  ɔ:klənd EPD,BBC,Schr.,Kruis.
  ɑ:klən(d) DSDu
Audlem/Chs
  ɔ:ləm PNChs III/82("loc.dial.")
         GlossChs,DSChs 17
  ɔ:dləm PNChs III/82,BBC
Audley/St
  ɔ:dli EPD,Schr.
Aughertree/Cu
  æfətri: PNCu 327,BBC,BCE,
          GlossCu xvii
  ɔfətri: BBC,BCE
Aughton/La (nr Lancaster)
  aftn PNLa 179
  æftn DEPN
  æftən BBC,BCE
  ɑ:ftn HL 1103
Aughton/La (nr Ormskirk)
  æftən PNLa(i) 16of.,PNLa(ii)
  ɔ:tn DEPN,HL 1103
  ɔ:t(ə)n BBC
  ɔ:tən BCE

Aughton/Nt
  aitən Hope
Aughton/W
  ɔ:tən PNW 344
Aughton/ERY
  ɔ:tn PNYE 237
  ɔ:t(ə)n BBC
  ɔ:tən BBC
Augill Castle/We
  'ɔ:gil BBC
Ault Hucknall/Db
  'ɔ:lt 'hʌknəl BBC
Aumser/Nf
  ɑ:nmə Hope
Aust/Gl
  ɔ:st PNGl III/127,BBC
Austby/WRY
  ɔ:stbi PNYW V/69
Austerson/Chs
  ɔstər-, ɔ:stərsən PNChs III,
Austin Canons/Bd
  ɔ:stin Schr.
Austwick/WRY
  ɔ:stwik, ɔstik BBC,BCE
Avebury/W
  olim ɔ:bəri PNW 293
  eibri DEPN
  eibəri PNW 293,BBC,Schr.,
         PNW(i) 17
  eivbəri PNW 293,EPD,BBC,
         Schr.,Kruis.,PNW(i):
  eivbri BBC
Aveley/Ess
  eivli PNEss 12o,BBC,BCE
Ave Maria Lane /Ldn
  ɑ:vi mə'ri:ə BBC
Avening/Gl
  eivniŋ PNGl I/86,BBC,BCE
Averham/Nt
  ɛ:rəm PNNt 181
  ɛərəm DEPN,BBC,BCE,Hope
  æərəm PNNt(i)4
Avery/K
  eivəri EPD
Aveton Gifford/D
  ɔ:tən dʒifəd PND 265,BBC,BC
         Hope
  ɔ:tn DEPN,BBC,BCE
  eivtən BBC,BCE
Avill/So
  ævil DEPN,BBC,BCE
Avington/Brk,Ha
  æviŋtən BBC
Avisford Ho/Sx
  hɛ:zfut PNSx 143
Avishays/Do (also spelt Avishaye
  'ævisheiz, 'æviʃeiz BBC
"The spelling Avishays and the fi
pron.apply to the historic house
the agricultural and sporting est
Avishayes,pron.either way,is appr
priate for the modern housing sit

13

Avon/D (r.n.)
 æv(ə)n   EPD,BBC
Avon/Gl,Le,Np,Wa (r.n.)
 eiv(ə)n   EPD,BBC
 eivn   Schr.,Kruis.
 "pron. by many with the ac-
 cent on the second syllable"
 (Mrs S.M.Woods of Bristol,
 Times,Aug.8,1977,p.15,
 letters)
Avon Carrow/Wa
 -eiv(ə)n 'kærou   BBC
Avoncliff/W
 olim ænklif   PNW 122
Avonmouth/Gl
 'eiv(ə)nmauþ   EPD,BBC
 -məþ   EPD
 eivənmauþ, æ-   Schr.521
Avon Tyrell/Ha
 'eiv(ə)n 'tir(ə)l   BBC
Avonwick/D
 æv(ə)nwik   BBC
Awbridge/Ha
 eibridȝ, ɑ:bridȝ   BBC,BCE
Awliscombe/D
 ɔ:liskəm   BBC
Awre/Gl
 ɔ:ər   PNGl III/25o
 ɔ: BBC
Awsworth/Nt
 ɔzwəþ   BBC
Axholme/Li (Isle of A.)
 'ækshoum   BBC,BCE
 æks(h)oum, -səm   EPD,Bchm.81
 "loc. called 'the Isle'"
          GlossM&C,s.n.Isle
Axminster/D
 æksminstə   EPD,Kruis.
Axmouth/D
 æksmauþ   BBC
Axworthy/D
 esəri   ROS
Ay/La (r.n.) ⟶ Eea
Aycliffe/Du
 jakli   PNNbDu 8
 jækli   Hope
 'eiklif   BBC
Aylburton/Gl
 'eilbə:t(ə)n   BBC
Aylesbeare/D
 eilzbiə   BBC,BCE
Aylesbury/Bk
 eilzb(ə)ri   EPD
 eilzbəri   Schr.
Aylesford/K
 eilzfəd   EPD,PNK,Schr.
 -lsf-   EPD

Aylesham/K
 eilzəm   PNK
Aylsham/Nf
 eilʃəm   EPD,BBC,BCE
 eilsəm   BBC,BCE
 elʃəm, elsəm   Hope
Aynho/Np
 'einhou   BBC,BCE
Ayot St. Lawrence/Hrt (or -tt)
 'eiət snt 'lɔr(ə)ns   EPD,BBC
 eijət   BCE
 eit   Hope
Ayr/Co (p.n. and r.n.)
 ɛə   EPD,Schr.
Aysgarth/NRY
 ɛəzgɑ:þ, e:ska   PNYN 262
 'eizgɑ:þ   BBC
Aythorpe Roding/Ess
 loc. eiþrəp   PNEss 491
 eiþrɔp   DEPN,EssDD 158
 (s. also s.n. Roothing)
Ayton
 eitn   EPD
Ayton/NRY (Gt and Lt A.)
 jætn, kæni jætn   PNYN 165[1]
 jatn   DSto
 kæni eitən, kæni jætən   Hope
Ayton/NRY (West A.)
 jætən   PNYN 1oo
 jatn   DSto
Azerley/WRY
 azələ, e:zələ   PNYW V/199
Azores/D
 æzəriz   PND 217,Alexander 3o5

1) "The popular appellation 'Canny' probably refers to its pleasant
 situation" (PNYN 165).

B

Babbacombe/D
  -ə- ESpr. 349
Babingley/Nf
  bevəli Hope
  bævəli PNNf
  ("vulgarly called BAVERLEY")
Babington/So
  bæbintən EPD,Kruis.
Babraham/Ca
  beibrəm PNCa loo, BBC
  beibr(ə h)əm ONCa 176
Bache/Chs
  batʃ PNChs III/147,IV/144
  beitʃ EPD
Bache/Chs (Blue B. Fm, The Bache,
         Butter B.)
  bætʃ PNChs III/lo3, III/314,
         IV/117
Bachelors/Wt
  bætʃə lərz PNWt 168
Backford/Chs
  bækfəd PNChs IV/174
Backstone Gill/WRY
  bakstn gil DDd 13
Bacup/La
  be:kəp PNLa 92
  beikəp DEPN,EPD,BBC,BCE,PNE&W
Baddeley/St
  bædəli,bædli EPD
Baddesley/Ha (South B.)
  bædzli, bædizli BBC
Baddesley/Ha (North B.)
  bædzli BBC
Baddesley Clinton/Wa
  bædzli klintən,bædizli BBC
Baddesley Ensor/Wa
  bædʒli PNWa 14
  'bædizli 'enzɔ:, bædzli BBC
Baddiley/Chs
  badili, badli PNChs III/124
Baddow/Ess
  bædə PNEss 233,EssDD 158
Badgworthy/D
  bætʃə ri Mawer(2)93
Badgworthy Cottage/D
  bædʒəri PND 59
Ba(d)gworthy Water/D (r.n.)
  bædʒəri wɔ:tə BBC,BCE
Badgworthy/Gl
  bædʒəri Hope
Badingham/Sf
  bædəgam Hope
Badlesmere/K
  bɑ:dsmiə,bæsmiə Hope
  bɑ:zmə, bædəlzmi:ə PNK
Badlingham/Ca
  bædliŋəm ONCa 176

Badminton/Gl
  bædmintən EPD,Schr.
Badmonden/K
  bædmənden PNK
Badsaddle Lodge/Np
  bætsædəl PNNp 129
Badsberry/La
  -dz- PNLa 148
Badsell/K
  bædsel PNK
Badworthy/D
  bædəvə PND 292
Bagendon/Gl
  bædʒəndən PNGl I/55
Baggrow/Cu
  bagrə PNCu 259
Baginton/Wa
  bægintən PNWa 155,DEPN(4),BBC
Bagleymoor/Sa
  bægəmur GlossSa 516
Bagnall/Nt,St
  bægnəl EPD,Bchm.9o
  bægnl EPD
Bagshaw/Db
  bægʃɔ: EPD
Bagshot/Sr,W
  bægʃɔt EPD,Schr.
Baguley/Chs
  bagili,beigli PNChs II/ix,
                  GlossChs
  bagli PNChs II/12
  bægəli,bægli BBC,BCE
Bagwich/Wt
  bægwidʒ PNWt 142
Bagworth/Le
  bægəþ Hope
Bagworthy/D (r.n.)
  bædʒəri EPD
Bagworthy Water/D → Badgworthy W.
Baildon/WRY
  be:ldən PNYW IV/ 158
  beildən Schr.
Bailey/Cu,La
  beili EPD
Bailiff Bridge/WRY
  'be:li 'brig PNYW III/79
  beli Hope
Bailrigg/La
  be:lrig PNLa 173
Bain/Li;NRY (r.n.)
  bein EPD
Bainbridge/NRY
  be:nbrig PNYN 262
  bein-,beimbridʒ EPD
Bainses/WRY
  be:nsiz DDd 15
Bainton/O
  beintən PNO(i)45
Baithley/Nf (now spelt Bale)
  beil Hope

Baker Street/Ldn (underground)
  baikə CPP 66
Bakewell/Db
  beikwel PNDb(i) I/173,BBC
  beikwəl PNDb(i) I/173,Schr.
  "bɔ:kwel ... may possibly
           exist" PNDb(i) I/173
Balambs/Wt
  bæ:ləmz PNWt 286
Balby/WRY
  bɔ:lbi BBC
Balcombe/Sx
  bɔ:kəm PNSx 255,Mawer(2)95
           ("still in common
           use"),PNK
  bɔ:lkəm BBC,BCE,Hope
Balderton/Chs
  bɔ:ldərtən, older local
  bɔ:ðərtən PNChs IV/xiv
Baldhu/Co
  bæl'dju: BBC[1]
  bɔ:l'dju: BBC,BCE
  bɔ:l'du: BBC
  bɑ:l'dju: BCE
  -æ- Jenner(2)3oo
  _ ɪ Jenner(2)3o4
Baldock/Hrt
  bɔ:ldɔk EPD,BBC
Bale/Nf
  beil Kruis.,Hope
  (s. also s.n. Baithley)
Balham/Sr
  bæləm PNSr 33,DEPN,EPD
Balk/NRY
  bɔ:k PNYN 189
Ballam/La
  bæləm BBC
Ballinger/Bk
  bælindʒə PNBk 154,BBC,BCE,
           Dodgson(2)362
Ballingham/He
  bæliŋəm, dial. -indʒəm DHe 43
  -indʒ- Dodgson(2)362 and
           (3)144,PNing 171
Balliol College/O
  beiliəl EPD,BBC,Kruis.
  beiljəl EPD,BBC
Balme Gn (in Sheffield)/WRY
  boum gri:n GlossSh 9
Balmer/Sx
  bɔ:mə PNSx 3o8
Balne/WRY
  bɔ:n PNYW II/14,PNSWY 65,BBC
Balney (Upr B.,Lwr B.,
        Badger's B.)/Ca
  bani PNCa 7

Balsall Heath/Wo (now in Wa)
  bɔ:səl PNWo 351
  bɔ:lsl BBC
  bɔ:lsəl BCE
Balsdean/Sx
  bɑ:zdi:n PNSx 312
Balsham/Ca
  olim bɔ:lsəm PNCa 114
  bɔ:lʃəm ONCa 176,BBC,BCE
  bɔlʃəm PNO 1i
Bamborough Castle/ERY
  bæmbərə Schr.,Kruis.
  bæmb(ə)rə EPD
Bamburgh/Nb
  bambri PNNbDu 1o
  bæmbərə BBC,BCE
Bamford/Db,La
  bæmfəd EPD
  bɔ:mfərt Ellis 442 (for B. in Db)
Bampton/D,O,We
  bæmtən Schr.
  bɑ:nən DWSo 9 (for B. in D),
           DWSO(i) (for B. in D)
  bæntən PNE'side 66 (for B. in
           We)
Banbury/O
  bæmbəri EPD
  bænbəri EPD,Schr.,Kruis.
Banbury Cross/La
  bɔmbri krɔs GlossR&R 21
Banbury Rd/Ldn
  _ _ _ ɪ MEG 157
Bandon Hill/Sr
  bændən Schr.
Banham/Nf
  bænəm EPD
Banhaw Wood/Np
  bænə PNNp 212
Bank Land/WRY (f.n.)
  baŋk land DDd 12
Banks
  bæŋks EPD,DDd 15 (for B. in
           WRY)
Bannerdale/Cu
  bænədəl PNE'side 74
Bannerdale Fell/We
  bænədəl PNE'side 76
Bannest Hill/Cu
  banəst PNCu 278
  bænəst hil PNE'side 75
Bannister Gn/Ess
  bʌnstə PNEss 421
  bænistə EPD
Bantham/D
  bæntəm BBC,BCE

---

1) "The dh in this name is not pron. as a soft th [i.e. ð]; the
   Cornish being bal du." (F.W.Jones 17, note 1).

Bapchild/K
    bæp-tʃaild   BBC
    bæb-tʃaild   PNK
Barber/Nf
    bɔːbə   Hope
Barbon/We
    bɑːbən   PNWe I/23
Barbury Hill/W
    bɑːbəri hil   Schr.
Barby Nortoft/Np
    nɔːtət   PNNp 25
Barcoe/Cu
    bɑːrkə   PNE'side 62
Barcombe/Sx
    bɑː'kuːm   PNSx 313
    bɑːkm   PNSx(i) 13
    bɑːkəm   BBC,BCE
Barcroft/WRY
    bɑːkrɔft,-krɔːft   EPD
Bardale/NRY
    bɑːdil   PNYN 263
Bardon/K
    bɑːden   PNK
Barden/WRY
    bɑːdin   PNYW VI/6o
Bardfield/Ess (Gt B., Lt B.,
                Bardfield Saling)
    bɑːfl   PNEss 5o4
Bardon/Le
    bɑːdən   Schr.
Bardsea/La
    bɑːdzə   PNLa 21o, PNLa(ii)
    bɑːdzi   PNLa 21o
Bardsley/La
    bɑːdzli   EPD
Bardwell/Sf
    bɑːdw(ə)l, -wel   EPD
Barfield/Cu
    bɑːfiːld   EPD
Barforth Hall/NRY
    bɑːfəþ   PNYN 298
Barfrestone/K
    bɑːsən, bɑːfrestən   PNK
    bɑːsn   Hope
    bɑːstən   Hope,WP 271
Bargh (s. also s.n. Barugh)
    bɑːf, bɑːk   H.A.(2)45
Barham/Ca,Hu,K,Sf
    bærəm   PNK,EPD (for B. in K),
                BCE (for B. in K),DEPN
                (for B. in K),BBC,
                Bchm. 1o5,Kruis.
    bɛərəm   PNK
    bɑːrəm   ONCa 176,Kruis.,Bchm.1o5
    bɑːhəm   Bchm 1o5
Barham Hall/Ca
    bærəm   PNCa 1o9
Barhaugh/Nb
    bɑːrəf   PNNbDu 11

Barholm/Li
    bærəm   BBC,BCE
Baring/NRY
    bæriŋ   EPD
    bɛəriŋ   EPD,Kruis.
Baripper/Co
    bə'ripə   BBC
Barkhouse/Cu
    bɑːkəs   GlossCu xvii
Barking/Ess,Sf
    bɑːkiŋ   Schr.
    bɔːkiŋ   EssDD 151,note 1
                (the Cockney pron.)
Barkisland/WRY
    bɑːslənd   PNYW III/57,BBC,BCE,
                Hope,Goodall 51
    bɑːkislənd   PNYW III/57,
                BBC,BCE
Barklye/Sx
    bɑːk'lai   BBC,BCE
Barkston/Li,WRY
    bɑːkstən   EPD,PNYW IV/53
    bɑːsən   Hope (for B. in Li)
    bɑːstən   PNYW IV/53
Barlaston/St
    bɑːləstən   BBC
Barlavington/Sx
    bɑːliŋtən, bɑːltən   PNSx 1oo
Barlborough/Db
    bɑːlbərə, bɑːbərə   BBC
    bælbrə   Hope
Barlestone/Le
    bɑːlstoun   BBC
Barlow/Db,Du,Sa,WRY
    bɑːlou   EPD,Schr.
    bɑːlə   PNYW IV/23
Barmby/ERY (two places)
    bɑːmbi   EPD
Barming/K
    bɑːmiŋ   PNK
Barmoor/Nb
    bɛəmuə   PNNbDu 11
Barmston/ERY
    bɑːms(t)ən   PNYE 83
Barnard Castle/Du
    bɑːni kasl   PNNbDu 12
    bɑːnəd kɑːsl   BBC,BCE
    bɑːni kæsəl   Hope
Barnard Gate/O
    bɑːnət jæt   PNO(i) 49
    bɑːnəd geit   BBC
Barnardiston/Sf
    bɑːnə'distən   EPD
    bɑːnɑː'distn   Kruis.
    bənstən   Hope
Barnborough/WRY (also spelt -brough
    bɑːmbə   Hope
Barnbow/WRY
    bɑːn'bou   BBC

Barnby
  ba:nbi   EPD
Barnby-on-Dun/WRY
  ba:mbi dʌn   Hope
Barnden/K
  ba:nden   PNK
Barnes/Du,Sr,Wt
  ba:nz   EPD,Schr.
  barnsiz   PNWt 64
Barnet/Hrt
  ba:nit   EPD,Schr.
Barnetby/Li
  ba:nəbi   Hope
Barney/Nf
  ba:ni   EPD
Barnham/Sf,Sx
  ba:nəm   PNSx(i) 14,EPD,Schr.
Barningham/Nf
  -inəm, -iŋəm   PNing 172
Barnoldswick/WRY
  ba:lik   PNYW VI/34,BBC,BCE,
          Hope,ONwick 363
  ba:'nouldzwik EPD,BBC,BCE
  ba:nəwik   Hope,ONwick 363
Barnskew/We
  ba:rnskə   PNE'side 63
Barnsely
  bæanslə   Hope (for B. in WRY)
  ba:nzli   EPD,Schr.
Barnsley Fm/Wt
  ba:rnzli   PNWt 52
Barnstaple/D
  ba:nstəpl   EPD,Schr.,Hope
  loc. ba:nstəbl   EPD
  bɛərəm   Hope
Barnston/Ess
  bænsn   PNEss 47o
  bænsən   EssDD 158
Barnwell/Ca,Np
  ba:nwəl   Schr.
Barr/St
  ba: EPD
Barrington
  bæriŋtən   EPD,Schr.,ONCa 24
  bærəntn   DSDu (for B. in Nb)
Barrock Pk/Cu
  bærik   PNE'side 75
  ba:rik   PNCu 2o1
Barrockside/Cu
  ba:rik   PNCu 2o1
Barron (as in B.'s Pk/Le
         B,'s Pike/Cu)
  bærən   EPD
Barrow (r.n.)
  bærou   Schr.
Barrow/Chs
  barə   PNChs III/261,GlossChs

Barrow Ho/WRY
  barə aus,barəs   DDd 15
Barrow-in-Furness/La
  barə   PNLa 2o4,GlossFu 62,s.n.
      Marra
  'bærou in 'fə:nis   EPD,BBC
         -nes   EPD
Barrow Moor/We
  bærə   PNE'side 63
Barrow-on-Trent/Db
  bærə   Hope
Barsham/Nf
  ba:ʃəm   BBC,BCE
  bæʃəm   Hope,PNNf,s.n.Basham
Barsham/Sf
  ba:ʃəm   BBC,BCE
Bartestree/He
  'ba:tistri: BBC
Barth/WRY
  baþ   DDd 13
Barthomley/Chs
  ba:təmli   PNChs III/5
  ba:þə mli   BBC
  ba:rtəmli   GlossChs
Barthorpe Bottoms/ERY
  ba:þrəp   PNYE 148
Bartle/La
  ba:tl   EPD
Bartlett's Fm/Wt
  bə:rtləts, ba:rtlits   PNWt 169
Barton
  ba:tən   Schr.,ONCa 15
  ba:tn   EPD
  ba:rtən   PNE'side 66 (B. in We)
Barton-in-Fabis/Nt
  ba:tən in feibis   BBC
Barton Blount/Db
  ba:ən [sic!] blʌnt   PNDb 524
Barton Manor/Wt
  ba:rtn   PNWt 236
Barugh/NRY
  ba:f   PNYN 74,DEPN,EPD
  ba:k   BBC,BCE
  (s. also s.n. Rook B.)
Barugh/WRY
  barə   PNYW I/316
  ba:k   BBC,BCE,Hope,PNSWY 68
  ba:f   EPD,Hope
  ba:rk   PNCuWe 11,s.n.Barkgate
Barwell/Le
  bærəl   Mawer(4)285 (this form
         of pron. is now lost)
Barwick
  bærik   EPD,Kruis., BBC (for B.
      in Hrt,Nf,So),BCE (for B.
      in Hrt,Nf),DEPN (for B.
      in Nf),Hope (for B. in
      Nf),ONwick 373 (for Nf)

Barwick/NRY
  barik   PNYN 171
Barwick in Elmet/WRY
  barik   PNYW IV/lo6
  bærik in elmit   BBC
  - - elmət   BCE
  bærik   DEPN
Baschurch/Sa
  bæstʃə:tʃ ₁ BBC
Basco Dyke/Cu¹
  baskədaik   PNCu 169
  bæskə   PNE'side 63
  baskədeik   PNE'side75
Basford/Chs
  basfəd   PNChs III/48
Basford/Nt
  beisfəd   PNNt 138,PNNt(i)9,
            DEPN,EPD,BBC,BCE,Hope
Basford/St
  bæsfəd   EPD,BBC,BCE
Bashingham/Nf
  beizingeim (?) Hope²
Basil Busk/WRY
  basl busk   DDd 12
Basildon/Brk,Ess
  bæzldən   BBC
Basing/Ha
  beisiŋ   DEPN
Basingstoke/Ha
  beizingstouk   EPD,Schr.,Hope
Basin Hill/Do
  ba:sən hil   DDo
Baslow/Db
  bazlə   PNDb 4o
  bæzlou   BBC
  bæslə   Thomp.7o
Bassenthwaite/Cu
  basnþət   PNCu 263
  bæsnþət   PNE'side 66
  bæs(ə)nþweit   BBC
  bæsənþweit,-þət   Schr. (for
            B. Lake)
Basset (as in B. Ho/W)
  bæsit   EPD
Bassetlaw/Nt
  'bæsit'lɔ: BBC
Bassingbourn/Ca
  'bæsiŋbɔ:n   BBC
  bæsiŋbən   ONCa 191
Bassingfield/Nt
  bæzinfi:ld   PNNt(i) 11
Basted/K
  beistəd   PNK
Bastonford/Wo
  bæst(ə)nfɔ:d   BBC
Bastwick/Nf
  ba:stwik   Hope,ONwick 373

Baswich/St (aslo called Berkswich)
  bæsidʒ   BEPN,BBC,BCE
  bæsitʃ   BBC,BCE
Baswick/ERY
  bazik   PNYE 72
Batchworth/Hrt
  olim bætʃə   PNHrt 81
Bath/So
  ba:þ   EPD,Schr.,Kruis.
  -þ   Dobson 944
  ba:f   DNSo 23
  bæ:þ   Ellis 79*
Bathampton/W
  baþ'æmtən, olim bætiŋtən
            PNW 227
  baþ'(h)æmtn, bed'(h)æmtn
            PNW(i) 2o
Bathealton/So
  bætltən   BBC,BCE
  bætltn   DEPN
Batheaston/So
  ba:þ'i:st(ə)n   BBC
  ba:'þi:stən   BCE
  bætistən   BBC,BCE
Batherton/Chs
  baþə(r)tn   PNChs III/5o
Bathford/So
  ba:þ'fɔ:d   BBC,BCE
Bathingbourne/Wt
  bænbərn   PNWt 143
Bathley/Nt
  bætli   PNNt(i) 11 ("not well
            authenticated")
Bathurst/Sx
  bæþəst   EPD,Schr.
  ba:þəst   Schr.
  bæþə:st   EPD,Kruis.
Batley/WRY
  bætli   BBC,Schr.,Haigh 22 (for
            B. nr Huddersfield)
  batlə   Haigh 22 (for B. nr
            Dewsbury)
Battersby/NRY
  bætəzbi   EPD
Battersea/Ldn
  bætəsi   EPD,BBC,Kruis.
  bætərsi   Schr.
Battisford/Sf
  bætisfəd   BBC
Battishorne/D
  bætshɔ:rn   PND 539
Battlesbridge/Ess
  'bætlzbridʒ   BBC
Baugh Fell/WRY (a mountain)
  ba:fl, bɔ:fl   DDd 17

1) The name is spelt Bascodyke in PNCu, Bascodike in PNE'side 75 and
   Basco Dyke ib. 63.
2) Hope's transcription is <u>Bazyngame</u>.

Baughurst/Ha
  'bɔ:ghə:st EPD
  -g- DEPN
Baumber/Li
  bɔ:mbə BBC
Baverstock/W
  bævərstɔk PNW 212
  bævə(r)stɔk PNW(i)2o
Bavinge/K
  bævindʒ PNK
Bawburgh/Nf
  beibə, bɔ:bərə BBC
  bɔ:bə Hope
Bawdeswell/Nf
  bɔ:dzwəl BBC,BCE
  ba:dsəl, bɔ:dsəl Hope
Bawdsley/Sf
  bɔ:dzi BBC,PNDVall 56
Baxenden/La
  bæksəndən (so pron.in Rochdale)
  bæʃəndən (so pron.in Rossen-
                  dale) GlossR&R
Baycroft/Wt
  beikrɔ:ft PNWt 146
Bayham Abbey/Sx
  beiəm PNK
Baylham/Sf
  beiləm BBC
Baynard's Castle/O
  beinədz Schr.
Baynard's (Gn)/O
  beina:dz gri:n BBC
  beiəz, bɛəz Hope
Baynards Pk/Sr
  bænədz PNSr 23o
Bayswater/Ldn
  beizwɔ:tə EPD,Schr.
Bazing/K
  beiziŋ PNK
Beach Fm, B.Hill, etc./Chs
  bi:tʃ PNChs III/188 and 2o6
Beachfield/Chs
  bi:tʃ PNChs III/188
Beachin Fm, B.Lane/Chs
  bi:tʃin PNChs IV/86
Beachy Head/Sx
  'bi:tʃi 'hed PNSx(i)15,BBC
  bi:ʃi 'hed Kruis.
  ˌ _ _ Schr.
Beaconsfield/Bk
  bekənzfi:ld PNBk 214,BCE,
                  Hope,Kruis.
  bek(ə)nzfi:ld EPD,BBC,MEG 124
  bekənsfi:ld Kruis.
  loc. beknzf(i:)ld Schr.
  loc. bekənzfld Hope
  -e- DEPN

bi:kənsfi:ld Kruis.
  -z- EPD(1),BCE,Schr.,
         Kruis.
  bi:k(ə)nzfi:ld BBC,MEG 124
Beadlam/NRY
  biədləm PNYN 67,PNNY 7
Beadnell/Nb
  bi:dlən [!] PNNbDu 13
Beaford/D
  bi:fəd BBC,BCE
Beal/Nb,WRY (in WRY also spelt
         Beaghall, cf. BG)
  bi:l EPD
Bealings/St
  bæləns, bi:- PNDVall 7
Beam Bridge/Chs
  bi:m PNChs III/153
Beam Heath/Chs
  bi:m PNChs III/36
Beaminster/Do
  beminstə DEPN,EPD,BBC,BCE,Chis.
  loc. bemistə EPD,Hope,Urlau 49,
               DDo,PNDo(i)262
  "bi:m- is sometimes heard from
  people unfamiliar with the place"
  (EPD)
Beamish/Du
  bi:miʃ EPD
Beanacre/W
  vulgo binəgər PNW 128
  bi(:)neikə(r) PNW(i)22
Beanthwaite/La
  bi:nþət PNLa 22o
Beaper Fm/Wt
  bi:pər PNWt 52
Beare/D
  biə EPD,BBC
Beare Gn/Sr
  bɛ:r PNSr 267
  'bɛə 'gri:n BBC[1]
Bearley/Wa
  bi:əli PNWa 198
  biəli BBC,BCE
Bearpark/Du
  'biə'pa:k BBC,BCE
  bi:ər PNNbDu 14
Bearsted/K
  ba:sted, bɛəsted BBC,BCE
  ba:stəd PNK
Bearstone/Sa
  biəstən BBC
Bearton Gn/Hrt
  bi:ətən PNHrt 9
Bearwardcote/Db
  barəkɔt PNDb 525
  bærəkət BBC

1) In fact, both sources mean the same sound, viz. a vowel as in 'there';
yet, in BBC this vowel is described as a diphthong, in PNSr as a
monophthong.

20

Beauchamp/Sx,Wt
    bi:tʃəm   PNWt 181; EPD,BBC,Kruis.,
               MEG 217,ESpr. 275
Beauchief/Db
    bi:tʃif   PNDb 2o8, BBC,BCE,Hope
Beauclerc/Nb
    bouklə:k, bouklɛ:ək   MEG 244
Beaudesert/Wa
    olim bju:dsɑ:t   PNWa 199
    bou'dezət   BBC,BCE
    boudi'zɛə   BBC
    belzə   BBC,BCE,Davy 23
    boudə'zɛə   BCE
Beaudesert Pk/St
    'boudizɛə pɑ:k   BBC
Beaufront/Nb
    bi:vrən   PNNbDu 15 (current in the
               18th c., but no longer
               used now)
Beaulieu/Ha (also spelt Bewley),Sx
    bju:li   EPD,BBC,BCE,EPD,Schr.,
              Kruis.,Chis.,Hope,MEG 26o,
              PNWo(i) 19,PNE&W,Mawer(4)
              284,DEPN
    bouli   Schr.,Kruis.
Beaulieu Wood/Do
    bju:li wud   Mayo
Beaumanor/Le
    bou'mænə   DEPN,BBC,BCE
Beaumont
    bi:mənt   BBC
    boumənt   EPD,Kruis.,MEG 244
    boumənt   Kruis.
Beaumont/Cu
    bi:mənt   PNCu 121,BCE,DEPN,GlossCu
               xvii
Beaumont/Ess
    boumənt   PNEss 327,DEPN,HL 557
Beaumont/La
    bo:mənt   PNLa 177
    boumənt   DEPN
Beaumont Otes/Ess
    bi:mən outs   PNEss 248
Beausale/Wa
    bouseil   PNWa 2oo
    bju:səl   PNWa 2oo,BCE
    bju:sl   BBC
    bju:-   DEPN
Beauvale/Nt
    bju:veil   PNNt 145
    bouveil   PNNt(i) 11
Beavan's Hill/He
    bev(ə)n   EPD
Beauworth/Ha
    bju:-   DEPN
Beauxfield/K
    bouzfi:ld   PNK

Beaworthy/D
    baueri   PND 129
    bauəri   BBC,BCE
    'bi:wə:ði   EPD,BBC,BCE
Beazley End/Ess
    bi:zli   EPD
Bebington/Chs
    bebiŋtən   PNChs IV/245
    bebitn   EDG § 273,RSp 135,
             DSChs 19
Beccles/Sf
    beklz   EPD,Schr.
Becconsall/La
    beknsə   PNLa(ii)
Beckbrooke/O → Begbroke
Beckces/Cu
    beksiz   PNCu 213,PNE'side 74
Beckcies/Cu → Beckces
Beckenham/K
    beknəm   EPD,PNK
Beckermet/Cu
    bek'ərmət   PNCu 337
    be'kɑ:mit   BBC
    be'kə:mət   BCE
Beckett/Brk
    bekit   EPD
Beckfellican/Cu
    bek'felikən   PNE'side 65
Beckfoot/Cu
    -fit   GlossCuWeNLa,s.n. fit
Beckford/Wo
    bekfəd   Kruis.
Beckhampton/W
    bek'hæmtən, olim bekiŋtən
                    PNW 294
Beckley/Ha,K,Sx
    bekli   EPD
Beck Mouray/We (f.n.)
    mɔ:rə   Simpson 281
Beckton/Ess
    bektən   EPD
Beckwith/WRY
    bekwiþ   EPD
Becky/D (r.n.)
    beki   EPD
Becontree/Ess
    bekəntri: EPD
Beda Fell/We
    beidə   PNE'side 62
Bedale/NRY
    bi:dəl   PNYN 236
    bi:dl   BBC,BCE,Hope
    bi:deil   BCE
    bi:-   DEPN
Bedales School/Ha
    bi:deilz   EPD,BBC,BCE
Bedchester/Do
    bedʒestə   PNDo(i) 23

Beddingham/Sx
 bediŋ'hæm PNSx 357,BBC,BCE,
    Mawer(4)285
Bedenham/Ha
 bed(ə)nəm BBC
Bedford/Bd,Le
 bedfəd EPD,BBC,Schr.,Kruis.
Bedfordshire
 bedfədʃə EPD,Schr.,Chis.
 -ʃiə EPD
 bedfɔːdʃair Chis.
Bedgebury/K
 bedʒbəri PNK
Bedham/Sx
 bed'hæm BBC,BCE
Bedingfield/Sf
 bedənfəld Hope
Bedlam/Ldn (a building),So,WRY
 bedləm Schr.(for Ldn),Gloss0
   (suppl.)99,s.n.Stunny
   (for B. in Ldn),EPD
Bedminster/So
 bedminstə Schr.
Bedruthan/Co (cliffs)
 bi'drʌðən BBC
Beds. (short for Bedfordshire)
 bedz EPD
Bedwardine/Wo
 bedwədiːn, bedwədin PNWo 89
Bedwell/Hrt
 bedw(ə)l, -wel EPD
Bedworth/Wa
 berəþ Hope
 bedəþ Ellis 487
Beeby/Le
 biːbi EPD
Beech/Ha,St
 biːtʃ EPD
Beechburn/Du
 bitʃbəːn PNNbDu 16
Beech Ho, B.Mill/Chs
 biːtʃ PNChs III/228
Beedale/NRY
 biədil PNYN 99
Beeford/ERY
 biːfəþ PNYE 76,Hope,GlossHol 17
Beela/We (r.n.;also called Beetha)
 biːlə RN 31,PNWe I/2
 (see also s.n. Belah)
Beeleigh/Ess
 biːliː, biːli BBC
Beeley/Db
 biːli PNDb(i) I/179
Beer/D,So
 biːr, biːə Schr.
Beesands/D
 'biːsændz BBC
Beeston/Bd
 biːsən PNBdHu 1o7

Beeston/Chs
 biːstən, bistən PNChs III/3o2
Beeston/Nf
 biːsən Hope
Beeston/Nt
 biːsən PNNt 139 ("vulgo"),
    Hope
Beetha/We (r.n.) ⟶ Beela
Beetham/We
 biːðəm PNWe I/66,DEPN,BBC,BCE
 biːþəm EPD
Beethoven Sq./Ldn
 biːt(h)ouvn EPD
Begbroke/O
 'begbruk BBC,BCE,Hope
Beggarsbush/Ess
 biglzbuʃ PNEss 182
Beggearn Huish/So
 'begəːn 'hjuːiʃ BBC
 - hjuiʃ BCE
Beighton/Db,Nf
 beitən PNDb 2o9,BCE
 beitn PNDb(i) I/18o
 baitən BCE
 beit(ə)n, -ai- BBC
Bekesbourne/K
 biːksbɔːn BBC,PNK
Belah (or Beela)/We (r.n.)
 biːlə PNWe I/3,RN 32,BBC
 beilə RN 32,PNE'side 63
Belas Knap/Gl
 'beləs 'næp PNGl II/5
Belaugh/Nf
 biːlɑː BBC,BCE
 biːlɔː BBC,BCE,EPD
 biːlou BBC,BCE,Hope,
    PNNf,s.n. Below
 biːluː BBC,BCE
Belbroughton/Wo
 bel'brɔːt(ə)n BBC
 bel'brɔːtən BCE
Belchamp Otten/Ess
 'belʃəm 'ɔt(ə)n BBC
Belchamp St. Paul's/Ess
 pɔːlz belʃəm PNEss 4o8
 'belʃəmp snt 'pɔːl BBC
Belgrave/Le,Wa
 belgreiv EPD
Belgrave Sq./Ldn
 belgreiv skwɛə Schr.
Belgravia/Du,Ldn
 bel'greiviə,
 belgreivjə EPD,Bchm.95
Bellasis/Du
 beləsis BBC
Belleau/Li
 'belou, 'belju: BBC,BCE
Belle Isle/Ldn,We,WRY
 'bel 'ail EPD

Belle Tout/Sx
  'bel 'tu:t   EPD,BBC
  _ ⌒ , ⌒ _   EPD
Bellevue
  'bel'vju:, ⌒ _   EPD
Bell Ho/Ess
  beləs   PNEss 481
Bell House Hill/Cu
  (f.n. nr Kirkoswald)
  beləs   Thorn. 62 and 79,
          note 1ol
Bellingham/Nb
  belindʒəm   DEPN,EPD,BBC,BCE,
          Schr.521,Kruis.,
    Hope,PNNbDu 16,PNing 17o,
    Zachr.(i)349,Ellis 64o,
    Dodgson(2)362,GlossSa
        xxxvii
Bellows (as in B.Cross/Do)
  belouz   EPD
Belmont
  belmɔnt, belmənt   Schr.,EPD
Belper/Db
  bilpə   Hope,Ellis 445
  belpə   Schr.
Belsay/Nb
  belsi   BBC
Belsham/Sx
  belʃəm   EPD
Belsize Lane/Ldn
  belsaiz lein   EPD,Schr.
Belstead/Sf
  belstid, -sted   EPD
Belswardine/Sa (-dyne)
  belzədain   Mawer(4)285
Belthorn/La
  'belþɔ:n   BBC
Beltinge/K
  beltindʒ   BBC,PNK
Beltingham/Nb
  beltindʒəm   EPD,BBC,BCE,PNing
          17o
Belton
  belt(ə)n   EPD
Belvedere/K
  belvi'diə   BBC,EPD
  ⌒ _ ⌒ , ⌒ _ _   EPD
  belvidi:r   Schr.
Belvoir/Le
  bi:və   DEPN,EPD,BBC,BCE,Hope,
        Schr.,Kruis.,HL 1222,
        PNE&W,Mawer(4)284
  beivə   ESpr.131f.
Belvoir (when used in London
  street names)
  belvwɔ:, -vɔə, -vɔ: EPD
  belvɔiə   EPD,HL 1222
  belwɔ: HL 1222

Belvoir (Vale of)/Nt
  bi:vər   PNNt 12
  bi:və, belvɔiə   PNNt(i) 13
Bembridge/Wt
  bimbridʒ   PNWt 34
  bembridʒ   PNWt 34,EPD
Bemerton/W
  bemərtən   PNW 225
  bemə(r)tn   PNW(i)24
  bemət(ə)n   EPD
  be-   DEPN
Benacre/Sf
  'beneikə   BBC
Benefield/Np
  benifi:ld   PNNp 211,DEPN,BBC,BCE
Benenden/K
  benəndən   EPD,BBC
  benən'den   BBC ("rarely used now
  beninden   PNK
Benfleet/Ess
  benfli:t   Schr.
Bengeo/Hrt
  bendʒou   PNHrt 215,DEPN,BBC,BCE,
        Dodgson(2)362
Bengeworth/Wo
  bendʒə:d   PNWo 95
  benʒə:d   Dodgson(2)363
  bendʒəþ, bendʒəd   GlossSEWo 81
Benhall/Sf
  benl   BBC
  bənəl   BCE
Benham Pk/Bkr
  benəm   EPD
Bennethead/Cu
  benət hi:d   PNE'side 75
Bennett (as in B.'s End/Bk)
  benit   EPD
Bennington/Hrt,Li
  beniŋtən   EPD
Ben Rhydding/WRY
  ben 'ridiŋ   BCE
Bensham/Du
  benʃəm   EPD,BBC,BCE
Bensington/O (now also spelt Benson)
  bensiŋtən   Schr.
  bensən   BCE,Hope,Schr.("loc."),
        EPN 86
  bens(ə)n   BBC
Benson/We (a hill)
  bensn   EPD
Benson/O → Bensington
Benthall/Sa
  bentɔ:l   BBC,BCE
Bentham/WRY
  bentəm   PNYW VI/237,EPD,Kruis.
  benþəm   EPD,Kruis.,Bchm.228,
        MEG 377
Bentham Ho/W
  bentəm   PNW 38

1)Hope gives two different transcriptions, viz. Bensun (p.1o) and Ben-
  sum (p.117);only the latter is quoted by PNO(i)52 and rendered
  [bensəm].

Bentley
  bentli   EPD,Schr.
  bentlei Schr.
Bentley/WRY
  bentlə DYorks 63
Benton/D,Nb
  bentən EPD
Benty Hough/WRY
  hɔf GlossSh 297
Benwick/Ca
  benik PNCa 246
Beoley/Wo
  biːli PNWo 186,DEPN,BBC
Bere
  biə EPD
Bere Alston/D
  'biər'ɔːlstən BBC
Bere Regis/Do
  'biə 'riːdʒis BBC
Beresford/St
  berəsfəd Kruis.
  beris-,berizfəd EPD
Bergh Apton/Nf
  bəːr'æptən BBC
Bergholt/Sf (East B.)
  'bəːghoult BBC
Bergholt/Ess (West B.)
  olim bɑːfould, bɑːfl
            PNEss 360
Berkeley/Gl,K
  barkli PNGl II/211
  bɑːkli PNGl II/211,DEPN,EPD,
         BBC,BCE,Schr.,Kruis.,
         MEG 197,Hope
  bəːkli BCE,Schr.,Kruis.,
         Bchm.2o ("rarely"),
         EPD ("rarely"),
         MEG 197
  bəːkliː CPhon
  -lei Schr.
Berkesden Gn/Hrt
  bɑːdən PNHrt 171
Berkhamstead/Hrt
  'bɑːkəmstid PNHrt 27("olim"),
         Potter 35
  bək'hæmstid Schr.
  'bɑːkəmsted BBC,BCE,Potter 35
  'bɑːkəmsted BBC,BCE
  'bəːkəm(p)stid, -sted EPD
  less commonly bɑːk- EPD
  'bəːkhəmsted Chis.
  bəːk'hæmstid Kruis.
  bəːk- DEPN
Berkley/So
  bɑːkli DEPN,BBC,BCE,HL 446
Berks. (short for Berkshire)
  bəːks EPD ("rarely"),Schr.
  bɑːks EPD
  -ɑː- , -əː- Koeppel 38

Berkshire
  bəːkʃə Schr.,Kruis.,Chis.
         MEG 197
  bɑːkʃə DEPN,BBC,Schr.,Kruis.,
         MEG 197,HL 475
  bɑːkʃiə,
  rarely bəːk- EPD,Bchm.211
  -ʃə EPD

  bəːrtʃər, bəːrkʃər DDo
  bəːkʃair Chis.
  bɑːkʃaiə Hope
  (see also Koeppel 38)

Berkswell/Wa
  bɑː(k)swəl PNWa 56
  bɑːkswel,bəːkswel BBC,BCE
  bɑːk- DEPN
Berkswich/St (also called Baswich)
  bɑːkswitʃ BBC
  bəːkswitʃ BCE
Bermondsey/Sr
  olim bɑːmzi PNSr 16
  'bəːmən(d)zi EPD,Bchm.22
  'bəːməndzi Schr.
Berners Roding/Ess
  loc. bɑːniʃ EssDD 158,Reaney(2)
         177,PNEss 492
  (see also s.n. Roothing)
Bernwood/Bk
  bəːnud, olim bɑːnwud
         PNBk 132 and note 1
Berrick Salome/O (also spelt Berwick)
  'berik 'sæləm PNO(i)177,BBC,BCE
Berry Barn/Wt
  bəːri barn PNWt 285
Berry Brow/WRY
  beri brɛə DHd 14
Berry Croft/Wt
  beri krɔːft PNWt 146
Berryl/Wt
  bəːrl PNWt 286
Berrynarbor/D
  beri'nɑːbə BBC
Berry Shute/Wt
  bəːri ʃeuːt PNWt 286
Berwick
  berik EPD,BBC,Schr.,Kruis.
Berwick/Sx
  bərwik PNSx 411
  berik Hope
  bəːwik DEPN
Berwick/WRY
  barik PNYW VI/65
Berwick Bassett/W
  barik PNW 254
  berik, bʌrik PNW (i)25
  bærik DEPN
Berwick Hall/Ess
  bærək PNEss 384

Berwick St. John/W
  'berik snt 'dʒɔn   BBC
Berwick-upon-Tweed/Nb
  'berik əpɔn twi:d   DEPN,BBC,
                   Hope
Besselsleigh/Brk
  'beslz'li: BBC
Bessingby/ERY
  beznbi   PNYE loo,Hope
Besthorpe/Nf
  besþɔ:p   BBC
  bestrəp   GlossSWLi
Bestwood Pk/Nt
  vulgo beskəd   PNNt 114
Beswick/La,ERY
  bezik   BBC,PNYE 159
  besik   GlossR&R,DSLa,Hope
Betchton/Chs
  betʃtən   PNChs III/18
Betham/So
  betəm   BBC,BCE
Bethecar Moor/La
  beþəkə   PNLa 218
Bethel/Co
  beþl   Schr.
Bethersden/K
  beþəzdən   BBC
  beðəsden   PNK
Bethnal Gn/Ldn
  beþnəl   EPD,Schr.,Kruis.,
            MEG 211,CPhon 85
  betnəl   CPhon 124
  beþnl   EPD
Betsham/K
  betsəm   BBC,BCE,PNK
Betteshanger/K
  'betshæŋə   BBC
  betsæŋə   PNK
Beulah Ho/We
  biu:li, -lə   PNE'side 73
Beult/K (r.n.)
  bʌlt   RN 33
  belt   PNK
Beversbrook/W
  bi:və(r)sbruk   PNW(i)26
Bevercotes/Nt
  'bevəkouts   BBC
Bevere Island/Wo
  bevəri   PNWo 111,BBC
Beverley/ERY
  bevələ   PNYE 192
  bevlə   PNYE 192,GlossHol 17,
        DYorks 63
  bevəli   EPD,Schr.,Kruis.
Bevington (Cock B.,Wood B.)/Wa
  beviŋtən   PNWa 22o
Bevis Marks/Ldn
  'bi:vis 'ma:ks   BBC

Bevois Fm/Wt
  bi:vəs   PNWt 184
Bewaldeth/Cu
  biwɔ:dəþ   PNCu 264 1
  bju:'ældəþ   BBC
  bju'ældəþ   BCE
  _ ⌐ _   DEPN
Bewcastle/Cu
  bju:kɑ:sl   Schr. 521
Bewclay/Nb
  bjukli   PNNbDu 19
Bewdley/Wo
  bju:dli   BBC,Schr.,Chis.
Bewholme/ERY
  biuəm   PNYE 77
  bju:ən [sic!]   Hope
Bewick/Nb
  bju:ik   PNNbDu 19,Kruis.
  bju(:)ik   EPD
Bewley/K
  bju:li   EPD
Bewley Castle/We
  biu:li kasl   PNE'side 73
Bexhill/Sx
  bækshil   PNSx 489,Hope
  'beks'hil   EPD,Kruis.,
  _ ⌐   EPD
Bexley/K
  beksli   EPD
Bexton/Chs
  bekstən, loc. beksn   PNChs II/72
Beyton/Sf
  beit(ə)n   BBC
Bibury/Gl
  baibəri   BBC
Bicester/O
  bistə   PNO 198,PNO(i) 53,DEPN,
        EPD,BBC,Kruis.,Hope,Schr.
        Chis.,BCE
  rarely baisistə   Schr.
Bickenhall/So
  biknəl   Bardsley,s.n.Bicknell
Bickenhill/Wa
  olim bignəl   PNWa 59
Bickerstaff/La (also -staffe)
  bikəsta:f   EPD,Kruis.
Bickerton/Chs,Nb,WRY
  bikətn   EPD
Bickford/St
  bikfəd   EPD
Bickleigh/D
  'bikli: BBC
  bikli   EPD
Bickley/Chs
  bikli   PNChs IV/6, EPD
Bicknor/K
  biknə   PNK

1) The transcription given in GlossCu xvii, viz. Bewodeth, is ambiguou

Bicton/Sa
  bikən   Hope
Bidborough/K
  bidbərə   PNK
Biddenden/K
  bid(ə)ndən   BBC
  bidnden   PNK
Biddenham/Bd
  bidnəm   PNBdHu 26,Hope
Biddestone/W
  bidstən   PNW 82,PNW(i) 26
  bidistən   BBC
Biddlesden/Bk
  bitəlzdən   PNBk 41
  bilzdən   BBC,BCE
Biddlestone/Nb
  bitlstən   PNNbDu 21
Biddulph/St
  'bidʌlf   EPD,BBC
  bidl [sic!]   DEPN
  bidəlf   EPD
Biddulph Moor/St
  bidl muə   Hope
Bideford/D (also spelt Bidde-)
  bidifəd   PND 87,PNND 34,DEPN,
           EPD,BBC,BCE,Kruis.
  bidəfəd   Chis.,BG
  baidfəd   Schr.("loc."),Hope
  bidifɔrd   Schr.
Bierley/Wt
  b(i)ər'lai   PNWt 252
Bierley (East B.,North B.)/WRY
  baiəli   BBC
  baiələ   PNYW III/8 (for North
         Bierley)
Bierton/Bk
  bi:ətən   PNBk 146
  biət(ə)n   DEPN,BBC
Bifrons/K
  baifrɔns   PNK
Bigbury/Wt
  bigbəri   PNWt 286
Biggerside/WRY
  bigəsət   DDd 13
Biggin/Ess
  bigin   CPhon 24
Biggleswade/Bd
  biglzweid   Chis.
Bigholme/WRY
  bigəm   DDd 16
Bignell Ho/O
  bignəl, -nl   EPD
Bigod (as in B.s Hall/Ess)
  baigɔd   EPD
Bilborough/Nt
  bilb(ə)rə   EPD
Bilbrough/WRY
  bilbrə   EPD
Bildeston/Sf
  bildistən   BBC
  bilstən   Hope

Billericay/Ess
  bil'riki   PNEss 146
  bilə'riki   EPD,BBC,BCE,
           EssDD 158
  - 'iki   DEPN
  'bilərikei   Chis.
Billesdon/Le
  bilzdən   BBC
Billing/Np
  biliŋ   EPD
Billinge Hill, High B., B.Gn/Chs
  bilindʒ   PNChs I/138, II/198,
           III/298, BBC,
           Dodgson(2)328
Billinge/La
  bilindʒ   PNLa 1o4,BBC,BCE,
           H.A.(1)178,Zachr.(1)
           348,Dodgson(2)327
Billingford/Nf
  belinfə,   beliŋfə   Hope
Billingham/Du
  biliŋhəm   BBC
  -indʒ-   Dodgson(2)363
Billingham Manor/Wt
  bilənəm   PNWt 217,PNing 171
Billingsgate/Ldn
  biliŋzgeit   EPD,Schr.
  -git   EPD
  -gət   Schr.
  bilinzgit   CPhon 129
Billington/Bd,La,St
  biliŋtən   EPD
Bilsington/K
  bilziŋtən   BBC,BCE,PNK
Bilsthorpe/Nt
  bilstrəp   PNNt 45
Bilston/St
  bilstən   EPD,Schr.
Bilstone/Le
  bilstən   EPD
Bilton/Nb,Wa,WRY,ERY
  bilt(ə)n   EPD
Bincknoll Castle/W
  bainəl   PNW 296
Binderton/Sx
  bindətn   PNSx(i) 22
  bindətən   BBC
Binegar/So
  binigə   EPD
Bineham/Sx
  bainəm   PNSx(i) 22
Bingham/Do,Nt
  biŋəm   EPD
Bingley/WRY
  biŋli   EPD
Binnegar/Do
  binəgə   PNDo I/146,
           PNDo(i) 144
Binney/K
  bini   EPD

Binsey/Brk,Cu,O
  binzi BBC,BCE (for B. in Brk)
Binsoe/NRY
  binsə PNYN 222
Binstead/Wt
  binsted, -stid EPD
Binsted/Ha,Sx
  binstəd PNSx(i)23
  binstid,-sted EPD
Birchall Bridge,B.Brook,B.Moss/Chs
  'bə:tʃɔ:(l) PNChs III/62
Bircham/Nf
  bɑ:tʃm Hope
Birchanger/Ess
  'bə:tʃæŋgə PNEss 518
Birchen Tree/WRY
  bə:tʃən trei DDd 14
Birchin Lane/Ldn
  bə:tʃin lein Schr.
Birchmore/Wt
  bə:tʃmɔ:r PNWt 8
Birchover/Db
  bə:tʃə PNDb 45,Hope,Walker 25
Birdbrook/Ess
  bʌbruk PNEss 411
Birdforth/NRY
  budfəþ PNYN 190
Birdgate/NRY
  bɔrgət PNYN 85
Birdingbury/Wa
  bə:bəri PNWa 126,PNE&W
Birdsall/ERY
  bodsəl PNYE 141
  bodsil Hope
Birkbeck College/Ldn
  'bə:kbek EPD,BBC,Bchm.113
Birkby/NRY
  bɔrkbi PNYN 211
Birkenhead/Chs
  bə:kən'ed, bərkən'ed

                       PNChs IV/313
  bə:k(ə)n'hed, ⟋ _ _ BBC,EPD
  'bə:knhed Schr.
  'bə:kənhed BCE,Chis.
  _ _ ⟋ BCE
  loc. _ _ ⟋ EPD

Birkett Mire/Cu
  bərkit PNE'side 71
Birk Rigg/WRY
  bək rig DDd 14
Birks/WRY
  bɔrks DHd 13
Birkthwaite/Cu (not in PNCu)
  bɔ:þət Hope
Birkwray/La
  bə:kre: PNLa 218
Birley/Db,He,Yorks.
  bə:li EPD,DHe 43

  bə:lə DHe (dial. in North Here
    fordshire)
Birling/K,Nb,Sx
  bə:liŋ EPD,PNK
Birlington/ERY (now spelt →
             Bridlington)
  loc.vulg. bɔlitən PNERY
Birmingham/Wa
  brʌmədʒəm PNWa 34 ("vulgo"),
    PNWa(i)29,PNE&W,DSLa
    Mawer(4)285
  bɛ:nigəm PNWa 34
  brʌmidʒəm GlossSEWo 81,GlossWa
    Schr.("vulgar"),MEG 2
    ("the popular form"),
    Zachr.(2)155 ("loc.")
  brumidʒəm Ellis 488
  brʌmidʒem Schr.
  bə:miŋəm EPD,BBC,BCE,Schr.,
    Kruis.,Chis.
  bə:migəm EDG §274
  bæmiŋgəm Wilde 29
  brʌm Hope (note: The newspaper
    the B. area of the
    National Union of St
    dents is called Brum
    Student)
Birstall/Le,WRY
  'bə:stɔ:l BBC
  bəstəl Ellis 489 (for B. in Le)
Birtley/Nb
  bɑ:tli PNNbDu 23
Biscovey/Co
  'biskəvei BBC
Bisham/Brk
  bisəm BBC
  bisən Hope
Bishampton/Wo
  biʃəmtən PNWo 97
  bisəpn GlossSEWo 81
Bishopsgate/Ldn
  biʃəpsgeit, -git EPD,Kruis.
  nearly always -geit MEG 254
  biʃəgit CPP (for the undergrou
    station,now Liverpool S
Bishopsgate Street/Ldn
  biʃəpsgeit,-get,-git Schr.
Bishopston/So
  biʃəpstən EPD,BBC
Bishopstone/W
  olim buʃtən PNW 286
Bishopsworth/So(=Bishport)
  biʃpɔ:t BG,PNE&W
Bishopsthorpe/Li,WRY
  biʃəpþɔ:p Schr.
Bishopswearmouth/Du
  'biʃəp'wiəmauþ BBC
  wiəməþ Hope
  -məþ more often heard than
  -mauþ Bchm.77

Bisley/Sr
  bizli   PNSr lo3,EPD
Bispham/La
  bispəm   EPD,BBC,BCE
Bissoe/Co
  bisou   BBC
Bittesby/Le
  bitsbi   BBC,BCE
Bitteswell/Le
  bitizwel   BBC
  bitswel, bitʃəl   BCE
Bivelham Fm/Sx
  bivəl'hæm   PNSx 382
Bixton/Nf
  biksn   Hope
Blaby/Le
  bleibi   BBC
Blackawton/D
  blæk'ɔːt(ə)n   BBC
Blackburn/La,WRY
  blegbərn   PNLa(ii),DSLa,
            Ellis 346 (for B.
            in La)
  blegbəːn   DAd 73
  blækbəːn   EPD
  blækbən   Schr.
Blackdown/Wt
  blækdaun   DWt,s.n.jaant
Blackford
  blækfəd   EPD
Blackfordby/Le
  bloufədbi   Hope
Blackfriars/Ldn
  'blæk'fraiəz   EPD,Schr.,Kruis.
  ˈ _ _   EPD
  blek-   CPP 66
Blackgang Chine/Wt
  blæ(k)gæŋ tʃain   PNWt 114
Blackhall/Cu
  blekəl   GlossCu xvii
Blackhall/La
  blækou   Bardsley,s.n.Blackow
Blackham/Sx
  blækəm   PNSx(i) 26
Blackheath
  blæk'hiːþ   EPD,Kruis.,Schr.,
            HSM 5
  ˈ _ , ˌ ˈ   EPD
Blacklands/Wt
  blæklənz   PNWt 237
Blackley/La,WRY
  bleikli   PNLa 37,DEPN,EPD,BBC,
            BCE,Bardsley
  blækli,blæklei   Schr.
Blackmoor
  blækmuə,-mɔə EPD,Bchm.83
  -mɔː   EPD
  -mɔːə   Bchm.83

Blackmoor/We
  blækmər   PNE'side 73
Blackmore/Ess,W
  'blækmɔː   EPD,Bchm.69
  -mɔə   EPD
Blackness/Gl,Sx
  blæk'nes   BBC
Blacko/La
  blakə   PNLa 67
Blackpool
  blækpuːl   EPD,Schr.
Blackrock/La
  blækrɔk   EPD
Black Rock Ledge/Wt
  blæk rak leidʒ   PNWt 36
Blackstone
  blækstən   EPD,Kruis.
Blackwall/Ldn
  'blækwɔːl   EPD,Schr.
Blackwater (r.n.)
  blæk'wɔːtə   BBC,Schr.
  ˈ _ _   EPD,DWt,s.n.jolterhead
Blackwell
  blækw(ə)l, -wel   EPD
  blækwəl   Schr.
  blekl   Schr.("loc."),Hope (for
            B. in Cu)
Blacon/Chs
  bleikən   PNChs IV/168,BBC
Blacon Barn/Bk
  bleikən   PNBk 18
Blacup/WRY
  bleikəp   PNSWY 76
Bladon/O
  bleidən   PNO 252,BBC
Blagrave/Brk
  blægreiv   EPD
Blaisdon/Gl
  bleizdən   BBC
Blake (as in B.Hall/Ess)
  bleik   EPD
Blakeden/Chs
  blek-   PNChs III/171
Blakehope/Nb
  bleikəp   BBC,BCE
Blakeley Brow/Chs
  bleikli   PNChs IV/227
Blake Mire/WRY
  bleːk maiər   DDd 16
Blakemore/Sa
  bliːkmər   GlossSa xxx
Blakeney/Gl,Nf
  bleikni   EPD,BBC,BCE (for B.
            in Nf)
Blakenhall/Chs
  'blækənɔːl,'blæknɔːl   PNChs III/51
Blakenham/Sf
  bleikənəm   BBC

Blake Rigg/WRY
  ble:k rig   DDd 16
Blakesley/Np
  breiksli [sic!]   PNNp 39
  bleiksli   BBC
Blanchland/Nb
  blænʃlənd   BBC,BCE
Bland/WRY
  blænd   EPD
Blandford/Do,So
  blɑ:nvərd   DDo
  blæn(d)fəd   EPD
Blands Gill/WRY
  blanz gil   DDd 12
Blandy (as in B.'s Hill/Brk)
  blændi   EPD
Blashenwell Fm/Do
  blæʃənwel   PNDo I/8,PNDo(i)118
Blaston/Le
  bleistən   BBC
Blawith/La
  blɑ:ð, blɑ:þ   PNLa 214
  blɑ:iþ   EPD
Blawith Rd/Ldn
  bleiwiþ   EPD
Blaydon Haughs/Du
  'bleid(ə)n 'hɔfs   BBC
Blaze Fell/Cu
  bli:zfl   PNE'side 75
  bli:z   PNCu 220
Blea- (as first element in pl.ns
    in Cu)
  bliə-   PNCu xli
Bleadon/So
  bli:d(ə)n   BBC
Bleak Down/Wt
  blik dæun   PNWt 147
Blea Moor/WRY
  blea mouər   DDd 17
  bli: muə   BBC
Blean/WRY
  blein   BBC
Blean, B.Forest/K
  bli:n   BBC,PNK
Bleansley/La
  bli:nzli   PNLa 222
Bleawick/We
  'bli:wik   PNWe II/221
Blechingley/Sr (so spelt in PNSr;
    it is spelt Bletchingly in
    Hope and Blechingly in Schr.)
  bletʃiŋ lai   Hope
  bletʃiŋli   Schr.
Bledington/Gl
  blediŋtən   PNGl I/213
Bledisloe/Gl
  bledislou   EPD

Blelham Tarn/La (a lake)
  bleləm   PNLa 192
Blemundsbury Ho/Ldn
  blemzbəri   BBC
Blencarn/Cu (also spelt -cairn)
  blen'kɑ:rn   RN 59,PNE'side 74
  -kɑ:n   DEPN
Blencathara/Cu (a mountain, which
    also called Saddleback)
  blen'kæðrə   BBC,BCE
Blenheim/Gl,O
  blenəm, blenim   Schr.
Blenheim Palace/O
  blenəm   EPD,BBC,Kruis.
  blenim   EPD
Blenkinsop/Nb (also spelt -pp)
  bleŋkinsɔp   EPD
Blennerhasset/Cu
  blin'reisit   /NCu 265
  blenəhæsit   EPD
  blinreisət   GlossCu xvii
Bletchenden/K
  bletʃinden   PNK
Bletchingly/Sr → Blechingley
Bletchley/Bk
  bretʃli   PNBdHu xxxviii
  bletʃli   EPD
Bletsoe/Bd
  bletsou   BBC
Bliby/K
  blaibi   PNK
Blidworth/Nt
  vulgo blidəð, blidəf   PNNt 115
  blidwə:þ   BBC
Blindcrake/Cu
  blin-kreiək   PNCu 266
Blindley Heath/Sr
  blaindli hi:þ   BBC
Blisland/Co
  blizlənd   BBC
Blisworth/Np
  blizwəþ   PNNp 143
  blizwə:þ   BBC
Blithfield/St
  'blifi:ld   BBC

Blofield/Nf
  bloufi:ld   BBC
Blo Norton/Nf(see also s.n. N.Belle
  'blou 'nɔ:tən   BBC
Bloodstone Copse/Wt
  blʌdstoun kɔ:ps   PNWt 52
Bloomfield/So,St
  blu:mfi:ld   EPD
Bloomsbury/Ldn
  blu:mzbəri   Schr.
  -b(ə)ri   EPD

Blore/St
  blɔ:, blɔə EPD
Blount (as in B.'s Ct,/O,W,
    B.'s Gn/St)
  blʌnt EPD,Kruis.
Bloxham/O
  blɔksəm EPD
Bloxwich/St
  blɔkswitʃ BBC
  blɔksidʒ Hope,ONwick 369
Bluethwaite/We
  bliuþət PNE'side 67
Blundeston/Sf
  blʌndistən BBC
Blunsdon St.Andrew, Broad B./W
  olim blʌnsən PNW 31
Bluntisham/Hu
  blʌntsəm,blʌntʃəm PNBdHu 2o4
  blʌntiʃəm, blʌntisəm BBC,BCE
Blyborough/Li
  blaibə GlossM&C,s.n.Cobble
Blyth/Nb,Nt,Wa
  blaið BBC,BCE (for B. in Nb),
          PNNt(i) 17
Blyth/Nb;Sf (r.n.)
  blaið RN 39 (for B. in Nb),
        DEPN (for B. in Nb),BBC,
  bleið Ellis (for B. in Nb)
Blythborough/Sf
  blaibrə DSf 249,BBC,Hope
  blaib(ə)rə EPD
Blythe/Wa
  blaið EPD
Blyton/Li
  blaitn EPD
Boarhunt/Ha
  'bɔ:hʌnt BBC
  bɔrənt BBC,BCE
  bo:hʌnt BCE
Boarzell/Sx
  bɔ:'zel PNSx 451
Boasley/D
  bouzli PND 174
Bobby (as in B.Hill/Sf)
  bɔbi EPD
Bobberstone/Wt
  babəsn, bɔbərstn PNWt 147
Bobbing/K
  bɔbiŋ PNK
Bobbingworth/Ess
  bɔbiŋwə:þ BBC
  bʌviŋə Hope
  boviŋə EssDD 158
(see also s.n. Bovinger/Ess)
Bochym/Co
  bɔtʃim Jenner(2)3o1
Bockhanger/K
  bɔkhæŋə PNK

Bocking/Ess,WRY
  bɔkən PNEss 413
  bɔkiŋ Schr.
Bockingfold/K
  bɔkiŋ fould PNK
Bocombe/Do
  bukəm Mayo
Boconnoc/Co
  bə'kɔnək BBC
  bo'kɔnək BCE
  _ ́_ DEPN (stress only)
Boden Hall/Chs
  boudən, budən PNChs II/3o7
Bodenham/He,W
  bɔd(ə)nəm PNW 393,BBC
  bɔdənəm DHe 43,BCE (for B. in He)
  -ɔ- DEPN (for B. in He)
  dial. bɔdnəm DHe 43
Bodgate/D
  bɔdʒət PND 158
Bodiam Mill/K
  bɔdiəm PNK
Bodiam/Sx
  bɔdʒəm PNSx 518,PNSx(i) 26,DEPN
  bɔdʒm Hope
  boudiəm EPD,BBC,BCE
  bɔdiəm BBC,BCE
  boudjəm EPD
Bodleian Library/O
  'bɔdliən EPD,BBC,Schr.
  bɔd'liən EPD,BBC
  bɔd'li:ən EPD,Schr.
Bodicote/O
  bɔdikʌt PNO 395
Bodlestreet Gn/Sx
  bu:dl PNSx 48o, Hope
Bodley/D
  bɔdli EPD
  bʌdli Zachr.(2)15o ("the etymol-
        ogically correct pron.")
Bodmin/Co
  bɔdmin EPD
Bodrugan's Leap/Co (or: Bodrigan)
  bə'drʌgən BBC
Bodsham/K
  bɔdsəm PNK
Bogden/K
  bɔgden PNK
Boggart Hole Clough/La
  'bɔgət 'houl 'klʌf BCE
Boggs/Cu (f.n. nr Kirkoswald)
  bougs Thorn. 7o and 81, note 171
Bognor/Sx
  bɔgnə PNSx(i)27,EPD
  bʌgnə PNSx(i) 27
Bohemia/Wt
  bou'eimi PNWt 148

Bohun's Hall/Ess
  bu:nz PNEss 3o5
  cf. EPD,s.n. Bohun: bu:n,bouən
Bohunt Manor/Ha
  bouhʌnt BBC
Bois/Bk
  bɔiz EPD
Bolam/Du,Nb
  bouləm BBC
Boldon/Du
  bouldən BBC,BCE
  boudən PNNbDu 27
Boldre/Ha
  bouldə EPD,BBC,BCE
Boldron/NRY
  bourəm, boudrən PNYN 3o3
Bolenow/Co
  bə'lenou BBC
Bolesworth Castle, B. Hill Fm/Chs
  boulzwəþ PNChs IV/15
Bolingbroke/Li
  buliŋbruk EPD ("old fash-
      ioned"),HSM 52
      note 74 ("old fash-
      ioned"),HL 1224 ("ob-
      solete"),MEG 334
  bɔliŋbruk HL 1224,MEG 334,HSM
      52,note 74,Kruis.
  -brouk HL 278 ("rarely")
  bɔlinbruk Kruis.
  bouliŋbruk EPD,Kruis.
Bolingey/Co
  bə'lindʒei BBC
  bo'lindʒi BCE
Bolitho/Co
  bə'laiþou BBC,EPD
  bo'laiþou BCE
  bɔ'laiþou EPD
  _ / _ GlossWCo xiv (stress)
Bollin/Chs (r.n.)
  bɔlin BBC
Bollingham/He
  bɔlindʒəm,
  bɔliŋəm BBC,BCE
Bollington/Chs (Macclesfield Hd)
  bɔlitn PNChs II/vii ("olim"),
      GlossChs
  bɔlintən PNChs II/vii
  bɔliŋtən PNChs II/vii,Hope
Bollington/Chs (Bucklow Hd)
  bɔliŋtən PNChs II/ix
  bɔlitn PNChs II/ix ("olim"),
      GlossChs,Hope
Bolney/O
  bou(l)ni BBC
Bolney/Sx
  bouni DEPN,BBC,BCE,PNSx 257,
      Mawer(2)95 ("still in
      common use")

boulni PNSx(i)27,BBC,BCE
Bolnhurst/Bd
  bounərs PNBdHu 13
  bounhə:st BBC
  -oun- DEPN
Bolsover/Db
  bauzə PNDb 214,GlossSh 24,Hope
      Walker 25,Schr. ("loc."
  bouzər Ellis 438
  'boulzouvə EPD,BBC,BCE
  'bɔlsəvə Schr.
Bolsover St/Ldn
  bɔlsəvə, bɔlsouvə EPD
Bolstone/He (also spelt -ston)
  bouls(ə)n BBC
Boltby/NRY
  boutbi PNYN 198
Bolt Head/D (a promontary)
  boult hed EPD,Schr.
Bolton
  boult(ə)n EPD
  boultən Schr.
Bolton/Cu
  boutən GlossCu xvii
Bolton/La
  boutn PNLa 45,Ellis 343,Hope
  bautn PNLa(ii),Hope
  boutən Brunner 167
Bolton/We
  boutən PNE'side 66
  boutn ib. 73
Bolton by Bowland/WRY
  'boultən bi 'bɔlənd PNYW VI/18
  'boult(ə)n bai 'bɔlənd,
    -      - 'boulənd BBC
  boultn bai bɔlənd,
    -      - boulənd BCE
Boltons/Cu
  boutən [sic!] PNCu 269
Bolventor/Co
  bɔl'ventə BBC
Bomere Heath/Sa
  'boumiə 'hi:þ BBC
Bonchurch/Wt
  'bɔntʃə:rtʃ PNWt 45
  bɔntʃə:tʃ EPD
Bonham/W
  bɔnəm EPD
Boningale/Sa (also spelt Boninghall
  'bɔniŋeil BBC
Bonington/Nt
  bʌniŋtən, bɔniŋtən PNNt 255
Bonsall/Db
  bɔnsl PNDb 345
  bɔnsə Hope
Bonscale/We
  bɔnskil PNE'side 68
Bonwick/ERY
  bɔnik PNYE 8o

Bonython/Co
  bə'naiþən, bɔ'naiþən EPD
  -'ai- Jenner(2)3ol
Booker/Bk
  bukə EPD
Boon (as in Boon Hill/St)
  bu:n EPD
Boonwood/Cu
  bi'u:n wud GlossCu xvii
Boosbeck/NRY
  biuzbek PNYN 145
  bu:zbek BBC
Boot/Cu
  bo:t PNCuWe 19
Booth/ERY,WRY
  buiþ PNYW III/72
  buið DHd 17
  bu:þ Kruis.
  bu:ð EPD
Bootham/Yorks.
  bu:ðəm DEPN
Boothby/Cu,Li
  bu:ðbi Kruis.,EPD
Booth Dean/WRY
  buiþ dein Hope
Booth Town/WRY
  buəs tɑ:n, buiþ tɑ:n Hope
Boothwaite/We (f.n.)
  olim bɔ:ðət Simpson 287
Bootle-cum-Linacre/La
  bu:tl EPD
  bu:tlkəm'linəkə Schr.
Boots Gn/Chs
  bu:ts EPD
Booze/NRY
  bu:z PNYN 295
Boraston/Sa
  bʌrəstən Hope
Bordeaux Fm/Ess
  bɔdəz PNEss 531
Borden/K
  bɔ:den PNK
Borderiggs/La
  bordərig [sic!],
  bɔ:drigz PNLa 222
Boreat/D
  bʌrjət PND 358
Boreatton/Sa
  brætn GlossSa 516
Boreham
  bɔ:rəm, bɔərəm EPD
Boresile/K
  bɔ:sail PNK
Boringdon/D
  bɔritən PND 252
The Borough/So
  vulg. ðə bʌrə MEG 257

Boroughbridge/WRY
  'bərəbrig PNYW V/82
Borough Gn/Ca
  bʌrə gri:n ONCa 197
Borrend Head/WRY
  bɔrən ied DDd 12
Borrowash/Db
  bɔrouwɔʃ PNDb 488,BBC [1]
  bʌrouwɔʃ DEPN,BBC,Hope [1]
  bɔrouæʃ BBC [2]
  bʌrouzæʃ Hope [2]
  bʌrowɔʃ,bɔroæʃ, bɔrowɔʃ BCE
Borrowby/NRY (in Langbargh East
                 Wapentake)
  bɔrəbi PNYN 136
Borrowby/NRY (in Allerton Wapentake)
  barəbi PNYN 2o5
Borrowdale/Cu,We
  bɔrədəl PNCu 349
  bɔrədl PNE'side 74
  bɔrədeil EPD,Schr.
  bɔroudeil EPD
Borstal/K
  bɔ:stl EPD,PNK
  bɔ:stəl CPhon 77
Borthwood Fm/Wt
  bu:ðwəd, bɔ:rþwud PNWt 53
Borwick/La
  bɔrik DEPN,EPD,BBC,BCE,Hope
Bosbury/He
  bɔsbəri, dial. bɔsbri: DHe 43
Boscar/NRY
  bɔskə PNYN 26
Boscastle/Co
  'bɔskɑ:sl EPD,BBC,BCE
  'bɔskæsl BBC
  _ ⹁ MEG 153
Boscaswell/Co
  bəs'kæzwəl BBC
Boscawen/Co
  bəs'kauən BBC
  bɔs'kouən, -kouin EPD
  bɔs'kɔ:in EPD,Kruis.
Boscobel/Sa
  'bɔskəbel BBC
Bose Hill/Cu (f.n. nr Kirkoswald)
  bu:əz Thorn. 61 and 79,note 118
Bosham/Sx
  bɔzəm PNSx 57,PNSx(i)29,DEPN,
               EPD,BBC,BCE
  bɔsəm EPD,BCE
  bɔs-həm Hope
  "A new pron. bɔʃəm is now sometimes heard" (EPD)
Boshaw/WRY
  bo:ʃei (?) DHd 1oo [3]

---

1) Hope's transcription <u>Burro Wash</u> is rendered [bʌrəwaʃ] in PNDb(i) I/185.
2) Hope's transcription <u>is Burros Ash</u>.
3) <u>Bo-shay</u> in DHd could also be [bou-].

Bosinney/Co (also spelt Bossiney)
   bə'sini   EPD,BBC,
              DEPN (stress only)
   bɔ'sini   EPD
Bosley/Chs
   bɔ:zli   PNChs I/54,GlossChs
Bosporthennis/Co
   bɔsp'renis   Jenner(2) 3o3
Bossall/NRY
   bɔsəl   PNYN 36
Bossinney/Co → Bosinney
Bostock/Chs
   bɔstɔk   EPD
Boston/Li
   bɔstən   Schr.,Kruis.
   bɔ:stən   Hope
   bɔst(ə)n   EPD
Bosullow/Co
   bə'sʌlou   BBC
Boswarth/Co
   _ ˊ   Jenner(2)3o4
Boswell/Li[1]
   bɔzwl, bɔzwel   EPD,Kruis.
   bɔzwəl   EPD
Bosworth (Market B.)/Le
   bɔzþ   GlossLe
   bɔzwəþ   EPD,BBC,Schr.,Kruis.
   bɔzwə:þ[2]   EPD
Botany Bay[2]
   bɔtəni bei   Schr.
Botesdale/Sf
   bædsdeil, bʌdsdeil   Hope
Bothal/Nb
   bɔtl   PNNbDu 28,DEPN
   bɔtəl   Hope
Bothamsall/Nt
   bɔtəmsəl, bɔðəmsəl   PNNt 69
   bɔtəmsɔ:l   Hope
   loc. bɔðmsəl, oth. bɔtmsəl
              PNNt(i) 19
   'bɔðəmsɔ:l   BBC
   - ð-   DEPN
Bothel/Cu
   bouəl, boul   PNCu 271
   bu:el   DEPN
   bu:əl   GlossCu
Bothel and Threapland/Cu
   'bɔþl ən(d) 'þri:plənd   BBC
Bothenhampton/Do
   bouþənhæmtən, olim bɔ:ntən
          PNDo(i) 255 and note 1
   bɔþ(ə)n'hæm(p)tən   BBC
   -ouþ-   DEPN
Botolph Claydon/Bk
   bɔtl   PNBk 131,DEPN
   bɔtɔlf, bɔtəlf   EPD

Botolphs/Sx
   bʌtəls   PNSx 222
   bʌtəlfs   PNSx 222,PNSx(i)29
Botterley Hill/Chs
   bɔtəli   PNChs III/142
Bottesford/Li
   bɔtisfəd, bɔtsfəd   BBC,BCE
   bɔtsəþ, bɔtsə:þ, bɔtswə:þ   Hope
   bɔdswə:þ (?)   GlossM&C
Bottisham/Ca
   olim bɔtisəm   PNCa 129
   bɔtsəm   PNCa 129,Hope
   bɔtʃəm   PNO li (add. and corr.)
   bɔtiʃəm   ONCa 177,BBC
Bottlesford/W
   bɔdl   DPew 99
Bottomroyd/WRY (f.n.)
   bumrɔid   DAl&Hd
Boughton
   bautn, bɔ:tn   EPD,Kruis.
Boughton (Gt B.,B.Hall,B.Heath)/Chs
   bɔ:tn   GlossChs
   boutən   PNChs IV/123
   bɔ:t(ə)n   BBC
Boughton/Hu
   baut(ə)n   BBC
Boughton/K
   bɔ:t(ə)n   BBC
   bɔ:tən   BCE
Boughton, B.Ho/Np
   bautən   PNNp 133,173,BCE
   baut(ə)n   BBC
Boughton/Np (nr Northampton)
   -au-   DEPN
Boughton/Nt
   bu:tn   PNNt(i) 2o
   bu:t(ə)n, baut(ə)n   BBC
   bu:tən, bautən   BCE
   -u:-   DEPN
Boughton Aluph/K
   'bɔ:t(ə)n 'æləf   BBC
   bɔ:tən æləf   PNK
   -ɔ:-   DEPN
Boughton Malherbe/K
   'bɔ:t(ə)n 'mæləbi   BBC
   bɔ:tən mæləbi   PNK
Boughton Monchelsea/K
   'bɔ:t(ə) 'mʌntʃlsi   BBC
   'bɔ:tn 'mʌntʃəlsi   BCE
   bɔ:tən mʌntʃəlsi   PNK
Boughton-under-Blean/K
   bɔ:tən ʌndə bli:n   PNK
Boughton-under-Bourne/K
   bɔ:tən ʌndə bɔ:n, bə:n, bʌn   PN
Boulby/NRY
   boulbi   PNYN 14o , EPD

1) A gypsy is called "Boswell" and pron.[bɔzl] in Lincs.(GlossM&C, s.
Boswell).   2) In the Lincs. saying "to send one to B.Bay" the
name is pron. [bɔtni bei] (GlossM&C, s.n. Bot'ny Bay).

Bould/O
    bould   PNO 357
Bouldnor/Wt
    bou(l)dnər, bo:dnər   PNWt 2o8
Boulge/Sf
    bu:ldʒ, bouldʒ   BBC,BCE
Boulmer/Nb
    bu:mə   PNNbDu 28,DEPN,BBC,BCE
Boultham/Li
    bu:təm   BBC,BCE
    bu:ðəm   BBC,BCE,Hope
Boulton/Db
    boun   PNDb 425
    boult(ə)n   BBC
    boultən, bu:tn   Hope
Boundstone/Sr
    'baundstoun   BBC
Bourchier's Hall/Ess
    bautʃəz   PNEss 3o5
Bourchiers/Ess (f.n.)
    boutʃəz   EssDD 159
Bourn/Ca
    bə:n   PNO li (add. and corr.)
    bɔn   ONCa 191
Bourne
    buən, bɔ:n, bɔən   EPD
Bournemouth/Ha
    bɔ:nməþ   EPD,Schr.,Kruis.,
        HL 495
    buən-, bɔən-   EPD
    -mauþ   EPD ("rarely"),Bchm.247
    -or-   ESpr 343
Bourn's/Ess (a farm)
    bounzəz   EssDD 158
Bournville/Wo
    bɔ:nvil, bɔən-, buən-   EPD
Bourton
    bɔ:t(ə)n   BBC
Bourton/Bk
    bu:ətən   PNBk 6o
    -uə-   DEPN
Bourton/Do
    bɔ:tən   PNDo(i) 3
Bourton/O (in Banbury Hd)
    bə:tən is commoner than
    bɔ:tən   PNO 414
    bo:tən   BCE
Bourton (Black B.)/O (in Bampton
        Hd)
    bɔ:tən is commoner than
    bə:tən   PNO 3o6
    bɔ:t(ə)n   BBC
    bɔ:tən   BCE
Bourton on Dunsmore/Wa
    bɔ:tən   PNWa 127
Bourton-on-the-Water/Gl
    bɔ:t(ə)nɔn ðə wɔ:tə   BBC
    -ɔ:-   DEPN

Bousfield/We
    bausfi:ld   EPD
Bouth/La
    bauð   PNLa 216, DEPN
Boveney/Bk
    bʌvni   DEPN,BBC,BCE,Hope
Boveridge/Do
    bovəridʒ   PNDo(i)loo
    -ɔ-   DEPN
Bovey/D (r.n.)
    bɔvi   RN 44
    bʌvi   PND 2
Bovey Tracey
    bʌvi   PND 466,DEPN,EPD,Schr.,Hope
    bʌvi treisi   BBC,BCE
    bɔvi   DEPN
Bovingdon/Ess,Hrt
    bɔvəndən   PNHrt 29
    bɔviŋdən, bʌviŋdən   EPD (for B.
        in Hrt),BBC,BCE (for B.
        in Hrt)
    bouviŋdən   BCE (for B. in Hrt)
    loc. -ʌ-   EPD (for B. in Hrt)
Bovinger/Ess
    bʌvindʒə   PNEss 52,Dodgson(2)364
        and (3)144,Hope
    (see also s.n. Bobbingworth)
Bovington/Do
    bɔviŋtən   BBC
Bovington Hall/Ess
    bʌviŋdən   PNEss 413
Bow/Brk,Cu,D,Ldn (i.e. Stratford-le-
        Bow)
    bou   BBC,Schr.
Bow Brickhill/Bk
    bou brikəl   PNBk 3o
Bow Bridge/Wt
    bou bridʒ   PNWt 286
Bowcombe/Wt
    bæukəm   PNWt 96
    bʌkəm   PNWt 96,DWt,s.n. dresh
Bowden
    baud(ə)n   BBC
    boudn, baudn   EPD
Bowden/Chs
    boudn   BCE
    -ou-   DEPN
Bowden Hd/Db
    boudn   PNDb(i) I/187
Bowden/Np
    baudən   PNNp lo
Bowder Stone/Cu
    'baudə stoun   BBC
Bowdon/Chs
    boudən   PNChs II/5
    boud(ə)n   BBC
Bower/Wt → Queen's Bower
Bower Bank/WRY
    bauə baŋk   DDd 15

Bowers Giffard/Ess
  dʒifəd   PNEss 144
  'bauəz 'gifəd   BBC
Bowerswain Fm/Do
  bouswein, bousən   PNDo(i) 92
Bowes/NRY
  bouz   PNYN 3o4,EPD,BBC
Bowes Pk/Ldn
  bouz pɑ:k   BBC
Bow Fell/Cu (a mountain)
  'bou 'fel   BBC
Bowforth/NRY
  boufəþ   PNYN 64
Bowland
  boulənd   EPD
Bowland/La (B.Forest)
  bɔlən(d)   PNLa 142
  bɔlənd   DEPN,BBC,BCE
  bɔlən   PNLa(ii)
Bowland/WRY
  bɔlənd   PNYW VII/112,DEPN,BBC
Bowling/WRY
  bouliŋ   PNYW III/244,EPD,BBC
Bowmont/Nb (r.n.)
  bou-   DEPN
Bowness on Windermere/We
  'bounes   PNWe I/185,EPD,BBC,
            BCE
  bu:-   DEPN
Bowness/Cu
  'bounes   DEPN,EPD,BBC,BCE
Bowood/Do
  bouwud   PNDo(i) 276
Bowood Ho/W
  bouwud   PNW 257
Bowscale/Cu
  bouskel   PNCu 181
  bouskil   PNE'side 68
Bow Scar/Cu
  bou skɑ:r   PNE'side 73
Bowsden/Nb
  bauzən   PNNbDu 28
Bowsear/K
  bouziə   PNK
Bowston/We
  boustən   PNWe I/152
Bowthorpe/ERY
  bouþrəp   PNYE 261
Bowyer Twr/Ldn
  boujə   BBC
Bowzell/K
  bouzel, bauzel   PNK
Boxgrove/Sx
  -grəv, -grouv   PNSx(i) 29
Boxmoor/Hrt
  'bɔksmuə,-mɔə,-mɔ:,
  loc. _ ′   EPD

Boxworth/Ca
  bɔkswə:þ   ONCa 184
Boyce (as in B.Ct/Gl)
  bɔis   EPD
Boyd/Gl (r.n.)
  bɔid   EPD
Boythorpe/ERY
  bɔiþrəp   PNYE 115
Boyton/Sf
  buitn   DSf 25o
  bɔitn   EPD
Bozeat/Np
  bouʒət   PNNp 189,DEPN,HL 1o81
  bouziæt   BBC
Bozenham Mill/Np
  bouznəm   PNNp 1oo
Brabourne/K
  breibɔ:n   EPD,BBC,BCE
  breibən   BBC,BCE
  breibɔən   EPD
  breibə:n   PNK
  brei-   DEPN
Bracebridge/Li,Nt
  breisbrig   GlossSWLi,Hope (for ?
              in Li),Schr.("loc.")
  breisbridʒ   Schr.
Bracelet/La
  bre:slət   PNLa 222
Bracey Bridge/ERY
  brɛ:sibrig   PNYE 9o
Brackenber/We
  brekinbər   PNE'side 76
Brackenbrough/Cu
  brekinbruf   PNE'side 7o
Brackenbrough Twr/Cu
  brikinbruf   PNCu 2o5
Brackensgill/WRY
  'braknz gil   DDd 15
Brackenslack/We
  brekinslæk   PNE'side 7o
Brackenthwaite/Cu,WRY
  brekənhwit   PNE'side 7o
Bracknell/Brk
  bræknəl, -nl   EPD
Bracon Ash/Nf
  'brækən æʃ   BBC
Bradbury/Du
  brædb(ə)ri   EPD
Bradenham/Bk,Nf
  brædnəm   PNBk 175
  brædənəm   BCE (for B. in Nf)
  -æ-   DEPN (for B. in Nf)
  bræd(ə)nəm   BBC
Bradenstoke-cum-Clack/W
  breidənstouk vulgo brædstɔk
              PNW 27o
  breidnstouk   PNW(i) 33
  brei-   DEPN

Bradfield
  brædfi:ld   EPD,Schr.
Bradford
  brædfəd   EPD,Schr.
  brætfəd   ED 97
Bradford/La
  brædfət   DSLa
Bradford/WRY
  bratfəþ   PNYW III/241
  brædfəþ   Hope,DA1 Hd
  bradfəþ   Ellis 367
Bradgate/WRY
  brædgit, -geit   EPD
Brading/Wt
  breidn   PNWt 49
  breidiŋ   EPD
  brei-   DEPN
  brɑ:dn (or breidn ?)[1] DWt,s.n.
            flick
Bradle Fm/Do
  breidl   PNDo(i) 132,PNDo
         I/88,DEPN
Bradley
  brædli   EPD,Schr.
Bradley/Cu
  brædlə   PNE'side 64
Bradley/St
  brɛ:dli   Ellis 48o
Bradninch/D
  bræniʃ   PND 555
  brædniʃ   PNND 9o
Bradshaw/Db,La,WRY
  loc. breiʃɔ: ROS 42 (for B.
              in WRY)
  brædʃɔ: EPD
Bradstone/D
  brasən   PND 173
Bradwell/Bk
  brædəl   PNBk 17
Bradwell/Db
  bradə   Ellis 426
Bradwell/O
  brædl   PNO(i) 61
Bradwell-juxta-Coggeshall/Ess
  brædl   PNEss 282
Bradwell-juxta-Mare/Ess
  brædəl   PNEss 2o9
Bradworthy/D
  brædəri   PNND 137,DHt1 8 [2]
Brafield on the Green/Np
  breifi:ld   PNNp 144,DEPN
Bragenham/Bk
  brægnəm   PNBk 83
Bragg's Hill/Wt
  brægz il   PNWt 54

Braham Hall/WRY
  brɛ:(ə)m   PNYW V/33
Braidmoor/Cu
  breimə   GlossCu(Suppl.) 1o,s.n.
           Braemer
Brailsford/Db
  breilsfəd   EPD
Brainshaugh/Nb
  breinzhɑ:f   BBC,BCE
Braintree/Ess
  breintri,brɑ:ntri   PNEss 415
  brɑ:ntri: EssDD 158
  brɑ:n-   DEPN
  breintri:, loc. -tri   EPD
Braithwaite/Cu,WRY
  brɛ:þət   PNCu 225, PNE'side 67
  breiþweit   EPD
Braithwell/WRY
  'breiþwel   BBC
  bru:əl   Hope
Brambletye Ho/Sx
  bræmbltai   BBC
  bræmbəltai   BCE
Bramcote/Nt,Wa
  bramkət   PNNt 14o
  bræmkət   PNNt(i) 22
  bræmkɔt   BBC
  braŋkət   Hope
Bramerton/Nf
  bræmət(ə)n   BBC
Bramery/Cu
  brameri   PNCu 17o
Bramfield/Hrt
  vulgo bræmfəl   PNHrt 1o8
Bramfield/Sf
  brɑ:mfild   DSf 25o
Bramford/Sf
  brɑ:mfəd   Hope
Bramhall/Chs
  bramə   PNChs II/vii ("olim"),
           GlossChs
  bramɔ:l   PNChs II/vii
  'bræmhɔ:l   BBC
Bramery/Cu,We
  bræməri   PNE'side 75 (for B. nr
           Penrith and B. nr
           Ainstable)
  brouməri   PNE'side 75 (for B. nr
           Plumpton)
  brɔməri   PNE'side (for B. in We)
Bramhope/WRY
  braməp   PNYW IV/195
  'bræmhoup   BBC
Bramley
  bræmli   EPD

---

1) The transcription in DWt is braadn.
2) The transcription in DHt1 is Bradery.

Bramling/K
  bræmliŋ PNK
Brampton
  bræm(p)tən EPD
  bræmtən Schr.
Brampton/Cu
  bræntən PNE'side,GlossCu
           xvii, Hope
  brantən Ellis 669
Brampton Brian/He
  bræmptən braiən, dial. brɔn
           DHe 43
  brɔːn Hope
Brancaster Staithe/Nf
  'bræŋkəstə 'steið BBC
Brancepeth/Du
  braːnspəþ BBC
Brandesburton/ERY
  branzbɔtn PNYE 74
Brandeston/Sf
  brændistən BBC
Brandis Corner/D
  'brændis 'kɔːnə BBC
Brandiston/Nf
  brændistən BBC
Brandlesholme/La
  'brændlzhoum BBC
Brandon
  brændən EPD,Schr.
Brandon/Sf
  brænd Hope
Brangehill/Ca
  -ndʒ- Dodgson (2)365 and
         (3)145
Brankelow/Chs
  brænkəlou PNChs III/94
Branksea Is/Do (also called
        Brownsea Is)
  "Two pronunciations survived,
  one with, another without
  syncope in the second syllable."   Tengstrand 98
Branksome/Do
  bræŋksəm EPD
Branston/Le,Li,St
  brænstən EPD
Branstone/Wt
  bræns(t)n PNWt 169
Brant Broughton/Li
  brænt bruːt(ə)n BBC
  - bruːtn BCE
  -uː- DEPN
Brantham/Sf
  brænðəm BBC
Branthwaite/Cu
  brænþət DDd 17,PNCu 276 and
        366
  brænðət GlossCu xvii
  brænþweit Kruis.

Brasenose College/O
  breiznouz EPD,Schr.,Kruis.
Brassey Gn/Chs
  bræsi EPD,Kruis.
  braːsi Kruis.
Brassington/Db
  bræsən PNDb 351
  bræsn Hope
Brasted/K
  'breisted DEPN,EPD,BBC,BCE
  breistəd PNK
  (see also s.n. Chart)
Brathay/La,We (r.n.)
  breːði RN 49,PNLa 192
  breiðə Hope
  -eið- DEPN
Bratoft/Li
  breitɔft DEPN,BBC,BCE
Braughing/Hrt
  braːfiŋ PNHrt 189,BCE
  bræfiŋ PNHrt,BCE,BBC,EPD,DEPN
Braunston/Np
  brɔːnsən, braːnsən PNNp 14
Braunstone/Le
  brɔːnstən BBC
Braunton/D
  braːntən PND 32
  brɔːntən BBC
Brawby/NRY
  brɔːbi PNYN 57
Brawith/NRY
  brewiþ PNYN 2o6
  -e- DEPN
Bray/Brk,D
  brei Schr.
Braysworth/Sf
  breisə Hope
Brea/Co
  brei BBC
Breaches Close/Db (f.n. in Ingleby
  today loc. called "British Close
          FnSDb 72
Breaday Heights/NRY
  'briəde PNYN 115
Breadsall/Db
  bredsl PNDb(i) I/195
Breadstone/Gl
  bredstən PNGl II/214
Breage/Co
  briːg DEPN,BBC,BCE
  breig BBC
Breamore/Ha
  bremə EPD,BBC,BCE
Brean/So
  briːn BBC
Brear/WRY
  breː PNYW III/98
Brearley/WRY
  brelə Gloss R&R (so pron. in
         Rossendale)

Brearton/Du
  bri:ə-   IPN II/8
Breaston/Db
  bri:stən   PNDb 43o,BBC
  bri:sən   Hope
  bri:stn   PNDb(i) I/196
Breazle/D
  breizəl   PND 174
The Breck/K
  bræk   PNK
Bredgar/K
  bredgɑː   PNK
Bredicot/Wo
  bredikət   PNWo 1ol
Bredon/Wo
  bri:d(ə)n EPD,BBC
  -i:-   DEPN
Bredwardine/He
  bredwə'dain   BBC
  'bredwədin, -wɔːdin,
  -wɑːdin   Förster
Breightmet/La
  'braitmit   BBC
  breitmit   DEPN,BBC
  braitmet, breitmet BCE (s.n.
                  Tonge-cum-B.)
  breitmət, braitmət, breikmət,
  bregmət   PNLa(ii)
  (see also s.n. Tonge-cum-B.)
Breighton/ERY
  breitən   PNYE 239
Breinton/He
  breintən   BBC,BCE
Bremeridge Fm/W
  bremridʒ   PNW 147
Bremhill/W
  olim brimbəl   PNW 86
Brenchley/K
  brentʃli   BBC
Brendon Hill/So
  buːrnən iːəl   DWSo 11 f.
Brenscombe Fm/Do
  brinskəm   PNDo I/9,PNDo(i)119
Brent/Hrt,Mx (r.n.)
  brent   EPD,Schr.
Brent Eleigh/Sf
  'brent 'iːli   BBC
Brentford/Bk,Mx
  breinfəd   PNBk 227
  breinfɔːd, brænfɔːd Hope
              (for B. in Mx)
  brentfəd   EPD,Schr.,Bchm.132
Brent Pelham/Hrt
  bəːnt peləm   PNHrt 184
Brentwood/Ess
  bəːntud   Hope
Brenzett/K
  brenzit   BBC
  brænzit   PNK

Brereton/Chs.St
  briət(ə)n BBC
  briətən   EPD
  brɛətən, briːətən Schr.
Brereton Gn, B.Hall/Chs
  briətən,loc.brɛətən PNChs II/274
Bressingham/Nf
  bresəŋən   [sic!] Hope
Bretforton/Wo
  brefət(ə)n,bretfət(ə)n BBC
Brettargh Holt/We
  'bretər'hoult BBC
Brewood/St
  bruːd   DEPN,BBC,BCE,Hope
Breydon Water/Nf
  'breid(ə)n 'wɔːtə BBC
Briaryhulme/Chs
  -juːm   PNChs II/237
Bricett/Sf
  braisit   BBC
  braiset   BCE
  -ai-   DEPN
Brickhill/Bk
  brikəl   PNBk 31 f.
Bricklehampton/Wo
  brikləm   PNWo 19o
  brikländ, brikldən GlossSEWo 82
Briddlesford/Wt
  bridlzvərd   PNWt 238
Bridekirk/Cu
  loc. braidkurk DLo 87
Bridestowe/D
  bridistou PND 177,DEPN,BBC
  bridstou   BBC
  bridəstou BCE
Bridewell Springs/W
  bridəl   PNW 15o
Bridge End/WRY
  brig end   DDd 16
Bridge Holme/NRY
  brigoum   PNYN 129
Bridgemere/Chs
  'bridʒmiːə(r) PNChs III/53
Bridgend
  bridʒ'end BBC
  ˊ -   Schr.
Bridgerule/D
  bridʒruːl EPD
Bridgetown
  bridʒtaun EPD,Schr.[1]
Bridgewater Canal/Chs,La[1]
  bridʒwɔːtə EPD,Schr.
Bridgnorth/Sa (also spelt Bridge-)
  'bridʒnɔːþ EPD,BBC,Schr.
Bridgwater/So
  bridʒwɔːtə EPD
Bridlington/ERY
  bridliŋtən EPD,BBC,Schr.,Chis.
  bridliŋtn Kruis.

1) The canal is called Duke's Cut in South Lancs. (DSLa).

local forms of pron.are:

bə:liŋtən Bchm.241,Schr., Chis.,H.A.(2)45, ScandPN 21

bɔlitən PNYE loo,Ellis 5ol, GlossHol 17

bɔliŋtən Schr.,Hope,H.A.(2)45

bɔlintən GlossHol 17

Bridport/Do
bridpɔ:t EPD

Bridstow/He
bridstou BBC,Förster

Bridzor Fm/W
bridzər PNW 197

Brierdene/Nb
bri:ədən PNNbDu 31

Brierley
braiəli EPD

Brierley Hill/St
braiəli hil BBC

Brigg/Li
brig EPD

Brigham/Cu,ERY
brigəm EPD,Schr.

Brigham Bank/We
brigəm bæŋk PNE'side 65

Brighouse/WRY
brigəs PNYW III/76,DHd 27, Hope
brighaus BBC

Brighstone/Wt
braisn,bri(k)stən PNWt 63
braistən PNWt 63,BBC,BCE

Brighthelmstone/Sx → Brighton

Brightholmlee/WRY
braitəmli BBC,BCE

Brightling/Sx
braitliŋ BBC

Brightlingsea/Ess
britlzi PNEss 33o,Zachr.(4)
britlsi Schr. 122
briklzi PNEss 33o,Zachr.(4) 122,DEPN,Hope
brikəlsi PNNbDu [!] 23
'braitliŋsi: EPD,BBC,BCE

Brightmans Hayes/D
brɑ:nsi PND lo6

Brighton/Sx
brait(ə)n BBC
braitən Schr.,Hope
braitn PNSx(i)33,EPD,Kruis., MEG 265

Brightstone/Wt (now spelt Brixton)
braisən DWt,s.n.┐chock-dog
braistoun EPN 87┘

Brightwell/Sf
braitwəl PNDVall 8

Brigmerston/W
brigmə(r)stn PNW(i) 36

Brignall/NRY
brignəl PNYN 3o2

Brigsteer/We
'brig'stiə PNWe I/lo9

Brigstock/Np
brigstok EPD

Brimpsfield/Gl
brimzfi:ld PNGl I/144

Brimstage/Chs
brimstidʒ PNChs IV/234

Brind/ERY
brind EPD

Brindle/La
brindl EPD

Briningham/Nf
brin- DEPN
-inəm, -iŋəm PNing 172

Brinkheugh/Nb
'briŋkhju:f BBC,BCE

Brinscall/La
brinskl BBC
brinskəl BCE

Brinsea/So
brinzi BBC,BCE

Brinsley/Nt
olim brʌnzli PNNt 117
brinzli EPD

Briscoe/NRY
briskə PNYN 3o6

Brislington/So
bʌstin ROS 42
bʌstən Hope

Bristol/Gl
bristl EPD,Bchm.188,MEG 297
bristəl Bchm.188,Schr.,MEG 297

Brisworthy/D
brisəri PND 229

Britain
britn EPD,Schr.,Kruis.,MEG 264 DSDu
britən EPD

Britford/W
bə:fəd PNW 22o

Britwell Salome/O
sɔləm PNO lo5
britwəl sæləm PNO(i)177,BBC,BC

Brixham/D
briksəm Schr.,Chis.

Brixton/D.Ldn
briksən PND 249
brikstən MEG 266, Schr.
brikst(ə)n EPD

Brixton/Wt → Brightstone

Brize Norton/O
braiz nɔ:tən PNO(i)64,BBC

1) The natives of B. are called "BrIsoner[s]" (EPN 29).

Broadbent/La
  brɔ:dbent   EPD
Broadclyst/D (also spelt Broad
                       Clyst)
  'brɔ:dklist   BBC,BCE
Broadfield/Cu
  brɛædfi:ld   PNE'side 72
Broadford/K,Sr
  brɔ:dfəd   Schr.
Broadford Bridge/Sx
  brɔ:dfəd   PNSx(i) 34
Broadhembury/D
  brɔ:d'hembəri   BBC
Broadhurst/Sx
  brɔ:dhəːst   EPD
Broadmoor/Brk,Sr,St
  brɔ:dmuə,-mɔə,-mɔ: EPD
Broadnymet/D
  -i-   DEPN,s.n.Nymet
Broad Oak/WRY
  bruəd uək   DHd 15
Broadoaks Fm/Ess
  brɛædəks   PNEss 547
Broadstairs/K
  brɔ:dstɛəz   EPD
Broadstone/Wt
  'brɔ:dstuən   PNWt 285
Broad Stones/WRY
  bruəd stuənz   DHd 15
Broadstruthers Barn/Nb
  bradstə   PNNbDu 31
Broadwas/Wo
  brɑ:dəs, brɔ:dəs   PNWo 1o3
  brɔ:dwəs   BBC
  brædis   Mawer(2)95
Broadwater/Sx
  brɔ:dwɔ:tə   PNSx(i) 34
Broadway
  brɔ:dwei   EPD,Schr.
Broadway/Wo
  brɔ:di   GlossSEWo 82
Broadwell/Gl,O,Wa
  bradəl   PNGl I/214
  brædl   PNO(i) 64
  brædəl   PNWa 139
Broadwood/Nb
  brɔ:dwud   EPD
Broadwoodwidger/D
  bradud   PND 179
  'brɔ:dwud'widʒə   BBC
Brocas/K
  brɔkəs   PNK
Brockdish/Nf
  broudiʃ, brɔ:diʃ   Hope
Brockenhurst/Ha
  brɔk(ə)nhəːst   EPD

Brockford/Sf
  brɔkfəd   Hope

Brockhall/Np
  brɔkəl   PNNp 8o
Brockhampton/Do,Gl
  brɔkətən   Mayo (for B. in Do)
  brɔkiŋtən   Hope (for B. in Gl)[1]
Brockholes/WRY
  brɔkhɔilz   Hope,DAl&Hd
Brockley
  brɔkli   EPD
Brockley Moor/Cu (=Brockleymoor)
  brɔkli   PNE'side 7o
Brockwell/Ldn
  brɔkw(ə)l   EPD
Brodsworth/WRY
  brɔdsəþ   Hope
Brogyntyn/Sa
  brɔ'gʌntin   BBC
Broke/K
  bruk   PNK
Brokerswood/W
  olim brɔkə:zwud   PNW 139
Bromborough/Chs
  loc. brumbərə   PNChs IV/237
  brɔmbərə   PNChs IV/237,BBC
  brʌmbərə   PNL'pool 8o,Hope
Brome/Sf
  bru:m   PNSf 12o,BBC,BCE
Bromeswell/Sf
  brʌmsəl   PNDVall 57
Bromford/Wa
  brɔmfəd   BBC
Bromham/Bd,Wa
  bruməm   PNBdHu 28,DEPN (for B. in
  brʌməm   BBC   Bd)
  brɔməm   EPD
Bromholm/Nf
  'brumhoum   BBC
Bromley
  brɔmli   EPD,Schr.,Bchm.2o5
               ("rarely")
  brʌmli   EPD,Schr.,Bchm.2o5,Chis.
               Zachr.(2)15o ("the [ety-
               mologically] correct
               pron.")
Bromley/Ess
  brɔmli   BBC
Bromley/K
  brʌmli   BCE,PNK ; brɔmli   BBC

  "The old pron. [brʌmli] [...]
  seems to have succumbed completely
  to the spelling pron."   BBC

Bromley/Mx
  brɔmli   BCE
  brʌmli   PNMx(i)
  -ʌ-   DEPN
Bromley/St (Abbots B.)
  brɔmli   BBC
  brʌmli   Hope

---

1) The name is spelt Brook- in Hope.

Brompton
   brʌm(p)tən, brɔm(p)tən EPD,[1]
                   Schr. 521
   brɔm(p)tən BBC
   brʌmtən Kruis.
   "B. used to be [brʌmptən], but
   is now more usualley pron.
   [brɔmptən]" Jones 85

Brompton/K
   brʌmptən Hope
   brʌmtən PNK
Brompton/Mx
   brʌmtən PNMx(i)
   -ʌ- DEPN
Brompton/NRY
   brumptən, brɔmptən PNYN 96
   brʌmptən, brʌntən
     (or -u- ?) Hope
   brɔm(p)tən BBC
Brompton Ralph/So
   'brɔm(p)tən 'rælf BBC
Bromsgrove/Wo
   brɔmzgrouv EPD,BBC
   brʌmzgrouv EPD,Chis.
Bromwich (Castle B./Wa,
              West B./St)
   brʌmidʒ DEPN,EPD,Schr.,
            Kruis.,Bchm.2o5,
            MEG 2o5
   brʌmitʃ EPD,Bchm.2o5,Chis.
   brɔmitʃ EPD,BBC,Kruis.,
            Bchm.2o5
   brʌmwitʃ Schr.
   brɔmidʒ EPD,Bchm.2o5,Kruis.
   brɔmwitʃ Bchm.2o5,Kruis.

for Castle Bromwich:
   brʌmidʒ PNWa 4o,Hope,BBC

for West Bromwich:
   brʌmidʒ BCE,GlossSEWo 82,
            ONwick 369
   brʌmitʃ, brɔmidʒ, brɔmitʃ BCE
Bromyard/He
   brʌmjɑːd, dial. brɔmjəd
                  DHe 43

Brook/K,Wt
   bruk PNK,PNWt 73,EPD
Brookfield
   brukfiːld EPD
Brookhampton/Wo
   brukən PNWo 269
Brookland/K
   bruklənd EPD,PNK
Brookside/Wt
   bruk zaid PNWt 285
Brookville/Nf
   brukvil Schr.

Brookwood/Ha,Sr
   brukwud EPD
Broomfield
   bru(ː)mfiːld EPD
Broomfield/Ess
   brʌmfəl PNEss 241,EssDD 158,
   -ʌ- DEPN
Broomfieldhall Fm/Ess
   blʌmfilz [sic!] PNEss 381
Broomfleet/ERY
   brumflit PNYE 222
Broomhall/Chs
   'bruːmɔːl PNChs III/114
Broseley/Sa
   brouzli BBC
Brotherilkeld/Cu
   olim butərilket PNCu 343
   bʌtərilkət Hope
   butərilket GlossCu xvii
Brotherton/WRY
   brɔðətən PNYW IV/45
   brʌðətən Schr.
Brotherwick/Nb
   brɔdrik PNNbDu 32
Brough
   brʌf EPD,Kruis.,Schr.
   -f Dobson 947
Brough/Db
   bruf HL 857
   brʌf DEPN,Hope,PNDb(i) I/147
Brough/Nt
   bruf HL 857,PNNt 2o4
   brʌf PNNt(i) 24 DEPN
Brough/We (see also s.n. B.under S
   bruf PNWe II/63
   brʌf BBC,BCE,MEG 287
   -f Ferguson 9
Brough/ERY
   bruf PNYE 22o
   brʌf BBC,BCE
Brough, B.Hall,B.Hill/NRY
   bruf PNYN 242,263,273,DEPN (
         B. nr Catterick [=PNYN
         and for B. nr Reeth [=
         PNYN 273])
   brʌf BBC
Broughall/Sa,Sf
   brɔfl BBC
Brougham/We
   bruːm PNWe II/127,BBC,BCE,EPD
         (the only form in EPD o
         1917/24),DEPN,Kruis.,Ho]
         MEG 237
   bruːəm EPD,Kruis.,MEG 376
   broum MEG 376
   brum EPD
   brouəm EPD,PNE'side 65

---

1) According to EPD -ɔ- is now more popular than -ʌ- (see EPD[1917/:
   EPD [1937] and EPD [1967]).

Brough-by-Sands/Cu (=Burgh b.S.)
   bruf   HL 857
Brough Sowerby/We
   'bruf 'sauəbi, - 'sɔəbi
               PNWe II/69
Broughton
   brɔ:tn   Kruis.,EPD (not for B.
   brɔ:tən   Schr.   in Np)
Broughton/Bk (two places)
   brɔ:tən   PNBk 32 (for B. nr
               Fenny Stratford),
               DEPN (for B. nr
               Bierton)
Broughton/Cu
   brɔ:tn, brautn   PNCu 274
   brɔ:t(ə)n   BBC
   brɔ:tən   BCE
Broughton/Db (Church B.)
   brɔ:tən   Hope
   brɔ:tn   PNDb (i)I/2oo
Broughton/Ha
   brɔ:t(ə)n   BBC
   brɔ:tən   BCE
Broughton/K
   brɔ:tən   PNK
Broughton/La (in Lonsdale Hd)
   brɔ:tn   PNLa 222
   brɔ:t(ə)n   BBC
   brɔ:tən   BCE
Broughton/Le (Nether B.)
   brɔ:t (ə)n   BBC
Broughton/Li
   brɔ:t(ə)n   BBC
   brɔ:tən   BCE
Broughton/Np
   brautən   PNNp 123,BCE
   braut(ə)n   DEPN,BBC
   brautn   EPD
Broughton/Nt (Upper B.)
   brɔ:tn   PNNt(i) 25
   brɔ:t(ə)n   BBC
   brɔ:tən   BCE
Broughton/O,St
   brɔ:t(ə)n   BBC
   brɔ:tən   BCE
Broughton/Sa
   brɔ:t(ə)n   BBC
Broughton/NRY
   brout n   PNYN 46
   brɔ:t(ə)n   BBC
   brɔ:tən   BCE
Broughton Astley/Le
   brɔ:t(ə)n æstli   BBC
   brɔ:tən   -   BCE
Broughton Gifford/W
   brɔ:tən dʒifərd   PNW 119[1]
Broughton-in-Furness/La
   brɔ:t(ə)n in fə:nis   BBC
   brɔ:tən in fə:nes   BCE
   broutn i fɔ:rnəs   Ellis 553

Broughton Pogges/O (also spelt Poggs)
   commonly called [pɔgz], but
   [poudʒis] is also heard   PNO(i)65
Brough-under-Stainmore/We
   'brʌf ʌndə 'steinmɔ: BBC
   bruf   GlossCu(re-arr)
   brʌf   DEPN
Brownhow/Cu,We,Brown How/Cu,
Brown Howe/We
   brounə   PNE'side 62
Brownrigg/Cu
   braunrig   EPD
Brownsea Is/Do —→ Branksea Is
Brow Road/WRY
   brɛə ruəd   DHd 14
Broxa/NRY
   brɔksə   PNYN 111
Broxbourne/Hrt
   vulgo brɔgzbən   PNHrt 219
Broxton/Chs
   brɔkstən   PNChs IV/12
   brɔksn   PNChs IV/12,GlossChs
Bruen Stapleford/Chs
   'bru:ən 'steipəlfəd   PNChs III/269
Brundall/Nf
   brʌndl   BBC
Brundholme/Cu
   brundəm   PNCu 32
Brundholme Beck/Cu
   brundəm   PNE'side 65
Brunshaw/La
   branʃə   PNLa (ii)
Brunswick/WRY
   brʌnzwik   EPD,Schr.
Brunthwaite/WRY
   brumfit   PNYW VI/19
Brunton
   brʌntən   EPD
Bruton/So
   bru:t(ə)n   EPD
Bryers (as in B.Brow/La)
   braiəz   EPD
Bryher/Co (Scilly Islands)
   braiə   BBC
Brynn Bank/Chs
   brin   PNChs III/198
Bubwith/ERY
   bubiþ   PNYE 239
Buckden/Hu,WRY
   bʌgdən   PNBdHu 252
   bukdin   PNYW VI/115
Buckenham/Nf
   bʌknəm   Schr.,Hope
   bʌkinəm   Schr.
Bucket's Copse/Wt
   bɔkəts kɑ:ps   PNWt 285
Buckfastleigh/D
   bʌkfəst'li: PND 293
   'bʌkfɑ:st'li: BBC

1) [dz-] in PNW is an apparent misprint.

Buckholme/We
    bukəm   PNE'side 65
Buckhurst
    bʌkhəːst, bʌkəːst   EPD
Buckhurst Pk/Sx
    bʌk-   PNSx(i) 36
Buckingham/Bk,Sx
    bʌkiŋəm   EPD,BBC,Schr.,Kruis.
    bʌkinim   Höfer 3ol
Buckingham Palace/Ldn
    bʌkinəm pælis   CPhon 129
Buckinghamshire
    bʌkiŋəmʃə   EPD,Schr.
    -ʃiə   EPD
Buckland
    bʌklənd   EPD,Schr.
Buckland/Hrt
    olim bʌkəldən   PNHrt 175
Buckland Filley/D
    'bʌklənd 'fili   BBC,BCE
Buckland Monachorum/D
    mə'nækərəm   PND 225
Buckland Tout Saints/D
    'bʌklənd 'tu: 'seints   BBC,BCE
Bucklersbury/Ldn (a street)
    bʌkləzbəri   Schr.
Bucklesham/Sf
    bʌkəlʃəm   PNDVall 27
Buckley
    bʌkli   EPD
Buckley's Fm/Ess
    bʌkləz   PNEss 4ol
Bucklow Hill/Chs
    buklou   PNChs II/ix
    bukli   PNChs II/ix ("olim"),
    bʌkli   Hope
    bukli il   GlossChs
Bucknall/Li,St
    bʌknəl, -nl   EPD
Bucknell/O,Sa
    bʌknəl, -nl   EPD
Bucknowle Ho/Do
    bʌknəl, bʌgnəl   PNDo I/89,
                            PNDo(i) 132
Bucks. (short for Buckinghamshire)
    bʌks   EPD
Bucksteep Manor/Sx
    bʌk-   PNSx(i) 36
Buckton/ERY
    buktən   PNYE lo3
Budbridge/Wt
    bʌ(t)bridʒ   PNWt 8
Buddle/Wt (nr Niton)
    bʌdl   PNWt 182
Buddlehole/Wt
    bʌtlou   PNWt 65
Bude/Co (also called Budehaven)
    bju:d   EPD,BBC,Schr.

Budle/Nb
    bju:dl   DEPN,BBC,BCE
    bʌdl   PNNbDu 33
Budleigh Salterton/D
    'bʌdli'sɔːltətən   BBC
    -    sɔːltətn   BCE
    bʌdli   EPD
Budley/D (in Exeter)
    bʌdli   HL 187
Budock/Co
    bju:dək   BBC
Budworth/Chs (Gt and Little B.)
    buduþ   PNChs II/ix (for Gt B.)
    'budəːþ   PNChs II/lo7 (for Gt B
    loc. 'budəːþ   PNChs III/184
                        (for Little B.)
    budəþ   GlossChs
Buerton/Chs
    bju:ə(r)tən, bu:ə(r)tən   PNChs
    IV/79 (for B. in Broxton Hd)
    b(j)u:ərtən   PNChs III/87 (for
                        in Nantwich Hd)
Buglawton/Chs
    'bug'lɔːtən   PNChs II/29o
Bugle/Co
    bju:gl   BBC
Bugsell Fm/Sx
    bʌg'sel   PNSx 458
Bugthorpe/ERY
    bugþrəp   PNYE 149
Buildwas/Sa
    bildəs, bilwəs   Hope
Bulbarrow/Do
    bu:əbər   DDo
Bulbridge/W
    bulbridʒ   PNW(i) 42
Bulcote/Nt
    bulkət   PNNt 156,BBC
    bu:kə   PNNt(i) 26
Bulford/W
    bulfə(r)d   PNW(i) 42
Bulkeley/Chs
    bukli   PNChs IV/17,DEPN,BBC,BC
    bulkli   PNChs IV/17
Bulkington/W
    bəlkiŋtn   PNW(i)42
    -ʌ-   DEPN
Bulkington/Wa
    bʌkiŋtən   Hope
Bullingham/He (also called B'hope)
    buliŋm, bulindʒəm   Hope
    -ndʒ-   Dodgson(2)366 and (3)i4
            PNing 171,DEPN
    (see also Zachr.(1)348 f.)
Bulls Wood/Wt
    bulz ud   PNWt 285

Bulmer/Ess,NRY
  boumə   PNYN 39
  bulmə   EPD
Bulpham/Ess
  bulvən   PNEss 144,BBC,Hope
  buləm [sic!]   Hope
Bulstrode/Bk
  bulstroud   PNBk 238,EPD
  bʌlstroud   EPD
Bulverhythe/Sx
  bulvə 'haið   BBC
Bulwell/Nt
  vulgo bulil   PNNt 141
  loc. buləl, oth. bulwel
          PNNt(i) 26
Bulwick/Np
  bulik   PNNp 151,BBC
Bunbury/Chs
  bunbəri,bunbri   PNChs III/305
  bumbəri   PNChs III/305 ("older local"),GlossChs
  bʌnbəri   Schr.
Bungay/Sf
  bʌŋgi   PNSf 22,EPD,BBC,Schr.
  bʌŋgei   Schr.
Bungdale/NRY
  bondil   PNYN 57
Bunhill Row/Ldn
  bʌnhil rou   Schr.
Bunkers Bottom/Wt
  bʌŋkərz   PNWt 225
Bunker's Hill
  buŋkəz hil   Schr.
Buntingford/Hrt
  vulgo bʌn(t)ifəd   PNHrt 182
Bunting's Gn/Ess
  bʌntnz   PNEss 380
Bunts Hill Fm/Wt
  bʌn(t)s il   PNWt 78
Bunwell/Nf
  bʌnwəl   BBC
  bʌnəl   Hope
Burbage/Db,Le,W
  bə:bidʒ
Burchell (as in B.'s Gn/Gl)
  bə:tʃ(ə)l   EPD
Burcombe Ivers/W
  aivərz   PNW 213
Burdale/ERY
  bodl   PNYE 132
  bodil   Hope
Burdett Rd/Ldn
  bə:'det   EPD,Kruis.
  bə'det   EPD
Burdon/D,Du
  bə:dn   EPD,Kruis.
Bure/Nf (r.n.)
  bjuə   BBC
  bju:r   Schr.

Bures, Mt B.,Little B./Ess
  bju- s   PNEss 363,420
  bjuəz   DEPN,BBC
Bures/Sf
  bjuəz   BBC
Burford/O,Sa,Sr
  bə:fəd   EPD,Schr.
Burgate/Ha,Sf,Sr
  'bə:geit   BBC
Burge (as in B. End/Hrt)
  bə:dʒ   EPD
Burgh
  bə:g   BBC
  bʌrə   Kruis.
Burgh/Cu
  brʌf   PNCu xliii
Burgh/Li
  bʌrə   EPD,PNWo(i)32,PNWa(i)37
  bə:g   Hope
Burgh/Sf
  bʌrə   DEPN,EPD,BCE,Hope
  bə:g   EPD,BCE
Burgh/Sr
  bʌrə   PNSr 69
Burgh-by-Sands/Cu
  brʌf bai sændz   PNCu126,DEPN,BBC,BCE
  bruf   HL 857
Burgh Castle/Sf
  'bʌrə 'ka:sl   BBC,BCE
Burghclere/Ha
  bə:klɛə   EPD,BBC
Burgh Heath/Sr
  bʌrə hi:θ   EPD,BBC
  bə: hi:θ   BBC
Burghfield/Brk
  bə:fi:ld   BBC,BCE
Burgh Ho/Ldn (in Hampstead)
  bə:g   BBC
Burgh-le-Marsh/Li
  'bʌrə lə 'ma:ʃ   BBC,BCE
Burghley/Np (= B.House)
  bə:li   EPD,Kruis.
Burgh St. Peter/Nf
  bʌrəsnt 'pi:tə   BBC
Burham/K
  bʌrəm   BBC,PNK
Burhouse/WRY
  burəs   DHd 27
Buriton/Ha
  berit(ə)n   BBC
  -e-   DEPN
  bəritən   BCE
Burleigh/Brk,Gl
  bə:li   EPD,Kruis.
Burlescombe/D
  bə:leskəm   PND 546
Burley
  bə:li   EPD

Burlingham/Nf
  bəːliŋəm Burl. 124
Burlington/La,Sa
  bəːliŋtən EPD,Schr.
(see also s.n. Bridlington)
Burlong's Mead/Ess (f.n.)
  bʌnsti, older
  bʌnstə griːn EssDD 158 f.
Burlongstye Gn/Ess
  bænistə EssDD 158
Burmantofts/WRY
  'bəməntɔps GlossMY,s.n. Tuft
Burnaston/Db
  bəːnəstən PNDb 543,BBC
Burn Butts/ERY
  bɔn buts PNYE 159
Burnby/ERY
  bɔmbi PNYE 18o
  bɔnbi Hope
Burneside/We
  'bəːnisaid PNWe I/153,BBC,
                BCE
  bəːnsaid BCE
Burneston/NRY
  bɔnistən PNYN 226
Burnett/He,Sa
  bə(ː)'net, bəːnit EPD
Burney Hill/We
  burnə PNE'side 62
Burngullow/Co
  bəːn'gʌlou BBC
Burnham
  bəːnəm EPD
Burnhope/Du
  'bəːnhoup BBC
Burniston/NRY
  bɔnistən PNYN 1o7
Burnley/La
  bəːnli Schr.
  bərnli Ellis 35o
Burnsall/WRY
  bənsəl PNYW VI/83
Burnt Ho/Wt
  bəːrnt (h)æus PNWt 1o
Burpham/Sx,Sr
  bəːfəm PNSx(i)37,BBC,
                BCE (for B. in Sx)
Burradon/Nb
  bɔːrdn PNNbDu 34
Burrator Reservoir/D
  bʌrətɔː BBC
Burrell Gn/Cu
  bʌr(ə)l EPD
Burrill/NRY
  bɔril PNYN 237
Burringham/Li
  bʌriŋəm BBC,BCE
Burroughs/Mx
  bʌrouz EPD,Kruis.

Burrows (as in B.Lea/Sr)
  bʌrouz EPD
Burscough/La
  bəːskou BBC,BCE
  bəːskə PNLa(ii),H.A.(2)36
Bursdon/D
  bəːzən PND 77
Bursea/ERY
  bɔsi PNYE 234
Burshill/ERY
  bɔsil PNYE 74
Bursledon/Ha
  bəːzldən BBC,BCE
Burslem/St
  bəːzləm EPD,BBC,Schr.
Burstow/Sr
  bʌstə PNSr 286
Burstwick/ERY
  bɔstwig PNYE 33,GlossHol 17
  boustwiːk Hope,ONwick 365
  brustwik GlossHol 17
Burtersett/NRY
  bɔtəsit PNYN 267
Burtholme/Cu
  bəːþəm PNCu 7o
Burton
  bəːtən Schr.
  bəːtn EPD,Schr.
Burton/Li
  bɔtən Hope,GlossM&C,s.n. Bott
Burton/Sf
  bɑːtn DSf 252
Burton/So → Flax Burton
Burton/ERY
  bɔtn Hope,GlossHol 17
  (so pron. in B.Constable,Brands
  burton; see also following
  entries)
Burton (Cherry B.)/ERY
  tʃeri bɔtn PNYE 191
Burton (Bishop B.)/ERY
  biʃi bɔtn PNYE 192
Burton Agnes/ERY
  bɔtn (agnəs), bɔʔn PNYE 88
  "Sometimes called Agnes Burton
  old people and, I think, somet
  Annies Burton"   (PNERY)
Burton Hill/WRY
  butn il DDd 13
Burton Lazars/Le
  'bəːt(ə)n 'læzəz BBC
Burton Pedwardine/Li
  'bəːt(ə)n 'pedwədain BBC
  bəːtn -   BCE
Burton Pidsea/ERY
  bɔtn PNYE 55,GlossHol 17
  bɔtən pidsə Hope
Burton Pynsent/So
  bəːt(ə)n pins(ə)nt BBC

Burtonwood/La
  'bə:t(ə)n'wud BBC
Burwains/La
  bo:winz, bə:winz PNLa 85
Burwardsley/Chs
  bə:wədzli PNChs IV/93,BBC,
                  BCE
  bə:wəzli,loc. bouəzli,
  bu:əzli PNChs IV/93
  bʌzli GlossChs
Burwarton/Sa
  bə:wət(ə)n BBC
  bərətn GlossSa 516
Burwash/Sx
  beriʃ PNSx 461
  bʌriʃ PNSx 461,PNSx(i)38,
        DEPN,Hope,Mawer(4)285,
        deBarri 43
  'bə:wɔʃ BBC
Burwash Weald/Sx
  bʌriʃ wi:l Hope
Burwell/Ca,Li
  'bə:wel BBC
  bə:wəl ONCa 189
Bur Well/Hrt
  bʌrəl PNHrt 112
Bury
  beri EPD,BBC,Schr.,Kruis.,
        Chis.
Bury/La,Sx
  beri PNSx(i)39,Brunner 168
      (for B. in La)
-bury (as a suffix)
  -bri, -brə ESpr. II/14
Bury Lane/Wt
  'bə:ri lein PNWt 286
Bury St. Edmunds/Sf
  beri DSf 252
  'beri snt 'edməndz BBC
  'berisənt'edməndz Schr.
  also called St.Edmundsbury:
  səntedməndzberi Schr.
Busby/NRY
  bʌzbi Kruis.
The Bush/K
  buʃ EPD
Bushaw/We
  buʃə PNE'side 62
Bushbury/St
  loc. biʃbəri PNSt 29
Bushey/Do,Hrt,Mx
  buʃi EPD
Bushton/W
  buʃtn PNW(i) 44
Busta Beck/Cu (or Bustabeck)
  bustə bek PNE'side 74
  bustəbek PNCu 244

Butley/Chs,St
  bʌtli BBC
Butterfield/WRY
  bʌtəfi:ld EPD
  butər- DHd 17
Butterleigh/D
  bʌtəli EPD
Butterley/Db,He,WRY
  bʌtəli EPD
  butər- DHd 17 (for B.in WRY)
Buttermere/Cu
  butrmi:r PNCu 355
  bʌtəmi:r Schr.
Butter Nab/WRY
  butərnæb DHd 17 and 72,DA1&Hd,
                  s.n. Nab
Butter Pots/WRY
  butəpɔts DDd 15
Buttershaw/WRY
  butər- DHd 17
Butterthwaite/WRY
  often pron. bʌtəfit PNSWY 89
Butterwick
  bʌtəwik,bʌtərik EPD,BBC
Butterwick/Cu (nr Ousby)
  butərik grɛ:nz PNE'side 69
Butterwick/Li
  bʌtəwi:k GlossM&C,s.n. Butter-
                  week
Butterwick/We
  butərik PNE'side 69
  bʌtəwik, bʌtərik BCE
Butterwick/ERY
  butəwik, butþərik PNYE 114
Butterworth/La,WRY
  butərwɔrþ DHd 17 and 153 (for B.
            in WRY)
  bʌtərəþ GlossR&R (for B. in La)
  bʌtəwə(:)þ EPD
Butthouse/He
  bʌtəs (StE and dial.) DHe 43
Buxhall/Sf
  bʌksɔ:l BBC
Buxted/Sx
  bʌk- PNSx(i) 39
Buxton/Db
  bʌkstən Schr.
  bʌkst(ə)n EPD
Buxworth/Db
  "... used to be ... pron. locally
  with medial [g] instead of [k], a
  pron. which may still be heard
  today" (Kuurman 8)
Byers Gn/Du
  baiəz EPD
  - grein DSDu
Byerworth/La → Byrewath

Byfleet/Sr
   baifliːt   EPD
Byker/Nb
   baikə   BBC
Bylaugh/Nf
   biːlou   BBC,BCE,Hope
   biːlɑ:,
   bailɑ:, bailou   BBC,BCE
Byley/Chs (B.Hall,Lwr B.,B.Fm,
          B.Hill)
   baili   PNChs II/233
Byng/Sf
   biŋ   EPD
Byram/WRY
   bɑːrəm, bairəm   PNYW IV/46
Byrewath/La (also spelt
         Byerworth)
   baiəwəþ   PNLa 163
Byshottles/Du
   'baiʃɔtlz   BBC
Bytham/Li
   baiþəm, loc. baitəm   Kruis.
   -þ-   Eminson(2)159
Bytham Fm/W
   bitəm   PNW 3o5
Byward Twr/Ldn
   baiwəd   BBC

C

Caber/Cu
 kɛabə PNCu 249
Cabourn/Li (also spelt -bourne)
 keibɔ:n DEPN,BBC,BCE
Cabus/La
 ke:bəs PNLa 165
 kei- DEPN
Cadbury/D,Gl,So
 kædb(ə)ri EPD
Cadeby/Li,WRY
 keidbi BBC,BCE
 kætbi Hope (for C. in WRY)
Cadenham/Ha
 kædnəm Hope
Cade Street/Sx
 vulgo kæt stri:t PNSx 464
Cadgwith/Co
 kædʒwið, -wiþ BBC
 -dʒ- Jenner(2)302
Cadishead/La
 kædizhed BBC
 kerised PNLa(ii)
Cadshaw/La
 kadʒə PNLa 7o
Caenby/Li
 keinbi, keiənbi BBC,BCE
Cage/WRY
 ke:dʒ DDd 16
Cairn/Co
 kɑ:n Hope
Caistor/Li,Nf
 keistə BBC
Caius College/Ca
 ki:z EPD,Kruis.,HL 288
Cakeham/Sx
 kækəm PNSx 88
Calbourne/Wt
 kɛ:bərn, kælbərn PNWt 75
 kɑ:bən DWt,s.n. show hackle[1]
 kɑ:lbən PNE&W
Calcot/Brk,Gl
 kælkət BBC,EPD (for C. in
    Brk),Bchm.1o (for
    C. in Brk)
Calcote Fm/W
 kɔ:kət PNW 251
Calcott/Brk,K,Sa
 kɔ:lkət EPD,Bchm.115
 kɔlkət EPD
Calcutt/W
 kɔ:kət PNW 42
 kɔ:lkət PNW(i)45
Caldbeck/Cu
 kɔ:bek PNCu 275
 kɔ:ldbek BBC,BCE

 kɔ:dbek BBC,BCE,DLo 22 and 73,
    GlossCu xvii
 kɔdbek BBC,BCE
 -ɔ- PNCu xli
Caldbergh/NRY
 kɔ:dbə PNYN 253
Cald Beck/Cu (also spelt Caldbeck)
 kɔdbek RN 59,PNE'side 75
 kɔ:dbek RN 59
Caldecot(e)
 kɔ:ldkət Schr.
Caldecote/Bd,Bk,Ca
 kɑ:kət PNBdHu 94
 kælkət PNBk 31
 olim kɔ:kət PNCa 156
 kɔ:ldikʌt PNO 1i (for C. in Ca)
 kældekɔt ONCa 194
Caldecote/Hrt
 loc. kɑ:kət PNW xxix
 kɔ:ldikət EPD
Caldecote/Nf,Np
 often called kɔkik PNNf
 kɔ:kət PNNp 95,Hope (for C.in Ca)
Caldecott/Chs,Np,Ru
 kɔ:ldikət EPD,BBC
 kɔl-, EPD
 loc. kɔ:kət PNYE 1iii (for C. in
    Np), GlossChs
 kɔ:di-, kɔ:dkət PNChs IV/ 62
Calder
 kɔ:ldə EPD
Calder/Cu;La;WRY (r.n.)
 kɔ:ldə Schr.
 kɔldə RN 59 (for C. in La)
 kɔ:dər PNLa(ii)
Calder/Cu
 kɔ:də PNCu 427
 kɔdə GlossCu xvii
Calders/WRY (a mountain)
 kɑ:ldəz DDd 17
Caldew/Cu (r.n.)
 kɔ:də RN 62,PNE'side,GlossCu xvii
Caldmore/St
 kɑ:mə BBC,BCE
Caldwell
 kɔ:ldw(ə)l, kɔl-, -wel EPD
Caldwell/NRY
 kɔ:dwel PNYN 299
 kɔ:ldə Hope
Caldy/Chs
 kɔ:ldi PNChs IV/282,BBC
Calebrack/Cu
 kɛ:lbrik PNE'side
Calehill/K
 keilhil PNK
Calenick/Co
 kə'lenik BBC

---

1) The transcriptions in DWt and PNE&W are <u>Caaburn</u> and <u>Kaalbourn</u>
resp.; the meaning of <u>aa</u> is not quite clear.

Calke,C.Abbey/Db
  kɔ:k   PNDb 626,BBC,BCE,Hope
Calkwell/Li
  kɔ:kwel BBC,BCE
Callaly/Nb (also spelt -ley)
  kæləli BBC,BCE
Callestick/Co
  kə'lestik BBC
  'klestik BBC,BCE
  kæ'lestik BCE
Callington/Co
  kæliŋtən BBC
Callisham Down/D
  kælisəm PND 229
Callow/Db
  kɔ:lə PNDb 354
Calloways/Wt
  kæləweiz PNWt 286
Callis Mill/WRY
  kælis BBC
Calne/W
  kɑ:n PNW 256,DEPN,EPD,BBC,
      BCE,Schr.,Kruis.,MEG
      293,GlossW 214,Grüning
      22,note 2
  vulgo kan PNW 256
  kæn PNW(i) 46
  kɔ:n Schr.,Kruis.,Grüning
      22,note 2
Calow/Db
  keilou PNDb 229,DEPN,BBC,BCE
  kɔ:lou BBC,BCE
Calshot/Ha
  kælʃɔt EPD,BBC
Calstock/Co
  kælstɔk BBC
Calstone Wellington/W
  vulgo kɑ:sən PNW 257
  kɔ:lstn PNW(i) 46
Calthorpe/Nf,O,Wa
  'kælþɔ:p BBC,EPD (for C. in
Calthorpe Ho/O   Wa)
  kɔ:lþɔ:p, kælþɔ:p PNO 412
Calthwaite/Cu
  kɔ:þət PNCu xli and 2o2,
      PNE'side 66,Hope,
      GlossCu xvii
Calton/WRY
  kɔ:tn PNYW VI/13o
Calva/Cu
  kɔ:və PNE'side 62
Calva Hall/Cu
  kɔ:və PNCu 367,GlossCu xvii
  kɔvə Hope
Calveley/Chs
  kɑ:vəli PNChs III/3o7
  kɑ:vli BBC,BCE,DEPN,GlossChs
  kɔ:vli BBC,BCE,DSChs 18

Calver/Db
  kɑ:və PNDb 54,DEPN
Calverhall/Sa
  'kælvəhɔ:l BBC
  kɔrə GlossSa 516
Calverley/WRY
  kɑ:vələ PNYW III/224
  kɑ:vəli EPD,BBC,BCE
  kɔ:vəli EPD
  kɔ:vli BBC,BCE
  kɔ:vlə Hope
  kɔ:vələ PNYW III/224,Ellis 39o
Calver Sough/Db
  'kɑ:və'suf PNDb 54
  - sʌf BBC,BCE
Calvert/Bk,NRY
  kælvə(:)t, kɔ:lvət EPD
Calverton/Bk
  kælvətən PNBk 18
  kælvət(ə)n, kɑ:vət(ə)n BBC
  kæl- DEPN
Calverton/Nt
  kɑ:vətən PNNt 158,BCE
  kɔ:vətən PNNt 158
  vulgarly kɔ:vətn,
  oth. kɑ:vətn,kælvətn PNNt(i) 29
  kælvət(ə)n,kɑ:vət(ə)n BBC
  kælvətən BCE
  -ɑ:v- DEPN
Calveshay/So
  klɑ:si Hope, H.A.(2)45
Calvington/Sa
  kævintən, kɔvitn GlossSa xxxix
Calvo/Cu
  kɔ:və PNCu 295
Cam/Gl
  kæm EPD,Schr.,Kruis.
Cam/Ca,Gl (r.n.)
  kæm EPD,BBC,Schr.,Kruis.
Camberley/Sr
  kæmb(ə)li EPD
Camberwell/Sr
  olim kæməwəl PNSr 17
  kæmbəwel EPD,Schr.
  kæmbəw(ə)l EPD
Cambo/Nb
  kamə PNNbDu 38
Cambois/Nb
  kæməs DEPN,BBC,BCE
  kaməs PNNbDu 38
  kæmis PNE&W,BBC,BCE
Camborne/Co
  'kæmbɔ:n EPD,BBC,BCE
  rarely -bən Bchm.69,EPD
Cambridge/Ca,Gl,WRY
  keimbridʒ DEPN (for C. in Ca),
      EPD,BBC,BCE (for C. in
      Gl),Schr.,Kruis.,Chis.

ONCa 195,Hope (for C. in Ca)
  kem- ESpr 133 (for C. in Ca)
Cambridgeshire
  keimbridʒʃ EPD,Schr.
    -ʃiə EPD,Schr.
  keimbridʃiə, -ʃə EPD
Cambs. (short for Cambridgeshire)
  kæm(b)z EPD
Camden/K
  kæmdən EPD
Camel/Co
  -æ- DEPN
Cameley/So
  keimli DEPN,BBC,BCE
Camelford/Co
  kæmlfəd BBC
  kæm(ə)lfəd EPD
Camer/K
  keimə PNK
Camerton/Cu,So,ERY
  kæmət(ə)n BBC
  kæmətən BCE (for C. in Cu)
  -æ- DEPN (for C. in Cu and
             ERY)
Campden/Gl
  kæm(p)dən EPD
  ᴵᴵ(see also s.n. Chipping C.)
Camps/Ca
  kæmps ONCa 197
Campsall/WRY
  kæmpsl BBC
Canewden/Ess
  kænədən, 'kænjudən,
  kænəndən PNEss 179
  kə'nju:d(ə)n BBC
Canford/Do,Ha
  kænfəd EPD
Cann/Do
  kæn PNDo 2o
Cannerheugh/Cu
  kænərhiuj, older
  kænərhiukhw PNE'side 71
Cannock/St
  kænək EPD
Cannon St /Ldn
  kenən stri:t CPP 66
Canonbury/Mx
  olim kæmbəri PNMx 125
  kænənbəri BBC,Schr.
Cantelows Gdns/Ldn
  kæntilouz BBC
Canterbury/K
  kæntəbəri BBC,Kruis.
  -beri EPD,Schr.,HL 195
  -b(ə)ri EPD,MEG 273
Cantsfield/La
  kansfi:ld PNLa 183
Canvey Is/Ess
  kænvi EPD

Canwick/Li
  kænik DEPN,BBC,BCE
  kænwik BBC,BCE
Cape Cornwall/Co
  keip kɔ:nw(ə)l BBC
Capel/K,Sf,Sr
  keipəl PNSr 264
  keipl BBC,BCE,PNK
  keip(ə)l EPD (for C. in Sr)
  -ei- DEPN
Capel Court/Ldn (a street name)
  keipl kɔ:t Schr.
Capel-le-Ferne/K
  'keipl lə 'fə:n BBC,BCE,PNK
Capenhurst/Chs
  keipənərst PNChs IV/ 2oo
  keip(ə)nhə:rst BBC
Capernwray/La
  ke:pnre: PNLa 187
  kei- DEPN
Capheaton/Nb
  kæp'hi:t(ə)n BBC
Caple (King's C.)/He
  kiŋz keipl DEPN,BBC,BCE
Caplestone/Do
  kɔplstən PNDo I/63,PNDo(i) 128
Capon Hall/WRY
  kapnə PNYW VI/138
Caradoc/Sa
  kwə:dək GlossSa 516
Caradoc Ct/He
  kə'rædək EPD
Caradon/Co
  kærəd(ə)n BBC
Carbis Bay/Co
  kɑ:bis bei BBC
Carburton/Nt
  kɑ:bət(ə)n BBC
  ɑ:bətən BCE
Car Colston/Nt
  koulstən PNNt 223
Carden/Chs
  kɑ:rdən PNChs IV/53
Cardew/Cu
  kɑ:dju: EPD
Cardington/Bd,Sa
  kæriŋtən PNBdHu 88
  kɑ:ditən Mawer(4)285 (this form
          of pron. is now lost)
Cardinham/Co
  kɑ:'dinəm BBC,Ellis 169
Cardiston/Sa
  kɑ:sn GlossSa 516
Carey/D,Do,He
  kɛəri PNDo I/158,PNDo(i)147,EPD
Carfax/O
  'kɑ:fæks EPD,Bchm.6o,HL 1o52
  -fəks Bchm.6o

Carham/Nb
  kærəm   DEPN,BBC,BCE
Carhampton/So
  kræmptən   PNEss [!] 41,Hope
Carlker mt(ə)n   Förster
Carholme Racecourse/Li
  kɑ:houm   BBC
Carhullan/We
  kɑ:r'hulən   PNE'side 65
  kɑ:r'ulən   PNWe II/189
Carisbrooke/Wt
  keizbruk   PNWt 93,Hope
  kiəz-,
  kæridʒ-, kæzbruk   PNWt 93
  kærisbruk   EPD,Schr.,Kruis.
  kærizbruk   EPD,Schr.
  ki:sbruk   DWt,s.n. Bide
Carlatton/Cu
  kɑ:'latn   PNCu 73
Carlcotes/WRY
  kɛərlkɔits   DHd 51
Carle (Band)/We
  kɑ:rlə (bænd)   PNE'side 63
Carleton/Cu,La,WRY
  kɑ:ltən   Chis.
  kɑ:lt(ə)n   EPD
Carleton Forhoe/Nf
  kɑ:lt(ə)n 'fɔ:hou   BBC
Carleton Rd/Ldn
  kɑ:'lit(ə)n   BBC
Carlett Cottage, C. Pk/Chs
  kærlet   PNChs IV/188
Carlinghow/WRY
  kɑ:liŋ'hau   BBC
Carlisle/Cu
  kɑ:'lail   BBC,BCE ("south-
           ern"),EPD,Kruis.,
           Chis.
  <u>ˈ</u> _   EPD,BBC,BCE ("northern")
  <u>ˈ</u> <u>ˈ</u>   EPD,MEG 155
  kɑ:rəl   GlossCu xvii
  kɛərəl   GlossCu xvii,Hope,
           PNCu 4o
  kə:lail   Hope
  karlail   Schr.,Lloyd 127
Carls Wark/Db (an earthwork nr
           Hathersage)
  tʃɑ:lzwɔ:k   GlossSh 3ol
Carlton
  kɑ:lt(ə)n   EPD
  kɑ:ltən   ONCa 15
Carlton Colville/Sf
  kɑ:lt(ə)n kɔlvil   BBC
Carlyon/Co
  kɑ:'laiən   BBC
  _ <u>ˈ</u> _   Jenner(2)3o4
Carnaby/ERY
  kɑ:nəbi   PNYE 86,EPD
Carn Brea/Co
  kɑ:n brei   BBC,BCE

Carnforth/La
  kɑ:nfɔ:þ   EPD
Carnkie/Co
  kɑ:n'kai   BBC
Carnmenellis/Co
  kɑ:nmi'nelis   BBC
Carnsew/Co
  kɑ:ndʒu:, -ju: Jenner(2)3o2
Carnyorth/Co
  kɑ:n'jɔ:þ   BBC
Carpenters/Wt
  karpəntərz   PNWt 54
  kæpəndərz   PNWt 285
Carperby/NRY
  kɑ:pəbi   PNYN 266
Carrath/We
  kæriþ   PNE'side 64
Carr Close/Db (f.n.)
  loc. kə:r   FnSDb 114,Fraser(1)34
Carrington/Chs,Li,Nt
  kariŋtən,olim
  k(j)aritn   PNChs II/ix
  kjaritn   GlossChs
  kæriŋtən   EPD
Carr Lane/WRY
  kar lɔin   Hope
Carrock Fell/Cu
  kærik   PNE'side 69
Carrock (Castle C.)/Cu
  kɑ:sl karik   PNCu 74
  kasl kærik   PNE'side 75
The Carrs/Db (f.n.)
  kɛəz   FnSDb 83
Carshalton/Sr
  kɑ:'ʃɔ:ltən   PNSr 41,BBC,BCE
  keis'hɔ:tən   PNSr 41 ("olim"),
           BBC,BCE,PNE&W,Hope
  keishɔ:ltən   PNE&W,Hope
  keiʃɔ:tən   Hope
  kə-, kɑ:ʃɔ:lt(ə)n   EPD
  keishɔ:lt(ə)n, -hɔ:tn,
  keiʃɔ:tn "old-fashioned loc.pron.
                    EPD
Carsington/Db,Nf
  kɑ:sən   PNDb 355,Hope (for C.
                  in Nf)
Carthorpe/NRY
  kɑ:þrəp   PNYN 226
Cartmel/La
  kɑ:tməl   BBC
Cartmell Fell/La
  ' kartm(ə)l 'fel   BBC
  kɑ:tmel   EPD
Cartworth/WRY
  kɑ:twəþ   Hope
Carus (as in C.Lodge/La)
  kɛərəs   EPD
Carwinnen/Co
  kɑ:'winən   BBC
Cary (Castle C.)/So
  kɑ:sl kɛəri   BBC
Casey Gn/NRY
  keisi   EPD

Cassia Gn, C. Lodge/Chs
  kɛ:ʃə   PNChs III/182
Cassio/Hrt
  kæsjou   PNHrt 1o4
  kæsiou   EPD
Cassiobury Pk/Hrt
  'kæsioubəri 'pɑːk   BBC
Castelnau/Ldn
  kɑːslnɔ:, kɑːslnou   EPD,BBC
Castle-an-Dinas/Co
  kɑːsl ən 'dainəs   BBC
Castledoor/Co
  kɑːsl'dɔ: BBC
Castleford/D,WRY
  kɑːslfəd   Schr.
Castlerigg/Cu
  kæstrig   GlossCu xvii
Castlethorpe/Li
  keistrəp   GlossM&C,s.n.Cais-
Castleton   trup
  kæsltən   Chis.
  kɑːslt(ə)n   EPD
Castletown
  kɑːsltaun   Schr.
Caston/Cu
  kɑːsən   Hope
Caston/Nf
  kɑːstən   BBC,BCE,DEPN
  kæs(ə)n   BBC
  kæsən   BCE
Castor/Np
  kɑːstə   PNNp 232,EPD
Caswell/Do,Np,So
  kæzw(ə)l,-wel   EPD
Catcleugh/Nb
  'kætklʌf, 'kætkliːf   BBC,BCE
Catcott/So
  kætkət   EPD
Caterham/Sr
  olim kætərəm   PNSr 311
  keitərəm   EPD
  -æ-   DEPN
Catesby/Np
  keitsbi   EPD
Catford/K
  kætfəd   EPD,PNK
Cathay/Gl
  kæ'þei, kə-   EPD
Catherine Tor/D
  kætən tɑː   DHtl
Catholes/WRY
  katlz   DDd 14
Catlow/La
  kætlə   PNLa(ii)
Caton/D
  keit(ə)n   BBC
Caton/La
  keːtn   PNLa 177
  keitən   BCE

keit(ə)n   BBC
  -ei-   DEPN
Cator/D
  keitə   EPD
Catsfield/Sx
  kætsful   PNSx 485,Hope
Catten Hall/Chs
  'katnɔ:l   PNChs III/24o
Catterall/La
  katərə   PNLa(ii)
Catterick/NRY
  kætrik, kæþərik   PNYN 242
Catterton/WRY
  katətən, kaþətən   PNYW IV/236
Cattistock/Do
  kætistɔk   BBC
Cattle Mire Tarn/We
  kætl mər   PNE'side 73
The Catwater/D
  'kætwɔːtə   BBC
Catwick/ERY
  katik   PNYE 73
  kætik   Hope,ONwick 365
Catworth/Hu
  kætəþ   PNBdHu 236
Caughall/Chs
  kɔːgəl   PNChs IV/14o
Caulcott/O
  kɔːkʌt, kɔlkʌt   PNO 219
  -ɔl-   PNO(i) 7o
Causeway End/Ess ⟶ Kerr's End
Causewayhead/Cu
  kɔːzə hiːd   PNCu 295
Causewell Fm/Hrt
  kæsl   PNHrt 56
Cautley/WRY
  kɔːtli   DDd 17
  kɔːtlə   PNE'side 63
Cavendish/Sf
  kændiʃ   MEG 39
  kævndiʃ   Kruis.,MEG 39
  kæv(ə)ndiʃ   EPD
Cavenham/Sf
  keinəm   Hope
Caversfield/O
  kiːrsfʌl   PNO 2o4
  keisfiːld   Hope
Caversham/Brk
  kævəʃəm   EPD,BBC
Caverswall/St
  'kævəzwɔːl   BBC
Cavil/ERY
  keːvil   PNYE 248
Cawkeld/ERY
  kɔːkəl   PNYE 159
Cawledge Pk/Nb
  kaliʃ   PNNbDu 42
Cawood/La ⟶ Arkholme

Cawood/WRY
  ke:wud PNYW IV/38
  keiwud BBC,BCE
  kauəd Hope
Cawsand/Co
  kɔːs(ə)nd BBC
Cawsand Beacon/D
  kɔsdən, kɔːzən PND 448
Cawston/Nf,Wa
  keisn ROS 42
  kɔːstən BBC
  kɑːsən Hope
Cawthorne/WRY
  kɔːþrən, kɔːþrəm Hope
Cawton/NRY
  kɔːtən PNYN 52
Caxton/Ca
  kækstən ONCa 15,Kruis.
  kækst(ə)n EPD
Caythorpe/Nt
  olim kat(ə)rəp PNNt 159
The Cearne/Sr
  sein PNSr 326
Celleron/Cu
  selərən PNE'side 65
Cerne Abbas/Do
  'səːn 'æbəs BBC
Cernel Bridge/Do
  loc. kəːnəl March 25
Cerney/Gl
  səːni PNGl I/58,BBC
  sarni PNGl I/58
  sɔːni GlossSEWo 82
Chaceley/Gl
  tʃeisli BBC
Chacewater/Co
  'tʃeiswɔːtə BBC
Chacombe/Np → Chalcombe
Chaddenwicke/W
  tʃædnwik PNW(i)47
Chaddesden/Db
  tʃædzdən BBC,BCE
  tʃædzən BBC
  tʃædzən BCE,Hope
Chaddesley Corbett/Wo
  tʃædʒli PNWo 234,Hope,DEPN,
      HL 811
Chaddlehanger/D
  tʃæliŋgər PND 185
  tʃadlhænə , tʃæliŋə BBC,BCE
Chadshunt/Wa
  tʃædz(h)ʌnt BBC
Chadstone/Np
  tʃædsən PNNp 143
Chadwell/Bk
  tʃædl Mawer(2)95
Chadwell/Ess
  tʃædl PNEss 15o

Chadwick/La,Wa,Wo
  tʃædwik EPD
  tʃerik DSLa,GlossR&R(for C. in I
Chagford/D
  tʃægfəd, tʃægivɔrd PND 424
Chaigley/La
  tʃeidʒli DEPN,HL 811
  tʃeːdʒli PNLa 141
Chailey/Sx
  tʃeili PNSx(i)4o
Chalbury/Do
  tʃɔːlbəri PNDo(i)78
Chalcombe/Np (also spelt Chacombe)
  tʃeikəm PNNp 5o,DEPN,BBC,BCE
Chaldon Herring/Do (=East Ch.)
  tʃɔːldən PNDo I/1o8,PNDo(i)138
Chaldon/Sr
  tʃɔːldən PNSr 42
  tʃɔːld(ə)n BBC
Chale/Wt
  tʃiəl, tʃeəl PNWt 112
  tʃiːl DWt,s.n. garbed-up
Chalfield/W
  vulgo tʃɑːvil PNW 115
Chalfont St.Giles, Ch. St Peter(s)/B
  tʃælfɔnt EPD
  tʃælfənt EPD,BBC,Bchm.8,Schr.
  tʃɑːf(ə)nt BBC
  tʃɑːfənt PNBk 218,BCE,Schr.
      ("loc."),EPD ("old
      fashioned")
  -ɑːf- DEPN

  -- snt piːtəz, -- snt dʒailz BBC
Chalford/Gl,O,W
  tʃælfəd BBC
Chalgrove/O
  tʃælgrouv BBC,Schr.
Chalk Beck/Cu (r.n.)
  ʃɔːk RN 74,DEPN
  tʃɔːk RN 74
Challacombe/D
  tʃɔləkum PND 6o
  tʃɔləkəm PNND 3
  tʃæləkəm BBC
Challenger Fm/D
  tʃæliŋgə PND 644
Challen Hall/La
  tʃalən hɔːl PNLa 19o
Challock/K
  tʃɔlək DEPN,BBC,BCE,PNK
Challock/Np
  tʃɔlək BBC
Challow/Brk
  tʃælou BBC
Chalvendon Hall/Ess
  olim tʃɑːltən PNEss 167

Chalvey/Bk
  tʃɑːvi   PNBk 234,DEPN,BBC,BCE
  tʃɑːlvi   BBC,BCE
Chalvington/Sx
  tʃɑːntən, tʃɔːtən   PNSx 398
  tʃɔːtn   PNSx(i)4o
  tʃɑːntn   DEPN
  tʃælviŋtən, tʃɑːlviŋtən
                  BBC,BCE
  tʃɑːsitən   Hope
Chambers (as in Ch. Ct/Wo)
  tʃeimbəz   EPD
Champion/Wt
  tʃæmpm   PNWt 1o
Chanctonbury Ring/Sx
  tʃæŋkbəri   PNSx 242
Chantmarle/Do
  tʃɑːntmaːl   PNDo(i) 195
Chapel/WRY ⟶ Low Chapel
Chapel-en-le-Frith/Db
  'tʃæpl en lə 'friþ   EPD,BBC,
                      BCE
  tʃæplənləfriþ   EPD
  tʃæpl friþ   Hope
Chapmanslade/W
  tʃæpmənsleid   PNW(i)48
Chard/So
  tʃɑːd   EPD
Charford/Ha,Wo
  tʃɑːfəd   Schr.
Charing/K
  tʃɛəriŋ   DEPN,BBC,BCE,Schr.,
             PNK
  tʃæriŋ   BBC,BCE,PNK
Charing Cross/Ldn
  tʃæriŋ   EPD,Kruis.,HL 732
  tʃɛəriŋ   EPD,DEPN,Schr.,
             HL 732

  krɔs   EPD,HL 732
  krɔːs   EPD,Schr.

  tʃɛərin krɔːs   CPP 66
  -in   Höfer 166
Charlbury/O
  tʃɔːlberi   PNO 415
  tʃɔːlbri   PNO(i) 72,Wyld 2o5
  -ɔːl-   DEPN
Charlecote/Wa
  ʃɑːlkət   PNWa 25o
  tʃɑːlkout   EPD
  tʃɑːlkət   Kruis.
Charlecote Pk/Wa
  tʃɑːlkout paːk   BBC
Charles/Do
  tʃɑːlz   EPD
Charles Head/Chs
  tʃulz jed   PNChs II/vii,
             GlossChs
  tʃɑːrlz ed, - jed
             PNChs II/vii

Charlestown
  tʃɑːlztaun   EPD,BBC,Schr.
Charlesworth/Db
  tʃɔːlzwəþ   PNDb(i) I/211
  tʃɑːlzwəːþ   EPD
Charleton/D,So
  tʃɑːlt(ə)n   BBC
  tʃɑːltən   BCE (for Ch. in So)
Charley/Le
  tʃɑːli   EPD
Charlton
  tʃɑːlt(ə)n   EPD
  tʃɑːltən   Schr.,PNK
  tʃɔːltən   PNHrt 9,PNW 54
  tʃɔltən   GlossSEWo 82
Charlwood/Sr
  tʃɑːliwud   PNSr 287
Charminster/Do
  tʃɑːrmistər   PNDo I/338,DDo
Charmouth/Do
  tʃɑːmauþ   BBC
  -məþ   Schr.
Charndon/Bk
  tʃɑːdən   PNBk 52
Charnock/La
  tʃɑːnɔk, -ək   EPD
Charrington St/Ldn
  tʃæriŋtən striːt   EPD,Schr.
Chart/K
  tʃɑːt   DK
Charterhouse/Ldn
  tʃɑːtəhaus   EPD,Kruis.
Chartershaugh/Du
  'tʃɑːtəzhaːf   BBC,BCE
Charwelton/Np
  tʃɑːltən   PNNp 17,Hope
Chater/Le,Ru (r.n.)
  tʃeitə   RN 74,EPD,DEPN
Chatham/K
  tʃætəm   EPD,Schr.,Kruis.,Chis.,
             HL 866,MEG 376,Hope
Chathill/Nb,Sr
  'tʃæt'hil   BBC
Chatsworth/Db
  tʃætswəþ   EPD,Schr.
  -wəːþ   EPD
Chatteris/Ca
  tʃætris, tʃɑːtris   PNCa 247
  tʃætəris   EPD
  tʃæt(ə)ris   ONCa 198
Chatterton/La
  tʃætətn   EPD,Kruis.
Chatterhope Burn/Nb
  tʃatləp   PNNbDu 43
Chatton/Nb
  tʃatən   PNNbDu 43
  ʃetn,ʃatn   Ellis 641
Chaul End/Bd
  'tʃɔːl 'end   BBC

Chaureth Hall, Ch.Gn/Ess
  "known loc. as Cherry Hall
  [and] Cherry Green"
    Reaney(1)257,note 5
    (cf. PNEss 471)
Chawleigh/D
  tʃɔ:li BBC
Chawney Leys/Wo (f.n. nr Feckenham)
  loc. called Chine Hill
         Davis 42
Chawston/Bd
  tʃɔ:sən PNBdHu 65
Chawton Fm/Wt
  tʃɔ:tn PNWt 286
Cheadle/Chs
  tʃi:dl Chis
  tʃedl GlossChs,DSLa
Cheadle Bulkeley, Ch. Moseley/Chs
  tʃi:dəl, older local
  tʃedəl PNChs I/246
  -i:- DEPN
Cheadle Hulme/Chs
  tʃi:dl ju:m PNChs II/vii
  tʃedl u:m PNChs II/vii
      ("olim"),GlossChs
  tʃi:dl hju:m, - hu:m BBC,BCE
  tʃedl ju:m Hope
  -i:- hju:m DEPN
Cheam/Sr
  tʃi:m PNSr 43
Cheapside/Ldn
  'tʃi:p'said EPD,Schr.,Kruis.,
             HSM 9
  _ˈ _ EPD
Chearsley/Bk
  tʃi:əzli PNBk 1o3
  tʃiəzli BBC
Cheaveley Hall Fm/Chs
  tʃi:vli PNChs IV/118
Chebbard Fm/Do
  tʃibəd PNDo 173
Cheddar/So
  tʃedə EPD,Schr.,Kruis.
Chedglow/W
  tʃedʒlou PNW(i)49,DEPN
Chedgrave/Nf
  tʃedgrəv Hope
Chediston/Sf
  tʃe:sn DSf 253
  tʃedistən BBC
Cheetham/La
  tʃi:təm EPD,Kruis.
Cheetham Hill/La
  'tʃi:təm 'hil BBC
Cheldon/D
  tʃeld(ə)n BBC
Chelfham/D
  tʃelfəm BBC,BCE

Chelford/Chs
  tʃelfərt PNChs II/vii ("olim")
             GlossChs
  tʃelfərd PNChs II/vii
Chellaston/Db
  tʃeləstən BBC
  tʃeləsən Hope
  tʃelistən Ellis 446
Chellington/Bd
  tʃiliŋtən PNBdHu 3o
Chelmer/Ess (r.n.)
  tʃelmə Schr.
Chelmerton/Db
  tʃelmə:tn PNDb(i)74
Chelmondiston/Sf
  tʃemtən PNSf 95
  tʃelmstən BBC
  tʃimstən PNE&W
  tʃemstən Hope
Chelmsford/Ess
  tʃemsfəd PNEss 245,DEPN,Hope,
            Schr.522,ESpr.388,
            EPD ("old-fashioned lo
            pron."),BBC
  tʃensfəd PNEss 245,EssDD 158
  tʃenʃfəd PNEss 245,EssDD 158,
            Reaney(2)177
  tʃendʒfəd PNEss 245
  tʃɔmsfəd EPD ("old-fashioned lo
            pron.")
  tʃelmsfəd EPD,BBC,HSM 64,note 2
  tʃelmzfəd Schr.,Kruis.
  tʃemzfəd Bchm.116 ("loc."),MEG
            228 ("sometimes")
Chelsea/Ldn
  tʃelsi EPD,BBC,Schr.,Kruis.
  -si: Schr.
Chelsham/Sr
  tʃelsəm PNSr 313
  tʃelʃəm BBC
Chelt/Gl
  tʃelt Schr.
Cheltenham/Gl
  tʃeltnəm PNGl II/1ol,EPD,Schr.
            MEG 376
  tʃeltənəm Kruis.,Chis.,MEG 376
Chelveston/Np
  tʃelsən PNNp 19o
  tʃel'vestən BBC,BCE
Chelworth/W
  olim tʃeləþ PNW 57
Chenies/Bk
  tʃeini, tʃi:ni PNBk 221,DEPN
  tʃeiniz, tʃi:niz EPD,BBC,BCE
Chenies St/Ldn
  tʃi:niz EPD,Schr.
Cheney/Sa,W
  tʃi:ni, tʃeini EPD

Chenil Galleries/Ldn
    tʃenil BBC
Chequerbent/La
    'tʃekəbent BBC,BCE
Chequers/Bk
    tʃekəz EPD
Cherhill/W
    tʃeril PNW 261,BBC
Cheristowe/D (also spelt -stow)
    tʃistɔ: DHtl 8
Cherkenhill Fm/Wo
    tʃɔknəl PNWo 2o5
Chertsey/Sr
    tʃə:tsi EPD,Schr.
Cherwell/Np,O (r.n.)
    tʃɑ:wəl PNO(i)75,DEPN,EPD,
              BBC,Kruis.,MEG 197
    tʃɑ:wel BCE
    tʃə:wl EPD,Schr.
    tʃə:wəl MEG 197
Chesham/Bk
    tʃesəm PNBk 223,DEPN,EPD
              ("old-fashioned loc.
              pron."),Schr.("loc."),
              Mawer(2)95 ("rarely"),
              BBC,BCE
    tʃeʃəm EPD,BBC,BCE,Schr.
Chesham Bois/Bk
    tʃesəm bɔiz PNBk 226,BBC,BCE
Cheshire
    tʃeʃə EPD,BBC,Schr.,Kruis.,
              MEG 127
Cheshunt/Hrt
    tʃesənt PNHrt 22o,BBC,BCE
    tʃesnt EPD,BBC,HL 816
    -s- DEPN
Chesil Beach/Do
    tʃezl bi:tʃ BBC
Chessell/Wt
    tʃesl PNWt 2o9
    tʃesəl DWt,s.n.nutten
Chester/Chs
    tʃestə EPD,Schr.
Chesterfield/Db,St
    tʃestəfi:ld EPD,Schr.
    tʃæstəfi:ld GlossSh 4o (for
              Ch. in Db)
Chesterford/Ca
    tʃestəfəd ONCa 186
Chester-le-Street/Du
    'tʃestə li stri:t BBC
    ˊ _ _ _ ˊ EPD
Chesterton
    tʃestətən EPD,ONCa 16
        -tn EPD
Chestham Pk/Sx
    tʃest'hæm PNSx 216

Cheswardine/Sa
    'tʃezwədain BBC
Cheswick/Nb
    tʃizik PNNbDu 44,DEPN,HL 732
Chetham/La
    tʃi:təm PNLa(ii)
Chetnole/Do
    tʃetnəl PNDo(i)222
Chettiscombe/D
    tʃeskəm PND 541,BBC,BCE
    tʃetiskəm BBC,BCE
Chetwode/Bk
    tʃitwud PNBk 62
    tʃetwud EPD
Chetwynd/Sa
    tʃetwind EPD
Cheveley/Ca
    tʃi:vli PNCa 125,ONCa 183,BBC
Chevening/K
    tʃi:vniŋ DEPN,EPD,BBC,BCE,PNK
Cheverden Fm/W
    tʃivədən PNW 9o
Cheverton/Wt (nr Shorwell),
Cheverton Fm/Wt (nr Brading)
    tʃivərtn PNWt 54, 218
Chevet/WRY
    tʃivit PNYW I/278
    tʃevit BBC
    tʃi:t Hope
The Chevin/WRY
    ʃivin PNYW IV/2o4
Chevington/Nb
    tʃeviŋtən BBC
    tʃivəntən PNNbDu 44
Cheviot Hills/Nb
    tʃiv(i)ət PNNbDu 44
    tʃiviət EPD
    tʃi:viət, tʃeviət EPD,BBC
    tʃevjət, tʃivjət EPD,BCE,Kruis.
    tʃi:vjət EPD,BCE
    -e- or -i- DEPN
Cheyne Walk/Ldn
    tʃein(i) EPD
Chichacott/D
    tʃisəkət PND 2o2
Chicheley/Bk
    tʃitʃili, tʃetʃli PNBk 33
Chichester/Sx
    tʃidəstə PNSx 1o
    tʃitstə PNSx(i)42
    sistə Schr.522 ("in clerical
              circles")
    tʃitʃistə EPD,Schr.,Wyld 262
    tʃitʃəstə Kruis.,Chis.
    tʃidstə Hope
Chicklade/W
    tʃikleid PNW(i)51

Chicksands/Bd
   tʃiksəndz, tʃiksən   PNBdHu 168
Chiddingly/Sx
   tʃitənlai   PNSx 398
   tʃidiŋ'lai   DEPN,EPD,BBC,BCE,
              Hope
   ˈ _ _   EPD
Chideock/Do
   tʃidik   PNDo(i)285,DEPN,Hope
   tʃidək   BBC,BCE
Chidlow/Chs
   tʃidlou   BBC
Chieveley/Brk
   tʃi:vli   PNBrk 72
Chigwell/Ess
   tʃigwəl   BBC
Chilbolton/Ha
   tʃil'boult(ə)n   BBC
Childerditch/Ess
   'tʃildədɪtʃ   BBC
Childerley/Ca
   tʃildəli   ONCa 183
Childer Thornton/Chs
   tʃildər   PNChs IV/196
   tʃildə þɔ:ntən   BBC,BCE
Childwall/La
   tʃilwəl   PNLa 112
   tʃildə   PNLa(ii)
   tʃilwɔ:l   BBC
   tʃildwɔ:l, -wəl   BCE
   -i-   DEPN
Childwick Bury/Hrt
   'tʃilikbəri   BBC
   olim tʃilik   PNHrt 91
Childwick Gn/Hrt
   tʃilik gri:n   BBC
Chilford/Ca
   tʃilfəd   ONCa 187
Chilfrome/Do
   tʃilfru:m   PNDo(i) 229
Chilgrove/Sx
   tʃilgrouv   PNSx 45
Chilham/K
   tʃiləm   BBC,BCE,PNK
Chilhampton/W
   tʃil'hæmtən, olim
   tʃiliŋtən   PNW 228
Chillenden/K
   tʃilindn   PNK
Chillerton Fm, Ch. Down/Wt
   tʃilərtn,
   tʃelərtn   PNWt 133
   tʃilətən   DWt,s.n.quealin
Chillesford/Sf
   tʃilzfəd   BBC
Chillingham/Nb
   tʃiliŋəm   EPD,BBC,BCE
   ʃiliŋəm   PNNbDu 45,Ellis 641[1]

Chillingwood/Wt
   tʃilnwud   PNWt 27
Chilsham/Sx
   -ʃəm , loc.-səm   PNSx add. 15?
Chiltern Hills, The Chilterns
   tʃiltən   BBC,Schr.
          -z   Schr.
   tʃiltə(:)n   EPD
Chilton
   tʃiltən   Schr.
   tʃilt(ə)n   EPD
Chilton Fm/Wt
   tʃiltn   PNWt 65
Chilton Foliat/W
   tʃilt(ə)n fouliət   BBC
Chilvers Coton/Wa
   'tʃilvəz 'kout(ə)n   BBC
Chine Cottage/Wt
   tʃain 'kɑ:tidʒ   PNWt 66
Chingford/Ess
   tʃiŋfəd   EPD
Chinnock/So
   tʃinək   EPD
Chinnor/O
   tʃinə   EPD
Chippenham/Ca,W
   tʃipnəm   EPD,Schr.
   tʃipənəm   EPD,Chis.,ONCa 177
   tʃipinəm   Schr.
Chipperfield/Hrt
   tʃipəfəl   EssDD 152
Chipping (as in Ch.Ongar/Ess,
                Ch.Warden/Np, etc.)
   tʃipiŋ   EPD
Chipping Camden/Gl
   tʃipiŋ kæmdən   BBC,Schr.
   kæmdin   GlossSEWo 82
Chipping Norton/O
   tʃipiŋ nɔ:t(ə)n   BBC
Chipping Ongar/Ess → Ongar
Chipping Sodbury/Gl
   tʃipiŋ sɔdbəri   BBC
Chipping Wycombe/Bk
   tʃipiŋ waikəm   Schr.
   wikəm   DEPN
Chipstead/K
   tʃipstəd   PNK
Chirbury/Sa
   tʃə:bəri   BBC
Chirdon/Nb
   dʒɔrdən   PNNbDu
Chisbridge/Bk
   tʃizbidʒ [sic!]   PNBk 178
Chishall/Ca
   tʃisəl   PNEss 52o (the place is
            now in Ca; cf. PNCa 373
Chisledon/W
   tʃizldən   BBC

_____

1) "[This is the] only Nb name in ingham,which is pron. [-iŋəm],all t
   others having [-indʒəm]" (Ellis 641).

Chislehurst/K
  tʃizlhə:st EPD,Schr.,Kruis.
  tʃisəlhə:st PNK
Chislet/K
  tʃislet PNK
Chiswick/Mx
  tʃizik PNMx 88,PNMx(i),EPD,
          BBC,BCE,Schr.,Kruis.,
          Hope,MEG 213,ONwick
          389,HL 755
  tʃisik ESpr.394
Chiswick Eyot/Mx (or Ch.Ait)
  'tʃizik 'eit BBC
Chithurst/Sx
  tʃidəst PNSx 33
Chittenden/K
  tʃitndən EPD
Chitterne/W
  tʃitə(r)n PNW(i)55
Chittlehamholt/D
  tʃitləmhoult BBC
Chittoe/W
  tʃitu: PNW 252
  tʃitu PNW(i)55,DEPN
Chitty/K
  tʃiti EPD
Chivenor/D
  tʃivnə BBC
Chobham/Sr
  tʃɔbəm BBC
Cholderton/W
  tʃouldətən, -tn EPD
Cholmondeley/Chs
  tʃoumli PNChs IV/21
  tʃumli GlossChs
  tʃʌmli PNChs IV/21,DEPN,EPD,
          BBC,BCE,Schr.,Kruis.,
          Hope,PNE&W,MEG 228,
          Mawer(4)284,GlossChs
          (i),s.n.Chumley,
          PNChs(i)9
Cholmondeston Gn, Ch.Hall/Chs
  tʃumstən,tʃoumstən,older local
  tʃə:mstən PNChs III/136
  tʃaumsən,tʃemsn PNDb(i) I/149
  tʃʌmsn PNChs(i)lo
  tʃə:rmstən GlossChs
  tʃɔms(ə)n BBC
  tʃɔmsən BCE
  tʃʌmstən Hope
Cholsey/Brk
  tʃoulzi EPD,BBC
Cholwich Town/D
  tʃɔlidʒ PND 269
Choppington/Nb
  tʃɔpəntn DSDu
Chorley/Chs
  tʃɔ:li PNChs III/115,EPD

Chorlton/Chs
  tʃɔ:rltən, older local
  tʃɔ:rtn PNChs III/59
Chosen/Gl (a hill)
  tʃouzn EPD,s.n.Churchdown
Chowbent/La
  tʃaubent PNLa(ii)
Chowley/Chs
  tʃouli, tʃauli PNChs IV/84
Chrishall/Ess
  krisəl PNEss 521
  'krishɔ:l BBC
Christchurch/Ca,Gl,Ha
  kraistʃə:tʃ, kraisttʃə:tʃ Bchm.131,
                         EPD
Christleton/Chs
  krisltən PNChs IV/lo7
  krislitn PNChs IV/lo7,GlossChs
  krislt(ə)n BBC
Christow/D
  kristou BBC
Chudleigh/D
  tʃʌdli EPD,Schr.,Chis.
Chulmleigh/D
  tʃʌmli PND 377,PNND 111,DEPN,
          BBC,BCE,HL 118o
Chunal/Chs
  tʃu:nə GlossChs
Churchdown/Gl
  tʃə:tʃdaun EPD[1]
  tʃouzən Hope
Churchill
  tʃə:tʃil EPD
Churchills/Wt
  tʃə:rtʃilz PNWt 2o9
Churchstow/D (also spelt -stowe)
  tʃə:stou PND 295
  'tʃə:tʃ'stou BBC,BCE
Churchtown
  tʃə:tʃtaun Schr.
Churt/Sr
  tʃi:ət PNSr 178
Churton/Chs,Sa
  tʃərtən PNChs IV/7o
  tʃə:tn EPD
Churwell/WRY
  tʃə:ril Hope
Chute/W
  tʃu:t PNW(i)57,EPD
Chyandour/Co (also spelt Chy-an-Dowr)
  ʃaiəndauə, 'tʃ- BBC,BCE
  tʃai- Jenner(2)3ol
  _ _ ı Jenner(2)3o4
Chyngton Fm/Sx
  tʃintən PNSx 364

---

1) "There was until recently a loc.pron. [tʃouzn] which is now probably
   obsolete as far as the village is concerned; it is preserved as the
   name of a hill near by,which is now written Chosen." (EPD)

Chypraze/Co
  tʃip'reiz   Jenner(2)3o1[1]
Chysoyster/Co
  tʃai'sɔ:stə BBC
Chytan/Co
  _ ˌ   Jenner(2)3o4
CinderyIs/Ess
  ðə sindri   PNEss 331
Cinque Port/K and Sx
  siŋk pɔ:t   PNK
Cippenham/Bk
  sipənəm   PNBk 217
  sip(ə)nəm   BBC
Cirencester/Gl
  sisitə   PNGl I/6o,DEPN,BBC,
           BCE,Schr.,Hope,
           Mawer(4)284,HL 1221,
           MEG 228,   EPN 86[2]
  sizitə   HL 1221,Kruis.,Hope,
           Moberly 123 ("before
           this generation")
  sistə   Hope,Kruis.
  sisistə   HL 1221,MEG 228
  sisəstə   WP 271
  sisestə   Kruis.
  sisətə   Chis. ("popularly"),
           Moberly 123 ("before
           this generation")

  'sairən'sestə   PNGl I/6o
  'saiər(ə)nsestə   BBC
  saierənsestə   Mawer(2)92
  saiərənsestə   BCE,HL 1222,
           Kruis.
  'sairənsestə   Schr.("rare"),
           Chis.
  sairinsestə   MEG 228

  sairən   PNGl I/6o,EPN 86
  serənsəstə   Hope
  srenstə   EPN 86

  zairnsestə   PNGl I/6o
  zairənsəstə   PNGl(i)169
  ziszətə   PNGl(i)169,GlossW
           2o8
Cisil Field/WRY
  sisil   GlossSh 3o2
Cissbury/Sx
  sisbəri   PNSx(i)46
Civer Hill/WRY
  si:və, seivə   GlossSh 3o2
Clacton/Ess
  klæktən   EPD

Claife/La
  kle:f   PNLa 219
Clamerkin/Wt
  klæmərkn   PNWt 78
Clannaborough/D
  klænəbərə   BBC
Clanricarde Gdns/Ldn
  'klænrikəd   EPD
Clapham/Ldn
  klæpəm   EPD,Schr.,Kruis.,Chis.
           HL 866,MEG 376
  klæpm   EPD
  -æ-   ESpr.312
Clapton
  klæptən   EPD,Schr.
Clapworthy/D
  klaperi   PND 347
  klæpəri   BBC,BCE
Clare/O,Sf
  klɛə   EPD
Clareborough/Nt
  klɑ:brə   PNNt(i)33
Claremont/So,Sr
  klɛəmɔnt, -mənt   EPD
Clarendon Pk/Le,We
  'klærəndən   Schr.,Kruis.
  klær(ə)ndən   EPD
Clarges St/Ldn
  klɑ:dʒiz   EPD
Clarke (as in C.'s Hill/La)
  klɑ:k   EPD
Clarks/WRY
  tlɑ:ks   DDd 15
Clatterford/Wt
  klætərfərd   PNWt 98
Claughton/Chs
  klɔ:tən   PNChs IV/316,BCE
  klɔ:t(ə)n   BBC
  klæftən   DEPN
Claughton/La (nr Caton)
  klaftn   PNLa 178,PNEss 334[!]
  klæftən   DEPN,BBC,BCE,H.A.(2)4
  klæftn   PNLa(ii)
Claughton-on-Brock/La (nr Garstang
  'klait(ə)n ɔn 'brɔk   BBC
  klaitən   BCE,PNLa 162
  -ai-   DEPN
Clavell's Copse/Wt
  kleivəlz kaps   PNWt 239
Claverdon/Wa
  klɑ:dən   PNWa 2o6,BCE
  klævəd(ə)n,klɑ:d(ə)n   BBC
  klævədən   BCE

1) "Educated people pronounce this vowel [i.e. the stressed vowel of
this name] as ay in may, but the ā, the natural elongation of ă, a
in man, is heard in the mouths of old people". (Jenner (2)3oo)
2) "Members of county families generally pron. ['sisitə],but the pron
most usually heard in the town is ['saiər(ə)nsestə](or [-stər] wi
the dial. retroflex r).An older pron. ['sizitər] may still be hea
in the country round." (EPD)

Claverham/So
  klævərəm BBC
Clavering/Ess
  kleivəriŋ BBC
Claverley/Sa
  klævəli BBC
  klɛəli Hope,PNWa(i)43
  klɑ:li GlossSa 516
Claverton/Chs,So
  klavərtən PNChs IV/16o
  klævət(ə)n BBC
  klævətən,kleivətən Schr.
Claxton/Du,Nf,NRY
  klækst(ə)n EPD
Claydon/Bk,O,Sf
  kleidən Schr.
Clayhanger/D
  'kleihæŋə EPD
Clayhidon/D
  kleihaid(ə)n BBC
  kleihaidən BCE
The Clays/Chs
  kleiz PNChs III/319
Clayton
  kleitn EPD,PNSx(i)48
Clearwell/Gl
  'kliə'wel, ◌ _, _ ◌ BBC,BCE
Cleasby/NRY
  kli:zbi PNYN 284
Cleator/Cu
  kli:tər PNCu 357
  kli:tə BBC,BCE
Cleckheaton/WRY
  klek'hi:t(ə)n BBC
Cleethorpes/Li
  kli:þɔ:ps EPD
Clegg/La
  kleg EPD
Clehonger/He
  klɔŋgə BBC,Hope
  klə'hɔŋgə,dial. kleɔŋgə
               DHe 43
Clenchwarton/Nf
  klenʃwɔ:t(ə)n BBC
Cleobury/Nf
  klibəri EPD
  klebəri EPD,Schr.
  kloubəri Schr.
Cleobury Mortimer/Sa
  and C.North/Sa
  'klib(ə)ri'mɔ:timə,
  'klib(ə)ri'nɔ:þ BBC
  klibəri PNSa,BCE,Schr.
  klebəri BCE,Schr.,Hope
  kloubəri Hope,Schr.
  -e- ,-i- DEPN
Clerkenwell/Mx
  klɑ:kənwel PNMx 94,Kruis.

  klɑ:knwel Schr.
  klɑ:k(ə)nw(ə)l,-wel EPD
  klɑ:k- PNMx(i)
Clermont/Nf
  klɔ:mənt Schr.
  klɛəmont, -mənt EPD
Clervaux Castle/NRY
  klɛəvou, klɛəvɔ:ks BBC,BCE
Clevancy/W
  kli'vænsi PNW 268
  kle'vænsi PNW(i) 58
Clevedon/So
  kli:vdən DEPN,EPD,BBC,Schr.,Kruis
Cleveland/NRY
  kli:vlənd PNYN 128,DEPN,EPD,Schr.
Cleveleys/La
  kli:vliz BBC
Cley-next-the-Sea/Nf
  klei BBC,BCE, DNf 42 ("telephone
          operators nowadays call it
          'Clay'")
  klai DEPN,DNf 42,Hope,BBC,BCE
Cliburn/We
  klibən, 'klaibə:n PNWe II/136
  'klibə:n BBC,BCE
  klibərən PNE'side 67
  -i- DEPN
Cliddesden/Ha
  klidizdən BBC
Cliffe
  klif EPD,Kruis.
Clifford/He,W (C.Bottom),WRY
  klifəd EPD,Schr.
  klifit PNW 228
Cliffords Mesne/Gl
  'klifədz 'mi:n BBC,BCE
Clifton
  kliftən Schr.
  klift(ə)n EPD
Clifton/Gl
  klifən Hope
Clifton-on-Teme/Wo
  klifn PNWo 43
Clifton Reynes/Bk
  kliftən reinz BBC,BCE
Clinch/Nb,W
  klin(t)ʃ EPD
Clints/WRY
  tlints DDd 14
Clipsham/Ru
  klipʃəm, klipshəm BBC
Clipston/Np
  klipsən PNNp 111
Clipstone/Np
  klipston BBC
Clissold Pk/Ldn
  klis(ə)ld, -ould EPD
Clitheroe/La
  kliðərou EPD,BBC,Schr.

'kliþərou   Chis.
Clive/Chs
    klaiv   PNChs II/234,EPD,
        Kruis.
Clive/Sa
    kliv   PNSa,Mawer(4)285
Cliveden/Bk
    klivdən   PNBk 232,DEPN,EPD,
        BBC
    kli:vdən   EPD
Cliviger/La
    tlivitʃər,
    tlividʒər   PNLa 84,Ellis 350
    klividʒə   DEPN
Clophill/Bd
    'klɔphil   BBC
Clopton/Ca
    klɔptən   ONCa 16
Close Ho/We
    kloəs hous   PNE'side 72
Closes (New C.)/WRY
    tluasiz   DDd 12
Clothall/Hrt
    klɔtəl   PNHrt 155
Clotton/Chs
    tlɔtn   GlossChs
Clotton Common, C.Hall,
C.Lodge/Chs
    klɔtən   PNChs III/271
Cloudesley/Wa
    klaudzli   EPD,Kruis.
Clough
    klʌf   EPD,Kruis.
    klu: EPD
Clough/St
    klʌf   PNSt 42
Clough/WRY (as in Harvey C.,
    Hell C.,Stainery C.)
    kluf   GlossSh 45
Clough/WRY (as in Crimble C.,
    Seller's C.)
    tluf   DHd 135
Clough/WRY (r.n.)
    klʌf   BBC
Clough/WRY (in Dentdale)
    tlɔf   DDd 16
Clougha Pike/La
    'klɔfə paik   PNLa 169,BBC,
        BCE
    kləfə   PNCuWe 36,s.n.
        Cloffocks, PNLa(ii)
Cloughfold/La (or Clough Fold)
    'klʌf'fould   BBC
Cloughton/NRY
    kloutən   PNYN 108,BCE,Hope
    klaut(ə)n,klout(ə)n   BBC
    klautən   BCE,Hope
Clough Wood/Chs
    klʌf   PNChs III/188

Clovelly/D
    klə'veli   EPD
    klou'veli   PND 70,DEPN,BBC,
        Chanter 523
    klauvali   PNND 26
Cloverley Hall/Sa
    klɔvəli   BBC
Clowes/Nf
    klu:z   EPD
Clowne/Db
    klaun   PNDb(i) I/216,BBC
Clumber Pk/Nt
    'klʌmbə 'pɑ:k   BBC
Clun/Sa (r.n.)
    klʌn   RN 89
Clun/Sa
    klʌn   BBC,BCE
Clunbury/Sa
    klʌnbəri   BBC,BCE
Clungunford/Sa
    klʌn'gʌnfəd   DEPN,BBC,BCE
    klʌngʌnə   GlossSa 516
Clunton/Sa
    klʌntən   BBC,BCE
Clutton/Chs,So
    klʌt(ə)n   BBC
    klʌtn   EPD
Clyffe Pypard/W (also spelt Cliffe
    olim kli:v pipər, vel pepər,
    nunc vero paipəd   PNW 266
    kli:v   PNW(i) 58
    klif paipɑːd   BBC,BCE
Clyst/D (r.n.)
    klist   PND 3,BBC,BCE
Coalbrookdale/Sa
    'koulbruk'deil   BBC,Schr.
Coates
    kouts   EPD
Coat Hill/Cu
    kouthil   PNCu 66
Coatley/WRY (nr.Sedbergh)
    ko:tli   DKe 6
Coatsike/We
    koət saik   PNE'side 72
Cobb (as in C.Croft/K)
    kɔb   EPD
Cobden (as in C.Edge/Db)
    kɔbdən   EPD
Coberley/Gl
    kubəli   PNGl I/152
    kʌbəli   DEPN,BBC,BCE
Cobham/Sr
    kɔbəm   EPD
Cobridge/St
    kɔbridʒ   BCE
Cockayne Hatley/Bd
    kɔkin ætli   PNBdHu 105
Cock Bevington/Wa → Bevington

Cockcroft/WRY
   koukrɔft,kɔkkrɔft EPD
Cocken/La
   kɔkin, kɔkn   PNLa 2o3
Cockenach/Hrt
   kɔknidʒ PNHrt 172
Cocker/Cu;La (r.n.)
   kɔkə EPD
Cockerel/Wt
   kɔ:krəl PNWt 174
Cockerington/Li
   kɔkəriŋtən BBC
Cockermouth/Cu
   kɔkəmaþ,-mauþ,
   (loc. only -məþ) EPD
Cockernhoe Gn/Hrt
   'kɔkənhou BBC
Cocking/Sx
   kɔkən PNSx 16
Cockleton/Wt
   kagltn PNWt 186
Cockley Cley/Nf
   kɔkli klai DEPN,BBC,Hope
Cocklock Scar/Cu
   kɔklə PNE'side 63
Cockshutt/Sa
   kɔkʃʌt BBC
Cockwood/D
   kɔkwud,loc.kɔkud EPD[1]
Coddington
   kɔdiŋtən EPD
Coddington/Chs
   kɔdintn PNChs IV/85
   kɔditn PNChs IV/85,GlossChs
Codicote/Hrt
   kʌdikət PNHrt 1o9
   koudikout EPD
   kɔdikət BBC
Codrington/Gl
   kɔdriŋtən EPD
Codsall/St
   kɔdsl BBC
Coffcott Gn/D
   kɔ:kət PND 139
Cogenhoe/Np
   kuknou PNNp 144,DEPN,BBC,BCE
   'kougənhou BBC,BCE
The Cogers/Ldn
   kɔdʒəz BBC
Cogges/O
   kɔgz PNO 333
Coggeshall/Ess
   kɔksl PNEss 365,DEPN,BBC
   kɔksəl,kɔgiʃəl BCE
   kɔksɔ:l PNEss 365,EssDD 158,
         Hope
   kɔgəshɔ:l Chis.

   kɔgiʃl BBC
   kɔgiʃ(ə)l EPD
   kɔkʃɔ:l, kɔgʃɔ:l Hope
   now usually 'kɔgiʃɔ:l PNEss 365
Coggin (as in C.'s Mill/Sx)
   kɔgin EPD
Cogill/NRY
   kɔgil PNYN 261
Cogshall/Chs
   kɔkʃl,kɔkʃəl PNChs II/ix,GlossChs
   kɔgsɔ:l PNChs II/1o9
   kɔkʃɔ:l Hope
Cokeham/Sx
   koukəm PNSx 2o1
Coker/Do,So
   koukə EPD
Cokethorpe Pk/O
   koukþɔ:p PNO 324
Colan/Co
   kɔlən BBC
Colaton Raleigh/D
   kɔlət(ə)n rɔ:li BBC
Colburn/NRY
   koubən PNYN 243
Colbury/Ha
   koulbəri BBC
Colby/Nf,We
   koulbi EPD,Hope(for C. in Nf)
   koubi PNWe II/96,PNE'side 73
Colcar Ing Wood/WRY
   koukə PNYW II/92
Colchester/Ess
   keutʃstə PNEss 367
   koutʃəstə Hope
   kaoʃəstə DEss.HL 9o3
   koultʃəstə BCE,Hope
   koultʃistə EPD,BBC,Schr.,Kruis.,
           MEG 225
   koultʃestə Schr.,MEG 224
   kɔltʃəstə Chis.
   kɔltʃistə Kruis.
Coldale/Cu
   koudəl GlossCu xvii
Coldbeck/We
   kɔdbek PNE'side 75
Colden/ERY
   koudn GlossHol 17
Cold Harbour/Li (a house in Northorpe)
   koud ha:bə GlossM&C,s.n.Coud
         harbour
Coldhesledon/Du (or Cold H.)
   'kould 'hesldən BBC,BCE
Coldhill Churn/WRY
   commonly called Crudhill Churn
         DA1&Hd,s.n.Loin
Coldred/K
   kouldred BBC,BCE,PNK

1) "[The loc. pron.] seems likely to become obsolete before long."(EPD)

Coldrum/K
  kouldrʌm PNK
Coldwaltham/Sx
  'kould'wɔːlþəm BBC
Cold Wold/ERY
  kɔːd wɔːd PNYE 172
Colebrooke/D
  koulbruk EPD
Coleby/Li
  koulbi EPD
Coleford/D,Gl,So
  koulfəd EPD,BBC
Colehill/Do
  'kɔlhil, 'koulhil BBC,BCE
Colemere/Sa
  kumər GlossSa xxvi and 516
  more modern koulmər
                GlossSa xxvi
  kuːmə, educated people
  call it koul miə PNSa
Coleorton/Le
  kɔl'ɔːt(ə)n BBC
  kɔl'ɔːtən BCE
Colerne/W
  kʌlərn PNW 93
  kʌlə(r)n PNW(i)6o
  kʌlən BBC,BCE
  -ʌ- DEPN
Coles (as in C.Hill/He)
  koulz EPD
Coleshill/Bk
  kousəl PNBk 227
  koulzhil BBC,Schr.
Coleward/Ess
  kɔləd PNEss 211
Coley/WRY
  kuːəli Hope
Colgate/Nf,Sx
  kɔlgeit,koul-,-git EPD
Colham Gn/Mx
  kɔləm PNMx 41
Colindale/Mx
  kɔlindeil EPD
Colkirk/Nf
  koulkəːk Hope
Collingbourne Ducis/W
  kɔliŋbɔːn djuːsis BBC
Collingham/Nt,WRY
  kɔliŋəm EPD,Schr.
Collingwood Ho/K,Nb,ERY
  kɔliŋwud EPD,Schr.
Collins (as in C.Gn/La)
  kɔlinz EPD
Collycroft/Wa
  kɔlikraːft Hope
Collyweston/Np
  kɔli'wesən PNNp 2oo
Colnbrook/Bk (or Colne-)
  kounbruk EPD,BBC,Kruis.,
                MEG 293

koulnbruk EPD,Bchm.119,Schr.
koulbruk Bchm.119,Schr.,Kruis
        MEG 293 ("rarely")
Colne
  kouln EPD,Chis.,Bchm.114
  koun EPD,Bchm.114,Kruis.
Colne/Ess;Bk,Hrt,Mx (r.n.)
  koun HL 9o3 (for C. in Ess),
        DEPN (for C. in Ess,Hrt,
        PNMx(i)
  kouln Schr.,HL 9o
Colne/Ess(C. Engaine,Wakes C.,
        White C.)
  kɔːən PNEss 379
  kounən'gein BBC
  koun 'engein BCE
Colne/La
  koːn PNLa 87
  kaun PNLa(ii)
  koun DEPN,BBC,BCE,Ellis 34o
Colne/WRY (r.n.)
  koun BBC,DHd 55
  kouln DHd 55
Colney/Hrt,Mx,Nf
  kouni EPD,BBC,PNHrt 67;
        for C. in Nf only: BCE,
        DEPN,Hope
Colney Heath/Hrt
  'kouni'hiːþ BBC
Coln St.Aldwyn/Gl
  'koun snt 'ɔːldwin BBC
Colsterdale/NRY
  koustədil PNYN 23o
Colsterworth/Li
  koutswəːþ Hope[1]
Colston-Basset/Nt
  kousn, or less frequently
  koulsn   PNNt(i) 36
  koulstən bæsit BBC
  koulst(ə)n EPD
Colt Close/Cu
  koət kloəs PNE'side 72
Colthouse/La
  kɔlthaus PNLa 219
Coltishall/Nf
  koultisəl, koultiʃl,
  'koultisɔːl, koulsl BBC
  koultsəl, koulsil Hope
Colton/La
  kɔltn, koːltn PNLa 216
Columbia Row/Ldn
  kə'lʌmbiə CPhon 52
Colveston/Nf
  kɔlstən Hope
  koulstən PNNf,s.n.Coulston
Colwall/He
  kɔlwəl BBC
Colwell/Nb
  kɔləl PNNbDu 51

---

1)Hope's second transcription <u>Coltseralt</u> looks very unlikely.

Colwell Bay/Wt
  kɔ:lwəl   PNWt 126
Colwich/St
  kɔlwitʃ   BBC
  kɔlidʒ   DEPN,Hope
Colwick/Nt
  kɔlik   PNNt 16o,PNNt(i)36,
          BBC,BCE,Hope,ONwick
          371
  kɔlwik   BBC,BCE
Colworth/Sx
  kɔlwə:ϸ   BBC
Coly/D (r.n.)
  kɔli   PND 3
Colyford/D
  kɔlifəd   BBC
Colyton/D
  kɔlitn   EPD
  kɔlit(ə)n   BBC
Combe
  ku:m   EPD,Kruis.,PNK
        BBC (for Castle C./W)
Combe-in-Teignhead/D
  'ku:m in tin'hed   BBC,BCE
Comb(e)pyne/D
  'ku:m'pain   BBC,BCE
Comberbach/Chs
  'kʌmbərbætʃ   PNChs II/111
  kʌmbəbætʃ   BBC
Comber Mare,
Combermere Abbey and Pk/Chs
  kumbə-, kʌmbə-   PNChs III/93
Comberow/He,So
  ku:mrou   BBC,BCE (for C. in
          So, also spelt
          Combe Row)
Comberton/Ca
  kʌmatən   PNO li (add. corr.)
  kɔmbatən   ONCa 16
Comberton/Wo
  kʌmatən   GlossSEWo 82
Combe Scar/WRY (a mountain)
  koum skɑ:r   DDd 17
Combestone/D
  kʌmstən   PND 3o2
Combley Fm/Wt
  kʌmli   PNWt 24o
  ku:mli   DWt,s.n.kite boughs
Combrook/Wa
  kɔmbruk   BBC
Combsies/So
  ku:mziz,kʌmziz   BBC,BCE
Combtonfield/Wt
  kumtnfild   PNWt 219
Combwich/So
  kʌmidʒ   DEPN,BBC,BCE
  kʌmitʃ,
  ku:midʒ,ku:mitʃ   BBC,BCE

Comforts/Wt
  kʌmfərts   PNWt 286
Comhampton/Wo
  kɔmən   PNWo 269
Commandry Fm/Wo
  kɔmɑ:ndəri   PNWo 316
Compstall/Chs
  kɔmpstɔ:(l),
  olim kɔmstɔ: PNChs II/vii
  kɔmstə   GlossChs
Compton
  kɔm(p)tən, kʌm-   EPD
  kɔmtən, kʌmtən   Schr.,Kruis.

  "to be pron. [kʌm(p)tən] rather
  than [kɔm(p)tən] which is a
  spelling form" (IPN II/2o)

  -ɔ-, -ʌ-   DEPN
Compton/Brk
  kɔm(p)tən   BBC
Compton/Ha
  kʌm(p)tən   BBC
Compton/Sr
  kʌmptə n   PNSr 194,BCE
  kɔmtən   BCE
Compton/Sx
  kʌmtən   PNSx 47
  kɔmtən   PNSx(i) 5o
Compton Abbas/Do
  kɔmtən   PNDo(i) 21
Compton Castle/D
  kɔm(p)tən   BBC
Compton Chamberlayne/W
  kɔm(p)tən tʃeimbərlin   BBC
Compton Fm/Wt
  kʌmtn   PNWt 126
Compton Pauncefoot/So
  'kɔm(p)tən 'pɔ:nsfut   BBC
Compton St/Ldn
  kɔm(p)tən   EPD
Compton Valence/Do
  'kɔm(p)tən 'væləns   BBC
Compton Wynyates/Wa (also spelt
          Wyniates and Winyates)
  loc. kɔm(p)tən winjeits,
  kʌm(p)tən winjeits   BBC
Condicote/Gl
  kundikət   PNGl I/216
  kɔndikət   BBC
Condover/Sa
  kʌndər   RN 99,GlossSa 516
  'kʌndouvə   BBC,BCE,Hope
  -ʌ-   DEPN
Conduit St/Ldn
  kɔndit, kʌn·   EPD
Coneysthorpe/NRY
  kunistrəp   PNYN 48
  -ʌ-   DEPN

Congerston/Le
ku:ndʒəsən   PNLe 76
Congleton/Chs
kɔŋərtn   PNChs II/ix
kɔŋgərtn   GlossChs
kɔŋətən   Hope

kɔŋltən,
kɔŋgltn   PNChs II/294
kɔŋgltən   EPD,Schr.
kɔŋgəltən   Chis.
Congresbury/So
kɔŋzbri   BBC[1]
ku:mzbəri   BBC,BCE
'kɔŋgresbəri   BCE
Congreve/St
kɔŋgri:v   Bchm.118,Kruis.,
kɔŋgri:v   EPD,Kruis.
-gri:v   HL 1o19
Coningsby/Li
kɔniŋzbi,kʌniŋzbi   BBC,BCE
Conington/Ca,Hu
kɔniŋtən   BBC,ONCa 25
kʌniŋtən   PNBdHu 182
Conisbrough/WRY (or -borough)
kɔnisbrə, kʌnisbrə   EPD
kɔnisbərə   BBC
kʌnzbrə   Kruis.
Coniscliffe/Du
kʌnzli   PNNbDu 51,Mawer(4)285
kunzli   PNBdHu 127 [!]
kɔnisklif   BBC
kʌnsklif   PNNbDu 51,Hope
kʌns-   DEPN
Conisholme/Li
kɔnishoum, kɔnizhoum,
kɔniʃoum   BBC,BCE
Coniston (Church C.)/La
kunistn   PNLa 215,PNLa(ii)
kɔnist(ə)n   EPD
-ʌ-   DEPN
Coniston Water/La
kɔnist(ə)n wɔ:tə   BBC
kɔnistən -   Schr.
Conningbrook/K
kʌninbruk   PNK
Connor Downs/Co
'kɔnə 'daunz   BBC
Cononley/WRY
kɔnənlə   PNYW VI/27
Consall/St
kʌnsɔ:l   Hope
Consett/Du
'kɔnsit,'kɔnset   BBC
Constable Burton/NRY
'kʌnstəbl 'bə:t(ə)n   BBC,Kruis.

Constantine/Co
kɔnst(ə)ntain   EPD,BBC
Conyer/K
kʌnjə,kɔnjə   BBC,BCE
Conyngham Ho/WRY
kʌniŋəm   EPD, Kruis.
Cooden/Sx
ku:dən, ku:'den   BBC,BCE
Cookridge/WRY
kukridʒ   PNYW IV/189
Cookspit Fm/Chs
kukspit   PNChs III/143
Cookwood/D
kukudə   DHtl 8
Coole Lane/Chs
ku:l   PNChs III/139
Coole Pilate/Chs
'ku:l 'pailat   PNChs III/138
Cooling/K,Sf
ku:liŋ   EPD
Coombe/Wt
ku:m   PNWt 66,EPD
Coombes/Sx
ku:mz   EPD
Coombswell Copse/Sr
ku:msəl   PNSr 2o6
Coopers nr Bembridge/Wt,
Coopers nr Chale/Wt
ku:pərz   PNWt 119 and 285
Coopersale/Ess
ku:pəseil   BBC
Copeland/Cu,Nb,We
kouplənd   EPD
Copley
kɔpli   EPD
Copped Hall/Ess,Hrt
kɔpt hɔ:l   BBC
Coppenhall/Chs
kɔpnɔ:l   PNChs III/22
kɔpnəl   PNChs III/22 ("older
local"), GlossChs
Coppidhall/Wt
kɑ:pidɔ:l   PNWt 29
Copplestone/D
koulstən   PND 424
kɔplstən   BBC
Copp (as in C.Street/K)
kɔp   EPD
Copped (as in C.Hall/Ess,Hrt)
kɔpt   EPD (see above s.n. C.Ha
Coppishull/Gl
gɔps hil   PNLe 66 (s.n.Gopsall
Coppull/La
kɔpl   BBC
kɔpəl   BCE
kɔp-pə(h)   DAd 4 and 74
Copt (as in C.Hall/Bd,Ess,Mx)
kɔpt   EPD

1) "The first is the loc. pron.; the [second] is said to originate i
   Bristol." (BBC)

Copthall Gn/Ess
 kɔpt(h)ɔ:l EPD
Coquet/Nb (r.n.)
 ko:kit, ko:kət RN 93
 kɔkət Chis.
 koukit PNNbDu 52,DEPN,BBC
 koukət BCE
Coquet Is/Nb (see also s.n.
 koukit BBC   Couquet)
Coram Street/Sf
 kɔ:rəm EPD
Corbridge/Nb
 kɔ:bridʒ BBC
Cornbury Pk/O
 kɔ:nbəri EPD
Corn Close/WRY
 kɔ:n tluas DDd 15
Corner Row/La
 kɔ:nəro: PNLa 154
Cornhill/Mx,
Cornhill-on-Tweed/Nb
 kɔ:nəl PNNbDu 54
 kɔ:n'hil EPD,BBC
 ˈ ˌ Kruis.
 ˌ ˈ EPD
Cornwall
 kɔ:nwəl BBC,Kruis.,Schr.
 kɔ:nwɔl Lloyd 115
 kɔ:nw(ə)l EPD
 kɔ:nwɔ:l EPD,Schr.,Chis.
Corpusty/Nf
 'kɔ:pəsti BBC
Corringales/Ess
 skrindʒəlz,
 kɔringeilz PNEss 4o
 skrindʒəls Dodgson(2)366
Corringham/Ess,Li
 kɔrənəm PNEss 151
 kɔriŋəm BBC
Corsham/W
 olim kɔsem PNW 95
 kɔ:ʃəm BBC
 kɔʃəm Hope
 kɔs- DEPN
Corston/W
 vulgo kɔ:rsən PNW 5o
Cortlingstock/Nt
 kɔstɔk Hope
Corve/Wt
 karv PNWt 114
Coryates/Do
 kɔrieits,
 kɔriəts PNDo(i)249
Coryton/D,Ess
 kɔritən PND 181,BCE (for C.
         in D)
 kɔrit(ə)n BBC
 kɔritn EPD
 kɔr- DEPN (for C. in D)

Cosca/We
 kɔskə PNE'side 63
Coseley/St
 kouzli BBC
Cosford/Sf,Wa
 kɔsfəd BBC
Cosham/Ha
 kɔsəm EPD,BBC,BCE
 kɔzəm BCE
 ku:əm Hope ('Cooham', a mis-
             print for 'Cosham' ?)
Cossall/Nt
 kɔsl PNNt 143,BBC
Cossington/Le,So
 kʌsiŋtən,kʌziŋtən BBC,BCE
Costessey/Nf
 kɔsi PNNf,s.n.Cossey, DNf 42,
      BBC,Hope
Costock/Nt → Cortlinstock
Coston/Le,Nf
 kousn BBC
 kousən PNNf,s.n.Coson, BCE (for
         C. in Le)
 -ou- DEPN (for C. in Le)
Cotcliffe/NRY
 kɔtlif PNYN 2o5
Cotehele/Co
 kə'ti:l, kət'hi:l BBC
 'kouthi:l BCE
Cote Hill/Cu
 koət hil PNE'side 72
Cotesbach/Le
 koutsbætʃ BBC
Cotescue Pk/NRY
 ko:tskiu PNYN 255
Cotgrave/Nt
 'kɔtgreiv EPD,BBC
Cotham/Nt,So
 kɔtəm PNNt 212,BBC
Cothelstone/So
 kʌɵlstən, kɔtlstən BBC
 kʌɵəlstən, kɔtəlstən BCE
Cotheridge/Wo
 kɔɵəridʒ BBC
Cotherstone/NRY
 kʌɵəstən BBC,Hope
Cothill/brk
 'kɔt'hil BBC
Cotmanhay/Db
 'kɔtmənhei BBC
Cotmaton/D
 kɔt'meitən PND 598
Coton
 kout(ə)n BBC
 koutn EPD
 koutən PNCa(i)8
 -ou- PNDb(i) I/144
 kouitən Hope (for C. in Wa)
         ("Cowiton")

The Cotswolds/Gl
  kɔtswouldz   BBC,EPD,HL 755
    -wəldz   EPD,HL 755
  kɔtswoul(z),-w(e)ld(z)
                 Bchm.251
  "the spelling pron. [...] has
  prevailed"   MEG 214
Cottam
  kɔtəm EPD
Cottenham/Ca
  kɔtnəm EPD,Hope
  kɔt(ə)nəm ONCa 177
Cotterdale/NRY
  kɔtədil PNYN 258
Cottered/Hrt
  kɔtred PNHrt 157
Cottesbach/Le
  kɔtəsbatʃ Ellis 489
Cottesbrooke/Np
  kɔtizbruk PNNp 67,BBC
Cottesloe/Bk
  kɔtslou EPD
Cottesmore/Ru
  'kɔtsmɔ: BBC,BCE
  kɔtʃmɔ:ə Zachr.(3)127,
             Ellis 256
Cottingham/Np,ERY
  kɔtiŋəm EPD
Cotton (Far C.)/Np
  kɔt(ə)n BBC
  kɔtən BCE
Cotton/Sa (also spelt Coton)
  koutən, an older pron. was
  kɔtən PNSa
Coughton/He
  kout(ə)n BBC
  koutən BCE
  -ou- DEPN
Coughton/Wa
  koutən PNWa 2o7,BCE
  kout(ə)n,kaut(ə)n BBC[1]
  kautən BCE
Coulby/NRY
  koubi PNYN 17o
Coulsdon/Sr
  koulzdən PNSr 44,EPD[2]
  koulzd(ə)n,ku:lzd(ə)n BBC
  ku:lzdən EPD
Coulston/W
  koulstən, vulgo
  koulsən PNW 14o
Coulton/NRY
  koutən PNYN 5o
  koult(ə)n EPD

Coumes Hills/WRY
  ku:mbs GlossSh 52
Coundon/Du,Wa
  kaundən PNDu,BBC,BCE (for C. ⚓
          Du),PNWa 159
Countersett/NRY
  ku:ntəsit PNYN 263
Countess Wear/D
  'kauntis 'wiə BBC
Countisbury/D
  kauntisbəri BBC
Coupland/Nb
  ku:pländ EPD,BBC,BCE
  kouplənd BBC,BCE
Coupland Beck/We
  kouplənd bek BBC
Couquet/Nb (r.n.) (see also s.n.
                 Coquet)
  koukit Mawer(2)92
Court/La ⟶ Le Court
Courtenay/Brk (= Sutton C.),
Courtney/O (= Nuneham C.)
  kɔ:tni, kɔətni EPD
Court in Holmes/Sx
  "The old inhabitants call it to
  this day C'rt'innoms (ex inf. Lⓔ
  Edward Gleichen)" PNSr xli
Courteenhall/Np
  kɔ:t(ə)nɔ:l PNNp 145
  kɔ:tn- DEPN
Couthy Butt/Wt
  kouði bʌt PNWt 286
Cove/Co,D,Ha
  kouv EPD,Schr.
Covehithe/Sf
  'kouv'haið BBC
Coven/St
  kouv(ə)n BBC
Coveney/Ca
  kouvni DEPN,BBC,BCE
Covenham/Li
  kouvənəm DEPN,BBC,BCE
Covenhope/He
  kɔnəp BBC,BCE
  kouv(ə)nhoup BBC
  kouvənhoup BCE
Covent Gdn/Mx (formerly called
             Convent Gdn)
  kɔmən gɑ:dən, kɔvənt - Hope
  kʌvənt gɑ:dn, kɔvənt - Schr.
  kɔv(ə)nt gɑ:d(ə)n EPD,BBC
  kʌv(ə)nt - EPD ("old fashioⓝ
            ed"),BBC
  kɔvnt Kruis.

1) "The first is usual for the National Trust property of Coughton
   Court." (BBC)
2) "[This is] the traditional loc. pron. People unfamiliar with the plⓐ
   generally pronounce ku:l-, as also do many new residents in the
   district." (EPD)

kɔvin   Höfer 3ol

Coventry/Wa
 kɔv(ə)ntri   EPD,BBC[1]
 kʌv(ə)ntri   EPD ("rarely"),
          BBC
 kɔvəntri   BCE,Schr.,Köppel 55
 kʌvəntri   Schr.,Chis.,
          Köppel 55
 kʌvntri, kɔvntri   Kruis.
 -ɔ-   DEPN,Dobson 584 ("the
          normal [...] pron.")

Cover/NRY (r.n.)
 kuər   RN loo
 kɔvə   RN loo,DEPN

Coverack/Co
 'kʌvəræk   BBC
 'kɔvəræk   EPD,BBC
 loc. also -rək   EPD

Coverham/NRY
 kuvərəm, kourəm   PNYN 254

Covington/Hu
 kʌviŋtən   EPD

Cowbit/Li
 kʌbit   BBC,BCE

Cowbridge
 kaubridʒ   Schr.

Cowden/K
 kau'den   EPD,BBC,BCE
 'kauden   EPD,PNK

Cowdham/K → Cudham

Cowdray Pk/Sx
 kaudri   PNSx(i) 51,EPD

Cow Dub/WRY
 kau dub   DDd 12

Cowen Head/We
 'kauwən 'ed   PNWe I/153

Cowes/Wt
 kæus   PNWt 119
 kauz   DEPN,EPD,Schr.,Kruis.,
          Chis.,DWt,s.n.needs

Cowesby/NRY
 kouzbi   PNYN 2ol

Cowfold/Sx
 kʌfəld   PNSx 2o9
 kaufould   PNSx(i) 52

Cowgill/WRY
 kɔ:gil   DDd 12,Ellis 559

Cow Hill/Db
 kou hil   PNDb(i) I/22o

Cowlam/ERY
 kauləm   PNYE 126

Cowlane/Cu
 ku:luən   GlossCu xvii

Cowldyke/NRY
 kouldaik   PNYN 58

Cow Lease/Wt   (or C.Leaze)
 kæu liəz   PNWt 286

Cowleaze Chine/Wt
 kæuli:z tʃain   PNWt 285

Cowley
 kauli   EPD,Kruis.

Cowley/Db
 kouli   PNDb (i) I/221

Cowley/O
 kauli   PNO(i) 86,BBC

Cowley/WRY
 kauli, kouli   BBC,BCE

Cowling/K
 ku:liŋ   PNK

Cowling/La
 kauliŋ,kouliŋ   BBC,BCE

Cowling/WRY
 kauliŋ   PNYW VI/12
 kouliŋ   BBC,BCE

Cowling/NRY
 koulin   PNYN 237
 kouliŋ   BBC,BCE

Cowlinge/Sf (also spelt Cooling)
 ku:lindʒ   DEPN,BBC,BCE,Hope,
          Dodgson(2)334

Cowlow/Db
 kau-   PNDb(i) I/142

Cowms/WRY
 kɛəmz, koumz   DHd 5o

Cowpe/La
 kaup   PNLa(ii),BBC

Cowpen/Nb
 ku:pən   DEPN,BBC,BCE

Cowpen Bewley/Du
 ku:pən bju:li   DEPN,BBC,BCE
 kaupən   PNDu

Cowper (Abbey C.)/Cu
 abəku:pə   PNCu 29o

Cowplain/Ha
 kauplein   BBC

Cowran/La
 kaurən   PNLa 211

Cowridge End/Bd
 skə:dʒend   PNBdHu 158

Cowrigg/Cu
 ku:rig   PNCu 247

Cowsden/Wo
 kouzən   PNWo 23o

Cowthorpe/WRY
 kouþrəp   PNYW V/22

Cowton/NRY
 ku:tən   PNYN 281
 kautn   EPD

Cowtray/We (also spelt Cotra)
 koutrei   Simpson 283

Coxtie Gn/Ess
 koksti   EPD

Cox's Corner/Wt
 'kɑ:ksiz 'karnər   PNWt 286

[1]) "Zwischen [ʌ] und [ɔ:],[ɔ] schwankt die heutige Aussprache."
 (ESpr.313)

Coxwold/NRY
    kukud   PNNY 12,PNYN 191
    kukwud   Schr.,Hope
Crabwall/Chs
    'kræb(w)ɔ:l   PNChs IV/169
Crackenthorpe/We
    krekinθrɔp   PNE'side 71
    kræk(ə)nþɔ:p   EPD
Cracoe/WRY
    kre:kə   PNYW VI/88
Cradle/La
    kredl   GlossR&R ("[a]
               pseudo-polite pron.")
Cradley/He
    krædli   BBC,BCE
    kreidli   EPD
Cradley/Wo
    kreidli   PNWo 294,DEPN,BBC,
             EPD
    krɛ:dli   Ellis 485
Cradley Heath/St
    kreidli hi:þ   BBC,BCE
Crafthole/Co
    krɑ:fthoul   BBC
Crag/WRY (a mountain)
    krag   DDd 17
Cragdale/NRY
    krægdil   PNYN 263
Cragg/Nb,WRY
    kræg   EPD
Craggs/WRY (also called C.Hill)
    krægziz   DDd 13
Crag Lough/Nb
    'kræg 'lɔf   BBC
Crake/La (r.n.)
    kre:k   RN 1o2,PNLa 191
Cralle Place/Sx
    krɔ:l   PNSx 469

Cramer's Gn/Ess
    krænməz   PNEss 4o1
Cramlington/Nb
    kræmliŋtən   EPD
    kræməltən   Mawer(2)94
Cranage/Chs
    krænidʒ   PNChs II/223
Cranborne/Do
    'krænbɔ:n   EPD,Bchm.69
      -bɔən   EPD
    (never -uə-   Bchm.51)
Cranbourne/Brk,Ha
    krænbən   Schr.
      -bɔ:n   EPD,Kruis.
      -bɔən   EPD
      -buən   EPD,Bchm.51
Cranbrook/K
    krænbruk   EPD,Schr.

Cranfield/Bd[1]
    krænfi:ld   PNBdHu 68
Cranford/D,Mx,Np
    krænfəd   EPD
Cranleigh/Sr → Cranley
Cranley/Mx,Sf,Sr
    krænli   EPD
Cranmer (as in C.Hall/Nf)
    krænmə   EPD
Cranmore/Wt
    kræ(n)mɔ:r   PNWt 2o9
Cranswick/ERY
    kranzik   PNYE 156
    krænzik   Hope
    krænsik   ONwick 365
Crantock/Co
    kræntək   Förster
Cranwich/Nf
    krænis   Hope
Cranworth/Nf
    krænwə:þ   EPD
    krænə   Hope
Craster/Nb
    kreistə   PNNbDu 57,DEPN
Craven Arms/Sa
    kreiv(ə)n ɑ:mz   BBC
Crawford/Do,La
    krɔ:fəd   EPD
Crawley
    krɔ:li   EPD,Kruis.
Crawley/Nb
    krala   PNNbDu 57
Cray/K
    krei   PNK
Crayford/K,WRY
    kreifəd   BBC,Schr.,PNK
Crayke/NRY
    krɔək   PNYN 27
Creacombe/D
    kreikəm   PND 379
    kri:kəm   BBC
Crease/D
    kreiz   Alexander 3o4
Creaton/Np
    kri:t(ə)n   BBC
Credenhill/He
    'kred(ə)nhil,kri:d(ə)nhil   BBC
    kredən-, kri:dən-   BCE
Crediton/D
    kə:rtən   PND 4o4
    kə:tən   Schr.("loc."),Hope
    kredit(ə)n   BBC
    kreditən   BCE,Schr.
    kreditn   EPD
Creeksea/Ess
    kriksi   PNEss 212

---

1) The pron. heard by the author was [krænfi:ld].

Creighton/St
   kraitn   EPD,Kruis.
Cremyll/Co
   'kremil   BBC
Crepping Hall/Ess
   kripən   PNEss 383
Creslow/Bk
   kris(t)lə   PNBk 77
Crespigny St/Ldn
   kres'pi:ni   EPD
Cressing/Ess
   krisn   PNEss 285
Cressingham/Nf
   kresindʒəm,
   krisəndʒəm   Hope
   -indʒ-, -iŋ-   Dodgson(2)367,
                  PNing 171
Cresswell/Nb,St
   krezw(ə)l, kres-   EPD,Bchm.
Cressy Hall/Li   124
   kresi   EPD
Creswell/Db
   kreswel, -wəl   BBC
   -zw-, -sw- (not so common)
Crewe/Chs   HL 1ol5
   kru: PNChs III/9,26
       and IV/73,EPD,Schr.,
       Chis.
Crewgarth/Cu
   kriugəþ   PNE'side 64
Crewkerne/So
   'kru:kə:n   EPD,BBC,BCE
   rarely _ ⁄   EPD

   krukhɑ:rn   DDo
   krukən   EPD
Crewood Common,C.Hall/Chs
   'kriwud   PNChs III/195
Cribden/La (a hill)
   kridən   GlossR&R
Crich/Db
   kraitʃ   PNDb 436,DEPN,BBC,
          BCE,Hope
Crichel Ho/Do
   kritʃ(ə)l   EPD
Cricket Malherbie/So
   'krikit 'mæləbi   DEPN,BBC
   krikət   -   BCE
Cricklade/W
   krikleid   PNW(i)66
   krikləd   PNSx(i)127
Cridmore/Wt
   kridmər, kridmɔ:r   PNWt 134
Crimble/WRY
   krimbl   DHd 56
   (see also above s.n. Clough/
    WRY)
Crimplesham/Nf
   krimplʃəm   BBC

Cringle Dyke/We
   krinl daik   PNE'side 74
Cringleford/Nf
   kriŋglfəd   BBC
Criol/K
   kri:-ɔl   PNK
Cripplegate/Ldn
   kriplgeit   EPD,Bchm.78
   -git   EPD
   kripəlgit   CPhon 53
Cripple Path/Wt
   kripl pæ:þ   PNWt 286
Croal/La (r.n.)
   kroul   BBC
Crocker End/O
   krɔkə   EPD
Crocker Lane/Wt
   krakərz [sic] lein   PNWt 184
Crockernwell/D
   krɔkənwel   BBC
Crockway Fm/Do
   krɔkwei   PNDo 233
Croft/Ca (r.n.) → Old Croft River
Croft/WRY → Double Croft
Croglin/Cu
   kə'rɔglən   PNE'side 65
Croglin Water/Cu (r.n.)
   kəroglən   RN 1o5
Croham Hurst/Sr
   'krou(ə)m 'hə:st   BBC
Cromer/Nf
   kroumə   DEPN,EPD,BBC,Schr.
Cromford/Db
   krumfəd   PNDb 358,Schr.,Hope
   krɔmfəd   BBC,Schr.
   -ʌ-   DEPN
   "The correct pron. was once [krʌm]
   but a spelling one [krɔm] now
   usually prevails."   IPN II/19
Cromhall Fm/W
   krɔməl   PNW 1oo
Crompton/La
   krʌm(p)tən   EPD,Bchm.2o5
   krɔm(p)tən   EPD
   krɔmptn   PNLa(ii)
Cromwell/Nt
   vulgo krʌməl   PNNt 185,PNNt(i)38
   krɔmwəl   PNNt(i)38 ("usually"),
              HL 1221,Kruis.
   krʌmw(ə)l, krɔm-, -wel   EPD,
                    Bchm.2o3
   krɔmwel   Kruis.
   -ʌ-   DEPN
   "The correct pron. was once [krʌm]
   but a spelling one [krɔm] now
   usually prevails."   IPN II/19
   (see also Zachr.(2)15o)

Cromwell Bottom/Nt
  krʌmil bɔðəm Hope
  krʌmil H.A.(2)46
Crondall/Ha
  krʌndl, krɔndl BBC
  krʌndəl, krɔndəl BCE
  -ʌ- DEPN
Crook/Du
  kruk DS Du
Crookdake/Cu
  kriukdeik GlossCu xvii
Crookdyke/We
  kriukidaik PNE'side 71
Crook of Devon/D
  kruk əv 'dev(ə)n BBC
Crooksby/NRY
  kriuksbi PNYN 268
Croom/ERY
  kru:m PNYE 127
Croome (Earls C.)/Wo
  krʌm PNWo 118
  kru:m EPD
Croome d'Abitot/Wo
  'kru:m 'dæbitou BBC
Cropredy/O
  krɔprədi PNO 419,BBC
  krɔpərdi PNO 419
  krɔpədi PNO(i)89
  krɔpredi BCE
Cropthorne/Wo
  kræptən GlossSEWo 82
Cropwell Bishop,C.Butler/Nt
  vulgo krɔpəl PNNt 234
Crosby/Cu,La,We,NRY
  krɔzbi PNLa(ii),EPD,BBC
  krɔsbi PNE'side,EPD
  krɔ:sbi EPD
Crosby Garrett/We
  'krɔzbi 'garət PNWe II/39
Crosby Ravensworth/We
  krɔsbi reəvnsit PNE'side 69
Cross Fell/Cu
  krɔsfel,krɔ:sfel Schr.
Crosshill/Db
  'krɔs'hil BBC
Cross Hills/WRY
  krɔslz DDd 12
Cross House/WRY
  krɔs aus DDd 13
Crossley/WRY
  krɔ(:)sli EPD
Crosthwaite/Cu (also spelt -ss-)
  krɔsþət PNCu 3o2,PNE'side 66
  krɔ(:)sþweit EPD
Crostwick/Nf
  krɔstwik BCE
  krɔstik BBC
  krɔsik BBC,DEPN,Hope,ONwick
    373

Crostwight/Nf
  kɔsit Hope
  kɔ:sit Hope,H.A.(2)45
Crotia Mill/Chs
  krouʃə PNChs III/76
Crouch
  krautʃ EPD
Crouch/Ess (r.n.)
  krautʃ DEPN
Crouch/K
  kru:tʃ BBC,BCE,PNK
Crouchmoor Fm/Hrt
  krɔtʃmə PNHrt 19
Croughton/Chs.Np
  kroutən PNChs IV/179,PNNp 51,
    BCE (for C. in Np),Hop
    (for C. in Np)
  krout(ə)n BBC
  -ou- DEPN (for C. in Np)
Crowan/Co
  krauən BBC
Crowborough/Sx
  kroubər PNSx 372
  kroubə Hope
Crowcombe/So
  kroukəm BBC,BCE
Crowden/Chs,D,Db
  kroud(ə)n BBC
  loc. krɔdn PNChs II/xxii
Crowe/Ha
  krou EPD
Crowhurst/Sr,Sx
  krouəst PNSr 315,PNSx(i)53
  krɔ:əst PNSx(i)53
  krouhə:st EPD
Crowland/Li
  kroulənd EPD,Schr.
  -ou- DEPN
Crowlas/Co
  krauləs BBC
Crowle/Li
  kroul BBC,BCE,Schr.
  kru:l BBC,BCE,DEPN,Hope
Crowle/We
  kroul BBC,BCE,Schr.
  kraul BBC,BCE
Crowley/Chs.D
  krouli EPD,Schr.
Crowndale/D
  kraundeil EPD
Croweast Ct/Wo
  krou nest PNWo 91
Crows-an-Wra/Co (or Crowsanwra)
  'krauz(ə)nrei BBC
  _ _ ╱ Jenner(2)3o4
Crowton/Chs
  krɔ:tən PNChs III/195
Croxdale/Du
  krɔksdəl BBC,BCE

Croxton/Ca,Chs
   krɔkstən   ONCa 17
   krɔkstən,
   krɔksn   PNChs II/236
Croxton/Li
   krɔkstən   BBC,BCE
   krous(ə)n   BBC
   krousən   BCE
Croxton/Nf
   krɔkstən   BBC,BCE
Croxton Kerrial/Le (or C.Keyrial)
   krous(ə)n keriəl   BBC
   krousən   -   BCE
Croxton Pk/Le
   krousn,
   kroustən,krouzən   Hope
Croxton (South C.)/Le
   krous(ə)n,
   kroust(ə)n,krouz(ə)n   BBC
   krousən,
   kroustən,krouzən   BCE
Croydon/Ca,So (a hill),Sr
   krɔidən   ONCa 188,Schr.
   krɔidn   EPD
Croyland/Li (or Crowland)
   kroulənd   BBC,BCE,GlossLi 239
Crudwell/W
   krʌdwel   BBC
Crummock Water/Cu
   krʌmək wɔ:tə   EPD,Schr.
Crundale/K
   krʌndl   PNK
Cruwys Morchard/D
   kru:z mɔ:tʃəd   PND 38o,PNND
                114,DEPN,BBC,
                BCE
Cruxton/Do
   krʌkstən   PNDo 233
Cubert/Co
   kju:bət   BBC
Cucket Nook/NRY
   kukit niuk   PNYN 136
Cuckfield/Sx
   kukfi:ld   PNSx 261,DEPN,EPD,
                BBC,BCE,BG,Hope,
                PNO(i)83
   kukful   PNSx 261, Hope (or
                kʌk- ?)
Cuckmere/Sx (r.n.)
   kukmi:ə   PNSx 4
   kukmiə   EPD,BBC,BCE
   -u-   PNO(i)83,DEPN
Cuckney/Nt
   kʌkni   BBC
Cuddesdon/O
   kʌdzdən   PNO 167,BBC,BCE
Cuddington/Chs
   kuditn   PNChs III/198
                ("older local"),
                GlossChs

Cudham/K
   kudəm   Hope,PNK
Cudlow/Sx
   loc. -lə   PNSx(i)54
Cudworth/WRY
   kudəþ   Hope
   kʌdəþ   Hope,Schr.,GlossR&R
   kʌdwəþ   Schr.
   kʌdwə(:)þ   EPD
   kʌdi   GlossR&R
Cuerden/La
   kju:ədn   PNLa 134
   kjuə-   DEPN
Cuffley/Hrt
   kʌfli   EPD
Culbone/So
   kʌlboun   BBC
   kʌlbɔ:ən   DWSo 23
Culcheth/La
   kʌltʃəþ   BBC
   kilʃəwud   PNLa(ii)
   ki:lʃa: Rose
   "The place is called Kilsha by the
   common people" (see Bardsley,s.n.
   Culshaw)
Culgaith/Cu
   kʌl'geiþ, kul'geiþ   BBC,BCE
   _ ´   DEPN (stress only)
Culham/Brk,O
   kʌləm   EPD,BBC
Cullercoats/Nb
   kʌləkouts   BBC
Culliford Tree/Do
   kʌlived   PNDo I/259
Cullompton/D (also spelt Collumpton)
   kʌlmptən   PND 56o
   'kʌləm(p)tən   BBC
   'kʌləmtən   BCE
   kə'ləm(p)tən   EPD
   kʌləpm   DWSo 17
Culm/D (r.n.)
   kʌlm   BBC
Culmington/Sa
   kʌmitn   GlossSa xxxix
Culmstock/D
   'kʌlmstɔk   BBC
Culpho/Sf
   -f-   PNSf 68f.
Culross St/Ldn
   'kʌlrɔs, _ ´   EPD
Culworth/Np
   kʌləþ   PNNp 52
Cumberland
   kʌmbələnd   EPD,BBC,Schr.,Bchm.85
   kʌmblənd   EPD,Bchm.85
   kumələn(d)   DSDu
   kumələn   GlossCu xvii,GlossFu 15,
                s.n. Copper
   kumərlənd   PNE'side 75

Cumberworth/WRY
  kʌmbəwəþ Hope
Cumdivock/Cu
  kumdivək PNCu 132
  kum'divik PNE'side 7o
  kʌm'divək BBC,BCE
  _ ╵ _ DEPN (stress only)
Cumerew/D
  kʌmeri PND 226
Cuming Museum/Ldn
  kʌmiŋ BBC
Cumnor/Brk
  kʌmnə EPD,BBC,Schr.
Cumrew/Cu
  kumri:u PNCu 77
  kum'riu: PNE'side 73
  kʌm'ru: BBC,BCE
  kum'rju: BCE
  _ ╵ DEPN (stress only)
Cumwhinton/Cu
  kʌm'(h)wintən BBC
  kʌm'hwintən BCE
  _ ╵ _ DEPN (stress only)
Cumwhitton/Cu
  kum'hwitən PNCu 78
Cundall/NRY
  kʌndl EPD
Cunliffe/La
  kʌnlif EPD
Cupernham/Ha
  kepənəm Hope
Current Cottage/Wt
  'kʌrənt katidʒ PNWt 286
Curry Rivel/So
  'kʌri 'raivl BBC
  -    raivəl BCE
Curthwaite/Cu
  kərþət PNCu 329,PNE'side
          66,GlossCu xvii
Curtisholme/Chs
  -ju:m PNChs II/237
Curwen Woods/We
  kə:win, -wən EPD
Curzon (as in C.Pk/Db)
  kə:zn EPD
Cury/Co
  kjuəri BBC
Cusgarne/Co
  kəz'gɑ:n BBC
Cuthbert/Co
  kʌþbət EPD
Cutnall Gn/Wo
  kʌtlənd [sic] PNWo 241
Cuxham/O
  kuksəm, kʌksəm BBC,BCE
  -u- DEPN

Cuxwold/Li
  kʌkswould BBC
Cwm/He
  kum BBC

Dacre/Cu (p.n. and r.n.)
   deəkər   PNCu 186,PNE'side 72
   deikə   EPD,Kruis.,
             DEPN (for the r.n.)
Dacre/WRY
   de:kə   PNYW V/139
Dadford/Bk
   dædfəd   PNBk 48
Dagenham/Ess
   dægnəm   PNEss 91,Hope
   -æ-   DEPN
Dalbury/Db (also spelt Dawbry)
   dɔ:bri   PNDb 548
   dɔ:lbəri   Hope
Dalbury Lees/Db
   'dɔ:lbəri 'li:z   BBC
Dalby
   dɔ:lbi,dælbi   EPD,Schr.,
             Kruis.,Bchm.9
Dalby/Le
   dɔ(:)lbi   BBC,BCE
Dalby/Li
   dɔ:lbi   BBC,BCE
Dalby/NRY
   dɔ:bi   PNYN 29
Dalditch/D
   deilitʃ   PND 582
Dalehead/Cu
   diəl hi:d   GlossCu xvii
Dalemain/Cu
   deəlmɛən   PNCu 186,PNE'side
             72
   loc. di'almi'an   PNO li
Dalington/Nt
   dælintn   PNNt(i) 4o
Dallam/La
   dæləm   EPD
Dalling (Field D.)/Nf
   fi:ld dɔ:liŋ   DEPN,BBC,Hope
Dallington/Sx
   dɔliŋtən   PNSx 473,DEPN,BBC,
             BCE,Hope
   dæliŋtən   PNSx(i)55,BBC,BCE
Dalscote/Np
   dɔ:lskət   PNNp 92
Dalston
   dɔ(:)lst(ə)n   EPD
   dɔ:(l)stən   Schr.
Dalston/Cu
   dɔ:stən   PNCu 13o,Hope,
             GlossCu xvii
Dalston/Mx
   dɔ:lstən   PNMx(i)21
Dalton
   dɔ:lt(ə)n,dɔlt(ə)n   EPD
   dɔ:ltən   Schr.,Chis.
Dalton/La
   dɔ:tn   PNLa 2ol,PNLa(ii)
   dɔltn   PNLa 2ol

Dalton/NRY
   dɔ:tən   PNYN 183 and 29o
   (see also s.n. North D.)
Dalwood/D
   daləd   PND 638
Damask Gn/Hrt
   dæmɔ:z   PNHrt 147
Damems/WRY
   dæməmz   BBC,BCE
Damerham/Ha
   dæmərəm   BBC
Danbury/Ess
   dænb(ə)ri   EPD
   dænbəri   Schr.
   deinbəri   Hope
Danby/NRY
   dænbi   EPD
Dandry Mire/WRY
   dandrə maiə   DDd 16
Dane/Chs (r.n.)
   dein   EPD,Schr.
Danthorpe/ERY
   da:nþrəp   PNYE 53
   danþrəp   GlossHol 17
Darby (as in D.End/Wo)
   da:bi   EPD
Darcy (as in D.Lever/La)
   da:si   EPD
Darent/K (r.n.)
   dærənt   BBC,Schr.
   dærən, da:n   PNK
Darenth/K
   dærənþ   EPD,BBC
   dærenþ   BCE
   dærən, da:n   PNK
Daresbury/Chs
   dɛ:rzbəri   PNChs IV/x
   da:rzbri   PNChs IV/x ("older
             local"),GlossChs
   da:zbəri   BBC,BCE,Hope
Darfield/WRY
   da:fi:ld   EPD
Darite/Co
   də'rait   BBC
Darlaston/St
   da:ləstən   EPD,BBC,Chis.
   darlisn   Ellis 484
Darley
   da:li   EPD
Darlington/Du
   da:liŋtən   EPD,BBC,Chis.
   da:litn   DSChs 19,EDG §273
   da:ntən   PNNbDu 6o,Schr.("loc."),
             Hope
   dæ:l(n)tn   DSDu
Darlton/Nt
   da:ltn   PNNt(i)41
Darnhall/Chs
   'da:nɔ:l, older local darn l
             PNChs III/168

Darsham/Sf
  dɑːʃəm BBC
Dartford/K,W
  dɑːtfəd EPD,Schr.
  dɑːfəd PNK
Dartmoor/D
  dɑːtmuə EPD,Schr.,Bchm.83
   -ecɔ EPD,Bchm.83
   -mɔː EPD
   -mɔːə Bchm.83
  dɑːtimɔː Schr.("loc."),Hope
Dartmouth/D
  dɑːtməþ EPD,BBC,Schr.
  dɑːtiməþ Schr.("loc."),Hope
Darton/WRY
  dɔːtn EPD
Darwell/Sx
  davəl PNSx add 153
Darwen/La (p.n. and r.n.)
  dɑːwin EPD,BBC,Schr.
  dɑːwən Schr.
  dɑːwen BCE
  dærən BBC,Schr.("loc."),
    GlossR&R (for r.n.)
  dæren BCE,DEPN (for r.n.)
Dassels/Hrt
  dɑːsəl PNHrt 19o
  dæslz BBC
Datchet/Bk
  dætʃit EPD,Schr.
Datchworth/Hrt
  dætʃər(þ) PNHrt 122
Dauntsey/W
  dɑːnsi PNW 68
  dɑːntsi PNW(i)68 [!]
   -ɑː- DEPN
Davenham/Chs
  deivnəm PNChs II/2o3
  deinəm PNChs II/ix,GlossChs,
    BBC,BCE,Hope,H.A.(2)
    45
  deiv(ə)nəm BBC
  deivən m BCE
   -ei- DEPN
Davenport/Chs
  davənpɔːrt,
  davn-, davm- PNChs II/ix
  deinpərt PNChs II/ix
    ("olim"),GlossChs
  dævnpɔːt, -vmp- EPD
  dævənpɔːt Schr.
  deimpərt DSChs 22
  dæmpɔːt H.A.(2)45
Daventry/Np
  deintri PNNp 18,DEPN,EPD
    ("old-fashioned
  local"),BBC,BCE,Schr.
  ("loc."),Hope,PNHu 35o,
  Mawer(2)91,ESpr.382
  ("loc."),MEG 39,EPN 88

  dɔːntri PNNp 18,Schr.("loc.")
    Hope
  dævəntri BCE,Horn,Mawer(2)91,
    Schr.
  dæv(ə)ntri EPD,BBC
  dævntri ESpr.382
Davidstow/Co
  'deividstou BBC
Davis Street/Brk
  deivis EPD
Davyhulme/La
  deivihuːm DEPN
Dawdon/Du
  dɔːdn EPD
Dawley/Sa,Mx; r.n. in Db
  dɔːli EPD
Dawlish/D
  dɔːliʃ EPD,Schr.
Daylesford/Wo
  deilzfəd, -lsf- EPD
Deal/K
  diːl EPD,Schr.,PNK
Dealtry Rd/Ldn
  deltri EPD
Dean/Sx ⟶ East Dean, West Dean
Dean/WRY ⟶ North Dean
Dean/Wt
  diːn,dein PNWt 286
Dean Row/Chs
  olim dein rɔː,
  now diːn rou PNChs II/vii
  dein rou GlossChs
Deans/Ess,La
  deinz PNEss 524
  diːnz EPD
Dean's Lane, - Cross/So
  deinz Hancock 194
Dearne/WRY (r.n.)
  diən PNYW VII/124
  dəːn PNYW VII/124,BBC
Debach/Sf
  debidʒ PNSf 5,DEPN,BBC,BCE,H
    Mawer(4)285,ON 56
  debitʃ BCE
Deben/Sf (r.n.)
  diːvn, diːbn RN 117
  diːb(ə)n BBC
Debenham/Sf
  debnəm EPD
  deb(ə)nəm BBC
Deddington/O
  dedintən EPD
Dedham/Ess,Gl
  dedəm PNEss 386,EPD
Dedswell Manor/Sr
  dedzəl PNSr 147
Dee/Chs;WRY (r.n.)
  dei DDd 17
  diː EPD,Schr.,Kruis.,Förster

Deepdale Head/WRY
  dipdl ied DDd 16
Deepdene/Sr
  olim dibdən,
  dipdən PNSr 275
Deerfold/He
  diəfould,dial. dɑ:vəl DHe 43
Deer Play Moor/La
  də:pli mɔə PNLa(ii)
Deighton/ERY,NRY,WRY
  di:t(ə)n BBC,DEPN (for D.in
  di:tn EPD   ERY)
  di:tən BCE,PNYN 2o9
  (see also below s.n. Kirk D.)
Delabole/Co
  'deləboul BBC,BCE
  _ _ � BBC
Delamere/Chs
  'deləmi:r,
  older local dæləmər PNChs III
  'deləmiə BBC,BCE
  �_ _ DEPN (stress only)
  daləmər,
  dalimər,dalimu:ər GlossChs
Delapre Abbey/Np
  'deləprei BBC
Delph/Ca,St,WRY
  delf BBC
Denardiston/Sf[1]
  denstən PNSf 98
Denby/Db,Gl,WRY
  denbi EPD
Denby Dale/WRY
  dembi deil Hope
Dendron/La
  dendərn PNLa 2o9
Dengie/Ess
  dendʒi PNEss 213,BBC
Denhall/Chs
  'denɔ:l, older local
  denə PNChs IV/22o
Denham/Bk,Sf
  denəm EPD,Schr.
Denholme/WRY
  denəm PNYW III/257,DEPN,Hope
  'denhɔlm BBC
Denshanger/Np
  dens-, dʌns-,dinsæŋə PNNp 1ol
Denston(e)/Sf → Denardiston
Dent/WRY
  dent DDd 17
Dent-de-Lion/K
  'dændilaiən BBC,BCE,PNK
Dent Head/WRY
  dent ied DDd 12
Denton
  dentən EPD,BBC

Denver/Nf
  denvə EPD,Schr.
Denwick/Nb
  denik DEPN,BBC,BCE
Deopham/Nf
  di:pəm BBC,BCE,Schr.,Hope
  di:fəm BBC,BCE
Deptford/D,K,W
  ditvəd PND 78
  detfə(r)d PNW(i)69
  detfəd DEPN (for D. in K and W),
              Hope (for D. in K),
              EPD,BBC,Schr.,Kruis.
  detfɔ:d Chis.
Derby/Db
  dɑ:bi PNDb(i) I/21o,s.n.Charles-
           town,DEPN,BBC,BCE,Kruis.,
           Hope,ESpr.333,BG,MEG 197,
           NED,HL 446,EPD,DSWY 47,Schr.,
  də:bi HL 475,MEG 197,Schr.,NED
  də:rbi DDo
  darbi DSWY 5o
  də:bi: CPhon 9o
  -ɑ:- , -ə:- Koeppel 38
Derbyshire
  dɑ:biʃə EPD,Schr.
  -ʃiə EPD
  dɑ:biʃə Schr.
Dereham/Bk,Nf
  diərəm DEPN (for D. in Nf),
           BCE (for D. in Nf),EPD,
           BBC
  dɛərəm Hope (for D. in Nf),Schr.
  di:rəm Schr.
Dering/K
  di:riŋ PNK
Deritend/Wa
  derit'end BBC,BCE
Derriards Fm/W
  olim derits PNW 9o
Derrill/D
  də:l PND 163
Dersingham/Nf
  də:ziŋəm BBC
Derwen/Sa
  dɛəwin BBC
Derwent/Cu,Db (r.n.)
  dɑ:rən GlossCu xvii
  darən PNDb 5
  də:wənt,-wint,dɑ:- EPD
  də:went EPD,Schr.
  -w- MEG 213
Derwenthaugh/Du (or Derwent Haugh)
  'dɛəwənthɑ:f BBC
  'də:wenthɑ:f BCE
Derwent Water/Cu
  'dɛə wəntwɔ:tə BBC
  'də:wənt, -went, -wint wɔ:tə EPD

---

1) This spelling is now obsolete; the name is spelt Denstone in PNSf
and Denston in BG.

Desborough/Np
  dezbrə   EPD
Desford/Le
  desfəd   BBC
Detchant/Nb
  detʃən   PNNbDu 62
Detling/K
  detliŋ   PNK
Devizes/W
  divaiziz   PNW 242,EPD,Schr.
  dəvaiziz   PNW(i)69,BG
  diːvaizəz   Chis.
  -vaiz-   GlossW 2o7
Devoke Water/Cu
  devək wɔːtə   BBC,BCE
  dʌvək   GlossCu xvii
Devon
  devn̩   EPD
  dev(ə)n   BBC
  devən   Schr.
  debm   DDo
Devon/Le,Nt (r.n.)
  diːvən,
  olim diːn   PNNt 3
  diːvn̩   RN 124,PNNt(i)41
  devən   Schr.
  -iː-   DEPN
Devonshire
  devnʃiə   EPD
  devnʃə   EPD,Kruis.
  devənʃə   Schr.
  debənʃiə   Hewett 163
Devonport/D
  devnpɔːt, -vmp-   EPD
  devənpɔːt   Schr.
Devoran/Co
  devərən   BBC,BCE
  devrən   BBC
Dewchurch/He
  djuːtʃəːtʃ   Förster
Dewlish/Do
  djuːliʃ, duːliʃ   PNDo(i)172,
               PNDo I/3o3
Dewsbury/WRY
  diuzbəri,
  dauzbəri   PNYW II/184
  djuːzb(ə)ri   EPD
  djuːzbəri   Schr.,Chis.
  djusbrə   Hope
Deyncourt/Bk
  diːnkɔːt,deinkɔːt   PNBk 198

Dibden Purlieu/Ha
  'dibdən 'pəːljuː   BBC,BCE
Didcot/Brk,Gl
  didkət   EPD
Didling/Sx
  didlən   PNSx 34
  didliŋ   PNSx(i)56

Didworthy/D
  didəvər   PND 291
Digby/Li
  digbi   EPD
Diggle/WRY
  digl   EPD
Diggory's Is/Co
  digəri   EPD
Diglis Lock/Wo
  digli   PNWo 162
  diglis   BBC
Dilhorne/St
  dilən, 'dilɔːn   BBC
Dillicar/WRY,We
  diləkə   DDd 15
  dilikə   PNWe I/31
Dilwyn/He
  dilin (StE and dial.)   DHe 43
Dimsdale Ho/St
  dimzdeil   EPD
Dinchope/Sa
  dintʃə p   BBC,Dodgson(2)368
Dinedor/He
  'dain'dɔː   BBC,BCE
  -ai-   DEPN
Dingle/La,Sf
  diŋgl   EPD,Schr.
Dingley/Np
  diŋli   EPD
Dinnington/Nb
  dintən   PNNbDu 63
Diptford/D
  dipfəd   PND 299,BBC
Dirt-hole/Cu
  dəːt hwɔːl   GlossCu xvii
Diseworth/Le
  'daizwəːþ   BBC
Disley/Chs
  disli   PNChs II/vii ("olim"),
               GlossChs
  now dizli   PNChs II/vii
Diss/Nf
  dis   EPD,BBC
Distington/Cu
  disiŋtən   PNCu 375
  disəntən   PNCu 375,GlossCu xvi
Ditchampton/W
  ditʃ'æmtən,olim
  ditʃiŋtən   PNW 219
  _ ˊ _   PNW(i)71,DEPN
Ditchling/Sx
  ditʃliŋ   EPD
Ditsworthy Warden/D
  ditsəri   PND 239
Dittisham/D
  ditsəm   PND 244 (for D. in
             Coleridge Hd),PND 322
             (for D. in Roborough H
             BBC,BCE,Hope

ditʃəm PND 322 (D. in C.Hd)
   ditisəm, ditiʃəm BBC,BCE
Ditton
   ditn EPD
   ditən Schr.,ONCa 17
Dixon (as in D.Gn/La)
   diksn EPD
Dobb (as in D.Pk/WRY)
   dɔb EPD
Docker/La,WRY
   dɔkə EPD
Docking/Nf
   dɔkən Hope
Dock Lane/Wt
   dak PNWt 184
Dockle Sike/WRY
   dɔkl saik DDd 15
Dockray/Cu,We
   dɔkrə PNE'side 63
Docton/D
   dɔkn DHtl 8
Doddenham/Wo
   dɔdnəm PNWo 46
Doddick/Cu
   dɔdik PNE'side 7o
Doddington
   dɔdiŋtən EPD,ONCa 25
   dɔriŋtən PNNbDu 65 (for D.in
Doddiscombsleigh/D Nb)
   daskəmzli: PND 494
   dæskəmli Mawer(2)93
Dodington/Gl,Sa,So
   dɔdiŋtən
Dodleston/Chs
   dɔdlstən PNChs IV/156
Dodman/Co
   dɔdmən BBC
Dodnor Fm/Wt
   dɑ:dnər PNWt 286
Dodpits/Wt
   dadpits PNWt 2o9
Dodwell/Wa
   dɔdw(ə)l, -wel EPD
Dodworth/WRY
   dɔdəþ Hope
Dogger [Bank]/North Sea
   dɔ:gə DSf 259
   'dɔgə 'bæŋk Kruis.
Dogsthorpe/Np
   olim dɔstrəp PNNp 226
Dolcoath/Co
   dəl'kouþ BBC
Dolcoppice/Wt
   'dɔ:kəps PNWt 149
Dolphinby/Cu (or Dolphen-)
   dɔfənbi PNCu 191,PNE'side 74
Dolphin Seat/We
   dousən fət PNE'side 67

Dolphin Sty/We
   dɔlfin stai PNE'side 74
Dolton/D
   doult(ə)n EPD,BBC
Don/WRY (r.n.)
   dɔn Förster
Doncaster/WRY
   dɔŋkəstə EPD,BBC,Schr.,Chis.
   dɔŋkistə Wyld 263
Doncombe/W
   dʌnkəm PNW 94
Donhead St.Andrew, - St.Mary/W
   vulgo dɔnət PNW 187
Donington/Le,Li,Sa
   dɔniŋtən BBC (for D. in Li,Sa),[1]
           BCE (for D. in Li)
   dʌniŋt(ə)n EPD
Donington-on-Bain/Li
   dɔniŋtən ɔn bein,
   dʌniŋtən - - BBC
Donkleywood/Nb
   duŋkli wud PNNbDu 65
   dʌŋkli - BBC,BCE
Donnington/Sa,Sx
   dɔnintən, dʌnitn GlossSa xxxvii
   dauntən PNSx 69
   dauntn DEPN (for D. in Sx)
   dɔniŋtən PNSx(i)57,EPD
Donyland/Ess
   dɔnilənd BBC
Dorchester/Do,O
   dɔ:tʃistə PNDo I/347,DDo,EPD,Schr.
   dɔ:dʒestə, dɑ:rtʃistər,
   dɑ:distər [sic!] PNDo I/347,DDo
Dore/He (r.n.),WRY
   dɔ:,dɔə EPD
Doreward's Hall/Ess
   də:wədz PNEss 414
Dorfold Hall/Chs
   dɔ:rfəld, older local
   dɑ:r- PNChs III/126
   dɑ:rfət DSChs 16
Dorking/Sr
   dɑ:rkiŋ (obsolescent) PNSr 269
   dɔ:kiŋ EPD
Dormstone/Wo (also spelt -ston)
   dɑ:msn GlossSEWo 82
Dorrington/Sa
   dɔri(n)tən Horn(Beiträge)32,
           GlossSa xxxvii
Dorset,Dorsetshire
   dɔ:sit EPD,BBC,Schr.,Kruis.,
           MEG 251
   dɑ:sət, dɑ:rsət DDo
   dɔsit ESpr.39o
   dɑ:set DHa 42
   dɔ:sitʃiə EPD
      -ʃə EPD,Schr.

1) Castle D./Le is pron.[dʌniŋtən](BBC,BCE,Hope),[dʌnitən](Hope),
   [dɔniŋtən](EPD,BCE).

Dorton/Bk
  du:ətən PNBk 123
  -uə- DEPN
Dorward's Hall/Ess
  də:wədZ PNEss 292
Doublebois/Co
  dʌblbɔiz EPD,BBC,BCE,EPN 87
Double Croft/WRY
  dubl krɔft,
  daubl - DDd 14
Doughton/Gl,Nf
  dautən PNGl I/111
  dʌftən BBC,BCE (for D.in Gl)
  -ʌf- DEPN (for D. in Gl)
Doulting/So
  doultiŋ,daultiŋ BBC,BCE
Dousland/D
  dauzlənd PND 244,BBC
Dove (r.n.)
  douv BBC
  dʌv Schr.
Dove/Db,St (r.n.)
  dʌv DEPN,EPD,BCE
  douv BCE
Dove/Sf (r.n.)
  dʌv RN 134
Dove/NRY (r.n.)
  duv RN 134
Dove Bank/La
  duv baŋk PNLa 22o
Dovedale/Db,St
  dʌvdeil EPD,BBC,Hope (for
       D. in Db),BCE (for
       D. in Db)
Dove Ford/La
  duf fɔ:d PNLa 22o
Dovenby/Cu
  dɔfnbi PNCu 284,PNE'side 74
  dʌv(ə)nbi BBC
Dovendale/Li
  dʌv(ə)ndeil BBC
Dover/K,La,Wt
  douvə EPD,BBC,Schr.,Kruis.
  dʌvər PMWt 196,GlossWt 46,
       W.H.Jones 163 (for D.
       in Wt)
Dover Beck/Nt
  douvə DEPN
Doverdeale/Wo
  dɔ:dəl PNWo 239
  dɔ:deil Mawer(2)93
  dɔ:- DEPN
Doverhay/So
  douvəri DEPN
Doveridge/Db
  dʌvəridʒ BBC,BCE
  -ʌ- DEPN
Dowber Lane/NRY
  du:bə le:n PNYN 188

Dowdeswell/Gl
  daudzwəl BBC
Dowerfield Fm/Do
  dauəfi:ld PNDo 239
Dowgate/Ldn
  daugit, -geit EPD
Dowgate Rd/Ldn
  daugət roud Schr.
Dowland/D
  daulənd PND 367,EPD,BBC
Down Close/Wt
  dæun kluəs PNWt 285
Down Ct/Wt
  dæun kɔ:rt PNWt 252
Downe/K
  daun EPD
Downend
  daun'end DWt,s.n. rig out, BBC
Downers/Wt
  dæunərz PNWt 119
Downham
  dæənəm PNLa(ii)
  daunəm ONCa 177,EPD
Downholme/NRY
  du:nəm PNYN 27o
Downs (a mountain range in S-England)
  daunz EPD,Kruis.
Downside/So,Sr
  daunsaid EPD
Downton
  dauntən EPD
Dowsby/Li
  dauzbi BBC,BCE
Dowsing/Li
  dauziŋ BBC
Dow's Place/Wt
  deu:z PNWt 15o
Dowthorpe Hall/ERY
  du:þrəp PNYE 47,Hope,GlossHol 1
  du:- PNERY
Dozmary Pool/Co
  'dɔzmri 'pu:l BBC
Dragley Beck/La (a hamlet!)
  draglə bek PNLa 212
Drakelow/Db,Nt,Wo
  dreiklou BBC
Drakelow Hall, D. Fm/Chs
  dreiklou PNChs II/198
Drake's Broughton/Wo
  dreiks brɔ:t(ə)n BBC
Draughton/Np
  drɔ:tən PNNp 112,BCE
  drɔ:t(ə)n BBC
  -ɔ:- DEPN
Draughton/WRY
  draftən PNYW VI/65
  dræftən BBC,BCE
Drax/Yorks.
  dræks EPD

Drayton
   dreitən   ONCa 17
   dreitn   EPD
Drayton Beauchamp/Bk
   bi:tʃəm   PNBk 92
Drayton Parslow/Bk
   pɑ:zlou   PNBk 66
Drellingore/K
   drelingɔ: BBC
Drewsteignton/D
   'dru:z'teintən   PND 431,BBC,
                  BCE
Drian Gallery/Ldn
   driən   BBC
Driby/Li
   draibi   BBC,BCE,DEPN
Driffield/Gl,ERY
   drifil,dðrifil   PNYE 153
   ðrifl   Hope (for D. in ERY)
   ðrifil   GlossHol 17
   drifi:ld   EPD,Chis.
Drighlington/WRY
   driglintən   PNYW III/19
   dri(g)lintən   BBC,BCE
   drig-   PNSWY 124
Dringhoe/ERY
   driŋə   PNYE 81
   ðriŋə   GlossHol 17
Droitwich/Wo
   drɔitwitʃ   EPD,Schr.,HL 969
   drɔititʃ   EPD ("rarely"),BG,
             Schr.("loc."),HL
             969
Dronfield/Db
   drɔnfi:ld   PNDb(i) I/231,EPD,
             BBC
Droylsden/La
   drɔilzdən   BBC,Chis.
Druce/Do
   dru:s   EPD
Druid Heath/St
   formerly dru:d   Duignan(1)5o
Drumburgh/Cu
   drʌmbrʌf   PNCu 124,Hav.loo
Drungewick/Sx
   -indʒ-   Dodgson(2)368 and
            (3)146
Drury Lane/Ldn
   dru:ri lein   Schr.
   druəri lein   EPD,Kruis.
Dryevers/We
   'drai'evəz   PNWe II/155
Dryholme/Cu
   draiəm   GlossCu xvii
Dubbens/Wt
   dʌbərz   PNWt 15o
Ducie Ave./Wt
   dju:si   PNWt 42

Duckerdale/We
   djukədl   PNE'side 71
Duckworth Fold/La
   dʌkwə(:)þ   EPD
   dʌkəþ   GlossR&R
Dudderwick/We
   dudərik   PNE'side 69
Duddeston/Wa
   dʌdistən   BBC
   dʌdstən   EPD
Duddington/Np,Wa
   dʌdiŋtən   EPD
Duddleswell/Sx
   dʌdlzwel   BBC
Duddlewick/Sa
   didlik   GlossSa 516
Duddon/Chs
   dud(ə)n,dʌd(ə)n   PNChs III/273
   dʌdn   EPD
Duddon/Cu;La (r.n.)
   dudən   PNCu 11
   dudn   PNLa 191
   dʌdn   EPD
Dudleston Heath/Sa
   diləsən jeþ   GlossSa 516
Dudley/La,Nb,Wo
   dʌdli   EPD,Schr.,GlossSt 27
Dudmire/We
   dudmər   PNE'side 73
Duffield/Db,ERY
   dʌfi:ld   EPD,Schr.
Dufton/We
   duftən   PNE'side 66
Dugdale/St
   dʌgdeil   EPD
Dukem Down, D.Copse/Wt
   deu:kəm   PNWt 99
Dukesfield/Nb
   duksfi:ld   PNNbDu 66
   dʌksfi:ld   BBC,BCE
Dukinfield/Chs (or Ducking-)
   dukinfi:lt   PNChs II/vii
   duknfilt   PNChs II/vii ("olim"),
             GlossChs
   dʌkənfelt   Hope
   dʌkinfi:ld   EPD,BBC,BCE
   -ʌ-   DEPN
Dullingham/Ca
   dʌliŋəm   ONCa 177,BBC
Duloe/Co
   'dju:lou   BBC
Duls Coppice/Ha
   du:kʌps   Hope
Dulverton/So
   dʌlvətən   Schr.
Dulwich/Sr
   dʌlidʒ   PNSr 19,DEPN,EPD,BBC,BCE,
            Schr.,Kruis.,MEG 213
   dʌlitʃ   BBC,EPD,Chis.,BG

Dumblar Rigg/Cu
    dumlə   PNCu 96
Dummah Crag/
    duməkræg   PNE'side 62
Dumpdon Hill/D
    dʌmdən   PND 642
Dunball/So
    'dʌnbɔ:l   BBC
Dunchideock/D
    dʌn'tʃidik   PND 495,DEPN
    'dʌntʃidək   BBC,BCE
Duncombe Pk/NRY
    dʌnkəm, dʌŋ-   EPD
Duncowfold/Cu
    duŋkəfɔ:ld   GlossCu xvii
Dundridge/Bk
    dʌnridʒ   PNBk 144
Dundry/So
    dʌndri   BBC
Dungee/Bd
    -ndʒ-   Dodgson(2)352 and
                (2)369
Dungeness/K
    dʌndʒi'nes   BBC
    dʌn(d)ʒi'nes, ◡ _ ◡   EPD
    dʌndʒ'nes   EPD,Chis.,Kruis.
    ◡ _   EPD
    dʌndʒənes   PNK
Dungeon Fm/Ess
    'dɔn'dʒɔnz   PNEss 436
Dungewood/Wt
    dʌndʒud, dʌndʒiwud   PNWt 219,
                      Dodgson(2)369
Dunham Massey, Dunhamtown/Chs
    dʌn-,dunəm   PNChs II/19
Dunham on the Hill/Chs
    dʌnəm   PNChs III/253
Dunhampton/Wo
    dʌnən   PNWo 270
Dunheved/Co
    dʌn-   Jenner(2)302
Dunholme/Li
    dʌnəm   EPD,BBC
Dunkeswell/D
    dʌŋkizwel   BBC
Dunkeswick/ERY
    duŋ'kezik   PNYW V/50
Dunmaile Raise/Cu and We
    dʌn'meil   EPD
Dunmallard Hill/Cu
    dunmɑ:lən   PNCu 187
    loc. dunmalək   PNO li
Dunmallet/Cu
    dun'mɔ:lən   PNE'side 65
Dunmore/Brk
    dʌn'mɔ: EPD,BBC
    ◡ _   Schr.

Dunmow/Ess
    dʌnmə   PNEss 474,EssDD 158
    dʌnmou   EPD,BBC,BCE
Dunnington/ERY
    dunitən   PNYE 77
Dunningworth/Sf
    dʌnərþ   Hope
Dunnose/Wt
    dʌnouz   PNWt 46
Dunsbury/Wt
    dʌnzbəri   PNWt 74
Dunsham/Bk
    dʌnsəm   PNBk 145
Dunsmore/Bk,Wa
    dʌnzmɔ: Schr.
Dunstable/Bd
    dʌnstəbl   EPD,Schr.
Dunstan/Nb
    dustən   PNNbDu 67
    dʌnstən   EPD
Dunstanburgh/Nb
    dʌnstənbərə   BBC,BCE
Duntisbourne Abbots/Gl
    dunzbɔrn   PNGl I/71
Duntisbourne Rouse/Gl
    'dʌntisbɔ:n 'raus   BBC
Duntish/Do
    dʌntʃ   Mayo
Dunwear/So
    dʌn'wɛə, dʌn'wiə   BBC,BCE
    _ ◡   DEPN (stress only)
Dunwich/Sf
    dʌnidʒ   DSf 261,Schr.,Kruis.,BG
    dʌnitʃ   DEPN,BBC,BCE,Schr.,Chis.
Dunwood/Ha,St
    dʌnwud   BBC
Dupath/Co
    dju:-   Jenner(2)302
Durham
    dʌrəm   BBC,Schr.,Kruis.,Chis.,
                MEG 377
    dʌr(ə)m   EPD
    dɔ:rəm, dɔ:m   Hope,Schr.("loc.")
Durkar/WRY
    də:kə   BBC
Durlston Bay/Do
    dɑ:rlstən   PNDo I/57
Durnford/W
    də:nfəd   EPD
Durrants/Wt
    durəns   PNWt 79
Dursley/Gl
    də:zli   BBC
Durton Fm/Wt
    də:tn   PNWt 10
Durtshot/Wt
    də:rtʃat   PNWt 67

Durweston/Do
   dʌrestən   PNDo(i)52,BCE
   dʌristən   BBC
Duryard/D
   deriəd   PND 436
Dutton/Chs,La
   dʌtn   EPD
Duxford/Ca
   dʌksə   PNCa 92
   dʌksfɔ:d   ONCa 185
Duxmore/Wt
   dʌksmər,dʌksmɔ:r   PNWt 241
Dyche Lane in Norton/WRY
   deitʃ lein   GlossSh 68
Dyer'S Fm/Wt
   daiərz   PNWt 169
Dyke/D,Li
   daik   EPD
Dyke Hall/WRY
   daik ɔ: DDd 16
Dymock/Gl
   dimək   PNGl III/168,DEPN,
             BBC,BCE
Dyrham/Gl
   diərəm   PNGl III/49
   dirəm   BBC

E

Eades Fm/Wt
  i:dz, i:diz   PNWt 21o
Ea Drain(Old E. D.)/Nt
  i: PNNt 32
Eagle/Li
  eikl G⎯ ɛⅼ ("now used only
        by old people")
Eakley Lanes/Bk
  i:əkli   PNBk 13
Eakring/Nt
  ekriŋ, eikriŋ   BBC,BCE
  i:-, olim ei-   DEPN
Ealing/Mx
  i:liŋ   EPD,Schr.,Kruis.
Ealingham/Nb
  -indʒ-   Dodgson(2)369,
         PNing 17o
Eamont/Cu,We (r.n.)
  iamən, jamənt, emənt   RN 139
  i:mənt   RN 139,PNCu 12,
         PNWe I/5,BBC,BCE
  jæmen   PNCu 12
  ɛəmən   PNE'side 72
  jæmənt   PNWe I/5,BBC,BCE
  i:-, jæ-   DEPN
Eamont Bridge/Cu and We
  jæmənt brig   PNWe II/2o5
  ɛəmən brig   PNE'side 65
Eanly Wood Fm/Chs
  i:nli, i:ənli   PNChs II/173
Earby/WRY
  iəbi   BBC,BCE
Eardington/Sa
  jə:tn   GlossSa 517
Eardishope/He
  jɑ:səp   GlossHe 38,s.n.Yarsop
Eardisland/He
  ə:dzlənd   DHe 43,BBC,BCE
  ə:dislənd   BCE
  dial. jə:zlənd   DHe 43,GlossHe
         38,s.n. Yersland
Eardisley/He
  ə:dzli   DHe 43,BBC,BCE
  dial. jə:zli   DHe 43,GlossHe
         38, s.n. Yersley
Eardiston/Wo
  jə:distən   PNWo 58
Eardley End/St
  ə:dli   EPD,Schr.
Eardswick/Chs
  'ɛ:rdzwik, olim
  jarzik   PNChs II/247[1]
  jɑ:sik   Hope
  jɑ:rzik   GlossChs[2]

Earith/Hu
  iəriþ   BBC
Earle/Nb
  jerl   PNNbDu 69
  dʒə:l   DEPN
  ə:l   EPD
Earley/Brk
  ə:li   BBC
Earls Cole/Ess
  ɑ:lz kɔ:ən   PNEss 381
  ə:lz koun   BBC,BCE
Earl's Court/Ldn
  ə:lz kɔ:t   EPD
Earlshaw Ho/Nt
  olim ɑ:lʃə: PNNt 184
Early Grove/Bd
  ɑ:li   PNBdHu 63
Earnley/Sx
  ə:nli   Schr.
Earnshaw/Chs
  ernʃɔ:, olim jernʃɔ: PNChs II/vi
Earnshaw/La
  jenʃi   GlossR&R 1oo
Earsdon/Nb
  jɔ:zən   PNNbDu 69
  ə:zdən   BBC,BCE
  iəzdən   EPD
Earsham/Nf
  ɑ:ʃən   Hope
  ə:ʃəm   BBC,BCE
Earswick/NRY
  i:əzwik   PNYN 12
  iə-   DEPN
Easby/NRY
  i:əzbi   DSto
Easdale/We (f.n.)
  eisdeil   Simpson 284
Easebourne/Sx
  ezbɔ:n   PNSx 16
  i:zbɔ:n, -bɔən   EPD
  ez-   DEPN
Eashing/Sr
  i:ʃiŋ   BBC
Easinghope Fm/Wo
  i:zənhoup   PNWo 47
Easington
  i:ziŋtən   BBC
  eizəntn   DSDu
  izintən   PNYE 17
  ezəntən   GlossHol 17 (for E. in
              WRY)
  eziŋtən,ezntən   Hope (for E. in
                  Yorks.)
Easingwold/WRY[3]
  i:əzinud   PNYN 24
  i:ziŋwould   EPD

1) The second form of pron. was archaic by 1886 (PNChs II/247).
2) "This pron. is not now heard much in conversation" (GlossChs).
3) Hope's transcription is Eseingwood (= [i:ziŋwud]?).

Easole/K
  i:soul,jeisəl PNK
Eastbourne/Du,Sx
  i:st'bɔ:n PNSx 426,Mawer(4) 285
  'i:stbɔ:n BBC,Schr.,Bchm.131
  i:s(t)bɔ:n EPD,Kruis.
  i:s(t)boən EPD
  i:stbən Schr.
  i:sbɔ:n Bchm.131
  i:sbən Bchm.7o,Schr.
Eastbury/Brk
  aisbəri Hope
Eastcheap/Ldn
  i:stʃi:p Schr.,Kruis.
  i:s(t)tʃi:p EPD
Eastcote/Np,Mx,Wa
  jeskət PNNp 93
  i:stkout BBC
Eastcotts/Bd
  i:stkəts PNBdHu 9o
Eastcourt/W
  eskət PNW 57
Eastdean/Sx
  i:stdein PNSx 417
East Dean/Sx
  i:zdi:n PNSx 47
Easter(Good E.,High E.)/Ess
  estə PNEss 478,DEPN
East Garston/Brk
  ɑ:gisən Hope
Eastham/Chs,Wo
  i:stəm PNChs IV/187,BBC
  i:st(h)əm EPD
Easthampstead/Brk
  'i:st'hæm(p)stid,
  'i:stəmsted BBC
Easthampton/He
  (')i:st'hæm(p)tən EPD
East Hill/Sr
  heist hil PNSr(i)15
Easthorpe/Ess,Nt,Yorks.
  i:stəp PNEss 388
  vulgo i:strəp PNNt 176
  i:sþrəp PNYE 232
  jiəstrəp PNYN 46
Easthwaite/Cu
  insþət PNCuWe 46
Eastleigh/D,Ha
  'i:st'li: EPD,BBC
  ◡ _ EPD
Easton
  i:stən EPD
Easton/Hu
  i:sən PNBdHu 238
Easton/Nf
  i:sən Hope

Easton/W
  i:zn DPew 99
Easton/Wt
  i:sn PNWt 127
Easton Maud(u)it/Np
  'i:stən 'mɔ:dit BBC
Easton Neston/Np
  i:sən nesən PNNp 98
Eastry/K
  i:stri PNK,BBC
Eastwick/Hrt
  i:stik PNHrt 191
Eastwood
  i:stwud EPD
  jestəd Crosl.51 (for E. in WRY)
Eatington/Wa
  etiŋtən PNWa 253
Eaton
  i:tən Schr.
  i:tn EPD
Eaton/Chs
  i:tən,eitn PNChs II/2o4 (for E. in Northwich Hd)
  i:tən,eitən PNChs III/289 (for E. in Eddisbury Hd)
  i:tən PNChs IV/148 (for E. in Broxton Hd)
Eaton (Castle E.,Water E.)/W
  olim jetən PNW 23 and 45
Eaton Socon/Bd
  'i:t(ə)n 'soukən BBC
Eau/Ca (r.n.) ⟶ South Eau
Eau/Li (r.n.)
  i: GlossM&C,P&RNLi 111
Eaudyke/Li
  oudaik BBC,BCE
Ebbor/So
  ebə Turner(2)155
Ebbs-Fleet/K (or Ebbsfleet)
  ebzfli:t EPD,Schr.
Ebernoe Ho/Sx
  ebənou BBC
Ebnal/Chs
  ebnəl PNCns IV/4o
Ebrington/Gl
  jæbətən PNGl I/242
  jʌbətn GlossSEWo 82
  jʌbətən B ("strictly local and used largely by older residents"),EPN 86
  ebriŋtən BBC,EPD
Ebsworthy/D
  ebsəri ROS 42
Ebury Hill/Sa
  i:bəri EPS
Ecchinswell/Ha (formerly in Brk)
  'etʃinzwel BBC,Hope

Eccles/K,La,Nf
   eklz   PNLa 38,EPD
   ekəls   PNK
Ecclesall/WRY
   eklzɔ:l   BBC
Ecclesfield/WRY
   eklzfi:ld   EPD
Eccleshall/St
   eklʃəl,eklʃɔ:l   BBC,BCE
Eccleston/Chs
   eklstən   PNChs IV/151
   eklstən   EPD
   eklistən   Ellis 457
Eccleston/La
   eklstən   EPD
Eccombsworthy/D
   ekəri   DHtl 8
Eckworthy/D → Eccombsworthy
Edale/Db
   i:deil   BBC
Edburton/Sx
   æbətən   PNSx 2o6
Edderside/Cu
   edərsid   PNCu 296
Eddington/Brk,K
   ediŋtən   EPD
Eddisbury/Chs
   edizbəri,
   edʒbəri   PNChs III/213
   edzbəri   PNChs III/213 ("older
           local"),GlossChs
Eddistone/D
   etsən   PND 72,DHtl 8
Eddlesborough/Bk
   loc. edʒbərə   Zachr.(3)129,
               Mawer(4)285
Eddlethorpe/ERY
   edlþrəp   PNYE 144
Eddystone/D (a lighthouse)
   edistən   Schr.,Kruis.
   edist(ə)n   EPD
Eden/Cu,We (r.n.); K,Sx
   i:dn   RN 142,DEPN (for E.
          in Cu,We),EPD,Kruis.
Edenbridge/K
   i:d(ə)nbridʒ   BBC
   idn-   EPD
Edenfield/La
   i:dnfi:ld   PNLa 64,EPD,
             Bchm.27
   i:d(ə)nfi:ld   BBC
   loc. ednfi:ld   Bchm.27
   i:-   DEPN
Edenhall/Cu
   i:dnəl   PNCu 19o ("olim"),
            GlossCu xvii,Hope
   i:dənhɔ:l   Schr.

Edensor/Db
   ensə   PNDb 9o,BBC,BCE,Hope,
          Bardsley,s.n. Ensor,
          PNDb(i) I/235
   enzə   BBC,BCE
   en-   DEPN
Edgbaston/Wa
   'edʒbəstən   PNWa 45,EPD,BBC,BCE
   edʒ'bɑ:stən   PNWa 45
Edgcumbe/Co,D
   edʒkəm   EPD,Kruis.
   -ku:m   EPD
Edgebolton/Sa
   edʒ'boult(ə)n   BBC
Edgehill/Wa (a hill)
   'edʒil   Schr.
   'edʒ'hil   Schr.,EPD,Kruis.
Edgeley Lodge/Chs
   edʒli   PNChs III/3o9
Edgerley/Chs
   edʒərli   PNChs IV/81
Edgerton/WRY → Egerton
Edgeware/Mx
   edʒwɛə   EPD,Schr.,Chis.
   edʒwə   Schr.
   -w-   MEG 213
Edgeware Rd/Ldn
   edʒwɛə roud, edʒwə roud   EPD
   edʒwə raud   CPP 66 (for the und
            ground station)
Edgeworth/Gl
   edʒwə:þ   EPD,Kruis.
Edial/St (also spelt Edjiall)
   'ediəl   BBC
   edʒəl   PNSt 55
Edingley/Nt
   ediŋli   PNNt 16o,PNNt(i)45
Edington/Nb,So,W
   i:diŋtən   BBC
   ediŋtən   EPD,PNW 14o
Edith Weston/Ru
   ediwestən   GlossLi 239
   ediwesən   GlossRu vii
Edlesborough/Bk
   edʒbərə   PNBk 92
Edleston/Chs
   edlstən   PNChs III/14o
Edlingham/Nb
   edlindʒəm   BBC,BCE,DEPN,PNNbDu
          PNing 17o,Dodgson(2)
Edmondsham/Do
   edmənʃəm,enʃəm   PNDo(i) 1ol
Edmonton/Co,Mx
   edməntən   EPD,Schr.,Kruis.,Chis.
Edmundsbury/Sf
   edməndzberi   Schr.
   (see also s.n. Bury St.Edmunds)

Edwalton/Nt
  edəltən   PNNt 246
  ed'wɔːltn, edltn   PNNt(i)46
  ed'wɔːlt(ə)n   BBC
  ed'wɔːltən   BCE
Edwinstowe/Nt
  vulgo edənstou   PNNt 75
  edwinstou   EPD
Eea/La (aslo spelt Ay)
  eː   PNLa 19o
Effingham/Sr
  efiŋəm   EPD
Egerton
  edʒətən   BBC,Schr.,PNChs IV/33,
               PNK,BCE(for E. in K),
               PNSWY 131 (for E. in
               WRY)
  edʒərtən,edʒərtn   PNChs IV/33
  edʒətn   EPD,Kruis.
  -dʒ-   DEPN (for E. in K)
  (the name is now spelt
   Edgerton in WRY)
Eggesford/D
  egzvəd   PND 369
  egzfəd   BCE,BBC
  egizfəd   BCE,BBC
Eggington/Bd
  egiŋtən   BBC
Egginton/Db
  egintən   BBC
Egglescliffe/Du
  iːglzklif,eksklif   Hope
Eggringe/K
  -ndʒ   H.A.(1)179
Eggworthy Ho/D
  ekəri   PND 244
Egham/Sr
  egəm   EPD,Schr.
Egley/Brk
  egli   PNBrk 74
Eglingham/Nb
  eglindʒəm   PNNbDu 72,DEPN,EPD,
               BBC,BCE,Hope,PNing
               17o,Dodgson(2)37o
Egliston/Do
  eglstən   PNDo I/1o2,PNDo(i)137
Egloshayle/Co
  egləs'heil   BBC
  eglɔs'heil   BCE
  _ _ ⟋   DEPN (stress only)
Egloskerry/Co
  egləs'keri   BBC
Egmanton/Nt
  'egməntən   BBC,BCE
  egməntn   PNNt(i)46
Egmere/Nf
  egmiə   BBC

Egremont/Chs
  egrimənt   BBC,BCE,EPD
  egrəmənt   EPD
Egremont/Cu
  occ. egaːməþ,egaːmət   PNCu 379
  egəməþ   GlossCu xvii
  egrimənt   BBC,BCE
  egrəmɔnt,egrimɔnt   EPD
  egri-   DEPN
Egton/La,NRY
  ektn   PNLa 213,DEPN (for E. in La)
  egtən   EPD
Ehen/Cu (r.n.)
  eːn   RN 143
  iːən   BBC,BCE
  ein   DEPN
  end   GlossCu xvii
Eighton Banks/Du
  eit(ə)n bæŋks, ait(ə)n b.   BBC
  eitən, aitən b.   BCE
Eisey/W
  aizi   PNW 45,PNW(i)78,DEPN
Elburton/D
  elbət(ə)n   BBC
Eldon/Du,Ha
  eld(ə)n   EPD
Eleigh/Sf → Monks E.
Elfordleigh/D
  elvəli   PND 253
Elham/K
  iːləm   EPD,BBC,BCE,PNK
Eling/Ha
  iːliŋ   BBC
Elkesley/Nt
  elzli   PNNt 78
  loc. el(k)sli,
  oth. elkəsli   PNNt(i) 47
  elksli   BBC
Elkington/Li,Np
  elkiŋtən   EPD
Ella (West E., Kirk E.)/ERY
  elə   EPD
Elland/WRY
  elənd   EPD,PNYW III/43
  jelənd   PNYW III/43,DHd 154,Hope,
             Smith(1)295,Crosl.51
  elən   EPD
Ellin/Cu (r.n.)
  elin   EPD
Ellenborough/Cu
  elinb(ə)rə   EPD
Ellerker/ERY
  eləkə   PNYE 222
Ellers/WRY
  eləz   DDd 15
Ellesborough/Bk
  elzbərə   BBC

Ellesmere/Sa
   elzmiə   EPD,BCE
   elzmi:r   Chis.
   elzmə   GlossSa xxvi
Ellesmere Port/Chs
   elzmi:r, older local
   elzmər   PNChs IV/xv
   elzmiə pɔ:t   BBC
   elzmər pɔ:rt   GlossChs
Ellinge/K
   elindʒ   PNK
Ellingham/Nb
   elindʒəm   EPD,DEPN,BBC,BCE,
           Dodgson(2)371,
           PNing 17o,PNNbDu 73
Ellishaw/Nb
   (e)liʃə   PNNbDu 73
Ellough/Sf
   elou   BBC,BCE
Elloughton/ERY
   elətən   PNYE 22o
Ellwood/Gl
   elwud   EPD
Elm/Ca
   eləm   PNCa 266
   elm   EPD
Elmdon/Ess
   eləmdən   PNEss 525
Elm Fm/Wt
   elm   PNWt 79
Elmham/Nf,Sf
   elməm   BBC
Elmhurst/So,St
   elmhə:st   EPD
Elmley/Wo
   embli   GlossSEWo 82
Elmore/Gl
   elmɔ:, -mɔə   EPD
Elmsall/WRY
   emsl   BBC
Elmscott/D
   emskət   PND 73
   emskit   DHtl 8
Elmsley Lodge/Nt
   emzli   PNNt 94
Elmswell/ERY
   emzil, emzəl   PNYE 154
Elmsworth Fm/Wt
   el(ə)mzər,elmzwərþ   PNWt 79
Elmwood/K
   elmwud   EPD
Elsecar/WRY
   elsi'ka: BBC,BCE
Elsenham/Ess
   elznəm   PNEss 527
   -z-   DEPN
Elsham/Li
   elʃəm   BBC
Elsing/Nf
   elziŋ   DEPN,BBC,BCE

Elslack/WRY
   el'slæk   BBC
Elsted/Sx (also spelt -stead)
   elsted   PNSx(i)64
Elston/Nt
   olim els(ə)n   PNNt 212
Elstow/Bd
   elstə   PNBdHu 7o
   elstou   EPD,BBC
Elstree/Hrt
   elstri:, elz-, -tri   EPD
Elstronwick/ERY
   elstþrənwig   PNYE 53
   elsþrənwig   GlossHol 17
Elswick/La,Nb
   elsik   PNNbDu 74,EPD ("loc.", fɔ
        E. in Nb),DEPN (for E. iɪ
        Nb),BBC,BCE (for E. in Nⁱ
        Kruis.
   elzik   PNNbDu 74,EPD ("loc.", fɪ
        E. in Nb),Kruis.
Elsworth/Ca
   elzwə:þ   ONCa 185
   -ə:-, rarely -ə-   Bchm. 67
Eltham/K
   eltəm   EPD,Schr.,Kruis.,HL 122o,
        MEG 377,BBC,BCE,Chis.,PNⱤ
   elþəm   EPD,Schr.,Kruis.,HL 122o,
        MEG 377
Eltisley/Ca
   elzli, eltzli   PNO li
   eltizli   BBC
   eltisli   ONCa 183
Elton
   elt(ə)n   EPD
   eltən   Schr.
Eltringham/Nb
   eltrindʒəm   DEPN,BBC,BCE,PNNbDu
        PNing 17o,Dodgson(2)
        371
Elveden/Sf
   elvdən, eldən   EPD,BBC,BCE
Elwick/Du
   elwik   BBC,BCE
Elwick/Nb
   elik   PNNbDu 75,BBC,BCE
Ely/Ca
   i:li   DEPN,EPD
   i:lai   Schr.,Miller 317 ("stran-
        gers sometimes say Elý")
Elyhaugh/Nb
   'i:liha:f   BBC,BCE
Emberton/Bk
   emətən   PNBk 35
Emblehope/Nb
   emləp   PNNbDu 75
Embleton/Cu
   eməltən   PNCu 383
Embley/Nb
   emli   PNNbDu 76

Embsay/WRY
   emsə   PNYW VI/67
Emley/WRY
   emli   EPD
Emmethaugh/Nb
   eimithɑːf   PNNbDu 76
Emmethill/Wt
   emətil   PNWt 286
Emsworth/Ha
   emswə(ː)þ   EPD
Enderby/Le,Li
   endə(ː)bi   EPD
Enfield/La,Mx
   enfiːld   EPD,Schr.,Kruis.
   enfild   Schr.
   enful, enfl   Ellis 235 (for
             E. in Mx)
Engeham/K
   endʒəm   PNK
   -dʒ-   PNing 171

England
   iŋglənd   Schr.,ESpr.274, MEG
            65,Chis.,Kruis.,RSp
            134,Lloyd 89
   iŋlənd   Schr.("dial."),MEG
            217,DLi 25,DLo 27
            and 78,DPe 192,DSDu
   iŋ(g)lənd   EPD,HL 135 and 1137
   iŋ(g)lən(d)   DSf 262
   iŋglən   HL 1113 ("dial.")
   iŋlən   DSto,DSDu
   iŋlnd   DHtl 35
   iŋlind   DBo,DSto
   iŋglænd   Schr.,Koeppel 36[1]
   iŋglɔnd   DOld 99

   eŋglənd   HL 1225
   eŋ(g)lənd   EPD ("rarely")
   eŋlən   DPew 39 and 8o
   eŋglænd   Koeppel 36

   hiŋlən   GlossM&C,s.n.What
   h-   CPhon 163
   (but: iŋ-   Höfer 96)

   "[ŋg] is normal in present StE,
   though [ŋ] is not at all un-
   common"   (Dobson 972)

Englefield/Brk
   eŋglfiːld   EPD
Enham/Ha → Knights Enham
Ensinge/K
   enzindʒ   PNK
   -indʒ   Dodgson(2)335

Entwistle/La
   entisl   PNLa(ii)
   tinsəl   Hope
Epperstone/Nt
   epəs(ə)n   PNNt 162
Epping/Ess
   epiŋ   EPD,Schr.
Epping Forest/Ess
   hepiŋ fɔrist   Höfer 3ol
Epsom/Sr
   epsəm   EPD,Schr.,BBC
Epworth/Li
   epwiþ   Hope
   epwəːþ   EPD
   epəþ   GlossM&C,s.n.Eputh
Ercall (High E.,Child's E.)/Sa
   ɑːkl   BBC
   ɑːkəl   BCE,GlossSa 517,Duignan(2)
   ɑː-   DEPN   pt l,p.8
Erchfont/W → Urchfont
Erdington/Wa
   olim jɑːrntən   PNWa 3o
   əːdiŋtən   EPD
Eresby/Li
   iəzbi   BBC,BCE
   iə-   DEPN
Erewash/Db,Nt (r.n.)
   eriwɔʃ   PNDb 7,PNNt 4,DEPN,BBC,
                BCE
Eridge Castle/Sx
   eridʒ   BBC
Eriswell/Sf
   eriswəl   BBC
Erith/K
   iəriþ   EPD,BBC,BCE
   iːriþ   PNK
   iː-   DEPN
Erle Hall/D
   əːl   EPD
Erlestoke/W
   əːlstouk   BBC
Ermine Street/Li
   coll. called Ramper or Owd Street
   = [oud striːt] (GlossM&C,q.nn.)
Erpingham/Nf
   əːpiŋəm   Schr.
   ɑːpiŋəm   Hope
   ɑː-   DEPN
   -inəm, -iŋəm   PNing 172
Eryholme/NRY
   erium   PNYN 28o
Escheat/Bd
   estʃiːt   PNBdHu 78

[1] "Aufgefallen ist mir bei meinem Zusammensein mit jungen Engländern, dass die [...] als pedantisch verpönte spelling pron. [eŋglænd] für [iŋglænd] in der That um sich zu greifen scheint." (Koeppel 36)

Escomb(e)/Du
  eskəm EPD
Escrick/ERY
  eskri:t ROS 42
  eskrit Hope,Goodall 51
Esh/Du
  eʃ BBC
Esher/Sr
  i:ʃə PNSr 92,EPD,DEPN,EPD,
        BBC,BCE,Chis.
  eʃə PNSr 92 ("olim"),Kruis.
Esholt/WRY
  eʃɔlt PNYW IV/144,BBC
Eshott/Nb
  eʃət PNNbDu 77,DEPN
Esk/ERY
  eʃ PNERY
Esk/NRY (r.n.)
  esk EPD,Schr.
Eskdale/Cu
  æʃdeil Hope
  occ. eʃdəl PNCu 388,GlossCu
        xvii
Esk Hause/Cu (a hollow)
  'esk 'hɔ:z BBC
Eskmeals/Cu
  eskmi:lz BBC
Essendine/Ru
  'es(ə)ndain BBC
Essex
  esiks EPD,BBC,Schr.,Kruis.
        MEG 251
  eseks MEG 251
  esəks Lloyd 83
Estcourt Ho/Gl
  estkɔ:t EPD
Estcourt Hill/W
  loc. often neskət PNNt xl
Esthwaite/La
  estwət PNLa 218
Esthwaite Water/La (a lake)
  esþweit wɔ:tə BBC
Etal/Nb
  i:təl PNNbDu 78,BBC,BCE
  i:- DEPN
Etchells/Chs
  ettʃəz PNChs II/vii ("olim"),
        GlossChs
  etʃəlz PNChs II/vii
Etchilhampton/W
  æʃəltən olim
  æʃliŋtən PNW 313
Etchingham/Sx
  etʃiŋ'hæm PNSx 455,BBC,BCE,
        Hope
  etʃiŋəm BCE
Etherington Hill/K
  eð(ə)riŋtən EPD

Eton/Bk
  i:tən DEPN,Schr.
  i:tn EPD,Kruis.,MEG 266
Etruria/St
  tru:riə, tru:ri Hope
  ətru:riə Chis.
Etton/ERY
  etn PNYE 19o
Etwall/Db
  etwɔ:l BBC
Euston/Ldn
  ju:stən BBC,Schr.
  ju:st(ə)n EPD
Euxton/La
  ekstən DEPN,BBC,BCE,PNLa 133
  ɔ:lstən, i:lstn PNE&W
  akstən, ekstn PNLa(ii)
Evedon/Li
  i:vdən BBC,BCE
Evegate/K
  i:vgeit PNK
Evenley/Np
  imli, emli, evənli PNNp 52
  i:mli Hope
  i:v(ə)nli BBC
Evenlode/Gl,Wo
  emloud,i:vənloud PNGl I/219
  emloud PNWo 123
Everden/K
  evədən PNK
Everley/NRY
  jiələ, evələ PNYN 115
Eversden/Ca
  evəzdən ONCa 188
Eversholt/Bd
  evəsɔ:l PNBdHu 123
  evaʃolt BBC
Eversley/Ha,We
  evəzli EPD,Kruis.
Everton
  evətən Schr.
Evesbatch/He (or -bach)
  ezbridʒ Hope
  esbætʃ PNHe 71
Evesham/Wo
  i:vʃəm EPD,Schr.,Kruis.,HL 81c
        MEG 377
  i:viʃəm EPD ("loc."),PNWo 262
  i:vʃem PNWo 262
  i:vzəm Schr.,Chis.,MEG 377
  i:vzhəm Chis.

  eisəm PNWo 262,GlossSEWo 82
  i:səm PNWo 262,Schr.,Hope,MEG
  i:zəm PNWo 262 ("olim")
  i:ʃəm PNWo 262,Schr.("dial."),
        Hope,Kruis.("loc.")
  i:sn Schr.("dial."),Hope
Evington/Gl,K,Le
  i:viŋtən BBC,PNK,BCE(for E.in

Ewart/Nb
   ju:ət   BBC,BCE
Ewbank/We
   ju:bæŋk   EPD
Ewegales/WRY
   jau-, jou ge:lz   DDd 14
Ewekene's Fm/Sr
   ju:kənz, ju:tənz   PNSr 265
Ewell/K,Sr
   ju:əl   PNSr 74,BBC,BCE (for E.
      in Sr)
   jouil   PNK
   ju(:)əl   EPD
Ewell Minnis/K
   minis   DK
Ewelme/O
   ju:əlm   BBC
   ju'elm   BCE
Ewen/Gl,W
   ju:ən   PNW 60
   ju(:)in   EPD
Ewen Close/We
   juənkloəs   PNE'side 72
Ewesley Burn/Nb
   u:zli   PNNbDu 79
Ewhurst/Sr
   ju:əst   PNSr 237
Ewias Harold/He → Ewyas H.
Ewstick/Co → Ustick
Ewood/La
   i:wud   PNLa 91,DEPN
Ewood Bridge/La
   i:wud bridʒ   BBC
Ewyas Harold/He   PNHe 72
   ju:is   PNHe 72
   ju:əs hærəld   DHe 43 (dial.
      and StE)
Exceat/Sx
   ek'set   PNSx 419
   'eksi:t   BBC,BCE
Exe/D,So (r.n.)
   eks   EPD,BBC,Schr.,Chis.
Exe/D → Up Exe
Exelby/NRY
   eʃəlbi   PNYN 226
Exeter/D
   eksitə   EPD,BBC,Schr.,Kruis.
   eksətə   EPD,Chis.
   ekstə   Schr.
   eksənz   Tanger
Exford/So
   'eksfɔ:d   BBC
Exmansworthy/D
   ekənzəri   PND 73
   ekənzri   DHtl
Exmoor/So
   eksmuə,-mɔə   EPD,Bchm.83
   -mɔ:ə   Bchm.83
   -mɔ: EPD
   -mu:ə   Schr.

Exmouth/D
   eksmauþ   EPD,BBC,Schr.,Bchm.77,
      HL 1177
   -məþ   EPD,Schr.,Bchm.77,HL 1177,
      MEG 128
   ("Both prons are heard loc."[EPD])
Exning/Ca
   eksniŋ   ONCa 196
Exton
   ekstən   EPD
Extwistle/La
   ekswisl muə   PNLa(ii)
Exwick/D
   ekswik   BBC
Eyam/Db
   i:m   PNDb 92,DEPN,BBC,BCE,Hope
   i:əm   EPD
   i:im   Ellis 442
Eydon/Np
   i:dən   PNNp 35,BCE
   i:d(ə)n   BBC
   i:-   DEPN
Eye/Le (r.n.),He,Np,Sf
   ai   RN 157,DEPN (for E. in Le,Sf),
      BBC (for E. in He,Np,Sf),Chis.
      BCE (for E. in Sf)
   ei   DEPN (for E. in Sf),BCE (for
      E. in Sf),Hope (for E. in Sf),
      Chis.
Eyford/Gl
   eifəd   PNGl I/198
Eyhorne/K
   eiən   PNK
Eyke/Sf
   aik   PNDVall 59,BBC,BCE
Eynesbury/Hu
   einzbəri   BBC
   i:nzbəri   ONCa 194
Eynsford/K
   einsfəd   EPD,BBC,BCE,PNK
Eynsham/O
   enʃəm   PNO 258,DEPN,BBC,BCE
   einʃəm   EPD,BBC,BCE
   ensəm   EPD ("loc."),H.A.(2)46
      ("formerly"),GlossO 114
      ("more modern")
   ainsəm   GlossO 114 ("heard at
      Barnard Gate near E.")
Eype/Do
   i:p   PNDo 293,DEPN,BBC,BCE
Eythorne/K
   'eiþɔ:n   BBC,PNK
Eythorpe/Bk
   i:þrəp   PNBk 139,DEPN
Eyton/He,Sa
   aitn   EPD (for E. in Sa)
   eitn   EPD (for E. in He)
   eit(ə)n   BBC
Eyton-on-the-Weald-Moors/Sa
   'ait(ə)n ɔn ðə 'wi:ld 'muəz   BBC

F

Faceby/NRY
  fɛəsbi   PNYN 176
Facit/La
  feisit   DEPN,BBC,BCE
  fe:sit   PNLa 6o
  fe:sit   PNLa(ii)
Faddiley/Chs
  fadili,fadəli,
  fadli   PNChs III/142
  fædili   EPD
Failsworth/La
  feilzwə:þ   EPD
Fairbroad Coppice/W
  vərbərt   PNW 17o
Fairburn/WRY
  fɛəbə:n   EPD
Fairfield
  fɛəfi:ld   EPD
Fairfields/Wt
  vɛərvildz   PNWt 286
Fairford/Gl
  fɛəfəd   EPD
Fairhaven/La
  'fɛəheiv(ə)n   EPD
Fairholme/ERY
  'fɛəhoum   EPD
Fairlee/Wt
  vɛərli   PNWt 241
Fairlight/Sx
  fɛəlait   EPD
  fɑ: lai   F.B.S.[1]
Fairlight/Sx (in Guestling Hd)
  fe:rlai   PNSx 5o7
Fairlight Fm/Sx (in East Grinstead)
  fɑ:r'lai   PNSx 332
  -lait   PNSx(i) 65
Fairnley/Nb
  fɑ:nli   PNNbDu 79
Fairwarp/Sx
  fɛəwɔ:p   BBC
Fairweather/WRY (a mountain)
  'fɛəweðə   EPD,Schr.
Fairy Pool/Cu
  fiul piul   PNE'side 71
Fakenham/Nf,Sf
  feiknəm   EPD
  feikənəm   BBC,BCE (for F.in
                 Nf),DEPN (for F. in
                 Nf)
Fal/Co (r.n.)
  fæl   EPD,DEPN
Falcutt/Np
  fɔ:kət   PNNp 47,DEPN
Faldingworth/Li
  fɔ:ldinwə:þ   BBC,BCE

Falfield/Gl
  fælfi:ld   BBC
Falhouse/WRY
  faləs   PNYW/II 212
Falkenham/Sf
  fɔ:knəm   PNDVall 29
Falkland/So
  fɔ:klənd   BBC,Kruis.
  fɔ:(1)k-   Schr.
Fallapit/D
  fæləpit   BBC
Fallen Cross/Cu
  fɔ:ən krɔs   GlossCu xvii
Falloden/Nb (or -don)
  fæloud(ə)n   EPD
  fælədən   BBC,BCE
  fæləd(ə)n   EPD
Fallowfield/La,Nb
  fæloufi:ld, fælə-   EPD
Falmer/Sx
  fɑ:mə   PNSx 3o8,DEPN,Hope
  fælmə   BCE
Falmouth/Co
  fælməþ   EPD,BBC,BCE,Schr.,Krui
             Chis.,Bchm.1o and 115
Falsgrave/NRY
  fɔ:zgrif   PNYN 1o7
  1oc.-grouv   GlossClv,s.n.Griff
Falstone/Nb
  fælstoun   BBC
Falstone Pond/W
  vɔlstən   PNW 345
Falthwaite/WRY
  loc. fɔ:lfit   PNSWY 135
Fambridge/Ess
  fɑ:mbridʒ   PNEss 214,Hope,Schr
                ("loc.")
  fæm-   Schr.
Fangfoss/ERY
  fæŋkis   Hope
Fanum Ho/Ldn
  feinəm   BBC
Farcet/Hu
  fæsət   PNBdHu 185
  fɑ:sit   BBC
Fareham/Ha
  fɛərhəm   Chis.
  fɛərəm   EPD
Farford/D
  værid   PND 73
  færəd   DHtl
Faringdon/Brk
  færiŋdən   Schr.
Farleigh,Farley
  fɑ:li   EPD,PNK
Farmington/Gl,O
  fɑ:miŋtən   EPD

1) "So pronounced by pilots in charge of ships between London River
and the Wight" (F.B.S.).

Farn/Chs
  farn Ellis 457
Farnborough
  fɑ:nb(ə)rə EPD
Farndon/Chs
  fɑ:rndən PNChs IV/73
  fɑ:rn GlossChs
Farne Is/Nb
  fɛ:rən,fə:n PNNbDu 8o
  fɑ:n Schr.,Chis.,Kruis.
Farnham
  fɑ:nəm EPD,Schr.
Farnley/WRY
  fɛənli Hope
Farnworth/La
  fɑ:nəþ PNLa(ii),DSLa,Hope,
           Parkinson
  fɑ:nwə:þ EPD
Farringdon/D,Ha,Ldn
  færiŋdən EPD,Schr.,Bau.
             (for F. in Ldn)
Farringdon Street/Ldn(underground
                        station)
  ferindən stri:t CPP 66
Farringford/Do,So,Wt
  færiŋfɔ:d Schr.
  -fəd EPD
  færənfərd PNWt 127
Farrington/Do
  færiŋdən PNDo 11
  -tən EPD,Schr.
Farrington Gurney/So (or Gournay)
  færiŋtən gə:ni EPD,BBC,BCE,
Farsley/Ess,WRY   Schr.
  fɔ:sli PNEss 297
  fɑ:zli EPD
Farthinghoe/Np
  fɑ:nigou PNNp 53,DEPN
Farthingstone/Np
  farəkstən PNNp 22
Fastbridge Fm/Sr
  vɑ:stbridʒ PNSr 222
Faugh/Cu
  fæf BBC,BCE
  fɑ:f PNCuWe 49,BBC,BCE
Faulkbourn/Ess (or -bourne)
  fɔ:bən PNEss 287
  fɔ:bo:n BCE
  fɔ:bə:n BBC,BCE
  fɔ:bɔ:n BBC
  fɔ:- DEPN
  foubən Hope
Faulstone/W
  fɔ:lstn PNW(i) 81
Faunstone/D
  vænstoun PNCu III/lxix
Faversham/K
  fævəʃəm EPD,BBC,BCE,Schr.,
            Chis.,Kruis.
  -æ- DEPN
  (see also s.n. Feversham)

Fawepark/Cu
  fɔ:- PNCu xli
Fawey/Co (r.n. and p.n.) → Fowey
Fawkham/K
  feikəm Hope,PNK
  fɔ:kəm PNK
Fawley
  fɔ:li EPD
Faygate/Sx (also spelt Fay Gate)
  feigeit EPD
Fazakerley/La
  fə'zækəli DEPN,EPD,BBC,BCE
Fazeley/St
  feizli BBC
Fea Faw/WRY
  fei fɔ: DDd 16
Fearby/NRY
  fiəbi PNYN 232
Fearnal Heath/Wo → Fernhill
Fearnall/Chs
  fə:rnəl PNChs III/318
Feasandford/La
  fezəntfuəd PNLa(ii)
Featherstone/Nb,St,WRY
  feðəstən EPD,Schr.
Feckenham/Wo
  feknəm PNWo 317,EPD
Feetham/NRY
  fi:təm PNYN 271
Feizor/WRY
  fe:zə, fi:zə PNYW VI/226
Felixstowe/Sf
  fi:likstou EPD,Kruis.,PNDVall 42
  -i:- DEPN
Felling/Du
  feliŋ EPD
Fell Side/Cu
  fel said PNE'side 69
Felmersham/Bd
  fensəm PNBdHu 31,Hope
  fenʃəm Hope
  felmaʃəm BBC
Felpham/Sx
  felpəm EPD,BBC
  felphəm, felfəm BBC
  felfm PNSx(i)66
Felstaed/Ess
  felstid, -sted EPD
Feltham/Mx,So
  feltəm PNMx 14,EPD,BBC,Schr.,
           Kruis.
  felþəm Potter 35
Felton
  feltən Schr.
  felt(ə)n EPD
Feltwell/Nf
  feltwel BBC
Fenay Bridge/WRY
  fini brig DHd 33
  feni bridʒ BBC

Fenchurch Street/Ldn
  fentʃətʃ striːt Schr.,EPD
  fentʃəːtʃ CPhon 21
Fenham/Nb
  fenəm EPD
Feniscowles/La
  'feniskoulz BBC,BCE
  feniskoːlz PNLa 74
Fenton
  fentən EPD,Schr.
Fenwick/Nb,WRY
  fenik EPD,BBC,Schr.,Kruis.
Feock/Co
  fiːək BBC
Ferney Bottom/Wt (f.n.)
  vɛəni bɔtəm DWt,s.n.bottom
Fernfield/Wt
  vəːrnvil PNWt 165
Fernhill Fm/Wt
  vəːrnil PNWt 174
Fernhill Heath/Wo
  fəːnəl PNWo 111,Hope
Fernhurst/Sx
  faːnəst PNSx 19
Fernyhalgh/La
  fəːnihʌf, -hælʃ BBC,BCE
Ferryhill/Du
  færijil DSDu
Fersfield/Nf
  faːsfiːld Hope
Feversham/K (an old spelling for
        Faversham)
  fevəʃəm EPD,Schr.,Kruis.
  fiːvəʃəm Schr.,Kruis.
  fevəzəm Kruis.
  "often fevəʃəm instead of
  fevəzəm" MEG 377
Fewston/WRY
  fiustən, foustən PNYW V/122
  faustən PNWRY 72
Fideoak/So
  fidiouk olim fidik Turner(1)
              116
Fifehead Magdalen/Do
  faif(h)ed mægdələn PNDo 4
Fifield/Brk,O,W
  faifiːld EPD
  faifi(ː)ld PNW(i) 81
Figheldean/W
  fai(ə)ldiːn olim
  fikəldiːn PNW 365
  faiəldi(ː)n PNW(i) 82
  faildiːn DEPN,BBC,BCE
Filey/ERY
  faːlə,failə PNYE 110
  faili DEPN,EPD,BBC,BCE
Fille Brook/Ess (r.n.)
  filibruk PNEss 7

Filleigh/D
  fili BBC
Filley/Co → Philley
Fillongley/Wa
  'filɔŋli PNWa 82,BBC,BCE
Fimber/ERY
  fimə PNYE 128,Hope
Finborough Parva/Sf (also called
              Little F.)
  finbərə paːvə BBC
Finchale/Du
  fiŋkəl PNNbDu 85,BCE
  fiŋkl EPD,BBC
  -k- DEPN
Finchingfield/Ess
  fintʃinfl PNEss 425
  'finʃiŋfiːld BBC
Finchley/Mx
  finʃli Schr.
  fin(t)ʃli EPD
Findern/Db
  findən BBC
Findon/Sx
  findən PNSx(i) 67,Schr.
Finedon/Np
  findən PNNp 181,DEPN
  faindən BBC,BCE
Finemere Wood/Bk
  fainmuːə PNBk 110
Fingest/Bk
  findʒəst,vindʒəst PNBk 176
  findʒist EPD,BBC
  -ndʒ- DEPN
Finghall/NRY
  fiŋgəl PNYN 247
Finglesham/K
  fiŋgləsəm PNK
Fingringhoe/Ess
  'fiŋriŋhou PNEss 315,BBC
Finney Hill, F. Ho/Chs
  fini PNChs III/240,EPD
The Finney/Chs
  fini PNChs III/240
Finningley/Nt
  finlə Hope
Finsbury/Ldn
  finzbəri Schr.
  finzb(ə)ri EPD
Finsbury Pk/Mx
  finzbəri paːk BBC
Firbank/We
  fəːbæŋk EPD
Firby/NRY
  fɔrbi PNYN 237
Firle/Sx (West F., F. Pk)
  fʌrəl PNSx 359,PNSx(i)68,DEPN,
            DSx,s.n.Crownation
  fəːl BBC,BCE

Firsby/Li,WRY
　fə:zbi　EPD
Fishbourne/Wt
　viʃbərn　PNWt 43
Fisherton Anger/W
　eindʒə　PNW 22
Fishwick/La
　fiʃwik　EPD
Fitzwilliam/WRY
　fits'wiljəm　EPD
Five Acres/Wt (f.n.)
　v-　DWt,s.n. gap
Flagdaw/We
　flegdə　PNE'side 62
Flagg/Db
　flæg　EPD
Flamborough/ERY
　flɛ:mbrə　PNYE 1o5
　flæmbərə　Schr.
　　-b(ə)rə　EPD
Flamstead/Hrt
　flæmstid,-sted　EPD
Flasco/We　(or Flascoe)
　flæskə　PNE'side 63
Flash/Db
　flas　Ellis 438
Flaska/Cu
　flaskə　PNCu 222
　flæskə　PNE'side 63
Flaskew/We
　flæskə　PNE'side 63
Flatbrooks/Wt
　flætbruks　DWt,s.n.pollard
Flawborough/Nt
　flɔ:brə　PNNt 214
Flawith/NRY
　flawiþ　PNYN 21
　flɔ:-iþ,flɔiþ　BBC,BCE
Flawns Cottages/Ess
　flɑ:nz　PNEss 492
Flax Burton/So
　flæks bə:t(ə)n　BBC
Flaxby/WRY
　flazbi,
　flaksbi　PNYW V/15
Flaxmoss/La
　flæsməs　GlossR&R
Fleam Dyke/Ca
　flem ditʃ　PNO 1i
Flecknoe/Wa
　fleknou　EPD
Fledborough/Nt
　fledbrə　PNNt 185
Fleecethorpe Fm/Nt
　vulgo fli:strəp　PNNt 82
The Fleet/Ldn (i.e. F. prison)
　fli:t　Bau.
Fleet/Nt (r.n.)
　fli:t　Schr.

Fleetlands/Wt
　fri:tlənz [sic!]　PNWt 285
Fleet Marston/Bk
　flit mɑ:sən　PNBk 136
Fleetprison/Ldn
　fli:tprizn　Schr. (see also s.n.
　　　　　　　　　The Fleet)
Fleetwood/La
　fli:twud　EPD,Schr.,Bchm.58
Fleggburgh/Nf
　flegbərə　BBC
Flendish/Ca (a hd)
　flendiʃ　ONCa 195
Fleswick Bay/Cu
　flezik　PNCu 429
Fletchamstead/Wa
　'fletʃəmsted　BBC
Fletching/Sx
　fletʃiŋ　PNSx(i)69
Flete Ho/D
　fli:t　EPD
Flitholme/We
　flitəm　PNE'side 65
Flitwick/Bd (also spelt Flitt-)
　flitik　PNBdHu 72,BBC,Hope,ONwick
　　　　　387
Flixton/La,Sf,ERY
　fli:sn　Hope (for F. in ERY)
　flikstən　EPD
Flockton/WRY
　flɔktən　EPD
Flodden/Nb
　flodən　Schr.
　flodn　EPD
Flook Ho/So
　fluk　EPD
Floore/Np (also spelt Flore)
　flu:ə　PNNp 82
　flɔ:　BBC
Flore/Np → Floore
Floshgate/Cu (also spelt Flosh Gate)
　flɔʃgɛ:t　PNE'side 76
Flotmanby/ERY
　flɔtnbi　Hope
Flusco/Cu
　flæskə　PNE'side 63
Flushing/Co
　flʌʃiŋ　EPD,Kruis.
Fluskew/Cu
　flæskə　PNE'side 63
　fluskə　PNCu 187,PNE'side 63
Foghanger/D
　fɔgnər　PND 215
Fold/La
　faut　PNLa(i)55 ("generally pron.
　　　　　　locally")
Foleshill/Wa
　fɔis-hil　Hope

Foley Lodge/Brk, F. Pk/Wo
  fouli   EPD
Folke/Do
  fouk   PNDo 214,BBC
Folkestone/K (or Folkstone)
  foukstən   EPD,BBC,Schr.,
              Kruis.,HL 1177
  foukstoun   Chis.
  fouksən   DK
Folking/Sx
  fɔ:kin,foukin   PNSx(i)66
Folkingham/Li
  fɔkiŋəm   DEPN,BBC,Hope
Folkington/Sx
  fouiŋtən   PNSx 411,Hope[1],
              DEPN,BBC,BCE
Folkstone/K → Folkestone
Folksworth/Hu
  olim fɔkswə:þ   PNBdHu 18o [2]
Follaton/D
  vɔlətən   Mawer(4)285
Folkton/ERY
  fautn   PNYE 115
  foutən   Hope (?)[1]
Font/Nb (r.n.)
  fɔnt   RN 16o,DEPN
Fonthill/Sx
  fɔnthil   EPD
Fonthill Bishop's,F.Giffard/W
  fʌnt(h)il   PNW 19o
  fɔnt-   DEPN
  fɔnthil   EPD
Font le Roi/Do
  fɔnt lə rɔi   PNDo 215
Fontmell Magna/Do
  fɔntməl   PNDo(i)22,[3] DEPN
Foolow/Db
  fu:lə   PNDb 1ol,Thomp.7o
  fu:lou   PNDb(i) I/242
Foots Cray/K
  'futs 'krei   EPD
Forbes Ho/Sr
  fɔ:bz, fɔ:bis   EPD
Forcewell/D
  fɔ:səl, fɔsəl   PND 73
  fousl   DHtl 8
Ford
  fɔ:d   EPD,Schr.
Ford Fm, F. Mill/Wt
  və:rd   PNWt 286
Fordcombe/K
  fɔ:dkəm   EPD
Forder/Co,D
  fɔ:də   EPD,ESpr.349

Fordham/Ca,Ess,Nf
  fɔ:dəm   EPD,ONCa 177
Fordingbridge/Ha
  fɔ:diŋbridʒ   EPD
Fordon/ERY
  fɔdn   PNYE 1o8
Fordwich/K
  fɔ:dwitʃ, fɔ:ditʃ   BBC,PNK
  fɔ:d(w)itʃ   BCE
  -ditʃ   DEPN
Fore Down/Wt
  vɔ:r dæun   PNWt 22o
Foreland/Wt
  vɔ:rlən(d)   PNWt 285
Forestall/K (Broken F. nr Buckley,
                Clare's F. nr Throwle
  fɔ:(r)stəl   DK
Forest Fm/Wt
  farist farm   PNWt 112
Forest Hill/O
  fɔ:stɔ:l, fɔ:stil   PNO 171
  fɔstl   PNO(i)1o9
Forhill/Wo
  fɔrəl   PNWo 333
Formosa/Brk (an island in the Tham
  fɔ:'mousə, -z-   EPD
Forncett St.Mary, F.St.Peter/Nf
  fɔ:nsit snt mɛəri, - - pi:tə
Fornside/Cu
  fɔrnsit   PNCu 312,PNE'side 75
Forrabury/Co
  fɔrəbəri   BBC
Forstal/K
  fɔstl   PNK
The Forstal/Sx
  fɔsəl   PNSx 378
Fosbury/W
  fɔzb(ə)ri   EPD
Foscott/O → Foxcott
Fosdyke/Li
  fɔzdaik, fɔs-   BBC,BCE
Foss/NRY (r.n.)
  fɔs   EPD
Fossdale/NRY
  fɔsdil   PNYN 259
Fothergill/Cu
  fɔðəgil   EPD
Fotheringhay/Np
  'fɔðəriŋgəi   PNNp 2o2,BBC,Kruis.
  'fɔðəriŋgei   Chis.
  'fɔðəriŋhei   BBC ("[This] is the
                     village pron. today
  The other is more usual for historic ~ Castle")

1) Hope's transcriptions are Fowington/Fowton resp.;they could repres
  either [au] or [ou].
2) [fɔx-] in PNBdHu is an apparent misprint for [fɔks-].
3) "This seems to be the only pron. heard nowadays,but old people hav
  told me that pronunciations such as [fʌntməl,fʌməl] were not uncom
  in their childhood." (PNDo(i)22,note 1)

Foulbridge/NRY
    foubrig   PNYN 98
Foulden/Nf
    fuːldən   BBC
    fouldən   EPD
    foudən   Hope
Foulk Stapleford/Chs
    fouk steipəlfəd   PNChs IV/1o5
Foulmire/Ca → Fowlmere
Foulness/Ess,ERY
    'faul'nes   EPD,BBC,Schr.
    ‿ _ , _ ‿   EPD
    loc. fuːni   RNY 23
Foulney/La
    foːlni   PNLa 2o4
    -ou-   DEPN
Foulridge/La
    foulridʒ   DEPN,BBC,BCE
    foːlridʒ   PNLa 88
    fourig   PNLa(ii)
Foulsham/Nf
    foulʃəm,fulʃəm   BBC
    foulsəm   DEPN,BBC,BCE,Hope
    foulʃ(ə)m   EPD
Foul Sike/WRY
    faul saik   DDd 15
Foulsyke/Cu
    fulsik   PNCu 296f.
Four Gates/La (also spelt F.Yates)
    jeits   PNLa(i)6o
Fovant/W
    fɔvənt   PNW 214,PNW(i)85,DEPN,
        BBC,BCE
Fowey/Co (r.n. and p.n.)
    fɔi   RN 164,DEPN (for r.n.);
        BBC,BCE,EPD,BG,Chis.
        (for p.n.)
Fowlmere/Ca
    faulmiːə   ONCa 194
Fownhope/He
    faunhoup   BBC
Fowrass/Cu
    fɔrəs   PNCu 24o
    fourəs   PNE'side 73
Foxboro' Hall/Sf
    fɔksb(ə)rə   EPD
Foxcott/O (or Foscott)
    fɔkskət,fɔskət   PNO(i)1o9
Foxearth/Ess
    fɔksəþ   PNEss 429
Foxfield/La
    fɔksfiːld   EPD
Foxhole/Co,Sx
    fɔkshoul   BBC
Foxley Henning/Cu (also spelt Fox
        le Henning)
    fɔksneilin   Hope
Foxton/Ca (or Foxeton)
    fɔkstən   Hope,ONCa 18

Foyle Fm/Sr
    fail   PNSr 333
Fraisthorpe/ERY
    frɛːzþrəp   PNYE 87
Framfield/Sx
    fræmfiːld [sic!]   PNSx 392
Framingham Earl, F. Pigot/Nf
    fræmiŋəm   BBC
    freimiŋəm   EPD
Framlingham/Sf
    fræmliŋəm   EPD
    fræmliŋhəm   Chis.
    fræmiŋəm   Hope
    frænigəm   DSf 266
Framlington/Nb
    framptən   PNNbDu 89
Frampton/Gl
    framptən   PNGl II/32
    fræm(p)tən   EPD
Frankby/Chs
    fræŋkbi   PNChs IV/287
Fransham/Nf
    frænsəm,frɑːnsəm   Hope
Frant/Sx
    fænt [sic!]   PNSx 373
    frænt   BBC,BCE
Frating/Ess
    freitiŋ   PNEss 338,BBC,DEPN
Fratton/Ha
    frætn   EPD
Frankland Hall/NRY
    fræŋklənd   EPD
Freemantle/Ha
    friː'mæntl   Kruis.
Freetown/La
    friːtaun   EPD
Fremington/D,NRY
    fremiŋtən   BBC
Frenchay/Gl
    frenʃei   BBC
French Hay/K
    -nʃ-   Dodgson(2)372
Frenchhurst/K
    -nʃ-   Dodgson(2)373
French Mill/Wt
    frentʃ mil   PNWt 15o
Frensham/Sr
    frʌnsəm   PNSr 177
    -s-   DEPN
Fresden Fm/W
    olim fristən   PNW 26
Fresdon/W
    frezdn   PNW(i)86
Freshwater/Wt
    'freʃwɔːdər   PNWt 122
    'freʃwɔːtə   EPD,Schr.,DWt,s.n.Leer
Fressingfield/Sf
    fresnfil,fresnfə   DSf 266
Fretherne/Gl
    freðən   PNGl II/178

Fridaythorpe/ERY
  fraidəþrəp,
  frɑ:dəþɔrp   PNYE 129
Friern Barnet/Mx
  fraiən bɑ:nit   BBC
  -    bɑ:nət   EPD,BCE
Friesden/Bk → Frithsden
Frieth/Bk
  friþ   BBC
Friezley/K
  fri:zli   PNK
Frimley/Sr
  frimli   EPD
Frindsbury/K
  frindzbəri   BBC
  frinsbəri   PNK
Fringford/O
  -ŋ-   Dodgson(2)374
Friskney/Li
  friskni   BBC
Friston/Sx
  frisən   PNSx 42o
  fristən   PNSx(i)71
Frithelstock/D
  fristɔk   PND 92,DHtl 8,BBC,
        BCE,PNND 37
  friþlstɔk   BBC
  friþəlstɔk   BCE
Frithsden/Bk (or Friesden)
  fri:zdən,frizdən   EPD,BBC
  friþsdən   EPD
Frittenden/K
  fritənden   PNK
Fritton/Nf,Sf
  fritn   EPD
Fritwell/O
  fritl   PNO 211
  fritəl   Hope [1]
Frizinghall/WRY
  fraiziŋɔ:l,
  fruzinlə   PNYW III/245
  'fraiziŋhɔ:l   EPD,BBC,BCE
Frizington/Cu
  friziŋtən   EPD,BBC,BCE
  fraiziŋtən   BBC,BCE
Frocester/Gl
  froustə   PNGl II/197
  frostə   DEPN,BBC,BCE,Hope
  frɔ:stə   Moberley 125
Frodingham/Li,ERY
  frɔdiŋəm   BBC,BCE
Frodsham/Chs
  fradsəm   PNChs III/221
        ("older local"),
        GlossChs

fratsəm   PNChs III/221 ("older
        local"),GlossChs
frodsəm   PNChs III/221
        ("older local"),Gloss(
frodʃəm   PNChs III/221,BBC,Chis
frodzəm   H.A.(2)46
frɔtsəm   H.A.(2)46,PNO(i)lo3
frædsəm   Hope (perhaps identica
        with [fradsəm] above)
Froghill/Wt
  vrɔgil   PNWt 286
Frogland/Wt
  frɔ:glən   PNWt loo
Frogmore
  frɔgmɔ: EPD,Schr.
  -mɔə   EPD
Froom/He (Bishop's F.,Canon F.)
  biʃəps fru:m   BBC,BCE,GlossHe
  biʃfroum   Hope

  kænən fru:m   BBC,BCE
  kænfru:m   Hope

  fru:m, dial. frum   DHe 43
Frome/So
  fru:m   EPD,BBC,BCE,Schr.,Kruis.
        PNE&W
Frome/Do;So,W (r.n.)
  fru:m   RN 166,DEPN,BBC,Schr.,Ho
Frome Vauchurch/Do
  fru:m voutʃə:tʃ   BBC,BCE
  -    vɔ:tʃə:tʃ   BCE
Frostenden/Sf
  frɔs(ə)ndən   BBC
  frɔsəndən   BCE
Frosthills/Wt
  vrɔstilz   PNWt 286
Froswick/We
  frɔzik   PNWe I/166
  frɔsik   BBC,BCE
Fryston/WRY (Ferry F.,Monk F.,New F
  fraistən   BBC
Fryton/NRY
  fritən   PNYN 5o
Fryup/NRY
  frai-up   PNYN 132
Fugglestone/W
  olim faulstən, now fʌgəl-   PNW
  faulstn   PNW(i)87,DEPN
Fuidge/D
  fju:dʒ   PND 447
Fulbourn/Ca
  fulbɔ:n   BBC
  fulbən   ONCa 191
Fulford
  fulfəd   EPD

1) Hope's transcriptions Frittel(l) are rendered [fritl] in
   PNO(i).
2) "The first and second pronunciations are still retained by a few o
   people;but the younger generation employ the last." (GlossChs)

Fulford/Wt (nr S.Arreton)
  vulvərd   PNWt 11
Fulford/Wt (nr Chale)
  fulfərd   PNWt 119
Fulham/Mx
  fuləm   PNMx 101,EPD,BBC,Schr.,
           Kruis.,MEG 334
Fulking/Sx
  fulkiŋ   BBC
Fullabrook/D
  -ə-   ESpr. 349
Fullerton Junction/Ha
  fulətn   EPD
Fullholding/Wt
  'vulhoudn   PNWt 285f.
Fullhurst Hall/Chs
  'fulə:st   PNChs III/122
Fulmer/Bk
  fulmə   EPD
Fulmodestone/Nf
  'fulmistən   BBC
Fulstow/Li
  fulstou   BBC
Fulwell
  fulwel   BBC
Fulwood
  fulwud   EPD
Fundenhall/Nf
  'fʌndənhɔ:l   BBC
Funtington/Sx
  fʌndən   PNSx 60,Hope
  fʌniŋtən   PNSx 60
Furnace/Sx
  fə:nis   BBC
Furness/La
  fə:nis   EPD,BBC,Schr.
  fə:nəs   PNLa 200
  fə:nes   EPD,Schr.
  fɔ:nəs   GlossFu 36,s.n.
          Forness
Furneux Pelham/Hrt
  fə:niks peləm   PNHrt 184,EPD,
                 BBC,BCE
  fə:nou   -   BBC,BCE
  fə:nu: -   EPD
Furzehill Fm/W
  vulgo fʌzl   PNNt xl (add.&
              corr.)
Fursey Butt/Wt
  vʌzi bʌt   PNWt 236
Furzyhurst/Wt
  'vʌzihʌst   PNWt 187
Fusedale/We
  fiuzdəl   PNWe II/216
  fiu:zdl   PNE'side 73
Fyfield/W
  faifi(:)ld   PNW(i)88
  faifi:ld   EPD,BBC

Fylde/La
  faild   DEPN,BBC,BCE,Ellis 358
Fylingdales/NRY
  failiŋdeilz   BBC

G

Gaddesby/Le
  gædzbi   BBC,BCE
Gaddesden/Hrt
  gædzdən   PNHrt 34,BBC,BCE
Gade/Hrt (r.n.)
  geid   EPD
Gadshill/K
  'gædʒhil   EPD,Schr.
  ˊ ˋ   Kruis.

  gædzil   Schr.
Gaggerhill/Wt
  gægəril   PNWt 68
Gagingwell/Do
  -edʒ-   DEPN
Gaines/He,Hu
  geinz   EPD
Gainsborough/Li
  geinzbərə   EPD,BBC,Schr.,
              Chis.,Kruis.
    -brə   EPD,Schr.
  geinzbə (or -s- ?) Hope
  -bərə   GlossM&C 3
G$_a$isgill/We
  geizgil   BBC
Gaitsgill/Cu
  gɛ:tskil   PNE'side 68
Galby/Le
  gɔ:lbi   BBC,BCE
Gale Garth/WRY
  ge:l gɑ:þ   DDd 15
Galfholme(s)/Li
  ðə gofəmz (a f.n. in North-
          pool)
  gɔ:fhoum (a f.n. in Scotton)
          P&RNLi 132
Galford/D
  gælvərd   PND 187
Galgate/La
  gɔ:lgeit   BBC
Galley Hill/O
  gjæli il   GlossO(suppl)84
Gallowsclough Fm, G.Hill/Chs
  -klʌf   PNChs III/218
Gallows Clough/Chs
  loc. gælʌskluf   PNChs II/xxii
Galmpton/D
  gæmptən   PND 3o4 (for G. in
          Stanborough Hd)
  gamtən   PND 511 (for G. in
          Haytor Hd)
  gæm(p)tən   BBC
  gæmtən   BCE
Galphay/WRY
  gɔ:fə   PNYW V/199
Galsham/D
  gɔ:lsəm   PND 73,EPD
  gɔlsəm   EPD

Galsworthy/D
  gælzəri   PND 88
  gɔ:lzwə:ði   PND 89,EPD,Kruis.
  gælz-   EPD
  gɑ:lz-,gɔlzwə:ði   Kruis.
Galton/Do
  gɔ:ltən   PNDo(i) 143,PNDo I/13⁕
  gɔ:lt(ə)n, gɔl-   EPD
Galtres/NRY
  gɔ:triz   PNYN 8
Galtres Forest/NRY
  gɔ:ltəz fɔrist   Schr.
Gamblesby/Cu
  gaməlzbi   PNCu 192
  gæməzbi   GlossCu xvii,PNE'side
  gæməlzbi   Hope
Gamlingay/Ca
  gæmliŋei   BBC
  gæmliŋgi   ONCa 18o
Ganstead/ERY
  gansti:əd   PNYE 48
Ganthorpe/NRY
  gonþrəp   PNYN 34
Ganton/ERY
  gantn   PNYE 118
Gap/WRY
  gap   DDd 14
Garboldisham/Nf
  gɑ:blʃəm   BBC,BCE
  gɑ:blsəm   BCE
  gɑ:blsm   DEPN
  gɑ:bli:səm   Hope
Garbridge/Cu
  gɑ:brid   Gordon 123 ("so pron.
Garbutt Hill/Nb   loc.'
  gɑ:bət   EPD
Garendon/Le
  gærəndən   BBC,BCE
  gæritən   Hope
  -æ-   DEPN
Gargrave/WRY
  gɑ:griv   PNYW VI/53
Garlinge Gn/K
  gɑ:lindʒ   BBC,H.A.(i)179,PNK
Garnett Bridge/We
  gɑ:nit   EPD
Garnons/He
  gɑ:nənz, dial. gɑ:nəlz   DHe 43
Garratt/Ldn
  gærət   EPD
Garrett/Ess
  gærət, -it   EPD
Garrick/Li
  gærik   EPD,Kruis.
Garriston/NRY
  gɑ:rəstən   PNYN 269
Garrowby/ERY
  garəbi   PNYE 13o

Garsdale/WRY
  gazdl   DKe 5
Garsden/W (or -don)
  gɑ:sdən   Anon.(2)
Garstang/La
  gjɑ:stin   PNLa(ii)
  gɑ:stəŋ   Chis.
Garston
  gɑ:stən   EPD,Anon.(1)(for G.
            in W)
  ðə gɑ:sən   Anon.(1) and (ii)
            (for G. in W)
  (see also s.n. East G.)
Garstons/Wt
  gæskinz   PNWt 137
Garth/WRY → Little G.
Garthorpe/Li
  gɑ:þrəp   GlossM&C,s.n.
            Dollups
Garveston(e)/Nf
  gɑ:vistən   BBC
Gascow/La
  gaskə   PNLa 212
Gasketh/Cu
  gasket   PNCu 4o2
Gastack Beck/WRY
  gastə bek   DDd 15
Gaston Fm/W
  gæsən   PNW 121
Gatacre/Sa
  gætəkə   EPD
Gatcliff/Wt
  gæklif   PNWt 151
Gatcombe/Wt
  gækəm   PNWt 132
  gætkəm   DWt,s.n. War'nt
Gateacre/La
  gætəkə   BBC,BCE
  -æ-   DEPN
Gate Helmsley/NRY
  ge:t emzlə   PNYN lo
Gatenby/NRY
  geətənbi   PNYN 227
  geitnbi   EPD
Gatesbury/Hrt
  gædzbəri   PNHrt 19o
Gætesgarth/Cu
  gækət   GlossCu xvii
Gatesgill/Cu
  gɛ:tskil   PNCu 133
Gateshead/Du
  geitshed   EPD,BBC,BCE,Schr.,
            Bchm.62
Gathurst/La
  gæþəst   BBC
Gatley/Chs
  gætli   EPD
Gatwick/Ess,Sr
  gætwik   EPD,BBC

Gaulter Cottages/Do
  goultə   PNDo I/96
Gavel Gn/Chs
  gavəl   PNChs III/172
Gaveston Place/Sx
  gævistən   EPD
  gævəstən   Kruis.
Gawsworth/Chs
  olim gɔ:zuþ, gɔ:zwərþ   PNChs II/vii
  gɔ:zəþ   GlossChs
Gawthorpe Hall/La
  gɔ:þrəp   PNLa(ii)
Gawthrop/WRY
  gɑ:þrəp   DDd 15
Gayhurst/Bk
  geiə:st   PNBk 4
Gaylock/We
  gɛ:lik   PNE'side 71
Gaythorn/We
  gɑ:rþərən   PNE'side 65
Gayton
  geit(ə)n   BBC
  geitn,geitən   PNChs IV/275
  gaitən   PNNf ("the vulgar pron.
           of the name"),Hope (for G.
           in Nf)
Gedding/Sf
  g-   PNSf 73
Geddinge/K (= Giddinge, q.v.)
  gedindʒ   BBC,BCE
Geddington/Np
  gediŋtən   BBC,BCE
Geffrye Museum/Ldn
  dʒefri   BBC
Geldeston/Nf
  geldstən, 'geldestən   BBC,BCE
  gelstən   BBC,BCE,PNNf,s.n.Gelston
Gelsthorpe/WRY
  gelsþrəp, -trəp   PNYW V/lo
Gembling/ERY
  gemlin   PNYE 91
Georgeham/D
  dʒɔ:dʒ 'hæm   PND 43,DEPN,PNND 19
  'dʒɔ:dʒhæm   BBC
Germoe/Co
  gə:mou   BBC,BCE
Gerrans/Co
  gerənz   BBC
Gerrard's Cross/Bk
  dʒerədz krɔs, -   krɔ:s,
  dʒerɑ:dz -   EPD
Gestingthorpe/Ess
  gestəp   PNEss 43o
Gestwick/Nf
  gestik   Hope,ONwick
Gibraltar
  dʒibrɔ:ltə   EPD,Schr.,Kruis.
  dʒibrɔltə   EPD,Kruis.

Gib's Hall/WRY
  gibz ɔ: DDd 12
Gidding/Hu
  gidiŋ   EPD,BBC
  g-   PNHu 33o,PNSf 73
Giddinge/K (= Geddinge)
  gidindʒ   PNK
  -indʒ   Dodgson(2)336
Gidea Pk/Ess
  gidi   PNEss 117
  gidiə   EPD
Giggleswick/WRY
  loc. gilzik   PNE&W
Gilberdyke (-dike)/ERY
  gilbədaik   BBC
Gilcambon/Cu
  _ ˈ _   DEPN
Gilcambon Beck/Cu (r.n.)
  gil'kɔ:mən   RN 171,PNE'side 65
Gilcrux/Cu (or Gill-)
  gilkru:s   PNCu 287,GlossCu
             xvii
  gilkru:z   DCu(i)198,DEPN,BBC,
             BCE
Gildersome/WRY
  gildəsəm   EPD,BBC
Giles/WRY
  dʒailziz   DDd 16
Gillamoor/NRY
  giləmuə   PNYN 64
Gillan Creek/Co
  gilən kri:k   BBC
Gillbent/Chs
  gil-   PNChs I/249f.
Gillcambon/Cu
  gilkɑ:mən   PNCu 196
  (see also above s.n. Gil-)
Gillerthwaite/Cu
  giləþət   Hope
Gillets Crossing/La
  'dʒilets 'krɔsiŋ   BBC,BCE
Gillhope/Sx
  dʒilʌp   PNSx 382
Gilling/NRY
  giliŋ   EPD,BBC,BCE
Gillingham/Do,Nf
  giliŋəm   PNDo 5,EPD (for
             G. in Do and Nf),
             BBC,BCE (for G. in
             Do and Nf)
Gillingham/K
  dʒiliŋəm   PNK,EPD,BBC,BCE
Gillman's/Wt
  gilmənz   PNWt 11
Gillow (as in G.Heath/Sx)
  gilou   EPD
Gills/K
  gilz   EPD

Gillscott/D
  gilskət   PND 365
Gill Yard/WRY (f.n.)
  dʒil jɑ:d   GlossSh 311
Gilscott/D
  gilskət   PND 85
Gilpin/We (r.n.)
  gilpin   EPD
Gilshaughlin Ho, G. Gill/We
  gil'ʃɔ:lin   PNWe II/136
Gilsland/Cu
  gilzlənd   BBC,BCE
Gilson/Wa
  dʒilsən, gilsən   EPD
Gilston/Hrt
  vulgo gilsən   PNHrt 192
Gilwell Pk/Ess
  gilwəl pɑ:k   BBC
Gimblett(as in G.'s Mill/Co)
  gim(b)lit   EPD
Gimingham/Nf
  gimiŋəm   BBC,BCE,PNing 172
  giminəm   PNing 172
  -i-   DEPN
Gimlets/Wt
  gimlits   PNWt 8o
Ginclough/Chs
  dʒinklʌf   BBC
Gingaford/D
  giŋgəfəd   PND 291
Ginge/Brk
  -ndʒ   Zachr.(1)348,H.A.(1)179
Gingerland/D
  gindʒ-   PND 556
Gipping/Sf (p.n. and r.n.)
  gipn   Hope
  gipiŋ   BBC,BCE (both for r.n.
             only)
Gipsey Race/ERY (r.n.)
  gipsə   PNYE 4
Girling's Hard/Sf (f.n. in Sutton)
  gælənz   PNDVall 71
Girlington Hall/NRY
  gɔrlintən   PNYN 3oo
Girsby/NRY
  gɔrzbi   PNYN 28o
Girtford/Bd
  gə:fəd   PNBdHu lo8
Girton/Ca,Nt
  gə:tən   ONCa 18,Schr.,PNNt(i)5
  gə:tn   EPD,Kruis.
Gisburn/WRY
  gisbə:n   BBC
Gisleham/Sf
  gizləm,gisləm   BBC,BCE
  -i-   DEPN
Gislingham/Sf
  gizliŋəm   BBC,BCE

Gisperdown/D
  gispədaun PND 292
Gissing/Nf
  gisiŋ EPD,BBC,BCE,Kruis.
Gittisham/D
  gitsəm PND 589,BBC,BCE
  gitisəm,gitiʃəm BBC,BCE
Givendale/ERY
  gindəl,
  gi:ndəl,geldən PNYE 177
Givendale/NRY
  gi:ndil PNYN 94
Givons Grove/Sr
  dʒivənz grouv BBC
Gladices/Wt
  'glædisi:z PNWt 114
Glaisdale/NRY
  gleizdeil EPD,BBC
  glɛ:əzdil DSto
  loc. gleizdl EPD
Glandford/Nf
  glænfə Hope
Glanville/Do
  glænvil EPD
Glapthorne/Np
  glæpþɔ:n EPD
Glaramara/Cu (a mountain)
  'glærəmɑ:rə BBC,BCE
  -æ- DEPN
Glasshampton/Wo
  glɑ:sən,gleizəntən PNWo 34
Glass Houghton/WRY
  'glɑ:s 'hautən BCE
Glasson/La
  glazən PNLa 171
  glazn PNLa(ii)
Glaston/Ru
  gleistən DEPN,BBC,BCE
Glastonbury/So
  glɑ:stənbəri BBC,Schr.,Kruis.,
                NED
  glɑ:st(ə)nb(ə)ri EPD
  glæstənbəri Schr.,Chis.
  glæst(ə)nb(ə)ri,
  glæsn- EPD,Bchm.131
  glɑ:snb(ə)ri Bchm.131
  glɑ:snbəri,glæsn- Schr.
Glaven/Nf (r.n.)
  glævn,gleivn RN 174
Glazebrook/La
  gleizbruk EPD
Glazebury/La
  gleizbəri BBC
Gleadthorpe Grange/Nt
  gli:dþɔ:p greindʒ BBC
  gledþɔ:p PNNt(i)56
Gleaston/La
  gli:stn PNLa 2o9
  -i:- DEPN

Glemsford/Sf
  glemsfəd EPD
Glencoin (Beck)/Cu,We → Glencoyne B.
Glencoyne/Cu,We
  gleŋ'kɔin,gleŋ'kiun PNWeII/222
  glen'kiun PNE'side 71
  glen'kiu:n GlossCu xvii
Glencoyne Beck/Cu,We (r.n.)
  glen kiun RN 178,PNCu 15
Glencoyne Pk/Cu
  glenki:un PNCu 254
Glendale/K
  gleindeil EPD
Glenderamackin/Cu
  _ _ _ _ ⁄ _ DEPN
Glenderaterra/Cu
  _ _ _ _ ⁄ _ DEPN
Glendue/Nb
  _ ⁄ DEPN
Glenelg/St
  glen'elg EPD,BBC
Glenridding/We
  glen'ridən PNWe II/222,
                PNE'side 65
Glen Ridding Beck/We (r.n.)
  glen ridən RN 18o
Glentham/Li
  glenþəm BBC
Glodwick/La
  glɔdik PNLa 51,DEPN
Glos. (short for Gloucestershire)
  glɔs EPD
Glossop/Db
  glɔsəp EPD
Gloster (as in G.Hill/Nb)
  glɔstə EPD
Gloucester/Gl
  glɔstə PNGl II/123,DEPN,EPD,BBC,
           PNE&W,Schr.,Kruis.,Chis.,
           NED,MEG 126,DHe 43
  glɑ:stər PNGl II/123
  glɔ:stə EPD,HL 67o,Moberly 124
  glɑ:stə DHe 43
  (see also note 1 below)
Gloucester Rd/Ldn
  glɔ:stə raud CPP 66
Gloucestershire
  glɔstəʃə EPD,Schr.,MEG 126f.
  glɔ:stə- EPD
  -ʃiə EPD
Glover's Fm/Wt
  glʌvərz varm PNWt 42
Glyme/O (r.n.)
  glaim BBC
Glympton/O
  glimtən PNO 264
  glim(p)tən BBC

1) "Older members of county families usually pronounce [glɔ:s-]"(EPD).

Glyn (as in G.Morlas/Sa)
  glin EPD
Glynde/Sx
  glain PNSx 352,DEPN
  glaind EPD,BBC,BCE
Glyndebourne/Sx (also spelt
               Glynde Bourne)
  glaindbɔːn BBC
  glain(d)bɔːn, -bɔən EPD
Glynleigh/Sx
  griːn'lai [sic!] PNSx 446
Glynn/Co
  glin BBC
Gnosall/St (also spelt -ss-)
  nouzl Schr.
  nousl EPD,BBC,Hope
  nousəl BCE
Goathland/NRY
  goːədlənd PNYN 81,DSto
  gouþlənd EPD,BBC
  -oud- DEPN
  guːədlənd DSto
Goathurst/So
  gouþəːst BBC,BCE,Hope
  -ouþ- DEPN
Gobowen/Sa
  gɔb'ouin BBC
Godalming/Sr
  'gɔdəlmiŋ PNSr 195,Schr.,BG,
               Chis.,Hope
  gɔdlmiŋ EPD,BBC,Kruis.
Goddard (as in G.'s Castle/K)
  gɔdəd, -dɑːd EPD
Godfrey (as in G.Ho/K)
  gɔdfri EPD
Godmanchester/Hu
  'gɔdmən'tʃestə BBC,BCE,Kruis.
  / _ _ _ _ EPD,Bchm.87
  'gʌmsestə BG
  gɔnʃistə Bchm.87
Godmanstone/Do
  gɔdmənstoun PNDo I/197
Godmersham/K
  gɔdməʃəm BBC,BCE
Godolphin/Co
  gə'dɔlfin EPD,BBC
Godrevy/Co
  gɔ'driːvi BBC,BCE
Godshill/Ha,Wt
  'gadzil PNWt 139
  gɔdzhil BBC,DWt,s.n.Lor a
          massey
Godwin (as in G.'s Halt/Hrt)
  gɔdwin EPD
Gogmagog Hills/Ca
  'gɔgməgɔg EPD
Golant/Co
  gou'lænt BBC
  go'lænt BCE

Golborne/La
  'goulbɔːn BBC
  goubən PNLa(ii)
Golborne Bellow, G.David/Chs
  gou(l)bɔrn,gou(l)bən (when used
  with affix) PNChs IV/88 and 9
Golcar/WRY
  goukə PNYW II/291,BBC,BCE,
               H.A.(2)45
  goukər DHd 43,Ellis 377
Golden/Co
  goulden Förster
Golding/Sa
  gouldiŋ EPD
Goldings/Wt
  guː(l)dnz PNWt 226
Golding's Fm/Wt
  guːdnz PNWt 286
Goldington/Bd
  gouldiŋtən BBC
Goldsborough/NRY,WRY
  gouldzb(ə)rə EPD
Goldsithney/Co
  'gould'siðni BBC
Goldthorpe/WRY
  gouþrəp Hope
Golton/NRY
  goutən PNYN 176
Gomeldon/W
  gʌməldən PNW 380
  gɔmild(ə)n BBC
Gomersal/WRY
  guməsəl PNYW III/21
  gɔməsl BBC
  gɔməs(ə)l EPD
Gomshall/Sr
  gʌmʃəl PNSr 248,BBC,BCE,EPD
  gɔmʃəl BBC,EPD
  gʌmʃl, gɔm- Bchm.205,EPD
  -ʌ- DEPN
Gonalston/Nt
  gʌnəlst(ə)n, gʌns(ə)n PNNt 16
  gʌnəsn PNNt(i)56
Gonerby/Li
  gʌnəbi Hope
Gonvena/Co
  'gɔnviːnə BBC
Gonville and Gaius College/Ca
  'gɔnvil ən(d) 'kiːz EPD,BBC,
                      Kruis.
Goodalls/Wt
  gudəlz, 'gudɔːlz PNWt 114
Goodameavy/D
  gudə'miːvi BBC
Gooderstone/Nf
  gudsən Hope
Goodge St/Ldn
  gu(ː)dʒ EPD
Goodmanham/ERY
  gudmədəm PNYE 230
  gudmədm Hope

Goodnestone/K
    gudnestən   BBC,BCE
    gudənstoun   PNK
    gʌnstən   BBC,BCE,PNK,Hope
    gɔdstən   Hope
Goodrich/He
    gudritʃ   EPD
Goodrington/D
    gɔrintən,gʌrintən   PND 517
Goodwin Sands/K (offshore)
    gudwin   EPD
    -w-   MEG 213
Goodwood/Sx
    gudəd   PNSx(i)72
    gudwud   PNSx(i)72,EPD,Bau.
Goodyear (as in G.'s Gn/Ha)
    'gudjə(:)   EPD
Goole/WRY
    gu:l   PNYW II/16,EPD,Chis.
Goonbell/Co
    gu:n'bel   BBC
Goonhavern/Co
    gə'nævən,gu(:)n'hævən   BBC
Goonhilly/Co
    gu:n'hili   BBC,Jenner(2)3o2
Goonhilly Downs/Co
    'gu:nhili   EPD
Goonvean/Co
    _ ∕   Jenner(2)3o4
Goonvrea/Co
    gu:n'vrei   BBC
Goosnargh/La
    gu:snə   BBC,BCE
    gu:znə   PNLa 149,DEPN
    gu:znər   PNLa(ii),Ellis 354
Goostrey/Chs
    gu:stri   PNChs II/ix,GlossChs
    gu:əstri   PNChs II/ix
Gopher Wood/W
    vulgo koufər   PNW 32o
Gordhayes Fm/D
    (The d is not sounded in the
    loc. pron.)   cf. PND 651
Gorhambury/Hrt
    'gɔrəmbəri   BBC
Goring/O,Sx
    gɔ:riŋ   EPD,BBC
Gorleston/Nf
    gɔ:lstən   EPD,BBC,BCE
Gorran Haven/Co
    gɔrən heiv(ə)n   BBC
Gorringe Pk/Sr
    gɔrin(d)ʒ   EPD
Gorse (Upper G.)/Db (f.n.)
    gɔs   FnSDb 135
Gorsecroft Fm/Chs
    gɔ:skrɔft   PNChs III/84
Gorstage/Chs
    gɔrstidʒ   PNChs III/2o2

Gorstella/Chs
    'gɔrstelə   PNChs IV/159
Gorton/La,St
    gɔ:tn   EPD
Gosberton/Li
    -z-   DEPN
Gosberton Clough/Li
    'gɔzbətən 'klau   BBC,BCE
Goscote/St
    'gɔskout   BBC
Gosfield/Ess
    gɔ:sfl   PNEss 431
Gosport/Ha
    gɔspɔ:t   EPD,Schr.
Gosport Clough/WRY
    loc. "Goseforth"   Smith(2)218
Gosset St/Ldn
    gɔsit stri:t   Schr.
Goswick/Nb
    gɔzik   DEPN,BBC,BCE
Gote Mill/Cu
    gwɔt mil   DLo 36
Gotham/Nt
    goutəm   PNNt 247,EPD,BBC,BCE
    gɔtəm   HL 762,Schr.
    goutm   PNNt(i)57
    -out-   DEPN
    gouþəm   Schr. (according to EPD,
        however,only used for G.
        in the U.S.A.)
Gotherington/Gl
    gɔðrintən   PNGl II/87
    gʌðətən,gʌðriŋtən   Hope
    gʌðətn   GlossSEWo 82
Gotten Leaze/Wt
    gatn li:z   PNWt 8o
Gotten Manor Fm/Wt
    gɔ:tn, gɑ:tn   PNWt 115
Goudhurst/K
    'gaudhə:st   BBC,BCE,PNK,Hope
    -au-   DEPN
Goulceby/Li
    goulsbi   BBC
Gover (as in G.'s Gn/Hrt)
    gouvə   EPD
Goverton/Nt
    gɔ:tən   PNNt 155
    gouvətn   PNNt(i) 57
Goveton/D
    gʌvit(ə)n   BBC
    gʌvətən   BCE
Gower/K
    gauə   EPD,Kruis.
Gowerdale/NRY
    jouwədil   PNYN 2o3
Gower's Fm (Little G.'s Fm)/Ess
    gɔ:əz   PNEss 547
Gower St/Ldn (underground station) [1]
    gauə   EPD,CPP 66

1) now Euston Underground Station.

Gowthorpe/ERY
  gɔːþrəp   PNYE 176
Gowy/Chs (r.n.)
  gaui   PNChs I/27,RN 182
Goxhill/Li
  gouzl   Hope
Goxhill/ERY
  gouzəl   PNYE 66,Hope
  gouzl   GlossHol 17
  gauzil   Hope
Grace Dieu/Le
  'greis 'dju: BBC,BCE
  greisdi   Hope (spelt
            Gracedieu)
Gradeley Gn/Chs
  greidli   PNChs III/134
Graffham/Sx
  græfəm   BBC
Grafham/Hu,Sr
  grɑːfəm   BBC (for G. in Hu)
  græfəm   BBC (for G. in Sr)
Grafton
  grɑːft(ə)n   EPD
  grɑːftən   Schr.
Grafton/Gl,Wo
  grɑːftən   PNGl II/43
  grɑːfn   GlossSEWo 82
Gragareth/WRY (a mountain)
  greːgərəþ   DDd 17
Grammerby Wood/D
  græməbai   PND 221
Grampound/Co
  'græmpaund   BBC
Gramskew/We
  græmskə   PNE'side 63
Granby/Nt
  grænbi   EPD
Grand Courts/Ess [1]
  grɔŋkəz   PNEss 423,EssDD 158
Grange
  grein(d)ʒ   EPD
Grange/Wt
  greindʒ,grændʒ   PNWt 68
Grangetown/Du,NRY
  grein(d)ʒtaun   EPD
Gransden/Ca
  grænzdən   ONCa 188
Gransmoor/ERY
  gransmə   PNYE 88
Gransmore Gn/Ess
  grismal [sic!]   EssDD 158
Granta/Ca (r.n., now usually
            called Cam)
  grɑːntə, græntə   Schr.
Grantchester/Ca
  grɑːntʃistə, græn-   BBC
  græntʃestə   ONCa 195

Grantham/Li
  grænþəm   EPD,BBC,BCE,Kruis.
  loc. græntəm   HL 122o,Schr.,Bͨ
                  EPD,Chis.,Kruis.
  grɑːntəm   Schr.,Kruis.,Bchm.2?
  -þ-   Eminson(2)159
Granville/Db
  grænvil   EPD,Schr.,Kruis.
Grappenhall/Chs
  grɔpnəl   PNChs II/ix,GlossChs,
            Hope
  grɔpnə   PNChs II/ix,GlossChs
  'grapənɔːl,grapnəl   PNChs II/ͨ
Grassington/WRY
  grasintən   PNYW VI/97
  gəːstən   PNYW VI/97,Hope
  grɑːsiŋtən   BBC
Gras(s)mere/We
  grɑːsmiə   EPD
  græsmiːə,grɑːsmiːə   Schr.,Kruiͧ
  -æ-   DEPN
  gəːsmə   Hope
Grassnop/Cu (also spelt Grass Knoͨ
  gərsnəp   PNCu 2o9,PNE'side 76
Grassthorpe/Nt
  gresþɔːp   PNNt(i)58
Grateley/Ha
  greitli   BBC
Graveley/Ca,Hrt
  greivli   BBC,ONCa 183
Gravelly Hill/Sr,Wa
  grævli hil   BBC
Graveney/K
  greivəni   PNK
  greini   PNK,Hope
Gravesend/K
  'greivz'end   EPD,Schr.
  'greiv'zend   EPD,Kruis.
  ◡ ─   Chis.
  ─ ◡   EPD,DEPN
Grayrigg/We
  grɛːr-rig   DKe 5
Graysouthen/Cu → Grey-
Greasby/Chs
  griːzbi   PNChs IV/291,DEPN,BBC
Greasley/Nt
  grezli   PNNt 144
  griːzli   PNNt(i) 58
Greatham/Du
  griːtəm   EPD,DEPN,BBC,BCE
Greatham/Ha
  gretəm   BBC
Greatham/Np
  gretəm   EPD,BCE
Greatham/Sx
  gritəm   PNSx 151,DEPN

---

1) The name is spelt Grandcourt's in EssDD.
2) cf. also PNChs(i)17: "Until recently spelt and pron. Greavesby."

gretəm   EPD,BBC

Great Huish/D
   gəːrtiʃ   PND 12o

Great Park/W
   gəːrt pɑːrk   PNWt 286

Great Salkeld/Cu
   gərt sæfl   PNE'side 74

Greatworth/Np
   gretwəːþ   PNNp 35
   -e-   DEPN

Greaves/La
   greivz   EPD,Kruis.
   griːvz   EPD

Green
   griːn   EPD

Greenfield
   griːnfiːld   EPD

Greenfield/La
   grinfilt   DSLa

Greenford/Mx
   griːnfəd   EPD

Greenhalgh/La
   griːnhæl(d)ʒ, griːnhɔː   EPD
   griːnhælʃ   EPD,BBC,BCE
   griːnhɔːlʃ   BBC,BCE
   griːnə   PNLa 154,DEPN

Greenhalgh Castle/La
   griːnə   PNLa 164
   griːnəl   PNLa(ii)

Greenhithe/K
   'griːnhaið   EPD,Chis.

Greenhow/Li
   griːnhou   P&RNLi 132

Greenlake/D
   grenlik   PND 78

Green Leighton/Nb
   griːnlaitən   PNNbDu 133
   -ai-   DEPN

Green Rigg/WRY
   grein rig   DDd 13

Greenses/Nb
   grinsiz   Ellis 645

Greensilhaugh/Nb
   'griːnsilhɑːf   BBC,BCE

Greenstead Hall, G. Gn/Ess
   grinsted   PNEss 437

Greensted/Ess (nr Ongar)
   grinsted   PNEss 57,DEPN

Greenthwaite/NRY
   griːnfit   PNYN 19

Greenthwaite Hall/Cu
   griːnþet   PNCu 198
   griːnhwɛːt   PNE'side 7o

Greenway Lane/Gl
   loc. grænə lein   PNGl II/xii

Greenwell/Cu,Du
   griːnw(ə)l, -wel   EPD

Greenwich/K
   grinidʒ   DEPN,EPD,BBC,BCE,Schr.,
            Kruis.,Hope,PNK,MEG 124,
            Dobson 94o,ONwick 39o,
            ESpr. 316 et passim
   grinədʒ   Bau.
   grinitʃ   MEG 213 ("rarely"),EPD,
            BBC,BCE,Chis.
   grenitʃ   EPD,BBC,BCE,Schr.("rare-
            ly")
   grenidʒ   EPD
   griːnitʃ   Schr.

Greeta/La,Yorks. (r.n.) (also spelt
                              Greta)
   griːtə   RN 185,DEPN,Schr.

Greetland/WRY
   griːtlənd   EPD

Grendon Underwood/Bk
   grindən   PNBk 1o3

Grenofen/D
   grenəfən   BBC

Grenoside/WRY
   grenousaid   BBC

Gresham/Nf
   greʃəm   EPD,BBC,Schr.,Kruis.,
            MEG 377,HL 816

Gresley/Db
   griːzli   DEPN,PNDb(i) I/143,Hope
   grezli   EPD

Gressenhall/Nf
   greslin, gresnel   Hope

Gressingham/La
   gresiŋəm   BBC

Gresty Bridge, G.Brook, G.Gn/Chs
   gresti   PNChs III/69

Greta/Yorks. → Greeta (r.n.)

Gretabridge/NRY
   griːtəbridʒ   BBC

Greta Hall/Cu
   griːtə hɔːl   BBC

Gretworth/O
   greitwəːþ, griːt-   Hope[1]

Grewelthorpe/WRY
   griuwilþrəp   PNYW V/2o6

Greygarth Fell/Yorks.
   gregriþ   PNE'side 64

Greysouthen/Cu (also spelt Gray-)
   'greisuːn   PNCu 397,BBC,BCE
   greːsuːn   PNCuWe 55
   greisiuːn   GlossCu xvii

Greystoke/Cu
   'greistɔk   DEPN,BBC,BCE
   greistik   GlossCu xvii
   grɛːstik   PNE'side 7o

Greywell/Ha
   'grei'wel, gruːəl   BBC,BCE

Gribbin Head/Co
   gribin hed   BBC

---

1) This p.n. is not listed in either BG or PNO; there is a Greatworth
   in Np.

Gridley (as in G.Corner/D)
  gridli   EPD
Grigshole/Wt
  grigzhoul   PNWt 174
Grimethorpe/WRY
  graimþɔ:p   BBC
Grimsargh/La
  grimzə   DEPN,PNLa 145
Grimsby/Co,Li
  grimzbi   EPD,Schr.
Grimscar/WRY
  'graimzkɑ: BBC,BCE
Grimston/Nf
  grimsən   Hope
Grimwith/WRY
  grimiþ   PNYW VI/79
Grindale/ERY
  grindl   PNYE lo4,BBC
  grindəl   BCE
Grindall/ERY
  grʌndil   Hope[1]
Grindley/Chs
  grindli   PNChs IV/47
Grindon/Du,Nb,St
  grindən   EPD
Gringley (Little G.)/Nt
  grinli   Hope
Grisdale/WRY,We
  graizdl   DDd 16
  'graizdeil   BBC,BCE (for G.
               in We)
Gris(t)mal Gn/Ess
  grizməl   PNEss 422
Gristhorpe/NRY
  grisþrəp   PNYN lo4
  graisþrəp   Hope,Hyde 39
Grizebeck/La
  graizbek   PNLa 221
Groby/Le
  gru:bi   BBC,BCE
  -ou-   DEPN
Groffa Crag/La
  grɔfə krag   PNLa 214
Groombridge/Sx
  'gru:m'bridჳ   BBC,BCE
Grosmont/NRY
  groumənt   DEPN,EPD,BBC,BCE
  groumɔnt   EPD
  grousmənt   EPD ("loc."),BBC,
               BCE
Grosvenor Pk, etc./Ldn
  grouvənə   Kruis.
  grouvnə   EPD
Groton/Sf
  grɔ:t(ə)n,grout(ə)n   BBC
  grɔ:tən, groutən   BCE
Ground/WRY → Low Ground

Grove
  grouv   EPD,Schr.
Grovehill/ERY
  grɔvəl   PNYE 198
Groveleys/Gl
  'grouv'li:z   PNGl II/16
Growen Fm/D
  grauən   PND 56o
Grub St/Ldn (later Milton St)
  grʌb stri:t   Bau.
Grumpley Hill/Cu
  grumplə   PNE'side 63
Grundisburgh/Sf (also spelt -bury)
  grʌndzbərə   BBC,BCE
  grʌnzbrə   DEPN,Hope
Guardhouse/Cu
  gɑ:dəs   GlossCu xvii
Guarlford/Wo
  gɔ:lfəd   PNWo 211
Gubeon/Nb
  gu:biən   PNNbDu 97
Guestwick/Nf
  gestik   DEPN,ONwick 373
Guilden Sutton/Chs
  gildən   PNChs IV/126
Guildford/Co,Sr
  gilfəd   DEPN,EPD,BBC,Schr.,Kru
               Chis.,MEG 223
  gildfəd   Chis.
Guildford Fm/Wt
  gilvərd   PNWt 286
Guilton/K
  giltən   PNK
Guisborough/NRY
  gi:zbrə   PNYN 149
  gizbrə   PNYN 149,DEPN
  gizbərə   BBC,BCE,Chis.
  gizb(ə)rə   EPD
  gisbrʌf   GlossWby,s.n.Bruff
Guiseley/WRY
  gɑ:zlə   PNYW IV/146
  gaizli   PNYW IV/146,DEPN,EPD,B
               BCE
Guist/Nf
  gaist   DEPN,BBC,BCE
Guiting Power/Gl
  gaitiŋ pauər   PNGl II/12
  gaitiŋ pauə   DEPN,BBC,BCE
Guldeford (East G.)/Sx (also spelt
               Guilford)
  gilfəd   PNSx 529,PNSx(i)75,PNK
               DEPN,BBC,BCE
  gʌl(d)fəd   PNSx(i)75
Gulliford/D
  sometimes gælifəd   Picken 149
Gulval/Co
  gʌlvəl   BBC,Jenner(2)3o2

1) Identical with Grindale (previous entry) ?

Gunby/ERY
   gumbi   PNYE 239
Gunhouse/Li
   gʌnəs   GlossM&C,s.n.Blashy
Gunnersbury/Mx
   gʌnəzb(ə)ri   EPD
Gunnerside/NRY
   gunəsit   PNYN 271
Gunnislake/Co
   gʌnizleik   BBC
Gunthorpe/Nt
   olim gʌntrəp   PNNt 167
   gʌnþɔ:p   PNNt(i)61
Gunthwaite/WRY
   gunfit   DHd 131
   gʌnfit   Hope
Gunthwaite Spa/WRY
   spɔ: PNSWY 264f.
Gunville/Wt
   gɔnvl   PNWt 286
Gunwalloe/Co
   gʌn'wɔlou   BBC
Gurnard/Wt
   gə:rnər   PNWt 187
Gurnards Head/Co
   gə:nədz hed   BBC
Gussage All Saints/Do
   gʌsidʒ, gisidʒ   PNDo(i)91
Guy's Hospital/Ldn
   short: gaiz   Bau.
Gweek/Co
   gwi:k   BBC
Gwennap/Co
   gwenəp   BBC
Gwinear/Co
   gwiniə   BBC,BCE
Gwineas Rock/Co
   gwiniəs   BBC
   (see also next entry)
Gwinges Rock/Co
   gwindʒiz   BBC
   (another name for above)
Gwithian/Co
   gwiðiən   BBC

H

Habergham/La
  abəgəm   Dodgson(2)374
  now habəgəm PNing 17o
  hæbəgəm DEPN
  once hæbədʒəm RD,s.n.
                       Habergham

Habergham Eaves/La
  æbəgm eivz,
  æbədʒm   PNLa(ii)

Habrough/Li
  heibərə BCE
  hei- DEPN

Haceby/Li
  heisbi BBC,BCE

Hacheston/Sf (also spelt -don)
  heisən Hope

Hackergill/WRY
  'akəgil DDd 14

Hacklestone/W
  hækstən DEPN

Hackney/Ldn
  hækni EPD

Hackthorpe/We
  hækþrɔp PNE'side 71

Hacra/WRY
  ɑːkərə DDd 13

Haddenham/Bk,Ca
  hædnəm PNBk 161
  hæd(ə)nəm ONCa 177

Haddington/Li
  hædiŋtən EPD,Schr.

Haddiscoe/Nf
  hædskou,hædskə Hope

Haddon
  hædn EPD

Haden Hill/St
  heidn EPD,Kruis.

Hades/La
  eːdz PNLa 57

Hadfield/Db
  hædfiːld EPD

Hadham/Hrt
  hædəm PNHrt 176

Hadleigh/Ess,Sf
  hædli EPD,Chis.

Hadley
  hædli EPD

Hadlow/Chs,K,Sx
  hædlou EPD

Hadlow Rd, H. Wood/Chs
  hadlou, older local adlə
          PNChs IV/232

Hadnall/Sa
  hædnəl BBC

Hadrian's Wall/Cu,Nb
  heidriənz wɔːl BBC

Hadston/Nb (also spelt -stone)
  hadsən PNNbDu 98

Hadzor/Wo
  hædzə BBC

Hagg/WRY (two farms nr Honley and
          Denby Dale resp.)
  æg DHd 3

Haggate/La
  hag geːt PNLa 85

Haggerston /Ldn,Nb
  hægəst(ə)n EPD

Haigh/La
  hei BBC,BCE,PNSWY 152

Haigh/WRY
  heig BBC,PNSWY 152

without reference to a
particular county:
  heig EPD,Kruis.
  hei EPD

Haighton/La
  hait(ə)n BBC
  haitən BCE

Haile/Cu
  hial PNCu 398
  hiəl GlossCu xvii

Hailes/Gl
  heilz EPD

Haileybury/Hrt
  heilib(ə)ri EPD

Hailsham/Sx
  helsəm PNSx 435,DEPN
  heilʃəm EPD,BBC,Chis.
  helʃəm Hope

Hainault Forest/Ess
  heinɔːt EPD,BBC
  heinɔ(ː)lt EPD

Haine/K
  hein PNK

Haisthorpe/ERY
  ɛəsþrəp PNYE 89

Hala Carr/La
  eːlə kɑː PNLa 174

Halam/Nt
  heiləm PNNt 167,DEPN

Halden/K (High H.)
  hai hɔːld(ə)n BBC
  hai hɔːldən BCE
  hɔːlden PNK

Haldon/D
  hɔːld(ə)n BBC
  hɔːldən BCE

Hale
  heil EPD
  (h)ɛəl PNWt 12

Haleacre Wood/Bk
  hɑːləkə PNBk 155

Halebarns/Chs
  heil'bɑːnz BBC

Hale Common/Wt
  hæl kɑ:mən PNWt 12
Hale Field/We
  t'hɛəl PNE'side 72
Hale Grange/We
  he:l gre:ndʒ Ellis 669
Hales
  heilz EPD
Halesowen/Wo
  heilz'ouin BBC
  heilz'ouwən Chis.
Halesworth/Sf
  heilzwə:þ EPD
  hɛ:lzwə:þ, holzə DSf 269
  hɑ:slə Hope
Halewood/La
  heil'wud BBC
Halford/D,So,Wa
  hɔ:lfəd EPD,Bchm.9 (for H.
    in D and Wa),BBC (for
    H. in Sa)
  hælfəd Bchm.9 (for H. in D
    and Wa),BBC (for H.
    in Wa),EPD
  hɑ:fəd BBC (for H. in Wa)
  holfəd EPD
Halhead Hall/We
  'hɔ:led PNWe I/154
Halison Hill/Nb
  hælid(ə)n EPD
  hælidən Schr.
Halifax/WRY
  hælifæks EPD,Schr.,Kruis.
  ɛəlifeks Ellis 367
  hælifeis Smith(2)228
  -ais DSWY 1o4 ("now ob-
    solete")
Hall/WRY → Low Hall,High Hall
Hallam
  hæləm EPD,Kruis.,BBC (for H.
  heiləm PNNt 62   in WRY)
Halland/Sx
  hɔ:l lænd PNSx 4oo
  hælənd BBC
Hallaton/Le
  hælət(ə)n BBC
Hallaze/Co → Chypraze
Hall Bank/WRY
  ɔ: baŋk DDd 13
Hall Bower/WRY
  o:lbɛər DHd 77
Hallen/Gl
  hælən BBC
Hallet Shute/Wt
  hælət PNWt 228
Hallin Crag/We
  hælən kræg PNE'side 65
Halling/K
  hɔ:liŋ BBC,BCE,DEPN,PNK

Halling/WRY
  hɔ:liŋ BBC
Hallingbury/Ess
  holiŋbri PNEss 34
  holiŋbəri,hɔ:liŋ- BBC,BCE
  -ɔ- DEPN
Halliwell/La
  hæliw(ə)l, -wel EPD
  hæliwəl Schr.
Hallon/Sa (also spelt Hallahon)
  hɔ:n Hope
Hall o' th' Hey/Chs
  (h)ei PNChs III/241
Halloughton/Nt
  hɔ:tən, hɔ:ʔn PNNt 168
  hɔ:tn PNNt(i)63,DEPN,Hope
Halloughton Hall/Wa
  hælətən PNWa 17
Hallow/Wo
  holou PNWo 129,DEPN
Hallsenna/Cu
  hɔ:senə PNCu 394,GlossCu xvii
  housenə Hope
Hallsteads/We
  hɔ:sti:dz PNE'side 75
Halmore/Gl
  hælmɔ: BBC
Halnaby Hall/NRY
  ɔ:nəbi PNYN 282,DEPN
Halnaker/Sx
  hænəkər PNSx 67
  hænəkə BBC,BCE
  hæn- DEPN
Halsall/La
  hɔ:lsl BBC
  hɔ:lsəl BCE
Halsbury/D (=Barton of H.)
  hɔ:lzb(ə)ri, hɔl- EPD
  hɔ:lzbəri Kruis.
Halse/Np,So
  hɔ:z PNNp 49,DEPN (for H. in Np)
  hæls, hɔ:s BBC,BCE
Halsetown/Co
  hɔ:lztaun BBC
Halsham/ERY
  ɔ:zəm PNYE 3o,Hope
  hɔ:nsəm [sic] Hope
  ɔ:səm GlossHol 17
Halshanger/D
  hɔ:sæŋər PND 464
Halstead/Ess,K,Le
  hælstid PNEss 433,EPD,Bchm.9
  hælsted BBC (for H. in Ess and K)
    BCE (for H. in Ess and K)
    EPD,Bchm.9,Chis.
  hɔ:lstid, -sted EPD,Bchm.9
  holsted, -stid EPD
  elsted EssDD 151,note 1
  ælsted Benham 17

Halstock/Do
  hælstək,
  hɔ:lstək   PNDo(i) 223
  hɔ:lstɔk   BBC,BCE
Halstow/K
  hælstou   BBC,BCE
Haltecliff/Cu
  hɔ:tlə   PNE'side 64
Haltcliff Hall/Cu
  hɔ:tli   PNCu 276
Haltemprice/ERY
  ɔ:təmpraiz   PNYE 2o8
  hɔ:ltəmprais   BBC
Halton/Chs
  hɔ(:)ltən   PNChs II/ix
  olim hɔ:tn   PNChs II/ix,
                GlossChs
  hɔ:tən   Hope
Halton/La
  hɔ:tn   PNLa(ii)
Halton/Li
  hɔ:tən, hu:tən   GlossM&C,s.n.
                Hawton,Hooton
Halton Hol(e)gate/Li
  hɔ:lt(ə)n houlgeit,
  -        hɔligeit   BBC
  hɔ:ltən   -   BCE
Haltwhistle/Nb
  ho:təsəl   PNNbDu 99
  hɔlt'usle,
  loc. hoat'usle   Mawer(1)99
Halvan/Co
  -æ-   Jenner(2)3oo
Halvean/Co
  "ī, as ee in see, is represent-
  ed by ea [...], but old people
  often sound ea as ay in may"
  (Jenner(2)3o1)
Halvear/Co
  _ _ ʹ   Jenner(2)3o4; see also
  s.n. Halvean
Halvergate/Nf
  hævəgeit (?)   PNNf[1]
Halwell/D
  hɔ:lwel   PND 323,BBC,BCE
  hælwel   BBC,BCE
Halwill/D
  hælwil,hɔ:lwil   BBC,BCE
Halwoon/Co
  hæl'u:n   Jenner(2)3o2
Ham (East Ham)/Ess
  'i:st 'hæm   EPD
Hamble/Ha
  hæmbl   EPD
Hambleden/Bk
  hæməldən   PNBk 177
  hæmbld(ə)n   EPD

Hambledon/Do,Ha,Sr
  hæmbld(ə)n   EPD
Hambleton
  hæmblt(ə)n   EPD
Hamel Close/K (f.n.)
  klous   DK
Hamel Down/D
  hæməldən   PND 527
Hameringham/W
  hæmərinəm   BBC,BCE
Hamerton/Hu
  hæmət(ə)n   EPD
Hamfallow/Gl
  hæm'fælou   BBC
Hamilton/Le
  hæm(i)lt(ə)n   EPD
  hæmiltən   Schr.,Kruis.
  hæmltən   Schr.
  hæmilt(ə)n   BBC
Hamlet/Do,Sa
  hæmlet   Kruis.
  hæmlit   Kruis.,EPD
Hammersmith/Ldn
  hæməsmiþ   EPD,Schr.,Bau.
  emə smiþ   CPP 66,Höfer 152
Hamond (as in H. Lodge/Nf)
  hæmənd   EPD
Hammoon/Do
  həmu:n   PNDo(i)53
  _ ʹ   DEPN
Hamoaze/D (an island)
  hæ'mouz   PND 2o
  'hæmouz   BBC
Hampden/Bk
  hæmdən   PNBk 151,EPD,Kruis.
  hæmpdən   EPD
Hampden Pk/Sx (in Eastbourne)
  hæmdən   BBC
Hampole/WRY
  hæmpoul   HL 278
Hampreston/Do
  hɑ:mprestn   DDo
Hampsfell/La (a ridge)
  hamsfel   PNLa 198
Hampsfield/La
  hamsfi:ld   PNLa 198
Hampshire
  hæmpʃiə   EPD,HL 48o
  hæmpʃə   EPD,BBC
  hæm(p)ʃə   MEG 222,Schr.
  hæmʃə   Kruis.
Hampstead/Ldn
  hæm(p)stid, -sted   EPD,BBC,MEG 22
  æmstid   Höfer 3o2
Hampstead Heath/Ldn
  'hæmpsted 'hi:þ   Bau.

1) "Mr. Gillett says H. is properly pron. HAVERGATE, from Haver, the
   old name for Oats; but we think not" (PNNf).

Hampsthwaite/WRY
 amstwit PNYW V/133
Hampton
 hæm(p)tən EPD,Schr.
 hæmtən Kruis.
 -mt- HSM 81
Hampton Ct/He,Mx
 hæm(p)tən kɔːt Schr.
Hamsey/Sx
 hæmsi PNSx 315
 hæmzi BBC
Hamstead/Wt
 (h)æmstid PNWt 21o
Hanbury/St,Wo
 hænbəri EPD
Handborough/O
 hænbərə PNO 268
Handforth/Chs
 olim hɔnfəːrt, handfərþ
     PNChs II/vii
 hɔnfərt GlossChs
Handley
 hændli EPD
 han(d)li PNChs IV/9o
Haney/Ca → Henney
Hangabank/WRY
 inə baŋk DDd 16
Hanging Shaw/We
 hiŋiʃə PNE'side 62
Hankelow/Chs
 hæŋkəlou,
 hæŋkəlɔː PNChs III/89
Hanley/St,Wo
 hænli EPD,Schr.
Hannah/Li
 hænə EPD
Hanningfield/Ess
 olim hænvəl PNEss 25o
Hannington
 hæniŋtən EPD
Hanover/Ess
 hænəvə EPD,Schr.
 'hænouvə EPD
Hannover Pt/Wt (or -n-)
 'hænəvər PNWt 128
Hanslope/Bk
 hænsləp PNBk 6
 hænsloup BBC
Hanson Grange/Db
 hʌnsdən PNDb(i) I/25o
Hants. (short for Hampshire)
 hænts EPD,Schr.
Hanwell/Mx,O
 hænw(ə)l, -wel EPD
Hanworth/Nf
 hænə Hope
Hanyard/St
 hænjaːd Förster

Happisburgh/Nf (also spelt Hasbr')
 heizbərə EPD,BBC,BCE,Hope,PNNf,
     s.n.Haisborough
 heizbrə EPD,DEPN,Hope
Hapton/La
 æptən PNLa(ii)
Harber Gill/WRY
 aːbə gil DDd 12
Harberton/D
 haːbət(ə)n EPD,BBC
Harbertonford/D
 'haːbət(ə)nfɔːd BBC
Harberwain/We
 harbərən PNE'side
 har'bɔrən PNCuWe 151
Harborough/Le,Wa
 haːb(ə)rə EPD
Harbour Ho/Du
 harbərəs PNNbDu 1ol
Harbreating/Sx
 haːbritiŋ PNSx(i)79
Harcourt/Co,Sa
 haːkət, -kɔːt EPD,Kruis.,Bchm.71
Hardcastle/WRY
 'haːdkaːsl EPD
Harden/St,WRY
 haːdn EPD,Förster
Hardenhuish/W
 harniʃ PNW 99
 haːniʃ PNW(i)95 ("loc."),DEPN,BBC,
     BCE
Hardhaugh/Nb
 haːdhaːf BBC,BCE
Hardingham/Nf
 haːdiŋəm Hope
Hardingshute/Wt
 hardnʃeuːt,aːrdiŋʃouːt PNWt 55
Hardisworthy/D
 ardzəri PND 78
 hardzəri PNND 28
 haːdzəri DHtl 8
Hardmead/Bk
 haːmiːd PNBk 36
Hardres/K
 haːdz EPD,DEPN,BBC,BCE,Kruis.
 haːds PNK
Hardrow/NYR
 aːdrə PNYN 259
Hardwick (in many counties)
 haːdik DEPN,Bchm.138,Schr.,PNBk
     79,PNDb(i)I/15o,Hope(for
     H. in Db),ONwick 371(for
     H. in Db)
 haːdwik EPD,Schr.,Bchm.138,
     ONCa 19o
 hærik Hope (for H. in Li),ONwick
     372 (for H. in Li)
 hædik Hope (for H. in Nf),ONwick
     373 (for H. in Nf)

Hardwick Hill/Li
 hædək GlossM&C
 hædik GlossM&C,P&RNLi 148f.
Hardwick Woods/Np
 hɑːd(w)ik wudz BBC,BCE
Hardy/La
 hɑːdi EPD,Kruis.
Hare (as in H.Gn/Ess, etc.)
 hɛə EPD
Harefield/Mx
 olim hɑːvəl PNMx 35
 hɛəfiːld BBC
Harehaugh/Nb
 hɛəhɑːf BBC,BCE
Haresceugh/Cu
 heskə PNCu 216
 'hɛəskjuːf BBC,BCE
 hæskə PNE'side 63
Haresceugh Castle/Cu
 hars- Thorn.55 and 8o,note
   131
Hareshaw/We
 hɛːrʃə PNE'side 62
Harewood/WRY
 hɛəwud PNYW IV/18o,EPD,[1] BBC
 hɑːwud PNYW IV/18o,EPD,BBC,
   BCE.Hope
Harewood End/He
 hɛəwud end,dial. hærəldz DHe 43
Harewood Grange/Db
 hærəd PNDb 44
Harewood Ho/WRY
 hɑːwud haus EPD
Harford/D,Gl,Nf
 hɑːfəd EPD
Hargham/Nf
 hɑːfəm DEPN,BBC,BCE,H.A.(2)
   45,Hope,PNNf,s.n.
   Harpham
Hargrave/Np
 hɑːgreiv PNNp 191
Hargraves/Ess
 hɑːgreivz EPD,Kruis.
Harlaxton/Li
 'hɑːləkstən BBC
 hɑːləstən Hope
Harlesden/Mx
 hɑːlzdən EPD,BBC,Kruis.
Harlesthorpe/Db
 "Halsthorpe" PNDb(i)I/251
Harleston/D,Nf,Sf
 hɑːlstən BBC,BCE (for H. in
   Nf)
Harlestone/Np
 hælsən PNNp 83
 hɑːlstən BBC

Harley
 hɑːli EPD
Harlow/Ess
 hɑːlou EPD,BBC,Schr.
Harlton/Ca
 hɑːltən ONCa 19
 hɔːltən PNCa 76
Harmer (as in H.Gn/Hrt)
 hɑːmə EPD
Harmondsworth/Mx
 olim hɑːmzwəːþ PNMx 38,PNMx(
 hɑːmzəþ PNMx(i)[2]
 hɑːməndzwəːþ BBC
Harmony/Ess
 ɑːməni,ɑːməri PNEss 422
Harpenden/Hrt
 olim hɑːdən, hɑːdiŋ PNHrt 37
 hɑːp(ə)ndən EPD
Harpham/ERY
 (h)ɑːpm PNYE 89
 hɑːpəm EPD
Harpole/Np
 ɑːpəl PNNp 84
Harraby/Cu
 hærəbi BBC
Harriet's Fm/Ess
 herjəts PNEss 414
Harrietsham/K
 hæriətʃəm, hæriʃəm BBC,BCE,PNK
 hærʃəm PNK
Harringay/Mx
 hæringei PNMx(i)
Harringe/K
 hærindʒ PNK
Harrington/Cu,Li,Np
 hærintən EPD
Harris (as in H. Barton/Gl)
 hæris EPD
Harriseahead/St
 'hærisiː'hed BBC
Harrogate/WRY
 hærəgit EPD,Kruis.
 hærəgeit,hærougit EPD
 hærəgət Schr.
 hærougeit EPD,Chis.
Harrop/Chs,Cu,WRY
 hærəp EPD
Harrow/Mx
 hærou EPD,BBC,Schr.,Kruis.
Harrowby/Li
 hærəbi, hæroubi EPD
Harrowden/Np
 hæroudən BBC
Harry (as in H.Hill/Gl)
 hæri EPD

---

1) "The village in Yorks. is now generally pron.['hɛəwud],though
 ['hɑːwud] may sometimes be heard from very old people there" (EPD)
2) This form is used "by the 'older people' of the neighbourhood,but..
 the 'younger generations' tend to 'pron. it as written'" (PNMx(i)).

Harston/Ca
   olim haːsən   PNCa 84
   haːstən   ONCa 19
Harswell/ERY
   ɑːswəl   PNYE 234
Hart/Du
   haːt   EPD
Hartfield/Sx
   haːtful   PNSx 365
Hartfoot Lane /Do
   haːrbət leːən   DDo
Hartford
   haːtfəd   EPD
   harfəd   PNNbDu 1o3 (for
         H. in Nb)
Hartfordbeach/Chs
   -biːtʃ   PNChs III/188
Hartham/W
   haːtəm   BBC
Harthay/Hu
   haːti   PNBdHu 234
Harthill/Chs
   haːrtil   PNChs IV/92
Harthill/Db (also spelt Hartle)
   haːtl   PNDb 1o8
Hartington/Db,Nb
   haːtiŋtən   EPD
   haːtiŋtn   Kruis.
Hartland/D
   haːtlənd   EPD
Hartlebury/Wo
   haːtlbəri   BBC
Hartlepool/Du
   haːtlipuːl   PNNbDu 1o4,EPD,
         BBC,BCE,Hope
  'haːtəlpuːl   Chis.
   haːtlpuːl   EPD
Hartley
   haːtli   EPD
   haːtlə   DYorks.63 (for H. in
         WRY)
   haːrtlə,haːklə   PNE'side 64
         (for H. in We)
Hartley Wespall/Ha
   haːtli wespɔːl   BBC
Hartsash/Wt
  '(h)aːrtsæʃ   PNWt 17o
Hartshead/WRY
   haːtʃit   Hope
Hartside/Cu
   haːrtsaid   PNE'side 69
Hartwell/Np
   haːtəl   PNNp 1oo
Harwich/Ess
   hæridʒ   PNEss 339,EPD,BBC,
        Schr.,Kruis.,Hope,
     DEPN,MEG 2o5,ONwick 376,
     ESpr.381,GlossEA,s.n.
     Harriage

   haːdʒ   PNEss 339
   hæritʃ   EPD,BBC,BCE,Schr.,Chis.,
        Kruis.,BG,EssDD 158
   hærədʒ   Bau.
   -dʒ   Dobson 94o
Harwood Dale/NRY (or Harewood D.)
   'ærəd dil   PNYN 113
   hærədeil,haːwud deil   Hope
Harwood/Du,La,Nb
   haːwud   EPD
   hærəd   DSLa,GlossR&R,Parkinson
        (for H. in La)
Harworth/Nt
   hærəp   PNNt(i)64,DEPN,Hope
Hasbury/Wo
   heizbəri   PNWo 294
Hascombe/Sr
   (h)aːskəm   PNSr 243
   haːskəm   Davies 25 [1]
Haselbech/Np
   heizəlbitʃ   PNNp 115
   -itʃ   DEPN
Haseley/O,Wa,Wt
   heizli   BBC
Haselor/Wa
   hæzlər   PNWa 211
   heizlɔː   BBC
Hasketon/Sf
   hæskitən   BBC
   hæskətən   PNDVall 9
Haslemere/Sr
   heizlmiə   EPD,BBC
   heizmiːr   Schr.
Haslett/Wt
   haːzlət,hæːzlit   PNWt 22o
Haslingdon/La
   hæzlindən   EPD,BBC,Chis.
Haslingfield/Ca
   hæzliŋfiːld   ONCa 192
   heizliŋfiːld   PNCa 77,BBC
Haslington/Chs
   hæzliŋ-   PNChs III/12
Hasluck (as in H.'s Gn/Wa)
   hæzlʌk, -lək   EPD
Hassall/Chs
  '(h)æsɔːl   PNChs III/21
   hæsl   EPD,Schr.,Kruis.
   hæsəl   Schr.
Hassobury/Ess
   haːsoberi [sic]   PNEss 55o
Hassocks/Sf,Sx,WRY
   hæsəks   EPD
   æzəks   DHd 5 (for H. in WRY)
Hastingleigh/K
   heistənlai,
   haːsənlai, heistiŋlai   PNK
Hastings/Sx,So
   heistiŋz   EPD,BBC,Schr.,Kruis.,
        Chis.

1) "still loc. pron. with great correctness HAASCOMBE" (Davies 25).

Hatch
  hætʃ EPD
Hatch Beauchamp/So
  'hætʃ 'biːtʃəm BBC,BCE
Hatfield
  hætfiːld Schr.,EPD
  hætfeld Hope (for H. in Hrt)
Hatfield Peverel/Ess
  'hætfiːld 'pevərəl BBC
Hatherleigh/D
  hæðəli(ː) EPD
Hatherley Ct/Gl
  hæðəli EPD
Hathern/Le
  hæðən DEPN,BBC,BCE
Hatherop/Gl
  heiðrəp PNGl I/36
Hathersage/Db
  (h)aðəsidʒ PNDb 111
  hæðəseidʒ BBC
  hæðəsidʒ, -sedʒ EPD
  aðərsitʃ Ellis 442
Hatherton/Chs,St
  haðətən PNChs III/62
  hæðətən EPD,Kruis.
  -tn EPD
Hatlex/La
  hatliks PNLa 186
Hatley/Ca
  hætli ONCa 184
Hatton
  hætən Schr.
  hætn EPD
Haugh/Li
  hɔː BBC,BCE
Haugh/WRY
  hɔːf BBC
Haugham/K
  hʌfəm BBC,BCE
Haugham/Li
  hæfəm BBC,BCE
Haughley/Sf
  hɔːli BBC,BCE
Haughmond Hill/Sa
  hɔːmənd hil, heimənd - BBC,
                             BCE
  eimən GlossSa 517
Haughton
  hɔːt(ə)n BBC
  hɔːtn EPD
  hɔːtən PNChs III/3o9,
          BCE (for H. in La)
  ɔːtn Ellis 48o (for H. in St)
Haughton-le-Skerne/Du
  'hɔːt(ə)n lə 'skəːn BBC
  hɔːtən - - BCE
Haulgh/La
  hɔf BBC,BCE

Haultwick/Hrt
  ɑːtik PNHrt 135
Haume/La
  ɑːm PNLa 2o6
Hause/Cu,We
  hɔːs PNE'side 75
Hautbois/Nf
  hɔbis DEPN,BBC,BCE,Hope,PNNf,s
      Hobbies
  hɔbəs Hope
Hauxley/Nb
  hɑːksli PNNbDu 1o6
Hauxton/Ca
  olim hɔːsən PNCa 85
  hɔːkstən ONCa 2o
Hauxwell/NRY
  hɔːkswel BBC
Havant/Ha
  hævənt EPD,DEPN,BBC,BCE
Haven Street/Wt
  hebm striːt,hevn - PNWt 32
Haverah Pk/WRY
  hævərə BBC
Havergate Is./Sf
  hævəgeit BBC
Haverhill/Sf
  heivril DEPN,BBC,BCE
  hævəril Schr.,Chis.,Bchm.18,
                MEG 377
  hævəhil MEG 377
  heivəril EPD,Bchm. 18
Haverigg/Cu
  hævərig BBC
Havering-atte-Bower/Ess
  heivəriŋ æti bauə BBC
Haveringland/Nf
  heivəriŋlənd BBC
  hævələnd Hope
Haversham/Bk
  hɑːʃəm PNBk 8
Haverstock Hill/Ldn
  hævəstɔk hil EPD,Schr.
Haverthwaite/La
  havəþət PNLa 217
Haverton Hill/Du
  'hævət(ə)n 'hil BBC
Hawcoat/La
  hɔːkɔːt PNLa 2o3
Hawes (in many northern counties)
  hɔːz EPD,Kruis.
  houz Hope (for H. in Cu)
  hɔːs PNE'side 75 (for H. in Cu
                and We)
  tɔːz PNYN 266
  hoːz DKe 5 (for H. in NRY)
  ɑːz DDd 17 (for H. in WRY)
Hawes Water/La (r.n.)
  ɔːz wɔːtə PNLa 169

Hawick/Nb
  'hɔ:-ik EPD,BBC,Schr.
  hɔik Hope
  hɔ:wik Kruis.
Hawkesbury/Gl
  hɔ:ksbəri Schr.
Hawkhill/Nb
  hɔ:kəl PNNbDu lo6
Hawk Hirst/Cu
  hɔ:krist PNCu 68
Hawkhope/Nb
  hɔ:kəp PNNbDu lo6
Hawkinge/K
  hɔ:kindʒ BBC,BCE,PNK,H.A.(1)
           178,Zachr.(1)348
Hawkshead/La
  hɔ:ksed, -səd PNLa 218
  hɑ:ksid PNE'side 69
  hɑ:ksəd DBo
Hawkwood/Ess
  hɔ:kwud EPD
Hawley
  hɔ:li EPD
Hawnby/NRY
  ɔ:mbi PNYN 2o3
Haworth/WRY
  auwəþ, ouwəþ PNYW III/261
  hɔ:wə:þ EPD
  hɔ:wəþ EPD,Schr.
  loc. hɔ:rəþ Schr.
  hauəþ, hɔ:əþ EPD,BBC,BCE
  heiwəþ, hɔ:þ Kruis.
  hɔriþ Hope(see note 1 below)
Hawridge/Bk
  hɔridʒ PNBk 95,DEPN
  coll. wɔridʒ PNBdHu 69,s.n.
           Wharley End
  hæridʒ BBC,BCE
Haws/Cu
  hɔ:s PNE'side 75
Hawsker/NRY
  ɔskə PNYN 121
Hawsker Bottoms/NRY
  ɔskə bɔdəmz PNYN 122
Hawthwaite/La
  ɔ:þət PNLa 222
Haxby/NRY
  asbi DYorks.63,GlossMY xix
Haxey/Li
  hæksi BBC
  hæksə GlossM&C,s.n.Haxa
Hay
  hei EPD
Haycock/Cu
  heikɔk EPD
Haycote/WRY
  e:kət DDd 15

Hayden/Gl
  heidn EPD
Haydock/La
  heidɔk BBC
  hædək PNLa(ii)
Haydon
  heidn
Haydor/Li ⟶ Heydour
Hayes
  heiz EPD,Kruis.
The Hayes/Db (f.n. in Flindern)
  ði i:ziz Fraser(2)74
Hayhead/Chs
  ei jed GlossChs
Haylands/Wt
  heilən(d)z PNWt 285
Hayle/Co
  heil BBC,Chis.
Hayles (as in H. Abbey/Gl)
  heilz EPD
Haymarket/Ldn
  heimɑ:kit EPD,Schr.
Haynes/Bd (old spellings: -ag-,-aw-)
  heinz PNBdHu 151,EPD,Hope
  hɔ:nz PNBdHu 151
Haynford/Nf (or Hain-)
  hænfə Hope
Hays/W
  heiz EPD
Haytor/D
  'hei'tɔ: BBC
  heitə EPD
Hayward/Brk,Ha
  heiwəd EPD
Haywards Heath/Sx
  hju:əds hɔ:ð PNSx 268
  hjuədz hɔ:ð Mawer(2)99,Hope
Hazelbadge/D
  -badʒ PNDb(i) I/257
Hazelbury/Do
  hɑ:zəlbər DDo
Hazeleigh/Ess
  heizli PNEss 215
Hazelford Ferry/Nt
  hæzlfəd PNNt(i)67
Hazel Grove/Chs
  olim azl grɔ:v PNChs II/vii,
                GlossChs
  heizəl grɔ:v PNChs II/vii
Hazelhurst/He,La,Sx
  heizlhə:st EPD
Hazelrigg/Nb
  hezlrig PNNbDu lo7
Hazlebadge/Db
  (h)azəlbadʒ PNDb 118
Hazledean/K
  heizldi:n EPD

---

1) Hope's transcription Horeth is rendered "probably [hɔriþ]" in Förster

Hazlerigg/Nb
  heizlrig EPD
Hazleworth/La
  hæzləþ DSLa
Hazlitt Gallery/Ldn
  hæzlit EPD,BBC
Heacham/Nf
  hetʃəm,hi:tʃəm BBC,BCE
  -e- DEPN
Head Down/Wt
  (h)ed dæun PNWt 182
Headingley/WRY
  hediŋli EPD,BBC
Headstone/Hrt
  hedstoun EPD
Headlam/Du
  hedləm EPD,Kruis.
Headon/Nt
  hedən PNNt 52
  hi:dn PNNt(i)67
  -i:- DEPN
Headon Hill/Wt
  hi:dn, hedn PNWt 228
Heage/Db
  i:dჳ PNDb 565
  hi:dჳ BBC,BCE,DEPN,PNDb(i)
        I/258 ("loc.")
Healam Ho, H. Beck/NRY
  i:ləm PNYN 22o
Healaugh/NRY,WRY
  i:lə PNYN 273
  hi:lə BBC,BCE (for H. in
        NRY),DEPN (for H. in
        WRY)
Healey/Yorks.,La,Nb
  i:lə PNYN 232
  jelə GlossR&R loo [1]
  jeli PNLa(i)112
  jeli wad PNLa(ii)
  hi:li EPD
Healey Castle/St
  hi:li EPD
Heamoor/Co
  heimↄ: BBC
Heane/K
  hein PNK
Heanor/Db
  heinə PNDb 469,BBC,BCE
  hi:nə BBC,BCE,EPD,Chis.
  'hi:ænə Chis.
Heanton Punchardon/D
  heintən PND 45
  hent(ə)n pʌnʃədən,
  heint(ə)n - BBC
  hentən, heintən - BCE
  -ei- DEPN

Hearnton Wood/Bk
  heriŋtən PNBk 2o8
Heasley/Wt
  heizli PNWt 13
Heath
  hi:þ EPD
  heþ PNWt 286
Heathcote/Db,Sr,Wa
  heþkət EPD,Kruis.
  hi:þkət EPD
Heathencote/Np
  hevənkət [sic] PNNp 1o4
Heather/Le
  hi:ðə DEPN,BBC,BCE
  heðə EPD
Heatherwick/Nb
  haðərwik PNNbDu 1o8
Heathery Cleugh/Du
  'heðəri 'klʌf BBC
  kliəf Ellis 617
Heathfield
  hi:þfi:ld EPD,BBC
  jefel Grüning 42
Heathfield/So
  hefl DEPN
Heathfield/Sx
  hefəl PNSx 463,PNSx(i)81,Hope,
        Keef 51
Heathfield Fm/Wt (nr Whippingham)
  heþfild PNWt 242
Heathfield/Wt (nr Colbourne)
  hæþfild PNWt 81
Heath Hill/Sa
  jeþil GlossSa 517
Heathpool/Nb
  heþpu:l PNNbDu 1o8,DEPN,BBC,BC
Heathrow/Mx
  'hi:þ'rou BBC
Heaton
  hi:tn EPD
Heaton(several places in La)
  hi:ətn,he:ətn PNLa(ii)
  jetən PNLa(i) 175
Heaton/WRY
  jetən Hope,DHd 155
  jetn, jiətn DHd 155
Heatree/D
  heitri: PND 481
Heawood/Chs
  heiwud BBC
Hebberdens/Wt
  (h)ebərdənz PNWt 81
Hebbinge/K
  -indჳ- Dodgson(2)339
Hebble/WRY (r.n.)
  jebl DHd 154

1) So pron. in Rochdale (GlossR&R).

Hebburn/Du,Nb[1]
 hebə:n   BBC,BCE (for H. in
                Nb)
 hebərən   PNNbDu 1o8 (for H.
                in Du)
 hebən   Böhm.67
Hebden/WRY (p.n. and r.n.)
 hebdən   EPD
Hebden Bridge/WRY
 'ebdin 'brig,
 t'brig   PNYW III/188
 jebdin brig   DHd 154
Heber (as in H.'s Ghyll/WRY)
 hi:bə   EPD
Hebron/Nb
 -e-   DEPN
Heckmondwike/WRY
 'hekmənwaik,
 hekənwɑ:k   PNYW III/24
 ekənwɔik,ekənwɔ:k   Ellis 403
 hekənwik   Hope
 hekməndwaik   BBC,BCE,Chis.
Hedgeford/St
 hedʒfəd,
 hetʃfəd   Zachr.(3)129
Hedgehope Hill/Nb
 hedʒəp   BBC,BCE
Hedgeley/Nb
 hedʒli   EPD,HL 811
 hidʒli   PNNbDu 1o9,DEPN
Hedgerley/Bk
 hedʒəli   EPD
Hedgrove/Nt
 hedgrouv PNNt(i)67
Hedingham (Castle H.,Sible H.)/Ess
 hinigəm   PNEss 438,PNW'stow
                17,Reaney(3)468
 hiningəm PNEss 438,DEPN
Hednesford/St
 hedʒfəd   BBC,BCE,HL 811
 henzfəd   HL 811
 hensfəd   BBC,BCE
 hedʒfɔ:d, hetʃ-   Hope
Hedon/ERY
 edn   PNYE 39
 hed(ə)n   BBC
 hedən   BCE
 -e-   DEPN
Hefferston Grange/Chs
 hefərsən PNChs III/2o3
Heggle Foot/Cu (or Hegglefoot)
 hegl fiut   PNE'side 71
Heggle Lane/Cu
 hegl loənin   PNE'side 72
Heigham/Nf
 heiəm   BBC,Hope
 haiəm   Hope,PNNf,s.n.Higham

Heighington/Du
 heiiŋtən BBC,BCE
 haiiŋtən,
 haintən   BBC,BCE,PNNbDu 11o
 eintən   Hope
 hai-   DEPN
Heighington/Li
 hei'iŋtən   BBC,BCE
 hei-   DEPN
Heighton (South H., H.Street)/Sx
 heitən   PNSx 361 and 363
 heitn   PNSx(i)83,EPD
 hei-   DEPN
The Heights/WRY
 ðə eits   DHd 29
Helhoughton/Nf
 hel'hout(ə)n,
 hel'haut(ə)n   BBC
 hel'houtən,hel'hautən   BCE
 helətn   Hope
Helks/WRY
 elks   DDd 14
Helland/Co,So
 helənd   BBC
Hellesdon/Nf (also spelt -den)
 helsdən   Hope
Hellifield/WRY
 (h)elifild   PNYW VI/158
Hellingly/Sx
 heliŋ'lai   PNSx 438,BBC,BCE,DEPN,
                Hope
 heriŋ'lai   PNSx 438,Hope
 'heliŋlai   EPD
Hellpool Bridge/Cu
 helpa   PNCu 444
Helmingham/Sf
 helmiŋəm BBC
Helmside/WRY
 eləmsət   DDd 13
Helms Knott/WRY (a mountain)
 eləmz nɔt   DDd 17
Helmsley/NRY
 emzlə   PNYN 71
 helmslə   DYorks.63
 helmzli   EPD,BBC
 hemzli   EPD ("loc."),BBC
 hemsli   ESpr.388
 hemz-   DEPN
 (see also s.n. Gate Helmsley)
Helperthorpe/NRY
 helpəþrəp   EDD,s.n.Thorpe
Helsby/Chs
 helzbi   PNChs III/235
Helsthorpe/Bk
 elstrəp   PNBk 88
Helston/Co
 helstən   EPD,BBC,Schr.

1) see also s.n. Hepburn/Nb.

Helstone/Co
  helstən EPD
Helvellyn/Cu
  hel'velin EPD,BBC,Chis.,
               DEPN (stress only)
Hemel Hempstead/Hrt
  olim hæməl hæmstid PNHrt 4o
  hem(ə)l hem(p)stid EPD
Hemerdon/D
  hemədən PND 253
Hemingbrough/ERY
  'hemiŋbrʌf BBC,BCE
Hemley/Sf
  hemli PNDVall 3o
Hempshill/Nt
  hemsəl PNNt(i)67
Hempstead/Hrt → Hemel H.
Hempton Wainhill/O
  hentən winɑ:l PNO 1o7
Hemswell/Li
  hemzwel BBC
Hemsworth/Do
  hemzud PNDo(i)1o8
Hemsworth/WRY
  himzwəþ Hope
Hemyock/D
  hemik PND 616
  hemjɔk BBC,BCE
  hemiɔk BBC
Henbury/D
  haiənbəri Bate 533[1]
Hendon/Du,Mx
  hendən EPD
Hendon Moor/D
  jenən PND 78
Hendrea/Co
  ◡́ _ Jenner(2)3o4

Henhull/Chs
  'henul PNChs III/145
Henlands Meadow/Db (f.n.)
  loc. endləndz FnSDb 56,s.n.
                 Endlands M.
Henley
  henli EPD,Chis.
Henney/Ca
  heni ONCa 181
Hennock/D
  henək PND 471
Hensingham/Cu
  hensigəm PNCu 4oo,GlossCu
                xvii
Henstead/Sf
  henstid BBC
Henwick/Brk,Wo
  henwik BBC
  henik PNWo 132

Hepburn/Nb (also spelt Hebburn)
  hebə:n EPD,BBC,BCE,MEG 231
  hebən EPD,Kruis.
  hepbə:n EPD,MEG 231
  hepbən EPD
  -eb- DEPN
Hepple Flats/Db (f.n.)
  æpl Fraser(2)74
Hepple Meadow/Db (f.n.)
  æpl FnSDb 57
Heptonstall/WRY
  epms(t)əl,epənstəl PNYW III/1
  hepənstəl Hope
  (see also s.n. Slack)
Hepworth/Sf,WRY
  hepwə:þ EPD
Herbert/Gl
  hə:bət EPD
Herculaneum/La
  hə:kju'leinjəm, -iəm EPD
Herdswick Fm/W
  hesik PNW 3o4
Hereford/He
  herifəd EPD,BBC,MEG 28o,DHe 4.
          Schr.
  herəfəd Chis.,Kruis.
  herəfət GlossHe 39,s.n.Ford
  dial. herifət DHe 43
  hə:rifəd DDo
Herefordshire
  herifədʃə EPD,Schr.
  -ʃiə EPD
Hereson/K
  hiəsən PNK
Hergest Ridge/He
  hɑ:gist BBC,DHe 43 (StE and di
  hə:gest, hɑ:gest BCE
Hermitage
  hə:mitidʒ EPD
The Hermitage/Wt
  hə:rmitidʒ PNWt 152
Herne/K
  hə:n EPD
Herriard/Ha
  heriəd BBC
Herstmonceux/Sx
  hərstmənsu: PNSx 479
  hə:stmən'su: BBC,BCE
  hə:stmən'sju: BBC
  hə:stmɔnsju: PNSx(i)84
  hə:s(t)mən'sju:, -mɔn-, -su: F
  -su: DEPN
  hɔsmaunsiz PNSx 479,PNSx(i)84,
             Hope
  hɔ:smaunsiz DSx,s.n. plum-heav

1) The transcription given in Bate 533 is <u>Hiarnbury</u>.

haːmaunsi PNSx(i)84
haːsmaunsi Hope
həːstmaunsiz PNSx(i)84,Hope
Hertford/Hrt
  haːfəd PNHrt 225,DEPN,EPD,
      BBC,BCE,Hope,Schr.,
      Kruis.,Chis.,MEG 197
  haːtfəd EPD,Bchm.,HL 1221
  həːtfəd Chis.
  haːtfɔd ESpr.333
  -aː- , -əː- Koeppel 38
Hertfordshire
  haː(t)fədʃ(i)ə ⎫EPD
  haːfədʃə   ⎭Schr.[1]
  haːfədʃ(i)ə MEG 225
Hertingfordbury/Hrt
  'haːtiŋfədberi BBC
Herts. (short for Hertfordshire)
  haːts EPD,Bchm.21,Schr.
  həːts EPD,Bchm.21
Hesketh/La
  heskiþ,-eþ,-əþ EPD
Hesketh-with-Becconsall/La ⟶
  Becconsall
Hesleden/WRY
  hesldən BBC
Hesledon/Du
  hesldən BBC,BCE
  (see also s.n. Coldhesledon)
Heslerton/ERY
  heslətən BBC
Hesley/We
  hezlə PNE'side 64
Heslington/ERY
  hezlətən Hope
Hessary Tor/D
  'hesəri tɔː BBC
Hessenford/Co
  hes(ə)nfəd BBC
Hessett/Sf
  hesit BBC
Hessle/ERY
  ezl PNYE 215
  hezl BBC,BCE
  hesl BCE
Hest/La
  hest PNLa 185
Heston/Mx
  vulgo hesən PNMx 25
  hestən BBC
Heswall/Chs
  hezwɔːl,
  dial. hesəl PNChs IV/276
  hezwəl PNChs IV/276,BBC
Hethel/Nf
  hiːþl, heþl BBC
  hiːþəl,heþəl BCE
  -iː-,-e- DEPN

Hethfelton/Do
  hefəltən PNDo(i)144,PNDo I/146
Hetton/WRY
  etn PNYW VI/92
Hetton-le-Hole/Du
  'hetnli'houl EPD
Heugh/Nb,Du
  hjuːf BBC (for H. in Nb),EPD
  hjuf PNNbDu 113
Heughscar/We
  hiuskə PNE'side 63
Heveningham/Sf
  hinigəm,henigəm DSf 271
  henigm Hope
Hever/K
  hiːvə BBC,PNK
Heversham/We
  evəsəm, iəsəm PNWe I/187
Hewaswater/Co
  hjuːəswɔːtə BBC
Hewett/Nf (a channel)
  hju(ː)it EPD
Heworth/Du,NRY
  hjuːiþ Hope
  (h)juːəþ, -wəþ, -wəːþ Förster
Hewthwaite/WRY
  jouþət DDd 14
Hexham/Nb
  heksəm EPD,Schr.,Chis.
  eksəm GlossMY,s.n. Hexam
Hexworthy/D
  hæksəri PND 194
Heydon/Ca,Nf
  heid(ə)n BBC
  heidən BCE (for H. in Nf)
Heydour/Li (also spelt Haydour)
  eisəlbi [sic] Hope (twice!)
Heyford/Np
  hefəd PNNp 85
  heifəd BBC
Heyford at Bridge/O (=Lwr H.)
  heifəd ət bridʒ,
  louə heifəd BBC
Heyford Warren/O (= Upper H.)
  heifəd wɔrən,
  ʌpə heifəd BBC
Hey Heads/Chs
  'eijedz,olim
  'ei 'jed PNChs II/viii
  loc. (h)ei edz PNChs I/xxii
Heyrod/La
  herəd BBC,BCE
Heys/Chs ⟶ Prior's Heys
Heysham/La
  hiːʃəm EPD,DEPN,BBC,BCE,PNLa 178,
      Potter 35
  hiːsəm PNLa(ii),BCE
  iːsəm Ellis 626

1) "Für [...] Hertfordshire wird jedoch Schriftaussprache nicht be-
   zeugt" (Schr.)

Heyshott/Sx
  hiːʃət PNSx 22
  heiʃɔt BBC
  hiː- DEPN
Heytesbury/W
  heitsbəri PNW 167,BBC,Chis.
  heitsb(ə)ri EPD
Heythrop/O
  hiːþrʌp PNO 271
  hiːþrəp BBC,BCE
  -iː- DEPN
Heywood
  heiwud EPD,BBC
  jeːwud Hope (for H. in La)
  loc. jaiəd PNLa(i)2o6,
               PNLa(ii)
  jeiwud GlossR&R 1oo
Hibaldstow/Li
  hiblstou BBC
  hibəstou,hibstou GlossM&C,[1]
    s.n. Hibberstow,Hibbestow
Hickling/Nf,Nt
  hikliŋ BBC
  ikliŋ PNNt(i)68
  hiklən Hope (for H. in Nf)
Hicks (as in H.Forstal/K)
  hiks EPD
Hickstead/Sx
  hikstiːd PNSx 279
Hide/Wt ⟶ Upper H.
Hield Brow,H.Ho,H.Lane/Chs[2]
  hiːəld PNChs II/1o2
Higham
  haiəm EPD
Higham/Db
  haiəm PNDb(i)I/259
Higham/K
  haiəm BBC,BCE,PNK
Higham/Sf (two places)
  haiəm, higəm BBC,BCE
Higham/WRY
  haiəm, hikəm BBC,BCE
  hikn Hope
Higham Ferrers/Np
  haiəm ferəz BBC,BCE
Higham Gobion/Bd
  haiəm goubiən BBC
  gaubiən,olim gʌbin PNBdHu 153
Higham's Pk/Ess
  haiəmz pɑːk BBC,BCE
High Bridge/Cu (or Highbridge)
  hiː brig PNE'side 76
Highbury   haibəri BBC
High Cap/Cu
  haikəp PNE'side 75

High Chapel/WRY
  tei tʃapl DDd 13
Highcliff/Wt
  aiklif PNWt 119
High Croft/WRY
  ei krɔft DDd 12
High Cup Gill/We
  haikəbl PNE'side 74
Highden/Sx
  haidn PNSx(i)86
Highdown/D
  juːdn DHtl 8
Highgate
  haigit EPD,BBC,Schr.,MEG 254[3]
  haigeit EPD,BBC,Schr.
  haigət Schr.
High Hall/WRY
  tei ɔː DDd 13
High Hat/Wt
  ai hæt PNWt 286
High Hat Castle/Cu
  hiːþət kasl PNE'side 67
High Hoyland/WRY
  heː huiilənd Hope ("Hegh Huyla
Highlands
  hailəndz EPD
Highrigg/Cu
  hiːrig PNE'side 75
High Street Kensington/Ldn
  ai striːt kenzintən CPP 66
Hightown/WRY
  hetɑːn Hope
Hilbre Is./Chs
  hilbri(ː) PNChs IV/3o3
Hildersham/Ca
  hildəʃəm ONCa 178
Hilderthorpe/ERY
  ildəþrəp PNYE 1o2
Hildyards/Wt
  hiljərdz PNWt 2o4
Hilgay/Nf
  hilgei BBC
Hillbeck/We (nr Brough)
  helbek PNE'side 74
Hillcross Fm/Wt
  ilkras PNWt 112
Hillesden/Bk
  hilzdən PNBk 62
Hillhampton/Wo
  hiləntən PNWo 52
Hillhead/Sr
  'hilhed EPD
Hillingdon/Mx
  hiliŋdən EPD

1) The name is spelt Hibbaldestowe in GlossM&C.
2) "Presumably there was a local dial. pron. [jeld] or [jiːld]"
   (PNChs II/viii).
3)"more rarely [-gət],but 'careful speakers' often retain [-geit]"
   (MEG 254).

Hillis Fm/Wt
  (h)iləs   PNWt 188
Hill Row/Ca
  hil rou   ONCa 198
Hillsborough/WRY
  hilzbərə   BBC
  hilzb(ə)rə   EPD
Hillside
  'hil'said, ⟋ _   EPD
Hill Top/WRY
  il tɔp   DDd 15
Hilmarton/W
  hil 'mɑːrtən   PNW 268
Hilton
  hilt(ə)n   EPD
  hiltn   DDo
  heltən   PNE'side (for H.in We)
Hinchliffe Mill/WRY
  hintʃlif   EPD
Hinckley/Le
  hiŋkli   EPD
Hindburn/La (r.n.)
  hainbən   PNLa 169
  hain-   DEPN
Hinderclay/Sf
  'hindəklei   BBC
Hinderskelfe/NRY
  indəskəl   PNYN 40
Hinderwell/NRY
  hindəwel   EPD,BBC
    -w(ə)l   EPD
Hind Harton/D
  hæn hɑːtən   DHtl 8
Hindhead/Sr
  haind-   DEPN
Hindle Fold/La
  hindl   EPD
Hindley/La,Nb
  hindli   BBC,Schr.,
           for H. in La:
           EPD,DEPN,BCE
  haindli   Schr.
  aindli   PNLa(i)112f.
Hindlip/Wo
  hindlip   EPD,DEPN,BBC,BCE
Hindolveston/Nf
  'hindl'vestən,
  'hilvistən   BBC
  hilvəstən,hindlstən   Hope
Hindringham/Nf
  -inəm, -iŋəm   PNing 172
Hingston/Co
  hiŋ(k)stən   EPD
Hining/WRY
  ainin   DDd 13
Hinksey/Brk
  hiŋksi   Schr.
Hinnegar/Gl
  (h)inigə   PNGl III/28

Hinton
  hintən   EPD,ONCa 2o
Hints/Sa,St
  hints   BBC
Hinwick/Bd
  hinik   PNBdHu 39,DEPN,BBC
Hinxton/Ca
  hiŋkstən   ONCa 2o
Hipperholme/WRY
  (h)iprəm   PNYW III/79
  hiprəm   Hope
Hirst/Nb,WRY
  həːst   EPD
Histon/Ca
  olim hisən   PNCa 153
  hisn   Hope
  histən   ONCa 21
Hitchenden/Bk ⟶ Hughenden
Hitchin/Hrt
  hitʃin   EPD,Schr.
Hither (as in H.Gn/Ldn)
  hiðə   EPD
Hoards Fm/Sx
  hɔːðz   PNSx 468
Hoath/K
  houþ   PNK
Hoathly/Sx
  huːəd'lai   PNSx 4oo
  hudlai   Hope
  houð'lai,formerly
  houdlai   PNSx add. 114
  houþ'lai   BBC,BCE
  'houþli   BCE
Hobby Binns/Ess
  hɔbi vainz [sic]   PNEss 458
Hobson/Du,Wo
  hɔbsn   EPD
Hobsons/WRY
  ɔbsənz   DDd 14
Hockenhull/Chs
  hɔk(ə)nul, -ʌl   PNChs III/274
Hockwold/W
  hɔkould   Hope
Hodder/La,WRY (r.n.)
  hɔdə   EPD
Hoddesdon/Hrt
  hɔdzdən   PNHrt 228,EPD,BBC,Chis.
  olim hɔdsən   PNHrt 228
Hodge (as in H.Beck/NRY)
  hɔdʒ   EPD
Hodnet Heath/Sa
  hɔdnət jeþ   PNSa
Hodson/W
  hɔdsn   EPD
Hodyoad/Cu
  hɔdjəd   Hope
Hoe
  hou   EPD
  hau   Hope (for H. in Nf)

Hoff/We
  hɔf PNWe II/97
Hogben (as in H.'s Hill/K)
  hɔgbən EPD
Hoggeston/Bk
  hɔgstən PNBk 67
Hog Hatch/Sr
  hɔgidʒ PNSr 176
Hoghton/La
  (h)ɔ:tn PNLa 132
  hɔ:t(ə)n BBC
  hɔ:tən BCE
  -ɔ:- DEPN
Hoghton Towers/La
  hɔ:t(ə)n tauəz,
  hout(ə)n - BBC
  hɔ:tən - ,houtən - BCE
Hogleaze Copse/Wt
  haglıəz PNWt 242
Hognaston/Db
  hɔgnəstən PNDb 376
Holbeach/Li,St
  hɔlbi:tʃ BBC
  houlbi:tʃ DEPN (for H. in Li)
Holbeck
  hɔlbek EPD,Bchm.37
  houlbek Bchm.37
  houbek H.A.(2)45,PNNt 83, Hope (for H. in Nt)
  hɔl- ESpr.332 (for H. in WRY)
Holbeton/D
  hɔbətən,houbətən PND 275
  houlbit(ə)n BBC
  hɔb- DEPN
Holborn/Db (f.n.)
  haubə:n GlossSh 110
Holborn/Mx
  houbən PNMx 113,PNMx(i),EPD, BBC,BCE,Schr.,Kruis., ESpr.332,MEG 293,Hope, Bau.
  houlbən EPD,BBC,Schr.524,Horn
  oubən PNE&W
  -oub- DEPN
Holbrook
  houlbruk EPD,BBC,Bchm.37
  hɔl- EPD,Bchm.37
Holburn/Nb
  houbə:n H.A.(2)45
Holcombe
  hɔlkəm BBC
Holcombe Burnell/D
  houkəm PND 442,DEPN
  - bə:nel BBC
  - bə:nəl BCE
Holcombe Rogus/D
  houkəm rougəs BBC,BCE
Holcot/Bd (also spelt -cut)
  hʌkət PNBdHu 127,DEPN,Hope

Holcot/Np
  houkət PNNp 139
Holcroft/La
  houlkrɔft EPD,Bchm.115
  -krɔ:ft EPD
Holden (as in H.Clough/WRY,H.Fold/
  hould(ə)n EPD
Holdenby/Np
  houmbi PNNp 85
Holden Fm/Wt
  hɔ:dn, ouldn PNWt 152
Holderness/ERY (a peninsula)
  'houldənes BBC
  ˊ _ _ ˊ Schr.
  houldənis Kruis.
  ouðərnes Ellis 532
Holdfast/Wo
  houldfɑ:st EPD
Holdsworth/WRY
  hɔldə,holdəþ Hope,Schr.
  houldzwə:þ EPD
  houldzwəþ Schr.,Kruis.
Hole (a common p.n. element)
  houl EPD
Holebiggerah/La
  (h)o:l bigre: PNLa 211
Hole House/WRY
  ɔ:l aus DDd 13
Hole Syke/WRY
  houl saik Hope
Holford/So
  houlfəd EPD,Bchm.37
  hɔl- Bchm.37,ESpr.332
Holincote/So
  hʌnikʌt Hope
Holker/La
  hɔ:kə PNLa 197
  hukə BBC,BCE,Hope
  oukər Ellis 627 (for Lwr H./L
  houkə DEPN
Holkham/Nf
  hɔlkəm BBC
  houlkəm BCE
Holland/Li
  hɔlənd EPD,Schr.
Holland Pk/Ldn
  hɔlm pɑ:k HL 1o18
Hollesley/Sf
  hauzli DSf 272
  houzli BBC,BCE,DEPN,Hope
Hollicondane/K
  hɔlikɔndein PNK
Hollies/St
  hɔliz BBC
Hollin Bush/WRY
  ɔlin busk DDd 15
Hollingworth/Chs
  (h)ɔliŋwərþ, olim
  ɔliŋwuþ PNChs II/vii
  ɔliŋwəþ GlossChs

Hollin Hall/WRY
  ɔlin   DHd 78
Hollins
  hɔlinz   EPD
  ɔlinz   DDd 12
Holloway
  hɔləwei   EPD,Schr.
  hɔluwei   EPD
Holly (as in H.Bank/Db)
  hɔli   EPD
Hollywell Ho/Chs
  olim hæli-   PNChs III/144
Holman (as in H.'s Bridge Bk)
  houlmən   EPD
Holmbury St. Mary/Sr
  'houmbəri snt 'mɛəri   BBC
Holmby Ho/Np
  houmbi   EPD
Holme
  houm   Schr.
Holme/Nf
  houm   BBC
  hɔlm   Hope
Holme/We
  houm   PNWe I/60
Holme/NRY
  oum   PNYN 224
Holme/WRY
  oun, oum   PNYW II/269
  oum   DHd 80
  houn   PNSWY 171
Holme/WRY (r.n.)
  houn   RN 199
  oum   DHd 80
-holme (see note below)
Holme Fell/WRY
  oum fel   Hedev.35
Holme Ho Fm, H.Bank,H.St/Chs
  houm   PNChs III/251 and 282
Holme Moss/WRY
  'houm 'mɔs   BBC
  oum mɔs   DHd 80
Holmer/He
  houmə   PNHe(i)143
  houlmə   EPD
Holmer Gn/Bk
  houmə   PNBk 155,DEPN,BBC
Holmes/La,Yorks.
  houmz   EPD,Schr.,Kruis.,
        MEG 293
Holmes Chapel/Chs
  ouəmz   PNChs II/ix
  houmz   PNChs II/278
  uːmz tʃapil   GlossChs
Holmesdale/K and Sr
  houmzdeil   EPD

Holme upon Spalding Moor/ERY
  oum   PNYE 234
Holme Stye/WRY
  oum stɔ:, older form:
  oum sti: DHd 80
Holme on the Wolds/ERY
  oum   PNYE 163
Holmewood Ho/Wt
  huːmwud   PNWt 285
Holm Field/WRY
  aum feild   DDd 15
Holmfirth/WRY
  'houm'fəːþ   BBC
  oumfɔrþ   DHd 80
Holm Hall/Nf
  houm   Hope
Holmpton/ERY
  umptən, umtən   PNYE 21
  umptn,umtn   GlossHol 17
  (h)ʌmptən   Hope
  houmtən   BBC
Holmston Hall/Chs
  houmstən   PNChs III/165
Holne/D
  houl   PND 301,DEPN
  hɔːl   HL 1111
  houn   BBC,BCE
Holnest/Do
  houlnest   PNDo(i)216
  hɔlnest   BBC
Holnicote/So
  hʌnikət   BBC
  hʌnəkət   Hancock 194
  l is silent   Elw.204
Holsworthy/D
  hɔlzəri   PND 146,DEPN
  houlzwəːði   BBC
  houlzəri   DHtl 8
Holt
  hoult   EPD,Schr.,Kruis.
  oult, out   DHd 80 (for H. in
                 Yorks. p.ns)
Holtby/NRY
  outbi   PNYN 9 and 239
  houltbi   EPD
Holtham/Ha
  houlþəm, houðəm   Bchm.229
Holthead/WRY
  oultjed   DHd 80
Holton
  houtn   DSf 272
  hɔltən, houltən   BCE (for H. in
                   Sf)
  hɔlt(ə)n, hoult(ə)n   BBC

_) "Holme, as a termination, is usually pron. 'am' [i.e. -əm]"
  (GlossCu(i)xvii).

Holton-cum-Beckering/Li
  hoult(ə)n kʌm bekəriŋ   BBC
  houltən   -   -   BCE
Holton Heath/Do
  hɔlt(ə)n hi:þ   BBC
Holtridge/Chs
  ɔ:tridʒ   PNChs III/1o9
Holtye Fm/Sx
  houl 'tai   PNSx 367,BBC,BCE
Holwell Fm/Do
  houlwel   PNDo(i)1oo
Holworth/Do
  hɔləd   PNDo(i)143,PNDo I/14o
  hɔl-   DEPN
  houlwə:þ   PNDo I/14o
Holybourne/Ha
  hɔlibɔ:n   BBC,BCE,HL 733
  hɔli-   DEPN
Holycross/Wo
  houlikrɔ(:)s   EPD
Holyport/Brk
  hɔlipɔ:t   BBC
Holystone/Nb
  houlistoun   BBC
Holywell
  hɔliwel   EPD,Schr.,MEG 126
    -w(ə)l   EPD
    -wl   Kruis.
Holywell/Bk
  hɔliul   PNBk 71
Holywell/Du
  hɔliwəl   PNNbDu 116
Holywell/Hu
  hɔliwəl   PNBdHu 2o9,DEPN
Holywell/Nb
  haliwel   PNNbDu 116
Holywell/O,So
  hɔliwel   PNO 21,BBC,BCE
          (for H. in So)
Holywell/Wo
  hɔliwɔ:l   PNWo 51
Holywell Gn/WRY
  hɔliwel gri:n   Hope
Holywell Row/Sf
  hɔliwel rou   BBC,BCE
Holywell St/Ldn
  hɔliwel   PNNbDu 116 (!)
Holywick/Bk
  hɔliwik,hæliwik   PNBk 179
Homer/Sa
  houmə   EPD,Kruis.
Homer Gn/Ldn
  houməgri:n   BBC
Homersfield/Sf
  hɔməzfi:ld,
  hʌməzfi:ld   BBC,BCE,HL 187
    -ʌ-   DEPN
Homerton/Ldn
  hɔmət(ə)n   EPD

Homildon/Nb ⟶ Humbleton
Homington/W
  hʌmiŋtən   PNW 223
Hondslough Fm/Chs
  hɔnslou, hɔnzlou   PNChs III/2?
Hone/Sx
  hu:n   Hope
Honeybourne/Wo
  hʌnibʌn   PNWo 264,GlossSEWo 8?
  hʌnibɔ:n, -bɔən, -buən   EPD
  -uə-   Bchm. 51
Honeycomb/Co
  hʌnikoum   EPD,Kruis.
Honey Head/WRY
  ɔnjərd, ɔnjəd   DHd 78
Honicknowle/D
  hʌniknoul   PND 237
  hɔniknoul   BBC
Honiley/Wa
  hʌnili: PNWa 213
  hɔnili   BBC
Honing/Nf
  houniŋ   BBC,BCE,DEPN
Honingham/Nf
  hʌniŋəm   BBC,BCE,DEPN
Honington/Sf
  honiŋtən, hʌniŋtən   BBC
Honington/Wa
  hʌniŋtən   PNWa 281
Honiton/D
  hʌnitən   PND 347 and 639,DEPN,
           BCE
  hɔnitən   BBC,BCE,Schr.,Chis.
  hɔnitn, loc. hʌnitn   EPD,Bchm.
Honley/WRY
  hɔnli   BBC
  ɔnli   DHd 78
Honley Head/WRY ⟶ Honey Head
Hoo/K
  hu: PNK
Hood Grange/NRY
  ud   PNYN 195
Hooe/D,Sx
  hu: BBC,BCE (for H. in Sx),
        PNSx(i)88
Hook/W,WRY
  huk   PNW(i)1o3,EPD
  hu:k, uk   PNYW II/2o
Hooke/Do
  huk   EPD
Hookedrise/D
  rukəraiz   PND 614
Hookney/D
  huknə   PND 47o
Hook Norton/O
  loc. hɔgz-   H.A.(2)46
Hoole/Chs
  hu:l   PNChs III/129

Hooley (as in H.Bridge/La)
 huːli   EPD
Hoon/Db
 huːn   PNDb(i) I/264
Hoo St. Werburgh/K
 huː snt wəːbəːg   BBC
 - sənt -   BCE
Hoose/Chs
 (h)uːs   PNChs IV/293
Hooton/Chs
 huːtən,huːtn   PNChs IV/189
Hooton Pagnell/WRY
 hutn panəl   PNYW I/87
 huːt(ə)n pægnəl,
 hʌt(ə)n pænl   BBC
 huːtən pægnəl   BCE
 hʌtən pænəl   BCE,Hope
Hope/Cu,Db
 houp   PNDb(i) I/144
 hwoup   GlossCu xvii
Hopebeck/Cu
 hɔbək   GlossCu xvii
Hopton
 hɔptən   EPD,Schr.
Hopwas/St
 hɔpwəs   BBC,BCE
 hɔpəs   BBC,BCE,DEPN,Hope
 ɔpəz   Ellis 482
Horbury/WRY
 hɔːbəri   EPD
Horcum/NRY
 ɔːkəm   PNYN 91
Horham/Sf
 hɔrəm   BBC,BCE,DEPN
Horkesley/Ess
 hɔsli   PNEss 392
Hormaly/Ess
 houm'lai   EssDD 159
Hornby/La
 hɔːnbi   PNLa(ii)
Horncastle/Bk,Li
 'hɔːnkaːsl   EPD
Horncliffe/Nb
 haːkli   PNNbDu 117
Horne/Sr
 hɔːn   EPD
Horner/So
 hɔːnə   EPD
Horninglow/St
 hɔːniŋlou   BBC
Horningsea/Ca
 olim hɔːnsi   PNCa 145,Hope
 hɔːniŋsi   ONCa 181
Horningsham/W
 olim hɔːrnisəm   PNW 168
Horningsheath/Sf (also called
       Horringer)
 -iŋz-   Dodgson(2)375

Hornsea/ERY
 hɔːnsiː   Chis.
Hornsey/Mx
 hɔːnzi   PNMx(i),EPD,BBC,Schr.
Horringer/Sf (also called Hornings-
                        heath)
 hɔrindʒə   Dodgson(2)375,BBC
Horringford/Wt
 harmvərd, (h)arimfərd   PNWt 13
Horrocks/La
 hɔrəks   EPD
Horscroft Copse/Wt
 haskraf kaps   PNWt 286
Horse/Cu,We
 hɔːs   PNE'side 75
Horseheath/Ca
 hɔːshiːþ   ONCa 194
Horsell/Sr
 hɔːsl   BBC
Horsepath/O
 hɔːspəþ   PNO(i)132
Horsewell/D
 hɔːswəl   Mawer(2)103
Horsey/Nf,So,Sx
 hɔːsi   BBC
Horseye/Sf
 hɔː'sai   BBC,BCE
Horsham/Sx,Wo
 hɔːsəm   PNWo 64,Mawer(2)94[1](for H.
              in Sx),MEG 377,PNSx 225
 hɔːʃəm   BBC,Schr.,Kruis.,MEG 377
 hɔːʃ(ə)m   EPD,Bchm.228
 hɔːshæm (rarely used)   Schr.,Bchm.
                                228
Horsham St. Faith/Nf
 hɔːʃəm snt feiþ   BBC
 -        - feiz   Hope
Horsley/Sr
 hɔːzli   BBC,EPD("loc. more fre-
                     quent")
 hɔːsli   EPD
Horslip Bridge/W
 hɔslip   PNW 295
Horsmonden/K
 hɔːsmən'den   EPD,BBC
 hɔːsn'den   EPD ("old-fashioned
                    loc. pron.")
 hɔːzmʌnden   PNK
Horstages/Ess
 hɔstidʒiz   PNEss 423
Horsted Keynes/Sx
 keinz   PNSx 336
 hɔːstid -   BBC
 hɔːstəd -   BCE
Horstow/Li
 hɔstou   Hope
Horton
 hɔːtən   Schr.
 hɔːtn   EPD

1) "now rarely pron. as Horsam" (Mawer(2)94).

Horton/Chs
   hɔːrtən   PNChs IV/xii
Horwich/La
   hɔridʒ   EPD,DEPN,Schr.,BCE,
            Kruis.,HL 969
   hɔritʃ   BBC,BCE,Schr.
Horwood/Bk
   hɔrud   PNBk 68
Hotham/ERY
   uðəm   PNYE 225
   hʌðəm   BBC
Hothersall/La
   ɔðəsə,ɔðəsl   PNLa 145
   hɔð-   DEPN
Hothfield/K
   hɔþfiːld   BBC,BCE
Hothorpe/Np
   houþɔːp   PNNp 115
Hoton/Le
   hout(ə)n   BBC
   houtən   BCE
   -ou-   DEPN
Hotwells/So
   hɔtwelz   BBC
Hough/Chs (see also s.n. Thornton
   hʌf   EPD,BBC,Schr.,   H.)
         MEG 287,Kruis.
   hɔf   EPD,Schr.
   uf   GlossChs
Hough (nr Alderly)
   ð uf   GlossChs 43o
The Hough (in Eddisbury Hd)
   þə 'huf   PNChs III/263
Hough, loc. The Hough (in Maccles-
              field Hd)
   þuf   PNChs II/vii
   t ʌf   PNChs I/221
Hough (in Nantwich Hd)
   (h)ʌf   PNChs III/64
Hough (Old H.) (in Northwich Hd)
   uf, ʌf   PNChs II/262
Hough/Cu
   hʌf   Hope
Hough/Li
   hɔf   GlossLi 237
Houghall/Du
   hɔfəl   PNNbDu 118,BCE
   hɔfl   EPD,BBC
   -ɔf-   DEPN
Hougham/K
   hʌfəm   EPD,DEPN,BBC,BCE,
         PNK,MEG 287
Hough Bridge/Chs (nr Bradley)
   huf   PNChs IV/11
Hough Bridge/Chs (nr Malpas),
Hough Fm/Chs
   hʌf   PNChs IV/4o

Hough End Hall/La
   huːzend   PNLa 31
Hough Green/Chs
   hʌf griːn   BBC,BCE
Hough-on-the-Hill/Li
   hʌf ɔn ðə hil,
   hɔf - - -   BBC,BCE
Houghpark/Db
   huf   PNDb 574
Hough's Bank/Chs
   uːks bɔŋk   GlossChs
Houghton
   hɔːtn, hautn   EPD,Kruis.
   houtn   EPD
   hautən,hɔːtən,houtən   Schr.
Houghton/Db (Stoney H.,New H.)
   hɔːtn   PNDb(i) I/266
Houghton/Ha
   hout(ə)n, haut(ə)n   BBC
   houtən, hautən   BCE
Houghton/Hu
   hout(ə)n   BBC
   houtən   BCE,PNHu 344[1]
   hautən   PNHu 344
Houghton/La
   hɔːt(ə)n, haut(ə)n   BBC
   hɔːtən, hautən   BCE
Houghton/Nf
   haut(ə)n, hout(ə)n   BBC
   houtən   BCE,Hope
   hautən   BCE
Houghton/Np
   houtən   PNNp 149,BCE
   hout(ə)n   BBC
Houghton/Sx
   houtən   PNSx 128,Hope
Houghton/WRY (Glass H.)
   haut(ə)n   BBC
Houghton/WRY (Gt H.,Little H.)
   hɔːtən   PNYW I/98,PNWRY lo4
   hautən   PNYW I/98
   hɔːt(ə)n   BBC
Houghton Bridge/Sx
   hout(ə)n bridʒ,
   haut(ə)n -   BBC
   houtən - , hautən -   BCE
Houghton Conquest/Bd
   haut(ə)n kɔŋkwest   BBC
Houghton-on-the-Hill/Le,Nf
   hout(ɔ)n ɔn ðə hil   BBC
Houghton Regis/Bd
   haut(ə)n riːdʒis   BBC
Houghton-le-Side/Du
   haut(ə)n lə said, - li -   BBC
   hautən lə said   BCE
Houghton-le-Spring/Du
   houtnlispriŋ   EPD

---

1) "It is usually called houtən by the inhabitants [...]. And som[e]
   call it hautən" (PNHu 344).

hout(ə)n lə spriŋ, - li - BBC
houtən lə spriŋ   BCE,Chis.
loc. hautn   EPD
hautən   GlossHtn viii
Houkler Hall/La
haukləhɔːl   PNLa 215
Houndsditch/Ldn
haunzditʃ   EPD,Schr.
haundzditʃ   EPD,Bau.
Hounslow/Mx
haunzlou   EPD,Schr.,Kruis.,
Chis.
Hounslow Gn/Ess
ɔnzlou   PNEss 47o
Housel Bay/Co
hauzl   EPD
Houtsay/We
huːtsə   PNE'side 62
Hove/Sx
huːv   PNSx 293,DEPN,Mawer(2)
99
houv   BBC
Hoveringham/Nt
hɔvriŋəm   PNNt 169
hɔvəriŋəm   BBC
- ɔ -   DEPN
Hoveton/Nf
hɔft(ə)n,
hʌft(ə)n, hɔvit(ə)n   BBC
hɔftən,hʌftən,hɔvətən   BCE
Hovingham/NRY
ɔvinəm,ouiŋəm   PNYN 51
hɔviŋəm   BBC,BCE
hɔviŋgəm   BCE
-ɔ-   DEPN
How/Co ⟶ Brown How(e)
Howa(r)th/La
hauəþ   PNLa 164
houəþ, -wəþ   Förster
Howbeck Bank/Chs
houbek   PNChs III/71
Howbrook Copse/Np
houbruːk   PNNp 154
Howden/ERY
oudn   PNYE 25o
haud(ə)n   BBC
haudən   Schr.
Howdon-on-Tyne/Nb
haud(ə)n ɔn tain   BBC
Howe
hau   EPD,Kruis.
ou   PNYN 224
Howell/Li
hauəl   EPD,Kruis.
Howgate Fm/Wt
hæugeit   PNWt 285
The Howgh/Db (f.n.)
hʌf   FnSDb 1o3

How Gill/We
haugil   DKe 145
Howgill/WRY
augil   DDd 14
hougil   Ellis 63o (for H. nr
Sedburgh)
Howgrave/NRY
ougriv   PNYN 22o
Howick/La,Nb
houik   PNNbDu 119,BBC,BCE (for H.
in Nb),DEPN (for H. in Nb)
hauik   EPD,Chis.
Howle/Sa
"pron. as a monosyllable"   PNSa
Howley/Gl,La,Sa
houli   BBC,BCE (for H. in So)
hauli   EPD
How Rigg/Cu (also spelt Howrigg)
hiurik   PNE'side 69,PNCu 331
(see also s.n. Hung Rigg)
Howsham/Li,ERY
hauʃəm,hauȝəm,hauzəm   BBC,BCE (for
H. in Li)
uːzəm   PNYE 145
Howthorpe/NRY
ouþrəp   PNYN 5o
Hoxall/Wt
(h)aksl, (h)ɔːksil   PNWt 166
Hoxne/Sf
hɔks(ə)n   BBC
hɔksən   PNSf 123,BCE,Hope
hɔksn   DEPN
Hoxton/Ldn
hɔkst(ə)n   EPD
Hoye's Fm/Wt
ɔiz   PNWt 184
Hoylake/Chs
'hɔileik   PNChs IV/299,EPD
Huby/NRY,WRY
iubi   PNYN 18,PNYW V/52
hjuːbi   BBC
Huccaby/D
hʌkəbi   BBC,BCE
Hucclecote/Gl
hʌklkout   BBC
Huckenden/Bk
hʌkiŋtən, hʌkiŋdən   PNBk 2o5
Hucklow/Db
hʌklou   PNDb(i) I/267
hʌklə   Thomp.68
Hucknall/Db ⟶ Ault H.
Hucknall/Nt
hʌknəl, -nl   EPD
Hucknall Torkard/Nt
uknətɔːkəd   PNNt 118
Hucknall under Huthwaite, also called
Dirty Hucknall/Nt
huþweit, dʌtiukn   PNNt 119
dʌti(h)ʌknə   PNNt(i)71

Huckworthy/D
 hʌkəri   PND 238
Huddersfield/WRY
 uðəzfild   PNYW II/295
 uðərsfild   Ellis 367,DHd 142
 uðəzfil   Ellis 367
 udərsfild   DHd 14o
 udəsfi:ld   Mawer(4)285
 ʌdzfi:ld   Lloyd 127
 hʌdəzfi:ld   EPD,Schr.,Chis.
 (see also note 1 below)
Huddisford/D
 ʌtsvə:d   PND 81
Huddlesceugh/Cu
 hudlskiuf   PNCu 216,PNE'side
                71
 hudlskə   GlossCu xvii
 older pro.: hudlskiukw
                PNE'side 71
Huddleston/WRY
 hʌdlstən   EPD
Hudscales/Cu
 hudskəlz   PNCu 279
 hudskilz   PNE'side 68
Huggate/ERY
 ugit   PNYE 173
 hʌgit   BBC
 hʌgət   BCE
Hugh Croft/WRY
 jou krɔft   DDd 13
Hughenden/Bk (also spelt
             Hitchenden)
 u:əndən   PNBk 182
 hiltʃəndəm [sic] Hope
 hitʃəndən   Schr.,Hope
 hju:əndən   EPD,Schr.
Hughley/Sa
 "with stress on the last sylla-
Hugill/We   ble"(PNSa)
 'hiugil   PNWe I/169
 hju:gil   BBC,BCE
Huish/D,So,W (also spelt Hewish)
 huiʃ, juiʃ   PNW(i)lo3
 hju:iʃ   BBC,BCE (for H. in D),
             Kruis.
 (see also s.n. Great H.)
Hulcott/Bk
 hʌkət   PNBk 151,DEPN
Hull/ERY (=Kingston upon Hull)
 ul   PNYE 2o9
 ɔl   DSEY 3o
 hʌl   EPD,Schr.
 hɔl   DSWY 113
 hul   GlossSWLi

Hull/ERY (r.n.)
 ʌl   Lloyd 127
 hɔl   DSh 48
 hul   DYorks.5o
 hʌl   EPD,Schr.
Hulland/Db
 hʌlənd   PNDb(i) II/268
Hullavington/W
 hʌliŋtən   PNW 71,PNW(i)lo4,DEPN,
             Hope,BBC,BCE
 hʌ'læviŋtən   BBC,BCE
Hulme
 hju:m   EPD,Schr.,Chis.
 hu:m   EPD
 hʌlm   Schr.
Hulme/Chs
 hu:m, hju:m   PNChs II/ix
Hulme (Church H.)/Chs
 hju:m   PNChs II/278
Hulme/La
 hju:m   PNLa 33,BBC,BCE
 hu:m   PNLa 33,Hope
Hulme/St
 hju:m, hu:m   BBC,BCE
Hulme Walfield/Chs
 hju:m wɔ:l-   PNChs II/3o2
Hulne/Nb
 hul   PNNbDu 12o,DEPN
 hʌl   HL 1111
Hulse/Chs
 hʌls   EPD
Hulverstone/Wt
 (h)ʌvərstn, (h)ʌlərstn   PNWt 74
 hʌlvəstən   DWt,s.n.hooast
Humber (p.n. and r.n.)
 hʌmbə   EPD,Schr.,Kruis.,Chis.
 umər   GlossHol 17
Humbleton/Nb (also called Homildon
             and Holmedon)
 hʌmbltən   Schr.
 hɔmildən   Schr.,s.n.Homildon
 houmdən   Schr.,s.n.Holmedon
 hɔm(i)ldən   EPD,s.n.Homildon
Humbleton/ERY
 uməltən   PNYE 54
 hʌməltən   Hope
Humshaugh/Nb
 hʌmzhɑ:f   BBC,BCE
Huncote/Le
 hʌnkout   BBC
Hungerford
 hʌŋgəfɔ:d   Schr.
 hʌŋgəfəd   Chis.

1) 'Uthersfield', the transcription given in PNSWY 178,is ambiguous
   as to the quality of the first vowel.

Hungerford Newtown/Brk
  hʌŋgəfəd nju:taun BBC
Hunger Hill/We
  huŋrəl,huŋəril PNE'side 68
Hungerton/Le,Li
  hʌŋgətən BBC
Hung Rigg/Cu
  hiurik PNE'side 69
Hungry Hill/Wt
  hʌŋgərhil PNWt 286
Hunmanby/ERY
  unənbi,
  umənbi,uməbi PNYE 1o8
  hʌnmənbi BBC
  hʌnənbi Hope
Hunning Hall/Wt
  hʌnihil PNWt 68
Hunnyhill/Wt
  hʌni hil DWt,s.n.Forest Ho
Hunsdon/Hrt
  hʌnzdən Schr.
Hunslet/WRY
  hʌnslit BBC
  hʌnslet BCE
Hunstanton/Nf
  hʌnstən EPD ("loc."),BBC,BCE,
           PNHu 35o,EPN 86,Hope,
           Bchm.85,HL 1o59,
           Kruis.,Schr.524
  hʌn'stæntən BBC,BCE,EPD,Schr.,
              Bchm.85
  'hʌnstæntən Schr.524
  hʌnstn DEPN
Hunstanworth/Du
  huntənwud PNNbDu 121
Hunsterson/Chs
  (h)unstəsn PNChs III/65
Hunter's Nab/WRY
  næb DA1&Hd,s.n.Nab
Hunsworth/WRY
  hʌnzwə(:)Þ EPD
Huntingdon/Hu
  hʌntiŋdən EPD,BBC,Schr.,Chis.
Huntingdonshire
  hʌntiŋdənʃiə, -ʃə EPD
Huntingford/Do,Gl
  hʌntiŋfəd EPD
Huntington
  hʌntiŋtən EPD,Schr.
Huntley/Gl,St
  hʌntli EPD
Hunton
  hʌntən EPD
Hunts. (short for Huntindonshire)
  hʌnts EPD
Huntsham/D
  hʌnsəm PND 54o
Huntshaw/D
  hʌnʃɔ: BBC,BCE

Huntspill/So
  hʌntspil BBC
Hunwick/Du
  hʌnwik BBC,BCE
Hunwick's Fm/Ess
  hʌnəks PNEss 412
Hurdcott/W
  hə:rkət PNW 384
Hurdsfield/Chs
  olim u:tsfilt,
  hərdz-, hərtsfi:ld PNChs II/vii
  utsfilt GlossChs
Hurleston/Chs
  (h)ərlstən PNChs III/146
Hurlingham/Ldn
  hə:liŋəm EPD
Hurlstone Point/So
  hə:lstən EPD
Hurst Gn/Ess
  ðə hə:st, hə:s PNEss 331
Hurstmonceux/Sx ⟶ Herst-
Hurtspierpoint/Sx
  'hə:stpiə'pɔint EPD,BBC
Husborne Crawley/Bd
  olim hʌzbənd PNBdHu 118
  -z- DEPN
Hussey Gn/Sf
  hʌsi EPD
Hussingtree/Wo
  hʌsəntri: PNWo 213
Husthwaite/NRY
  ustwit PNYN 191
Hustley Mire/Cu
  huslə maiər PNE'side 63
Huthwaite/Nt
  hʌÞweit PNNt(i)72,BBC,BCE
  hju:Þweit BBC,BCE
  hu:Þweit EPD
  -ʌ- DEPN
  (see also s.n. Hucknall)
Huthwaite/NRY,WRY
  iuÞwit PNYN 177
  (for transcriptions in BBC and EPD
  see s.n. Huthwaite/Nt)
Hutton
  hʌtən Schr.
  hʌtn EPD
Hutton/ERY
  jutn Hope
Hutton Buscel (or H. Bushel)/NRY
  hʌtən buʃəl BCE,Hope
  hʌt(ə)n buʃl BBC
Hutton Cranswick/ERY ⟶ Cranswick
Hutton-le-Hole/NRY
  'hʌt(ə)nli'houl BBC
Hutton Roof/Cu,We
  ri:əf PNCu 21o
  (h)utn ru:f PNWe I/35
  hutn riuf PNE'side 71

Hutton Sceugh/Cu
   hutn skiuf   PNCu 279,
               PNE'side 71
Hutton Soil/Cu
   hutən sjul   GlossCu xvii
Hutton Wandesley/WRY
   (h)utn wanzlə   PNYW IV/253
Huxley/Chs
   hʌksli   EPD,Kruis.
Huyton with Roby/La
   hait(ə)n wið roubi   BBC
   haitn   PNLa 113
   haitən   BCE
   -ai-   DEPN
Hyam/W
   haiəm   EPD
Hyde
   haid   EPD
Hyde/Chs
   olim ei:d, haid   PNChs II/vii
Hyde Pk/Ldn
   'haid'pɑːk, ⌐   EPD
   _ ⌐   EPD,Kruis.

   aid pɑːk   CPhon 164
Hykeham/Li
   haikəm   BBC
Hylton/Du
   hilt(ə)n   EPD
Hyson Gn/Nt
   haisn   EPD
Hythe/K
   haið   EPD,DEPN,Schr.,Chis.

I

Ibberton/Do
  ebərtn   DDo
Ible/Db
  ibəl   PNDb 38o
Ibstone/Bk
  ipstən   PNBk 185
Ickham/K
  ikəm   PNK
Icklesham/Sx
  ikəlsəm   PNSx 51o
  iklʃəm   BBC,BCE
Ickleton/Ca
  ikltən   ONCa 25
Icknield Street (Roman Road)
  ikni:ld   EPD
Ickornshaw/WRY
  'ikɔnʃɔ: PNYW VI/13
  'ikɔ:nʃɔ: EPD
Icomb/Gl
  ikəm   PNGl I/22o,BBC,BCE
Iddesleigh/D
  idʒli   PND 93,Mawer(2)94,
         Zachr.(3)13o
  idzli   EPD,BBC,Schr.,Kruis.,
         Bchm.78
  idzlei   Bchm.78
  idəzli   Schr.
Iddinshall/Chs
  idənʃɔ:(1),
  idinʃɔ:l,idnʃɔ:(1)
            PNChs III/286
Ide/D
  i:d   PND 497,EPD,DEPN,BBC,BCE
Ideford/D
  idifəd   PND 474,DEPN
  idfəd   BBC
Iden/K,Sx
  aidn   EPD,PNSx(i)93
  aid(ə)n   BBC
  aidən   PNK,BCE (for I. in Sx)
  ai-   DEPN (for I. in Sx)
Idle/Li,Nt (r.n.)
  ai-   DEPN
Idle/WRY
  aidl   BBC,BCE
Idlecombe/Wt
  aidə(l)kəm   PNWt 1ol
Idless/Co
  i:dlis   BBC
Idridgehay/Db
  iðəsi   PNDb(i) I/143
  iðəsə   Brushf.67
  iðəsi: Hope
  iðəsei   BCE
  'aidridʒhei   BBC,BCE
Iffley/O
  ifli   EPD

Ifield/K
  aifi:ld   BCE,PNK
  ai-   DEPN
Ifield/Sx
  aivəl   PNSx 2o7
  aifi:ld   PNSx(i)93
Iford/Sx
  aivərd   PNSx 317
  aifəd   PNSx(i)94,BCE
  ai-   DEPN
Ightenhill Pk/La
  aitn(h)il   PNLa 82
  ait-   DEPN
Ightham/K
  aitəm   EPD,DEPN,BCE,PNK,Kruis.
Iken/Sf
  aikən   BCE,DEPN
Ilam/St
  ailəm   BBC
Ilchester/So
  iltʃistə   EPD,BBC,Schr.
  iltʃəstə   Chis.
Ilford/Ess,So,Sx
  ilfəd   EPD,BBC
Ilfracombe/D
  ilfrəku:m   EPD ($\prime$ _ _ , _ _ $\prime$);
          Schr. ($\prime$ _ $\prime$),Kruis.;
          Chis.($\prime$ _ _);Hope
Ilkeston/Db
  ilkistən   BBC
  ilkestən   BCE
  ilkəstən   Chis.
  ilsn   Hope,Ellis 445
Ilketshall/Sf
  ilkiʃɔ:l   BBC
Ilkley/WRY
  ilklə, formerly also
  i:flə   PNYW IV/21o
  i:Þlə   Hope
  ilkli   EPD,Schr.
Illingworth/WRY
  ilinwə(:)Þ   EPD
Ilminster/So
  ilminstə   EPD,Chis.
Illmire/Bk → Ilmer
Illogan/Co
  i'lʌgən   BBC,BCE,DEPN
  i'lougən   EPD
Ilmer/Bk (also spelt Illmire)
  ilmə   BCE
Ilsley Walton/Le
  i:zli wɔ:tən   Hope
Immingham/Li
  iminhəm   BBC
Impington/Ca
  impintən   ONCa 25

Ince/Chs,La
   ins   PNChs III/251,EPD
Inditch/Db (f.n.)
   indaik   FnSDb 74
Ing/WRY ⟶ Round Ing
Ingatestone/Ess
   iŋgətstən   PNEss 253
   'iŋgeitstoun   EPD,BBC
   'in-   EPD
Ingbirchworth/WRY
   bə:tʃwəþ   Hope
Ingelburne/W
   iŋgəlbərn   PNW(i) lo6
Ingestre/St
   iŋgəstri:,iŋgstə   Schr.
   iŋgestri   EPD
Ingham/Li,Nf,Sf
   iŋəm   EPD,Schr.,Kruis.
Ing Hill/We
   iŋ hil   PNE'side 68
Ingleborough/Nf,WRY
   iŋglb(ə)rə   EPD
Ingleborough Mountain/WRY
   iŋglbərə   Schr.,Chis.
   -bʌrə   Schr.
Ingleby/Db,Li,NRY
   iŋglbi   EPD
Inglesham/W
   iŋgəlsəm   PNW 28
   iŋgəls(h)əm   PNW(i)lo6
Inglewood/Cu
   iŋglwud   EPD,Schr.
Ingoldmells/Li
   'iŋgomelz   BCE
Ingoldsby/Li
   iŋg(ə)l(d)zbi   EPD
   iŋgldzbi   Schr.
   iŋgəl(d)zbi   Kruis.
Ingram/Nb
   iŋgrəm   EPD,Schr.,Kruis.
Ingrebourne/Ess (r.n.)
   'iŋgribɔ:n   EPD,BBC
   -bɔən   EPD
Ingrow/WRY
   iŋgrə   PNYW VI/4
Inholms Gill/Sx
   gil   PNSx 2o3
Inkerman/Nt
   'iŋkəmən   EPD
   'inkə'mæn   Schr.
Inny/Co (r.n.)
   ini   Schr.
Instow/D
   instou   BBC
Intack/WRY
   intak   DDd 12
Intake/WRY
   intæk, intək   DHd 126

Inwardleigh/D
   inəli, iŋəli   PND 149
Inwood/So
   inwud   EPD
Iping/Sx
   aipiŋ   PNSx 22,PNSx(i)95
   ai-   DEPN
Ipplepen/D
   iplpen   BCE
Ippolitts/Hrt ⟶ St. Ippolyts
Ipswich/Sf
   ipsidʒ   DSf 274,MEG 213[1]
   ipswitʃ   EPD,Schr.,Kruis.,Chis
          HL 969,ONwick 375,Hop
          MEG 213,ESpr.381
   ipsitʃ   Hope,ONwick 375
Irby/Chs,Li
   ə:rbi   PNChs IV/264,BCE (for I
          Li)
   iəbi   BCE (for I. in Li)
Irby Manor/NRY
   ɔrbi   PNYN 218
Irchester/Np
   ɑ:tʃestə   PNNp 192
Ireleth/La
   aiələþ   PNLa 2o5
   ai -   DEPN
Ireley Fm/Gl
   aiərli   PNGl II/16
Ireton/Db ⟶ Kirk I.
Irlams o' th' Height/La
   'ə:ləmz o 'ðait   BCE
Irnham/Li
   ə:nəm   BCE
Irthing/Cu,Nb (r.n.)
   ə:ðiŋ   RN 212,DEPN
Irthlingborough/Np
   ɑ:təlbərə, jɑ:təlbərə   PNNp 1
   ə:þliŋbərə   BBC
   ɑ:tlbərə   DEPN
Irton/NRY
   ɔrtən   PNYN lol
   hɔtn   Hope
Irwell/La (r.n.)
   ə:wel   BBC
   ə:wəl   Schr.
Isel/Cu (also spelt Isell)
   aisəl   PNCu 267,BCE
   ai-   DEPN
Isfield/Sx
   izvəl   PNSx 396
   isfi:ld   BBC
Isham/Np
   aisəm   PNNp 127,DEPN
   aiʃəm   BCE,BG
Isington/Ha
   iziŋtən   BBC

1) "The old pron. [ipsidʒ] is now disappearing" (MEG 2o5).

Isis/O (r.n.)
   aisis   EPD,DEPN,Schr.,Kruis.,
               BCE
Isle Fm/Chs
   aiəl, ail   PNChs IV/58
Isleham/Ca
   izləm   PNCa 192
   aizləm   ONCa 178,DEPN,BCE
Isle of Wight
   'ail əv 'wait   BBC
   _ _ ◡   MEG 153

Isleworth/Mx
   aizəlwa:þ   PNMx 27,PNE&W
   aizlwə(:)þ   EPD
   aizlwa:þ   DEPN,BBC,BCE,Hope
   aizəl-   PNMx(i)
   ilswa:þ, aislwa:þ   Hope
Islington/Ldn,Nf,WRY
   izlintən   EPD,BBC,Kruis.,
              Chis.,DEPN (for I.
              in Ldn),Schr, (for
              I. in Ldn)
   izlintən   CPhon 129
Islip/Np,O
   ai(s)lip,islip   Schr.
   izlip   BBC

   for I. in Np:
   aizlip   PNNp 183,DEPN
   aislip   BCE,Hope,Ellis 219

   for I. in O:
   aislip   PNO 221,PNO(i)137,BCE,
           DEPN,EPN,Meiklejohn
           17o(note)
   ailip   Bchm.232
Itchall/Wt
   i:tʃəl   PNWt 286
Itchen/Ha;Wa (r.n.)
   itʃin   EPD
   itʃən   Schr.
Itchen/Ha
   itʃin   EPD
Itchenor/Sx
   itʃinɔ: BBC
Itonfield/Cu
   aitnfi:ld   PNE'side 76
Itteringham/Nf
   -inəm, -iŋəm   PNing 172
Ittinge/K
   -indʒ   Dodgson(2)34o
Ivel/Bd,Hrt (r.n.)
   ai-   DEPN
Ivelet/NRY
   aivlət   PNYN 272
Iver/Bk
   aivə   EPD,DEPN
   ivə   Mawer(4)284[1]

Iveston/Du
   aistən   PNNbDu 213
Ivinghoe/Bk
   'aiviŋhou   Chis.
Ivington/He
   iviŋtən   DEPN,BCE
Ivybridge/D
   aivibridʒ   EPD
Iwade/K
   'ai'weid   BCE,PNK
Iwerne/Do (r.n.)
   ju:-   DEPN
Iwerne Courtney, I. Minster/Do
   ju:ən   PNDo(i) 1o and 26
   ju:ə:n   BCE
   ju:ə:n kɔ:tni   BBC

1) "[...] can now no longer be traced" (Mawer(4)284).

J

Jacobstow/Co
　dʒeikəbstou　BBC
Jacques Hall/Ess
　dʒeiks　PNEss 329
Jaggard (as in J.'s Ho/W)
　dʒægəd　EPD
Jarrow/Du
　dʒærou　EPD,Schr.,Kruis.
　dʒærə　DSDu
Jarvis (as in J.Brook/Sx)
　dʒɑːvis　EPD
Jaspers (as in J.Gn/Ess)
　dʒæspəz, rarely -ɑː-　EPD
Jay/He
　dʒei　EPD
Jaywick/Ess (or Jay Wick)
　dʒeiwik　BBC
Jeckyll's Fm/Ess
　dʒiglziz　PNEss 427
Jenkin/Chs
　dʒeŋkin, dʒen-　EPD
Jennings/K
　dʒeniŋz　EPD
Jenny (as in J.Gn/La)
　dʒeni,dʒini　EPD
Jervaulx/NRY
　dʒɑːvis　PNYN 25o,PNE&W,BBC[1]
　　　　DEPN,Kruis.,Smith(1)293[2],
　　　　MEG 197
　dʒəːvou　PNYN 25o[3],EPD,DEPN,BBC,
　　　　BCE
　dʒɑːvou　EPD,BCE
　dʒəːvis　Kruis.
Jobsons/Wt
　dʒabsənz　PNWt 286
Jodrell Bank, J.Hall/Chs
　dʒɔdril, -əl,
　olim dʒɔːdril,
　dʒɔːðril, dʒɔɔðril　PNChs II/viii
　dʒɔdr(ə)l　EPD
Johnby/Cu
　dʒounbi,
　dʒwouənbi　PNCu 197
　dʒuːənbi　GlossCu xvii
　dʒoənbi　PNE'side 72
Johnny Gate/Db
　dʒounə geit　GlossSh 119
Jolby/NRY
　dʒoubi　PNYN 283

Joldwynds/Sr
　dʒouldwindz　BBC
Jolliffe (as in J.Row/Sr)
　dʒɔlif　EPD
Jordan/D
　dʒɔːdn　EPD
Jordanthorpe/WRY
　dʒəːdinþɔːp　GlossSh 12o
Julian Bower/We
　dʒiliən bouər　PNE'side 74
Jurston/D
　dʒesən　PND 425

1) "It appears that an old pron. [dʒɑːvis] is still used by some lo⸱
　speakers" (BBC).
2) "I have never heard the pron. Jervaulx as [dʒɑːvis], except at H⸱
　a little village at the head of the dale" (Smith(1)293).
3) "The usual modern pron.of the name is [dʒəːvou]; this is simply ⸱
　spelling pron. The dial.pron. [dʒɑːvis] is rapidly passing into
　disuse" (PNYN 251).

K

Kaber/We
  ke:bə PNWe II/5
Kateridden/NRY
  ke:t ridin PNYN 147
Kea/Co
  ki: BBC
Keadby/Li
  ki:dbi BBC
  kidbi GlossM&C,s.n.Kidby
Kearby/WRY
  kiəbi PNYW V/4o
Kearsley/La,Nb
  kə:zli BBC,EPD ("loc.")
  kiəzli EPD
Kearsney/K
  kə:zni EPD,BBC,BCE,PNK
Kearstwick/We
  kiəstwik PNWe I/43
Kearton/NRY
  kiətn, kə:tn EPD
Keckwick/Chs
  kekwik, olim
  k(j)egwidჳ PNChs II/ix
  kjegwidჳ GlossChs ("by old
            people")
Kedington/Sf (= Ketton)
  kediŋtən, ket(ə)n BBC[1]
  ketən BCE
Kedleston/Db
  kədlstn PNDb 58o
  'kedlstən EPD,BBC,Kruis.
  kelsn Hope
Keekle Beck/Cu (r.n.)
  ki:kl RN 223
Keele/Cu,St
  ki:l BBC
Kehelland/Co
  ki'helənd BBC
Keighley/WRY
  ki:þlə PNYW VI/2,Ellis 367
  keiþlə,keilə (obs.) PNYW VI/2
  keiþli PNE&W
  ki:þli PNWRY 111,PNSWY 187,
          EPD,DEPN,BBC,BCE,Hope,
          Kruis.,Chis.,MEG 285,
          BG,ESpr.389,Wyld 289
  ki:li PNWRY 111,PNSWY 187,
          Kruis.,Hope
  kaili Kruis.
  ki:χli MEG 286 (see also
          note 2)

Keigwin/Co
  kegwin EPD
Keinton Mandeville/So
  'kentən 'mændivil BBC
Keisby/Li
  keizbi, keisbi BBC,BCE
Keisley/We
  keisli PNE'side 7o
Kelbarrow/Cu,We
  kelbərə PNCu 183,PNE'side 67
Kelham/Nt
  keləm PNNt 187
Kellet/La
  kelt PNLa(ii)
Kelmscott/O
  kemzkɔt, kelmzkɔt PNO 325
  kemskət PNO(i)138,BBC,BCE
Kelsall/Chs
  kelsɔ:l,
  loc. kelsəl PNChs III/276
  older kelsə PNChs III/276,Hope
Kelsey
  kelsi,kelzi EPD
Kelshall/Hrt
  kelʃɔ:l, kelsi: PNHrt 159
Kelsick/Cu (also spelt -wick)
  kelsik ONwick 361,Hope
Kelvedon/Ess
  keldən EssDD 158 ("old-
      fashioned"),PNEss 29o
  kelvidən BBC
  kelvədən BCE
Kelvedon Hatch/Ess
  keldən hætʃ Hope
Kelynack/Co (also spelt -nach)
  ke'lainək,
  klainək BBC,BCE
Kemble/Gl
  kembl EPD
Kemp (as in K.'s Corner/K)
  kemp EPD
Kemerton/Gl
  kemətən PNGl II/59
Kemphill/Wt
  kem(h)il PNWt 33
Kemplah/NRY
  kemplə PNYN 151
Kempley/Cu
  kemplə PNE'side 64
Kempsey/Wo
  kemsi,kemzi BBC,BCE
Kemptown/D,Sx
  kemptaun BBC

1) "Older residents use only the second pron." (BBC).
2) "It is not called Keeley, as might be supposed, but as if written
  Keihley, wherein there seems to be a relic of a guttural sound"
  (DAl&Hd) and "[...] the younger generation of the district [are]
  no longer using the sound [viz. χ]" (Wyld 289).

Kemsing/K
  kemziŋ   PNK
Kenardington/K
  kenətən,
  kenədiŋtən   PNK
Kendal/We
  kendl   DKe 143,EPD
  kendəl   Schr.
Kenidjack/Co
  ki'nidʒæk   BBC
  kə'nidʒæk   BCE
  _ ˏ _   DEPN
Kenilworth/Wa (=Killingworth)
  ken(i)lwə(:)þ   EPD
  kenəlwəþ   Kruis.
  kenəlwə:þ   Schr.
  kiliŋwə:þ   Hope,Schr.,s.n.
           Killingworth
Kennardington/K
  ken'ɑ:diŋtən   BBC,BCE
Kennel (as in K.Cove Tarn/We)
  kenl   EPD
Kennerley/Wt
  kenərli   PNWt 153
  kenəli   EPD
Kennet/Brk,W (r.n.),Ca (p.n.
         and r.n.)
  kenit   EPD,Schr.
  kenət   ONCa 198
Kennet/La (r.n.)
  kʌnət   J.D.222
Kenninghall/Nf
  kenigl   Hope
Kennington/Brk,K,Ldn
  keniŋtən   EPD,Schr.
The Kennington Oval/Ldn
  ouvəl   Bau.,s.n.Oval
Kenny/So
  keni   EPD
Kennythorpe/ERY
  keniþrəp   PNYE 141
Kensal (as in K.Gn/Ldn)
  kensl   EPD
Kensham Gn/K
  -nʃ-   Dodgson(2)380
Kensington/Gl,La,Ldn
  kenziŋtən   EPD,Schr.,Kruis.
Kensington (South K.)/Ldn
  (underground station)
  kenzintən   CPP 66
Kent (county and r.n. in We)
  kent   EPD,BBC,Schr.
Kentchurch/He
  kentʃə:tʃ   Förster
Kenwick/Li,Sa
  kenik   BBC,BCE (for K. in Li)
Kenwood (as in K.Pk/WRY)
  kenwud   EPD

Kenworthy/Chs
  kenədi, kenə:ði   PNChs I/235
Kenwyn/Co
  kenwin   BBC
Kenyon/La
  kenjən   EPD,Schr.,Kruis.
  keniən   EPD
Kepier/Du
  ki:pjə   BBC,BCE
Kepwick/NRY
  kepik   PNYN 2ol,DEPN
Keresley/Wa (also spelt Kersley)
  kɛ:əzli   PNWa 174
  kɑ:zli   DEPN,BBC,BCE
  kɑ:sli   Hope
Kermincham/Chs
  k(j)ermidʒəm   PNChs II/ix
  kjermidʒəm   GlossChs
  kə:rmintʃəm, older local
  -idʒəm   PNChs II/281
Kern/Wt
  kə:rn   PNWt 56
Kernsham/D
  kə:nsən   DHtl 8
Kernstone/D
  kə:msən   PND 74
  kə:nsən   DHtl 8
Kerridge/Chs
  keridʒ   PNChs I/188
Kerr's End/Ess (now currently
         Causeway End)
  by old people: kɑ:z i:nd
                  EssDD 1
Kersal/La
  kə:zl   BBC
Kersal Moor/La
  kɑ:si muə   DSLa
  kæsə muə   DSLa,GlossR&R
Kersey/Sf
  kə:zi   EPD,Schr.
Kershope/Cu
  kə:səp   PNCu 61,BBC
  kɑ:səp   PNCu 61
Kersoe/Wo
  kesə   GlossSEWo 82
Kesgrave/Sf
  kezgreiv   BBC
Kesteven/Li
  'kestivən   BBC
  'kesti:vən   BCE
  -'i:-   DEPN
  kes'ti:v(ə)n   EPD
Keston/K
  kestn   PNK
Keswick/Cu
  kezik   EPD,Schr.,Kruis.,Chis.
         MEG 213
  kezwik   Chis.

Keswick/Cu
    kezik   PNCu 3ol,GlossCu xvii,
              PNE'side 7o,ONwick 361,
              DEPN,BBC,BCE,Hope
Keswick/Nf
    kesik   ONwick 374,Hope
    kezik   BBC
Keswick/WRY
    kezik   PNYW IV/184
Kettering/Np
    ketəriŋ   EPD,BBC
Kettle (as in K.Corner/K)
    ketl   EPD
Kettleshulme/Chs
    olim kjetlsum,
    ketəlzju:m   PNChs II/vii
    kjetlsəm   GlossChs
Kettleside/Cu
    ketlsaid   PNE'side 69
Kettlethorpe/ERY
    ketlþrəp   PNYE 225
Ketton/Sf ⟶ Kedington
Kew/Sr
    kju: EPD,Schr.,Kruis.,Chis.
Kew Gdns/Ldn
    ku: gɑ:dənz   CPhon 144
Kexb(o)rough/WRY
    kespə   Hope
Key/W (r.n.)
    ki: EPD
Keybridge Fm/Wo
    keibridʒ   PNWo 3o5
Keyhirst/Nb
    kɑ:(h)əst   PNNbDu 126
Keyingham/ERY
    kenigəm   PNYE 32,GlossHol 17
    keniŋəm   PNYE 32,Hope
    keniŋgəm   GlossHol 17
    keniŋhəm,
    keiiŋhəm, keninhəm   BBC
Keymer/Sx
    kaimə   PNSx 276,BBC,BCE,Hope,
              PNSx(i)97
    -ai-   DEPN
    ki:mə   BBC,BCE
Keynor Fm/Sx
    kainə   PNSx 86
Keynsham/So
    keinʃəm   BBC,BCE
Keysoe/Bd (also spelt Keyso)
    keisou   PNBdHu 14,DEPN,Hope
    ki:sou   BBC
Keyston/Hu
    olim kestən   PNBdHu 243

Keyworth/Nt
    loc. kjuəþ, otherwise
    ki:wə:þ   PNNt(i)73[1]
    ki:əþ   Hope
    kju:-   DEPN
Kidburngill/Cu
    kiprəngil   GlossCu xvii
Kidderminster/Wo
    kidi   Hope
    kidəminstə   EPD,Schr.,Chis.
    kidimistə   GlossSEWo 82
Kielder/Nb
    ki:ldə   BBC,BCE
Kilburn/Db,Ldn
    kilbən   EPD,Bchm.67,BBC (for K.
              in Ldn)
    kilbə:n   BBC (for K. in Db and
              Ldn),BCE (for K. in Db)
              EPD,Bchm.67
Kildale/NRY
    kildeil   EPD
Kildwick/WRY
    kildwik   BBC
Kilham/Nb,ERY
    kiləm   PNYE 97,EPD
Kilkhampton/Co
    kilk'hæm(p)tən   BBC
    kilkətən   DHtl 8
Killamarsh/Db
    'kiləmɑ:ʃ   BBC
Kill Croft/WRY
    kil krɔft   DDd 15
Killingholme/Li
    kiliŋhoum   BBC
Kilndown/K
    kilndaun   BBC
Kilnsea/ERY
    kilsi   PNYE 15,GlossHol 17
Kilnsey/WRY
    kilsə   PNYW VI/86
Kilnwick/ERY
    kilik   PNYE 16o,GlossHol 17
Kilnwick Percy/ERY
    kilik pə:si   Hope
    - piəsi   PNYE 179
Kilve/So
    kilv   BBC
Kimberley/Nt
    vulgo kimli   PNNt 148
    kimbəli   EPD,Schr.
Kimbolton/He,Hu
    olim kiməltən   PNBdHu 243,Schr.
    kim'boult(ə)n   EPD,BBC
    kim'boultən   Schr.

---

1) "The polite pron. is based entirely on the written form, whereas loc.
the etymologically correct form survives" (PNNt(i)74).

Kimmeridge/Do
   kiməridʒ   EPD
Kinder Scout/Db (a mountain)
   kində skaut   BBC
Kinderton/Chs
   kind-   PNChs II/236
Kineton/Gl,Wa (=Kington/Wa)
   kaintən   BBC
   kintən   PNWa 282,Schr.(for
                K. in Wa)
   ki:tn   Hope (for K. in Wa)
Kinfare/St ⟶ Kinver
Kingates Fm/Wt
   kiŋgəts   PNWt 183
Kingcombe/Do
   kiŋkəm   PNDo(i) 236
Kinglyvale/Sx
   kindəveil   Hope
Kingsbury
   kiŋzb(ə)ri   EPD
King's College/Ldn
   ˈ ˈ , but
   K.C.London: ˈ _ _ ˈ _   EPD

Kingscote/Gl,Sx
   kiŋzkət, -kout   EPD,Bchm.8o
King's Cross/Ldn
   kiŋz krɔ:s, ŋz krɔ:s   CPP 66
Kingskerswell/D
   kiŋzˈkə:zwəl   BBC
   ˈkiŋzˈkə:zwel   BCE
Kingsland/He
   kiŋzlənd, dial.
   kinzlənd   DHe 43
Kingsley
   kiŋzli   PNChs III/239,
             EPD,Kruis.
Kingsnympton/D
   kiŋz nimtən   BBC,BCE
Kingsteignton/D
   kiŋzteintən   BBC,BCE
Kingsterndale/Db
   kiŋˈstə:ndeil   BBC
Kingsthorpe/Np
   kiŋzþrəp   EDD,s.n.Thorpe
Kingston
   kiŋkstən,kiŋstən   EPD
   kiŋztən   Schr.

   kiŋstən   ONCa 21
   kiŋ(k)stn   PNWt 163
   kiŋstən   DWt,s.n.Lor a massey
Kingston Bagpu(i)ze/Brk
   kiŋstən bægpju:z   BBC,BCE
Kingston Blount/O
   kiŋstən blʌnt   BBC,BCE
Kingstone
   kiŋstən,kiŋkstən   EPD

1) "KYINE" in GlossSEWo 82.

Kingston-upon-Hull/ERY
   kiŋstən əpən hʌl   EPD
Kingstown/Cu
   kiŋztaun   EPD,Schr.
   kiŋstən,kiŋkstən   EPD
Kingsway/So
   kiŋzwei   EPD
Kingswear/D
   kiŋzwiə   BBC,BCE
Kingswinford/St
   kiŋˈswinfəd   BBC,BCE
Kington
   kiŋtən   Schr.
   kintən   DHe 43 (for K. in He)
   kaintən   PNW 8o and 1oo (for W
             K. and K.St.Michael/W
             PNWo 33o
   kain (?) GlossSEWo 82[1]
Kinoulton/Nt
   ki'nault(ə)n   BBC
   kin'aultən   BCE
Kinver (also spelt Kinfare)/St
   kinvou   Wilde 29
Kinwarton/Wa
   kinətən   PNWa 214,BCE,Hope
   kinətn   DEPN
   kinət(ə)n,kinwət(ə)n   BBC
   kinwətən   BCE
Kipling Cotes/ERY
   kipliŋ kouts   BBC,EPD
Kirby
   kə:bi   EPD,Schr.,BBC
           PNChs IV/294
Kirby Bedon/Nf
   kə:bi bi:d(ə)n   BBC
   - bi:dən   BCE
Kirdford/Sx
   ka:dfu:rd,keifu:rd   PNSx 1o2
   kə:dfuəd   Hope
   kə:dfəd   PNSx(i)98
Kirk (as a prefix)
   kə:k   EPD, DSDu
Kirkbampton/Cu ⟶ Kirkbanton
Kirkbanton/Cu
   kə:kbæntən   GlossCu xvii
Kirkbarrow/Cu
   kərbərə   PNE'side 67
   kəbərə   PNCu 21o
Kirkbarrow/We
   kərkbərə   PNE'side 67
Kirkbride/Cu
   kə:k'braid   BBC
Kirkburn/ERY
   kɔkbɔn, kərkbən   PNYE 166
Kirkburton/WRY
   kə:k'bə:t(ə)n   BBC
Kirkby
   kə:bi   EPD,DEPN,BBC,Kruis.,Sc
           524,Bchm.113

Kirkby/La
  kə:bi   BCE
Kirkby/We
  kərbi   PNE'side 68
Kirkby (South K.)/WRY
  sauþ kə:bi   BBC
Kirkby-in-Ashfield/Nt
  kə:kbi in æʃfi:ld   BBC
Kirkby Ireleth/La
  kə:bi   PNLa 22o
Kirkby Lonsdale/We
  kə:bi lɔnzdeil   BBC,BCE
  kə:kbi -   Chis.
  kə:bi lɔnzdl   DKe 5
Kirkby Malham/WRY
  kə:bi mæləm   BBC
Kirkby-in-Malhamdale/WRY
  kə:bi in mæləmdeil   BBC
Kirkby Mallory/Le
  kə:kbi mæləri   BBC
Kirkby Malzeard/WRY
  kə:bi mælzəd   BBC,BCE
Kirkby Moorside/NRY
  kə:bi muəsaid   BBC,BCE
Kirkby Overblow/WRY
  kə:bi ouəblɔ: PNYW V/42
Kirkby Stephen/We
  'kə:kbi - ,
  'kə:bi 'stevn   PNWe II/8
  kərbi stebən   PNE'side 65
  kə:bi sti:v(ə)n   BBC
  - sti:vn   BCE
Kirkby Thore/We
  kə:bi þɔ: BBC
  - þju   Hope
  - þɔ:ə   BCE
  kərbi fiuər   PNE'side 71,
               Ellis 63o
  kərbə fiur   Ellis 669
Kirkcambeck/Cu
  kərkɑ:mək   PNCu 56
Kirkdale/La,NRY
  kə:kdeil   EPD
  kə:tə   PNLa(ii)
Kirk Deighton/WRY
  kək'di:tən   PNYW V/23
  kə:k'di:t(ə)n   BBC
Kirkham/La,ERY,NRY
  kə:kəm   EPD
  kɔkəm   PNYE 143
Kirkhaugh/Nb
  'kə:khɑ:f,kə:khɔ: BBC,BCE
Kirkheaton/Nb,WRY
  kə:kji:tən,
  ji:tən   Hope (for K. in WRY)
  kə:k'hi:t(ə)n   BBC
Kirk Ireton/Db
  aiətən   EPD

Kirkland
  kə:klənd   EPD
Kirk Leavington/NRY
  kiltən [sic]   Hope
Kirklees/WRY
  kə:kles   Hope
Kirklington/Nt
  kit-   DEPN
Kirkoswald/Cu
  kə:ku:zl   PNCu 215
  kə:ki:zl   PNCu 215,Hope
  kə:kuzl   Hope
  loc. kerkuzld   PNO li
  kərk'uzld   PNE'side 75
  kə:k'ɔzwəld   BBC
Kirksanton/Cu
  kʌrsantən   PNCu 415
  kə:sæntən   GlossCu xvii
Kirkstall/WRY
  'kə:kstɔ:l   EPD,BBC
  rarely kɔ:kstl   Bchm.9o
Kirkstone Pass/We
  kə:kstən   BBC
Kirkstyle/Cu
  kurksti:l   DLo 87
Kirkthorpe/WRY
  kiþrəp   Hope
Kirkthwaite/Cu,WRY
  kə:þət   GlossCu xvii
  kiþət   DDd 12
Kirsgillhow/Cu
  kə:skilə   GlossCu xvii
Kirtling/Ca
  olim kætlidʒ   PNCa 126
  kə:tliŋ   ONCa 197
Kirton/Li (two places)
  ketn   Hope
  ketən   GlossM&C,s.n.Ketton (for
               K. in Lindsey)
Kirton/Sf
  kə:tn   PNDVall 31
Kismeldon/D
  kesiŋtən   PNEss lvi
Kismeldon Bridge/Co
  kiz'meld(ə)n   BBC
Kitbridge Fm/Wt
  kitbridʒ   PNWt 286
Kite Hill/Wt
  kait il   PNWt 43
Kits Croft/WRY (f.n.)
  kit krɔft   DDd 13
Kitshowe Bridge/We
  'kits hau   BBC
Kitson (as in K.Hill/WRY)
  kitsn   EPD
Kitts (as in K. End/Mx)
  kits   EPD

Kiveton/WRY
  kivit(ə)n   BBC
  kivətən   BCE
Knaith/Li
  neiθ,neiþ   BBC,BCE
Knapside Fell/Cu
  nɛ:psit   PNE'side 69
Knapton/Nf
  næptn   Hope
Knapton/WRY
  naptən   PNYW IV/230
  næpn   Hope
Knapwell/Ca
  næpwəl   ONCa 189
Knaresborough/WRY
  neizbrə,
  nɛəzbrə   PNYW V/110
  nɛəzbərə   BBC,Schr.,Kruis.,
           Chis.
  nɛəzb(ə)rə   EPD
Knaresdale/Nb
  na:zdəl   PNNbDu 129
  na:z-   DEPN
Knayton/NRY
  ne:tən,ni:ətən   PNYN 206
Kneesall/Nt
  ni:sə   PNNt(i)78,Hope
  -s-   DEPN
Kneeton Hall/NRY
  ni:tən   PNYN 285
Kneller (as in K.Hall/Mx)
  nelə   EPD
Knepp Castle/Sx
  nep   PNSx(i)98
Knighton
  naitn   EPD
Knighton/Ha
  ki'nait(ə)n   BBC
  kə'naitən   BCE
Knighton Fm/Wt
  naitn   PNWt 170
Knightsbridge/Ldn
  naitsbridʒ   EPD,Bau.
Knights Enham/Ha
  naits enəm   BBC
Knightshulme/Chs
  -ju:m   PNChs II/237
Knipe/We
  naik   PNWe II/191
Kniveton/Db
  neitn   PNDb 383
  naivtən   BBC,BCE
  niftən   BBC,BCE,Hope
  niftn   DEPN,PNDb(i) I/275
Knock/We
  nɔk   PNE'side 75,BBC
Knockholt/K
  nɔkhoult   BBC

nɔkoult   PNK
nɔkl   Hope
Knodishall/Sf (also spelt -dd-)
  nədiʃəl   BBC
Knole/K,So,Sx
  noul   BBC,PNK
Knook/W
  nuk   PNW 171,PNW(i)109,DEPN
Knottingley/WRY
  nɔtiŋli   Chis.
Knoutberry Hill/WRY
  nautbəri il   DDd 17
Know/WRY (a mountain)
  nou, nau   DDd 17
Knowesgate/Nb (or Knowe's Gate)
  nauzgeit   BBC,BCE
Knowle
  noul   BBC
Knowles
  noulz   EPD
  nɔ:lz   PNWt 183
Knowl Gn/La
  noul gri:n   PNLa 145
Knowlton/K
  noultən   PNK
Knowsley/La
  nouzli   BBC,BCE,H.A.(2)33
  nauzli   PNLa(ii),H.A.(2)33
          ("loc.")
Knowsley/WRY
  nouzli   DEPN,BBC
Knowstone/D
  naustən   PND 340,DEPN
Knox/K,WRY
  nɔks   EPD
Knoyle/W
  nɔil   PNW 175
Knuston/Np
  nʌstən   PNNp 192,BBC
Knutsford/Chs
  nutsfərt   PNChs II/ix,GlossChs
  nutsfərd   PNChs II/73
  nʌtsfəd   EPD,Schr.,Kruis.,Chis
Knypersley/St
  naipəzli   BBC
Krumlin/WRY (a hill)
  krumlin   DHd 57
Kuggar/Co
  kʌgə, kigə   BBC,BCE
Kyle/NRY (r.n.)
  kail   EPD
Kynance/Co
  kainəns   BBC
  kainæns   EPD
Kynaston/He,Sa
  kinəstən   EPD
Kyo/Du
  kaiou   BBC

Kyre Brook/Wo (r.n.)
 kiər   RN 233
 kiə   Hope
Kyre Magna/Wo
 ki:ər   PNWo 55
 -i:-   DEPN

L

La Belle Sauvage Yard/Ldn
 lɑ: 'bel 'sou'vɑ:ʒ   BBC
Lacey Gn/Bk,Chs
 li:əsi   PNBk 173
 leisi   EPD
Lach Dennis/Chs
 latʃ   PNChs II/186
Lache/Chs
 latʃ   PNChs IV/162
Lackenby/NRY
 lækənbi   BBC
Lacock/W (also spelt Lay-)
 leikɔk   PNW 1o2,PNW(i)11o,BBC
 -ei-   DEPN
Lacon/Sa
 leikən   EPD
Laconby/Cu
 leikənbi   PNCu 396
Lacra/Cu
 lɑ:krə   Hope
 lɑ:krɑ: PNCuWe 72
Lacy Gn/Bk → Lacey Gn
Ladbroke/Ldn,Wa
 lædbruk   EPD
Ladbroke Rd/Ldn
 lædbruk roud   Schr.
Ladock/Co
 lædək   BBC,BCE
Ladthwaite/We
 lædfət   PNE'side 67
Laggers Bank/Chs
 lagəz   PNChs III/76
Laindon/Ess
 leindən   BBC
Laindon Hills/Ess (also called Lang-
                    don H.)
 leindən hilz   BBC
Lainger Ho/WRY
 le:ndʒəraus   PNYW VI/81
Laira/D (an island)
 lɛ:rə   PND 2o
 lɛərə   BBC
Laitha/We
 lɛ:ðə   PNE'side 76
Laithes/Cu (also spelt Laiths)
 lɛəðz   PNE'side 72
 -i:ə-   PNCuWe 72 (!)
Laithwaite/Cu
 leiþət   PNCu 362
Lake/Wt
 leik   PNWt 286
Lake Cottage/Wt
 leik   PNWt 153
Lakehouse Fm, L.Grove/Ess
 leikəz   PNEss 511
Lakenham/Nf
 leikənəm   BBC

Lakenheath/Sf
  'leikənhi:þ   BBC
La Lee Fm/Do
  ləli: PNDo(i)67
Laleham/Mx
  leiləm Kruis.
Lamarsh/Ess
  læmiʃ   PNEss 444
  lɑ:'mɑ:ʃ, læməʃ   BBC
  læ-   DEPN
Lamas/Nf → Lammas
Lamb Beck Ing,
Lambecking/Cu
  læmbek'iŋ   PNE'side 68
Lambeth/Ldn
  læmbəþ   EPD,BBC,Schr.,Kruis.,
           Chis.
  -beþ   EPD
Lambfoot/Cu
  lamfit   PNCu 384
Lamb Paddock/WRY
  lam parək   DDd 12
Lambsceugh/Cu
  lamskiuf   PNCu 2o3
  læmskiuf   PNE'side 71
Lambsleaze/Wt
  læmzli:z   PNWt 81
Lambton/Du
  læmtən,læmptən   EPD
  læmtn Kruis.
Lambwath/ERY
  laməþ, lɑ:miþ   PNYE 7o
  lamiþ   GlossHol 17
Lamerton/D
  læmətən   PND 185,DEPN,BBC
Lamesley/Du
  leimzli   BBC,BCE
Lammas/Nf
  læməs   DEPN,EPD,BBC,BCE,Hope
Lamorbey/K
  læməbi   BBC,BCE,PNK
Lamorna (Vale of L.)/Co
  læ'mɔ:nə   BBC
Lamorran/Co
  læ'mɔrən   BBC,BCE,DEPN
Lamplugh/Cu
  lamplə   PNCu 4o4
  'læmplu: EPD,BBC,BCE
  læmplə   BBC,BCE
Lancashire
  læŋkəʃə   EPD,BBC,Schr.,Kruis.,
           Chis.
  læŋkəʃiə   Bchm.2lo
  læŋkiʃə   EPD,DSLa
  læŋkiʃiə   EPD
  læŋkəʃaiə   Chis.
  lɔŋkəʃə, laŋkəʃiə   Brunner 163

Lancaster/La
  læŋkəstə   EPD,BBC,Schr.,Kruis.,
           Chis.
  læŋkistə   DSLa
Lancaut/Gl
  læŋ'kɔ:t   PNGl III/263
  læŋ'kout   BBC
Lancing/Sx
  lɑ:nsiŋ   PNSx(i)99,EPD,BBC,Schr.
Lancs. (short for Lancashire)
  læŋks   EPD,Bchm.2lo
Landbeach/Ca
  lændbi:tʃ   ONCa 192
Landewednack/Co
  lændi'wednək   BBC,BCE,Förster
  _ _ _ ⸍   DEPN
  the Cornish pron. is
  lanəd'wednak   Förster
Landguard Manor/Wt
  læŋgərd   PNWt 57
Landican/Chs
  landikən   PNChs IV/266
Landkey/D
  læŋki   PND 341
Landmoth/NRY
  lanməþ   PNYN 2o6
Landrake/Co
  læn'dreik   BBC
Land's End/Co
  'lændz'end   Schr.,Kruis.
  'læn(d)z'end   EPD
Landsfoot/Cu
  lænfuts [sic]   PNE'side 75
Landulph/Co
  læn'dʌlf   BBC
Laneast/Co
  _ ⸍   Jenner(2)3o4
Lanefoot/Cu
  lɔninfiut   GlossCu xvii
Lanehead/WRY
  lɔinhed   Hope
Lanercost/Cu
  'lænəkɔst   BBC,BCE
Langar/Nt
  laŋgə   PNNt 227
  læŋgə   BBC
Langbaurgh/NRY (also spelt -barugh)
  'lænbɑ:f   EPD,BBC,BCE,GlossClv,
           s.n. Bargh
Langbridge/Wt
  læŋbridʒ   PNWt 81 and 17o
Langdale/Du,We,NRY
  læŋdeil   EPD
Langdon Hills/Ess (also called
           Laindon H.)
  læŋdən hilz   BBC

Langenhoe/Ess
 'læŋgənhou BBC
Langford/Nf
 læɲfə Hope
Langham
 læŋəm EPD,Schr.
Langho/La
 læŋou BBC
Langland/Cu
 læŋglənd EPD,Schr.,Kruis.
Langley
 læŋli EPD,Schr.
Langmere/Nf
 læŋmiə EPD
Langney/Sx
 læŋli [sic] PNSx 447
Langold/Nt
 'læŋgould BBC
Langridge/D,So
 læŋgridʒ EPD
Langrish/Ha
 læŋgriʃ EPD
Langstone/D
 læŋstən BBC
Langstrothdale/WRY
 laŋstədil PNYW VI/117
Langthorpe/NRY
 læŋþrəp PNYN 18o
Langton
 læŋtən EPD,Schr.
Langton Matravers/Do
 læŋtən mə'trævərz BBC
Langwathby/Cu
 laŋənbi PNCu 218,Ellis 561
 læŋənbi PNE'side 74,DEPN,
 Hope
Lanherne Nunnery/Co
 læn'hə:n BBC
Lanhydrock/Co
 læn'haidrək BBC,BCE,DEPN
Lanivet/Co
 læn'ivit BBC
 læn'ivət BCE
 _ ⁄ _ DEPN
Lanjeth/Co
 læn'dʒeþ BBC
Lankaber/We
 'læŋ'ke:bə PNWe II/155
 laŋkəbər PNCuWe 16o
Lanlivery/Co
 læn'livəri BBC
Lanreath/Co (also spelt -reth)
 læn'reþ BBC,BCE,DEPN

Lansdown/Gl,So
 lænzdaun EPD
Lanteglos/Co
 læn'teglɔs,
 læn'teiglɔs BBC,BCE
 _ ⁄ _ DEPN
Lanyon/Co
 loc. læng̩nain,
 StE læng̩njən Jenner(1) 142
 and Jenner(2)3o4[1]
Lanyon Cromlech/Co
 læng̩njən krɔmlek BBC
Lanyon Guvit/Co
 lenain gʌvit Hope
Lapal/Wo
 læpəl PNWo 298,DEPN
Laployd/D
 læpləd LCo 142,note 54
Laployd Barton/D
 læpləd PND 423
Lapwing Hollow/Db (f.n.)
 læpiŋ FnSDb 49
Larden Gn/Chs
 lardən PNChs III/143
Lark/Ca,Sf (r.n.) (also spelt Larke)
 lɑ:k Schr.
Larkrigg/We
 lɑ:krig PNWe I/1o9
Lartington/NRY
 lɑ:tintən Smith(1)292,note 1
Larton/Chs
 lærtən, lɑ:rtən PNChs IV/3oo
Lasham/Ha
 læsəm, læʃəm EPD,BBC[2]
Latham/ERY,WRY
 leiþəm Dobson 944,HSM 7o
 leiþm,læþm,leiðm Kruis.
 (see also note 3)
Lathbury/Bk
 læþbəri EPD
Lathe Bank/WRY (f.n.)
 leaþ baŋk DDd 14
Lathom/La
 leiðəm EPD,DEPN,BBC,BCE
 leiþəm EPD
Latimer/Bk
 lætimə EPD,Kruis.
Laughern(e)/Wo
 lɔ:n PNWo 93,DEPN,BBC,BCE
Laughton-en-le-Morthen/WRY
 laitniŋ in ðə mɔ:niŋ Hope
Laughter Hole, L. Torr/D
 lɑ:tər PND 195

---

1) "Young people are now taking to call ist Lan-yón" (Jenner(2)3o4).
2) "The first is the traditional village pron. The second is familiar
 to those using the Gliding Centre" (BBC).
3) "Generally [leiþəm] in South of England; always [leiðəm] in North"
 (EPD).

Laughterton/Li
   loutətən   Hope
Laughton/Le,Li,Sx,WRY
   lɔːtn   EPD
   lɔːt(ə)n   BBC
   lɔːtən   BCE (for L. in
             Le,Li and WRY)
   lɔfn   Hope (for L. in Li)
   lɑːftən, lɑːtən   PNSx 4o2
   lɑːftn   PNSx(i)loo
   læftn   PNSx(i)lol
Launcells/Co
   lɑːnslz, lænslz   BBC
Launceston/Co
   lɔːnsestn   Kruis.
   lɑːnstən   EPD ("loc."),BBC,
             BCE,Schr.,Chis.,
             HL 1142
   lɑːnstn   DEPN
   lɔːnsən   BCE,HL 1142
   lɑːns(ə)n,lɔːns(ə)n   BBC
   lɑːnsən   BCE,HL 1142
   lænsn   Hope,Schr.,Kruis.
             ("loc.")
Laundon/Bk ⟶ Lavendon
Laund's Fm/Ess
   lændz   PNEss 4o7
Launton/O
   lɔːntən, lɑːntən   PNO 228
Lavant/Sx (p.n. and r.n.)
   lævənt   BBC,BCE
   -æ-   DEPN (for r.n.)
Lavender's Fm/Wt
   'lævəndərz   PNWt 286
Lavendon/Bk
   lɑːndən   PNBk 9
   lɔːndən   BCE,Hope
   lɑːn-   DEPN
   læv(ə)ndən   BBC
   lævəndən   BCE
Lavenham/Sf
   lævənəm   BBC,BCE,DEPN
   lænəm   PNSf 56
Laver/Ess
   leivə   PNEss 61,DEPN
Laver/WRY (r.n.)
   lɑːvə   BBC
Laverstock/W
   olim lɑːrstɔk   PNW 381
   lævə(r)stɔk   PNW(i) 112
   lævəstɔk   BBC
   -æ-   DEPN
Laverstoke/Ha
   lævəstouk   BBC
Laverton/WRY
   lɑːtən,
   lɛətən, lavətən   PNYW V/211
Lavington/Li (now called Lenton)
   lentən   Hope

Lavington/Sx,W
   læviŋtən   PNSx(i)lol,EPD,BBC
             PNW 24o
Lawes (as in L. Bridge/D)
   lɔːz   EPD
Lawford/Ess,So,Wa
   lɔːfəd   EPD
Lawhitton/Co
   lɔː'(h)wit(ə)n, lɑː-   BBC
   lɔː'hwitən, lɑː-   BCE
   _ ́ _   DEPN
Lawshall/Sf
   lɔːʃl   BBC
Lawton/Chs,He,Sa
   lɔːtn   EPD
Laxfield/Sf
   læksfild   DSf 277
Laxton/Nt ⟶ Lexington
Laycock/W,WRY
   leːkɔk   PNYW VI/7
   leikɔk   EPD
Layer Breton/Ess
   leiə bret(ə)n   BBC
Layer-de-la-Haye/Ess
   leiə də lɑː hei   BBC
Layham/Sf
   leiəm   BBC
Layrus/NRY
   lɛərəs   PNYN 256
Laysthorpe/NRY
   lɛəsþrəp   PNYN 54
Layton/La,NRY
   leːtən   PNYN 3oo
   leitn   EPD
Lazenby/NRY (two places)
   lɛəzənbi   PNYN 16o and 21o
   leiznbi   EPD
Lazonby/Cu
   leiz(ə)nbi   BBC
Lea/Ldn (r.n.)
   rivə liː   Bau.
Lea/Chs
   liː   PNChs III/67, IV/175,EPD,
             Kruis.
Leadenhall St/Ldn
   'led(ə)nhɔːl   BBC
   lednhɔːl striːt   EPD,Schr.
Leadenham/Li
   ledənəm   BBC,BCE
   le-   DEPN
Leaden Roding/Ess
   loc. liːdn   PNEss 493
   liːdən   EssDD 158
   -iː-   DEPN
Leadgate/Cu,Du
   ledgit   BBC
   ledgət   BCE (for L. in Du)
Leadington/Gl
   lediŋtən   PNGl III/169

Leadon/He,Gl,Wo (r.n.)
   ledn   PNGl I/1o,RN 241,DEPN
Lea Fm/Wt
   li: varm   PNWt 57
Leahall Fm/Chs
   'li:'ɔ:l   PNChs IV/119
Leake/NRY
   li:k   PNYN 2o7,EPD
Leakses/WRY
   lieksiz   DDd 13
Lealholm/NRY
   li:ləm   PNYN 133,DEPN
Leam/Np,Wa (r.n.)
   lem   RN 243,DEPN
   li:m   Schr.
Leam Hall/Db
   li:m, liəm   PNDb(i) I/277
Leamington/Wa (=Royal L. Spa)
   lemiŋtən   EPD,BBC,BCE,Schr.,
                  Kruis.,Chis.,BG
Leamington Hastings,L.Priors/Wa
   -e-   DEPN
Lea Newbold/Chs
   'li: 'nju:bould   PNChs IV/119f.
The Leas/K (f.n.)
   li:z   DK (see note 1)
Leasingthorne/Du
   li:ziŋþɔ:n   BBC
Leasowe/Chs
   li:zou   PNChs IV/332
   li:sou   BBC,BCE
Leatherhead/Sr
   leðəhed   EPD
Leathley/WRY
   li:þlə, leiþlə   PNYW V/54
Leavening/ERY
   li:vniŋ   BBC
Leavesden/Hrt
   li:vzdən   BBC
Leavington/NRY ⟶ Kirk L.
Lea Yeat/WRY
   lei jet   DDd 12
Lechlade/Gl
   letʃleid   PNGl I/4o,EPD,BBC,
                  BCE
Leckhampton/Gl
   lækiŋtən,lekiŋtən   Hope
   'lekhæm(p)tən   EPD
Leconfield/ERY
   lekənfild   PNYE 189
   lek(ə)nfi:ld   EPD,BBC
Le Court/Ha
   'li: 'kɔ:t   BBC
Ledburn/Bk
   lebə:n   PNBk 81

Ledbury/He
   ledb(ə)ri   EPD
   ledbəri   Schr.,DHe 43
   ledbri (dial.)   DHe 43
Ledge/Wt ⟶ Ship Ledge
Ledsham/Chs
   ledʃəm   PNChs IV/217
   ledsəm   PNChs IV/217,H.A.(2)46
   letsəm,ledzəm   PNO(i)1o3
Ledsham/WRY
   ledsəm   PNYW IV/49
Lee/K (r.n.)
   li: EPD,Schr.
Leece/La
   li:s   PNLa 2o9
Leechmore Pond/Wt
   læʃmər   PNWt 153
Lee Cottages/Chs
   li: PNChs IV/119
Leeds/K,WRY
   li:dz   EPD,BBC,Schr.,Lloyd 127
   leidz   DSto (for L. in WRY)
Leedstown/Co (or Leeds Town)
   li:dztaun   BBC
Lee Fm/Wt
   li: PNWt 21o
Leek/St
   li:k   EPD,Schr.
Lees
   li:z   EPD
Leese/Chs
   li:s   PNChs II/229
Lefevre Galleries/Ldn
   lə'fɛ:vr   BBC
Leger Galleries/Ldn
   ledʒə   BBC
Legh (High L.)/Chs
   li: PNChs II/45,EPD,BBC,Hope
Leicester/Le
   lestə   DEPN,EPD,BBC,Schr.,Kruis.,
             Chis.,MEG 121,PNE&W,BG
Leicestershire
   lestəʃə   EPD,Schr.
   lestəʃiə   EPD
Leigh
   li: EPD,DEPN,Schr.,Chis.,Kruis.
   lai   EPD,DEPN
   lei   Schr.
Leigh(Little L.)/Chs (formerly L.
                juxta Bartington)
   li: PNChs II/115
Leigh (North L.)/D
   li: BBC (see also s.n. South-
                      leigh)

---

1) "[This] is the name given at Folkestone to the fine open space of
common at the top of the cliffs" (DK).

Leigh/Do
    laɪ   PNDo(i)79 and 224,EPD,
           BBC,BCE
Leigh/Ess
    liː   PNEss 188,EPD,BCE
Leigh/Gl
    liː   PNGl II/83
Leigh/K
    laɪ   EPD,BBC,BCE,PNK
Leigh/La
    liː   EPD,BBC,BCE,BG
    leitʃ   Hope
    leiþ   PNSWY 187,PNLa(ii),
           Parkinson,Hope
           (see also note 1)
Leigh (North L.)/O
    liː   BBC,BCE (see also s.n.
                 Southleigh/O)
Leigh/Sr
    laɪ   PNSr 297,EPD,BBC,BCE,
           Hope
Leigh/St
    liː   BBC
Leigh/W,Wo
    laɪ   PNW 46,PNWo 2o4
Leigham Ct/Sr
    olim laɪm   PNSr 34
Leigh Ct/So,Wo
    laɪ kɔːt   BBC
    laɪ koːt   BCE (for L.Ct in Wo)
Leigh Delamere/W
    laɪ dælimɔːr   PNW 1o6
    liː deləmiə   BBC
    liː delɑːmiə, laɪ -   BCE
Leigh Gn/Bk,K
    liː griːn   BBC,BCE (for L.Gn
                in K)
Leigh Hill/W
    laɪ   PNW 254
Leigh-on-Mendip/So
    laɪ ɔn mendip   BBC,BCE,Hope
    liː - -   BBC,BCE
Leighs/Ess
    liːz   PNEss 256,DEPN
Leigh-on-Sea/Ess
    liː ɔn siː   BBC
Leigh Sinton/Wo
    laɪ sintən   BBC,BCE
Leighton
    leit(ə)n,let(ə)n   BBC
    leitn   EPD,Kruis.
Leighton/Chs
    lɛːtən,leitən   PNChs IV/218
                 (for L. in
                 Wirral Hd)

    letən,leitən   PNChs III/28 (for
                  in Nantwich Hd)
    leit(ə)n,let(ə)n   BBC
    leitən, letən   BCE
Leighton/Db
    leitn   PNDb(i) I/277
Leighton/La
    leːtn   PNLa 189
Leighton/Nb → Green L.
Leighton/Sa,NRY
    leitn   GlossSa xxvii
    liːtən   PNYN 232
Leighton Buzzard/Bd (formerly spelt
                    L.Beaudesert)
    leitən bʌzɑːd   Chis.
    - bʌzəd   Hope
Leintwardine/He
    'lentwədain,
    'lentwədiːn, lænt diːn   BBC,BCE
    læntwɑːdain   Hope
    lent-   Hope,DHe 43
    -e- , -ain   DEPN
Leire/Le
    liə, leə   BBC,BCE
Leiston/Sf
    leist(ə)n   EPD
    leistən   BBC,BCE
    leisən   Hope,BG
    -ei-   DEPN
Leith/We (r.n.)
    liːþ   PNWe I/9, RN 248,DEPN,EPD,
           BBC
Lelant/Co
    le'lænt   BBC,BCE,DEPN (stress
                    only)
Leman/D (r.n.)
    lemən   Schr.
Leman St/Ldn
    lemən, formerly li'mæn   EPD
Lenacre/K
    lenəkə   PNK
Lenborough/Bk
    lembərə   PNBk 61
Lench (Abbot's L.)/Wo
    "known as Hob-Lench" GlossSEWo ?
    (the name is spelt Ab Lench in B?
Lenham/K
    lenəm   PNK
Lenthall/Yorks.
    lenþɔːl   EPD,Bchm.229
    -əl   EPD,Bchm.7o
    -l   EPD
Lenton/Li → Lavington

---

1) "It is said that the original guttural pron. of Leigh is still retained by the natives" (PNL'pool 51); "The nearest approach is [...
Leght" (Rose) and: " lecχ heard by Mr Sephton" (PNLa(ii)).

Leominster/He
  lemstə   DEPN,EPD,BBC,BCE,BG,
             Schr.,Kruis.,Chis.,
             Hope,Bchm.87,GlossHe
             42,DHe 43 (dial. and
             StE),PNHu 35o
  leminstə EPD,Bchm.87
Leonard's Bridge, L.Fm/Chs
  lenərdz   PNChs II/119
Lesnes/K ⟶ Lessness
Lesnewth/Co
  lez'nju:ϸ BBC,BCE
  _ ⁄   DEPN

Lessland/Wt
  leslən PNWt 154
Lessness/K
  lesnis BBC
  lesnez PNK
Letchworth/Hrt
  vulgo litʃwə:ϸ PNHrt 132
  letʃwə(:)ϸ EPD
Letheringsett/Nf
  laːnset Hope
Letty (as in L. Gn/Hrt)
  leti EPD
The Level of Hatfield Chase/WRY
  "commonly called 'the Levels'"
    GlossM&C,s.n. Levels
Levells/Nb
  "loc.called Linnolds"
    Heslop 21f.
Leven/ERY
  levən, liːvən PNYE 72
  liːv(ə)n BBC
  levn Schr.,Kruis.
Leven/La and We (r.n.)
  liːvən, levən BCE
  levn Schr.
Levens/We
  levənz PNWe I/9o,BCE
  lev(ə)nz BBC
  -e- DEPN
Levenshulme/La
  levenzuːm PNLa 31
  lev(ə)nzhjuːm BBC
  levnzuːm DEPN
Lever/La
  liːvə EPD,KRuis.
Leverstock Gn/Hrt
  levəstɔk griːn BBC
Leverton/Nt
  levət(ə)n BBC
Leverton/Li
  levətən BCE

Levisham/NRY
  liusəm, levisəm PNYN 92
Lew/D (r.n.)
  luː   RN 253,DEPN
Lewannick/Co
  lə'wɔnik BBC
  le'wɔnik BCE
  _ ⁄ _ DEPN

Lewarne/Co
  lə'wɔːn BBC
Lewdown/D (also spelt Lew Down)
  'luː'daun BBC
Lewell/Do
  luːəl PNDo I/2o7,PNDo(i)154,
        DEPN
Lewes/Sx
  luːis PNSx 318,PNSx(i)1o2,DEPN,
        BBC,BCE,Kruis.
  luːs PNSx(i)1o2
  luis EPD,Hope
  luːiz Hope,BCE
  lju(ː)is EPD
  ljuəs Chis.
Lewisburn/Nb (r.n.) (or Lewis Burn)
  luzbɔːrn PNNbDu 134
Lewisham/K
  lu(ː)iʃəm,lju(ː)-,-isəm EPD[1]
  luːiʃəm Schr.,Kruis.,Bchm.241,
        HL 815,MEG 377
  luiʃəm Chis.,Potter 35
  loc. often luisəm HL 815
  loc. luːisəm Bchm.241,MEG 377
  ljuisəm ("at the turn of the
        century") Potter 35
  ljuiʃəm Potter 35
Leworthy/D
  ljuəri PND 82
Lewtrenchard/D (or Lew T.)
  trænʃəd PND 187
  'luːtrenʃəd BBC
Lexington/Nt (also called Laxton)
  leksiŋtən EPD,Schr.
Ley/Co,D,Gl
  liː EPD,Kruis.
Leybourne/K
  'leibɔːn EPD,BBC,PNK
  -bɔən EPD
Leyburn/NRY
  leːbən, leibən PNYN 257
  leibəːn EPD,BBC
Leycett/St
  liːset, laiset BBC,BCE
Leycourt/Hu
  legət PNBdHu 258

---

1) "Many residents in L. say [-isəm]" (EPD[1917,1924]); "Some residents [etc.]" (EPD [1937]); "Former pronunciations [lu(:)isəm] and
[luːsəm] are probably now obsolete or nearly so" (EPD[1967]).

Leyhill/Bk
'leihil BBC
Leyhill/Db
'li:hil BBC
Leyland/Co,La
leilənd EPD,BBC,Chis.,
Picken 186 (for L.
in Co)
lɛ:lən Ellis 345 (for L.in
La)
Leys (as in L. Hill/He)
li:z EPD
Leysdown/K
leizdaun BBC,BCE,PNK
Ley Seat/We
leisit PNE'side 69
Leyton/Ess
leitn PNEss 1o1,EPD,Kruis.
leit(ə)n BBC
Leytonstone/Ess
let(ə)nstoun BBC
Lezant/Co
le'zænt BBC,BCE
_ ∠ DEPN
Leziate/Nf
'leziət BBC,BCE
ledʒit BBC
ledʒət BCE,Hope
ledʒet DEPN
Lichfield/St
litʃfi:ld EPD,Schr.,Chis.
Lidford/D
lidfəd Schr.
Lidgate/Db,Sf,WRY
lidgeit BBC
lidgət Schr.
Lidsey/Sx
lidzi PNSx(i)1o2
Lidsing/K
lidsiŋ PNK
Lifford/Wa
lifəd EPD,Schr.
Lightcliffe/WRY
li:tklif Hope
Lighthorne/Wa
laithɔ:n PNWa 255
Lilleshall/Sa
liliʃəl BBC,BCE
linsəl Hope
linsil (obs.) GlossSa 517
and xxxix
Lilliput/Do
lilipʌt, -put, -pət EPD
Lilly Garth/WRY
lili gɑ:þ DDd 14
Limbersey/Bd
liməsi PNBdHu 81

Limehouse/Ldn
laimhaus EPD,HL 122o
loc. liməs HL 122o,Bchm.35
Limerstone/Wt
limərstn PNWt 68
Limpenhoe/Nf
limpənhou BBC
Linacre/La
linəkə EPD,Kruis.
Lincoln/Li
liŋkən DEPN,EPD,BBC,Schr.,Kruis.
Chis.,Hope,HL 896,MEG 2
-ŋk- Dobson 952
Lincolnshire
liŋkənʃiə EPD,GlossM&C,s.n.
Linc'nsheer
liŋkənʃə EPD,Schr.
liŋkiʃiə GlossM&C,s.n. Linc'n-
sheer,Linkisheer
liŋkiʃə RSp 135,EDG §267
leŋkəʃiə DSEY 29
Lincs. (short for Lincolnshire)
liŋks EPD
Lindal/La
lindl PNLa 2o7
Lindale/La
lindou Bardsley,s.n.Blackcow
Linden/He,La,Nb
lindən EPD
Lindon End/Ca
lindən ONCa 188
Lindfield/Sx
linvəl PNSx 34o
Lindisfarne/Nb (an island)
lindisfɑ:n EPD,BBC,Schr.,Kruis.
Lindley/Le,WRY
lindli BBC,Kruis.
lin(d)li EPD
linli DHd 62 (for L. in WRY)
Lindley Murrey/Li
limli GlossLi 24o
Lindow/Chs
lində PNChs II/vii ("olim"),
GlossChs
lindou PNChs II/vii
Lindow End/Chs
olim lində ɛ:nd,
lindou end PNChs II/vii
lində i:nd GlossChs
Lindsey/Ess,Li,Sf
lin(d)zi EPD
Lineham/O
lainəm PNO(i) 148
Lineholt/Wo
linjəl PNWo 271
Linewath/Cu
lainwəþ PNE'side 66
lainwiþ PNE'side 64

Lingen/He
   liŋgən EPD
Lingham/Chs
   liŋgəm,liŋəm PNChs IV/319
Ling Stubbs/Cu
   liŋstubz PNE'side 68
Linhope/Nb
   linəp BBC,BCE
Linkhowe Syke/Cu (f.n.)
   liŋkə Thorn.67 and 79,note
      116
Linkinhorne/Co
   'liŋkinhɔ:n BBC
Linley/He,Sa
   linli EPD
Linmouth/Nb ⟶ Lynmouth
Linnet/Sf (r.n.)
   linit EPD
Linslade/Bk
   lintʃeid, linsleid PNBk 79
   linzleid BBC
Linstone Chine/Wt
   lintʃən tʃain PNWt 129
Linthorpe/NRY
   linþrəp PNYN 161
Linthwaite/WRY
   linfit PNYW II/273,DHd 62,
      Hope
   linþwət EPD
Linton
   lintən EPD,ONCa 21
Lions Lane/Sr
   lainz PNSr 234
Liscard/Chs
   'liskɑ:rd PNChs IV/324
   lis'kɑ:d EPD
Liscow/Cu
   liskə PNE'side 63
Liskeard/Co
   lis'kɑ:d EPD,Chis.,BBC,BCE
   _́ _ DEPN,BG
Lisle Ct/Ha
   lail EPD,Schr.
Lissett/ERY
   lisit PNYE 77
Lisson Grove/Ldn
   lisn EPD
Lister (as in L. Hills/WRY)
   listə EPD
Liston/Ess
   list(ə)n EPD
Litchfield/Ha
   litʃfi:ld EPD,Schr.
Litchurch/Db
   litʃə:tʃ PNDb 452
   li:tʃətʃ Hope,PNDb(i) I/279
Lithersgate Common/Sx
   lizgət PNSx 127

Litlington/Ca,Sx
   litlintən ONCa 25
   liliŋtən PNSx 412
Littleborough/La,Nt
   litlbruk GlossR&R,DSLa
   litlbruf DSLa
   litlbrə BBC
Littlecote/Bk
   lidkət PNBk 72
Little Dale/Cu
   lɑ:l deəl PNE'side 72
Littlehampton/Sx
   litəl'hæmptən Chis.
   'litlhæm(p)tən EPD
   _́ _ _́ _ EPD
Littlemore/O
   litlmɔ:ə Kruis.
Littleover/Db
   litlə ROS 42; cf. also Bardsley,
      s.n. Littler
Littleport/Ca
   litlpɔ:t ONCa 193
Little Puddle Fm/Do
   lidl pidl PNDo I/311,DDo
Littler/Chs
   litlər PNChs III/172
   litlə EPD
Little Salkeld/Cu
   lal sæfl PNE'side 74
Littlestone-on-Sea/K
   litlstən ɔn si: BBC
Littleton
   litltən Schr.,Kruis.
   litlt(ə)n EPD
Little Town/WRY
   lail taun DDd 14
Little Weighton/ERY
   lɑ:tl wi:tn PNYE 2o5
Litton
   litn EPD
Litton Cheney/Do
   lit(ə)n tʃeini BBC
Liverpool/La
   livəpu:l EPD,BBC,Schr.,Kruis.,
      Chis.,Bau.,Lloyd 117
   livəpul CPhon 82
   lə:pl Hope
   livəpi:əl DSto
   lə:pu: DSLa
   lə:poul H.A.(2)45 ("old pron.
      of L.")
Liversedge/WRY
   livəsedʒ BBC
Livesey/La
   livzi, livsi EPD,Bchm.35
   laivzi Bchm.35
Liza/Co (r.n.)
   laizə EPD
   -i- DEPN

The Lizard, L. Point/Co,
Lizard/Sa
  lizəd   EPD,BBC,Schr.
  'lizɑːd   Chsi.
Llanthony Priory/Gl
  'læn'touni,
  'læntəni   PNGl II/138
  lænt-houni   Förster
Lobscombe Corner/W
  lɔbzkəm   BBC
Lock
  lɔk   EPD
Lockinge/Brk
  lɔkindʒ   PNBrk 67,BBC,H.A.(1)
        179,Zachr.(1)348,
        Dodgson(2)341,
        PNWa(i)28
Lockington/ERY
  lɔkitən   PNYE 160
Lock's Green/Wt (or Locksgreen)
  lɔks griːn   DWt,s.n. ram-
          shackled
Lockwood/WRY
  lɔkəd   Hope,DHd 140,
  lɔkwud   EPD,Schr.
Loddiswell/D
  lɔdzwəl   PND 306
  lɔdizwel   BBC
Loddon/Nf
  lɔdən   Chis.
Loddon/Ha,Brk, (r.n.)
  lɔd(ə)n   BBC
Lodge
  lɔdʒ   EPD,Kruis.
Lodore (as in L. Falls/Cu)
  lɔ'dɔː, -dɔə,lə-   EPD
Lodsworth/Sx
  lʌdzwəþ   PNSx 26
  lɔdzwəþ   PNSx(i)104
Lofshaw Hill/Cu
  lɔfʃə   PNE'side 62
Lofthouse/NRY,WRY
  lɔftəs   PNYW II/136,DHd 27,
        Hope,EPD,Bchm.105
  lɔfthaus   EPD,Bchm.105 (for
Loftus/NRY,WRY   L. in WRY)
  lɔftəs   EPD,Bchm.105 (for L.
         in NRY)
Lofty Gn/Ess
  lʌfti   PNEss 484,EssDD 158
Lois (as in Weedon L./Np)
  louis   EPD
Lollesworth Fm/Sr
  luːzəþ   PNSr 141
Lolworth/Ca
  loulə   PNCa 180,Hope
  lɔlwəþ   ONCa 185

Lombard St/Ldn
  lɔmbəd striːt   Schr.
Lomeshay/La
  lɔmiʃi   PNLa 86
Londesborough/ERY
  lounzbrə   PNYE 231
  lɔnzb(ə)rə   EPD
London
  lʌndən   EPD,Schr.,Kruis.,Chis.,
        Bchm.253,HL 1130,Bau.,
        Lloyd 113,CPhon 24,Hope
        MEG 265 ("now [lʌndən]
        rather than [-dn]")
  lʌndn   HL 1130,MEG 265 (but see
        above)
  lʌnən   Bchm.253 ("dial. and vul
        gar"),Hope,DEss,DSx,s.n.
        Leetle,DWt,s.n. zet up,
        GlossHa xii,GlossO(suppl.)9
        s.n.Old,GlossR&R,GlossW 215
        GlossWCo,s.n.Church-town,
        Hewett 14
  lʌn(ə)n   MEG 223 ("dial. and
        vulgar")
  lʌnn   DSf 278,HL 1130, cf. also
        EDG §301
  lundən   DBo,DHd 142,s.n. up,
        DLa 9,DLi 89
  lunən   Brunner 169,DOld 23,DSLa
        DSChs 17,DSto,GlossWby,s
        Consate
  lun(ə)n   DSDu
  lɔnən   GlossW 207
  lənən   GlossM&C,s.n.Lunnon

London (Little L.)/Li
  lʌnən   GlossM&C,s.n. Little L.
London Colney/Hrt → Colney
London Fm/Wt
  lʌn(d)n   PNWt 82
Londonthorpe/Li
  lʌnənþɔːp   Hope
Lonethwaite/La
  loːnþət   PNLa 219
Longdown/Wt
  lɔŋdæun   PNWt 16
Longford
  lɔŋfəd   EPD,Schr.
  laŋfəd,lagənfɔːd   PNDb(i)
Longframlington/Nb → Framlington
Longham/Do,Nf
  'lɔŋ'hæm   BBC,BCE (for L. in Do)
Longhirst/Nb
  laŋəst   PNNbDu 136
Longhorsley/Nb (or Long H.)
  'lɔŋ 'hɔːsli   BBC
Longhoughton/Nb
  'lɔŋ'haut(ə)n, -'hout(ə)n   BBC
     -hautən, -houtən   BCE

Longlands/Wt
   lɔŋlənz   PNWt 285
Longleat/So,W
   lɔŋliːt   EPD,BBC
Longlevens/Gl (or -leavens)
   'lɔŋ'lev(ə)nz   BBC
Long Marton/We
   læg mɑːrtin   PNE'side 7o
Longmynd/Sa
   -i-   DEPN
Longney/Gl
   lɔŋni   BBC
Longnor/Sa,St
   lɔŋnə   BBC
Longridge
   lɔŋgridʒ   EPD
Long Sallows/Db (f.n.)
   seləz   FnSDb 75
Longsleddale/We
   laŋ'sledəl   PNWe I/16o
   lɔŋ'slidl   BBC
Longstow/Ca (a hd)
   lɔŋstou   ONCa 199
Longton/La,St
   lɔŋtən   EPD,Schr.,Chis.
Longtown/Cu
   lɔŋtuːn   PNCu 53
Longwathby/Cu
   lænənbi   GlossCu xvii
Longwood/WRY
   lɔŋəd   Hope
Lonscale Fell/Cu
   lɔnskil   PNE'side 68
Lonsdale/La,We,NRY
   lounzdil   PNYN 165
   lɔnzdeil   EPD
Lonton/NRY
   luntən   PNYN 3o7
Looe/Co
   luː   EPD,BBC,BCE
Loose/K (r.n.)
   luːz   RN 259,PNK
Loose/K (the village)
   luːz   BBC,BCE,Hope,DEPN
Loose Howl/NRY
   luːsou   PNYN 8o
Loosley Row/Bk
   'luːzli 'rou   BBC,BCE
Loppington/Sa
   lɔpitn   PNSa 13o,s.n.ington.
          PNSa 146,GlossSa xxxvii
   lɔpintən   GlossSa xxxvii
   læpitən   PNSa 13o,s.n.ington
Lorden Copse/Wt
   lɑːrdn, lɔːrdn   PNWt 22o
Lordine Ct Fm/Sx
   lɔː'dain   PNSx 519

Loscars/We
   lɔskəz   PNE'side 75
Loseley Pk/Sr
   louzli   BBC
Lostock Gralam/Chs
   'lɔstɔk 'greiləm   PNChs II/189
Lostock Hall/La
   'lɔstɔk hɔːl   BBC
Lostwithiel/Co
   lɔst'wiþiəl   EPD,BBC,BCE
   lɔswiþiəl   EPD,PNE&W
   lɔst'wiðil   EPD,Schr.
   lɔstwiþəl   Chis.
   -iþ-   DEPN
   also spelt Lest- and pron.
   lest'wiðil   Schr.
   lɔs(t)wiþjəl   EPD
Lothbury/Ldn
   lɔþbəri, louþ-   BBC
   lɔþb(ə)ri, louþ-   EPD
Loudwater/Bk
   'laudwɔːtə   EPD
Loughborough/Le
   lʌfbərə   BBC,BCE,Kruis.,Chis.,Hope,
          BG,DEPN,Schr.,MEG 287
   -b(ə)rə   EPD
   lufbərə   Ellis 489
Loughrigg/We
   lufrig   PNWe I/2o9
   lʌfrig   DEPN,BBC,BCE
Loughton/Bk,Ess
   lautən   PNBk 2o,BCE
   lautn   PNEss 64,EPD,Kruis.
   laut(ə)n   BBC
   -au-   DEPN
Loups/NRY
   loups   PNYN 3o7
Louth/Li
   lauþ   DEPN,EPD,BBC.BCE
   lauð   Schr.(see note 1)
   lauəþ   GlossSWLi,Hope,Ellis 3o9
Lovell (Minster L.)/O
   minstə lʌvl   BBC
   -    lʌvəl   BCE
Loverley Fm/Do
   lʌvəli   PNDo(i)93
Loverston Fm/Wt
   lʌvərs(t)n   PNWt 137
Low Abbey/We
   lɔː æbə   PNE'side 62
Lowca/Cu
   laukə   PNCu 4oo,BBC
Low Chapel/WRY
   t lɑː tʃapl   DDd 13
Lowdham/Nt,Sf
   laudm   PNNt(i)84
   laudəm   BBC

1) According to EPD [-ð] only applies to the place in Ireland.

Lowe
  lou   EPD
Lower Bache Fm/Chs
  bɛːtʃ   Ellis 176
Lowes Hill/Db,Wo
  louz   PNDb(i) I/284,EPD
Lowesby/Le
  louzbi   DEPN,BBC,BCE
Lowestoft/Sf
  loustɔft   EPD,BBC,BCE,Schr.,
                Chis.
  loustɔf   BG
  loustəf   EPD,BBC,BCE
  loustəft   EPD,BBC
  louəstɔft   Chis.
  louistɔft   EPD,Schr.,Kruis.
  louəstɔf   DSf 278
  louistəf   EPD
  lestɔf   Hope
  -ous-   DEPN
Loweswater/Cu (a lake)
  lauzwɔtə   PNCu 4lo
  louzwɔtə   Schr.
  louzwɔːtə   BBC,BCE
  -ouz-   DEPN
Lowey/K (f.n.)
  loui   DK
Low Ground/WRY
  lɑː grund   DDd 16
Low Hall/WRY
  t lɑː ɔː   DDd 13
Lowick/La,Nb,Np
  louik   EPD,Schr.
Lowick/La
  louik   DEPN,BBC,BCE
  loːik   PNLa 213
Lowick/Nb
  louik,lauik   BBC,BCE
  -ou-   DEPN
Lowick/Np
  louik   PNNp 185,DEPN,BBC,BCE
  lʌfik   PNNp 185,DEPN
Low Maslack Pasture/We (f.n.)
  mæslək   Simpson 287
Lownthwaite/Cu,We
  lounþət   PNE'side 66
Lowood/La
  louwud   EPD,Schr.
Low Scales/Cu
  laskəlz   PNCu 416,GlossCu xvii
Lowther/We
  lauðə   PNWe II/182,BBC,BCE,
           Schr.,EPD,Kruis.
Lowther/We (r.n.)
  lauðə   PNWe I/9,RN 266,DEPN,
           Schr.,EPD,Kruis.
Lowthorpe/ERY
  louþrəp   PNYE 93,GlossHol 17,
           EDD,s.n.Thorpe

Lowthwaite/Cu
  louþət   PNCu 317,PNE'side 67
Lowton/La,So
  lout(ə)n   BBC
  loutn   EPD
  lɔːtn   PNLa(ii)
Loxley/St,Wa,WRY
  lɔksli   EPD
Lozells/Wa
  lou'zelz   BBC
  lo'zelz   BCE
Lubenham/Le
  lʌbənəm   BBC,BCE
Luccombe/So,Wt
  lʌkəm   BBC,BCE (for L. in So),
           PNWt 47
Lucerne Street/K
  luː'səːn, ljuː-,lu-   EPD
Lucketts/Wt
  lʌkits   PNWt 211
Lucyclose/Cu
  lusti kluːəz   GlossCu xvii
Lud/Li (r.n.)
  lʌd   EPD
Luddenden Foot/WRY
  ludndin fuit, t fuit   PNYW III,
    "abbreviated 'The Foot' and
    pron. þfuit "   DUCd 16
Luddenham/K
  lʌdnəm   PNK
Luddesdown/K
  lʌdzdaun   BBC
Ludford/Sa
  lʌdfət   GlossHe 39,s.n.Ford
Ludgate/Ldn
  lʌdgit, -geit   EPD
  lʌdgət   Schr.,Kruis.
Ludgershall/Bk,W
  ləːgəsəl   PNBk lo4,Mawer(2)95
  ləːg-   DEPN (for L. in Bk)
  lʌgərʃɔːl   PNW 367,PNW(i)117
  lʌg-   DEPN (for L. in W)
  lʌ(d)gəʃəl   BCE (for L. in W)
  lʌ(d)gərʃəl   BBC
  lʌdgəzhɔːl,lʌgəʃɔː: [sic] Schr.
Ludgvan/Co (also spelt Ludjan)
  lʌdʒən   BBC,BCE,Jenner(2)3o3
  lidʒən   Hope
Ludlow/Sa
  lʌdlou   EPD,BBC,Schr.,Chis.
Lugwardine/He
  'lʌgwədiːn   BBC
   ／　　／   DHe 43
The Luham/Cu
  lium   PNE'side 71
Lullington/Sx
  liŋkən   PNSx 417

Lulsgate/So
  lʌlzgeit BBC
Lulworth/Do
  lʌlwə:ɸ, lʌləɸ,
  lɔlwə:ɸ, lauwə:ɸ PNDo I/123
Lumley/Du,Sx
  lʌmli EPD
Lund (in northern counties)
  lund PNYE 163,EPD
Lunds/WRY
  lunz DDd 13
Lundy Is/D
  lʌndi EPD
Lune (r.n.)
  lu:n BBC
  l(j)u:n Schr.
Lune/La,We (r.n.)
  lu:n PNWe I/9,PNLa 167
  liun PNWe I/9,PNLa 167,
        RN 27o
Lune/Yorks. (r.n.)
  liun PNYN 4,RNY 11,DDd 17,
        PNE'side 71
Lune Dale/NRY
  liundil PNYN 3o8
Lune's Bridge/We
  liunz brig DKe 145
Lurgashall/Sx
  lə:gəsəl, -'seil PNSx 111
  lə:gəʃəl BBC
  lʌdʒəʃɔ:l PNSx(i)1o5,Hope
Lustleigh/D
  lʌstli BBC
Luton/Bd,D,K
  lu:tn EPD
  lu:t(ə)n BBC
  lu:tən BCE (for L. in Bd)
  -u:- DEPN (for L. in Bd)
  l(j)u:tən Schr.
  lutən Chis.
Luton Fm/Wt
  lu:tn PNWt 286
Lutterworth/Le
  lʌtəwə(:)ɸ EPD
  -wə:ɸ Schr.,Kruis.
  litlwə:ɸ Hope
  loc. litlwəɸ Schr.
Lytwyche Hall/Sa
  lʌtwitʃ EPD
Luxulyan/Co (also spelt -ian)
  lʌk'siljən BBC,BCE,DEPN,
        Jenner(2)3o2
  lʌk'sʌljən BBC,BCE
Lydd/K
  lid EPD,BBC,PNK
Lydden/K
  lid(ə)n BBC
  lidn PNK

Lydeard (Bishop's L.)/So
  lidiəd BBC
Lydford/D,So
  lidfəd Schr.
Lydgate/Sf,WRY
  lidgit, ligit BBC
  lidgət Kruis.
  lidgeit,-git EPD (for L. in Sf)
  lidʒit EPD (a lane in Sheffield)
Lydiard Pk/W
  lidiəd BBC
Lydiate/La
  lidiət BBC
Lydney/Gl
  lidni BBC
Lyells/Wt
  laiəlz PNWt 174
Lyghe/K
  lai EPD
Lymage/Hu
  -idʒ Dodgson(2)342
The Lyme/Chs
  laim PNChs I/2
Lyme Regis/Do
  laim ri:dʒis EPD,BBC,BCE,Chis.
Lyminge/K
  limindʒ BBC,BCE,DEPN,PNK
  laimindʒ BBC,BCE
  -ndʒ H.A.(1) 179
Lymington/Ha
  limiŋtən EPD,DEPN,BBC,Schr.,
        Kruis.,Chis.
Lyminster/Sx
  limstə DEPN,PNSx 169
  laiminstə PNSx(i)1o6
  liminstə BBC
  linstə Hope
Lymm/Chs
  lim PNChs II/36,BBC,BCE
Lymn/Li (r.n.)
  lim RN 243,DEPN
Lympne/K (also spelt Lymme)
  lim DEPN,EPD,BBC,BCE,PNK
Lympstone/D
  lim(p)stən BBC
Lynch/K (f.n.),Wt
  lintʃ DK,PNWt 286
  lin(t)ʃ EPD
Lyndhurst/Ha
  lindhə:st EPD
Lyndon/Ru
  lindən EPD
Lyne/Nb (r.n.)
  lain Schr.
Lyneal/Sa
  liniə [sic] GlossSa 517
Lyneham/D,O
  lainəm BBC

Lyneham/W
   lain(h)əm   PNW(i) 119
Lynemouth/Nb (= Linmouth)
   lainmauþ   BBC
Lynher/Co (r.n.)
   lainə   RN 275,DEPN,BBC,BCE
Lynmouth/D
   linməþ   EPD,BBC,Schr.
   loc. liməþ   Bchm.119
Lynn (King's L. or L. Regis)/Nf
   kiŋz lin   Schr.
   lin ri:dʒis   Schr.,Chis.
Lynn (in other counties)
   lin   EPD,Schr.
Lynn Fm/Wt
   lin   PNWt 286
Lynnhouse Bridge, L. Fm/Chs
   lin-   PNChs III/19
Lynstead/K
   linsted   PNK
Lynton/D
   lintən   EPD
Lynwick Ho/Sx
   linik   PNSx 157
Lyons/Du
   laiənz   Schr.,Kruis.
Lypiatt Fm/W
   lipjət   PNW 96
Lytchett Matravers/Do
   litʃət mə'trævəz   PNDo(i)112
   litʃit   -   BBC
   litʃət   DDo
Lyth/We
   laið   PNWe I/81
   laiþ   DEPN,BBC,BCE
   li:þ   DEPN
Lytham St. Annes/La
   liðəm snt ænz   BBC,BCE,DEPN,EPD
                  PNLa 155
   leðəm   PNLa 155
Lythe/Sr,NRY
   laið   EPD
Lyttleton/Ldn
   litltən   EPD,Schr.
   -tn   EPD
Lyveden/Np
   livdən   BBC
   livden   EPD
Lyvennet/We (r.n.)
   li'venit, li'venət   RN 276
   lai'venit   PNWe I/lo
   _ ´ _   DEPN

M

Mabe/Co
  meib BBC
Mablethorpe/Li
  meiblɔ:p EPD
Macclesfield/Chs
  olim maksfilt. maksilt
    PNChs II/vii,GlossChs
  makslt GlossChs
  mækslt Hope
  mæksfilt DSLa,Schr.("loc."),
    Hope
  mæksfi:ld GlossChs(i),s.n.
    Maxfield,Hope,
    Schr.("loc.")
  now makəlsfi:ld PNChs II/vii
  mæklzfi:ld EPD,BBC,Schr.,
    Chis.
  mæklsfi:ld EPD
Macefen/Chs
  meisfen PNChs IV/37
Machpelah/WRY
  mæk'pi:lə BBC
Macketts Fm/Wt
  mækits PNWt 16
Mackworth/Db
  mækwə:þ BBC
Madehurst/Sx
  mædəst PNSx 129
  -æ- DEPN
Madeley/Sa,St
  meidli BBC,DEPN,BCE (for M.
    in Sa),EPD (for M. in Sa)
  mɛ:dli Ellis 483 (for M. in
Madingley/Ca   Sa)
  mædiŋli PNCa 181,ONCa 184,EPD
Madresfield/Wo
  mædəzfi:ld PNWo 2o9,DEPN,BBC,
    BCE
  mætʃfi:ld GlossSEWo 82
Madron/Co (also spelt Maddern)
  mædrən DEPN,BBC,BCE,Hope
Maer/Co,St
  mɛə BBC,BCE (for M. in St)
Maesbury/Sa
  (see note 1 below)
Maesfen/Chs
  meisfen PNChs IV/37
Magdale/WRY
  meig- PNSWY 3o9
Magdalen/Nf,Yorks.
  mægdəlin BBC,Förster (for
    M. in Yorks.)

Magdalen College/O,
Magdalene College/Ca
  mɔ:dlin EPD,BBC,Förster,Kruis.,
    Schr.(for M.C. in O)
Magdalen Hill/ERY
  mɔ:dlin il GlossHol 17
Magdalen Ho/ERY
  mɔ:dlin u:s PNYE 41
Maggra Pk/NRY
  mɑ:grə PNYN 166
Maghull/La
  mə'gʌl PNLa 119,EPD,DEPN,BBC,BCE
  megul PNLa 119
  me:l PNLa(ii) (see also note 2)
  olim meil DEPN,PNL'pool 52
Magna Charta Is/Sr
  mægnə kɑ:tə EPD
Maida (as in M.Hill,M.Vale/Ldn)
  meidə EPD
Maidenhead/Brk
  meidnhed EPD,Bchm.62,Schr.
  -h- ESpr.416
Maidstone/K
  meidstən EPD,BCE,Schr.,Bchm.29,
    Kruis.,MEG 124,HL 727
  loc. medstən Schr.,Hope,PNK,
    MEG 124,HL 727
  rarely spelling pron.:
  meidstoun EPD,BBC,HL 727,Bchm.8o
Maindea/D
  mendə PND 175
Maisemore/Gl
  meizmɔ: BBC
Maitland Pk/Ldn
  meitlənd EPD,Schr.,Kruis.
Makeney/Db
  makni PNDb 589
Malborough/D
  mɔ:lbərə PND 3o7,BBC,BCE,DEPN,
    HL 1o51
Malcomb Place/K
  mælkəm Kruis.
Malden/Sr
  mɔ:ld(ə)n EPD,BBC
  mɔ:ldən BCE,Schr.
  mɔld(ə)n EPD
  mɔ:ldn Kruis.
Maldon/Ess
  mɔ:ldən PNEss 218,BCE,Schr.
  mɔ:ld(ə)n EPD,BBC
  mɔld(ə)n EPD
  mɔldn Kruis.
Malford (Christian M.)/W
  kristjən mɔ:lfəd BBC

1) "English people, I think, pron. Maesbury, Mayzbury (Meiz), but
   Welsh people nearly Mizebury or Marzbury (Maiz or Mɑ̄iz)" (PNSa)
   (i.e. [meizbəri, maiz-, mɑ:z-]).
2) "The old pron. [me:l] is not forgotten" (PNLa 119).

Malham/WRY
  mɔ:m, maləm   PNYW VI/133
  mɔ:n [sic] Hope
Malins Lee/Sa
  meilinz EPD
Malkin Twr/La
  mælkin EPD,Bchm.lo
The Mall/Ldn
  ðə mæl EPD,BBC
  mɔ:l EPD[1917/24,1937][1]
Mallerstang/We
  maləstæŋ PNWe II/11
  fromerly mɔ:stən PNWe II/11,
                  PNE'side 65
Malling/K
  mɔ:liŋ EPD,DEPN,BBC,BCE,
        Hope,PNK
Malling Without/Sx
  mɔliŋ PNSx 354
  mɔ:liŋ PNSx(i)lo6
  ma:liŋ Hope
Mallow Ghyll/Du
  mælou gil BBC,BCE
Mallows Gn/Ess
  mæləz PNEss 553
Malmesbury/W
  mɑ:mzbəri BBC,BCE,DEPN,Chis.,
        Kruis.,MEG 297,BG
  -zb(ə)ri EPD
  mɑ:msb(ə)ri Schr.
Malpas/Chs
  mɔ:pəs PNChs IV/38 ("older
        local"),GlossChs(i),
        s.n.Mawpus,GlossChs,
        PNE&W,H.A.(2)45,EPD,
        BBC,BCE,Bchm.9,Hope
  mɔ:lpəs PNChs IV/38,DEPN,EPD,
        BBC,BCE,Bchm.9
  mælpəs PNChs IV/38,EPD,BBC,
        BCE,MEG 291,Bchm.9
Malpas/Co
  moupəs EPD,BBC,BCE,PNE&W
Malpergis Fm/Ess (alias Mellow
  mɔlipɑ:dʒis PNEss 81 Purgess)
Malsis Hall/WRY
  mɔ:sis PNYW VI/26
Maltby/NRY
  mɔ:tbi PNYN 171
Malton/NRY
  mɔ:lt(ə)n EPD,BBC
  mɔlt(ə)n EPD
  mɔ:ltən Chis.,Hope
Malvern/Wo
  mɔlvə:n PNWo 2lo,EPD
  mɔ:və:n PNWo 2lo
  mɔ:lvən EPD,BBC,BCE,Chis.,
        HL 1222

mɔ:vən EPD ("loc."),BBC,BCE,
      HL 1222,MEG 291,Hope,
      GlossSEWo 82
mɔ:lvə:n EPD,HL 1222
mɔlvən EPD,Hope
Malvern Hills/He and Wo
  mɔ:vən, mɔ:lvən,
  mælvən ("incorrect") hilz   Sc
  mɔ:(l)vən hilz   Kruis.
Malwood (Castle M.)/Ha
  mɔ:lwud BBC
Manaccan/Co
  mə'nækən BBC,BCE,DEPN (stress
                        only)
Manaton/D
  mænətən PND 481,BBC,BCE
Mancetter/Wa
  mænsətə Hope
Manchester/La
  mæntʃestə BBC
  mæntʃəstə Chis.,Bau.
  mæntʃistə BBC,Kruis.,Wyld 262
              DSLa
  mæn(t)ʃistə EPD,Schr.
  mæn(t)ʃestə,-(t)ʃəstə EPD
  mɑ:n(t)ʃistə Schr.
  mantʃəstə Brunner 163,Lloyd 1
  mantʃstər, mantʃtrər [sic]
              Lloyd 127
Manea/Ca
  meini BBC,BCE
  -ei- DEPN
Manesty/Cu
  manəsti PNCu 353
  mænəsti PNE'side 7o
Mangerton/Do
  mæŋgətən PNDo (i)278
Mangotsfield/Gl
  'mæŋgətsfi:ld BBC
Manhood Hd/Sx
  ðə mænud PNSx 79
Manley/Chs
  mænli EPD,Schr.
Manningham/WRY
  mæniŋəm Schr.
Manning (as in M.'s Heath/Sx)
  mæniŋ EPD
Manningtree/Ess
  mæniŋtri: Schr.
Mansell/He
  mænsl EPD
Mansergh/We
  manzə PNWe I/49
  mænzə BBC,BCE
  mænsə EPD
  -zə DEPN

---

1) "früher und [...] heute noch oft [mɔl], jetzt aber zunehmend [mæl]
   (ESpr.332).

Mansfield/Nt
    mansfild   PNNt 123
    mænsfiːld   EPD,Schr.,Kruis.
Mansfield Woodhouse/Nt
    vulgo wudəs   PNNt 127
Manshead/WRY
    mɔːnzed   PNSWY 2o7
Mansion House/Ldn
    mænʃ(ə)n haus   EPD
    menʃən aus   CPP 66
    vulg. mʌntʃiŋ (h)aus, -in
            Bau.,s.n.Munchin(g) H.
Manthorpe/Li
    mæntrəp   Hope
Manuden/Ess
    'mænjudən   PNEss 551 [1],BBC
Manwood/Sx
    mænud   Mawer(2)lo3
Mapledurham/O
    meipl'dʌrəm   PNO(i)15o
Mapledurwell/Ha
    meipl'dəːwel   BBC
Maplescombe/K
    meipləskuːm   PNK
Mapleton/Db (also spelt -pp-)
    mapltən   PNDb 387
    meipltən   PNDb(i) II/99,BBC
    mæpltən   BBC
Mapleton/K
    meipltən,mæpltən   BBC,BCE
Maplin Sands/Ess
    meiplin   PNEss 18
    mæplin sændz   BBC
Mappleton/ERY
    mapltən   PNYE 63
Marazion/Co
    mærə'zaiən   EPD,BBC,BCE,
               Jenner(2)3o4
    mærə'zain   DEPN
    mæ'rɑːziən   Chis.
Marbury/Chs
    mɑːbəri   PNChs III/lo6
March/Ca
    mɑːtʃ   EPD,BBC,Schr.,ONCa 198
Marden
    mɑːd(ə)n   BBC
Marden/K
    mɑː'den   EPD ("old-fashion-
           ed"),BCE,PNK
    mɑːd(ə)n   EPD
Marden/Sx
    mɑːrn   PNSx 51

Mare Fen/Ca
    mɑːfn   PNO li
Mareham/Li (i.e. M.-le-Fen,M.-on-the-
           Hill)
    meərəm   DEPN,BBC,BCE
Maresfield/Sx
    mɛːrzfəl   PNSx 349
Marfleet/ERY
    mɑːflit   PNYE 213,GlossHol 17,
             Hope
Margaretting/Ess
    mə'gritən   PNEss 258
    mɑːgə'retiŋ   BBC
    mɑːgetiŋ   Hope
Margate/K
    mɑːgit   EPD,Schr.,Kruis.,HL 1177,
             MEG 254
    mɑːgeit   EPD ("loc."),BBC,
             Schr.,Chis.
    mɑːgət   Schr.,Chis.,MEG 254 [2]
Margery/Sr
    mɑːdʒ(ə)ri   EPD
Marham/Nf
    mærəm   BBC[3],EPD,BCE,DEPN
    mɑːrəm   BBC,EPD
Marhamchurch/Co
    'mærəmtʃəːtʃ   EPD,BBC,BCE
Marholm/Np
    mærəm   PNNp 237,DEPN,BBC,BCE
Mariansleigh/D
    mɑːli, mɛːri ænzliː   PND 382
Marishes/NRY
    mæriʃiz   EPD
Mark/So
    mɑːk   EPD
Markby/Li
    mɑːkbi   EPD
Markeaton/Db
    mɑːtn   PNDb 481,DEPN,Hope
Market Weighton/ERY
    mɑːkit wiːtən   PNYE 229
    - wiːt(ə)n   BBC,PNE&W
    mɑːkət wiːtən   BCE
    wiːtn   Ellis 5ol
    -i:-   DEPN
Markham/Nt
    mɑːkəm   EPD
Mark Lane/Ldn (underground station,now
    mɑːk lain   CPP   Twr Hill)
Marklye/Sx
    mɑːk'lai   BBC,BCE

1) "There was considerable variation locally in the pron. as late as
the nineties when [mɑːndən], [mæləndain], [mæləntain] and
[mælindən] could be heard" (PNEss 552).
2) "more rarely [-gət], but 'careful speakers' often retain [-geit]"
(MEG 254).
3) "The first is the traditional loc.pron. The second is used for the
R.A.F. station by R.A.F. personnel" (BBC,cf. EPD).

Marks (as in M.Gate/Ess)
  mɑːks EPD
Markshall/Ess
  'mɑːkshɔːl BBC,BCE
  mɑːksl BBC
  mɑːksəl BCE
Marksteakes Fm/Sx
  mɑːstiks PNSx 297
Marks Tey/Ess ⟶ Tey
Markyate/Hrt
  mɑːkit PNHrt 47
Markyate Street/Hrt
  mɑːkjeit striːt BBC
Marlborough/W
  mɔːlbərə PNW 297,BBC,BCE,
            Schr.,Hope,MEG 291
  mɑː(r)lbərə PNW(i) 123
  mɔːlbrə BBC,Schr.,BG
  mɔːlb(ə)rə, mɑːl- EPD[1]
  mɔːl- DEPN,Dobson 992
  mɑːlbərə Schr.
Marlborough Ho/Ldn
  mɔːlbrə, -bərə BBC
Marlborough Place, M.Rd/Ldn
  mɑːlbərə HL 1222 (see also
            note 1 below)
Marley
  mɑːli EPD
Marlingford/Nf
  mɑːlnfəd Hope
Marling Pk/Mx
  mɑːliŋ EPD
Marlow/Bk,He
  mɑːlou EPD,BBC,Schr.,Chis.
Marlston/Chs
  mɑːrlstən PNChs IV/163
Marnham/Nt
  (see note 2 below)
Marnhull/Do
  mɑːnəl PNDo(i)42,BBC
Marple/Chs
  olim marpə,
  mɑːrpəl PNChs II/vii
  mɑːrpə GlossChs
Marsden/Du,La,WRY
  mɑːzdin PNLa 86
  mɑːzdən EPD
Marsett/NRY
  mɑːsit PNYN 264
Marsh
  mɑːʃ EPD
Marshalsea/Do
  mɑːʃ(ə)lsi(ː) EPD

Marsham/Nf,Sx
  mɑːʃəm BBC,PNSx(i)lo8
Marsh Baldon/D
  mɑːʃ bɔːldən BCE
  -    bɔːld(ə)n BBC
Marshgreen/Wt
  meʃgriːn PNWt 69
Marsh Ho/Wt
  mɑːrʃ PNWt 57
Marske/NRY
  mask PNYN 154 and 293
Marston
  mɑːst(ə)n EPD
  mɑːstən, mɑːsn Schr.
Marston/He
  mɑːsn GlossSEWo 82
Marston/WRY
  loc. mɑːrsn,
  mɑːsn; mɑːstən HL 1221
Marston-on-Dove/Db
  mɑːsn PNDb(i) II/lol,Hope
Marston Gill/Cu (f.n.)
  mɑːstin gil, mɑːsən gil
     Thorn.7o and 76,note 3o
Marston Jabbett/Wa
  mæsn Hope
Marston Mersey/W
  vulgo mɑːsən PNW 29
Marston Moor/Yorks.
  mɑːstən muːə Schr.
Marston Moretaine/Bd
  mɑːsən mɔːtən PNBdHu 79
Marsworth/Bk
  mɑːzəþ PNBk 98
Marthall/Chs
  marþə PNChs II/ix
  mɑːrþə GlossChs
  martɔːl PNChs II/82
Martham/Nf
  mɑːþəm DEPN,BBC,BCE
  mæþəm Hope
Martinhoe/D
  still pron. loc.
  mætinhou Chanter 523
Martinsthorpe/Ru
  mɑːstrəp GlossRu vii
Martlesham/Sf
  mɑːdlzəm DSf 28o
  mɑːtəlʃəm PNDVall 12
  mɑːtlʃəm BBC,BCE
Marton/We ⟶ Long M.
Martonsands/Chs
  mɑːtn sæːnz PNChs III/182

1) "[mɔːlb(ə)rə]is the usual pron. of the name of the town in Wilts.
   [...]. [mɑːl-] is not infrequently heard in names of London stre
   (EPD).
2) cf. the Lincs. saying 'Marnum hole' which refers to Marnham/Nt
   (GlossM&C,s.n. Marnum hole).

Martyr Worthy/Ha
   mɑ:t wə:þi   BBC
Marvell Fm/Wt
   mɑ:rvəl   PNWt 1o2
Marylebone/Mx
   a) with [l]:
   "now the l is often sounded"
               MEG 228
   mærələbən   BBC,HL 122o
   mærələboun   HL 122o
   mær(ə)ləboun   EPD
   mær(ə)ləbən   EPD
   mærləbən   HL 122o
   mæriləbən   PNMx(i)6o
   mæriləboun   Zachr.(2)149
   mærəlboun, -bən   Schr.
   mɛəriliboun   Schr. ("rarely")
   mɛəriləboun   Chis.
   mɑ:libən   EPD,BBC,HL 122o
   b) without [l]:
   mæribən   PNMx 137 ("olim"),
           EPD,BBC,Schr.,Kruis.,
          Chis.("popularly"),
          Zachr.(2)149f. (see
          note 1 below),MEG
          125,HL 1221
   mæriboun   MEG 125,Schr.,Hope
   mærəbən   EPD,HL 1221,Bau.
   mærouboun   Hope,H.A.(2)46
   mæribɔn   MEG 228
Maryport/Cu
   mɛəripɔ:t   EPD,Schr.
Mary Tavy/D
   mɛəri teivi   BBC,BCE
Masbrough/WRY
   mæzbərə   BBC,BCE
   mæzbrə   Hope
   -æz-   DEPN
Masham/NRY
   mæsəm   PNYN 234,EPD,DEPN,BBC,
          BCE,Schr.
   mæʃəm   Schr.,Kruis.
Mashbury/Ess
   mæʒbri   PNEss 488
   mæʒbəri   EssDD 158
Mason/Nb
   meisn   EPD
Masson/Db (a hill)
   mæsn   EPD
Mastock/Sx
   mæstik   Hope
Mathon/He
   -eið-   DEPN
Mathon/Wo
   meiðən   PNWo 65,DEPN
Matlaske/Nf
   'mætlæsk   BBC

Matlock/Db
   mætlək   Schr.
   mætlɔk   EPD
Matravers/Do
   mə'trævəz   PNDo(i)258,EPD,BBC
   _ ⏌ _   DEPN
   (see also s.n. Lytchett M. and
   Langton M.)
Mattersey/Nt
   olim mɑ:si   PNNt 86
   mætəsi   BBC
Mattishall/Nf
   mætsəl   Hope
   mætsl   Ellis 273
Maudlin/Sx
   mɔ:dlin   PNSx(i)1o8
Maugersbury/Gl
   mɔ:gəzberi   PNGl I/222
   mɔ:zbəri   BBC,BCE
Maughenby/Cu (also spelt Maughan-
           and Maughon-)
   mɑ:hwənbi   PNCu 194
   mafnbi   PNCuWe 77
   mæfnbi   DEPN
   mæfənbi   BCE,Hope
   mæf(ə)nbi   BBC
   mɔfənbi   Hope
   mæhwənbi   PNE'side 75
Maulds Meaburn/We
   'mɔ:dz 'mi:bən   PNWe II/156
Mauleverer (as in Allerton M./WRY)
   mɔ:l'evərə   EPD
Maunby/NRY
   mɔ:nbi   PNYN 274
Maunsell Ho/So
   mæns(ə)l   EPD
Mautby/Nf
   mɔ:bi   BBC,Hope
Mavis Enderby/Li
   meivis   EPD
Mawkinherds/Ess
   mɔkinhə:dz   PNEss 47o
Mawnan/Co
   mɔ:nən   BBC
Mayfair/Ldn
   meifɛə   EPD
Mayfield/Sx
   meivul   PNSx 381,Hope
   mefəl   PNSx 381
Maynard (as in M.'s Gn/Sx)
   meinəd, 'meinɑ:d   EPD
Mayon/Co (also spelt Mean)
   mein   BBC,BCE
Meaburn/We
   miəbərən,
   meibərən   PNE'side 67

---

1) "The etymologically correct pron. is being ousted by spelling prons."
   (Zachr.(2)149f.).

Mead/D,Ha
  miːd EPD
Meaford/St
  mefəd DEPN,BBC,BCE
Meagre/Hu
  megri PNBdHu 264
Mean/Co ⟶ Mayon
Mears Ashby/Np
  mɛːəz æʃbi PNNp 137
  miəz EPD
Measand/We
  miːzən(d) PNCuWe 163
Measand Beck/We
  meizən bek PNE'side 65
Mease/Db,Le,St (r.n.)
  miːs RN 28o,DEPN
Measham/Db
  miːʃəm PNDb(i) II/1o3
Meathop/We
  miːþəp PNCuWe 164,BBC
Meaux/ERY (= Melsa)
  mius PNYE 43
  mjuːs BBC,DEPN,Hope
Meavy/D
  meivi PND 229,DEPN
  miːvi DEPN,BBC,BCE
Meddon/D
  meidən PND 75,DHtl 8
Meden/Nt (r.n.)
  olim meidən PNNt 6
  miːdn PNNt(i)92,RN 283
  -iː- DEPN
Medham/Wt
  medəm PNWt 286
Medhurst Row/K
  medhəːst Schr.
Medina/Wt (r.n.)
  midiːnə Schr.
Medley/O
  medli EPD
Medlock/La (r.n.)
  medlɔk EPD
Medmenham/Bk
  mednəm PNBk 19o,BBC,Hope
  medənəm Hope
Medomsley/Du
  medəmzli BBC,BCE
Medway/K,Sx (r.n.)
  medwei EPD,Schr.,Kruis.
Meeth/D
  miːþ BBC
Meir/St
  miə BBC,BCE
Melbourn/Ca
  melbən ONCa 191
Melbourne/Db,ERY
  melbɔːn EPD,Kruis.,Bchm.7o
  melbən EPD,Schr.,Kruis.,
        Bchm.7o

Melbury Abbas/Do
  melbəri æbəs BBC
Melcombe/Do (i.e. M.Horsey,M.Regis
  melkəm EPD
  melkəm riːdʒis Schr.
  milkəm haːrsi DDo
Meldreth/Ca
  meldrəþ ONCa 193
Melford/Sf
  melfəd Schr.
Melhuish Barton/D
  meliʃ PND 452,EPD,Kruis.
  melhjuiʃ, meljuiʃ EPD
Melishaw/La
  meliʃɔː, meliʃə PNLa 176
Melkinthorpe/We
  melkinþrɔp PNE'side 71
Melksham/W
  melksəm, melsəm PNW 128
  melkʃəm BBC
Mellingey/Co
  me'lindʒi BBC,BCE
Mellis/Sf
  melis BBC
Mellor/Chs,La
  melə, melɔː EPD
Mellow Purgess Fm/Ess ⟶ Malpergis
Melmerby/Cu,NRY
  melərbi PNCu 223,GlossCu xvii,
        PNE'side 74,Hope (for
        in Cu)
  meləbi DEPN (for M. in Cu),BBC
  melənbi ROS 42
  melməbi BBC
Melsa/ERY ⟶ Meux
Meltham/WRY
  melþəm BBC
  meltəm Hope,DHd 68
Melton
  meltən Schr.
  melt(ə)n EPD
Melton/Sf
  meltn PNDVall 61
Melton Constable/Nf
  melt(ə)n kʌnstəbl BBC
Melton Mowbray/Le
  melt(ə)n moubrei BBC
  meltən - BCE,Chis.
  moubri Kruis.
Menabilly/Co
  menə'bili BBC
Mendip Hills/So
  mendip hilz EPD,Schr.
Menheniot/Co (= Menhynnet)
  mən'heniət BBC
  men'heniət BCE
  _ ∕ _ DEPN
Menthorpe/ERY
  menþrəp PNYE 261

Menwith/WRY
   meniþ PNYW V/135
Meole Brace/Sa
   mi:l breis PNSa,BBC,BCE,Hope
   -i:- DEPN
Meols/Chs
   mels PNChs IV/296,DEPN,BBC,
       BCE
Meolz/La
   mi:lz DEPN,BBC,BCE
Meon/Ha (r.n. and p.n.)
   mi:ən BBC
Meopham/K
   mepəm EPD,DEPN,BBC,BCE,PNK,
       Hope
   mefəm Hope
Mepal/Ca
   mepəl PNCa 237
   mi:pl BBC
   mi:pəl BCE
   -i:- DEPN
Meppershall/Bd
   mepʃul PNBdHu 17o
   mepsəl Mawer(2)93
   mepəʃəl BBC
Merchistoun Hall/Ha
   mə:tʃistən BBC
Mere/W
   miə(r) PNW(i)125
   miə DEPN
Meredith/Gl
   meridiþ EPD,MEG 28o
   merədiþ EPD
Merevale/Wa
   merivəl PNWa 87,BCE
   meriveil BBC
   meri- DEPN
Mereworth/K
   meriwə:þ BBC,BCE,PNK
Meriden/Wa
   meridən BBC
   miədən (?) Hope[1]
Merley/Wt
   mə:li PNWt 286
Merrington/Du
   mær(ə)ntən DSDu
Merrivale/D
   meriveil EPD
Merry Gardens/Wt
   meri girdənz PNWt 2o4
Merryl Cottage/Wt
   mə:rl PNWt 286
Mersea/Ess (also spelt -ey)
   olim mɑ:si PNEss 319,DEPN
   mə:zi BBC
   meisi Hope

Mersey/Chs,La (r.n.)
   mə:zi RN 289,EPD,Schr.,Kruis.,
       Chis.
   mɑ:zi DSto
   -z- DEPN
Mersham/K
   mə:zəm PNK
Mersham/Sx
   (see note s.n. Chilsham)
Mersley Fm, M. Down/Wt
   mezli, mə:rzli PNWt 171
Merstham/Sr
   mə:stəm PNSr 300,BBC
   mə:stəhæm PNSr 3oo
   meistrəm Hope
Merston Manor/Wt
   mesn, mə:stn PNWt 16
   mesən DWt,s.n.jolterhead
Merton
   mə:tən Schr.
   mə:tn EPD,Kruis.
Merton/Nf
   mɑ:tən Hope
Meshaw/D
   'meʃɔ: BBC,BCE
Metham/ERY
   metəm, mi:ðəm PNYE 254
Methley/WRY
   meþli BBC
   often pron.
   medli PNDu,s.n.Medomsley
Methwold/Nf
   meþəld, mjuəl Hope
Mevagissey/Co
   mevə'gisi, -'gizi BBC,BCE
   _ _ ´ _ DEPN
Mexborough/WRY
   meksb(ə)rə EPD
Meynell Langley/Db
   menl, meinl EPD
   menəl Kruis.
Michaelchurch/He
   mʌltʃə:tʃ Hope
Michaelstow/Co
   'maiklstou BBC
Michelcombe/D
   mʌtʃikəm PND 3o2
Micheldever/Ha
   'mitʃldevə BBC
   'mitʃ(ə)ldevə EPD
Micklebring/WRY
   miklbrin BBC
Mickleham/Sr
   mikləm PNSr 81
Mickleover/Db
   -ouvə PNDb(i) II/1o6

---

1) Hope's transcription is 'Mere-den'.

Middlesb(o)rough/NRY
  midəlzbruf   PNYN 16o
  midlzbrʌf   ESpr.355
  -bruf   DEPN
  midlzbrə   EPD,BBC,ESpr.355
  midlzbərə   Schr.
  midəlzbrou   Chis.
Middlesceugh/Cu
  midlskiuf   PNCu 224,PNE'side
  midlskə   GlossCu xvii   71
Middlesex
  midlseks   EPD,Schr.,Kruis.
Middlethorpe/Li
  þelþrəp   Hope
Middleton
  midltən   EPD,Schr.,Kruis.
Middleton Tyas/NRY
  midltən taiəs   BBC
Middletown/Cu,So
  midltaun   BBC
Middlewich/Chs
  midlwitʃ   PNChs II/ix and 24o,
               BBC,BCE,Kruis.,
               GlossChs (so pron.
               in W. Chs)
  midlweitʃ   PNChs II/ix and
               24o,GlossChs (so
               pron. in E. Chs)
  midlwaitʃ   PNChs II/ix and 24o,
               GlossChs
Midhurst/Sx
  midəst   PNSx 27,PNSx(i)1o9
  midhə:st   EPD
Midsomer Norton/So
  midsʌmə nɔ:t(ə)n   BBC
Milburn/Sr,We
  milbən   Schr.
Mildenhall/W
  mainəl   PNW 3o1,Hope
  mainɔ:l   DEPN,BCE,Hope
  mild(ə)nhɔ:l   BBC (see note 1
  mildənhɔ:l   BCE   below)
Mildmay/Ldn
  maildmei   EPD
  mɑ:mei   CPhon 71
Mile (as in M. End, etc.)
  mail   EPD
Mile End Road/Ldn
  mɑ:l en roud   CPhon 7o
Miley Pk/NRY
  milə paik   PNYN 2o4
Milford
  milfəd   EPD,Schr.
Milford/D
  milvəd   PND 75
Millbank/K,Ldn,WRY
  milbæŋk   EPD
Millbay/D
  mil'bei   BBC

Mill Beck/WRY
  mil bek   DDd 15
Mill Dyke/Cu
  mel   Thorn.74 and 77,note 49
Millichope/Sa
  militʃə p   Dodgson(2)381
Millington/Chs
  miliŋtən   PNChs II/ix
  olim militn   PNChs II/ix,
               GlossChs
Millington/ERY
  militən   PNYE 178
Millom/Cu
  miləm   EPD
Mills (as in M.Hill/La)
  milz   EPD
Millwall/Ldn
  'mil'wɔ:l, milwəl   BBC,BCE
Milnrow/La
  mildrou   GlossR&R,DSLa
Milnthorpe/We
  milþrəp   PNWe I/95,PNE'side 71
  milþəp   Chis.
  milþɔ:p   MEG 2o8
Milton
  miltən   Schr.
  milt(ə)n   EPD
  miltn   Kruis.
Milton/Ca
  miltən   ONCa 21
Milton Ernest/Bd
  ɑ:nist   PNBdHu 24
Milton Hyde, M. Street/Sx
  miltən   PNSx(i)11o
Milton Keynes/Bk
  ki:nz   (heard by the author)
Mimran/Hrt (r.n.)
  mimræn   BBC
Mincing Lane/Ldn
  minsiŋ lein   Schr.
Minehead/So
  mainhed   Kruis.
  ◡ _ , _ ◡   EPD
  minjəd   Hope
  -h-   ESpr.416
Minety/Gl,W
  minti   PNGl I/77,PNW 61
  mainti   EPD,BBC
Miningsby/Li
  miniŋzbi   BBC,BCE
The Minories/Mx
  minəriz   PNMx 153
Minsceugh/We
  minskə   PNE'side 63
Minshull Vernon, Church M./Chs
  minʃəl   PNChs III/154
  minʃl və:nən   BBC

1)"Sometimes spelt MINAL and pron. [mainɔ:l]" (BBC).

Minsmere/Sf (r.n.)
  minzmiə BBC
Minster/Co,K
  minstə EPD
Mirables/Wt
  mə:rəblz PNWt 253
Mire Garth/WRY
  'maiə gɑ(:)þ DDd 16
Mire House/WRY
  maiər aus DDd 12 and 13
Mirfield/WRY
  mə:fild Hope
Miserden/Gl
  mizədin PNGl I/129
  mizədən BBC
  misədən, maizədən BCE
  (see also note 1 below)
Missenden/Bk
  misndən EPD
Misson/Nt
  miz(ə)n PNNt 87
  -z- DEPN
  (see also note 2 below)
Mistley/Ess
  misli PNEss 343,DEss
Miswell/Sx
  mizwəl PNSx(i)llo
Mitcham/Sr
  mitʃəm EPD,BBC
Mitchell(as in M.Pk/Sx)
  mitʃ(ə)l EPD
Mitford/Nb
  mitfəd EPD
Mithian/Co
  miðiən BBC
Moat/Cu
  muɔ:t GlossCu xvii
Mockerkin/Cu
  mouəkin GlossCu xvii
Moggerhanger/Bd (or Mugger-)
  mɔ:rhæŋə PNBdHu 91,DEPN,Hope
  muəhæŋə BBC
Mohun's Ottery/D
  mu:nz'ɔtəri PND 642
Moira/Le
  mɔi(ə)rə EPD
  mɔiərə BBC
Molash/K (also spelt Moldash)
  moulæʃ DEPN,BBC,BCE,Schr.,
      Hope,PNK
  mɔliʃ PNK
  (see also s.n. Moldash)
Mold (as in M.Gn/WRY)
  mould EPD

Moldash/K (also spelt Molash)
  mouldæʃ, moulæʃ Schr.
Mole/D;Sr,Sx (r.n.)
  moul Schr.
Molesdon/Nb
  mouzdən PNNbDu 143
Molesey/Sr
  moulzi EPD,BBC
Molesworth/Hu
  olim mʌlzwəþ PNBdHu 246
  moulzwə(:)þ EPD
Mollington/Chs
  mɔlitn GlossChs
Mollington Banastre /Chs (=Little M.)
  banəstər PNChs IV/171
Mollington Torold/Chs (= Gt M.)
  'tɔroud PNChs IV/177
Molton/D
  moultən Schr.
  moult(ə)n EPD
  (see also s.n. South M.)
Molyneux (as in M.Brow/La)
  mɔlinju:ks, mʌlin-, -ju: EPD
Monckton/Do,WRY
  mʌŋ(k)tən EPD
  (see also s.n. Tarrant M./Do)
Moncrieff's/Wt
  mɔŋkri:f PNWt 260
Mondrum/Chs ⟶ Aston-juxta-M.
Monewden/Sf
  mʌnidən Hope
  mɔnəden BCE
Mongeham/K
  mʌndʒəm DEPN,BBC,BCE,Dodgson(2)
      382,PNK,PNing 171
Mongewell/O
  mʌnɡwel PNO 48,BBC,BCE,Dodgson(2)
      382
  mʌndʒəl PNO(i)155,DEPN
Monkham/Wt
  mʌŋkm PNWt lo3
Monkhams Fm/Ess
  mʌŋkəmz PNEss llo
Monkhouse/St
  mʌŋkhaus EPD
Monks/Sx
  mʌŋks PNSx(i)llo
Monks Eleigh/Sf
  mʌŋks i:li BBC
Monkton
  mʌŋ(k)tən EPD
Monkton/D
  mʌŋktən BCE

1) "always pron. by the common people Miserdine" (Moberly 126).
2) Hope's transcription 'Mizen' could be [maizən].

Monkwearmouth/Du
 mʌŋk'wiəmauþ EPD,BBC
 wiəməþ Hope
 (see also note 1 below)
Monnow/He (r.n.)
 mʌnou BBC
Montacute/So
 'montəkju:t BBC,Schr.
Montford/Sa
 mounvərt,mʌmfərt GlossSa 517
Montreal/K
 montriɔ:l EPD,Schr.,Kruis.
 montri:əl,
 vulg. montri:l Schr.
The Monument/Ldn
 monimnt CPP 66
Monyash/Db
 'mʌniæʃ BBC
Moon's Fm/Ess
 mu:nziz PNEss 436
Moordale/NRY
 modəl PNYN 151
Moor Divock/We
 mouər'divik PNE'side 7o
Moore/Chs
 muə EPD
 mɔ:ə, mu:ə Kruis.
Mooredge/D
 mʌridʒ PND 576
Moor Fm/Wt
 muər PNWt 155
Moorfields
 mu:əfi:ldz Schr.
Moorgate/Ldn,Nt,WRY
 muəgit, mɔə-, mɔ:-, -geit EPD
 (cf. Bchm. 78)
Moorgate Street/Ldn (underground
       station)
 mɔ:git stri:t CPP 66
Moorhouse/Cu
 marəs PNCu 334
Moorsley/Du
 mausli GlossHtn,s.n.Lonning
Moorthorpe/WRY
 moðərəp Hope
Moortown/Wt
 muərtæun PNWt 285
 muətaun DWt,s.n. pitchen
       prong
Moorwinstow/D
 məːstɔ: DHtl 8
Moota/Cu
 mju:tə GlossCu xvii
Moray Hill/Cu
 murə PNE'side 63
Morchard/D ⟶ Cruwys M.
Morden/Ca
 mɔ:dən ONCa 189

Mordiford/He
 mɔ:difəd BBC,DHe 43
 dial. mɔ:difət DHe 43,GlossHe
       s.n.Ford
More/Sa
 mɔ:, mɔə EPD
Morebath/D
 mɔ:bɑ:þ BBC,BCE
Morecambe/La
 mɔ:kəm EPD,Schr.,Chis.
Moredon/W
 mɔ:(r)dn PNW(i)128
Moreleigh/D
 mɔ:li BBC,BCE
Moresby/Cu
 morizbi PNCu 421
 morisbi DEPN,BBC,BCE
Moreton
 mɔ:tn EPD
Moreton/Chs
 mortən PNChs IV/319
Moreton Morrell/Wa
 mɔ:t(ə)n morəl BBC
Morgan's Lane/Wt
 mɑ:rgnz PNWt 286
Morland/We
 mouərlən PNE'side 74
Morley
 mɔ:li EPD,Schr.,Kruis.
 loc. mɑ:li Schr.
Morley Pk/Db
 mɑ:li pɔ:k Hope
Mornington Crescent/Ldn
 mɔ:niŋtən EPD
Morpeth/Nb
 mɔ:pəþ EPD,BBC,BCE
 -piþ Schr.
 -peþ EPD
 morpəþ Chis
Morphany Hall Fm/Chs
 mɔ:rfəni PNChs II/154
Morrell Roding/Ess
 mʌr(ə)l, mə'rel EPD
 mʌrəl Kruis.
 (see also s.n. Roding,Roothing)
Morris (as in M.Ct/K)
 moris EPD
Mort(e)hoe/D
 mɔ:thou BBC,BCE
Mortham/NRY
 mɔ:təm PNYN 3o1
Mortimer/Brk
 mɔ:timə EPD,Kruis.
Mortlake/Sr
 mɔ:tleik EPD,BBC,Schr.
Morton
 mɔ:tən Schr.
 mɔ:tn EPD,MEG 265

1) [-məþ] is heard more often than [-mauþ], as pointed out in Bchm.7

Morton/Li
  mɔtən   GlossM&C,s.n.Motton
Morton/Wt
  mɑːrtn, mɔːrtn   PNWt 58
Morvah/Co
  mɔːvə   BBC
Morwenstow/Co
  mɔːwinstou   BBC
Morwick/Nb
  mɔrik   PNNbDu 145,DEPN
Mosedale/Cu
  mouzdəl   PNCu 3o4
Mosedale/We
  moːzdəl   PNWe II/169
  moəzdl   PNE'side 72
Moseley/Gl,St,Wo
  mouzli   EPD
Moser/We
  moːzə   PNWe I/149
Moser Hill/WRY
  mɔːzər il   DDd 14
Moses (as in M.Gate/Ldn)
  mouziz   EPD
Mosley Common/La
  mɔsli   BBC
  mɔzli, mouzli   EPD
Moss/WRY
  mɔs   EPD
Mossford/Chs
  mɔsfət   DSChs 16
Mossley/Chs,La
  mɔsli   BBC
  məzli   PNLa(ii)
  mɔːsli   DSLa
Mossley/WRY
  mɔzli   DHd 7o
Mostard/WRY
  mɔstədz   DDd 16
Moston/Chs
  mɔstən   PNChs IV/141
Mothecombe/D
  mʌdikum   PND 277
  mʌðikəm   BBC
Mottistone/Wt
  mat(i)stn,
  mɔːtsn, matəstn   PNWt 164
  mɔtistən, -stoun   EPD
  mɔtsən   DWt,s.n.Lor a massey
Mottram/Chs
  mɔtrəm   EPD
Mouldsworth/Chs
  mouldzwəːþ,
  mouldzwəþ   PNChs III/279

Moulham/Do (also spelt Mowlem)
  mɔləm   PNDo I/55,PNDo(i)127
Moulsecoombe/Sx (see note 1 below)
  mauskəm   PNSx 294,DEPN
  moulskuːm   BBC
  maulskm   PNSx(i)111
Moulsford/Brk
  moulzfəd   BBC
Moulsham/Ess
  moulʃəm   PNEss 246,BBC
  mulsəm, mulʃəm,
  muːsəm,mausəm   PNEss 246
  maulsəm   EssDD 158
  -u-   DEPN
Moulsoe/Bk
  mʌlsou   PNBk 36,DEPN[2]
  moulsou   BBC,BCE
Moulton
  moultən   Schr.
  moult(ə)n   EPD
  moultn   Kruis.
Moulton/Chs
  moultən,
  mou(l)tn, mouʔn   PNChs II/2o7
  moult(ə)n   BBC
  muːətn   DSChs 18
Moulton/Li
  moult(ə)n   BBC
  moultən   BCE
Moulton/NRY
  moutən   PNYN 286
Moulton Eaugate/Li
  moult(ə)n iːgeit   BBC
  moultən -   BCE
Mount/Co,WRY
  maunt   EPD,Schr.
Mt Caburn/Sx
  kɔːbəːn, kɑːbəːn   PNSx 353
Mountfield/Sx
  mʌntfəl   PNSx 474
Mountjoy/Co
  maunt'dʒɔi, ⟋ _   EPD
Mountnessing/Ess
  mʌnt'nisən,
  'mʌnəsiŋ   PNEss 26o
  mʌnisiːn, mʌnisend   Hope
  mʌnəziːn   GlossEss vi,note 1
Mt Sorrel/W
  maunt 'sɔrəl   BBC
Mousehold/Nf
  maushould   BBC,BCE

---

1) This is the spelling used in PNSx; different spellings have been
   found in BBC (-coomb), BG (-comb) and PNSx(i) (-combe).
2) Only this form was heard by the author in the neighbouring villages
   in Beds.

Mousehole
   mauzl   BBC
   mausl,maushoul   Schr.
Mousehole/Co
   mauzl   EPD
   mauzəl   BCE,Hope,Pezzack l,
      note l
   maushoul   BCE
Mousehole/Wt
   mæushoul   PNWt 174
Mousell/La
   mo:zəl   PNLa 2o6
Mouse Sike/WRY
   maus saik   DDd 16
Mouthlock/We
   mouðlik   PNE'side 71
Mowbray/NRY,WRY
   moubrei, -bri   EPD
   (cf. also Bchm. 78)
Mow Cop/St (= Mowcop)
   mau kɔp   DEPN,BBC,BCE
Mowlem/Do ⟶ Moulham
Mowsley/Le
   mauzli   DEPN,BBC,BCE
   mouzli   BBC,BCE
Mowthorpe/ERY,NRY
   mouþrəp   PNYE 125,PNYN 35
   mu:þrəp   Hope (for M. in ERY),
      PNERY
Moxby/NRY
   mouzbi   PNYN 29
Muchelney/So
   mʌtʃəlni   BBC
Mudeford/Ha (= Muddiford)
   mʌdifəd   BBC,BCE
Mugginton/Db
   mʌgintən   BBC
Muggleton Lane/Wt
   mʌgltn   PNWt 69
Muker/NRY
   miukə   PNYN 272
Mulgrave/NRY
   mougriv   PNYN 137
   mʌlgreiv   EPD
Mullion/Co
   mʌliən   EPD,BBC
   -jən   EPD
Mundesley/Nf
   mʌnzli   BBC,Hope
Mundford/Nf
   mʌndfəd   BBC
   mʌnfə   Hope
Mungrisdale/Cu (also spelt -grise-)
   mʌŋraizdəl   PNCu 226
   loc. muŋraizdəl   PNO li
   mən'graizdl   PNE'side 75
   mʌn'graizdeil   DEPN,BCE
   mʌŋ'graizdeil   BBC

Munsley/Wt
   mʌnzli   PNWt 17
Muntham/Sx
   mʌntəm   PNSx 177 and 198
Murcott/Np,W
   mə:kət   EPD
   mə:(r)kət   PNW(i) 128
Murdishaw Wood/Chs
   mə:diʃə   PNChs II/181
Mursley/Bk
   mə:zli   PNBk 7o
Murton/We
   murtən   PNE'side 66
Murton/NRY
   muətən   PNYN 2o3
Musgrave/We
   mʌzgreiv   EPD
   muzgrə   PNE'side 63
Muska/Cu (two places)
   muskə   PNE'side 63
Muston/Le,ERY
   mʌs(ə)n   BBC
   mʌsən   BCE (for M. in ERY)
   mʌstən   BBC,BCE (for M. in ERY)
Muswell Hill/Mx
   mʌzəl, mʌzwəl   PNMx 123
Mutley/D
   mʌtli   BBC
Muzwell/Bk
   mɔzəl   PNBk 177
Myerscough/La
   maiəskou   EPD,BCE
   maskə   PNLa(ii)
Mylor/Co
   mailə   BBC
Mynd/Sa (i.e. Long M., a hill range)
   lɔŋ mind   BBC
Myne/So
   mi:n   DEPN
Myrtle Cottage/Wt
   mə:rtl   PNWt 174
Mystole/K
   maistoul   PNK
Mytchett/Sr
   mitʃit   BBC
Mytholm/WRY
   maiðəm   BBC,BCE
Mytholmroyd/WRY
   mɑ:ðəmrɔid,'maiðəm-   PNYW III/.
   maiðəm'rɔid   BBC,BCE
   'miðəmrɔid   EPD
Mythop/La
   miþɔp   BBC
Myton-on-Swale/NRY
   mitən   PNYN 23,DEPN

ɟ

Nab/WRY
 næb   DHd 72,DAl&Hd
Nabal's Fm/W
 næbəlz   PNW 74
Naddle Beck,N.Ho/We
 nadl   PNWe II/169
Nafferton/ERY
 nafətən   PNYE 94
Nailinghurst Fm/Ess
 næniglz   PNEss 417
Nailstone/Le
 nelsən   Hope,PNLe 76
Naish/So
 næʃ   EPD
Nancegollan/Co
 nænsi'gɔlən   BBC
Nancekuke/Co
 næns'kju:k   BBC
Nancledra/Co (or -ea)
 næn'kledrə   BBC,BCE
Nanjizal Bay/Co
 næn'dʒizl   BBC
 næn'dʒizəl   BCE
Nantwich/Chs
 næntwitʃ   PNChs III/3o,EPD,
            BBC,BCE,Kruis.,Chis.
 næntwaitʃ   PNChs III/3o,BBC,
            EPD ("loc.")
 næntitʃ   Chis.
 næn?witʃ, older
 næntweitʃ   PNChs III/3o
 nənt'waitʃ   Schr.525 ("every-
            where in Chs")
 nantwitʃ   (so pron. in WChs),
 nantweitʃ   (so pron. in EChs),
 nantwaitʃ   GlossChs
Naphill/Bk
 næpəl   PNBk 184
Narford/Nf
 nɑ:fə   Hope
Narsmeer/Co
 _ ́   Jenner(2)3o4
Naseby/Np
 neizbi   DEPN,EPD,Schr.,Chis.,
            Kruis.
Nash
 næʃ   EPD,Kruis.
Natcot/D ⟶ Nattacot
Nateby/We
 ne:tbi   PNWe II/2o
 nɛətbi   PNE'side 72
Nattacot/D
 nædikit   DHtl 8

Naunton/Gl
 nɔ:ntən   Schr.
 nɑ:ntən,nɔ:ntən   PNGl II/35 (for
            N. in Lwr Kiftsgate Hd)
 nɑ:ntən   PNGl I/199 (for N. in
            Lwr Slaughter Hd)
Naunton Beauchamp/Wo
 nɔ:n   GlossSEWo 81[1]
Navenby/Li
 neiv(ə)nbi   BBC
 neivənbi   BCE
 neiənbi   Hope,GlossSWLi[2]
 -ei-   DEPN
Naworth Castle/Cu
 nɑ:waþ   PNCu 67
 nauəþ, nɑ:wəþ   BBC,BCE
 neiwəþ, neiəþ   Schr.
 nɔ:wəþ   Schr.525
Nawton/NRY
 nɔ:tən   PNYN 65
The Naze/Ess (a promontory)
 ðə neiz   EPD,Schr.
Nazeing/Ess
 neiziŋ   EPD,BBC
Neadon/D
 neidən   PND 482
Neasden/Mx
 ni:zdən   PNMx 163,EPD
Neasham/Du
 ni:səm   PNNbDu 147
 -i:-   DEPN
Neatishead/Nf
 ni:tstid, ni:tished   BBC[3]
 ni:tshed   Hope
Neaton/Nf
 neitən   Hope
Neaum/We
 ni:əm   PNWe I/211
Nechells/Wa
 ni:tʃlz   BBC
Nedging/Sf
 nedʒiŋ   PNSf 74
Needham Market/Sf
 li:dəm [sic] Hope (found twice in
 ni:dəm   EPD   Hope)
Needingworth/Hu
 ni:dinə:þ   PNBdHu 2o9
Nelson/La
 nels(ə)n   BBC
 nelsn   EPD,Kruis.
Nene/Np (r.n.)(also spelt Nen)
 nen   PNNp 3,EPD,BBC,BCE,DEPN,Schr.
 ni:n   PNE&W,DEPN,EPD,BBC,Chis.,
            PNSr xliii ("also heard
            locally")

1) loc. also called 'Dirty Naun' (GlossSEWo 81).   2) "The old clipped
forms are mostly retained by the upper classes"(GlossSWLi). 3) "The
first is the traditional village pron. The second is used by Service
personnel for the local R.A.F. Station" (BBC).

Neopardy/D
  nepədi PND 4o6
Nesbit/Nb,Nesbitt/Du,Nb
  nezbit EPD
Nesfield/WRY
  nesfi:ld EPD
Ness/Chs,NRY
  nes EPD
Neston/Chs
  nestən PNChs IV/222
  nesn PNChs IV/222,GlossChs
Neswick/ERY
  nezik PNYE 165
Netheravon/W
  neðəreiv(ə)n BBC
Nethercote/Gl,O,Wa
  neðəkət BBC
Netherfield/Sx
  neðifəl Hope
Netherhampton/W
  olim neðərigtən PNW 217
Netherland/St
  neðələnd EPD
Netherne/Sr
  neðən BBC
Netherscales/Cu
  nedərskɛəlz PNE'side 72
Netherthong/WRY
  neðərþɔŋ DHd 129
Netley/Ha,Sa,Sr
  netli EPD
Netteswell/Ess
  netswəl PNEss 46
  netswel BBC,Hope
  nets- DEPN
Nettlecombe/Wt
  nedlkm PNWt 254
Nettlestone/Wt
  netlstn PNWt 198
Nevendon/Ess
  nɛ:ndən PNEss 164
  nev(ə)ndən BBC
Nevill (as in N.Holt/Le)
  nev(i)l EPD
Newall/WRY
  niuwil PNYW IV/2o4
Newark/Gl,Np,Nt
  nju:ək BBC,Schr.
  nju(:)ək EPD (for N. in Nt)
Newbald/ERY
  niubɔ:d PNYE 226
Newbarn Down/Wt
  nju:barn dæun PNWt 82
  nu:bərn - PNWt 286
  nju:bɑ:n DWt,s.n. pill

Newbiggin
  nju:'bigin Schr.
  ∕ _ _ EPD
Newbiggin/Cu
  nibikən PNCu 188,PNE'side 65
        DEPN
Newbold
  nju:bould EPD
Newbold-on-Stour/Wo
  noubəld PNWo 173
Newborough/Np,St
  nju:bərə BBC
Newbourne/Sf
  nju:bɔn PNDVall 15
Newbridge
  nju:bridʒ Schr.
Newbridge/Wt
  nu:bridʒ PNWt 211
Newbrough/Nb
  'nju:brʌf BBC,BCE
Newburgh/La,NRY
  nju:bərə Kruis.
  nju:b(ə)rə EPD
Newbury
  nju:bəri Schr.,Chis.
  nju:b(ə)ri EPD
Newcastle/Nb,St (-on-Tyne,-under-)
  'nju:kɑ:sl EPD,Schr.,Kruis.,
        Mawer(2)91,BCE (for
        N. in Nb)
  _ ∕ Kruis.,Ellis 645
  nju:'kæsl BCE (for N. in Nb
  loc. nju'kæsl EPD (for N. i
        Schr.
  'nju:kæsəl Chis.,Mawer(4)28
  'nju:kɑ:sl əpən tain,
  nju:'kæsl - - BBC[1]
  'nju:kɑ:sl ʌndə'laim BBC
Newchurch/Wt
  niutʃərtʃ PNWt 167
  nju:tʃə:tʃ DWt,s.n.rudder
New Cut (a street name)/Ldn
  vulg. 'Recent Incision' Bau.
Newdigate/Sr
  nju:digeit EPD,Schr.
  -git EPD,Schr.,Kruis.
  -gət Schr.
Newent/Gl
  niuwənt PNGl III/173
  nju:ənt Chis.
Newfound/Ha
  nju:faund BBC

---

1) "The second, being the loc. pron., should normally take precedenc
over the other. Here, however, is a case where the first is firml
established national usage" (BBC).

Newgate/Ldn
   nju:git EPD,Kruis.
   nju:geit EPD,Bau.
   vulg. nu:gət Bau.
   short: The Gate Bau.,s.n.Gate
Newham/Ess
   nju:(h)əm BBC
Newham/Nb
   nju:əm BBC
Newhaven/D,Db,Sx
   'nju:heiv(ə)n BBC
   nju:'heivn Schr.
   _ ⌐ , ⌐ _ EPD
   nju(:)'heivn EPD
Newington
   nju(:)iŋtən EPD
Newington/O
   nu:tən PNO 277 and 4ol
Newland
   'nju:lænd BBC
Newland/Gl
   nju:'lænd BCE
Newlyn/Co
   nju:lin BBC
Newman Lane/Wt
   'niu:mən lein PNWt 115
Newmarket
   'nju:ma:kit EPD,BBC
   _ ⌐ _ Schr.
   nju:ma:kət Bau.(for N.in Sf)
Newnes/Sa
   nju:nz EPD,Kruis.
Newnham
   nju:nəm EPD,Schr.,Kruis.
Newnham Fm/Wt
   ninəm PNWt 43
Newport
   'nju:pɔ:t EPD,Schr.
Newport/St
   nu:pərt Ellis 478
Newport/Wt
   'nipərt DWt 16 and passim,
            PNWt 175 (see also
            note 1 below)
Newport Pagnell/Bk
   nju:pət pænəl PNBk 21
   nju:pɔ:t pægnəl BBC
Newquay/Co (or New Quay)
   'nju:ki: BBC,BCE
   ⌐ _ EPD
Newsham/Cu (several places)
   niusəm PNE'side 65

Newsham/Nb
   nju:səm PNNbDu 15o
   nju:ʃəm Potter 35
Newsome/WRY
   nju:zəm BBC,BCE
Newstead
   nju:stid EPD,Schr.,Bchm.62
   rarely -sted Bchm. 62
Newstead Abbey/Nt
   'nju:stid 'æbi Schr.
Newthorpe/Nt
   njutrəp PNNt 146
Newtimber/Sx
   nju:timbə PNSx(i)116,BBC
Newton
   nju:tən Schr.
   nju:tn EPD,Kruis.
Newton Flotman/Nf
   nju:t(ə)n flɔtmən BBC
Newton Kyme/WRY
   - kaim BBC
Newton Morrell/NRY
   - mɔr(ə)l BBC
Newton Purcell/O
   - pə:sl BBC
Newton Reigny/Cu
   - reini BBC
   nju:tən - BCE
   niu:tən PNE'side 73
Newton St. Cyres/D
   - snt saiəz BBC
Newton St. Loe/So
   - snt lou, snt lu: BBC
   nju:tən sənt lou, sənt lu: BCE
Newtown
   'nju:taun EPD,Schr.
Newtown/Wt
   niu:tæun PNWt 82
Neyland/Nf
   neilənd BBC
Nibthwaite/La
   nibþət PNLa 217
Nidderdale/WRY
   niðədil PNYW V/76
   neðədil GlossMY,s.n.Rant
Nidon/So
   naidən BCE
   naid(ə)n BBC
Ninezergh/We
   nainzə PNWe I/92
Ninfield/Sx
   ninfəl PNSx 487,Hope
   ninvəl Hope
Ningwood/Wt
   niŋwud PNWt 211

1)"The loc. pron. of the last century was ['nipərt], which may still
  be heard occasionally from old people" (PNWt 175).

Ninham/Wt
  ninəm PNWt 58
Niton/Wt
  nitn,naitn,nɔitn PNWt 18o
  naitən BCE
  nait(ə)n BBC
  -ai- DEPN
Nixon/Cu
  niksn EPD
Noctorum/Chs
  'nɔk'tourəm PNChs IV/269
Nod Hill/Wt
  nɔd EPD
Noneley/Sa
  nʌnəli BBC
Nonington/K
  nɔniŋtən,nʌn- PNK
Nonsuch Palace/Sr
  'nʌnsʌtʃ, 'nɔn- BBC¹
Nonsuch Pk/Sr
  (see note 1 below)
Noonstones/Cu
  ni:ənstæns PNCu 178
Norbury/Chs
  -bəri PNChs III/1o9
The Nore (a sandbank in the
  nɔ:ə EPD   Thames)
  nɔ: EPD,Schr.
Norfolk
  nɔ:fək EPD,Schr.,Kruis.,
          HL 9o4,MEG 257
  nɔrfək Chis.
Norham/Nb
  nɔrəm EPD,DEPN,BBC,BCE,Schr.,
         MEG 377
  nɔ:rəm EPD
Norland/WRY
  nɔ:lənd EPD
Normanby/Li,NRY
  nɔrənbi Hope (for N. in Li)
  nɔrəmbi GlossSWLi,GlossM&C,
           s.n.Norumby
  nɔ:mənbi EPD
Normandy/Sr
  nɔ:mandi, loc.
  nɔ:'mændi EPD
Normans/Wt
  nɔ:rmənz PNWt 83
Normanton
  nɔ:məntən EPD,BBC,Schr.,BCE
             (for N. in WRY)
  nɑ:məntən Hope (for N.in Le)
             PNLe 78

Norice Field/WRY
  nɔris fi:ld GlossSh(suppl)41
Norsworthy/D
  nɔzwə:ði, nɔzəri PND 245
Northallerton/NRY
  nɔ:'θælətn EPD,DEPN (stress
                            only
  nɔrθ'ælətən Chis.,Schr.
Northam/D,Ha
  nɔ:ðəm BBC,BCE (for N. in D)
Northampton/Np
  nɔ:'þæm(p)tən,
  nɔ:þ'hæm(p)tən EPD,BBC
  loc. nə'þæm(p)tən EPD,Bchm.2...
  nɔ:þ'æmptən BCE,Kruis.
  nɔrþæmptən Chis.
  nɔrþ'æmtən Schr.
Northamptonshire
  nɔ:'þæm(p)tənʃə EPD,Schr.
          -ʃiə EPD
  (for further variants see preceding entry)
Northants. (short for Northampton-
  nɔ:'þænts EPD   shire)
Northbourne/K
  nɔ:þbɔ:n PNK
Northbrook
  nɔ:þbruk EPD,Kruis.
Northbrook End/Ca
  noubəkən Hope
North Burton/ERY
  nɔþ bətn PNYE 112
Northcote Ho/D
  nɔ:þkət EPD,KRuis.
  -kout EPD
North Dalton/ERY
  dɔltn PNYE 168
  nɔ: dɔtn Hope
North Dean/WRY
  nɔ:di:n Hope
Northenden/Chs (also spelt Norther...
  nɔ:rðəndən, older
  nourðin, -ən PNChs I/234
  nɔ:ðəndən BBC
  nɔ:ðən Hope
  nɔ:ð(ə)n EPD (if spelt Northe...
  nɔ(:)rðin GlossChs
Northfield
  nɔ:þfi:ld EPD
Northfleet/K
  nɔ:þfli:t EPD
Northiam/Sx
  nɔrdʒəm PNSx 522

1) "The first of these is usual among scholars. Locally, however, at
Nonsuch Park, where the site of the original Tudor palace is to b...
found, the second is current today" (BBC).

nɔ:dʒəm PNSx(i)114,DEPN
nɔ:ðiəm BBC
Northill/Bd
  norɔl PNBdHu 93
Northland Ho/W
  nɔ:þlənd EPD
Northleigh/D (in Braunton Hd)
  nɔ:þli:, nɔ:li: BBC,BCE
Northleigh/D (in Colyton Hd)
  nɔ:rli: PND 628
  nɔ:þli: BBC,BCE
Northleigh/O
  nɔrlai GlossO(suppl)74
Northolme/Li
  nɔ:þoum BBC,BCE
Northorpe/Li
  nɔþərəp GlossM&C,s.n.Heaps
  nɔþrəp ibidem,s.n.Nothrup
Northowram/WRY
  nə'þauərəm BBC
  nɔ:þərəm Hope
Northrepps/Nf
  'nɔ:þreps BBC
Northsceugh/Cu
  norskə PNCu 79,PNE'side 63
  nɔ:þskju:f BBC,BCE
North Sea
  nɑ:rf se: DDo
Northstow/Ca (a hd)
  nɔ:þstou ONCa 199
Northumberland
  nɔ:'þʌmbələnd EPD,BBC,Kruis.
  rarely nə- EPD,Bchm.69
  -blənd EPD
  nɔrþʌmbələnd Schr.,Chis.
  nə'þumələn(d) DSDu
Northwich/Chs
  nɔ:þwitʃ PNChs II/ix,DOld 97,
    EPD,BBC,BCE,Schr.,
    Kruis.,EPN 88
  -weitʃ, -waitʃ PNChs II/ix
  nɔ:ðwitʃ (so pron. in WestChs),
    -weitʃ (so pron. in EChs),
    -waitʃ GlossChs
Northwick/Wo
  nɔ:ðik PNWo 113
Northwold/Nf
  nɔrəl [sic] Hope
Northwood
  nɔ:þwud EPD
Northwood/Wt
  nɔrþwud,
  nɔ:rðud PNWt 185
Norton
  nɔ:tn EPD
Norton/D
  nɔ:dən PND 136
Norton/So → Midsomer N.

Norton Belleau/Nf (now called Blo N.)
  blou nɔ:tən Hope
Norton Folgate/Ldn
  nɔ:t(ə)n fɔlgit CPhon
Norton Hawkfield/So (sometimes -ville)
  nɔ:t(ə)n hɔ:kfi:ld BBC
  nɔ:tən - BCE
Norwell/Nt
  nɔrəl PNNt 193
Norwich/Nf
  nɔridʒ DEPN,EPD,BBC,BCE,Schr.,
    Kruis.,Hope,ONwick 374,
    MEG 2o5
  nɔritʃ EPD,BBC,Schr.,Chis.
Norwood
  nɔ:wud EPD,Schr.
  nɔrəd PNYW V/124
Norwood Gn/WRY
  nɔrəd gri:n Hope
The Nothe Promontory/Do
  nouð BBC
Notley/Ess
  nɔ:tli PNEss 293
Nottingham/Nt
  nɔtiŋəm PNNt 13,EPD,BBC,Schr.,
    Chis.,Hope,MEG 376
  vulgo nɔtigəm PNNt 13
  nɔtigəm EDG §273,RSp 135
  nɔtinəm Hope (see note 1 below)
  nɔtindʒəm PNE&W,s.n.Birmingham
Nottinghamshire
  nɔtiŋəmʃiə EPD
    -ʃə EPD,Schr.
Notting Hill/Ldn
  nɔtiŋ hil EPD
Notting Hill Gate/Ldn (underground
             station)
  nɔtin il gait CPP 66
Notts. (short for Nottinghamshire)
  nɔts EPD
Nova Scotia/Du,La,WRY
  nouvə skouʃə EPD
Noverton/Gl
  nɔvətən PNGl II/llo
Nower Hill/Mx
  nauə PNMx 65
Nowton/Sf
  noutən BCE
  nout(ə)n BBC
  -ou- DEPN
  -au- PNSf 1o5
Nox/Sa
  nɔks EPD
Nunburnholme/ERY
  nun'bɔnəm PNYE 18o
Nuneaton/Wa
  nʌn'i:tn EPD,Kruis.
  nʌn'i:t(ə)n BBC

1) Another transcription given in Hope is 'Nottingyum'.

nʌn'iːtən   Schr.,BCE,Chis.,
               DEPN (stress only)
'nʌniːtən   Schr.
jiːtən   Hope
nuniːtn   Ellis 487
Nuneham Courtenay/O
   njuːnəm kɔːtni   EPD,BBC,BCE,
                   Kruis.
Nun House/WRY
   nun aus   DDd 15
Nunneys Wood/Wt
   nʌniz wud   PNWt 212
Nunthorpe/NRY
   nunþrəp   PNYN 166
   nʌnþrəp   EDD,s.n.Thorpe[1]
   -þrəp   GlossClv,s.n.Thorp
Nunwell/Wt
   nʌnəl   PNWt 58
Nunwick/Nb
   nʌnik   DEPN,BBC,BCE
Nursling/Ha ⟶ Nutshalling
Nurstead/K
   nʌstid   PNK
Nutbourne/Sx
   nʌtbən   PNSx(i) 115
Nuthall/Nt
   vulgo nʌtl   PNNt 149,PNNt(i)lol,
                 BBC
   nʌtəl   BCE
Nuthampstead/Hrt
   vulgo nʌtstid   PNHrt 183
Nutshalling/Ha
   nəːsliŋ   H.A.(2)46,Hope
Nuttall/La,Nt
   'nʌtɔːl   EPD,Bchm.7o
   nʌtou   GlossR&R
Nyetimber/Sx
   naitimbə   PNSx(i)116
Nyland/Do
   nailənd   PNDo(i) 12,DEPN
Nymans/Sx
   naimənz   BBC
Nymet/D
   -i-   DEPN
Nymet Rowland/D
   nimit roulənd   BBC
   nimet   -   BCE
Nymet Tracey/D
   nimit treisi   BBC
Nympton (Bishop's N.)/D
   biʃəps nimtən   BBC

1) 'Nunthrup' in EDD could also be [nun-].

O

Oadby/Le
   oudbi   BBC

Oakbank/We
   ɛːkbænk   PNE'side 75

Oak Dale/NRY
   jagdil   PNYN 214

Oakeley/Sa
   oukli   EPD

Oakenclough/La
   oukənkljuː,
   -klau, -klʌf   BBC,BCE

Oakengates/Sa
   wʌkn jæts, - jiəts   GlossSa 517

Oakerthorpe/Db
   ou-   PNDb(i) II/119

Oakes/WRY
   ouks   EPD

Oakham/Ru
   uːkəm   DEPN,Hope,Ellis 256,
               Mawer(4)285,GlossRu 24
   jekm   PNE&W
   oukəm   EPD,Schr.,GlossRu 24

Oakhampton/D → Oke-

Oakhampton/Wo
   'ouk'hæm(p)tən, _ ˌ _   EPD

Oakington/Ca
   ouki̯ntən   ONCa 26

Oaklands
   oukləndz   EPD

Oakleigh/La,Sx
   oukli   EPD

Oakley
   oukli   EPD,Schr.
   olim ɔkli   PNBdHu 24

Oakley Purlieus/Np
   pəːliz   PNNp 17o

Oakmere/Chs
   older local
   -mɛːr   PNChs III/217
   ɔːkmɛːr   GlossChs

(The) Oaks
   ouks   EPD

Oakshaw/Cu
   jækʃə   GlossCu xvii

Oakworth/WRY
   oukwə(ː)þ   EPD

Oare
   ɔː   Schr., PNK
   ɔːə   DWSo 23
   ɔː(r)   DK

Oare Fm/W
   olim hwəːr   PNW 262

Oath/So
   ouð   BBC,BCE

Oatlands/Cu,Sr
   outləndz   EPD

Oaze Deep (a channel in the Thames
   ouz diːp   BBC   estuary)

Obleigh/So → Ubley

Oby/Nf
   oubi   BBC

Occlestone/Chs
   ɔkəlstan [sic]   PNChs II/252

Ock/Brk (r.n.)
   ɔk   Schr.

Ockbrook/Db
   ɔkbruk   PNDb(i) II/12o

Ockenden Rd/Ldn
   ɔkindən roud   Schr.

Ockham/Sr,Sx
   ɔkəm   EPD,Schr.

Ockley
   ɔkli   EPD

Ocklynge/Sx
   ɔklindʒ   PNSx 432,EPD,BBC

Ocle Pychard/He
   oukl pitʃəd   BBC,BCE
   ou-   DEPN

Oddendale/We
   oudldɛəl   PNE'side 72

Odell/Bd (also spelt Woodhill)
   wʌdəl, oudəl   PNBdHu 34
   wʌdl   Hope,DEPN
   ou-   DEPN
   ou'del, ə'del   EPD

Odham/D
   ɔdəm   EPD

Odiam/K
   ɔdiəm   PNK

Odiham/Ha
   oudi(h)əm   EPD
   oudiəm   BBC,BCE,Hope
   hɔdʒeəm, ɔdʒhəm   Hope
   ou-   DEPN

Odin Mine/Db
   oudin   EPD

Odsal/WRY
   ɔdzl   BBC

Offenham/Wo
   ʌfənəm   PNWo 266,GlossSEWo 82

Offham/K
   oufəm   DEPN,Hope
   ʌfəm   PNK

Offham/Sx
   ɔfəm, oufəm   BBC,BCE
   ɔfəc   PNSx 142 (for O. in
                     Avisford Hd)
   ouf'hæm   PNSx 316 (for O. in
                     Barcombe Hd)

Offoxey/Sa
   called ʌŋkət   GlossSa 517

Ogden/La,WRY
   ɔgdən   EPD,Schr.

Ogle/Nb
   ougəl   PNNbDu 152

Oglebird Scar/Cu
  uklbər skɑːr   PNE'side 74
Oglethorpe/WRY
  ouglϸɔːp   EPD
Ogwell/D
  ougwel   PND 461,BBC,BCE
  ou-   DEPN
Okehampton/D (also spelt Oak-)
  ɔkiɣtən   PND 2o2,Hope
  ɔkəntən   PND 2o2 (see note 1)
  ouk'hæm(p)tən   BBC,EPD
  ˌ ˈ _   EPD
  oukhæmptən   Chis.
Olantigh/K
  ɔlæntei   PNK
Olantigh Towers/K
  'ɔlənti tauəz   BBC,BCE
Oldbury
  ouldb(ə)ri   EPD
Oldbury-on-Severn/Gl
  ouldbəri ɔn sevən   BBC
Oldcastle/Chs
  ouldkɑːsl   EPD,Schr.
  oulkɑːsl   Schr.
Oldcoates/Nt
  eilkouts   Hope²
  ouldkouts   PNNt(i)1o2
Old Croft River/Ca (r.n.)
  ould krɑːft   PNCa 9
Oldfield
  ouldfiːld   EPD
  oufəl   PNNp 91
  oudfild,oufild   DHd 79 (for
                O. in WRY)
Oldfield Plantation/Hrt
  oufəl   PNHrt 117
Old Ford/Ldn
  oulʔ fɔːʔ   CPhon 117
  'ould'fɔːd   PNMx(i)
Oldham/La
  audəm   Hope,PNLa(ii)
  oudəm   GlossR&R,DSLa,H.A.(2)45
  ouldəm   EPD,Schr.,Kruis.,Chis.
Old Malton/NRY
  ɔːd mɔːtən   PNYN 43
  (see also s.n. Malton)
Oldpark/Wa
  ouldpɑːk   BBC
Oldscale/Cu
  æskəl   GlossCu xvii

Old Sleights/NRY
  ɔːd   PNYN 151
Old Street Hill/Ess
  hɔlstəz hil   PNEss 43
Ollerton
  ɔlətn   EPD
  ɔlərtən, olim
  uːlər-, oulərtn, -tən   PNChs II/
  uːlərtən   GlossChs
  oulətən   Hope
Olmstead/Ca
  ɔmstid, ʌmstid   Bchm.62
  ɔmsted   Bchm.62,EPD
Olney/Bk
  ouni   EPD,PNBk 12,DEPN,BBC,BCE,
          Bchm.37,Mawer(4)284
  oulni   EPD,BBC,Bchm.37,HL 896
  ɔlni   EPD [1917/24],BCE,Kruis.,
          Chis.,Schr.,HL 896
Olton/Wa
  oultən   BBC
Ottinge/K
  -ndʒ   H.A.(1)179
Olveston/Gl
  oulvistən, oulstən   BBC
Olympia/Ldn
  ɔ'limpiə   CPhon 52
Ombersley/Wo
  ɔmbəzli   BBC
Onecote/St
  ɔnkət   DEPN,BBC,BCE
Ongar (High O.,Chipping O.)/Ess
  ɔŋgə   PNEss 71
  'ɔŋgɑː   BBC
Onibury/Sa
  ɔnibəri   BBC
Onley/Np
  (w)ɔnli   PNNp 14
Onny/He,Sa (r.n.)
  ɔni   RN 31o (for O. in Sa),BBC
Onslow
  ɔnzlou   EPD
Onston/Chs
  ɔnstn, loc. ɔnsn   PNChs III/2oo
Openshaw/La
  ɔpnʃə   PNLa(ii)
  oup(ə)nʃɔː   EPD,BBC
  oupənʃɔː   Chis.
Orchard
  ɔːtʃəd   EPD

1) "the loc. pron. [see above] still survives among old people in the
   district" (PND 2o2).
2) "The transcription of the loc. pron. furnished by Hope [scil. Ale-
   cotes] is very ambiguous; if it is interpreted in accordance with
   the ordinary principles of ModE spelling it would mean [eilkouts].ᴵ
   spite of inquiries instituted in the locality itself a pron. devi-
   ating from the spelling could not be traced" (PNNt(i)1o2).

Orcop/He
  ɔ:kɔp, dial. ɑ:kəp DHe 43
Ord/Nb
  ɔ:d EPD
Ordsall/Nt
  vulgo ɔ:rsəl PNNt 9o
Ore/Sf (r.n.), Sx
  ɔ: EPD
Oreston/D
  ousn Hope
Orfold Fm/Sx
  ɑ:- PNSx 134
Orford/Ess,La,Li,Sf
  ɔ:fəd EPD,Schr.,DSf 285
Orfordness/Sf (a promontory)
  'ɔ:fəd'nes BBC
Orgarswick/K
  ɔ:gəswik PNK
Orlestone/K
  ɔ:lstən BBC,PNK
Orleton/He,Sa,Wo
  ɔ:ltən BBC,BCE (for O. in He)
Orlingbury/Np
  olim ɔ:libi:ə PNNp 128
Ormathwaite/Cu
  ɔ:rmþət PNCu 322
  ɔmþət PNE'side 67
Ormesby/Nf,NRY
  ɔ:mzbi EPD,Schr.
Ormsby/Li
  ɔ:mzbi EPD
  ɔrmzbi Chis.
  ərmzbi DLi 42
Ormside/We
  ɔ:msaid, ɔ:msit PNWe II/89
  ɔrmsit PNE'side 69
Ormskirk/La
  ɔ:mzkə:k EPD
  -kək Schr.
  ɔrmzkək Chis.
Orpington/K
  ɔ:piŋtən EPD
Orrell/La
  ɔrəl BBC
  ɔr(ə)l EPD
Orston/Nt
  olim ɔ:s(ə)n PNNt 227
Orston Spa/Nt
  spɔ: PNMx xxxii[1]
Orton/Cu,Np,We
  wɔrtən PNE'side 66
  o:tn DKe 5
  ɔ:tn EPD
Orton Longueville/Hu
  ɔ:t(ə)n lɔŋvil BBC
  (see also s.n. Overton)

Orwell/Ca,Sf; also r.n. in Sf
  olim ɔrəl PNCa 79
  o:wəl ONCa 189
  ɔ:w(ə)l EPD
  ɔ:wel EPD,Schr.(for r.n. in Sf)
Orwell Wood/Co
  ɔ:vəl wud Picken 19o ("so pron.
                    locally now")
Osbaldeston/La
  ɔzbəldestn, ɔ:bistn PNLa 7o,DEPN
  ɔzbəl'destən BBC
Osbaldwick/NRY
  ɔzbəwik PNYN 1o
Osbaston/Le,Sa
  trɔsbən PNSa,GlossSa 517
  trɔspən GlossSa 517
  ɔzbəstən BBC,BCE (for O. in Le)
  ɔz- DEPN (for O. in Le)
Osborne/Wt
  azbərn PNWt 244
  ɔzbən, -bɔ:n EPD,Schr.,Bchm.69
  ɔz- DEPN
Oscroft/Chs
  ɔskrɔft PNChs III/281
Osea Is/Ess
  ouzi, ousi BBC
Osgathorpe/Le
  æsgəɔ:p Hope,PNLe 7o
Osgodby/ERY
  ɔzgəbi PNYE 261,Hope
Osleston/Db
  ɔslistn PNDb 593
Osmaston/Db
  ɔzməstən BBC
Osmond Croft/Du
  uzmənkrɔft PNNbDu 152
Osmotherly/La,NRY
  ɔzmuðəli PNLa 213
  ɔzmələ PNYN 213 [sic]
Osney/O (an island in the Thames)
  ouzni BBC,BCE
Ospringe/K
  ɔsprindʒ BBC,BCE,PNK
  -n(d)ʒ EPD
Ossett Spa/WRY (also spelt -t)
  ɔsit EPD,BBC,Hope
  spɔ: PNSWY 264f.
Ost End/Ess (also spelt Ostend)
  ɔ:st PNEss 427
Osterley/Mx
  ɔstəli EPD
Oswaldtwistle/La
  ɔzw(ə)l(d)twisl EPD
  ɔsətwisl GlossR&R
Oswestry/Sa
  'ɔzwəstri EPD,BBC

1) "The old pron. is still heard locally" (PNMx xxxii).

ɔzwistri   EPD
'ɔzwestri   EPD,BCE
'ɔzistri   BBC
ɔzəstri   Chis.,GlossSa 518
ɔgəstri: Hope
ɔdʒəstri   GlossSa 518
ɔz-   DEPN
Oteley/Sa
  outli   PNSa
Otham/K,Sx
  ɔtəm   BBC,BCE (for O. in K)
  outəm   PNK
Otford/K
  ɔtfəd   EPD,Schr.
  outfəd   PNK
Otherey/So
  ouðəri   BBC
Otherton Fm/Wo
  ɔðətən   PNWo 117
Otley/Sf,WRY
  ɔtlə   PNYW IV/2o3
  ɔtli   EPD
Otley Chevin/WRY
  ɔtli ʃevin, - ʃivin   BBC,BCE
  (see also s.n. The Chevin)
Otter/D (r.n.)
  ɔtə   Schr.
Otterburn/Nb,WRY
  ɔtəbə:n   EPD,Schr.
  ɔtəbən   Chis.
Otterham/Co
  ɔtərəm   BBC
Ottery/D
  ɔtəri   EPD,Schr.
  (see also s.n. Up O.)
Ottery St. Mary/D
  ɔtəri snt mɛəri   BBC
Ottinge/K
  ɔtindʒ   BBC,BCE,PNK,H.A.(1)
Ottringham/ERY   179
  utriŋəm   Hope
Oubrough/ERY
  oubrə   PNYE 48
Ouchthorpe/WRY
  autʃþəp   PNYW II/157
Oughterby/Cu
  autərbi   PNCu 143
Oughtershaw/WRY
  autəʃɔ: BBC
Oughterside/Cu
  u:tərsed   PNCu 3o6
  autəsaid   BBC,BCE
  aut-   DEPN
Oughtibridge/WRY
  'u:tibridʒ   BBC,BCE,GlossSh
    166
  auti-, ɔ:ti- , outi-   BBC,BCE
Oughton Head/Hrt
  ɔ:tən   PNHrt 1o
  autn,ɔ:tn   EPD

Oughtrington/Chs
  u:triŋtən   PNChs II/37,DEPN,BBC,
    BCE,Hope
Oulston/NRY
  oulstən, oustən   PNYN 192
Oulton/Chs
  u:ltən, oultən   PNChs III/165
    and 185
  older local u:tn PNChs III/ 165
    and 185,GlossC
Oulton/Cu
  u:tən   PNCu 3o7,GlossCu xvii
Oulton/Nf
  oultən   DEPN,Hope
Oulton/Sf,St,WRY
  oult(ə)n   BBC
  oultən   BCE (for O. in Sf and WR
  ou-   DEPN (for O. in Sf)
Oulton Broad/Sf
  oult(ə)n brɔ:d   BBC
Oulton Pk/Chs
  oult(ə)n   BBC
Oundle/Np
  aundəl   PNNp 213,Chis.
  aundl   EPD,BBC,BCE
  au-   DEPN
Ousby/Cu
  u:zbi   PNCu 228,DEPN,BBC
  ouzbi   PNE'side 73
Ousden/Sf (= Owsden)
  auzdən   DEPN,BBC,BCE
Ouse (or Gt Ouse)/East Midlands (r.n.
  u:z   RN 313,DEPN,EPD,Schr.,Kruis
Ouse/NRY (r.n.)
  u:z   PNYN 5,RN 314,EPD,Schr.,
    Kruis.
Ouse/WRY
  u:z   PNYW VII/134,EPD,Kruis.
Ousefleet/ERY
  ʌslət, auzfli:t   Hope
Ouseley Lodge/Brk
  u:zli   EPD,Kruis.
Ousethorpe/ERY
  u:sþrəp   PNYE 181
Oussaborough/D
  ɔsəbʌrə   PND 53
Ouston/Du,Nb
  austən   EPD,BBC,BCE (for O. in Du
Ouston Fm/WRY
  oustən   PNYW IV/238
Outhwaite/Cu,La
  ouþət   PNCu 235,PNE'side 67
  u:þweit, ou- , au-   EPD
Outlane/WRY
  ɛətlɔin   DHd 8o
  autlein   BBC
  (see also s.n. Slack)
Outrake Foot/WRY
  autrək fut   DDd 15

Outwood/WRY
  εatwud DHd 8o
Ovangle/La
  o:faŋgl PNLa 176
Ovenden/K,WRY
  ɔv(ə)ndən BBC
  ʌvəndən PNK
  ɔvəndən BCE (for O. in WRY)
Over/Ca
  u:və PNO 1i
  ouvə ONCa 198
Over/Chs
  ouvə PNChs III/17o,BBC
Over/Gl
  u:və BBC
Overbury/Sf,Wo
  ouvəb(ə)ri EPD
Overby/Cu
  auərbi PNCu 296
Overcombe/Do
  ouvəku:m BBC
Oversley/Chs
  olim ɔ:ərzli, u:əzli,
  ou(v)ərzli PNChs II/vii
Oversley Ford/Chs
  u:zli fɔ:d Hope
  -    fɔ:rd GlossChs
  ɔ:rzli -   GlossChs
Overstrand/Nf
  ouvəstrænd EPD
Overthwaite/We
  wɔrfət PNE'side 67
  wɔ:fət Hope
Overton
  ouvətən BBC,Schr.
  ouvətn EPD,Bohm.2o7
  ɔvətən BBC
  ɔ:tən H.A.(2)45
Overton/Chs
  ɔvərtn, uvərtn GlossChs
Overton/Ha
  ouvətən, ɔvətən BCE
Overton/Hu (see note 1 below)
  ɔ:tən Hope
Overton/La
  ɔvətn PNLa 175,PNLa(ii)
  o:vətn PNLa 175
  ɔ-, ou- DEPN
Overton (Market O.)/Ru
  ɔ:tən GlossRu vii
Overton/NRY
  ouətən PNYN 15
Oving/Bk,Sx
  ouviŋ BBC,BCE

u:viŋ PNSx 75,PNSx(i)117,DEPN,
    Hope(for O. in Sx),BCE
    (for O. in Sx),PNBk 1o7
Ovingdean/Sx
  u:viŋdi:n PNSx 311,PNSx(i)118,
    DEPN
  ouviŋdi:n Schr.
  ɔviŋdi:n EPD
Ovingham-on-Tyne/Nb
  ɔvindʒəm PNNbDu 154,PNing 17o,
    Dodgson(2)383,DEPN,BBC,
    BCE,EPD,Ellis 64o
Ovington-on-Tees/Du
  uviŋtən PNNbDu 154
Ovington/Nb
  ɔviŋtən PNNbDu 154,DEPN
Ovington/Nf
  ouvitən EPD,BBC,BCE
  ouvətən Hope
Ovington/NRY
  ouvintən PNYN 299
  ɔviŋtən EPD,BBC,BCE
Ovis/D
  ɔfis PND 58
Ower/Do,Ha
  auə PNDo I/16,PNDo(i)12o,EPD
Owermoigne/Do
  ɔ:rmɔin PNDo I/138,PNDo(i)142
  ouəmɔin BBC,BCE
  ɔ:- DEPN
The Owers/Sx
  oərz PNSx 83f.
  auəz BBC
Owersby/Li
  auəzbi BBC,BCE
Owlands/NRY
  ouləndz PNYN 294
Owler Bar/WRY
  oulə ba: BBC,BCE
Owlers Close/Db (f.n.)
  u:ləz FnSDb 8o
Owlerton/WRY
  oulətən BBC,BCE
Owlett (as in O.'s End/Wo)
  aulit, -let EPD
Owlswick/Bk
  elsik PNBk 172
Owmby/Li
  oumbi BBC,BCE,Hope
Owsden/Sf ⟶ Ousden
Owslebury/Ha
  ʌslbəri BBC,BCE
  ʌzlbəri BBC,BCE,DEPN
  ʌsəlbəri Shore 24o

1) Now spelt Orton; the spelling above is still used for the railway-
   station (cf. BG).

Owsthorpe/ERY
  ouzþrəp   PNYE 247
Owthorne/ERY
  uːþrən   PNYE 28
  þɔːn   Hope
Owthorpe/Nt
  ouþɔrp, ouþrəp   PNNt 238
Oxcliffe/La
  ɔkslif   PNLa 176
Oxenden (as in O. Corner/K)
  ɔksndən   EPD
Oxenham (as in O. Manor/D)
  ɔksnəm   EPD
Oxenhope/WRY
  ɔksnəp   Hope
  ɔksnhoup   EPD
Oxenstand/We
  ousən stænd   PNE'side 65
Oxenthwaite/We
  ousənþət   PNE'side 65
Oxford/O
  ɔksfəd   EPD,BBC,Schr.,Kruis.,
          Bau.
Oxfordshire
  ɔksfədʃə   EPD,Schr.
   -ʃiə   EPD
Oxley/Ess,St,Sx
  ɔksli   EPD
Oxney's Fm/Ess
  ɔksnz   PNEss 423,EssDD 158
Oxon. (short for Oxfordshire)
  ɔksɔn   EPD,Bchm.63
  ɔks(ə)n   EPD
Oxshott/Sr
  ɔkʃɔt   PNSr 95,EPD
Oxspring/WRY
  ɔkspriŋ   DHd 80
Oxton/Chs
  ɔkstən,ɔksn   PNChs IV/269
Oxton/Nt
  vulgo ɔks(ə)n   PNNt 172
Ozengell Grange/K
  ouz(ə)ngel greindʒ   BBC

P

Pachesham/Sr
  olim pætsəm,
  et vulgo plætsəm   PNSr 8o
Packer (as in P.'sHill/Do)
  pækə   EPD
Padanaram/Wt
  pæd'nɛərəm   PNWt 285
Paddington/Ldn
  pædiŋtən   EPD,Schr.,Bau.
Paddock/WRY
  pædək   EPD,DHd 81
Padgham/Sx
  pædʒəm   Dodgson(3)171
Padiham/La
  pædiəm   BBC,BCE
  pædihəm   Chis.
Padmore/Wt
  pædmər   PNWt 245
Padstow/Co
  pædstou   EPD,BBC,Schr.
Pagham/Sx,Wt
  pæ:gəm   PNWt 18
  pægm   PNSx(i)118
  pægəm   BBC
Paghill/ERY → Paull
Paglesham/Ess
  pækəlsəm,pægəlʃəm,
  peglʃəm   PNEss 189
Paignton/D
  peintən   EPD,BBC,Chis.
Pailton/Wa
  peltən   Hope
Painshaw/Du
  -e-   DEPN
  (see also s.n. Penshaw)
Painsthorpe/ERY
  penzþrəp   PNYE 131
Painswick/Gl
  peinzwik   EPD,BBC
Painter (as in P.'s Gn/Hrt)
  peintə   EPD
Pakenham/Sf
  pækənəm   EPD,BBC,Kruis.
  pæknəm   EPD,Bchm.87
Paley Street/Brk
  peili   EPD
Palfrey/St
  pɔ(:)lfri   EPD
Palgrave/Nf,Sf
  pælgreiv   EPD,BBC,Bchm.8
  pɔ:lgreiv   EPD,Schr.,Kruis.,
            Bchm.8

Palling/Nf
  pɔ:liŋ   DEPN,BBC,BCE
Pallion/Du
  pæliən   BBC
  pæljən   BCE
Pall Mall/Ldn
  'pæl'mæl   EPD,BBC,Schr.,Kruis.,
           ESpr.332 ("rarely")
  'pel'mel   EPD,BBC,Schr.,Kruis.,
           ESpr.332 ("usually"),
           Ellis 233 ("generally")
  ⊥ _   EPD[1]
  pal mal   Ellis 233
Palmer (as in P.'s Gn/Hrt)
  pɑ:mə   EPD
Palmersbrook/Wt
  pælmərzbruk   PNWt 286
Palstre Ct/K
  pɔ:lstə   PNK
Pamington/Gl
  pæmintən   PNGl II/54
Pampisford/Ca
  pɑ:nzə   PNCa 111,Mawer(4)285,
           Hope
  pɑ:ntʃə,pɑ:nsə,pɔ:nsə   Hope
  pæmpisfəd   ONCa 185,BBC
Pan (Black P.)/Wt
  blæk pæn   PNWt 2o4
  pæn   EPD
Pancras/So
  pæŋkrəs   EPD,Schr.
Pan Fm (Great P.Fm)/Wt
  gə:rt pæ:n   PNWt 286
Panfield/Ess
  pænfl   PNEss 448
Pangbourne/Brk
  pæŋbɔ:n, -buən,
        -bɔən,-bən   EPD
Pannal/WRY
  pænl   BBC
Panshill/Bk
  pænsəl, pænsɔ:l   PNBk 117
Pant/Ess (r.n.)
  loc. pɔnt   PNEss 9
Panton/Li
  pæntən   Schr.
Panxworth/Nf
  pɑ:nsə   DNf 43
Papplewick/Nt
  vulgo papəlwig   PNNt 13o
Papworth Everard/Ca
  loc. pɑ:pə   PNE&W
  pæpwəþ   ONCa 185

---

1) "The pron. with [e] is generally employed by members of West End
   Clubs. With other Londoners the pron. with [æ] is common" (EPD).

Par/Co
  pɑ: EPD
Paradise
  pærədais   EPD
Parah Gn/Chs
  para   PNChs III/54
Paramour Street/K
  pærəmɔ: PNK
Parbold/La
  pə:bət   PNLa(ii)
Pardshaw/Cu
  pɑ:rdzə   PNCu 367,GlossCu
                   xviii
Parham/Sf
  pærəm   DEPN,BBC,BCE
Parham/Sx
  pærəm   PNSx 152,BBC,Hope
  pɛərəm   BCE
Park, Park Fm/Wt
  pɑ:rk   PNWt 59 and 1o4
Parke/D
  pɑ:k   EPD
Parker's Lane/Sf
  loc. called 'Park Lane'
               PNDVall 34
Parkeston Quay/Ess
  pɑ:kstən ki: BBC
Parkgate
  'pɑ:kgeit   BBC
Parkhurst Forest/Wt
  pɑ:rkərst vɔrəst   PNWt 1o5
Park Riding/WRY
  pɛərk rɔ:din   DHd 82
Parks/WRY
  pɑ:ks   DDd 16
Parkstone/Do
  pɑ:kstən   EPD,BBC
Parley/Do,Ha
  pɑ:li   EPD
Parley Beams Fm/Ess
  pɑ:li bi:nz [sic] PNEss 436
Parme Fm/Chs
  pɑ:m   PNChs II/251
Parr/La
  pɑ: EPD
Parracombe/D
  'pærəku:m   BBC
Parret/Do,So (r.n.)
  pærət Schr.
Parsonage Fm/Wt
  pæ:snidʒ,pɑ:rsnidʒ   PNWt 171
Partington/Chs
  partiŋtən,olim
  partitn   PNChs II/ix
  pɑ:rtitn   GlossChs
  pɑ:tiŋtən   EPD
Parton/Cu,He
  pɑ:tn   EPD

Partridge Gn/Sx
  pɑ:tridʒ   EPD
Parwich/Db
  paritʃ   PNDb 4o3
  pæritʃ   DEPN,ONwick 371,Hope
  -dʒ   PNDb(i) II/127
Pashley/Sx
  pæʃli   PNSx(i)119
Passenham/Np
  pɑ:znəm   PNNp 1ol
Passfield/Ha
  pæsfi:ld, pɑ:s-   EPD
Paston
  pæstən   EPD
  rarely -ɑ:- Bchm. 15
Paston/Nf
  pɑ:sn Hope
  -ɑ:-   DEPN
Paston/Nb
  pɔ:stən   PNNbDu 155,DEPN
Paston/Np
  pɑ:stən   PNNp 24o,DEPN
Pateley Bridge/WRY
  pɛətlə brig   PNYW V/149
  peitli   EPD
Paternoster Row/Ldn
  'pætə'nɔstə rou   EPD,Bau.
  short: The Row Bau.,s.n.Row
Patford Bridge/Np
  pæpfəd bə:dʒ   PNNp 66
Patmore/Hrt
  pætmɔ:ə   EPD,Kruis.
  -mɔ: EPD
Patricroft/La
  pætrikrɔft Chis.
Patrington/ERY
  patþrintən   PNYE 25
  pæþriŋtən Hope
  pætrintən   GlossM&C,s.n.Chech-
  pætriŋtən   BBC   maiste
Patrixbourne/K
  'pætriksbɔ:n   BBC
Patterdale/We
  pætədeil   EPD
Patteson Ct/Sr
  pætisn   EPD
Pattingham/St
  pætindʒəm   PNWa(i)28,PNE&W,PNin
                17o,PNSt 114,Dodgson
                (2)384
Pattishall/Np
  pætʃə:l   PNNp 92
  pætiʃl   BBC
Pattiswick/Ess
  pæsik   PNEss 397,EssDD 158
Paul/Co
  pɔ:l   EPD

Paulerspury/Np
  pɔ:ləzpəri BBC,BCE
Paull/ERY
  pɔ:l PNYE 36,GlossHol 17
Pauperhaugh/Nb
  pepəhɑ:f PNNbDu 155
  pɔ:pəhɑ:f BBC
Pavenham/Bd
  pe:ətnəm,pævənəm,
  olim peikənəm PNBdHu 36
  peivənəm BBC
  peitən Hope
Paxton/Hu
  pækstən EPD
Pay Down/Wt
  pæi dæun PNWt 212
Paynter (as in P.'s Cross/Co)
  peintə EPD
Peacock Hill/Wt
  peikɔk hil PNWt 42
Peagham Barton/D
  pegəm PND 12o
The Peak/Db
  ðə pi:k EPD,Schr.
Peakyclose Copse/Wt
  pikiklous PNWt 59
Pearson (as in P.'s Gn/K)
  piəsn EPD
Peartree/Wt
  peərtri:,pə:rtri: PNWt 171
Peascod/Brk
  peskəd EPD
Peasemoor/Brk
  peismə Hunt.21
Peasmarsh/Sx
  pi:zmeʃ PNSx 531
Pebmarsh/Ess
  pedmiʃ [sic] PNEss 449
Pebsham/Sx
  see note s.n. Chilsham
Pebworth/Wo
  pebəþ GlossSEWo 82
Peckham/K,Ldn
  pekəm EPD,BBC,Schr.,PNK,
          Chis.
Peckingell/W
  pekindʒel PNW 1o5,Dodgson(2)
          385
Pedlinge/K
  pedlindʒ, -liŋ PNK
  -ndʒ H.A.(1)179
Peel/Chs,La
  pi:l EPD,Schr.,Kruis.
Peele/Chs
  pi:l
Peel Hall/Chs
  pi:l PNChs III/241
Peggles Wright/WRY
  peglz reit DDd 13

Pegsdon/Bd
  pegsən PNBdHu 175
Pelaw/Du
  pi:lə, pi:lɔ: BBC,BCE
  -i:- DEPN
Pelham/Ha
  peləm EPD,Schr.
Pelham/Hrt
  peləm EPD,Schr.
  (see also s.n. Brent P. and
               Furneaux P.)
Pelly (as in P.Port/Co)
  peli EPD
Pelutho/Cu
  peləte PNCu 297
  pelidə PNCu 297,GlossCu xviii
Pelynt/Co
  pə'lint BBC,BCE
  plint BBC,Jenner(2)3ol
  pe'lint BCE,DEPN (stress only)
Pemberton/La
  pembət(ə)n EPD
Pembridge/He
  pembridʒ EPD
Pembroke College/Ca,O
  pembruk BBC
Penberth/Co
  pen'bə:þ BBC
Pencalenick/Co
  penkə'lenik BBC
Pencalinick/Co
  -'ai- Jenner(2)3ol and 3o4
Pencombe/He
  pæŋkəm Hope
Pencoys/Co
  pen'kɔiz BBC,BCE
Pencraig/He
  'pen'kreig BBC
Pendarves/Co
  pen'dɑ:vis BBC
Pendeen/Co
  pen'di:n EPD,BBC,BCE
Pendell Ct/Sr
  pendl kɔ:t BBC
Pendennis/Co
  pen'denis EPD,BBC,Kruis.,Förster
Pendlebury/La
  pembri Hope,Parkinson
  pendlb(ə)ri EPD
Pendle Hill/La
  penl il Ellis 34o
Pendleton/La
  pendltən EPD
Pendomer/So
  pen'doumə DEPN,BBC,BCE
Pendragon/We
  pen'drægən EPD,DEPN (stress only)
Pendrea/Co (also spelt -dray)
  pen'drei BBC,BCE

Penfound Ho/Co
   pən'faund haus   BBC
Penge/K
   pendʒ   Chis.,PNK
   pen(d)ʒ   EPD
Pengegon/Co
   pen'gegən   BBC,BCE
Pengersick/Co
   pen'gə:sik   BBC,BCE
Pengy Mill/Ess
   pendʒi   Reaney(3)469
Penistone/WRY
   'penistən   BBC,Schr.,DHd 122
Penjerrick/Co
   -dʒ-   Jenner(2)302
Penketh/La
   peŋkiþ, peŋkit   PNLa(ii)
Penlee/Co
   pen'li: BBC
Penn/Bk,St
   pen   EPD
Pennaton/D
   peniŋtən [sic]   PND 247
Pennenden Heath/K
   penənden   PNK
The Pennines
   penainz   EPD,BBC
Pennington/Ha,La
   penitn   PNLa 210
   piniŋtən   Rose (for P. in La)
   penintən   EPD
Penny Gn/Ess
   peri [sic]   PNEss 449
Penponds/Co
   pen'pondz   BBC
Penquit/D
   pænkit   PND 272
Penrice/Co
   pen'rais   BBC
Penrith/Cu
   penriþ   PNCu 229,EPD,BBC,BCE,
       Chis.
   ˈ_,_ˈ   EPD
   pi:əriþ   PNCu 229
   pi:riþ   PNCu 229,PNE'side 64
   piərəþ   DKe 6
   pi:rəþ   PNO 1i,GlossCu xviii
Penrose/Co
   pen'rouz   EPD
Penrose/D
   pen'ru:z   PND 159
Penruddock/Cu
   pen'rudik   PNE'side 70
Penryn/Co
   pen'rin   BBC,BCE,DEPN
   ˈ_   Chis.

Pensby/Chs
   penzbi   PNChs IV/271
Penselwood/So
   pen'selwud   BBC,BCE,DEPN (stres
                        only)
Penshaw/Du
   penʃə, 'penʃɔ: BBC,BCE
Penshurst/K
   penzhə:st   EPD
Pentewan/Co
   pen'tju:ən   BBC,BCE
Pentire/Co
   -ai-   Jenner(2)301
Pentire Head/Co
   pen'taiə   BBC
Pentlowend/Ess
   pæntl i:nd   PNEss 483,EssDD 158
Penton/Cu
   pen'tɔn   BBC,BCE
Pentonville/Ldn
   'pentənvil   EPD,BBC
Pentreath/Co
   (see note s.n. Halvean)
Pentre Uchaf/Sa
   pentrə iχəv   BBC
Pentrich/Db
   pentritʃ   BBC
   -dʒ   PNDb(i) II/127
Penwith/Co
   'penwiþ, never _ˌ   Jenner(2)30
Penwortham/La
   'penwəðəm   BBC,PNLa 135
   -ð-   DEPN
Penyghent/WRY
   'penigent   BBC
Penzance/Co
   pen'zæns   EPD,BBC,BCE,Chis.,Kru
                      Bchm.58
   pən-   EPD
   _ˌ   EPD,Jenner(2)304
   loc. pen'za:ns   Bchm.58,Schr.
   loc. pən'za:ns   EPD
Peopleton/Wo
   pipəltən   PNWo 216
   -i-   DEPN
Peover/Chs
   pi:vər   Schr.,GlossChs,PNChs II,
             85,90 and 220
   pi:və   DEPN,BBC,BCE,Hope,PNChs(
             5,Bardsley,s.n.Littler
Peper Harrow/Sr
   'pepə'hærou   PNSr 207,DEPN,BBC,
Percy/Nb
   pə:si   EPD
Perdiswell Hall/Wo
   pə:dzəl   PNWo 113
Perdiswell Pk/Wo
   pə:diswəl   BBC

Perham/W
　perəm　EPD
Perio Barn, P.Mill/Np
　periou　PNNp 207
Perivale/Mx
　periveil　EPD
　-e-　DEPN
Perlethorpe/Nt
　olim peilþɔ:p　PNNt 91,Hope
Perranarworthal/Co
　perənə'wɑ:ðl　BBC
Perranporth/Co
　perən'pɔ:þ　BBC
　-'po:þ　BCE
Perranuthnoe/Co
　perən'ju:þnou　DEPN,BBC[1],BCE
　perən'ʌþnou　BBC
Perranwell/Co
　perən'wel　BBC
Perranzabuloe/Co
　perən'zæbjulou　BBC,BCE
　-zæbju:lou　DEPN
Perreton Fm/Wt
　perətn, pə:rətn　PNWt 18
Pershore/Wo
　pɑ:ʃər　PNWo 217
　pɑ:ʃə　Hope
　pɑ:ʃɔ:　PNWo(i)127
　pɔ:ʃɔ:　Hope
　pə:ʃɔ:　Chis.
　pə:ʃə, pɔ:ʃə　GlossSEWo 82
Pershore Rd (Birmingham)
　pæʃə raud　Wilde 24
Pertenhall/Bd
　pɑ:tnəl　PNBdHu 16
Peterborough/Np
　pi:təbərə　EPD,BBC,Schr.,
　　　　　Chis.,Kruis.
　-b(ə)rə　MEG 257
　-brə, bʌrə　EPD
Petersfield/Ha
　pi:təzfi:ld　EPD,Schr.,Chis.
Petersham/Do,Sr
　pi:təʃəm　EPD,BBC
Petertavy/D (or Peter Tavy)
　pi(:)təteivi　PND 231
　pi:tə　-　BBC,BCE
Petham/K
　petəm　BBC,BCE,PNK
Petherton/So
　peþətən　Chis.
Petrockstow/D
　'petrɔkstou　BBC,BCE
Pett/Sx
　pet　EPD

Pettaugh/Sf
　petə　Hope
Petteril/Cu (r.n.)
　petərəl　PNCu 23,RN 323,PNE'side 68
Pettistree/Sf
　'petistri:　BBC
Petworth/Sx
　petəþ　PNSx 114
　petwəþ　Schr.
Pevensey/Sx
　pemzi　PNSx 443,PNSx(i)122,Hope,
　　　　　DSx,s.n.Mesh
　pinzi　Hope ("Pinsy")
　loc. pemsi, pinsi　Schr.
　pev(ə)nzi　EPD,DEPN,BBC
　pevnsi　Schr.,Kruis.
　pimzi　PNSx 443,PNSx(i)122
Peveril Castle/Db
　pevəril　EPD
Pewitt Is/Ess
　pju:it　BBC
Pewsey/W
　pju:zi　DEPN,BBC,BCE
Pewsham/W
　pju:ʃəm　BBC
Phillack/Co
　filək　BBC,Chis.
Philleigh/Co (or Filley)
　fili　BBC,BCE
Philpot/Ess
　filpɔt　EPD
Philpots/Sx
　filpɔts　EPD
Phips Fm/Ess
　pips [sic]　PNEss 318
Phoenice Fm/Sr
　fi:nis　PNSr 100
Picardy/K
　pikədi　EPD
Piccadilly/Ldn
　pikədili　EPD,BBC,Schr.,Kruis.,
　　　　　Bau.
　_́ _́ , _́ _ , _ _́　EPD
Pickenham/Nf
　piknəm　Hope
Pickering/NRY
　pikərin　DSto
　pikəriŋ　EPD,Schr.
Pickford/Wa
　pikfəd　EPD
Pickles/WRY
　piklez　DHd 84
Pickthall/Cu
　pikthɑ:　GlossCu xviii

1) "Although the second is used extensively in the West Country, the
first is the local pronunciation" (BBC).

Pickt Hatch/Ldn (now obs.)
  pikt hætʃ Bau.
Pickwick/W
  pikwik EPD,Kruis.
Picton/Chs,NRY
  piktən PNChs IV/132,EPD,
Picthall/La   Schr.
  pikɔ:l PNLa 215
  piktɔ: Bardsley,s.n.
          Blackcow
Picts Hill/Bd
  pikshil PNBdHu 46
Piddinghoe/Sx
  pidənhu: PNSx 324
  pidiŋ'hu: DEPN,BBC,BCE,Hope
Piddlehinton/Do
  pidl hɛəntən PNDo I/3o9
  pidl he:ntən DDo
Piddletrenthide/Do
  pidl'trentaid BBC,BCE
  pidltre:ntei(d) DDo
Pidford/Wt
  pidfərd, -vərd PNWt 19
  pidfəd DWt,s.n.war'nt
Piercebridge/Du
  'piəs'bridʒ BBC,BCE
Pigeon Coo/Wt
  pidʒn ku: ,
  - keu: PNWt 212
Pighill/ERY
  pigəl PNYE 2oo
Pigtail/Wt
  pigteil PNWt 212
Pike How/We
  paikə PNE'side 62
Pike Stile/WRY (a hill)
  pɔ:k stɔ:l, older form
  pi:k sti:l DHd 82
Pilkington/La
  pilkitən DSLa
Pillaton/Co,St
  pilətən BBC
Pilling/La (p.n. and r.n.)
  pilin PNLa 165,PNLa(ii),
         RN 326
Piltdown/Sx
  piltdaun EPD
Pimlico/Ldn
  pimlikou EPD,Schr.,Chis.
Pimperne/Do
  pimpən BBC
Pind Hill/We
  paind hil PNWe II/78
Pinhoe/D
  pinhou PND 443,BBC

Pipewell/Np
  pipwəl PNNp 175
  pipwel BBC
Pirbright/Sr
  pə:brait EPD,BBC
Pitsea/Ess
  pitsi: BBC
Pitt
  pit EPD,Kruis.
Pitts
  pits EPD
Plaish/Wt
  plæʃ PNWt 286
Plaistow
  pleistou Schr.
  plæstou Chis.
Plaistow/Db
  plastou PNDb 437
  pleistou BBC
  (see also s.n. Plaistowe Gn)
Plaistow/Ess
  (see below s.n. Plaistow/Ldn)
Plaistow/He
  pleistou BBC
Plaistow/K
  plæstou PNK
  plɑ:stou, pleistou BBC
Plaistow/Ldn
  plɑ:stou PNEss 96,DEPN,EPD (1
  plæstou EPD,BBC,BCE
Plaistow/Sx
  plæstou BBC
Plaistow Gn/Db (also spelt Plaisto
  pleistou PNDb(i) II/129
Plaitford/Ha (formerly in Wilts)[1]
  plætfəd PNW 383
  pleitfəd BBC,BCE
Plaster (Chapel P.)/W
  pleistər PNW 83
Platt/K,WRY
  plat DDd 15
  plæt EPD
Platting/La
  plætiŋ BBC
Playstall/Ess
  plɑ:səl EssDD 159
Pleasington/La
  plezintən DEPN,BBC,BCE
Pleasley/Db
  plesli PNDb 292
  plezli DEPN,BBC,BCE,Hope
  pli:zli PNDb(i) II/129
Plemstall/Chs
  plemstɔ:l, plemstou,
  older local plimstən [sic]
              PNChs IV/135

1) transferred to Hants. in 1895 (see PNW 383,note).

plimstən   GlossChs,Hope
plinstə   PNChs IV/135,GlossChs
plemstəl   Hope
Pleshey/Ess
  plʌʃə   PNEss 488
  plʌʃi   EssDD 149
  pleʃi   BBC
Plockwoods/NRY
  plɔkudz   PNYN 72
Plompton/WRY
  plumptən   PNYW V/3o
Ploughley Hill/O
  plauli   PNO 236
Plowden/Sa
  plaudn   EPD
Plucka Tarn/We
  plukə tarn   PNE'side 62
Pluckley/K
  plʌkli   EPD
Plumbland/Cu
  plimlən   PNCu 3o9,GlossCu
        xviii
Plummer (as in P.'s Plain/Sx)
  plʌmə   EPD
Plumpton
  plʌmtən   Schr.
  plʌm(p)tən   EPD
  dial. plʌntən   Schr.
Plumpton/Cu
  pluntən   PNE'side 66,Hope,
        GlossCu xviii
Plumpton Wall/Cu
  pluntən   PNCu 234
Plumstead/Ldn,Nf
  plumstid,-sted   EPD,Bchm.62
Plungar/Le
  'plʌŋgə: BBC
Plurenden/K
  pluərinden   PNK
Plymouth/D
  pliməþ   EPD,BBC,Schr.,Kruis.,
        Chis.,MEG 257
  never -mauþ   Bchm.77
Plymtree/D
  plimtri: BBC,BCE
Plymyard/Chs
  plimjɑ:d   PNChs IV/187
Pockley/NRY
  pɔklə   DYorks 63
Pocklington/ERY
  pɔklintən   PNYE 182
  pɔkliŋtən   EPD
Podington/Bd
  pʌdiŋtən   PNBdHu 37
  pɔdiŋtən   BBC
Podlinge/K
  pɔdlindʒ, -liŋ   PNK
Pokerly/Du
  pɔkəli   PNNbDu 158

Poland/Ha
  poulənd   EPD
Polapit/Co
  'pɔləpit   BBC
Polbathic/Co
  pɔl'bæþik   BBC
Polden Hill/So
  pould(ə)n hil   BBC
Poldhu/Co (=Poldew)
  pɔl'dju: BBC,BCE
  ◡ –   EPD
  loc. pɔldʒu:, StE: pouldhu:
        Jenner(1)142
Polegate/Sx
  poulgeit   BBC,BCE
Polehanger/Bd
  olim puliŋgə   PNBdHu 171
Pole Moor/WRY
  poul muər   DHd 88
Polgear/Co
  -g-   Jenner(2)3o2
Polglaze/Co
  – ◢   Jenner (2)3o4 (see also s.n.
        Chypraze)
Pol Hill/K
  pɔl hil   BBC
Poling/Sx
  pouliŋ   PNSx(i)126,BBC
Poljew/Co
  -dʒ-   Jenner(2)3o2
Polkerris/Co
  pɔl'keris   BBC
Polperro/Co
  pɔl'perou   BBC,BCE,DEPN (stress
        only)
Polruan/Co
  pɔl'ru:ən   BBC
Polstead/Sf
  'poulsted   BBC
Poltimore/D
  poultimɔ: BBC
  poultimo: BCE
Polwarra/Co
  – ◢ –   Jenner(2)3o4
Polwhele/Co
  pɔl'wi:l   BBC
Polzeath/Co
  pɔl'zeþ   BBC,BCE,EPD
  -'zi:þ   EPD
  loc. -'zɛ:þ   EPD
Pomer Sick/Db (a valley)
  poumə sik   GlossSh(suppl.)45
Pondclose Copse/Wt
  pɔn(d)kluəs kaps   PNWt 212
  paund klous   DWt,s.n.grippen
Ponsanooth/Co
  pɔnz'nu:þ   BBC

Ponsbourne/Hrt
  pʌnzbən   PNHrt 128
Ponsonby/Cu
  pʌnsnbi   EPD
  pʌns(ə)nbi,pɔns(ə)nbi   BBC
  pʌnsənbi   BCE,Schr.,Kruis.
  pɔnsənbi   BCE,Schr.
  punsəbi   GlossCu xviii
  -ʌ-   DEPN
Pontefract/WRY
  pɔmfrət   PNYW II/76,Bardsley,
             s.n.Pomfret,Chis.
  poumfrət   PNYW II/75
  pəmfrat [sic]   PNYW II/75
  pʌmfrit   ESpr.132,Kruis.,EPD[1],
             BBC (see note 2)[2]
  pɔmfrit   Kruis.,Schr.,BBC[2],
             Hope
  po:mfrit   DHd 86
  pɔntifrækt   PNYW II/76,EPD,BBC,
             BCE,Schr.,Kruis.,
             Chis.
Ponteland/Nb
  pɔnt'i:lənd   DEPN,BBC,BCE
Pontesbury/Sa
  pɔntizbəri   BBC
  pɔnsbəri   Hope
Pontesford/Sa
  pɔnsət   GlossSa 518
Ponton/Li
  pɔntən   BBC
Pontop/Du
  'pɔntɔp   BBC
Pontop Pike/Du (a hill)
  pɔntɔp paik   BBC
Pontrilas/He
  pɔnt'railəs   BBC,BCE
Pontshill/He
  pʌntzl   DHe 43 (dial. and StE)
Pool/WRY
  pu:il   Hope
Poole
  pu:l   EPD,Schr.,Chis.,
          PNChs III/148,
          PNYW IV/47
  puil   PNYW IV/47
Poole Keynes/Gl
  pu:l keinz   PNGl I/79
Poole Keynes/W
  keinz   PNW 64
Pooley (as in P.Hall/Wa)
  pu:li   EPD
Pooley/We
  poulə   PNE 'side 64
Poolfoot/Cu
  pu:fu:ət   GlossCu xviii

Popham/D,Ha
  pɔpəm   EPD
Poplar/Hrt,Ldn
  pɔplə   EPD
Porchester/Nt
  pɔ:tʃə stə   Chis.,EPD
  pɔ:tʃistə   EPD
  (see also s.n. Portchester)
Porchfield/Wt
  pɔ:rtʃfild   PNWt 83
Poringland/Nf
  pɔ:riŋlænd,pɔ:lænd   BBC,BCE
Porkellis/Co
  pɔ:'kelis   BBC
Porlock/So
  pɔrlək   Chis.
Porsham/D
  pɔ:rsəm   PND 242
Portesham/Do (= Portisham,see below
  pɔ:tiʃə m   BBC
Portgate/Nb
  pu:rtgət   PNNbDu 159
Porthallow/Co
  pɔ:þ'ælou   BBC
Porthcuel/Co
  pɔ:kju:əl   Jenner(2)3o3
Porthcurno/Co
  pɔþ'ka:nou   BBC
Porthgwarra/Co
  pɔ:þ'gwɔrə   BBC
Porthleven/Co
  pɔ:þ'lev(ə)n   BBC
Porthmear/Co
  (see s.n. Halvean)
Porthmellin/Co
  _ ́ _   Jenner(2)3ol
Porthoustock/Co
  pɔ:'austɔk, praustɔk   BBC,BCE
Porthpean/Co
  pɔ:þ'piən   BBC
Porthscatho/Co
  pɔ:skæþou   Jenner(2)3o3
Porthtowan/Co
  pɔ:þ'tauən   BBC
Portisham/Do (=Portesham, see abov
  pɔsəm   Hope
Portishead/So
  pɔ:tished   EPD,BBC,Schr.
  loc. pɔsit   Schr.
  pɔsət   BG ("popularly"),PNE&W,
Portland/Do
  pɔ:tlənd   EPD,Schr.,Kruis.
Portland Rd/Ldn
  pɔ:tlənd raud   CPP 66
Portloe/Co
  pɔ:rt'lou   BBC

1) "An old loc. pron. ... now obsolete" (EPD).
2) "old local form[s]" (BBC).

Portman Sq./Ldn
  pɔ:tmən EPD
Portobello
  pɔ:tə'belou EPD,BBC,Schr.
  pɔ:toubelou EPD
Portquin/Co
  pɔ:t'kwin BBC
Portreath/Co (also spelt
             Porthtreath)
  pɔ:'tri:þ BBC,BCE,Jenner(2)
        304 (stress),Chis.
  (see also s.n. Halvean)
Portscatho/Co
  pɔ:t'skæþou BBC
  (see also s.n. Porth-)
Portsea/Ha
  pɔ:t'si: EPD,Schr.
  ˈ_ EPD
  'pɔ:tsi EPD,Chis.
Portslade/Sx
  -leid PNSx(i)126
Portsmouth/Ha
  pɔ:tsməþ EPD,Schr.,Kruis.,HL
        627,MEG 128
  never -mauþ Bchm.77
  pɔ:tsmauþ,pɔrtsməþ Chis.
  -þ Dobson 944
Postlethwaite/Cu
  pɔslþweit EPD
Possingworth/Sx
  vulgo -fəd PNSx 407
Postcombe/O
  poustkəm BBC,BCE
Postgate/NRY
  pous(t)geit EPD,BBC
  -git EPD
Postling/K
  poustliŋ BBC
  pɔstliŋ, pɔzliŋ PNK
Postwick/Nf
  pɔzik BBC
  pɔsik DEPN,ONwick 374,Hope
Pott/NRY
  pɔt EPD
Potter Heigham/Nf
  pɔtə heiəm, haiəm, hæm BBC,BCE
The Potteries/St
  ðə pɔtəriz EPD,Schr.
Potterne/W
  pɔtə(r)n PNW(i)136
Potterspury/Np
  pɔtəzpəri BBC,BCE
Pott Shrigley/Chs
  olim pɔt sigli PNChs II/vii,
                GlossChs
  pɔt ʃrigli PNChs II/vii
Poughill/Co
  pɔfil PNO 322,EPD,BBC,BCE
  pʌfil DEPN,BBC,BCE,Hope

Poughill/D
  pauəl PND 415,DEPN
  pauil BBC,BCE
  pɔfil EPD
  pʌfil PNND 109
Poulders/K
  pouldəs PNK
Poulner/Ha
  paunə, paulnə BBC,BCE
Poulshot/W
  poulʃət PNW 130,PNW(i)136
  poulʃɔt BBC,BCE
  -ou- DEPN
Poulter/Nt (r.n.)
  pautə PNNt(i)109
Poultney/Le
  poultni EPD,BBC,Schr.
Poulton
  poult(ə)n EPD
Poulton/Chs (in Broxton Hd)
  pu:ltən PNChs IV/153
Poulton/Chs (in Wirral Hd, formerly
          P. Lancelyn)
  poultən, pu:ltən PNChs IV/250
Poulton/Chs (in Wirral Hd, formerly
          P.-cum-Seacombe)
  poultən, olim
  pu:tən, pu:ltən PNChs IV/329
Poulton in the Fylde/La
  pu:lt(ə)n lə faild BBC
  pu:ltən - - BCE
  pu:tn i þ faild Ellis 354
Poulton/K
  poultən PNK
Pound/D,K (The Pound),Wt
  paund EPD
  pæun PNWt 19
Pounds/D,Gl
  paundz EPD
Poundstock/Co
  'paundstɔk BBC
Poundswick/Chs
  olim pɛ:inzwik, paunz-,
  paiənzwik PNChs II/vii
  painzwik GlossChs
Pouparts Junction/Ldn
  pu:pɑ:ts EPD,BBC
Povey's Cross/Sr
  pouviz krɔs BBC
Povington/Do
  pɔviŋtən PNDo I/103,PNDo(i)137,
               DEPN
Powburn/Nb
  'paubə:n BBC
Powell (as in P.'s Gn/Hrt)
  pouəl, -il, -el, pau- EPD
Powerstock/Do
  pauəstɔk, earlier
  pɔ:stɔk PNDo(i)240

Powick/Wo
  pɔ-ik PNWo 223[1]
  pouik DEPN,BBC,BCE
Powis Sq./Ldn
  pauis EPD
Pow Maughan/Cu (r.n.)
  po: mafan PNCu 24
  po: mafən RN 331
Pownall Hall/Chs
  paunl EPD
Poxwell/Do
  poukswəl PNDo(i)143
Poynatts/Bk
  painəts PNBk 179
Poynings/Sx
  pʌninz PNSx 286,DEPN
  pʌnənz PNSx 286
  pʌniŋz PNSx(i)127[2],Hope
  pɔiniŋz PNSx(i)127,EPD
Poyning's Town/Sx
  pʌniŋz PNSx 364
Poynton/Chs,Sa
  olim pɛ:əntn, peintn
      PNChs II/vii
  peintn GlossChs
  pɔintən EPD,PNChs II/vii
Praed Street,Paddington/Ldn
  praid stri:t pedintən CPP 66
  preid EPD,Kruis.
Prah Sands/Co
  prei sændz BBC,BCE
Pratt (as in P.'s Bottom/K)
  præt EPD
Praugnells [sic]/Wt
  præŋgəlz,prægnəlz PNWt 19
Praze/Co
  preiz BBC
Predannack/Co
  'predənæk, prednæk BBC,BCE
Preesall/La
  pri:zə PNLa(ii)
  (see also note 3 below)
Prendwick/Nb
  prendik BBC,BCE
Prescot/La
  preskət EPD,Chis.
Prescott/D,Gl,Sa
  preskət EPD
Presford/Wt
  prisfərd, presfərd PNWt 221
Preshute/W
  'preʃu:t PNW 3o7
  preʃət PNW(i)137.DEPN

Prestbury/Chs
  pres(t)bəri, -buri,
  -beri, olim pres- PNChs II/vi
  presbəri GlossChs
Presteigne/Sa
  pres'ti:n DEPN,Schr.
  -tein Schr.
Preston
  prest(ə)n EPD,BBC
  prestən Schr.
Preston/La,ERY
  presən DSLa
  prustn GlossHol 17
Prestwich/La
  prestwitʃ EPD,Schr.
  prestitʃ DSLa
Prestwick/Nb
  prestik PNNbDu 16o,BBC,BCE
Prideaux/Co
  pridəks BBC,BCE
  pri(:)dou EPD,Kruis.
Priestfield/Ess (f.n.)
  pristi EssDD 158
Priestley/Bd
  prestli PNBdHu 74
  pri:stli EPD
Princelett/Wt
  prinslit PNWt 171
Princetown/D
  prinstaun EPD,BBC
Prinknash Abbey/Gl
  prinidʒ BBC
Prinknash Pk/Gl
  priŋknæʃ, priniʃ PNGl II/17o
Prior's Heys/Chs
  praiəz, praiərz PNChs III/284
Privett/Ha
  privit BBC
Probus/Co
  proubəs BBC
Prudhoe-on-Tyne/Nb
  prudə PNNbDu 161
  prʌdou, prʌdhou BBC,BCE
Prussia (as in P.Cove/Co)
  prʌʃə EPD
Psalter Lane/Db ⟶ Salter L.
Puckaster/Wt
  'pʌkəstər PNWt 184
Puck Fm/Wt
  pu:k PNWt 171
Puckwell Fm/Wt
  pʌkl PNWt 184

1) cf. the transcription given in GlossSEWo 82: PWOYK.
2) "The polite pron. [pɔiniŋz] is purely bogus, and is merely due to the accidental preservation of the spellings in -oy-" (PNSx(i)127
3) "[-ow is] the usual pron. in the north of names ending in -all; c Preesow for Preesall" (Bardsley, s.n. Priestnall).

Pudding Lane/Ldn
    pudiŋ lein   Bau.
Puddle Fm/Do ⟶ Little P.Fm
Puddletown/Do,So
    pʌdltaun   PNDo I/314,PNDo(i)
                    175,BBC
    pidltaun   PNDo I/314,PNDo(i)
                    175
    pidltoun   DDo
Pudlicote/O
    pʌdlikʌt   PNO 378
Pudsey/WRY
    pudsə   PNYW III/236
    pʌdsi   BBC,BCE,Chis.,EPD
           ("loc.")
    -s-   DEPN
    pʌdzi   EPD
    pudzə   Mawer(4)285
Pulborough/Sx
    pulbər   PNSx 152
    pulbrə   PNSx(i)129
    pulbərə   MEG 334
Puleston/Sa
    pulistən, loc. also
    pilsn   EPD
Pulloxhill/Bd
    puləkshil   BBC
Pulverbatch/Sa
    paudəbætʃ, pauðə-,
    pauðəbitʃ   GlossSa 518
Pumpfold Lane/Wt
    pɔmpvəl   PNWt 285
Puncknowle/Do
    pʌnəl   PNDo(i)251,DEPN,BCE
    pʌnl   BBC
Purbeck (Isle of)/Do
    ail əv 'pə:bek   EPD,Schr.
    pə:bək   Chis.
Purfleet/Ess
    pə:fli:t   Schr.,Chis.
Puriton/So
    pjuəritən   BBC
Purleigh/Ess
    pə:li   BBC
Purley/Brk,Sr
    pə:li   EPD,BBC
Purton/Ess,Gl,W
    pə:tn   EPD
Pusey/Brk
    pju:zi   EPD,Kruis.
Puseydale/Chs
    pu:si-   PNChs III/68
Puslinch/D
    pʌzlidʒ   PND 282

Purshall/Wo
    pə:səl   PNWo 291
Putney/Ldn
    pʌtni   EPD,BBC,Schr.,Chis.
    pʌʔni   CPhon 128
Puttenham/Hrt,Sr
    pʌt(ə)nəm   HL 19o
    pʌtnəm   EPD
Putteridge Bury/Hrt
    pʌtəridʒ beri   BBC
Pye (as in P.Bridge/Db)
    pai   EPD
Pyecombe/Sx
    'paiku:m   BBC,BCE,Hope,PNSx(i)124
Pye Corner/Ldn
    pai kɔ:nə   Bau.
Pyle/Wt
    pail   PNWt 19 and 116,BBC
Pylle/So
    pil, pail   BBC,BCE
Pymore/Do
    paimə   PNDo(i)255
Pyon (Canon P.)/He
    kænən paiən   BBC,BCE
    (see also note 1 below)
Pyrford/Sr
    pə:fəd   BBC,BCE
Pytchley/Np
    paitʃli   PNNp 13o,EPD,BBC,BCE,
             DEPN,HL 811,Zachr.(3)
             127,note 2
Pythingdean/Sx
    petiŋdi:n   PNSx 154

1) "The loc. pron. was (and with old people still sometimes is)
Pyoun" (PNHe 159); Hope's transcription <u>Progown</u> seems very unlikely.

Q

Quadring/Li
  kweidriŋ DEPN,BBC,BCE
Quainton/Bk
  kweintən PNBk 1o8
Quaker Bridge/La
  kweikə EPD
Quantock Hills/So
  kwɔntɔk BBC
  kwɔntək EPD,Bchm.17,Schr.526
  kwæntɔk Chis.
Quantock Street/Ldn
  kwɔntɔk EPD
  kwɔntək EPD,Bchm.63
  kwæntɔk Bchm.63
Quarles/Nf
  kwɔ:lz EPD,BBC
Quarley/Ha
  kwɔ:li BBC
Quarmby/WRY
  kwɔ:mbi EPD
  kwɑ:rmbi,kwɛərmbi DHd 58
Quarndon/Db
  kwɔ:ndən BBC,BCE,Schr.
  kwɔ:n Hope,Schr.("loc.")
Quarr Abbey/Wt
  kwɔ:r æbi PNWt 44
  kwɔ:(r) BBC
  kwɔ: EPD
Quatt Jarvis, Q.Malvern/Sa
  kwɔt BBC
Quay (New Q.)/K
  nju: ki: Hope
Queastybirch Hall, Little Q.Fm/Chs
  kwi:sti PNChs II/15o
Quebec/Du
  kwibek Kruis.
  _ ´ EPD,Schr.

  kwə'bek EPD
Quedgeley/Gl
  kwedʒli BBC
Queenborough/K
  kwi:nbərə BBC,Schr.
    -b(ə)rə EPD
Queenhill/Wo
  kwinəl PNWo 155
Queen's Bower/Wt
  kwi:n bæuər [sic] PNWt 172
Queensbury/WRY
  kwi:nzb(ə)ri EPD
Queensland/Ha
  kwi:nzlənd EPD,Schr.,Kruis.
    -lænd EPD
Queens Rd, Bayswater/Ldn
  kwi:nz raud baizwɔ:tə CPP 66
  (now called Bayswater Underground station)

Queenstown/La
  kwi:nstaun Schr.
  kwi:nztaun EPD
Quemerford/W
  kʌməfəd DEPN,BBC,BCE
Queniborough/Le
  kwenibərə BBC
Quenington/Gl
  kwenintən PNGl I/44
  kweniŋtən BBC
Quernmore/K,La
  wɔ:mə PNLa 173
  kwɔ:mə, kwɑ:mə BBC,BCE (for Q.
Quethiock/Co   in L
  kweðik, kwiðik BBC,BCE
  kweþik BBC
Quex/K
  kweks EPD,PNK
Quidhampton/W
  kwid'hæmtən, olim
  kwidiŋtən PNW 226
Quin/Hrt (r.n.)
  kwin EPD
Quinton/Gl,Np,Wa
  kwintən EPD,BBC
Quoiseley/Chs
  kɔizli PNChs III/1o6
  kweizli DSChs 26
Quorn/Le (also spelt Quorndon)
  kwɔ:n EPD,BBC,Hope,PNLe 78
Quy/Ca
  kwai PNCa 133,ONCa 181,EPD,BBC
    BCE

R

Raan's Fm/Bk
   reinz   PNBk 211
Raans Moor/Bk
   reinz   BBC
Raby/Chs
   reibi   PNChs IV/228,EPD
Rackenthwaite/WRY
   rakənþət   DDd 16
Radcliffe/La,Nb,Nt
   ræklif   Hope (for R. in La)
   rætlif   PNNt(i)1o9,Hope (for
           R. in La)
   rædklif   EPD,BBC,Kruis.
Radclive/Bk
   rætli   PNBk 46
Radfield/Ca
   rædfi:ld   ONCa 192
Radford
   rædfəd   EPD
Radford Semele/Wa
   simili   PNWa 178
   rædfəd semili   BBC
Radipole/Do
   rædipoul, -pu:l
          PNDo(i)157,PNDo I/239
Radley/Brk,Ess,Nt
   rædli   EPD
Radnor/Chs
   rædnə   EPD,BBC,Förster
   rædnɔ: EPD,Förster
Radway Gn/Chs
   rædə   PNChs III/7
Radwell/Bd
   rædəl   PNBdHu 32
Radworthy/D
   radəri   PND 6o
Raeburn/La
   reibə:n   EPD,Kruis.
Rahere Street/Ldn
   rə'hi:ə stri:t   Schr.
   rəhiə   -   EPD
Rainors/Cu
   renərɑ: PNCuWe 9o
Rainow/Chs
   reinə(r)   GlossChs
Rains Grove/Wt
   reindʒ grouv   PNWt 286
Rainworth/Nt
   reinə:þ,renə:þ   PNNt 116
Raisdale/NRY
   rɛəzdil   PNYN 69
Raisthorpe/ERY
   rɛ:zþrəp   PNYE 132
Raisthwaite/La
   re:stət   PNLa 221
Raleigh Ho/D
   rɔ:li   PND 55,DEPN,HL 516,EPD,
         Schr.,Kruis.

   rɑ:li, ræli   EPD,Schr.,Kruis.
   reili   Schr.
Ralph Cross/NRY (a hill)
   rɑ:lf krɔs,
   rælf   - , - krɔ:s   EPD
Rame/Co
   reim   BBC
Ramillies Cove/D
   ræmiliz   EPD
Rampisham/Do
   ræmpiʃəm   PNDo(i)234,BBC
   rænsəm   PNDo(i)234,Hope,BG ("pop-
         ularly")
Rampside/La
   ramsaid   PNLa 2o3
Rampton/Ca,Nt
   ræm(p)tən   ONCa 21,BBC
Ramsden
   ræmzdən   EPD,Schr.
Ramsden Bell Ho/Ess (or R.Balhouse)
   ræmzdən bæləs   Hope
Ramsdown/Wt
   ræmzn   PNWt 286
Ramsey/Ess,Hu
   ræmzi   ONCa 181 (for R. in Hu),
         EPD,Schr.,Kruis.,Chis.
   ræmsi   Kruis.
Ramsgate/K
   ræmzgeit   BBC
   -git   EPD,Schr.,Kruis.
   loc. -geit   EPD
Ramsholt/Sf
   ræmshɔlt   PNDVall 65
Rancombe/Wt
   rænkəm   PNWt 221
Rand/Li
   rænd   Kruis.
Raneleigh/D
   rænəli   PND 261
Rannelow/Li
   "R. is pron. Ranyelho"   P&RNLi 215
Ranworth/Nf
   rænə   Hope
   renəþ   Schr.526
   rænwə:þ   EPD
Raphael Pk/Ess
   reifl   BBC
Rasen (Market R.)/Li
   mɑ:kit reiz(ə)n   BBC
Rash/WRY
   raʃ   DDd 14
Raskelf/NRY
   ræskil   PNYN 26
Rastrick/WRY
   ræstrik, re:strik   PNYW III/38
Rat/Wt
   ræt   PNWt 285
Ratcheugh/Nb
   rætʃəf   BBC,BCE

Ratcliff/Ldn
  rætklif EPD,Schr.
Ratcliff High Way/Ldn
  rætklif hai wei Bau.
Ratcliffe/Le,Nt
  rætklif EPD
Rather Heath/We
  ræðəriþ PNWe I/154
Ratlinghope/Sa
  dial. rætʃʌp Dodgson(2)385,
  rætʃəp GlossSa 518,Hope
  rætʃoup Mawer(4)285
Ratten Clough/WRY
  ræt(ə)n klʌf BBC
Raughton Head/Cu
  raftn PNCuWe 91
  rɑːft(ə)n,rɔft(ə)n hed BBC
  rɑːftən, rɔftən hed BCE
  -ɑːf- DEPN
  rɑːhwt heid PNE'side
Raunds/Np
  rɑːns PNNp 194,DEPN
  rɔːndz BBC
Raven (as in R.Crag/Cu)
  reiv(ə)n EPD
Ravendale/Li
  reiv(ə)ndeil BBC
  reivəndeil BCE
Ravenglass/Cu
  reiv(ə)nglɑːs BBC
  rebnglɑːs GlossCu xviii
Ravenhill/Wo
  ræfəl Hope
Raveningham/Nf
  ræniŋəm DNf 42 ,Hope,BBC
  ræv(ə)niŋəm,
  ræviŋəm ("particularly associ-
    ated with R. Hall") BBC
Raven's Bank/Chs
  older local
  rɑːnz- PNChs III/86
Ravensbourne (p.n. and r.n.)/K
  reivnzbɔːn, -bɔən EPD
Ravenscroft/Chs
  olim riːnskrɔft PNChs II/ix,
          GlossChs (so pron.
          in Northwich)
  reivəns-,
  reiənskrɔft PNChs II/ix
  reivnzkrɔːft Schr.
Ravensden/Bd
  rɑːnzdən PNBdHu 61,DEPN
Raven's Hall/Ca
  rænsɔːl PNCa 116
Ravensham
  rɑːnsəm H.A.(2)45
Ravensmeols/La
  reːvn miːlz PNLa 125

Ravensmoor/Chs
  reivnzmɔːr PNChs III/134
  ranmər PNChs III/134 ("older
    local"),DSChs 22
  ramnər PNChs III/134,GlossChs
    (so pron. is South Chs)
  ramnə PNDb(i) II/132
Ravenspur/ERY
  reivnspə: Schr.
Ravensthorpe/Np
  rɔːnstrəp PNNp 87
  rænstrəp EDD,s.n.Thorpe
Ravensthorpe Manor/NRY
  reːnzþrəp PNYN 198
Ravenstone/Bk
  rɔːnstən PNBk 12
  rɑːnsən Hope
Ravenstone/Db
  rɑːnstən Hope
Ravenstone/Le
  rɔːnsən Hope,PNLe 76
Ravenstonedale/We
  risəndeil Hope
  risndəl PNE'side 74
  rasndl DDd 17
Ravenstone Rd Copse/Np
  rɑːnsən PNNp 154
Ravenswood/Brk,Sx
  reivnzwud Schr.
Raventhorpe/Li
  rænþrəp GlossM&C,s.n.Ranthrup
Raw/WRY
  rɑː DDd 281
Rawcliffe/La
  rɔkli PNLa(ii)
Rawcliffe/WRY
  rɔːklif PNYW II/22
Rawcroft/NRY
  roːkrɔft PNYN 271
Rawdon/WRY
  rɔːdən PNYW IV/152,EPD,Schr.
Rawnpike Oak/St
  ræmpik PNSt 125
Rawreth/Ess
  rɔːrəþ BBC
Rawridding/WRY
  rɑːridinz DDd 13
Rawtenstall/La
  rɔ(ː)t(ə)nstɔːl BBC
  rædənstl GlossR&R (so pron. in
                Rossendale)
Rawthey/We,WRY (r.n.)
  roðə, rɔːðə RN 335
  rɔðə PNE'side 62
  rɔːði BBC
  rɑːðə DDd 17
Rawtonstall/WRY
  rɔtnstəl, rɔːtnstɔːl PNYW III/

Ray/Bk,O;W (r.n.)
  rei   EPD
Rayleigh/Ess
  reili   EPD,BBC,Kruis.,ROS 42
Rayseat/We
  re:sit PNE'side 69
Rayside/WRY
  rea said DDd 12
Rea/Sa;Wa,Wo (r.n.)
  rei BBC,BCE (for R. in Wa),
     EPD
  riə, ri: EPD
Reading/Brk (see also note 1)
  rediŋ DEPN,EPD,BBC,PNE&W,BG,
     Schr.,Kruis.,Chis.,Hope
Rease Heath,
Reaseheath Hall/Chs
  ri:s- PNChs III/153
Reasby Moor/We
  rezli PNE'side 7o
Reculver/K
  ri'kʌlvə EPD,BBC,Schr.
  ri:kʌlvə Hope
  'rekʌlvə Hope,Schr.("loc.")
  rə'kʌlvə EPD,BBC,DEPN (stress
     only)
  reikʌlvə PNK
Redbourn/Hrt
  redbən PNHrt 78
Redcar/NRY
  redkɑ: Chis.
Redcliffe/Gl
  redklif EPD
Redditch/Wo
  reditʃ EPD,Chis.
Rede/Nb (or Reed) (r.n.)
  ri:d Schr.
Redenhall/Nf
  'red(ə)nhɔ:l BBC
  'redənhɔ:l BCE
  -e- DEPN
Redesdale/Nb
  ridzdəl PNNbDu 163
Redfern/Wa
  redfə:n EPD
Redfield/Bk,Gl
  redfi:ld EPD
Redheugh/Du
  'redhju:f BBC,BCE
  redju:f BBC
Redheugh/Nb (in Newcastle)
  redjəf EPD
Redhill/Wt
  'ridil PNWt 156
  'red'hil EPD
Redisham/Sf
  retsəm DSf 29o
  rediʃm Hope

Redmain/Cu
  ri:dmian PNCu 267
  ri:dmiən GlossCu xviii
Redmarley D'Abitot/Wo
  ridmɑ:li PNWo 156,DEPN
Redmire/Cu
  reidmər PNE'side 73
Redmire/NRY
  redmɑ: PNYN 257
Redmoss/La (also spelt Red Moss)
  'red 'mɔs BBC
Redruth/Co
  red'ru:þ DEPN,BBC,BCE,Schr.
  _́ _ EPD,Schr.,Chis.,BG
Redway/Wt
  redwei, ridwei PNWt 2o
Reed/Nb (r.n.) ⟶ Rede
Reepham/Li,Nf
  ri:fəm BBC,BCE,DEPN (for R. in
     Nf),Hope (for R. in Nf)
Reeth/NRY
  ri:þ PNYN 273
Reeth Lodge, R. Bay/Wt
  ri:þ PNWt 184
Reeve (as in R. Castle/D)
  ri:v EPD,Kruis.
Regis (an affix to place-names)
  ri:dʒis EPD
Reigate/Sr
  raigeit PNSr 3o4,Chis.
  raigət PNSr 3o4,Schr.
  raigit EPD,BBC,Schr.,Kruis.
  raiget Schr.
  rai- DEPN
Reighton/ERY
  ri:tən PNYE 1o7,Hope
  ri:t(ə)n BBC
  -i:- DEPN
Reigny/Cu
  reini EPD
Reinow/Chs
  olim reinə(r), now
  reinə, reinou PNChs II/vii
The Reins/WRY
  t' reinz DHd 92
Rejerrah/Co
  ri'dʒerə BBC
Relubbas/Co (also spelt -us)
  ri'lʌbəs BBC
Renhold/Bd
  renəld PNBdHu 62
  renld BBC
Renishaw/Db
  'reniʃɔ: BBC
Renwick/Cu
  renik PNCu 235,EPD,BBC,Kruis.
  renwik EPD,BBC,BCE

1) Sometimes incorrectly spelt Readins and pron. [redinz] (Schr.).

Repps-with-Bastwick/Nf → Bastwick
Repton/Db
  reptən   EPD
  repn   Ellis 427
Reskadinnick/Co (or Resku-)
  rəskə'dinik   BBC
Restormel Castle/Co
  ri'stɔːməl   BBC
Restronguet/Co
  ri'strɔŋget   BBC
  re'strɔŋget   BCE
  -ŋg-   DEPN
Retford/Nt
  redfəd   Hope
  retfəd   EPD,Chis.
Revel End/Hrt
  revəl   Schr.
Revelstoke/D
  'revlstouk   BBC
  rev(ə)lstouk   EPD
Revesby/Li
  riːvzbi   BBC,BCE
Rewe/D
  ruː   BBC
Rew Fm/Wt
  ruː   PNWt 156
Rewstreet Fm/Wt
  ruːstriːt   PNWt 286
Reybridge/W
  reibəːrdʒ   PNW 1o3
Reydon/Sf
  reid(ə)n   BBC
Reymerston/Nf
  reməstən   DEPN,BBC,BCE
Rhee Wall/K
  riː   PNK
Rhenish Twr/D
  reniʃ   BBC
Rhewl/Sa
  (h)reul   BBC
Rhodes/La
  roudz   Schr.
Rhuddall Heath/Chs
  'rudɔːl   PNChs III/296
Rhyll/Db
  ril   Hope
Rialton Priory/Co
  'raiəltən   BBC
Ribbesford/Wo
  ribzfəd   Chis.
Ribble/La,Yorks. (r.n.)
  ribl   Schr.
Ribblesdale/Yorks.
  riblzdeil   Schr.
Ribchester/La
  'ribtʃəstə   Chis.
Ribston/WRY
  ribst(ə)n, -z-   EPD

Richborough/K
  ritʃbərə   Schr.,Chis.,PNK
Richmond/Sr,NRY,WRY
  ritʃmənd   EPD,BBC,Schr.,Chis.
Ricket's Hill/Wt
  rikits il   PNWt 59
Rickmansworth/Hrt
  rikmənzwaːþ   EPD,BBC,Chis.
Ridding Ct/Sr
  ridiŋ   EPD
Riddings/Ess
  ðə ridnz   PNEss 47
Riddlesay/We
  ridlsə   PNE'side 62
Ridge
  ridʒ   EPD
Ridgeway
  ridʒwei   EPD
Ridgewell/Ess
  redʒwəl   PNEss 453,DEPN
Ridgmont/Bd
  rigmənt   PNBdHu 82
Ridgmont/ERY
  ridʒimənt   PNYE 34
  ridʒiment   GlossHol 17
Ridgway
  ridʒwei   EPD
Riding/Yorks.
  rɔːdin   DHd 91
  raidiŋ   EPD
Riding Ct/Bk
  rediŋ, raidiŋ   PNBk 235
Ridley/Chs,K
  ridli   EPD
Rievaulx/NRY
  rivis   PNYN 73,Smith(1)293,Hop
  rivəz   PNYN 73,Smith(1)293,Hop
        DEPN,EPD,BBC,Kruis.,
        Mawer(4)284
  riːvou   DEPN,EPD ("the usual l
        pron."),BBC,BCE,Hope
  riːvouz   EPD
Rigby Hall/Wo
  rigbi   EPD
Rigdyke/Cu
  rigdeik   PNE'side 75
Rigg End/WRY
  rig end   DDd 16
Riley/Db
  raili   PNDb(i) II/136,EPD
Rileybank/Chs
  raili-   PNChs III/224
Rill,R.Cottage,R.Fm/Wt
  ril   PNWt 138 and 172
Rillington/ERY
  rʌliŋtən, rʌlitn   Hope
Rimington/WRY
  rimintən   PNYW VI/176
  rimiŋtən   BBC,BCE

Rimswell/ERY
   rimzil   PNWE 28,GlossHol 17,
           Hope
Ringash/D → Ashreigny
Ringsend/Ca
   riŋz'end   BBC
Ringsfield/Sf
   riŋsfil   DSf 291
Ringshall/Bk,Sf
   rinʃ(ə)l   EPD
Ringway/Chs
   riŋwei   PNChs II/ix
   rundʒə,
   rundʒi   PNChs II/ix,GlossChs,
           Hope (see note 1 below)
Ringwould/K
   riŋwould   PNK
Ringwood
   riŋwud   Schr
   riŋu:d   DDo
Rinsey Head/Co
   rinzi   BBC
Ripley
   ripli   EPD,Schr.
Ripon/WRY
   rip(ə)n   EPD,BBC
   ripən   Schr.,Kruis.,BG
   -i-   DEPN
Ripponden/WRY
   ribndən   GlossR&R
   ripəndən   Chis.
Risborough/Bk
   rizbərə   Schr.,Chis.
   rizb(ə)rə   EPD
Rise Hill/WRY
   raizl   DDd 17
Riseley/Bd,Bk
   raizli   BBC
Rishangles/Sf
   riʃæŋə   Hope
Rishworth/WRY
   ruʃəþ   PNYW III/71
   rʌʃwə:þ   Hope
Rising (Castle R.)/Nf
   -aiz-   DEPN
Risley/Db,La
   rizli   BBC
Risp Howe/We
   rispə   PNE'side 62
Rivacre Wood/Chs
   rivikər, rivəkər,
   'riveikə   PNChs IV/19o
Rivar/W
   raivə   PNW 355
Rivelin/WRY
   rivəlin   BBC,BCE

Rivenhall/Ess
   rivnɔ:l   PNEss 295
   -i-   DEPN
Rivington/La
   riviŋtən   EPD
   rivitn   Parkinson
Rivling/WRY
   rivlin   DDd 14
Roa/La
   ro:ə   PNLa 2o5
Roanhead/La
   rɔnəd   PNLa 2o6
   rɔnhed, rounhed   BBC,BCE
Roantree/WRY
   'rantrei   DDd 13
Robberby/Cu
   rɔbəbi   PNE'side 74
Robertsbridge/Sx → Rotherbridge
Roborough/D
   roubərə   BBC
Roby/La
   roubi   BBC
Rocester/St
   roustə   DEPN,BBC,BCE,Schr.,Hope
   rɔsistə   Schr.
   rɔ:stər   Ellis 444
Roch/La (r.n.)
   ro:tʃ   RN 344,PNLa 28
   routʃ   DEPN,BBC
Rochdale/La
   rætʃdə   PNLa(ii),Mawer(4)285,Hope,
           Brunner 167,Parkinson,
           GlossR&R (so pron. in R.),
           DSLa
   rætʃdl   GlossR&R (so pron.in
               Rossendale)
   ratʃdə, ratʃit   PNLa 54,Ellis 322
   rɔtʃdeil   EPD,BBC,Schr.,Chis.
Roche/Co
   routʃ   EPD,BBC
Rochester/K,Nb
   rɔtʃistə   EPD,BBC,Schr.,Kruis.,
               PNK
   rɔtʃəstə   Chis.
Rochford/Ess
   rɔtʃfəd   PNEss 196,BBC,Schr.
Rockbeare/D
   rɔkbiə, rɔkbə   BBC,BCE
Rockcliff/Cu
   rouklə   GlossCu xvii
Rockhampton/Gl
   rɔk'hæmtən   Schr.
Rockingham/Np,WRY
   rɔkiŋəm   EPD
Rocking Stone/WRY
   rɔgin stuən   DHd 94

---

1) Hope's transcrption 'Run-' could also represent [ʌ].

Rockwell End/Bk
  rɔkəl   PNBk 18o
Rockwoods/Ess
  rʌkəts   EssDD 159
Rodbaston/St
  rɔdbəstən   BBC
Rodey Lane/Chs
  roudi   PNChs III/241
Rodgebrook/Wt
  radʒbruk   PNWt 1o6
Roding/Ess (r.n.)
  rɔdiŋ   Chis.
Roding/Ess (also spelt ⟶Roothing)
  roudiŋ   EPD,BBC
  ruːðiŋ   DEPN.EssDD 158,BBC:

"The second, the historical pronunciation, has gradually given way, although not entirely succumbed, to the former. The group of villages known as The Rodings includes Abbess Roding, Aythorpe Roding, Beauchamp Roding, Berners Roding, High Roding, Leaden Roding, Margaret Roding, and White Roding or Roothing. Except in the last case, where Roothing has been retained in the name of the civil parish, it appears that Roding is now accepted as the standard spelling."

  loc. generally ruːdiŋ EPD[1]
  (see also s.n. Roothing)
Roding (High R.,White R.)/Ess
  roudiŋ   EssDD 158
Rodmersham/K
  rɔdməʃəm   BBC,BCE
  rɔdməsəm   PNK
Rodney Stoke/So
  rɔdni   EPD,Schr.
Rodway/So
  rɔdwei   EPD
Roe Beck/Cu (r.n.)
  roː bek   RN 346
  rɔː bek   PNE'side 74
Roeburn/La (r.n.)
  roːbən   PNLa 169
Roecliffe/WRY
  rɔːklif   PNYW V/86
Roedean School/Sx
  'roudiːn   BBC
Roehampton/Ldn
  rou'hæm(p)tən   EPD,BBC
  rə-   EPD
  rouhæmptən   Schr.526
Roel/Gl (also spelt Rowell)
  rouwəl, roːl   PNGl II/21
  rauəl, rouəl   Bchm.225
Roffey/Sx
  rʌfi   PNSx(i)133
Rogate/Sx
  rougeit   PNSx(i)133
Rogersceugh/Cu
  rɔdʒərskʌf   PNCu 126
Rohall/La ⟶ Rowall

Rokeby/NRY
  roukbi   EPD,BBC,Schr.,Kruis.,Ch
Roker/Du
  roukə   EPD
Rollesby/Nf
  roulzbi   DEPN,BBC,BCE
Rolleston
  roulst(ə)n   EPD
Rolleston/Le
  roulstən   BBC,BCE,Hope
  roulstn   DEPN
Rolleston/Nt
  roulstn   PNNt(i)113,DEPN
  roulstən   PNNt 173,BBC
Rolleston/St
  roulstən   BBC,BCE
Rollestone/W
  roulstn   PNW(i) 14o
  roulstən   BBC
  raulstən   Hope
Rolleylane Bridge/Ess
  rouli   PNEss 292
Rolvenden/K
  rɔlv(ə)ndən   BBC
  rɔlvəndən   BCE,Chis.
  rɔvinden   PNK
  rɔl-   DEPN
Romaldkirk/WRY
  rʌməldkəːk   Hope
Romanby/NRY
  roumənbi   BBC
Romford/Do,Ess,K
  rʌmfəd   PNEss 117,DEPN (for R.
    Ess),Hope (for R. in Es
    BBC,BCE (for R. in Ess
    and K),EPD,Schr.
  rɔmfəd   BBC,BCE (for R. in K),B
    (for R. in Ess),EPD ("o
    fashioned"),Dobson 593
    (for R. in Ess)
Romansleigh/D
  rʌmzli   PND 391,DEPN
Romney/K
  rɔmni   EPD,BBC,Schr.,Kruis.
  rʌmni   EPD,BBC,BCE,DEPN,Schr.,
    Kruis.,PNK
Romney Marsh/K
  rʌmni maːʃ   DK ("It is simply
    called the Marsh in
    East Kent")
  rɔmni maːʃ   BBC
Romsey/Ha
  rʌmzi   DEPN,PNE&W,BBC,BCE,Schr.
    Hope (listed s.n. Kent)
  rʌmsi   Chis.

---

1) "The pron. [roudiŋ] is being encouraged by the county council, and
   will doubtless become the accepted form before long" (EPD).

Rook Barugh/NRY
  riukbɑːf, riukbarə PNYN 58
Rookley/Wt
  rukli PNWt 2o,DWt,s.n.jack-
        assen about
Rookwith/NRY
  riukwiþ PNYN 235
Rookwood Hall/Ess
  rʌkits PNEss 75
Roos/ERY
  ruːəz,rus,rɔːz PNYE 56
  rɔs Hope,GlossHol 17
  ruːs BBC,BCE
Roose/La
  ruːz, ruːs PNLa 2o2
Roothing/Ess (also spelt→Roding)
  ruːðiŋ PNEss 49o,Hope
  (see also s.n. Aythorpe Roding,
  Berners R. and Leaden R.)
Rope/Chs
  roup PNChs III/68
Roppa/NRY
  rɔpə PNYN 72
Roscroggan/Co
  rɔs'krɔgən BBC
Roseacre/La
  roːzeːkə PNLa 152
Roseberry/D
  rouzb(ə)ri EPD
    -bəri Kruis.
Rosedale/NRY
  roːzdil PNYN 8o
  ruːəzdil DSto
Rosedown/D
  ruːzən PND 75
  ruːzn DHtl 8
Roseground/Chs
  rɔːz- PNChs III/116
Rose Hill/NRY
  roːzil PNYN 196
Rosevear/Co
  _ _ ´ Jenner(2)3o4
Rosewain/Cu
  rɔznən Hope
Roseworthy/Co
  rouz'wəːði BBC
Rosgill/We
  rɔskil PNE'side 68
Rosherville/K
  rouʃəvil, rɔzəvil BBC,BCE
  rɔʃə(ː)vil EPD
Roskestal/Co
  rɔs'kestl BBC
Roskruge/Co
  loc. rɔskriːg,
  St.E. rɔskruːdʒ Jenner(1)142
Rosley/Cu
  rɔsle PNCu 33o
  rɔsl PNE'side 64

Roslin/Wt
  rɔːzlən PNWt 138
Ross/He,Nb,St
  rɔs EPD,Schr.
  rɔːs Schr.
Rossall School/La
  rɔsl BBC
Rossendale/La
  rɔs(ə)ndeil BBC
  rɔsəndə DSLa
Rossendale (The Forest of R.)/La
  rəsəndə GlossR&R
Rostherne/Chs
  rɔstərn PNChs II/ix,GlossChs
  rɔstəːn PNChs II/56,Hope
  rɔstən Schr.
Roston/Db
  rɔsn PNDb 591
Rothamsted/Hrt (or -stead)
  'rotəmstid PNHrt 39
  'rɔþəmsted EPD,BBC
Rothay/We (r.n.)
  rɔþei BBC
  rouðei Chis.
Rothbury/Nb
  rɔtbəri PNNbDu 169
  rɔþbəri DEPN,BBC,BCE
Rother/Db,WRY;Ha,Sx;K,Sx (r.n.)
  rɔðə BBC (for R. in Yorks.).
        Schr.
  rouðə PNK
Rotherbridge/Sx (also called Roberts-)
  rɔðəbridʒ PNSx(i)132
Rotherfield Greys,R.Peppard/O
  rɔðəfiːld PNO(i)174
  - pepaːd BBC
Rotherfield/Sx
  rʌdəfəl PNSx 376
  rʌdəvəl PNSx 376,Hope,PNSx(i)134
Rotherham/WRY
  rɔðərəm EPD,BBC,Schr.,Kruis.,
        Chis.
Rotherhithe/Sr (also spelt -hide)
  olim redrif PNSr 28,DEPN,Schr.,
           ESpr.4o7,MEG 386
  rɔðəhaið EPD,Schr.,Chis.,Bchm.
        2o7,MEG 386,ESpr.4o7
  rɔdriþ MEG 386
  rʌðəhiþ seems to have dis-
        appeared MEG 386
  rɔðə- Koeppel 56
Rothersthorpe/Np
  þrʌp PNNp 151 ("The short form
        of the name is still used
        locally")
  rɔðəsþrəp EDD,s.n.Thorpe
Rotherwick/Ha
  rɔðərik, rɔðəwik EPD
Rothley/Le
  rouþli BBC,BCE,DEPN

Rothmire/Cu
   roumə   GlossCu xviii
Rothwell
   rɔþwəl, rauəl.
   loc. rɔdil   Schr.
Rothwell/Li
   rɔþwel   BBC
Rothwell/Np
   rouəl   PNNp 118,BBC,BG
   rouel   DEPN,BCE
   rɔþwel   BBC,BCE
Rothwell/WRY
   rɔþwel   BBC
   rɔþil   GlossR&R
   rɔdil, rauəl   Hope
Rotsea/ERY
   rɔtsə, ratsə   PNYE 157
Rotten Row/Ldn
   rɔtn rou   Schr.,Bau.
   short: The Row   Bau.,s.n.Row
Rottingdean/Sx
   rɔtiŋdi:n   EPD,BBC,Kruis.
Roud/Wt
   ræud   PNWt 156
Roudsea Wood/La
   raudzi   BBC
Rougemont/WRY
   'rudʒmɔnt   PNYWV/51
Rougham/Nf,Sf
   rʌfəm   BBC,BCE
   -ʌf-   DEPN (for R. in Nf)
Roughdown/Ha
   raudaun   BBC,BCE
Roughdown/Hrt
   raudaun   PNHrt 43,BBC
Roughey/Sx ⟶ Roffey
Rough Hill/We
   rufəl   PNWe II/192
Roughlee/La
   'rʌf'li: BBC
Roughlee Booth/La
   ruf li:, ðə ruf li: PNLa 81
Roughton
   rautən   Schr.
Roughton/Li
   ru:t(ə)n   BBC
   ru:tən   BCE
   -u:-   DEPN
Roughton/Nf
   rautən   Hope,BCE
   raut(ə)n   BBC
   -au-   DEPN
Roughton/Sa
   raut(ə)n   BBC
Rough Tor/Co
   'rau 'tɔ: EPD,BBC,BCE
Rough Tor/D
   rautər   PND 199
   rau tɔ: BBC

Roundhay Pk/WRY
   raundei   BBC
Round Ing/WRY
   raund iŋ   DDd 16
Roundthwaite/We
   rounþət   PNE'side 66
Rousdon/D
   rauzdən   PND 647,DEPN,BBC,BCE
   ru:zdən   BBC,BCE
Rousham/O
   rauʃəm   PNO 278,BBC
   rausəm   BBC
Rous Lench/Wo
   'raus 'lenʃ   BBC
Routen/Cu
   ru:tn   Hope
Routh/ERY
   ru:þ   PNYE 71,DEPN,Hope
   rauþ   EPD,Kruis.
Rowall/La (also spelt Rohall)
   ru:ə   PNLa 163 ("The pron. is s
                    to be 'Rooa'")
Rowant/O
   rauənt   EPD
Rowarth/Db
   rauəþ   BBC
Rowborough/Wt
   roubrə, ræub(ə)rə   PNWt lo7
Rowborough Fm/Wt
   ræubrə   PNWt 6o
Rowde/W
   roud   PNW 246,PNW(i)141,DEPN
   raud   BBC
Rowden
   raud(ə)n   BBC (for R. in D and
   raudn   EPD
Rowditch/Db
   rauditʃ   PNDb(i) II/141
Rowdown Lane/Wt
   ræudæun   PNWt 285
Rowdown Wood/Sr
   rʌfdaun   PNSr 4o
Rowe/Co,So,NRY
   rou   EPD
Rowell/Np ⟶ Rothwell
Rowell/We
   rauəl, rouəl   EPD
Rowhedge/Ess
   'rouhedʒ, rau-   BBC,BCE
Rowington/Wa
   rauiŋtən   PNWa 217
Rowland/Db,Sf
   roulənd   PNDb(i) I/14o,EPD
   rouln   DSf 292
Rowlands Fm, R. Wood/Wt
   ræulənz   PNWt 33
Rowledge/Ha,Sr
   raulidʒ   BBC,BCE

Rowley
    rouli   EPD,Kruis.
    rauli   Kruis.
Rowley/WRY
    ru:li   DHd 96
Rowley Regis/St
    rauli ri:dʒis   BBC
    raulei   -   Chis.
    -au-   PNSt 128
Rowling/K
    rouliŋ   PNK
Rowner/Ha
    raunə   DEPN,BBC,BCE
Rowney (as in R.Abbey/Hrt)
    rouni, rauni   EPD
Rowrah/Cu
    ru:rə   DEPN,Hope
Row Ridding/La
    rau ridn   PNLa 221
Rowridge/Wt
    ræuridʒ   PNWt 108
    rauridʒ   BBC
Rowsham/Bk
    rauʃəm   PNBk 89
    -au-   DEPN
Rowsley/Db
    rouzli   DEPN,BBC,BCE,Hope
    rauzli   PNDb(i) II/142
Rowston/Li
    raustən   DEPN,BBC,BCE
Rowthorn/Db
    rau-   PNDb(i) I/138
Rowton/Chs,Sa
    rautən   PNChs IV/114,BCE (for
    raut(ə)n   BBC   R.in Chs)
    rautn, rɔ:tn   EPD
    rɔ:tən   Schr.
    -au-   DEPN (for R. in Chs)
Rowton Fm/ERY
    ru:tən   PNYE 50
Roxby/NRY (in Pickering Lythe
               Wapentake)
    rouzbi   PNYN 90
Roxby/NRY (in Langbargh East
               Wapentake)
    rouzbi   PNYN 139,GlossClv xlv
    rousbi   Ump.30
Roxwell/Ess
    rɔkswel   BBC
The Royals/Chs
    rɔiəlz, older local
    raiəlz   PNChs III/102
Royal's Gn/Chs
    rɔilz, older local
    raiəlz   PNChs III/97
Royalswood Fm/Chs
    rɔiəlz, older local
    raiəlz   PNChs III/102

Royston/Hrt,WRY
    vulgo raistən   PNHrt 161
    rɔist(ə)n   EPD
    rɔistən   Schr.,PNYW I/284
Royton/La
    rɔit(ə)n   BBC
Ruanlanihorne/Co (also spelt Ruan L.)
    ruən'lænihɔ:n   BBC
Ruardean/Gl
    'ru:ədi:n,
    'ruərə'di:n   PNGl III/240
    ruədi:n   BBC
Rubery/Wa,Wo
    ru:bəri   BBC
Ruckinge/K
    rʌkindʒ   BBC,BCE,Dodgson(2)343,
               H.A.(1)179,PNK
    rʌkiŋ   PNK
Rudding/Cu
    rudiŋ   PNCu xlii
Rudge
    rʌdʒ   EPD
Rudgwick/Sx (also spelt Rudge-,Ridge-
               in PNSx(i))
    ridʒik   PNSx 156,PNSx(i)129
    rʌdʒik   PNSx(i)129,BBC,Hope,
               ONwick 392
    rʌdʒwik   BBC
Rudhall/He
    'rʌdɔ:l   BBC
Rudston/ERY
    ruds(t)ən   PNYE 98
Rudyard/St
    rʌdjəd   EPD,Kruis.
Rue Cliffs/WRY (f.n.)
    ru: klifs   GlossSh 329
Rufford/Nt
    rʌfə:d [sic] PNNt 94
Rugby/Wa
    rʌgbi   EPD,BBC,Schr.,Kruis.,Chis.,
           Bau.
Rugeley/St
    rʌdʒli   DEPN,Chis.,Hope [1]
    ru:dʒli, ru:ʒli   EPD
    rudʒli   BBC
    ridʒli   Ellis 463,PNSt 129 ("The
               natives keep up the old
               pron.")
Ruishton/So
    ru:iʃtən   BBC,BCE
    raiʃn   DWSo 7
Ruislip/Mx
    raislip   PNMx 46,PNMx(i),DEPN,EPD,
               BBC,BCE
    raizlip   EPD
Ruloe/Chs
    ru:lou   PNChs III/196

1) Hope's transcription 'Rudgley' could also mean [u] (cf. BBC).

Rumford/Co
  rʌmfəd   EPD,Schr.
Rumworth/La
  raməþ   PNLa(ii)
Runcorn/Chs
  rʌnkɔrn   Schr.
  rʌŋkɔ:n   EPD
  rʌŋkən   Chis.
Runhall/Nf
  rʌnəl   Hope
Runnymede/Sr (or Runny Mead)
  rʌnimi:d EPD,Schr.,Chis.
Runswick/NRY
  runsik   DSto
Runswick Bay/NRY
  runzik   PNYN 139
Runton/Nf
  rʌntən   EPD
Rushall/He,St
  rʌʃɔ:l   BBC
Rushall/Nf
  ru:ʃil   Hope
  rʌʃhɔ:l   BBC
Rushall/W
  rəʃl   PNW(i)141
  rʌʃəl   BBC
Rushdon/Hrt
  vulgo rizdən PNHrt 163
  rʌʃdən   ONCa 188 (for R.
                      in Hrt)
Rushden/Np
  rʌʒdən   PNNp 195
Rushmere/Sf
  rʌʃmiə   EPD
Rusholme/La
  rʌʃhoum   EPD,BBC,Bchm.81
  rʌʃəm   EPD,Bchm.81,Chis.
Rusholme Grange, R.Hall/WRY
  rusəm   PNYW IV/14
Rushton
  rʌʃtən   EPD
  risn   Hope (for R. in So)
Rushyford/D
  'rʌʃi'fɔ:d BBC,BCE
Rusland/La
  ruzlən(d)   PNLa 217
  rʌzlənd   BBC,BCE
  -z-   DEPN
Rusper/Sx
  rʌspə   PNSx(i)136,EPD
Russell (as in R.Hill/Sr)
  rʌsl   EPD,Kruis.
Russia Fm, R.Hall/Chs
  ruʃə   PNChs IV/95
Rusthall/K
  'rʌsthɔ:l BBC
  rʌstɔ:l   PNK
Ruston Parva/ERY
  lɑ:tl riəstən PNYE 93
  litl ri:stən Hope

Ruswarp/NRY
  ruzəp   PNYN 125,DEPN,EPD
  rʌzəp   EPD,Bchm.71
  rʌsəp   BBC,PNE&W,BCE
  rʌzwɔ:p   EPD,Bchm.7o
Ruswick/NRY
  ruzik   PNYN 241
Ruthwaite/Cu
  rʌþweit, rʌþət BBC,BCE
Rutland
  rʌtlənd   EPD,BBC,Schr.
Rutlandshire
  rʌtləndʃiə EPD
  -ʃə   EPD,Schr.
Ruyton-Eleven-Towns/Sa
  rait(ə)n i'lev(ə)n taunz BBC
  raitən i'levn taunz BCE
Ryarsh/K (also spelt Riarsh)
  'raiɑ:ʃ   BBC
  ri:æʃ   PNK
  ræʃ   Hope,PNK
Rydal/We
  raidəl   PNWe I/2o8,Schr.,Chis.
  raidl   BBC,Kruis.
Ryde/Wt
  raid   PNWt 193,EPD,Chis.
Rye/Sx (p.n.),NRY (r.n.)
  rai   EPD,Schr.,Chis.(for R. in
Ryhope/Du
  raiəp   BBC,BCE
Rylah/Db
  rai-   PNDb(i) II/136
Ryle/Nb
  rail   EPD
Rylstone/WRY
  rilstən   PNYW VI/93,EPD
  rilstoun EPD
  railstən Kruis.,Chis.
Ryme Intrinseca/Do
  raim in'trinsikə BBC
Ryton
  raitən   Schr.
Ryton-on-Dunsmore/Wa
  rait(ə)n ɔn 'dʌnzmɔ: BBC

S

Saberton/Gl
  sabətən PNGl II/43
Sacombe/Hrt
  seikəm PNHrt 137,BBC
Sacriston Heugh/Du
  sækristən hju:f BBC,BCE
Sadberge/Du
  'sædbə:dʒ BBC,BCE
Saddleback/Cu (a mountain)
  sædlbæk EPD,Schr.
Saddlescombe/Sx
  sælskum PNSx 286
Saddleworth/La
  sædlə þ DSLa
Saffron Hill/Ldn
  sæfən il CPhon 14o
Saffron Walden/Ess
  sæfrən wɔ:ld(ə)n BBC
  - wɔ:ldən Schr.,Chis.
Saham/Nf
  seim Hope
Saham Tony/Nf
  seiəm touni BBC
Saighton/Chs
  seitən PNChs IV/121,BCE
  seit(ə)n BBC
  -ei- DEPN
Sainham/Wt
  sɛ:nəm PNWt 286
Saint (a prefix)
  snt, sənt, sint EPD
  seint, sint ("coll.") Chis.
  sænt (so pron.in WRY) DAl&Hd,
                   s.n.Sant
St. Agnes/Co
  snt ægnis BBC
St. Albans/Hrt
  snt ɔ:lbənz EPD,BBC,Hope
  sənt - BCE,Schr.
St. Aldates/O
  səntouldz PNO(i)37,Hope
  snt'ouldz BBC,EPD ("old-
                fashioned")
  snt ɔ:ldits BBC
  ɔ:ldeits, ɔl-, -dits EPD
St. Andrew/Wo
  snt ændru: EPD
St. Anstell/Co
  snt ænsl Hope
St. Anthony in Meneage/Co
  snt 'æntəni in mi'ni:g,
  - - - mineig BBC
  sənt æntəni in meni:dʒ BCE
St. Austell/Co
  snt ɔ:stl EPD,BBC
  snt ɔ:sl EPD ("loc."),BBC,
              Bchm.43 ("loc.")
  ɔ:st(ə)l, rarely ɔst(ə)l
                   Bchm.43

St. Bees/Cu
  sn(t) bi:z EPD,DEPN
St.Bees Head/Co (a promontory)
  sən(t) bi:z hed Schr.
St. Benet's Abbey/Nf
  snt benits BBC
St. Blazey/Co
  sn(t) bleizi EPD
St. Botolph's Bridge/Ess
  bʌtlz PNEss 377,DEss
St. Breock/Co
  snt bri:ək BBC
St. Breward/Co
  snt bru:əd BBC
St. Briavels/Gl
  sənt 'brevəlz PNGl III/242,BCE
  snt brevlz BBC
  -e- DEPN
St. Budeaux/D
  bʌdəks PND 236
  snt bju:dou BBC
St. Buryan/Co
  snt bʌriən, beriən BBC
  sənt -, - BCE
St. Catherine/So,
St. Catherine's/Wo
  sn(t) kæþ(ə)rin(z) EPD
St. Catherine's Down/Wt
  sn(t) kæþərinz dæun PNWt 116
St. Chloe/Gl
  'siŋkli PNGl I/98
  snt kloui BBC
  sənt - BCE
St. Clement Danes/Ldn
  snt 'klemənt 'deinz BBC
St. Clements/Co
  snt klemənts BBC
St. Clether/Co
  snt kleðə BBC
St. Cloud/Wo
  snt klu: BBC
  sənt - BCE
St. Columb/Co
  snt kʌləm, kɔləm BBC
  sənt -, - BCE
  sn(t) kɔləm EPD
St. Cross Cottage/Wt
  'siŋkrɔs PNWt 1o8
St. Dennis/Co
  snt denis BBC
St. Dominock/Co
  snt dɔminik BBC
St. Ebbes/Co
  stæbs Hope
St.Endellion/Co
  snt en'deliən BBC
  sənt en'deljən BCE
  _ ∕ _ DEPN

St. Enoder/Co
  snt 'enədə   BBC
St. Enodoc/Co
  snt enədɔk   BBC
St. Erth/Co
  snt ə:þ   BBC
St. Eval/Co
  snt evl   BBC
St. Ewe/Co
  snt ju: BBC
St. Feock/Co
  snt 'fi:ɔk   BBC
St. Gelly/Co
  sti:vəngeli   Hope
St. Gennys/Co
  snt genis   BBC
  sənt - , dʒenis   BCE
St. George/So
  sn(t) dʒɔ:dʒ   EPD
St. George's Down/Wt
  sn 'dʒɔ:rdʒiz 'dæun   PNWt 21
St. Germans/Co,Nf
  snt dʒə:mənz   BBC
St. Giles/D,Do
  sn(t) dʒailz   EPD
St. Gluvias/Co
  snt glu:viəs   BBC
St. Gor(r)an/Co
  snt gɔrən   BBC
St. Helens
  sənt helinz   EPD
  - helənz   Schr.
  snt 'elənz   PNWt 195
St. Helen's Well/WRY
  sæntelin   DAl&Hd
St. Hilary/Co
  snt hiləri   BBC
St. Ippolyts/Hrt
  snt ipəlits   BBC
St. Issey/Co
  snt izi   BBC
St. Ive/Co
  snt i:v   PNE&W,BBC,DEPN
  sənt -   BCE
St. Ives
  snt aivz   BBC (for St.I. in
      Co and Hu),EPD
  sənt -   BCE (for St.I. in Hu)
  snt i:vz   Hope (for St.I. in
      Co)
  səntaivz, loc. senti:vz   Schr.
  sintaivz   Chis.
St. James
  sn(t) dʒeimz   EPD
St. James's Pk/Ldn
  sn dʒaimsiz pɔ:k   CPP 66
St. John
  səndʒɔn   EPD,Schr.
St. John's Wood/Ldn
  _ ⁄ ⁄   MEG 158

St. Juliot/Co
  snt dʒu:liət, dʒilt   BBC
St. Just/Co
  səndʒʌst   Hope
St. Just in Penwith/Co
  snt 'dʒʌst in pen'wiþ   BBC
St. Kenelms/Wo
  kenələmz   Hope
St. Keverne/Co
  snt kevən   BBC
St. Keyne/Co
  snt kein, ki:n   BBC
  sənt - , -   BCE
St. Lawrence
  snt lɔr(ə)ns   EPD
  snlɔrəns   PNWt 2ol
St. Leonards
  sənt'lenədz   EPD
  sən(t)'lenədz   Schr.
  sint lenɑ:dz   Chis.
St. Leonards-on-Sea/Sx
  snt lenədz ɔn si: BBC
St. Levan/Co
  snt lev(ə)n   BBC
  snt levən   EPD
St. Mabyn/Co
  snt meibin   BBC
  sənt -   BCE
  -ei-   DEPN
St. Margaret
  sn(t) mɑ:g(ə)rit   EPD
St. Martin in Meneage/Co
  snt mɑ:tin in mi'neig,
  - - - mi'ni:g   BBC
St. Mary
  sn(t) mɛəri   EPD
St. Mary Axe/Ldn
  snt 'mɛəri 'æks   BBC
  sn(t) - -   EPD
  siməri æks   BBC,EPD ("old-
        fashioned")
St. Mary-le-Bone/Ldn
  sn(t) mɛərilə'boun   EPD
  snt 'mærələbən   BBC
  (see also s.n. Marylebone)
St. Mary-le-Strand/Ldn
  snt 'mɛəri lə 'strænd   BBC
St. Mary Woolnoth/Ldn
  snt 'mɛəri 'wulnɔþ   BBC
St. Mawes/Co
  snt mɔ:z   BBC,DEPN
  sn(t) -   EPD
  sənt -   BCE
St. Mawgan in Meneage/Co
  snt mɔ:gən in mi'ni:g,
  - - - mi'neig   BBC
St. Mawgan in Pydar/Co
  snt mɔ:gən in paidɑ: BBC
St. Merryn/Co
  snt merin   BBC

St. Mewan/Co
  snt mju:ən BBC
St. Michael
  sn(t) maikl EPD
St. Michael Penkivel/Co
  snt maikl pen'kivl BBC
St. Neots
  snt ni:əts BBC
  sənt ni:ts, loc.
  sənt nauts,sni:ts,snouts Schr.
St. Neots/Co
  snt nouts, sni:ts Hope
St. Neots/Hu
  sənt ni:ts PNBdHu 265,BCE,
              Hope
  snouts PNBdHu 265,Hope
  sni:dz PNBdHu 265
  sənt niəts BCE
  sn(t) ni:ts,ni:əts EPD
St. Nicholas
  sn(t) nikələs EPD
St. Olave's/Ldn
  snt ɔlivz, ɔləvz EPD
St. Olaves/Sf
  snt ɔlivz EPD,BBC
  - ɔləvz EPD
St. Osyth/Ess
  snt ouziþ, ousiþ EPD,BBC
  tu:zi PNEss 347,DEPN
  sənt ousiþ BCE
St. Pancras/Mx
  olim pæŋkridȝ PNMx 140
  snt pæŋkrəs BBC
  sən(t) pæŋkrəs EPD,Schr.
  smpæŋkrəs EPD
St. Paul
  sən(t) pɔ:l EPD,Schr.
St. Paul's/Ldn
  sn(t) pɔ:lz EPD,Schr.
St. Paul's Churchyard/Ldn
  _ ´ _ ´ MEG 158
St. Paul's Walden Bury/Hrt
  snt 'pɔ:lz 'wɔ:ld(ə)n'beri
              BBC
St. Pinnock/Co
  snt pinək BBC
St. Roche's Chapel/Cu
  rauks PNCu 297
St. Teath/Co
  snt teþ BBC,DEPN
  sənt - BCE
St. Thomas/St
  sn(t) tɔməs EPD
  sentiməs Hope
St. Tudy/Co
  snt tju:di BBC
St. Weonards/He
  snt wɔnədz Hope,DHe 43
              (dial. and StE)

  snt wenədz BBC,DHe 43 (dial.)
  sənt - BCE
  -e- DEPN
Salcey Forest/Np
  sɑ:si PNNp 1
  sɔ:lsi BBC
Salcombe/D
  sɔ:lkəm, sɔlkəm EPD,BBC,BCE
Salcott/Ess
  sɔ(:)kət PNEss 322
Salden/Bk
  sɔ:ldən PNBk 71
Sale/Chs
  seil BBC
Salem/Np
  seilem EPD,Schr.
  seiləm EPD,Kruis.
Sales/La
  se:lz PNLa 217
Salesbury/La
  se:lzbri PNLa 70
  seilzbri DEPN
  seilzb(ə)ri EPD
  sɔ:lzb(ə)ri MEG 280
Sale Wheel/La
  se:lwi:l PNLa 70
Salford
  sɔ:lfəd EPD,Schr.,Chis.,Bchm.114
  sɔ:fəd,sælfəd, loc. sæfəd Schr.
  sɔlfəd EPD
Salford/Bd
  sɑ:fəd DEPN,PNBdHu 131
  sæfəd BBC,Hope
Salford/La
  sɔlfəd DEPN,BBC,BCE
  sɔ:vəþ GlossR&R
Salford Ct Fm/Wo
  sɔ:lfəl [sic] PNWo 45
Salford Priors/Wa
  sɔ:lfəd PNWa 220
Salisbury/W (see also s.n. Sarum)
  sɔ:lzbəri PNW 18,BBC,Schr., EPD,
              Chis.,MEG 280,Kruis.
  sɔ:lzbri BBC,DEPN,Schr.,MEG 280,
              EPD
  sɔlzb(ə)ri EPD
  sɔ:lsberi Hope
Salkeld/Cu
  sɔ:kəl PNCu 236,Hope
  safl(t) PNCu 236
  sæfəlt Powley 276
  sɔ:kld PNO li
  sɔ:lkeld BBC,BCE
  (see also s.n. Little S. and Gt S.)
Sall/Nf (also spelt Salle)
  sɔ:l DEPN,BBC,BCE,Hope
Sally Wood/WRY
  sæli wud DHd 97

Salmesbury/La
  sɑːmzbəri BBC,BCE
  seimzbəri Hope
Salmonby/Li
  sæmənbi DEPN,BBC,BCE
  sælmənbi BBC,BCE
Salome Wood/Hu
  sɔləm PNBdHu 246
Salop (a county, also short
    for Shropshire)
  sæləp EPD,BBC,BCE,Schr.,Chis.
  incorrect: seiləp Schr.
Salph End/Bd
  sɑːf end PNBdHu 64
Saltaire/WRY
  sɔːl'teə BBC
Saltash/Co
  sɔːlt'æʃ BBC,BCE
  'sɔ(ː)ltæʃ EPD,Schr.,526
Saltburn/NRY
  sɔːtbən PNYN 143
Salter/Cu
  sɔːtə GlossCu xviii
Saltcoats/Cu
  sout kwɔːts GlossCu xviii
Saltcote/Sx
  sɔːkət PNSx 533
Salter Lane/Db
  suːət lein GlossSh(suppl)55[1]
Salter/Cu
  sɔːtə PNCu 432
  sɔ(ː)ltə EPD
Salterton/D,W
  sɔ(ː)ltət(ə)n EPD
Saltfleet/Li
  sɔːflit Hope
Saltfleetby/Li
  sɔləbi BBC,BCE,Hope,EPD
    ("loc.")
  sɔːltfliːtbi EPD,BBC,BCE
Saltford/So
  sɔːlfəd Turner(2)157
Salthouse/La,Nf
  sɔːlthaus BBC
  sɔːtəs GlossFu 89,s.n.Sotus
  sæləs Hope (for D. in Nf)
Salthrop Ho/W
  sɔːltrəp PNW 279
Saltley/Wa
  sɔːltli BBC
Saltmarsh/He
  sɔ(ː)ltmɑːʃ EPD
Salton/NRY
  sɔːtən PNYN 57
  [ɔ] beside [ɔː] Dobson 789

Saltwick/Nb,NRY
  sɔːltik ONwick (for S. in Nb),
    Hope (for S. in NRY)
Salwarpe/Wo
  sɔlwʌp, olim sæləp PNWo 3o6
  sɔlwɔːp Schr.
Salwarpe/Wo (r.n.)
  sɔlwɔːp Schr.
  sæləp Mawer(2)95
Salwick/La
  sælik, sælwik BBC
Samber Hill/Wt
  zæmbər il PNWt 222
Samlesbury/La
  sæmzbəri, sɑːmzbəri BBC,BCE
  samzbəri Ellis 346
Sampford Courtenay/D
  sæm(p)fəd kɔːtni BBC
Sampford Spiney/D
  sæmfəd spaini BBC,BCE
  -ai- DEPN(3)
Samson Is/Co (Scilly Islands)
  sæms(ə)n BBC
  sæm(p)sn EPD
Sancreed/Co
  sænkrəd, sæŋkris Hope
  sæŋ'kriːd BBC
Sancton/ERY
  santən PNYE 227
Sandal Magna/WRY
  sændəl Schr.
Sandbach/Chs
  sanbitʃ PNChs II/ix,GlossChs
  sanbætʃ PNchs II/269
  sændbætʃ BBC,BCE
  sæn(d)bætʃ EPD
Sanderstead/Sr
  sɑːndəsted EPD
Sandford
  sænfəd EPD
  sæn(d)fəd Schr.
  zæmvərd, sæmfərd PNWt 158
  sænfəþ PNE'side 67 (for S. in
Sandfordhall Gn/Ess
  stæmfəd PNEss 362
Sandgate/K,Sx
  sængit EPD
  sændgit Schr.
  sængeit EPD,PNK
Sandhills/Wt
  zændhilz PNWt 1o9
Sandhurst/Brk
  'sændhəːst EPD,BBC,Schr.,Chis.
Sandiacre/Db
  sendʒikə Hope
  sændieikə BBC

---

1) "Now vulgarly written Psalter Lane" (GlossSh(suppl)55).

Scagglethorpe/ERY
  skaglþrəp   PNYE 139
Scaitcliffe/La
  skatklif   Whiteh.75
Scalby/NRY
  skɔ:bi   PNYN 1o8,Hope,BBC,BCE
  skɔ:lbi   BBC,BCE
Scalderskew/Cu (or Sk-)
  skoudəskə   Hope
Scald Fell/We
  skɔ: fel   PNE'side 74
Scaldwell/Np
  skɔ:ldwəl   PNNp 131
Scaleby/Cu
  skiəlbi   GlossCu xviii
Scale Gill/WRY
  skeal gil   DDd 12
Scales/Cu
  skiəlz   GlossCu xviii
Scalesceugh/Cu
  skelskə   GlossCu xviii
Scales Hall/Cu
  skɛəlz hɔ: PNE'side 72
Scalford/Le
  skɔ:fɔ:d   DEPN,Hope
  skɔ:lfəd, skɔ:fəd   BBC,BCE
Scalthwaite Rigg/We
  skɔ:þət rig   PNE'side 66
Scar, S.End, S.Top/WRY
  skɑ:r   DHd 1o6
Scarborough/NRY
  skɑ:bərə   EPD,Schr.,Kruis.,
             Chis.
  skɑ:brə   EPD,Schr.
  skarbrə   Lloyd 127
  skɑ:brʌf   GlossWby,s.n.Bruff
Scargill/NRY
  skɑ:gil   PNYN 3o3
Scarisbrick/La
  ske:zbrik   PNLa 124
  skɛəzbrik   DEPN,BBC,BCE
Scarrington/Nt
  vulgo skæritn   PNMx xxxii
Scarrowhill/Cu
  skarə   PNCu 79
Scarrowmanwick/Cu
  skarə'manik   PNCu 25o
Scarside/We
  skɑ:rsaid   PNE'side 69
Scartho(e)/Li
  'skɑ:þou   BBC,BCE
Scathwaite/La
  skaþət   PNLa 213
Scawfell/Cu → Sca Fell
Scawton/NRY
  skɔ:tən   PNYN 56
Sceugh/Cu
  skiuf   PNCu 191,PNE'side 71
Sceugh Dike/Cu
  skiuf daik   PNE'side 71

Sceugh Head/Cu
  skiuf hi:d   PNCu 2o6,PNE'side 71
Schofield/La
  skuəfil   GlossR&R (so pron. in
             Rochdale)
Scholar Gn/Chs
  skɔlə(r)   PNChs II/3o8
Scholefield/La
  sko:lfi:ld   PNLa 86
Scholes/La,WRY
  skoulz   BBC,BCE (for S. in WRY),
             EPD
Scilly Is, The Scillies/Co
  sili   EPD,BBC,Schr.,Chis.
  siliz   EPD
Scissett/WRY
  si'set   BBC
Scole/Nf
  skoul   BBC
Scolt Head/Nf (or Scolthead)
  skɔlt   BBC
Scopwick/Li
  skɔpwik   BBC,BCE
  skɔ:bi   Hope,ONwick 372
Scorborough/ERY
  skɔ:brə   PNYE 162
Score Crag/We (f.n.)
  skou   Simpson 289
Scorrier/Co
  skɔriə   BBC
Scorton/La
  skɔ:tn   PNLa 164
Scotby/Cu
  skɔtbi   BBC
Scotchells Brook/Wt
  skɔ:tʃəlz bruk   PNWt 6o
Scotchergill/WRY
  skɔtʃəgil   DDd 13
Scothern/Li (sometimes spelt -thorn)
  'skɔþə:n   BBC,BCE
  -ɔþ-   DEPN
  loc. skɔþən   Eminson(1)183
Scothwaite/Cu
  skɔ:þət   GlossCu xviii
Scotland Fm/Wt
  skatlənd   PNWt 286
Scottow/Nf
  skɔtə   Hope
  skɔtou   BBC
Scoulton/Nf
  skoutən   Hope
Scow/WRY
  skou   DDd 12 and 16
Scrafield/Li
  skreifi:ld   BBC,BCE
Scrainwood/Nb
  skɑ:nwud   PNNbDu 172,DEPN
Scratchmill Scar/Cu
  skrætʃmə skɑ:r   PNE'side 75

Scremerston/Nb
  skraməsən PNNbDu 172
Screveton/Nt
  skri:t(ə)n PNNt 229,BBC
  skreitn PNNt 229
  skri:tn PNNt(i)119,DEPN
  skri:tən BCE
  skrevitən BBC,BCE
Scrithwaite/La
  skraiþət PNLa 223
Scrivelsby/Li
  skrivlzbi, skri:lzbi BBC,BCE
  sə:səlbi, sə:səlsbi,
  skri:lsbi Hope
Scriven/WRY
  skrivin PNYW V/114
  skriv(ə)n EPD
Scroby/Nf
  skroubi BBC
Scropton/Db
  skrɔpn Hope (spelt Scrapton)
Scruton/NRY
  skriutən, skru:tən PNYN 238
Scumsceugh/Cu
  skumskə PNE'side 63
Scunthorpe/Li
  skʌnþrəp GlossM&C,s.n.Thrup
Seabach/Sx
  sibidȝ PNSx 68
Seacombe/Chs
  si:kum PNChs IV/329
  si:kəm Chis.
Sea Dike/Cu
  sidik PNCu 295
Seaford/Sx
  si:'fu:əd PNSx 363,Hope
  si:fəd EPD,BCE,Mawer(2)91
  si:'fɔ:d BBC,BCE
  'si:fɔ:d BBC,EPD
  zi:'vu:əd Mawer(2)91,Mawer(4)
      285 (stress only)
Seaforth/La
  si:fɔ:þ EPD
Seaham/Du
  si:əm BBC,BCE
Seahouses/Nb (or Sea Houses)
  'si:hauziz BBC
Seasalter/K
  'si:sɔ:ltə BBC
  si:sæltə PNK
Seascale/Cu
  'si:skeil BBC
Seathwaite/Cu,La
  si:hwæ:t PNCu 351
  si:þət, si:hweit GlossCu
        xviii
  si:þweit BBC
Seaton
  si:tn EPD
  si:tən Schr.

Seaton/Ru
  seitən GlossRu vii
Seaton Carew/Du
  si:t(ə)n kə'ru: BBC
  si:tən - BCE
  Carew: _ / DEPN
Seaton Delaval/Nb
  si:t(ə)n deləvəl BBC
  si:tən - BCE
Seattle/La
  se:tl PNLa 199
Seaville/Cu
  sevil BBC,BCE
Seavington/So
  seviŋtən DEPN,BBC,BCE
Sebergham/Cu
  sebrəm PNCu 15o,DEPN,Hope
  sebərəm PNCu 15o,Hope,BBC,BCE,
      PNE'side 65
Sedbergh/WRY
  sebə PNYW VI/263
  sedbə PNYW VI/263,DEPN,BBC,BCE,
      EPD,Hope,Bardsley,s.n.
      Thornbarrow
  sedbrə PNYW VI/263
  sedbə:g PNYW VI/263,BBC,Chis.
  sedbərə BCE
  sebə(r) DDd 17
  sedbər DKe 6
  sebər DKe 145,Ellis 559
Sedbergh School/WRY
  sedbə EPD
  sedbə:g EPD,BCE
Sedgeberrow/Wo
  sedȝiberou PNWo 164
Sedgebrook/Li
  saidbruk Hope
Sedgefield/Du
  sedȝfi:ld EPD
Sedgehill/Nb → Seghill
Sedgehill/W
  sedȝhil, sedȝl BBC
Sedgemoor/So
  sedȝmɔ:, -muə, -mɔə EPD,Bchm.83
    -mɔ:ə Bchm.83
  sedȝmɔ:r Schr.
  sedȝmu:r Schr.,Chis.
Sedgewick Castle/Sx
  sedȝik PNSx 231,PNSx(i)139
  sedȝwik Bchm.138
Sedgley/St
  sedȝli EPD,Schr.
Sedgwick/We
  sedȝwik EPD
Sedlescombe/Sx
  selzkəm PNSx 524,Hope
  sedlskəm EPD
Sedsall/Db
  -ds- PNDb(i) II/147

Seend/W
 olim si:n   PNW 131
 si:nd   BBC
Seething/Nf
 "SENGES, by which name the
 place is sometimes called,
 appears to be a strange cor-
 ruption of SEETHING" (PNNf)
Segenhoe/Bd
 segnou, olim
 sedӡnou   PNBdHu 84
Seghill/Nb
 seghil   BBC,BCE
Segry/W
 olim segəri   PNW 72
Seifton/Sa (or Siefton)
 si:fn   DEPN
Seighford/St
 saifəd   DEPN,BBC,BCE,Hope
Seisdon/St
 si:zdən   DEPN,BBC,BCE
Selborne/Ha
 selbɔ:n   EPD,Schr.,Bchm.69
 -bən   EPD,Schr.,Kruis.,
Selby/WRY   Bchm.69
 selbi   EPD,Schr.
Seldon's Fm/Ess
 selənd   PNEss 513
Selham/Sx
 si:ləm, seləm   BBC
Sellack/He
 selək   BBC
Sellinge/K —→ Sellindge
Sellindge/K
 selindӡ   BBC,PNK,Dodgson(2)
            345,H.A.(1)179,
            Zachr.(1)348
Selling/K
 seliŋ   PNK
Selly Oak/Wa
 seli ouk   BBC
Selmeston/Sx
 simsən   PNSx 338,SxArchSoc
 simsn   DEPN
 simpsən   Hope
 selmztən   BBC
Selscombe/Sx
 selskəm   PNSx(i)156
Selsea Bill/Sx (= Selsey B.)
 selsi: bil   Schr.
 selsi bil   BBC,Schr.
 selzi bil   BBC
Selsey/Gl,Sx
 selzi   BBC
 selsi   EPD
Selside/We
 selsit   PNE'side 69
Selston/Nt
 vulgo selsən   PNNt 131

Semele (family-name affixed to p.n.)
 semili   EPD
Semer Water/NRY
 seməwætə   PNYN 264
 semə   DEPN
Semington/W
 semintən   PNW 143,BBC
Senlac/Sx
 senlæk   EPD
Sennen/Co
 senən   BBC
Serlby/Nt
 sɑ:lbi   Hope
Seseley/K
 sisli   PNK
Sessay/NRY
 sesi   PNYN 187
Setmabanning/Cu
 setəne'baniən   PNCu 313
 setənə'bæniən   PNE'side 65
Setterah/We
 setərə   PNE'side 63
Seven/NRY (r.n.)
 sevn   RN 358,DEPN
 sevən   Kruis.
The Seven Dials/Ldn
 sevn daiəlz   Bau.
 short: The Dials (Bau.,s.n.Dials
Sevenhampton/W
 seniŋtən   PNW 27,PNW(i)145,
                PNGl(i)136
Sevenoaks/K
 sevnouks   EPD,Schr.,Bchm.138
 sevənouks   Chis
 olim snu:ks   DEPN(3)
 (cf. HL 747: "die altertümlichste
  Lautung ist [snu:ks]")
Severn/Wo (r.n.)
 sevən   DEPN,BBC,Schr.,Chis.
 sevə(:)n   EPD
 sivən   GlossSEWo 82
 sevn   Times,August 8,1977,p.15,
            letters to the editor
Sevington/K
 seviŋtən   PNK
Sewardsley/Np
 ʃouzli   PNNp 99
Sewborwens/Cu
 siubɔrənz   PNCu 228
 siu:bɔrənz   PNE'side 67
Sewell/Bd
 sju:əl, sjuəl   EPD
Sewell/O
 sju-   cf. PNO(i)181
Sewerby/ERY
 siuwəbi   PNYE lo4
 sju:bi   Hope
 su:əbi   BBC

Sewing Shields/Nb
   sju:iŋ ʃi:lz PNNbDu 174
Seymour (as in S.Ct/Bk)
   si:mə EPD,Kruis.
Sezincote/Gl
   'si:ziŋkout PNGl I/257
   'si:z(ə)nkət BBC
Shadwell/Ldn
   ʃædwəl Schr.
   -w(ə)l, -wel EPD
Shaftesbury/Do
   ʃɑ:ftsbəri BBC,Schr.,Kruis.,
              Chis.
     -b(ə)ri EPD
   loc. ʃæstən Schr.,Hope
Shakenhurst/Wo
   ʃækənhə:st PNWo 4o
Shakerley/La
   ʃækəli BBC
Shalbourne/W
   ʃælbə(r)n, ʃɔ:l- PNW(i)145
Shalcombe/Wt
   ʃɑ:kəm, ʃɔ:-, ʃæl- PNWt 212
Shalden/D,Ha
   ʃɔ(:)ld(ə)n BBC
   ʃɔ(:)ldən BCE
Shalfleet/Wt
   ʃæ(:)flət PNWt 2o5
   ʃɑ:flət DWt,s.n.Lebb'n o'
             clock
Shalford/Ess,Sr
   ʃɑ:fəd PNEss 455
   ʃælfəd BBC,BCE
Shallcross Hall/Db
   cf. Bardsley,s.n. Priestnall:
    "[-ow is] the usual pron. in
    the north of names ending in
    -all; cf.[...]Shawcross for
    Shallcross."
Shalmsford St/K
   ʃælmzfəd stri:t BBC
   ʃɑ:msfəd PNK
Shalstone/Bk
   ʃɔ:lstən PNBk 47
Shandy Hall/NRY
   ʃændi EPD,Kruis.
Shanklin/Wt
   ʃæŋklin(d) PNWt 214
   ʃæŋklin EPD,BBC
Shanks Ho/So
   ʃæŋks EPD
Shap/We
   ʃæp PNWe II/164
   ʃap DKe 5
Shapwick/Do,So
   ʃæpik BBC
Shardeloes/Bk
   ʃɑrlouz PNBk 211
Sharnbrook/Bd
   ʃɑ:mbruk PNBdHu 39

Sharpenhoe/Bd
   'ʃɑ:pinou BBC
Sharples Hall/La
   ʃɑ:plz EPD
Sharpness/Gl
   ʃɑ:pnis BBC
Sharrow Bay/We (on Ullswater)
   ʃærəbe: PNE'side 63
Shate Fm/Wt
   ʃeit PNWt 7o
Shaugh/D
   ʃei PND 258
Shaugh Prior/D
   ʃɔ: praiə BBC,BCE
   ʃei Mawer(2)96
Shavington/Chs
   ʃævintən, loc. ʃentən PNChs III/69
Shaw/La
   ʃei GlossR&R
Shawforth/La
   ʃeivəþ GlossR&R
Shawhall/Chs
   ʃei ɔ: PNChs I/317
Sheaf/Db,WRY (r.n.)
   ʃi:f BBC,Schr.
Shealy Spring/Ess
   ʃeili PNEss 298
Sheard's Copse/Wt
   ʃiərds kaps PNWt 222
Shearsby/Le
   ʃiəzbi BBC
Sheat/Wt
   ʃeit PNWt 138
Shebbear/D
   ʃebiə BBC
Sheepridge/Bk
   ʃipridʒ PNBk 189
Sheepscombe/Gl (also spelt Sheps-)
   ʃepskəm PNGl I/133,BBC,BCE
   ʃi:pskəm BCE
Sheepshed/Le (also spelt Sheps-)
   ʃepʃəd Hope
Sheepstones/NRY
   ʃi:əpsti:ənz Ump.31
Sheepwash/Wt
   ʃi:pwɔʃ PNWt 158
Sheering Hall/Ess
   ʃə:nhɔ:l PNEss 455
Sheerness/K
   'ʃiə'nes, ͵ _ EPD
   _ ´ EPD,Kruis.
   ʃi:rnes Schr.,Chis.
Sheffield/WRY
   ʃefi:ld EPD,BBC,Schr.,Chis.
   -fild EPD ("loc."),NED
   ʃæfəld GlossSh xxxiii
Sheinton/Sa (also spelt Shine-)
   ʃaintən PNSa

Sheldon/D,Db,Wa
  ʃeld(ə)n EPD
Sheldwich/K
  selwidʒ PNK
Shelfanger/Nf
  'ʃelfæŋgə BBC,BCE
Shelfield/St
  ʃelfil PNSt 134
Shelford/Ca
  ʃelfəd ONCa 187
Shelland/Sf
  ʃelənd BBC
Shelley/Ess,WRY
  ʃeli EPD,Schr.
Shelsley Beauchamp/Wo
  biːtʃəm PNWo 76
Shengay/Ca → Shingay
Shenstone/St,Wo
  ʃenstən EPD
Shephalbury/Hrt
  ʃeplbəri BBC
Shephall/Hrt
  ʃipɔːl PNHrt 115
  ʃepl BBC
Shepherdine/Gl
  'ʃepədain BBC
Shepherd's Chine/Wt
  ʃepərds tʃain PNWt 7o
Shepherd's Well/Sx → Sibertswold
Shepley/WRY
  ʃepli Schr.
Sheppey (Isle of)/K
  ʃepi Schr.,DK (the Isle of S.
        is called 'The Island'
        in North Kent; cf.DK,
        s.n. Marsh)
Shepreth/Ca
  ʃepriþ BBC
  ʃeprəþ ONCa 194
Shepscombe,Shepshed → Sheeps-
Shepton/So
  ʃepən Hope
Shepton Beauchamp/So
  ʃeptən biːtʃəm BBC,BCE
Shepton Mallet/So
  ʃeptən mælit BBC
  popularly ʃepən BG
Sheraton/Du
  ʃerətn EPD
Sherborne
  ʃəːbən BBC,BCE(for S.in Do),
        EPD,Schr.
  -bɔːn EPD
  ʃəːrbən DDo (for S. in Do),
        Urlau 5o
Sherbrooke/Sr
  ʃəːbruk EPD
Shere/Sr
  ʃiə EPD,BBC

Sherfield-on-Loddon/Ha
  'ʃəːfiːld ɔn 'lɔd(ə)n BBC
Sheringham/Nf
  -inəm, -iŋəm PNing 172
  ʃeriŋəm BBC
  -e- DEPN
Sherington/Bk
  ʃəːtən, tʃəːtən PNBk 38
Sherlock Street,Birmingham
  tʃælɔk Wilde 27
Shermanbury/Sx
  ʃəːmənbəri BBC
Sherston/W
  olim ʃɑːs(t)ən PNW lo9
Sherwood/Nt
  ʃəːwud EPD,Schr.
Sheviock/Co
  ʃeviək BBC
Shibden/WRY
  ʃibdin Hope
Shide/Wt
  ʃaid PNWt 179
Shield Gn/Cu
  ʃilgrin PNE'side 74
Shields (North S.)/Nb,
Shields (South S.)/Du
  ʃiːldz BBC,Schr.,Chis.
  ʃeildz DNDu 3o
Shillingstone/Do
  ʃilənstn DDo
Shillington/Bd → Shitlington
Shiloh/La
  ʃailou EPD,Schr.
Shilvinghampton/Do
  ʃilviŋtən PNDo(i)249
Shincliffe/Du
  ʃiŋkli PNNbDu 178
  ʃiŋklə DSDu
  ʃiŋklif BBC,BCE
Shineton/Sa → Sheinton
Shingay/Ca
  ʃeŋgi, ʃiŋgi ONCa 181
Shinybricks/Wt
  ʃainibriks PNWt 163
Shipbourne/K
  ʃibəːn BBC,BCE,PNK
  ʃibən PNK
Shipdham/Nf (or Shipdam)
  ʃindəm Hope
  ʃipdəm, ʃipəm BBC,BCE
Shiplake/O
  ʃipleik EPD,BBC
Ship Ledge/Wt
  ʃipli PNWt 285
Shipley
  ʃipli EPD,Schr.,PNSx(i)143
  ʃiplə PNYW III/267,DEY 8
Shippea Hill/Ca
  ʃipi BBC,BCE

Shipston-on-Stour/Wa
  'ʃipstən ɔn 'stauə BBC
Shipton
  ʃiptən EPD,PNYN 15
Shipton Bellinger/Ha
  ʃiptən belindʒə BBC
Shirburn/O
  ʃəːbən PNO(i)185
Shireoaks/Nt
  ʃaiərəks Hope
Shirle Hill/WRY
  ʃəːl hil GlossSh 211
Shirley
  ʃəːli EPD,Schr.
Shish Ford Cottage/Wt
  ʃiʃfərd PNWt 286
Shitlington/Bd (now Shilling-)
  ʃiliŋtən Hope
Shitterton/Do
  ʃidərtn PNDo I/276,DDo
Shobrooke/D
  ʃoubruk BBC
Shocklach (Church S.)/Chs
  ʃɔklatʃ PNChs IV/63,
              GlossChs
  ʃɔklitʃ BBC
Shocklach Oviatt/Chs
  ʃɔklatʃ ouvjət PNChs IV/63
Shoebury/Ess
  ʃuː- DEPN
Sholden/K (or Shoulden)
  ʃould(ə)n BBC
  ʃouldən PNK
Sholing/Ha
  ʃouliŋ BBC
Shoolbred/WRY (f.n.)
  'ʃoulbred DDd 13
The Shore/WRY
  ʃuər DHd 1o2
Shoreditch/Ldn,So
  ʃɔːditʃ Schr. (for S. in
              Ldn),EPD,CPhon 76
  ʃɔə- EPD
Shoreham/K,Sf
  ʃɔːrəm EPD,Schr.,Chis.
  ʃɔə- EPD
Shorncliffe/K
  ʃɔːnklif EPD
Shorncote/Gl,W
  ʃɑːŋkət PNGl I/83
  vulgo ʃɑːŋkət PNW 47

Shoeburyness/Ess
  'ʃuːbəri'nes BBC,Kruis.
  'ʃuːbərinəs Chis.
  'ʃuːb(ə)ri'nes EPD
  ʃuː- DEPN
Shortlanesend/Co (or Shortlane End)
  ʃɔːtleinz'end BBC
Shorton/D
  ʃɔːtən PND 518
Shorwell/Wt
  ʃɔrəl PNWt 215,Ellis 1o7
  ʃɔːwel BBC
Shotesham/Nf (S.All Saints,S.Mary)
  ʃɔtsəm BBC,Hope
  - ɔːl seints, - snt mɛəri BBC
Shottisham/Sf
  ʃɔtsəm BBC
  ʃɔtisəm PNDVall 66
Shotwick/Chs
  ʃɔtwik PNChs IV/2o6,BBC,PNL'pool
              94
  loc. ʃɔtik PNChs IV/2o6,
               PNChs(i)16
Shoulden/K → Sholden
Shouldham/Nf
  ʃouldəm BBC
Shouldham Thorpe/Nf
  ʃouldəm þɔːp BBC
Shoulthwaite/Cu
  ʃoulþət PNE'side 67
Shovelstrode Fm/Sx
  "No trace of the old pron. [ʃuːl]
  seems to have survived"(PNSx 333)
Showell/O → Sewell
Shoyswell/Sx
  ʃouzwəl PNSx 457
Shrawardine/Sa
  ʃreidən, sreidən Hope
  ʃreidn GlossSa 518
  ʃreiwədain BBC
Shred/WRY
  ʃred, ʃriəd DHd 1o2
Shrewbridge/Chs
  ʃruːbridʒ PNChs III/131
Shrewsbury/Sa
  ʃrouzbəri DEPN,BBC,BCE,Kruis.,
              Schr.("loc."),MEG 95,
              GlossSa 519 ("classi-
              cal and educated
              pron."),Mawer(4)284,
              Hope

1) "[ʃrou-] is the pron. used by those connected with Shrewsbury School
and by many residents in the neighbourhood,especially members of
county families. The form [ʃruː-] is used by outsiders, and is the
common pron. heard in the town" (EPD).
"Diese Aussprache [viz. ʃruːz-] ist auch in der Stadt bereits die
übliche; [ʃrouz-] wird noch von vielen Leuten gesprochen. die in
der Nachbarschaft der Stadt wohnen" (Bchm. 241f.).
"... both [viz. ʃrouz- and ʃruːz-] are used in the town" (BBC).

ʃrouzb(ə)ri EPD
ʃru:zbəri EPD,BBC,Schr..
      Kruis.,Chis.,MEG 95
ʃru:zb(ə)ri Bchm.241
srouzbri ("semi-refined
     pronunciation"),
souzbri ("the pron. of the
     country folk"),
su:zbri ("a vulgarism")
     GlossSa 519
sro:zbri, ʃro:zbri HL 814
sousbri Hope
Shrewton/W
ʃru:t(ə)n BBC
Shrivenham/Brk
ʃriv(ə)nəm BBC
Shropshire
ʃrɔpʃə EPD,Schr.
  -ʃiə EPD
Shroton/Do
ʃrɔ:tən PNDo(i) 1o
ʃrout(ə)n BBC
ʃɔtən Urlau 5o
ʃu:dən Urlau 46
Shuart/K
ʃouɑ:t PNK
Shuckburgh/Wa
ʃʌkbərə BBC,Schr.
ʃʌkbrə EPD
sʌkbrə Hope
Shude Hill in Sheffield/WRY
ʃu:d hil GlossSh 213
Shugborough/St
ʃʌkbərə PNSt 138
Shulbrede Priory/Sx
ʃulbri:d BBC
Shunner Howe/NRY
ʃunərou PNYN 13o
Shurlach (Hr S.,Lwr S.,S.Fm)/Chs
'surlaʃ PNChs II/ix
'ʃurlatʃ PNChs II/21o
surləʃ GlossChs
sə:ləʃ Hope ("Surlash")
Shustoke/Wa
ʃʌstək PNWa 92
Shute/D
ʃu:t EPD
Shutlanger/Np
'ʃʌtlæŋə PNNp 1o6
Sibdon Carwood/Sa
sibdən kɑ:wud BBC
Sibdown/Wt
zibdən PNWt 158
Sibertswold/K (also called
     Shepherd's Well)
ʃepədzwel Hope
Sible Hedingham/Ess
sibl hediŋəm EPD,BBC
(see also s.n. Hedingham)

Sicklesmere/Sf
siklzmiə BBC
Sidbury Hill/W
vulgo ʃedbəri PNW 243
Sidcup/K
sidkʌp, sidkəp BBC
Siddington/Chs
olim siðitn PNChs II/vii,
        GlossChs
sidiŋtən PNChs II/vii
Sidebight/La (also spelt -beet)
-bi:t PNLa 73
Sidelong (as in S.Hill/Wo)
saidən Davis 38
Sidestrand/Nf
saidstrænd, saidistrænd BBC,BCE
Sidford/D
sid'fɔ:d BBC,BCE
'sidfɔ:d BBC
Sidlesham/Sx
sidəlsəm PNSx 85
sidlsəm BBC,BCE
-i-,-s- DEPN
Sidmouth/D
sidməþ EPD,BBC,BCE,Chis.
Sidon Hill/Ha
saidn EPD,Kruis.
Siefton/Sa → Seifton
Sigglesthorne/ERY
si:lsþrən PNYE 68
sigistən, silstən Hope
Sike Fold/WRY
saik fɑ:ld DDd 14
Silchester/Ha
siltʃistə EPD,Schr.
Silcombe Lane/Wt
silkəm PNWt 13o
Sileby/Le
sailbi BBC
Silkstone/WRY
silkstoun BBC
Sillery Sands/D
siləri EPD
Silloth/Cu
siləþ BBC,PNE'side 64
Silpho/NRY
silfə PNYN 115
Silsoe/Bd
silsə PNBdHu 161
silsou BBC
Silver Band/We
silvərə bænd PNE'side 63
Silverley/Ca
silvəli ONCa 184
Silverstone/Np
silsən PNNp 43
silstən Hope
Silvertown/Ess
silvətaun EPD

Simonsbath/So
  'simənzbɑːþ BBC,BCE
Simonsham/D
  senzəm PND 136
Simonside/Nb
  saimən- DEPN
Simonstone/La,NRY
  'simənstoun BBC,BCE (for S. in La)
  simən- DEPN (for S. in La)
Simpson/Bk,D
  sim(p)sn EPD
Sinderby/NRY
  sinəbi PNYN 225
Sindlesham/Brk
  sindlʃəm EPD
Singleborough/Bk
  siŋklbʌrou PNBk 69
  siŋkl- DEPN
Singleton/La,Sx,We
  siŋglt(ə)n EPD
Sinodun Hill/Brk
  sinədən BBC
Sion (as in S. Ho/Mx)
  saiən EPD,Kruis.
Sisland/Nf (or Size-)
  saizlənd BBC,BCE,DEPN,Hope
Sissinghurst/K
  'sisiŋhəːst BBC
Siston/Gl
  saistən, sais(ə)n BBC
  -ai- DEPN
Sithney/Co
  siþni BBC
Sittingbourne/K
  sitiŋbuːrn Chis.
  -bɔːn, -bɔən EPD
Sizergh/We
  saizə PNWe I/110,DEPN,BBC,
       BCE
Sizewell/Sf
  saizwəl BBC
Skalderskew/Cu ⟶ Sc-
Skarrow Hill/Cu
  skærə PNE'side 63
Skarrowmanwick/Cu
  skærə'mænik PNE'side 63
Skeeby/NRY
  skiːbi PNYN 288
Skeels/Cu
  skiːlz PNE'side 74
Skegness/Li
  'skeg'nes, ⟋ _, _ ⟋ EPD
Skelcies/We
  skelsiz PNE'side 74
Skell/WRY (r.n.)
  skel BBC

Skelmersdale/La
  'skelməzdeil, skeməzdeil BBC
  skjəməzdə PNLa(ii)
Skelsmergh/We
  skelzmə PNWe I/143,BBC,BCE
  skelzmiə BBC,BCE
Skelton/Cu,Yorks.
  skeltən Schr.,Kruis.
  skeltn EPD
Skelwith/La
  skeliþ PNLa 219,DEPN,BBC,BCE
  skeləþ PNLa(ii)
Skerne/ERY
  skiːən Hope
Skerton/La
  skəːtn PNLa 177
  skiːətn PNLa(ii)
Sketchley/Le
  sketʃli EPD
Skewsby/NRY
  skiuzbi PNYN 3o
Skeynes/K
  skeins PNK
Skeyton/Nf
  skait(ə)n BBC
  skaitən BCE
  skaitn Hope
  -ai- DEPN
Skiddaw/Cu (parish and mountain)
  'skidɔː EPD,Chis.,Schr.(for the
       mountain)
  loc. -də EPD,PNE'side 62
  skidi Hope
  _ ⟋ DEPN
Skinburness/Cu
  skinbərniːz PNCu 294,GlossCu
       xxviii
  skinbə:'nes BBC,BCE,DEPN (stress
       only)
Skinner (as in S.'s Bottom/Co)
  skinə EPD
Skinners/Wt (nr South Arreton)
  skinərz PNWt 285
Skinner's Hill/Wt
       (nr Newchurch)
  skinərz il PNWt 172
Skinningrove/NRY
  skinigrif Ump.31
Skiprigg/Cu
  skiprig PNE'side 76
Skippool/La
  skipə Hope
Skipsea Brough/ERY
  skipsi bruf PNYE 81
Skipton/NRY,WRY
  skiptən EPD
Skipwith/ERY
  skipiþ PNYE 262

Skircoat/WRY
  skə:kɔit   Hope
Skir-Gut/D
  skə:gə:t   Bate 529
Skirlaugh/ERY
  skelə   PNYE 49,GlossHol 17,
       Hope
  skə:lou   BBC
Skirlington/ERY
  skelitən   PNYE 8o
  skelətən   Hope
Skirlington Hill/ERY
  skelitən il   GlossHol 17
Skirpenbeck/ERY
  skɔpmbek   PNYE 15o
Skirsgill/Cu
  skirskəl   PNCu 189
  skuskil   PNE'side 68
Skirwith/Cu
  ski:riþ   PNCu 242
  skəriþ   PNCu 242,PNE'side 64
  skiriþ   Hope
  loc. skerit   PNO li
Skitwath Beck/Cu
  skitwəþ bek   PNE'side 66
  skitwiþ bek   PNE'side 64
Skye (as in S. Gn/Ess)
  skai   EPD
Skygarth/We
  skaigəþ   PNE'side 64
Slack/WRY (as in Heptonstall S.,
       Outlane S., etc.)
  slæk   DHd 1o8f.
Slack/La,WRY
  ðə slak   PNLa 199
  slak   DDd 16
Slaithwaite/WRY (two places,one nr
    Huddersfield,the other nr
    Thornhill)
  slauwit   PNYW II/3o7 (for S.
       nr H.)
  slauit   PNSWY 261,DAl&Hd
       (for S. nr H.),BBC,
       BCE,Goodall 51,Ellis
       377 (for S. nr H.),
       Hope,EPD ("loc.")
  slæwit   DHd (for S. nr H.)
  slouit   BCE
  slɔ:it   Hope,H.A.(2)36
  slæþwət   EPD
  slæþweit   BBC,BCE
  sleiþweit   BCE
Slakes/We
  slɛəks   PNE'side 72
Slape Ho/Do
  sli:p   PNDo(i)279
Slape Wath/NRY
  slɛə pwaþ   PNYN 147
Slapton Ley/D
  lei   PND 33o

Slater (as in S.'s Bridge/We)
  sleitə   EPD
Slaugham/Sx
  slæfəm   PNSx 277,BBC,BCE,Hope
  slæfm   PNSx(i)145
  -æf-   DEPN
  slɑ:fəm   BBC,BCE
Slaughdon/Sf
  slɔ:d(ə)n   BBC
Slaughter/Gl
  slɔ:tə   PNGl I/2o6,BBC
  slɑ:tə   PNGl I/2o6
Slaughter Hill/Chs
  slɔ:tər, older local
  slɑ:ðər   PNChs III/1o
Sleaford/Li
  sli:fəd   BBC,Chis.
Sleagill/We
  sli:gil   PNWe II/148
Sleap Magna/Sa
  loc. sleip   PNSa
Sleddale/We → Long S.
Sledmore/ERY
  sledmiə   BBC
Sleight/Do
  slait   EPD
Sleightholme/NRY
  sli:təm   PNYN 3o5
  -i:t-   DEPN
Sleightholme Dale/NRY
  sleitumdil   PNYN 62
Sleights/NRY (in Whitby Strand Wapen
  sli:ts   PNYN 12o,DEPN   take
  slaits   EPD,BBC,BCE
  (see also s.n. Old S.)
Sleights Ho/NRY
  sleit u:s   PNYN 63
Slepe/Do
  slip   PNDo(i)13o,PNDo I/73
Sloane Sq/Ldn
  slaun   CPP 66
  sloun   EPD
Slough/Bk,K
  slau   PNBk 243,DEPN (for S. in
       Bk),BBC,BCE (for S. in Bk)
       EPD,Schr.,Chis.,BG (for S.
       in Bk)
Slyne/La
  slain   PNLa 185,PNLa(ii),DEPN
Smaithwaite/Cu
  smiəþwæ:t   PNCu 314 and 4o7
  smiəþweit   GlossCu xviii
  -iə-   PNCu xli
Smallbridge/La
  smoubrig   GlossR&R (so pron. in
       Rochdale)
Smallbrook Fm/Wt
  'zmɔ:lbruk   PNWt 285
Smalley/Db
  smɔ:li   PNDb(i) II/155,EPD,BBC,
       BCE

Smallhythe/K
   smæli(d)   PNK
Smallmoor/Wt
   smɔ:(l)mɔ:r   PNWt 223
Smallthwaite/Cu
   smɑːəhwæ:t   PNCu 419
   smɑːhweit   GlossCu xviii
   smɔːþət   PNE'side 67
Smallwood/Chs,St,Sf
   smɔːlwud   EPD
Smanhill Covert/Np
   smænəl   PNNp 48
Smarden/K
   'smɑːd(ə)n   BBC
   smɑː'den   BBC,BCE
   smɑːden   PNK
Smeardon Down/D
   smə:n   PND 232
Smeaton/NRY,WRY
   smi:tn   EPD
   smi:tən   Schr.
Smeaton Hall/Chs
   smi:tn   PNChs III/97
Smeatonwood Fm/Chs
   smi:tn   PNChs III/97
Smeeth/K,Nf
   smi:ð   BBC,PNK,BCE (for S.
        in K)
Smethwick/St
   smeðik   DEPN,EPD,BBC,BCE,EPD,
        Schr.,Chis.
   smerik   GlossSEWo 82,ONwick
        37o,Schr. ("loc."),
        Hope
Smethwick Gn, S.Hall, S.Lane/Chs
   smeðik   PNChs II/275
Smite/Le,Nt (r.n.)
   smait   RN 373
Smitha/D
   smiðə   PND 386
Smithdown/La
   smedn   PNLa(ii),PNDb(i) I/248
Smithfield/Ldn,Cu
   smiþfi:ld   EPD,BBC,Schr. (for
        S. in Ldn),Bau.
        for S. in Ldn)
   vulgo smifl   MEG 227
   smifi:ld   Bau.,s.n.Smiffield
Smith(e)sby/Db
   the place is also called and
   spelt Smisby (cf.BG and PNDb(i)
   II/155)
Smorthwaite/WRY
   smɔ(:)þət   DDd 16
Snabdaugh/Nb
   snapduf   PNNbDu 182
   'snæbdʌf   BBC,BCE
Snailslinch Fm/Sr
   snɑːznidʒ   PNSr 173

Snailwell/Ca
   snailwəl   ONCa 19o
Snaizholme/NRY
   sne:zəm   PNYN 267
Snainton/NRY
   snɛəntən   PNYN 97
Snape Bank, S.Fm, S.Hollow/Chs
   sneip   PNChs III/76
Sneinton/Nt (also spelt Snenton)
   snentən   PNNt 174,Hope,BBC,BCE
   sne?n   PNNt 174
   snentn   PNNt(i)125
   -e-   DEPN
Snelshall Priory/Bk
   snelsəl   PNBk 74
Snelston/Db
   snəlstn   PNDb 6o2
Snenton/Nt ⟶ Sneinton
Snettisham/Nf
   snetʃəm,
   snetisəm   BBC,BCE,HL 811
   snetsəm   BBC,BCE,HL 811,Hope
   sni:zəm   ROS 42
Sneyd/St
   sni:d   DEPN,EPD,BBC,BCE
Snoad/K
   snoud   PNK
Snodland/K
   snɔdlənd   BBC
   -lænd   PNK
Snowden Bridge/Li
   snoudn   EPD
Snowhill/Bd,Sr
   snouhil   Schr.
Snowshill/Gl
   snouzəl   PNGl II/21,PNGl(i)143
Soar/Nt,Wa (r.n.)
   sɔ: BBC
   sɔ:r   Schr.,Chis.
Sockbridge/We
   sɔkbərt   PNE'side 73
Sockenber/We
   sɔkinbər   PNE'side 7o
Sodom/W
   sɔdəm   EPD
Sofla Ring/WRY
   sɔflə   GlossSh(suppl.)54
Soham/Ca
   olim soum   PNCa 196
   su:m   DSf 299
   souhəm   Chis.
   souəm   ONCa 178,BBC
Soho/Ldn
   souou   CPhon 93
   'souhou   EPD,Kruis.,Bau.
   _ ⸍   EPD,Kruis.
Soke of Peterborough/Np
   souk əv pi:təbərə   BBC

Sole Bay/Sf
  saulbei   DSf 299
  soulbei   Kruis.
The Solent/Ha
  ðə soulənt   EPD,DEPN,BBC,
               Schr.,Chis.
Solihull/Wa
  olim silil   PNWa 67,Hope
  souli'hʌl   BBC,BCE,Chis.
Solinger/Bk
  sɔːliŋgə, sæliŋgə,
  sæligə   PNBk 164
Solomon's Fm/Ess
  sæmənz   PNEss 154
Solton/K
  soultən   PNK
Solway Firth/Cu
  sɔlwei fəːþ   DEPN,EPD,BBC,
               Schr.
  - friþ   GlossCuWeNLa,s.n.
      frith
Somborne (King's S.)/Ha
  kiŋz sɔmbɔːn   BBC
Somerby/Le,Li
  sʌməbi   BBC,BCE (for S. in Li)
Somercotes/Db,Li
  sʌmə kouts   BBC,BCE (for S. in
                  Li)
  -ʌ-   DEPN (for S. in Li)
Somerford Hall, S.Pk, S. Fm/Chs
  sumər-, sʌmər-   PNChs II/318
Somerford Keynes/Gl,W
  suməfəd keinz   PNGl I/83
  keinz   PNW 46
Somerleyton/Sf
  sʌmələit(ə)n   BBC
  - leitən   BCE
  -ʌ-   DEPN
Somersby/Li
  sʌməzbi   BBC,BCE
Somerset
  sʌməsit   EPD,BBC
  sʌməset   BBC,Schr.,Kruis.
  sʌməsət   Chis.
  loc. zʌməzit   HL 934
  zʌməzet   DNSo 23,DWSo 22
Somersetshire
  sʌməsitʃiə, sʌməset-, -ʃə   EPD
  sʌməsetʃə   Schr.
  zəməzetჳiːr   DWSo 2o
Somersham/Hu,Sf
  sʌməsəm   PNBdHu 222
  sʌməʃəm   BBC,BCE (for S. in
                  Hu)
  -ʌ-   DEPN (for S. in Hu)
  sʌməzhəm   Chis.
  "now rarely pron. as
  Somersam"   Mawer(2)95

Somerton
  sʌmətən   Schr.,Kruis.
  -tn   EPD
Somerton/Nf
  sʌmət(ə)n   BBC
Somerton/Wt
  zʌmərtn   PNWt 19o
Somerville/Chs
  sʌməvil   EPD
Sompting/Sx
  sauntiŋ   PNSx 2ol,DEPN
  sʌmtiŋ   PNSx 2ol
  sʌm(p)tiŋ, sɔm(p)tiŋ   BBC
  sʌmət, sountiŋ (or -au- ?)   Hop
Songar Grange/Wa
  sʌŋə   PNWa 215
Sonning/Brk
  sʌniŋ, sɔniŋ   EPD,BBC
  sʌniŋ ɔn temz   BCE
  -ʌ-   DEPN
Sookholme/Nt
  sʌkm   PNNt(i)126,DEPN
  suːkəm   PNNt 97
Soper Lane in Dronfield/Db
  soupə lein   GlossSh 229
Sotterley/Sf
  sɔtəli   BBC
Soudley/Gl,Sa
  suːdli   BBC
The Soughan's/Chs, Soughan's Fm/Chs
  sʌfənz   PNChs IV/65
Sough Brook/Db
  sʌf   PNDb(i) II/16o
Soulbury/Bk
  sʌlbəri   DEPN,PNBk 82
  soulbəri   EPD
Soulby/Cu,We
  soulbi   BBC,BCE (for S. in Cu)
  suːlbi   PNWe II/22
Souldern/O
  souldən   BBC
Souldrop/Bd
  suːldrəp   PNBdHu 42
  souldrɔp   BBC
Soulton/Sa
  loc. suːtn   PNSa
Sound/Chs
  saund   PNChs III/121
Sour Bank/WRY
  saː   PNYW VI/12
Sourthwaite/WRY (f.n.)
  sauəþət   DDd 13
Sourton/D
  suːrtən   PND 2o6
  sɔːt(ə)n   BBC
Soutergate/La
  sautəgeːt   PNLa 221
Souter Point/Du
  suːtə pɔint   EPD,BBC,BCE

Southall/Mx
  sauþɔːl EPD,DEPN,BBC,BCE
  -ð- EPD
Southam/Gl,Wa
  sauðəm PNGl II/89,PNWa 144,
          BBC,Schr.
Southampton/Ha
  sauþ'hæm(p)tən,
  sau'þæm(p)tən EPD,BBC
  sə'þæm(p)tən EPD
  sauþ'hæmptən BCE
  sauþ'æmptən BCE,MEG 148,Chis.
  sauþæmtən, səþ'æmtən,
  familiar -ð- Schr.
  sau'þæmptən Kruis.
Southburn/ERY
  suːþbɔn PNYE 167
  suːbn Hope
Southcott/Bk
  səːkət PNBk 8o
Southdown/D,Do,Co
  zaudn DHtl 8 (for S. in D)
  sauþdaun EPD
South Down/Wt
  zæu(þ) dæun PNWt 116
South Eau/Ca (r.n.)
  sauði PNCa 1o and 21o
Southend-on-Sea/Ess
  'sauþ'end, ◡ ‿ EPD

  ‿ ◡ DEPN,EPD,Chis.

  sɑːfend EssDD 151,note 1
Southerey/Nf (= Southery, below)
  -ʌð- DEPN
Souther Gill/Cu
  þʌtərgil PNCu xliii
Souther Fell/Cu
  suːðəfəl PNCu 227
Southerfield/Cu
  suːtər fild PNCu 29o
Southerham Fm/Sx
  sautərəm PNSx 355
Southernby/Cu
  suːðərənbi PNCu 246
  suðərənbi PNE'side 75
Southery/Nf (= Southerey,above)
  sʌðəri BBC,BCE
Southey/WRY
  sauði, sʌði EPD,Kruis.
Southford/Wt
  zæuþfərd PNWt 255
  zʌþfərd PNWt 286
Southgate/Mx
  sauþgit BBC,MEG 125,Bchm.55
Southill/Bd
  sʌðil PNBdHu 96
Southlands/Wt
  zæuþlənz PNWt 119

Southleigh/D
  sauli PND 631
  sauliː, 'sauþ'liː BBC,BCE
South Leigh/O
  saulai Hope
Southminster/Ess
  'sauþ'minstə BBC
South Molton/D
  zaumoultən PND 346
Southowram/WRY
  sauþ'aurəm PNYW III/89
  sauþ'auərəm BBC
  sɑːþərəm Hope
Southport/La
  'sauþpɔːt EPD,Schr.
Southrepps/Nf
  'sauþreps BBC
Southrey/Li
  sʌðri DEPN,BBC,BCE
Southrop/Gl
  sauþrəp PNGl I/45
Southsea/Ha
  sauþsi(ː) EPD
South View Ho/Wt
  sæuþ veu PNWt 119
Southwaite/Cu
  suþət Hope
  souþət PNE'side 66
Southwark/Sr
  sʌðək PNEss lix[1],DEPN,BBC,Kruis.,
        Schr.,Wyld 263,ESpr.394,
        MEG 125,EPD,Hope
  sauþɑːk, coll. sʌðɑːk Chis.
  sauþwɔːk MEG 125
  sauþwək MEG 213,HL 755,EPD,
        ESpr.394
Southwark Bridge/Ldn
  sʌðəkbridʒ, less usually
  sauþwək bridʒ
  S.B.Rd appears to be, however,
  more usually
  'sauþwək 'bridʒ 'roud
             Jones 85,note 67
Southwell/Nt
  sʌðəl PNNt 175,BCE,Hope,MEG 125,
        Schr.("loc."),GlossSWLi
  sʌðl EPD ("loc."),DEPN,BBC,BG,
        HL 733,Bchm.54 ("loc.")
  sʌðə PNNt(i)126
  sauþwəl MEG 125,Schr.
  sauþw(ə)l EPD
  sauþ(w)əl Bchm.54
  sauþəl BCE
  suðil Ellis 45o
Southwick
  sauþwik EPD,Schr.,MEG 125,
        Bchm.54
  sʌðik Schr.,MEG 125,Bchm.54

1) correcting [suþək], which is given in PNSr 29.

Southwick/Du,Np
   sauþwik, sʌðik   BBC,BCE
   sudik   PNNbDu 185
Southwick/Np
   sauðik   PNNp 2o6
   sʌðik   BBC,BCE
Southwick/Nt
   sudik   Zachr.(5)llo,note
Southwick/Sx,W
   sʌðik   PNSx(i)147
   sauðik   PNW 144
   sauþwik   BBC,BCE
Southwold/Sf
   seuþwould   ISf 3oo
   sauþwould   EPD,BBC
   sauþwold   BCE
Sow/St,Wa (r.n.)
   sau   Schr.
Sowber Hill/NRY (or Solberge)
   soubəril   PNYN 275
Sowerby
   sauəbi, loc. souəbi   Schr.
Sowerby/Cu
   sɔ:bi   Hope
Sowerby/La
   sauərbi   PNLa 161
Sowerby/WRY
   sɔəbi   PNYW III/144,Hope
   sɔ:bi   PNYW III/144
   sauəbi   PNYW III/144,EPD
   souəbi   EPD
Sowerby/NRY
   sauəbi   BBC,EPD
   old-fashioned sɔ:əbi   EPD
Sowerby Bridge/WRY
   sɔ:bi brig   PNYW III/14o[1]
   sɔ:bi bridʒ   BCE
   souəbi bridʒ   BBC,BCE
   sauəbi bridʒ   BBC
Sowerby Hall/La
   sauərbi   PNLa 2o3
Sown Pit Sick/WRY (a valley)
   soun   GlossSh 23o
Sowton/D
   saut(ə)n   BBC
   sautən   BCE
Soyland/WRY
   swilənd   Hope
Spa (affixed to place-names)
   spɑ: EPD
Spa Bottom/WRY
   loc. spɔ: PNSWY 264f.
Spadeadam/Cu
   spi:di:dəm   PNCu 96,PNE'side 65
   speid'ædəm   BBC

Spalding/Li
   spɔ:ldiŋ   EPD,BBC,BCE,Chis.
   spɔldiŋ   EPD
Spaldinvton/ERY
   sparətən   PNYE 241
Spaldwick/Hu
   spɔ:ldik   PNBdHu 247,Mawer(2)95
Spalford/Nt
   spɔ:lfəd   BBC
Span Fm/Wt
   spæ:n   PNWt 16o
Sparham/Nf
   spærəm   DEPN,BBC,BCE
Sparket/Cu ⟶ Sparkhead
Sprakhead/Cu
   spɑ:rkit   PNE'side 71
Sparsholt/Brk,Ha
   spæsit   Hope (for S. in Brk)
   spɑ:ʃoult   BBC,BCE
Spaunton/NRY
   spɔ:ntən   PNYN 61
Spa Wood/WRY
   spɔ: PNSWY 264f.
Speedwell/Db,Gl
   spi:dwel, -w(ə)l   EPD
Speen/Bk,Brk
   spi:n   EPD
Speke/La
   spi:k   BBC
Spencer (as in S. Grange/Ess)
   spensə   EPD
Spettisbury/Do (or Spetis-)
   spetsbəri   PNDo(i)76,BBC
Spice Gill/WRY
   spais gil   DDd 12
Spicers/Wt
   spaisərz   PNWt 285
Spillsill/K
   spilzil   PNK
Spilsby/Li
   spilzbi   Chis.
Spital
   spitl   PNChs IV/251,BBC
   spitəl   PNChs IV/251,BCE (for S in Li)
Spitalfields/Ldn
   spitlfi:ldz   EPD,BBC
   spitəlfi:ldz   Chis.,Bau.
Spital Tongues/Nb
   spitl tʌŋz   BBC
Spithead/Ha
   'spit'hed   EPD,BBC,Kruis.
   ◜ _   EPD,Chis.
   _ ◝   EPD

1) Hope's transcription 'Soervy Brig' may be a misprint for
  'Soer̲by Brig' (= sɔəbi

Spitlye/Sx
   spit'lai   PNSx 383
Spofforth/WRY
   spɔfəþ   PNYW V/33,EPD
   -fɔːþ   EPD,Bchm.69
Spondon/Db
   spɔndən   BBC,BCE
   spuːndən   BBC,BCE,Hope
   -uː-   DEPN
Spooner (as in S. Row/Nf)
   spuːnə   EPD
Sporle/Nf
   spɔːl   BBC
Sporle with Palgrave/Nf
   spɔːl wið pælgreiv   BBC
Spotley Corner/Np
   spɔtlə: PNNp 155
Springe Lane/Chs
   sprindʒ, spriŋ   PNChs III/125
Springfield
   spriŋfiːld   EPD,BBC,Schr.
Sproatley/ERY
   sprɔːtlə   PNYE 52,DYorks 63
Sproston/Chs
   sprousn   PNChs II/ix
   sprɔstən,
   sprɔsn   PNChs II/254
   sprɔːsn   GlossChs
Sproughton/Sf
   sprɔːt(ə)n   BBC
   sprɔːtən   BCE
Sprowston/Nf
   sproustən   BBC
Sproxton/Le
   sprousn, spraustən   Hope
Sproxton/NRY
   sproustən   PNYN 7o
Spruce Gill Beck/NRY
   sprius gil   PNYN 233
Spurlands End/Bk
   spɑːliŋgz   PNBk 13o
Spurn/ERY
   spɔn   Hope,GlossHol 17
   spəːn   EPD
Spurn Head/ERY
   spəːn hed   Schr.
Spurrig End/We
   spudik   PNE'side 7o
Spurstow/Chs
   spəːstou   Schr.
Spynes Barn/Sr
   spinz   PNSr 311
Stacey/WRY
   steisi   EPD
Stadhampton/O
   stædəm, stɔdəm   PNO 154
Staffield/Cu
   stafl   PNCu 248
Stafford
   stæfəd   EPD,BBC,Schr.

Staffordshire
   stæfədʃə   EPD,Schr.
   -ʃiə   EPD
Staffs. (short for Staffordshire)
   stæfs   EPD
Stagden Cross/Ess
   stægn   PNEss 482
   stægən   EssDD 158
Stages Platt/Chs
   steidʒis   PNChs III/29o
Stagshaw/Nb
   stadʒi, steinʃə   PNNbDu 187
Stainborough/WRY
   steːnbrə   PNYW I/312
Staine/Ca → Stane
Staines/Mx
   steinz   BBC,EPD,Schr.
Stainmoor/We (or -more)
   stænmər   PNE'side
Stainton/Cu
   stentən   PNCu 188,PNE'side 66
   loc. stɛːntn   PNO li
Stainton/La
   stentn   PNLa 21o
Staithes/NRY
   stiəz   PNYN 139
   steiðz   EPD,BBC,Schr.528
   stiːəz   DSto
Stakehill/La (or Stake Hill)
   steik hil   BBC
Stalbridge/Do
   stɔːlbridʒ   EPD,BBC
   stɔl-   EPD
Staley/Chs → Stayley
Stalham/Nf
   stæləm   BBC
Stalisfield Gn/K
   loc. stɑːtʃfəl   PNE&W, PNK
   stɑːsfiːld   PNK
   stælisfiːld   BBC
Stallingborough/Li
   stɑːliŋbərə   BBC
Stalling Busk/NRY
   stɔːlin busk   PNYN 264
Stalmine/La
   stɔːmin   PNLa(ii)
Staleybridge/Chs
   steilibridʒ   EPD,BBC,BCE,Schr.,
              Chis.
Stambridge/Ess
   stɑːmbridʒ   PNEss 2o2,Hope
Stamford
   stæmfəd   EPD,Schr.
   stɑːmfəd   GlossLi 239
Stamfordham/Nb
   stanətən   PNNbDu 187
   stæmfədəm   EPD,BBC,BCE
   stænətən   BBC,Ellis 654 ("former-
              called and still known to
              the peasantry as Stannerton")

Stanah/Cu
  stænə PNE'side 62
Standal's Fm/Bk
  stændəlz PNBk 166
Standedge/WRY
  stænedʒ BBC,BCE
Standen/Wt
  stændən, stænn PNWt 21
Standish/Gl,La
  stændiʃ EPD,Schr.
Stane/Ca
  stein ONCa 198
Stanesgate Abbey/Ess
  stænzgeit PNEss 227
Stanfield/Nf
  stænfiːld EPD
Stanford
  stænfəd EPD,Schr.
Stanford/Nf
  stænfə Hope
Stanford-le-Hope/Ess
  stænfədli'houp BBC
  olim stæmvət PNEss 170
Stanghoe/NRY (or -how)
  staŋə Ellis 519
Stanhill/La
  stænhil BBC
Stanhoe/Nf
  stænə Hope,Ellis 264
  stænou BBC,BCE
Stanhope/Du
  stænəp EPD,BBC,BCE,Kruis.,
          MEG 125,Bchm.105
  -houp Bchm.105,MEG 125,
Stanhope Close/Db (f.n.)
  stænhoup Fraser(2)78[1]
Stanion/Np
  stænjən BBC
Stanley
  stænli EPD,BBC,Schr.,Kruis.
Stanlow Abbey/Chs
  stanlou PNChs IV/185
Stanmer/Sx
  stæmə PNSx 312
Stanmore/Brk,Mx,Sa
  stænmɔːr Chis.
Stanney/Chs (Little S.)
  stani PNChs IV/180
Stanney/Chs (Great S.)
  stæni PNChs IV/182
Stansfield/Sx
  stænzfiːld, -s- EPD
Stanstead/Hrt,Sf,Sx
  stænsted Chis.
Stansted Mountfitchett/Ess
  stænsted maunt'fitʃit BBC

Stanton
  staːntən EPD,Schr.,Kruis.,
          Bchm.12
  stæntən EPD,Schr.,Bchm.12
Stanton/Ca,Gl
  stæntən ONCa 22
  staːntən PNGl II/23
Stanton-by-Bridge/Db
  stæntən bai bridʒ BBC
Stanton St. John/O
  sindʒən PNO(i)195
Stanton's Fm/Ess
  staːntnz PNEss 294
Stanway/Gl
  stæni GlossSEWo 82
Stanwell Fm/Wt
  stænwl, stænəl PNWt 39
Stanwick/Np
  stænik PNNp 196,DEPN,BBC,BCE
Stanwick St. John/NRY
  stænik snt'dʒɔn BBC
  - sənt - BCE
Stanwix/Cu
  staniks PNCu 108
  stæniks BBC,BCE,GlossCu xviii
  stænwiks MEG 213
Stapeley/Chs
  steipəli, steipli PNChs III/71
Stapenhill/Db
  steipənil PNDb 662
Staple
  steipl EPD
Stapleford/Ca,Chs,Nt
  steiplfəd ONCa 187
  staplfərt GlossChs
  stæplfəd PNNt(i)129
Stapleford Abbots, S. Tawney/Ess
  steiplfut PNEss 79
Staplers/Wt
  stæplərz PNWt 247
Stapleton
  steipltən EPD,Schr.,Chis.
  stiəpəltən GlossCu xviii
Stapley/So
  stæpli, steipli EPD
Staploe, Staplow/Ca
  stæplou ONCa 195
Starbotton/WRY
  staːbɔtn PNYW VI/108
Stareton/Wa
  staːt(ə)n BBC
  staːtən BCE
  -aː- DEPN
Starnhill Ho/Nt
  staːnəl PNNt 222
Starr (as in S.'s Gn/Ess)
  staː EPD

---

1) "This is the pron. given [...] to me".

Startforth/NRY
  stɑ:tfəþ PNYN 3o4
Start Point/D (a promontary)
  stɑ:t pɔint Schr.
Statham/Chs
  steiþəm, -ð- EPD
Stathern/Le
  'stæthə:n BBC,BCE
  -æþ- DEPN
Staughton/Bd
  stɔ:tən PNBdHu 2o
  stɔ:t(ə)n BBC
Staughton Gn,S.Highway,S.Moor/Hu
  stɔ:t(ə)n gri:n,
  -    haiwei,
  -    muə BBC
Staunton
  stæntən Schr.
  stɑ:ntən MEG 3o2
Staunton/Gl
  stɑ:ntən PNGl III/186 and
Stauvin/La   247
  stauvin PNLa 182
Staveley/Db
  steivli PNDb(i) I/143,BBC,
        Chis.
Staveley/We
  steivəli BBC
  stɛ:vli DKe 5
  steivli Chis.
Staverton
  stɑ:tən Schr.
Staverton/Gl
  stævətən,
  stɑ:vətən PNGl II/84
  stævət(ə)n BBC
Staverton/Np
  stɛ:ətən PNNp 28
  stɑ:tən PNSr xliii,Hope
  stævət(ə)n BBC
  -ɛə- DEPN
Staverton/Sf
  loc. stævəndʒə PNDVall 59
Staverton/W
  stævətən PNW 133
  stævə(r)tn PNW(i)152
  -æ- DEPN
Stavordale Priory/So
  stævədeil BBC
Staward/Nb
  stɑ:wəd BBC,BCE
Stawell/So
  stoul Hope
Stayley/Chs
  steili Chis.
Staythorpe/Nt
  olim statrəp PNNt 196
  stei- PNNt(i)13o
  steiþɔ:p BBC

Stead/WRY
  sted EPD
Stean/WRY
  stiən PNYW V/215
Steart/So
  sti:ət BBC
Stechford/Wa
  stetʃfəd BBC
Steele/Sa
  sti:l EPD
Steelgate/Cu
  sti:l jet PNE'side 76
Steep Holmes Is/So (also called
  sti:p houmz Chis. S.Holme)
Steeple Aston/O
  sti:pl ɑ:stən PNO 247
Steeple Grange/Db
  sti:pl PNDb(i) II/167
Stella/Du
  stelə EPD
Stelling Minnis/K
  steliŋ miniz BBC
Stenalees/Co
  stenə'li:z BBC
Stenbury Fm/Wt
  stembəri PNWt 161
Steng-a-Tor/D
  stiŋkətɔ:r PND 2o6
Stenigot/Li
  stenigɔt BBC
Stenkreth/We
  stenkriþ, steŋkriþ PNE'side 64
Stepney/Ldn
  stepni EPD,Schr.,Kruis.,Chis.
Stert/W
  stə:rt PNW 314
Stetchworth/Ca
  stetʃwəþ ONCa 185
Stevenage/Hrt
  sti:vənidʒ, stivnidʒ PNHrt 137,
                  EPD
  sti:vəneidʒ Chis.
  -i:- DEPN
Stevens Crouch/Ess
  sti:vnz krautʃ EPD
Stevenstone/D
  stensən PND 456
Steventon/Brk,Ha
  sti:v(ə)ntən BBC
Stevington/Bd
  stefən, stiviŋtən PNBdHu 46
  steviŋtən BBC
  stefn DEPN,Hope
Stevington End/Ess (or Steventon E.)
  steviŋtən PNEss 5o7
  -ev- DEPN
Stewnor/La
  stju:nə PNLa 2o7

Steyne/Mx,Sx
    stiːn   EPD,BBC,BCE (for S.
        in Mx)
Steyne Ho, S. Wood/Wt
    stiːn   PNWt 117 (for S.Wood
        nr Chale),PNWt 285 (for
        S. Wood nr Bembridge)
Steyning/Sx
    steniŋ   PNSx 234,PNSx(i)148,
        DEPN,EPD,BBC,BCE,Hope,
        Schr.("loc.")
    steiniŋ   Schr.,BG
Stibbard/Nf
    _ ′   DEPN
Sticelett/Wt
    staislət   PNWt 191
Stickworth Hall/Wt
    stikwərþ   PNWt 22
Stiffkey/Nf (r.n.)
    stjuːki   RN 377
Stiffkey/Nf
    stjuːki   DEPN,EPD ("old-fash-
        ioned loc.pron."),
        Hope,DNf 42,PNNf,BBC[1]
    stuːki   BBC
    stifki   EPD,BBC,BCE
    stifkiː   EPD
    stiki   Hope
Stile Ho/Wt
    stail hæus   PNWt 285
Stilton/Hu
    stilt(ə)n   BBC
    stiltən   EPD,Schr.
    stiltn   EPD
Stinchcombe Hill/Gl
    "still emphatically called
    'The Hill' in that neighbour-
    hood"   GlossCots 22
Stiperstones/Sa
    'staipəstounz   BBC
Stirchley/Sa
    stætʃlei   Wilde 24
Stirchley Street/Wo
    stretli   PNWo 357
Stisted/Ess
    staistid   PNEss 460
    staisted   BBC,BCE
    -ai-   DEPN
Stithians/Co
    stiðiənz   BBC
Stittenham/NRY
    stitnəm   PNYN 33
Stitworthy/D
    stitəri   PND 70
Stivichall/Wa (or Styvechale)
    staitʃəl   PNWa 179,DEPN,BCE
    staitʃl   BBC

staitʃɔːl   BBC
staihəl   BCE
Stoborough/Do
    stoubərə   BBC
Stocia/Chs
    stouʃə   PNChs II/viii
Stockbridge/Ha,Sx,WRY,Wt
    stɔkbridʒ   Schr.
    stakbridʒ   PNWt 255
Stockdalewath/Cu
    stɔglwaþ   PNCu 246,PNE'side 73
Stocken/Ru
    stɔkiŋ   GlossRu vii
Stockham/Chs
    stɔkʌm   PNChs II/179
Stockleigh Pomeroy/D
    stɔkli pɔmərɔi   BBC
Stockport/Chs
    stɔpərt   PNChs II/vii ("olim"),
        GlossChs ("the old pron."
    stɔpət   Bchm.58,Schr.
    stɔkport   PNChs II/vii
    stɔkpɔːt   EPD,Schr.,Bchm.69
    stɔpfəd   ROS 43
    stɔpərþ   DHd 120
Stockton
    stɔktən   EPD,Schr.
Stockwell/Gl,Ldn
    stɔkwəl   BBC
    -w(ə)l, -wel   EPD
Stoddah/Cu
    studə   PNE'side 62
Stodday/La
    stɔdə   PNLa(ii)
Stodfold/WRY
    stɔtfəd   Hope
Stody/Nf
    stʌdi   DEPN,BBC,BCE
Stoford/W
    stoufə(r)d   PNW(i)155
Stogumber/So
    stou'gʌmbə   EPD,BBC,BCE
    'stɔgʌmbə   BBC,BCE
    stə'gʌmbə   EPD,DEPN (stress only)
Stogursey/So
    stou'gəːzi   BBC,BCE,DEPN (stress
        only)
    (see also s.n. Stoke Courcy)
Stoke
    stouk   Schr.
Stoke/Chs.Do
    stɔːk, older local
    stɔːək   PNChs III/151 (for S. in
        Nantwich Hd)
    stouk, formerly
    stuːək   PNChs IV/181 (for S. in
        Wirral Hd)
    stoːk   DDo

1) "[stuːki and stjuːki] are rarely heard today" (BBC).

Stoke Bruern/Np
   stouk bruːǝn   BBC
Stoke Courcy/So
   stǝ'gǝːzi, stou-   EPD
   sǝːgǝːsi (?) Hope[1]
   (see also s.n. Stogursey)
Stoke d'Abernon/Sr
   stouk 'dæbǝnǝn   EPD,BBC
Stoke Damerel/D
   stouk dæmǝrǝl   BBC
Stoke Dry/Le,Ru
   also called 'Drystoke'
                GlossRu vii
Stoke Gifford/Gl
   'stouk 'gifǝd   PNGl III/14o
Stoke Hammond/Bk
   stouk hæmǝn   PNBk 25
Stoke-in-Teignhead/D
   stoukǝntini(d)   PND 46o
   -tinid   DEPN
   stouk in tinhed   BBC,BCE
Stoke Mandeville/Bk
   stouk mændivil   BBC
Stokenchurch/Bk
   stou-   DEPN
   stɔkǝntʃǝːtʃ   Mawer(4)284
            ("can now no
            longer be traced")
Stoke Newington/Ldn
   _ ˊ _ _   MEG 153

Stokenham/D
   stoukǝn'hæm   PND 331,BCE
   stouk(ǝ)n'hæm   BBC,DEPN
            (stress only)
   'stoukǝnǝm   BBC,BCE
Stoke Pero/So (also spelt Stock)
   stouk piǝrou   BBC,DEPN
   stɔk piːrou   DWSo 23
Stoke Pogis/Bk
   poudʒis   PNBk 243
   poudʒiz   EPD
Stokesley/NRY
   stouzlǝ   PNYN 169,DYorks 6o,
              DSto
   stouzli   Schr.,Hope,GlossClv
   stouksli   Schr.   xliv
Stokke/W
   stɔk   PNW(i) 155
Stonar/K
   stɔnǝ   DEPN,BBC,BCE,PNK
Stondon Massey/Ess
   stoundǝn   PNEss 81
Stone
   stoun   Schr.
Stone/Wt (nr South Arreton)
   stuǝn, stoun   PNW 23

Stone/Wt (nr Bembridge)
   stuǝn   PNWt 285
Stonea/Ca
   stouni   BBC,BCE
Stoneaston/So (also spelt Ston Easton)
   stɔn'iːstǝn   BBC
Stonebow/Li (the name of the archway
          of the Guildhall at L.)
   stænbou   GlossSWLi
Stonebrook/Wt
   stuǝnbruk   PNWt 286
Stoneclough/La
   stounklʌf   BBC
Stonedge/Db (also spelt Stone Edge)
   stounedʒ, stænedʒ   BBC,BCE
Stoneferry/ERY
   stiǝnferi, stuǝnferi   PNYE 214
   stiːǝnferi   GlossHol 17
Stonegarthside/Cu
   steingǝrsiːd   PNCu 1o5
Stonehall/Wo
   stʌnǝl   PNWo 146
Stonehenge/W
   stoun'hendʒ, earlier and more
   popular -edʒ, olim stɔnidʒ
                    PNW 36o
   stounhentʃ   PNW(i)155
   archaic stounhin(d)ʒ   Schr.
   'stounhendʒ   Chis.
   'stoun'hendʒ   BBC,Kruis.
   'stounhen(d)ʒ   EPD,Schr.
   _ ˊ , ˊ ˊ   EPD
Stonehouse
   'stounhaus   EPD,Chis.
Stonehouse/WRY
   stean aus   DDd 12
Stonehurst/Ess
   stɔnǝdz   PNEss 23
Stoneleigh/Sr
   'stoun'liː   BBC
Stoneleigh/Wa
   'stounli   BBC
Stonely/Hu
   olim stɔnli   PNBdHu 244
Stoneley Gn/Chs
   stounli   PNChs III/135
Stonesfield/O
   stʌnzfiːld, stounzfiːld   PNO 283
Stoneshell/Wt
   stuǝnʃil   PNWt 23,DWt,s.n. rig
            out
Stonestar/La
   stoːn stɛːr   PNLa 223
Stonesteps/Wt
   stounsteps   PNWt 84

1) Hope's transcription is 'Sergursey'.

Stoney (prefixed to place-names)
    stouni   EPD
Stonham (Earl S.,Little S.)/Sf
    stɔnəm   BBC
Stonham Aspal/Sf (or Aspall)
    'stɔnəm'æspɔ:l   BBC
Stonor/O
    stɔnə   BBC,BCE
Stonyheugh/Cu
    stiəni hju: GlossCu xviii
Stopham/Sx
    stɔpəm   BBC
Storeton/Chs
    stortən   PNChs IV/253
Stortford/Ess
    stɔ:tfəd   Bchm.131
    stɔ:fəd   EssDD 158,Bchm.131
Stortford/Hrt (Bishop's S.)
    vulgo stɑ:fəd   PNHrt 2ol
    stɔ:fəd   PNHrt 2ol,EPD,BBC,BCE
    stɔ:tfəd   EPD,BChm. 131
Storwood/ERY
    stɔrəd   PNYE 236
Stot Scales/WRY
    stɔt skealz   DDd 14
Stottesdon/Sa
    stɔtizdən   BBC
    stɔðərtn   GlossSa 519
Stoughton/Le
    stout(ə)n   BBC
    stoutən   BCE
    stoutn   EPD
    -ou-   EPD
Stoughton/So
    stɔ:t(ə)n   BBC
    stɔ:tn   EPD
Stoughton/Sr
    stautən   PNSr 151
    staut(ə)n   BBC
    stautn   EPD
    -au-   DEPN
Stoughton/Sx
    stɔ:tən   PNSx 54,PNSx(i)151
    stoutn
    stout(ə)n   BBC
    stoutən   BCE,Hope
    stɔ:tn   Hope
    -ɔ:-   DEPN
Stoughton Cross/So
    stɔ:t(ə)n krɔs   BBC
Stoulton/Wo
    stoutən   PNWo 166
    stoutn   DEPN,GlossSEWo 82
    stoult(ə)n   BBC
Stoupe Brow/NRY
    stoup bru: PNYN 118
Stour/Do
    stauə   EPD,PNDo(i)16

Stour (r.n.)
    stu:r   Schr.
    staur   Chis.
Stour/Do,Ha,W (r.n.)
    stauə   RN 379,EPD,DEPN,BBC,BCE
    stuə   EPD,BBC,BCE
    stour   Urlau 37
Stour/K (r.n.)
    stu:ə   RN 378,PNK
    stauə   RN 378,BBC,EPD
    stuə   EPD,BBC
    -au-, -u:-   DEPN
Stour/Ca,Ess,Sf (r.n.)
    stauə   PNEss 379,RN 379,DEPN
    stuə   EPD,BBC
Stour/St,Wo (r.n.)
    stauə   RN 38o,DEPN,BBC,BCE
    stouə   BBC,BCE
Stour/Gl,O,Wa,Wo (r.n.)
    stauə   PNGl I/11,PNWa(i)1o9,
          RN 38o,DEPN,EPD,BBC,BCE
    stouə   EPD,BBC,BCE
Stourbridge
    stu:ə-, stɑ:-, stɔ:-   Schr.
    stə:bridʒ   Schr.,Chis.
    stauə-   EPD,BBC
    stouə-   BBC
Stourbridge/Ca (also called Stir-)
    stə:bridʒ   PNO li (for S. in Ca
Stourbridge/Wo
    stə:bridʒ   PNWo 311,DEPN,Hope,
          Ellis 485
    stɑ:bridʒ, stɔ:-   Hope
Stourhead nr Stourton/W
    stauəhed, stuəhed   BCE
Stourhead Ho/W
    stɔ:hed, stauəhed   BBC
Stourmouth/K
    stauəmauþ   EPD,BBC
    stuəmauþ   BBC,EPD ("rarely")
    "Although the first of these is
    more usual locally for the plac
    name, it is interesting that th
    neighbouring River Stour is mor
    often pron. [stuə]"   BBC
Stourpaine/Do
    stauəpein   PNDo(i)58
    stouərpein   DDo
Stourport/Wo
    stɑ:-, stə:-, stɔ:pɔ:t   Schr.,H
    stauəpo:t   Schr.,Hope,BBC
    stuəpɔ:t ɔn sevən   BBC
    stauəpo:t, stuəpo:t   BCE
Stour Provost/Do (also spelt Stower
    stauə prɔvəst   BBC,BCE
Stour Row/Do
    stauə rou   BBC,BCE
Stourton/W
    stɔ:rtən   PNW 181,BCE

stə:(r)tn PNW(i)156
stə:t(ə)n, stɔ:t(ə)n BBC
stə:tən BCE
stə:tn EPD
-ə:- DEPN
Stourton/WRY
  stə:t(ə)n BBC
Stourton Caundle/Do
  stɔ:tən kɔ:ndl,
  stə:tən kændl, kɑ:ndl
         PNDo(i)39 and note 1
  stɔ:t(ə)n kɔ:ndl BBC
Stoven/Sf
  stʌv(ə)n BBC
  stʌvən BCE
Stow
  stou EPD,Schr.,Chis.
Stow/Ca,Hu
  stou BBC
Stow Bedon/Nf
  stou bi:d(ə)n BBC
Stowe
  stou EPD,Kruis.
Stowell/Gl,So
  stouəl, stoul BBC,BCE (for
             S. in So)
Stower ⟶ Stour
Stowey/So
  stoui EPD,BBC,Chis.,Kruis.,
      s.n. Nether S.
Stowford/Chs
  stoufəd PNChs III/76,BBC,BCE
Stowford/D
  stoufəd PND 2o8,DEPN,BBC
Stow Maries/Ess
  stou 'mɑ:riz BBC
Stowmarket/Sf
  stau DSf 3o2
  'stoumɑ:kit BBC
  'stoumɑ:kət Chis.
Stow-on-the-Wold/Gl
  stou ɔn ðə would BBC
Stowting/K
  stautiŋ BBC
Stradbroke/Sf (or -brooke)
  strædbruk BBC
  strʌbək DSf 3o2,Hope
  stræbruk DSf 3o2
Stradishall/Sf
  strædiʃɔ:l BBC
  strædʒil Hope
Straits/Ka,La,St
  streits EPD
Stramongate/We (in Kendal)
  stramənge:t PNWe I/117
Strand/Ldn
  strænd EPD
Strangeways/La
  streindʒweiz PNLa 33,BBC

Strangford/He
  stræŋfəd BBC,Schr.
Stratfieldsaye Ho/Brk
  'strætfi:ldsei BBC
Stratford
  strætfəd EPD,Schr.
Stratford-le-Bow/Mx
  'strætfəd lə 'bou BBC,Schr.
Stratford upon Avon/Wa
  'strætfəd əpɔn 'eiv(ə)n BBC
  - ʌpɔn 'eivən Schr.,Chis.
Strathfieldsaye/Ha
  stræþ'fi:ldsei Chis.
Strathwell/Wt
  strædl PNWt 255
Stratton
  stræt(ə)n BBC
  strætən Schr.
  strætn EPD
Streatham/Sr,Sx
  stretəm PNSr 33,PNSx 219,EPD,
      BBC,Schr.,Kruis.,Po-
      gatscher (for S. in Sr)
  stretn Hope (for S. in Sr),
      Schr. ("loc.")
  -e- DEPN (for S. in Sr)
Streatley/Bd
  stretli BBC
  stri:tli EPD
Streatley/Brk
  stri:tli DEPN,BBC,EPD
Streethay/St
  'stri:thei BBC
Street Hill/Ess ⟶ Old Street Hill
Strenshall/NRY
  strensl BBC
  strensəl GlossMY,s.n.Strensal
Strensham/Wo
  strensəm PNWo 229,DEPN
Strethall/Ess
  stretəl PNEss 534
  'strethɔ:l BBC
Stretham/Ca
  stretəm BBC,ONCa 178
Stretton
  stretən Schr.
Stretton Sugwas/He
  'stret(ə)n 'sʌgəs BBC
  stretən - BCE
  (see also s.n. Sugwas)
Strickland/We
  striklənd EPD,Schr.
Strickland Ketel/We
  striklənd ketl PNWe I/151
Strixton/Np
  striksən PNNp 197
Strode/Do
  stroud PNDo(i)279

Strood
   stru:d   EPD,BBC,Chis.
   striud   PNK
Stroud/Gl,Ha
   straud   PNGl I/139,BBC,BCE,
             EPD,Schr.,Chis.,DEPN
             (for S. in Gl),BG
             (for S. in Gl)
Stroud Gn/Mx
   straud   PNMx(i)
Stroudgreen/Wt
   stræudgri:n   PNWt 117
Stroudwater Canal/Gl
   straudwɔ:tə   Chis.
Stroxton/Li
   strɔ:s(ə)n, strous(ə)n   BBC
   strɔ:sən   BCE,Hope
   strousən   BCE
   strɔ:sn   DEPN
Strumpshaw/Nf
   strʌmʃə   BBC,BCE
Strutt (as in S.'s Pk/Db)
   strʌt   EPD
Stublach/Chs
   -latʃ   PNChs II/viii
Stubbings/WRY
   stubinz   DHd 122
Stubbs/WRY
   stʌbz   EPD,Kruis.
Studdah/NRY
   studə   PNYN 247
Studdal/K
   stʌdl   BBC
Studfold/WRY
   studfəld   Ellis 619
Studley
   stʌdli   Schr.
Studley Garth/WRY
   studli gɑ:þ   DDd 12
Stukeley/Hu
   stju:kli   BBC,Schr.
Stuntney/Ca
   stʌntni   ONCa 182
Sturba Nook/Cu
   sturbəniuk   PNE'side 62
Sturgate/Li
   stə:geit   BBC
Sturminster Marshall, S.Newton/Do
   stə:minstə mɑ:ʃl,
   -   nju:t(ə)n   BBC
   stə:rmistər   DDo,Urlau 49
Sturry/K
   stʌri   BBC,PNK
Sturston/Nf
   stʌsən   Hope
Sturton/Li
   stə:t(ə)n   BBC
Styal/Chs
   olim staiə   PNChs II/vii,GlossChs

   staiəl   PNChs II/vii,BBC
Styche Hall/Ess
   staitʃ   EPD
Styvechale/Wa ⟶ Stivichall
Subberthwaite/La
   subəþət   PNLa 214
Sudbury/Db,Mx,Sf
   sʌdbəri   Schr.,Chis.
   sʌdb(ə)ri   EPD
Sudeley Manor/Gl
   su:dli, siudli   PNGl II/26
   sju:dli   EPD
Sud Moor/Wt
   zʌdmər   PNWt 167
Suffolk
   sʌfək   DSf 3o3,EPD,BBC,Schr.,
             Kruis.,Chis.,MEG 257,
             HL 9o4
Sugwas/He
   sʌgəs   DEPN,DHe 44 (dial. and
             StE)
Sugwas Pool/He
   sʌgəs pu:l   BBC
Sugworth Fm/Sx
   sʌgərz   PNSx 265
Sulham/Brk
   sʌləm   BBC
Sulhampstead/Brk
   sʌl'hæm(p)stid   BBC
Sullens/Wt
   zʌlənz, sʌlinz   PNWt 23
Summerfield
   sʌməfi:ld   EPD
Summersbury/Wt
   zʌmərzbəri   PNWt 161
Sunbiggin/We
   sunbigən   PNE'side 65
Sunbrick/La
   sunbrik   PNLa 2o8f.
Sunbury/Mx
   sʌnb(ə)ri   EPD
Sunderland/Cu,Du,La
   sʌndələnd   EPD,BBC,Schr.
   -lænd   Schr.
   sunələn(d)   DSDu
Sunk Is/ERY
   sʌŋk   Hope
Sunningdale/Brk
   sʌniŋdeil   EPD
Sunnyside
   sʌnisaid   EPD
Surbiton/Sr
   sə:bit(ə)n   BBC
   sə:bitən   Schr.,Chis.
   sə:bitn   EPD
Surrey
   sʌri   EPD,BBC,Schr.,Kruis.,Chis
          HL 463

Susacres/WRY
  'siuzakəz,
  'suse:kəz PNYW V/lo7
Sussex
  sʌsiks EPD,BBC,Schr.,Kruis.
  sʌsəks Chis.,Lloyd 83
Sutherland/D,NRY
  sʌðələnd EPD,Schr.,Kruis.
   -lænd Schr.
Sutterland/D
  sitəlænd PND 79
Sutton
  sʌt(ə)n BBC,Schr.
  sʌtn EPD
Sutton/Ca,Sf,Wt
  sʌtən ONCa 22
  sʌtn PNDVall 69 (for S. in
  zʌtn PNWt 71   Sf)
Sutton Coldfield/Wa
  sʌt(ə)n kouldfi:ld BBC
Sutton Courtenay/Brk (or S.Court-
  sʌt(ə)n kɔ:tni BBC   ney)
  sʌtən   -   BCE
Sutton Scotney/Ha
  sʌt(ə)n skɔtni BBC
Sutton Veny/W
  veni PNW 154
  sʌt(ə)n vi:ni BBC
Sutton/Chs → Guilden S.
Swaby/Li
  sweibi DEPN,BBC,BCE
Swadlincote/Db
  swɔdlinkout BBC
Swaffham Bulbeck, S.Prior/Ca
  (= Gt and Lt.S.)
  swɔfəm PNCa 133,ONCa 178,BBC
  olim sɔfəm PNCa 133
  -ɔ- DEPN
  swæfəm Chis.
Swaffham/Nf
  swɔfəm BBC,BCE
  swæfəm Chis.
Swafield/Nf
  sweifi:ld BBC,BCE
  -ei- DEPN
Swainby/NRY
  swɛənbi PNYN 225
Swains Ho, S.Villas/Wt
  sweinz PNWt 4o
Swainston/Wt
  zwɔnsn PNWt 85
Swalcliffe/O
  sweiklif PNO 425,BBC,BCE
  olim sweikli PNO 425
  -eik- DEPN
The Swale/K
  swɑ:l PNK
Swale/NRY (r.n.)
  swiəl RNY 15

sweil Chis.
swial Ellis 557
Swalecliffe/K
  swɑ:lklif, sweikli PNK
Swaledale/NRY
  loc. swɔ:dil PNYN 269
  swɔ:dl Ellis 557
Swallowcliffe/W
  olim sweikli PNW 192
Swalwell/Du
  swɔlwel BBC,BCE
Swanage/Do
  swɔnidʒ PNDo I/52,PNDo(i)126,
           EPD,Schr.
Swanbach Bridge,S.Fm,S.Grange/Chs
  swɔnbatʃ PNChs III/84
Swanbourne/Bk
  swɔnbɔ:n BBC
Swanley Hall Bridge,S.H.Cover/Chs
  swɔnli PNChs III/135
Swanlow Fm, S.Lane/Chs
  swɔnlou PNChs III/169
Swanscomb Fm/Ess
  swɔnskinz PNEss 365
Swanton Novers/Nf
  swɔntən nouvəz BBC
Swanwick/Db,Ha
  swɔnik BBC,BCE (for S. in Ha),
           DEPN (for S. in Db),EPD,
           Schr.,Chis.
Swanwick Gn/Chs
  swɔnik, swɔni?,
  swɔnə gri:n PNChs III/lo9
Swarbrick Hall/La
  swɑ:brik PNLa 153
Swardeston/Nf
  swɔ:stən BBC,BCE
  swɔ:stn DEPN
Swarkeston/Db
  swɑ:sn PNDb(i) II/177
  swɔ:sən Hope
  swɔ:kstən BBC
Swarling/K
  swɔ:liŋ PNK
Swarth Fell/WRY (a mountain)
  swɑ:fl DDd 17
Swarth Gill/WRY
  swaþ gil DDd 16
Swarthmoor Hall/La
  swɑ:þmuər PNLa 212
Swarthaite/WRY
  swɑ:þət DDd 14
Swathling/Ha
  -eið- DEPN
Swaton/Li
  sweit(ə)n BBC
  sweitən BCE,Schr.
Swavesey/Ca
  sweisi Hope

sweivzi   BBC,ONCa 182
Swayfield/Li
    swefi:ld   Hope
Sweeney/Sa
    swi:ni   EPD
Swefling/Sf
    swefliŋ   BBC
Swepstone/Le
    swepsən   PNLe 76
Swerford/O
    swɑ:vɔ:d   Hope
Swettenham/Chs
    swetnəm   PNChs II/ix,GlossChs,
                EPD
Swift/Le,Wa (r.n.)
    swift   EPD
Swimbridge/D → Swym-
Swinburn/Nb
    swinbə:n,-bən   Bchm.67
Swindon
    swindən   EPD,Schr.
    swinən   GlossW 213
Swine/ERY
    swain   BBC
Swine Redding/WRY
    swain ridin   DDd 17
Swinesale/NRY
    swinsɔ: PNYN 11o
Swinescales/Cu
    swainskilz   PNE'side 68
Swineshead/Bd,Li
    swinzhed   PNBdHu 2o
    swainzhed   BBC
Swinesherd/Wo
    swenzhəd   PNWo 161,GlossSEWo
                82
Swineside/Cu
    swainsit   PNE'side 69
Swinford
    swinfəd   Schr.
Swingfield Minnis/K
    minis   DK
Swinsow/NRY
    swinsə   PNYN 145
Swinstead/Li
    swinstid, -sted   Schr.
Swinton
    swintən   Schr.
Swymbridge/D (or Swim-)
    swimbridʒ   BBC
Swyre Head/Do
    swaiə   PNDo I/19,PNDo(i)121
Sydenham/Ldn
    sid(ə)nəm   BBC
    sidənəm   Schr.,Chis.
    sidnəm   EPD,Schr.
Syderstone/Nf
    saidəstoun   BBC

Sydling St. Nicholas/Do
    sidliŋ snt nikələs   BBC
Sydney/Chs
    sidni   PNChs III/24,EPD
Syerston/Nt
    saiəstn   PNNt(i)135
    saiəstən   BBC
Syke Bottom/WRY
    sɔ:k   DHd 98
Symond (as in S.'s Gn/Hrt)
    saimənd   EPD
Symondsbury/Do
    simənzbəri   PNDo(i)291,BBC,BCE
    -i-   DEPN
Symonds Yat/Gl
    simənz jæt   PNGl III/212
    siməndz jæt   BBC,EPD
Syon Ho/Mx
    zaiən   PNMx 28
    saiən   BBC
Syrencot Ho/W
    sirənkʌt, olim
    sisənkət   PNW 366
Syresham/Np
    saisəm   PNNp 59,DEPN,Hope
    sə:rsəm, sairəsəm   PNNp 59
Syston/Gl
    sais(t)ən   BCE
Syston/Le,Li
    saistən   BBC,BCE (for S. in Le),
    -ai-   DEPN (for S. in Le)
    sɔistən   Ellis 489 (for S. in Le
Sytchampton/Wo
    sitʃən   PNWo 272
    'sitʃhæm(p)tən   BBC
Syward Lodge/Do
    saiwəd   PNDo(i)187,PNDo I/36o
Sywell/Np
    saiəl   PNNp 139,DEPN
    saiwel   BBC

T

Tardebigge/Wo
  olim tɑ:bik PNWo 362

Tacolneston(e)/Nf
  tæklstoun Hope
  tæklstən BBC,PNNf,s.n.
           Tackelston
  tæklstn DEPN

Tarporley/Chs
  tarpəli, older local
  tarpli PNChs III/294
  tɑ:pəli BBC,BCE,Chis.
  tɑ:pli BBC,BCE
  tɑ:rpli GlossChs

Tadcaster/WRY
  'tædkæstə EPD,BBC
  'tædkəstə EPD,Schr.,Chis.

Tarleton/La
  tɑ:ltən EPD

Taddington/Db
  tadntən Eliis 426

Tarrant Keynston/Do
  tærənt keinstən PNDo(i)6o,BBC,
                 BCE

Tadlow/Ca
  tædlou ONCa 192

Tarrant Monckton/Do
  mʌŋktən EPD

Tailbert/We
  tɛəlbərt PNE'side 72 and 73

Tarring/Sx
  tæriŋ PNSx 194,BBC

Takeley/Ess
  teikli BBC

Tasburgh/Nf
  teizbrə Hope
  teizbərə BBC
  teiz- DEPN

Talaton/D
  tælətən PND 571,BBC

Talbot/Do,Gl
  tɔ(:)lbət, tæl- EPD

Tate Gallery/Ldn
  teit EPD,BBC

Tale/D (r.n.)
  teil RN 388

Tathall End/Ca
  tætəl PNBk 7

Talkin/Cu
  tɔ:kin PNCu 88,GlossCu xviii,
          BBC,BCE

Tatham/La
  teitəm DEPN,BBC,BCE
  teiþəm EPD

Talkin Tarn/Cu
  tɔ:kin tarn PNE'side 7o

Tattenhall Hall/Chs
  'tætnɔ:l, older local
  tætnə PNChs IV/97
  tatnə DSChs 18,GlossChs

Tamar/D,Co (r.n.)
  teimə EPD,BBC,Kruis.
  teimɑ: Chis.

Tattersall's/Ldn
  tætəsælz Bau.

Tame/St,Wa;Chs,La,Yorks. (r.n.)
  teim Schr.,Chis.,HL 758
  ti:əm DSto (for T. in Yorks.)

Tattershall/Li
  tætəʃəl BBC,BCE,Schr.

Tamerton (Kings T.)/D
  kiŋz tæmət(ə)n BBC

Tattingstone/Sf
  tætiŋstən BBC

Tamerton Foliott/D (or -ll-)
  tæmət(ə)n fouliət BBC

Tauldeley/Chs
  loc. tɔləri PNChs I/xxii

Tamworth/St
  tæmwə:þ BBC,EPD
  tæməþ BBC
  tæmwəþ EPD,Schr.
  taməþ Ellis 482

Taunton/So
  teintən, tæntən Hope
  tɔ:ntən BBC,BCE,Schr.,MEG 3o2,
             Chis.
  tɑ:ntən BBC,BCE,Schr.,MEG 3o2,
             EPD ("loc.")
  tɑ:ntn DWSo 6
  tɑ:nən DWSo 6,DWSo(i)

Tanfield/Du,NRY
  tænfi:ld EPD

Tangmere/Sx
  tæŋmiə BBC

Taverham/Nf
  teivərəm BBC,BCE
  -ei- DEPN
  tæbərəm Hope

Tanhouse Spa/WRY
  spɔ: PNSWY 264f.

Tanner (as in T.'s Gn/Wo)
  tænə EPD

Tavistock/D
  tævistɔk EPD,Schr.,Chis.
  -æ- DEPN

Tantobie/Du
  tæn'toubi BBC

Tavy/D (r.n.)
  teivi RN 393,DEPN,BBC,BCE

Taplow/Bk
  tɔplou PNBk 231

Taw/D (r.n.)
  tɔ: Schr.

Tapnell Fm, T. Down/Wt
  tæ:pnəl PNWt 227,DWt,s.n.
          nutten

Tawton/D
  tɔːt(ə)n BBC
Taxal/Chs
  olim taksə PNChs II/vii,
              GlossChs
  taksəl PNChs II/Vii
Tayler's Copse/Wt
  teilərs kaps PNWt 86
Tealby/Li
  tiːlbi BBC
Tean/St (p.n. and r.n.)
  tiːn BBC
Teathes/Cu
  tiːz Hope
Tebay/We
  tiːbei PNWe II/5o,EPD,BBC,
           BCE
  tiːbi PNWe II/5o
  tiːbə DKe 5
  -iː- DEPN
  tibi DDd 17
  teibə DKe 145,PNE'side 62
Tebworth/Bd
  tebəþ BBC
Tedburn St. Mary/D
  tedbəːn snt mɛəri BBC
Teddington/Gl,Mx
  tediŋtən EPD
Tees/Cu,Du,We,Yorks. (r.n.)
  tiːz DEPN,RN 395,EPD,Schr.,
        Chis.
  tiːəs Ump.32
Teesdale/Du and NRY
  tiːzdeil EPD
  tɛəzdl PNE'side 72
Teeson/K ⟶ Teston
Teffont Evias/W
  olim tefənt juːəs,
  nunc vero iːvaiəs PNW 193
Tehidy Ho/Co
  ti'hidi BBC
Teigh/Ru
  tiː DEPN,BBC,BCE
Teign/D (r.n.)
  tiːn RN 397,DEPN,PND 14,
        EPD,BBC,BCE,Schr.
  tin RN 397,DEPN,PNE&W,BBC,
       BCE,Schr. ("loc.")
  tein Chis.
Teigngrace/D
  tiŋ'greis PND 486,DEPN
  'tiːngreis BBC,BCE
Teignmouth/D
  tinməþ PND 5o3,DEPN,EPD,BBC,
       BCE,Schr.,Kruis.,
       Chis.,Hope
  teinməþ Hope
  tiːnməþ BBC
  loc. also tiŋməþ EPD

Teignton/D (as in Bishopsteignton,
             Drews-, Kings-/D)
  teintən EPD
Teise/K (r.n.)
  tiːz BBC,PNK
Telscombe/Sx
  tælz'kum PNSx 326
  telskəm PNSx(i)156,BBC,BCE
Teme/He,Sa,Wo (r.n.)
  tiːm RN 398,EPD,Chis.
Temple/Ldn
  tempəl CPP 66
  templ EPD
Temple Balsall/Wa
  bʌsl templ Hope
Temple Guiting/Gl
  templ gaitiŋ BBC
Temple Sowerby/We
  templ sauəbi, - sɔːbi BBC,BCE
Templeton/Brk,D
  templtən Schr.
  templt(ə)n EPD
Tenbury/Wo
  tembəri RN 4oo,GlossWWo
  tembri Hope
  tenb(ə)ri EPD
  tenbəri Chis.
Tenterden/K
  tentədən BBC,Chis.
  tentəd(ə)n EPD
  tendədən PNK
Ter/Ess (r.n.)
  tɑː EPD,BBC,BCE
Terling/Ess
  tɑːliŋ EPD,BBC,BCE,PNEss 296
  tɑːlən PNEss 296
  -ɑː- DEPN
  təːliŋ EPD,BBC,BCE
Terry (as in T.'s Gn/Wa)
  teri EPD
Terwick/Sx
  terik PNSx 42,DEPN,BBC
Test/Ha (r.n.)
  test EPD
Teston/K (also spelt Teeson)
  tiːs(ə)n BBC
  tiːsən BCE,PNK
  tiːsn DEPN,Hope
Tetbury/Gl
  tetbəri Chis.
Tetchwick/Bk
  tetʃik PNBk 1o6,DEPN,Dodgson
         (2)386
  tʌtʃik PNBk 1o6
Tettenhall Regis/St
  'tet(ə)nhɔːl BBC
  tetənhɔːl riːdʒis Chis
Teversall/Nt
  olim təːrsəl, tiːəsə PNNt 135

Teversham/Ca
  tevaʃəm ONCa 179
Tewin/Hrt
  tju(:)in EPD
Tewit/Cu (a lake)
  teiɑ:fit PNCu 35
Tewkesbury/Gl
  'tiuksberi,
  tʃuksbəri PNGl II/61
  tju:ksbəri Schr.,Kruis.,Chis.
  tju:ksb(ə)ri EPD
Tey/Ess
  tei PNEss 4oo,BBC
Teynham/K
  tenəm EPD,DEPN,BBC,BCE,PNK,
    Hope
  teinəm BBC.BCE
Thacka Beck/Cu (or -ey) (r.n.)
  þakə bek PNCu 28
  þækə bek PNE'side 62
Thackley/WRY
  þækli EPD,BBC
  faklə DWdl 91
Thakeham/Sx
  þækəm PNSx 18o,DEPN
  þeikəm BBC
Thame/O
  teim PNO 146,EPD,BBC,BCE,
    Schr.,Chis.,Hope
Thame/Bk,O (r.n.)
  teim DEPN,Schr.,HL 758
Thames (r.n.)
  temz RN 4o2,DEPN,EPD,BBC,
    Schr.,Kruis.,Chis.,
    DBo,MEG 45,ESpr.4ol
Thanet/K
  þænit EPD,Schr.,Kruis.,PNK,
    Bchm.194,HL 795,ESpr.
    268
  þænət Chis.
  tænət PNK
  -æ- DEPN
  The Isle of Th. is called 'The
  Island' in East Kent (DK,s.n.
  Marsh)
Thatcher (as in T.Stone Is/D)
  þætʃə EPD
Thaxted/Ess
  þæksted Chis.
Theakston/NRY
  þi:kstən PNYN 228
Theale/Brk,So
  þi:l BBC
Thearne/ERY
  þən, þɔn PNYE 2ol
Theddlethorpe/Li
  þelþrəp Hope
Theescombe/Gl
  t- PNGl(i)153

Thelnetham/Sf
  þel'ni:þəm BBC
  -þ- Eminson(2)159
Thelwall/Chs
  þelwɔ:l PNChs II/ix
  olim ðelwəl PNChs II/ix,
    GlossChs
Theobalds Pk/Hrt
  þiəbɔ:ldz BBC,EPD
  tibl(d)z EPD
  tiblz HL 1222
  "[t] is usual in the p.n. Theobalds in Herts." HSM 82,note 2
Theobalds Rd/Ldn
  þiəbɔ:ldz BBC,EPD
  tibəldz BBC
  formerly tibl(d)z EPD
Therfield/Hrt
  þɑ:rfəl PNHrt 166
Thetford/Ca,Li,Nf
  þetfəd ONCa 187,Chis.
  þetfə Hope (for T. in Nf)
Thevelby/Li
  þi:lbi Hope,H.A.(2)45
Theydon Bois/Ess
  þeid(ə)n bɔiz PNEss 82,BBC
  þeidən - BCE
  þeidn - EPD
Thimbleby/NRY
  þiməlbi PNYN 214
Thingwall/Chs
  þiŋwɔ:l PNChs IV/273
Thirkleby/ERY
  þɔtlbi PNYE 125,Hope
Thirlby/NRY
  þɔrlbi PNYN 199
Thirley Cotes/NRY
  þɔrlə PNYN 114
Thirlmere/Cu (a lake)
  þelmər PNE'side 73
Thirn/NRY
  þɔrn PNYN 235
Thirsk/NRY
  þɔsk, þrusk PNYN 188
  þə:sk EPD,BBC,Chis.
Thirston/Nb
  þrustən, þristən PNNbDu 195
  þrʌstn DEPN
Thistle Holm/WRY
  þisl aum DDd 12
Thistlewood/Cu
  þislwəd, vulgo olim
  þislhwət PNCu 246
Thixendale/ERY
  þisəndil PNYE 133,Hope
Thoby Priory/Ess
  toubi PNEss 261

Tholthorpe/NRY
  þouþrəp   PNYN 21
  þɔlþrəp   EDD,s.n.Thorpe
Thomley/O
  þʌmli   PNO 189,PNO(i)2o6,
          DEPN
Thong/WRY → Upperthong,
            Netherthong
Thonock/Li
  þɔnək   BBC
Thoresby/Li,Nt,Yorks.
  þɔ:zbi   BBC,Schr.
  þo:zbi   BCE (for T. in Li)
Thorganby/ERY
  þɔgəmbi   PNYE 263
Thorley/Wt
  þɔ:rli   PNWt 225
Thormanby/NRY
  þɔnəmbi   PNYN 26
Thornaby/NRY
  þɔ:nəbi   EPD,Chis.
Thornbarrow/Cu,We
  þɔrnbərə   PNCu 2o6,PNE'side 67
Thornbury
  þɔ:nbəri   BBC
Thorn Cottage/Wt
  ðə:rn kɔtidӡ   PNWt 286
Thorncross/Wt
  ðə:rnkrɔ:s   PNWt 285
Thorndon/Sf
  þoundən   Hope
Thorne
  þɔ:n   EPD,BBC,Chis.
  þoun   Hope (for T. in WRY)
Thorness/Wt
  þɔ:rnis   PNWt 191
  ðə:rnəs   PNWt 286
  þɔ:'nes   BBC
Thorney/Ca
  þɔ:ni   ONCa 182
Thornford/Do
  ðɑ:rnvərd   DDo
Thorngumbald/ERY
  gumbəþɔn   PNYE 38
  gumbəþɔ:n,
  þɔ:nəgumbɔ:ld   GlossHol 17
  gʌmbəþɔ:n,
  þɔ:nəgʌmbɔ:l [sic]   Hope[1]
Thornham/K (or Thurnham),Nf
  þɔ:nəm   BCE (for T. in K),
           BBC (for T. in Nf)
Thornham Fm/ERY
  þɔnəm   PNYE 96
Thornham Magna, T. Parva/Sf
  þɔ:nəm mægnə, - pɑ:və   BBC

Thornhaugh/Np
  þɔ:nhɔ: BBC
Thornhill
  þɔ:nhil   EPD,Schr.,Chis.
Thornholme/ERY
  þɔnəm   PNYE 9o
Thornthorpe/ERY
  þɔnþrəp   PNYE 143
Thornthwaite/Cu,We
  þɔ:nþət   PNCu 371
  þɔ:rnþət   PNE'side 66
Thornton (see also s.n. Childer T.)
  þɔ:ntən   EPD,Schr.
Thornton Heath/Sr
  þɔ:ntən hi:þ   BBC
Thornton Hough/Chs
  þɔrntən ʌf   PNChs IV/23o
  þɔ:ntən hʌf   BBC,BCE
Thoroton/Nt
  þʌrətən   PNNt 229
Thorp/La,WRY
  þɔ:p   EPD
Thorpe
  þɔ:p   EPD,Schr.
Thorpe/Yorks.
  þɔrp   DHd 129 (for T. in WRY)[2]
  in the East Riding: þrʌp
Thorpe/We
  þɔ:rp   PNE'side 76
Thorpe Malsor, T.Mandeville/Np
  þ rʌp   EDD,s.n.Thorpe
Thorpe Morieux/Sf
  þɔ:p mə'ru: BBC
  - mə'rju: BCE
  Morieux: _ ╱   DEPN
Thorpe-le-Soken/Ess
  þɔ:p lə souk(ə)n   BBC
Thorpe Wood/WRY
  þarp wu:d   GlossMY,s.n. Howgates
Thorp Perrow/NRY
  þɔ:p pɔrə   PNYN 229
Thorrington/Ess
  þɔriŋtən   BBC
Thrandeston(e)/Sf
  frænsn   Hope
Thrapston/Np
  þræpsən   PNNp 22o
Threadneedle Street/Ldn
  'þred'ni:dl stri:t   Schr.
  _ ╱ _   EPD
Threapland/WRY
  þri:plənd   BBC
  (see also s.n. Bothel-and-Threap-
  land)

---

1) Hope's transcriptions could also represent [u] instead of [ʌ].
2) "'Thorpe' in the East Riding is always pron. 'thrup'" (Cole 1o4);
   "on the Wolds invariably pron. 'thrup'" (ScandPN 6).

Threapwood/Chs
  'þri:pwud PNChs IV/61
Threckingham/Li (also spelt
               Threek-)
  þrekiŋəm BBC,BCE,Hope
  þri:kiŋəm BCE
  -i:- DEPN
Three Road/WRY
  þrei roud DDd 16
Threlkeld/Cu
  þrelkəl PNCu 252
  olim þrelkət PNCu 252,
             Powley 276,
             GlossCu xviii
  loc. trelkət PNO li
  þrelkit PNE'side 7o
Threshthwaite Crag/We
  þreʃit PNWe I/191
Threxton/Nf
  treksən Hope
Thrigby/Nf
  trigbi Hope
Thringstone/Le
  þriŋsən Hope
Throckmorton/Wo
  'þrɔk'mɔ:tən, þrɔg- Schr.
  frɔgmɔ:tn GlossSEWo 82
Throope Fm, T.Hill/W
  tru:p PNW 393
Throstle Hall/WRY
  þrɔsl ɔ: DDd 15
Througham/Gl
  þrufəm, drufəm PNGl I/12o
  drʌfəm PNGl(i)154
  þrʌfəm DEPN,EPD,BBC,BCE
Throwleigh/D
  þru:li PND 453
  -u:- DEPN
Throwley/K,St
  þrouli, þrauli BBC,BCE (for
               T. in K)
Throxenby/NRY
  þrɔsənbi PNYN 11o
  -ɔs- DEPN
Thrup/O
  þrʌp PNO(i)2o7
Thrushel/D (r.n.)
  þrʌʃəl RN 4o6
Thrushgill/We
  þruskil PNE'side 68
Thrushton Closes/Db (f.n.)
  þrʌʃtən Fraser(2)79
Thruxted/K
  drʌstəd Hope
Thrybergh/WRY
  þraibə, þraibərə BBC,BCE
Thuborough/D
  loc. stil sometimes
  fi:bə PNEss lvi (for T. in D)

Thulston/Db (old spelling: Thurle-
  þʌlsn Hope   stone)
Thurcaston/Le
  þru:ksn PNLe 76
Thurgarton/Nf
  'þə:gət(ə)n BBC
Thurgarton/Nt
  þə:gətən, þə:gəʔn PNNt 178
  'þə:gɑ:t(ə)n BBC
  'þə:gɑ:tən BCE
Thurgoland/WRY
  'þə:goulənd BBC
Thurlaston/Le,Wa
  þru:lsn PNLe 76
  þə:lstən PNWa 147
Thurlbear/So(also spelt -beer)
  dilbərə DWSo 6
Thurleigh/Bd
  þə:'lai PNBdHu 47,DEPN,BBC,
          Mawer(3) (stress only)
Thurlow/Sf
  þə:lou EPD,Schr.
Thurloxton/So
  þə:'lɔkstən BBC,BCE
Thurlstone/WRY(also spelt Thurle-)
  þə:lstn Hope
  -stən DHd 122
Thurmaston/Le
  'þə:məstən BBC
  þru:msn PNLe 76
Thurne/Nf
  þə:n BBC
Thurnham/La
  þə:nəm BBC
  (for Thurnham/K → Thornham)

Thurnscoe/WRY
  þrʌnskə Hope,H.A.(2)45
  þə:nzkou BBC
Thursby/Cu
  þɔ:sbi GlossCuWeNLa,s.n.Thor
  þju:əsbi GlossCu xviii
Thurstaston/Chs
  'þə:stæstən PNChs IV/279
Thurston/Db (f.n.),Sf
  þrʌʃtən FnSDb 61,s.n.Thrushton
  þə:st(ə)n EPD
Thurstonfield/Cu
  þrusənfi:ld PNCu 128
  þrʌstənfi:ld BBC
Thurstonland/WRY
  þə:slənd Hope
  þɔrslənd DHd 13o
Thwaite/Nf,Sf
  tweit Hope
-thwaite
  "usually ... pron. [þət]"
                    IPN II/6o

Thwing/ERY
  þwiŋ PNYE 112
  wiŋ PNYE 112,Hope
  twiŋ Hope
Tibenham/Nf
  tib(ə)nəm BBC
Tibthorpe/ERY
  tibþrəp PNYE 167
Ticehurst/Sx
  taisəs PNSx 450
  taisəst PNSx(i)157
  taishə:st EPD
Tichborne/Ha
  titʃbɔ:n EPD,BBC,Kruis.
  -bən EPD,Bchm.69,Chis.
Tickhill/WRY
  tikhil BBC
Ticknall/Db
  tiknəl BBC
Tiddingford Hill/Bk
  tidnfut, tinfut PNBk 81
Tideford/Co,D
  tidifəd BBC,BCE (for T.in Co)
  taidifəd PND 320
Tidenham/Gl
  tidnəm PNGl III/264
  tid(ə)nəm BBC
  tidənəm Chis.
Tideswell/Db
  tidzə PNDb 172,PNDb(i)
    II/184,de Barri 43,
    Mawer(4)284,Ellis 442
  tidsə PNDb 172,Hope,Brushf.67
  tidzəl DEPN,BCE,HL 811
  tidzl BBC
  taidzwel BBC,BCE
  taidzwəl HL 811,Schr.,Chis.
Tidkinhow/NRY
  tiŋkinou PNYN 148
Tidworth/W
  tedwəþ PNW 370
Tiffield/Np
  tifəl PNNp 93
Tiger Bay/Ldn
  taigə bei Bau.[1]
Tilberthwaite/La
  tilbəþət PNLa 216
Tilbury/Ess
  tilbəri EPD,BBC,Schr.,Chis.
Tilehurst/Brk
  tailhə:st EPD
Tilley/Ha,Sa
  tili EPD
Tilmanstone/K
  tilmənstoun BBC
Tilshead/W
  tilzhəd, olim tilzed PNW 236
  tilz'hed BBC

Tilston/Chs
  tilstən PNChs IV/xiii
  older local tilsn PNChs IV/xii
    GlossChs
Tilstone/Chs
  tilstən PNChs III/317
Timberscombe/So
  timbəzku:m BBC
Tindale/Cu,Du
  tindl EPD
Tingewick/Bk
  tindʒik PNBk 65,DEPN,Dodgson
    (2)386
  tiŋik Hope,ONwick 387
  tindʒwik BBC
Tingrith/Bd
  tiŋgriþ BBC
Tinker's Lane/Wt
  "laan" DWt,s.n.harl
Tinsley/La,
Tinsley Bongs ⟶ Tyldesley
Tintagel/Co
  tintædʒəl BCE,Schr.,Hope,Förste.
  tin'tædʒl BBC,DEPN (stress only
  -(ə)l EPD
  loc. dəndædʒəl Förster
Tintinhull/So
  tintnəl Turner(1)122
Tintwistle/Chs
  loc. tinsl PNChs I/320
  tinsil GlossChs
  'tintwisəl Chis.
Tipthorpe/ERY
  tipþrəp Hope
Tipton/St
  tiptən Schr.
  tipn Hope
Tipton St.John/D
  tiptən sənt dʒɔn BBC
Tiresford/Chs
  taiərz- PNChs III/320
Tirril/We
  tirəl PNWe II/208
  tərəl PNE'side 68
Tisbury/W
  tizbəri PNW 194
Titchfield/Ha
  titʃfi:ld Schr.,Chis.
Tithby/Nt
  tiðbi PNNt 242
Titley/He
  dial. titlə DHe 44
Tittenley/Chs
  titnli, older local
  titli PNChs III/90
Tittensor/St
  tit(ə)nsɔ: BBC
Tittleshall/Nf
  titsɔ:l Hope
  titlʃɔ:l BBC

---

1) "Name eines früher sehr berüchtigten Londoner Matrosenviertels".

Tiverton
  tivət(ə)n BBC
  tivətən Schr.,Chis.
  tivətn EPD
Tiverton/Chs
  tivərtn PNChs III/32o
  older local
  tiːərtn PNChs III/32o,
    GlossChs
  təːtən H.A.(2)45
Tiverton/D
  tivətən PND 541
  -i- DEPN
Tivetshall/Nf
  tivitshɔːl BBC
  titsəl PNNf(i)14
Toadhole/Cu
  tiədəl GlossCu xviii
Tocketts/NRY
  tɔkits PNYN 153
Tockholes/La
  tɔkhoulz BBC
Tockwith/WRY
  tɔkiþ PNYW IV/25o
  tɔkwiþ BBC
Todber/Do
  tɔdbə PNDo(i)18
Todd Hills/Du
  tɔd EPD
Toddington/Bd,Gl
  tʌdiŋtən PNBdHu 135
  tɔdiŋtən Chis.
  tɔdintən PNGl II/28
Todhole/Cu
  tiədəl PNCu 4o7
  tiədəl GlossCu xviii
Todlawmoor/Nb
  'tɔdli'muə BBC,BCE
Todmorden/WRY
  'tɔdmədin PNYW III/174
  'tɔdmədən EPD,BBC,BCE
  'tɔdmɔːdən PNYW III/174,BCE,
    GlossR&R
  tɔdmɔːd(ə)n BBC
  tɔd'mɔrdən Chis.
  tɔdmɔːdn EPD
  tɔːmɔːdən DSLa,s.n.Tawmorden
Toft/Ca
  tɔft ONCa 199
Tofts/WRY
  tɔfts DDd 15
Tolcarne/Co
  tɔl'kɑːn BBC
Tolgullow/Co
  tɔl'gʌlou BBC
Toll/K
  toul PNK
Toller Fratrum, T.Porcorum/Do
  tɔlə PNDo(i)235,DEPN

Tollerton/NRY
  toulətən PNYN 22,DEPN
Toller Whelme/Do
  tɔlə welm PNDo(i)272
Tollesbury/Ess
  toulzbəri PNEss 3o4,BBC,BCE
  -b(ə)ri EPD
Tollesby/NRY
  touzbi PNYN 163
Tolleshunt d'Arcy, T.Knights,
    T. Major/Ess
  toulzn(t) PNEss 3o6
  'toulzhʌnt EPD,BBC
  dɑːsi, naits, meidʒə BBC
  toulznt DEPN
  tousənt Hope
Tolpuddle/Do
  toulpʌdl PNDo(i)179
  toupidl PNDo I/331
  toːpidl DDo
  'tɔlpʌdl, -pidl BBC
Tolskithy/Co
  tɔl'skiþi BBC
Tolworth/Sr
  tɔlwəþ, toul- BBC
Tonbridge/K
  tʌnbridʒ DEPN,EPD,BBC,BCE,PNK
  tʌmbridʒ EPD,Bchm.116
Tone/So (r.n.)
  toun BBC
Tong/Sa
  tʌŋ PNSa ("[so] called by the
           working class")
Tonge/K,La,Le
  tɔŋ BBC,BCE (for T. in Le),
    PNK
Tonge-cum-Breightmet/La
  tɔŋ kʌm breitmet,
  - - braitmet BCE
Tonge Fold/La
  tɔŋ fould BBC
Tongue End/WRY
  tuŋ end DDd 16
Tooley St/Ldn
  tuːli striːt EPD,Schr.
Toot Baldon/O
  tuːt bɔːld(ə)n BBC
  - bɔːldən BCE
Toot Hill/Cu
  tjut hil GlossCu xviii
Tooting Graveney/Ldn
  tuːtiŋ greivni BBC
Too To Hill/WRY
  tuːədɔil PNYW III/13o
Topham/WRY
  tɔpəm EPD
Toppesfield/Ess
  tɔpəzfl PNEss 463
  tɔp(i)sfiːld BBC,BCE

Topsham/D
  tɔpsəm   PND 454,EPD,BBC,BCE,
               Chis.
Tor Bay/D
  'tɔ:'bei   EPD,Schr.
  _ ˌ , ˌ _   EPD,Kruis.
  tɔr'bei Chis.
Torkington/Chs
  olim tɔrkitn   PNChs II/vii,
                  GlossChs
  tɔrkiŋtən,
  tɔrkintən PNChs II/vii
Torksey/Li
  tɔ:ksi BBC
  tɔ:si Hope,GlossSWLi
Toronto/Du
  tə'rɔntou EPD
Torpenhow/Cu
  trə:'penə,
  Þrə:'penə PNCu 325
  tɔ:'penə PNCu 235,BCE
  trə'penə EPD("very common"),
              BCE,GlossCu xviii
  tɔr'penə PNE'side 62
  tɔ:'penou BCE,EPD ("some-
             times")
  tri'penə, tɔ:p(ə)nhau BBC
  'tɔ:pənhau EPD
Torpoint/Co
  tɔ:'pɔint BBC
Torquay/D
  tɔ:'ki: PND 524,BBC,BCE,Schr.,
          Chis.,MEG 98,Hope,
          DEPN (stress only)
  ˌ ˌ EPD,Kruis.
  tɔkei Hope
Torridge/D (r.n.)
  tɔridჳ Schr.
Torrington/D,Li
  tɔriŋtən EPD,Schr.,Chis.
Torrisholme/La
  tɔrisəm PNLa(ii)
Tortington/Sx
  tɔ:tən PNSx 143
Tortolacate/Cu
  tɔ:tləkeit GlossCu xviii
Torworth/Nt
  tɔrəÞ PNNt loo
  tɔriÞ PNNt(i) 14o
Tosside/WRY
  tɔsaid, tɔsid, tɔsit BBC,BCE
Totham/Ess
  tɔtəm PNEss 31o,BBC
Tothill/Li
  tɔthil EPD,Bchm.1o5
  tɔtil EPD
Totland/Wt
  tɔ:tlən PNWt 227
  tɔtlənd EPD

Totley/WRY
  tɔtli BBC
Totnes/D (also spelt -ness)
  tɔtnəs PND 334,Chis.
  tɔtnis EPD,BBC,Schr.
  tɔt'nes BCE
  'tɔtnes BCE,EPD,Schr.
Toton/Nt
  toutən PNNt 152
  tout(ə)n BBC
Tottenham/Du,Mx
  tɔt(ə)n m BBC
  tɔtnəm EPD,Schr.
  tɔtənəm Chis.
Totteridge/Bk,Hrt
  tɔtəridჳ EPD
Totternhoe/Bd
  tɔtənhou BBC
Tottington/La,Nf
  tɔtiŋtən Chis.
Totton/Ha
  tɔt(ə)n BBC
Toulston/WRY
  toulstən BBC
Tout/Sx → Belle Tout
Tovil/K
  tɔvil BBC,BCE,PNK
  tɔvl BBC
Towcester/Np
  toustə PNNp 94,DEPN,EPD,BBC,BCE
          Schr.,Hope
  taustə DEPN,Schr.,Chis.
  tɔstə Hope
Towcet/We
  tousit PNE'side 69
Towednack/Co
  tou'wednək BBC
  to'wednək BCE,DEPN (stress only)
Tow Law/Du
  'tau 'lɔ: BBC,BCE
Towler Hill/NRY
  taulə EPD
Town/WRY → Little T.
Townsend
  'taunzend EPD
Townshend/Co
  'taunz'end BBC
  ˌ _ EPD,Schr.,Kruis.
  'taunzənd Schr.
Towthorpe/ERY,NRY
  touÞrəp PNYE 134,PNYE 232,
          PNYN 13
Towton/WRY
  tautən Schr.
  tautn EPD,Kruis.
Toxteth/La
  tɔksteÞ EPD
  -əÞ EPD,BBC
Tracy (as in T.Pk/Gl)
  treisi EPD

Trafalgar Ho/W
   træf(ə)lgɑː   EPD
   træfl'gɑː   BBC,Kruis.
   trə'fælgə   BBC,Kruis.,MEG 158
   formerly ∕ ∕ MEG 158

Trafalgar Sq./Ldn
   trə'fælgə skwɛə   EPD,Schr.

Tranmere/Chs
   trænmiə, formerly and dial.
   tranmə   PNChs IV/257
   trænmiːr   Chis.

Trawden/La
   trɔːdin   PNLa 88

Treable Fm/D
   tribəl   PND 429

Treales/La
   treːlz   PNLa 152
   trelz   PNLa(ii)
   treilz   DEPN,BBC,BCE

Trebarwith/Co
   tri'bɑːwiþ   EPD,BBC
   trə-   EPD
   tre-   BCE
   tribæriþ   Bchm.138 ("old-
                  fashioned")

Trebehor/Co
   tri'biə   BBC

Trebelzue/Co
   olim tribi'dʒuː   Jenner(2)
                     3o2

Trebraze/Co
   see note s.n. Chypraze

Trebullet/Co
   tri'bulit   BBC

Trebursye/Co
   tri'bəːzi   BBC

Treby/D
   triːbi   PND 262

Trecarrel/Co (or -ll)
   tri'kærəl   BBC

Tredown/D (in Black Torrington
                         Hd)
   trə'daun   PND 146

Tredown/D (in Lifton Hd)
   trədaun   PND 181

Tredrea/Co
   -ei   Jenner(2)3o1

Treemaines/Sx
   triməns   PNSx 338

Trefnant/Sa
   trevnænt   BBC

Trefonen/Sa
   tri'vɔnin   BBC

Trefusis Pt/Co
   tri'fjuːsis, trə-   EPD

Tregadillett/Co (or -et)
   tregə'dilit   BBC

Tregajorran/Co
   tregə'dʒɔr(ə)n   BBC

Tregaminian/Co (or -on)
   tregə'miniən   BBC
   'tregə'minjən   BCE

Treganthe/Co
   tre'gænþi   BCE
   tri-   BBC

Tregavethan/Co
   tregə'veþ(ə)n   BBC
   'tregə'veþən   BCE
   _ _ ∕ _   DEPN(1)

Tregear/Co
   tri'giə, trə-   EPD

Tregelles/Co
   -g-   Jenner(2)3o2

Tregember/Co
   -g-   Jenner(2)3o2

Tregenna Castle/Co
   tri'genə   BBC,Jenner(2)3o4
               (stress only)

Tregeseal/Co
   tregi'si(ː)əl   BBC
   'tregi'siəl, 'tregi'siːl   BCE

Tregolls/Co
   tri'gɔlz   BBC

Tregonetha/Co
   tregə'neþə   BBC

Tregonissey/Co
   tregə'nisi   BBC

Tregony/Co
   'tregəni   BBC,BCE

Tregrehan/Co
   tre'grein   BBC,BCE

Tregurrian/Co
   tri'gʌriən   BBC

Trekenner/Co
   tri'kenə   BBC

Trelawney/Co
   tri'lɔːni, trə-   EPD
   _ ∕ _   GlossWCo xiv

Treleigh/Co
   tri'lei   BBC
   tre'lei   BCE

Treligga/Co
   tri'ligə   BBC

Trellick/D
   trelik   PND 76

Trelugga/Co
   tre'ligə   BCE

Treluggan/Co
   tri'lʌgən   BBC

Tremaine/Co
   -ei-   Jenner(2)3o1

Trematon/Co
   'tremətən   BBC

Trenance/Co
   tri'næns   BBC

Trenant/Co
   tri'nænt   BBC
   tre-   BCE

Treneglos/Co
  tri'negləs BBC
  tre'negləs BCE,DEPN (stress
            only)
Trengwainton/Co
  trin'gweintən BBC
Trenowth/Co
  tri'nauþ BBC
Trent (r.n.)
  trent EPD,BBC,Schr.,Kruis.
Trentbridge/Nt
  'trent'bridʒ BBC
Trentham/St
  trentəm EPD
  -þ- Eminson(2)159
Trentishoe/D
  trentiʃou BBC
Trentworthy/D
  trentəri PND 134
Trereif(e)/Co
  tri:v Hope
Trerule Foot/Co
  tri'ru:l fut BBC
Treryn Dinus/Co (or T. Dinas)
  tri:n BBC,BCE,Hope
  trə'ri:n BBC
  tri:n dainəs BBC
Tresco/Co (Scilly Is)
  treskou BBC,Chis.
Tresillian/Co
  tri'siliən BBC
Treskillard/Co
  tris'kiləd BBC
Tresmeer/Co
  trez'miə EPD,BBC
Treswell/Nt
  vulgo trʌsw(ə)l PNNt 61
Treswithian/Co
  tri'swiðiən BBC
Trevague/Co
  tre'veig Jenner(2)3o5
Trevarrack/Co
  tri'værək BBC
Trevalla/Co
  tri'velə BBC
Trevanyon/Co
  tre'vænjən Jenner(2)3oo and
             3o3
Trevear/Co
  _ ´ Jenner(2)3o4
Trevelga Head/Co
  tri'velgə, trə- EPD
Trevena/Co
  tri'vi:nə BBC
Treverbyn/Co
  tri'və:bin BBC,Jenner(2)3o1
Trevose Head/Co
  tri'vouz BBC

Trew/Co
  tru: EPD,BBC
Trewavas Head/Co
  tri'wɔvəs, trə- EPD
Trewellard/Co
  tri'weləd BBC
Trewhitt/Nb
  trufit PNNbDu 199
Trewidland/Co
  tri'widlənd BBC
Trewin Ho/Co
  tri'win, trə- EPD
Trewoofe/Co
  trouv Hope
Trewoon/Co
  tru:ən BBC,BCE
Treyarnon Bay/Co
  tri'jɑ:nən BBC
Treyford/Sx
  tri:fəd PNSx 43,DEPN
  trefəd PNSx 43,PNSx(i)159
Trimingham/Nf
  triminəm BBC
Trimley/Sf
  trimli PNDVall 35
Tring/Hrt
  triŋ EPD,BBC
Trinkeld/La
  triŋkəld, triŋ-keld PNLa 212
Triplow/Ca
  triplou ONCa 193
Trispen/Co
  trispən BBC
Troon/Co
  tru:n Schr.
Troopers/Wt
  tru:pərz PNWt 225
Trotterscliff/K (or -cliffe)
  trɔsli BBC,BCE,Hope,WP 271,
             Shell 218,
  trɔzli PNK
  trɔksli DK,Hope
  trɔtisklif BBC,BCE
Trottiscliffe/K ⟶ Trotterscliff(e
Troughend/Nb
  trufend PNNbDu 2o1
Trouts Dale/NRY
  tru:tsdil PNYN 98
Troway/Db
  troui BBC
Trowbridge/W
  troubridʒ PNW 133,EPD,BBC,BCE,
             Schr.,Chis.
  trau- Bchm.225,Schr.,Chis.
  tru:- Schr.
Trowell/Nt
  trauəl PNNt(i)143,BBC,BCE
  trouəl EPD,BBC,BCE

Trow Fm, T. Down/W
   trou   PNW 2oo
Trowle Fm,T.Common,T.Bridge/W
   troul   PNW 117
Trowlesworthy Warren/D
   trɔlzeri   PND 259
Trowse Newton/Nf
   trous   DEPN,BBC,BCE
Troy/WRY
   trɔi   EPD
Troytown/Do
   traitoun   DDo
Truckells/Wt
   trʌklz   PNWt 61
True Street/D
   tru: EPD
Truleigh Fm/Sx
   tru: 'lai   PNSx 2o7
Trumper (as in T.'s Crossing/Mx)
   trʌmpə   EPD
Trumpington/Ca
   trʌmpiŋtən   ONCa 26
Trunch/Nf
   trʌnʃ   BBC
Truro/Co
   truərou   EPD,BBC
   tru:rou   Schr.
Trusham/D
   trisəm   PND 5o3,DEPN,BBC,BCE,
           Chanter 53o
   trʌsəm   BBC,BCE
Trusthorpe/Li
   trʌsþɔ:p   BBC
Trysull/St
   tri:sl   BBC
   tri:zl   PNSt 156,DEPN,BBC
   tri:səl, tri:zəl   BCE
Trysull/St (r.n.)
   tri:zl   RN 419
Tub Hole/WRY
   tubl   DDd 14
Tudeley/K
   tju:dli, tu:dli   BBC,BCE,PNK
Tudhoe/Du
   tʌdou   BBC,BCE
Tuelldown/D
   tu:əl   PND 216
Tufnell Pk/Ldn
   tʌfnl, -nəl   EPD
Tulse (as in T.Hill/Ldn)
   tʌls   EPD
Tunbridge/K,WRY
   tʌnbridʒ   EPD,Schr.,Chis.
   tʌm-   EPD
Tunbridge Wells/K
   tʌnbridʒ welz   Schr.
   (see also preceding entry)
Tunstall
   tʌnstl   Schr.

tʌnstɔ:l   Chis.
Tunstall/Du,Sf
   tʌnstəl   BBC,BCE
Tunstall/Nf
   tʌnstɔ:l   BBC
Tunstall/St
   tʌnstəl   BBC,BCE
   tuənstil   Hope
Tunstall/ERY
   tunstəl   PNYE 57
Tunstead/Db,La,Nf
   tʌnstid   BBC
Turchington/D
   titʃiŋtən   PND 19o
Turnditch/Db
   tə:nditʃ   Hope
Turner (as in T.'s Gn/Sx)
   tə:nə   EPD
Turnham/Mx,ERY
   tə:nəm   EPD
Turnmill St/Ldn
   tə:nmil stri:t   Schr.
   also called 'Turnbull St':
   tə:nbul   Schr.
Turpin (as in T.Gn/La)
   tə:pin
Turweston/Bk
   tə:stən,'tawestən   PNBk 49
   tʌsən   PNBk 49,Mawer(4)285
   tə'westən   PNBk 49,BBC
   tə:stn   DEPN,Mawer(4)285
   tə:westən   Mawer(4)285
Tushingham Hall, T.Ho/Chs
   tuʃiŋəm   PNChs IV/47
Tutbury/St
   tʌtbəri   Schr.,Chis.
   tidbəri   Ellis 482
Tuxford/Nt
   tʌksfəd   BBC
Tweed/Nb (r.n.)
   twi:d   RN 421,EPD,BBC,Schr.
Tweedmouth/Nb
   twed-   PNNbDu 2o2,DEPN
   -mauþ   Bchm.77
   twedmaþ   HL 733
   twi:dməþ, -mauþ   EPD
Twickenham/Mx
   twiknəm   PNMx 29,EPD,Schr.
   olim twitnəm   PNMx 29,Hope,
                Schr.("loc.")
   twikinəm   Schr.
   twikənəm   Kruis.,Chis.
Twinaways/Co
   twi:nəweiz   Picken 195
Twineham/Sx
   twainəm   BBC,BCE
Twinhoe/So
   twinou   BBC,BCE

Twisley/Sx
  twiz'lai   BBC
Twitham/K
  twitəm   PNK
Twizell/Nb
  twaizl   BBC
  twaizəl   BCE
Twyford
  twaifəd   EPD,Chis.
Twyning/Gl
  twiniŋ   PNGl II/71
  -ai-   DEPN
Twyssenden/K
  twisenden   PNK
Tyberton/He
  tibət(ə)n   BBC
  tibətən   BCE
Tyburn/Mx
  taibə:n   EPD,Kruis.
  taibən   BBC,Schr.,Bau.
  -ai-   DEPN
Tyburnia/Ldn
  tai'bə:nəɑ: Bau.
Tydd Gout/Ca (or T. Gote)
  tid gout   Hope
  tid   BBC
Tyldesley/La
  tildzli   DEPN,EPD,BBC,BCE,
             Schr.
  tilzli   BBC,BCE,Schr.
  tinzli   PNLa(ii),PNLa(i)116f.
             ("a common dialect
              pron.")
  The place is also called Tinsley
  Bongs; cf.Hope,Rose,Parkinson
Tyler (as in T.'s Gn/Ess)
  tailə   EPD
Tylney Hall/Ha
  tilni   BBC
Tymparon Hall/Cu
  timpərən   PNCu 188
Tyndall (as in T.'s Pk in Bristol)
  tindl   EPD
Tyne/Du,Nb (r.n.)
  tain   EPD,BBC,Schr.,Kruis.,
          HL 733
Tyne Hall/Wt
  tain hɔ:l   PNWt 285
Tyneham/Do
  tainəm   PNDo I/1o1,PNDo(i)136
Tynemouth/Nb
  tinməþ   PNNbDu 2o2,EPD[1]("old-
            fashioned"),BBC,BCE,
            Schr.,Kruis.,Chis.,HL
            733,MEG 123,Bchm.35

  tainməþ,   EPD,Schr.,Kruis.,Chis.,
              BCE,HL 733,MEG 123
  tainmauþ   EPD,BBC,Bchm.35
  tinmauþ   Mawer(4)284
  tin-   DEPN
Tyntesfield/So
  tintsfi:ld   BBC
Tyringham/Bk
  tiriŋəm   PNBk 14,DEPN
Tyrrell (as in T.'s End/Bd)
  tir(ə)l   EPD
Tyseley/Wo
  taizli   PNWo 234,BBC
Tysoe/Wa
  taisou   BBC
Tythby/Nt
  tiðbi   PNNt(i)144,DEPN
Tytherington/Chs
  olim tiþitn, now triðrin-,
  tiðriŋtən   PNChs II/vii
  tiðitn   GlossChs
Tyttenhanger Pk, T.Grn/Hrt
  olim titnæŋə,
  tinæŋə   PNHrt 85
Tytup Hall/La
  taitəp   PNLa 2o7
Tywardreath/Co
  taiwə'dreþ   BBC,BCE
  -'eþ   DEPN,Jenner(2)3o4 (stress
                            only)

1) "Both pronunciations [viz. tinməþ and tainmauþ] are heard
   locally" (EPD-4); "The pron. [tinməþ] is now nearly obsolete"
   (EPD-13).

U

Ubley/So (also spelt Obleigh)
Λbli   BBC
Uckfield/Sx
Λkfl , ukfəl   PNSx 396
Λkfi:ld   EPD
Uckinghall/Wp
Λkindʒəl   PNWo 16o
Λkindʒel   Dodgson(2)388
Udiam/Sx
Λdʒəm   PNSx 52o
Udimore/Sx
Λdimər   PNSx 516
Λdimə   Hope
'ju:dimɔ:, 'Λdimɔ: BBC,BCE
Λ-   DEPN
Uffculme/D
Λfkəm   PND 537,BBC
Uffington/Brk,Li,Sa
Λfiŋtən   Chis.
Ufford/Sf
Λfəd   PNDVall 77
Ufton/Brk,K,Wa
Λftən   Schr.
Ugglebarnby/NRY
ugəlbɑ:nbi   PNYN 121
'Λgl'bɑ:nbi   BBC
Ugley/Ess (also spelt Oakley)
Λgli   BBC
Ugthorpe/NRY
'ugþrəp   PNYN 138
Λgþɔ:p   BBC
Ulcat Row/Cu
ulkit   PNCu 257
ulkitə   PNE'side 62
Ulceby/Li
u:sbi   BBC,BCE,Hope
Λlsbi   BBC,BCE
Ulcombe/K
ju:kəm   Hope
Λkəm, ulkəm   PNK
Λlkəm   BBC
Uldale/Cu
uldəl   PNCu 327
Uley/Gl
ju:li   PNGl II/253,BBC
jiuli   PNGl II/253
Ulgham/Li,Nb
ufəm   PNNbDu 2o3
Λfəm   EPD,BBC,BCE (for U. in
        Nb),DEPN (for U. in Nb),
        Hope (for U. in Nb),BG
        (for U. in Nb) (but see
        note 1 below)
Ulleskelf/WRY
uskəl, 'ul(ə)skelf   PNYW IV/67
ulskeld   Hope

Ullesthorpe/Le
Λlisþɔ:p   BBC
Ullingswick/He
Λliŋzwik, dial. Λlinzwik   DHe 44
Ullswater/Cu and We
Λlzwɔ:tə   EPD,BBC,Chis.
Λlzwɔtə   Schr.
hulzwatər   PNE'side 74
Ulpha/Cu
u:lfə   PNCu 437
u:fə   PNCu 437,GlossCu xviii
Ulpha/We
ouvə   PNWe I/76
Ulrome/ERY
u:ərəm   PNYE 84,GlossHol 17,
         PNERY
ulrəm   PNYE 84
u:rəm   Hope ('Ooram')
Ulshaw Bridge/NRY
ulʃə , ousə   PNYN 249
Ulverston/La (also spelt -stone)
u:stən   PNLa(ii),PNE&W,Hope,BG,
         GlossCu xviii,GlossFu 3,
         s.n. An',
u:stn   DEPN
oustən   PNE'side 66
Λlvəstən   EPD,BBC,Chis.
Umberleigh/D
Λmbəli   BBC
Underhill/Wo
Λndəhil   EPD
Underwood/WRY
'undəwud   DDd 15
Unstone/Db
unstən   PNDb 319
Λnstn   PNDb(i) II/188
Λnstən   BBC
Unsworth/La
A jocular name for this village is
'Gawbyshire' (cf.DSLa,s.n. G.)
Uny/Co
ju:-   Jenner(2)3o2
Uny Lelant/Co ⟶ Lelant
Upavon/W
'Λpeiv(ə)n   BBC
hɔpebm   DPew 97
Upcott/D,He
-kət,-kɔt   EPD, Bchm.64
Up Exe/D
Λbəks   PND 445
'Λpeks   BBC,BCE
Uphall/Do,Nf
Λp'hɔ:l   BBC
Upham/Ha
Λpəm   EPD,Schr.,Kruis.
Uphampton/Wo
Λpətən, Λpən   PNWo 272

1) The transcriptions given in Hope ('Uffum') and BG ('Uffham')
could also represent [ufəm].

Uplowman/D
  ʌp'loumən   BBC,BCE
Upminster/Ess
  'ʌpminstə   EPD
Up Ottery/D
  ʌp'ɔtəri   BBC,BCE
Uppark/Sx
  'ʌp-pɑːk   BBC
Upper Hide/Wt
  ʌpər haid   PNWt 56
Upperthong/WRY
  uvərþɔŋ   DHd 129
Uppingham/Ru
  ʌpiŋəm   EPD
Upton
  ʌptən   EPD,Schr.,Chis.
Upton Helions/D
  ʌptən 'heliənz   BBC
Upton Lovell/W
  lʌvəl   PNW 171
Upton Snodsbury/Wo
  snɔdʒbəri   PNWo 23o
  ʌptən snædʒbəri   GlossSEWo 82
Upwaltham/Sx
  ʌpwɔltəm   PNSx(i)162
Upwey/Do
  'ʌpwei   EPD,BBC
Urchfont/W (also spelt Erch-)
  ʌʃənt, ərʃənt   PNW 315
  əːtʃfɔnt   BBC
Ure/NRY,WRY (r.n.)
  (j)iuə   PNYW VII/141
  juə   EPD,BBC
  juːə   Schr.,Kruis.
  jiuə   Smith(1)292
Urmston/La
  əːmstən   BBC
Urswick/La
  ɔːsik   PNLa(ii)
  əːzwik, əːzik   BBC,BCE
Ushaw/Du
  ʌʃə, ʌʃɔː   BBC,BCE
Usselby/Li
  ʌslbi   BBC
Ustick/Co (also spelt Ewstick)
  juː-   Jenner(2)3o2
Uswayford/Nb
  'ʌzweifɔːd   BBC
Usworth/Du
  ʌzwəːþ   BBC
Utkinton/Chs
  utkintən   PNChs III/298
  older local
  utkitn   PNChs III/298,GlossChs

Uttoxeter/St
  ʌksitə   EPD,BBC,BCE,Schr.,Kruis.
       Hope
  ʌksətə   PNE&W
  ʌksetə   DEPN
  ʌkstə   Schr.,BCE,Hope
  ʌstə   Bchm.86
  ʌtʃətə   Hope,Zachr.(3)128
  ʌtʃitə   BCE,Schr.
  ʌtʃetə   DEPN,Bchm.86
  ʌt'ɔksitə   EPD,BBC,BCE,Schr.,
       Kruis.
  ʌ'tɔksətə   Chis.
  'tʌksitə   Schr.,Hope
  juː'tɔksitə   EPD,BBC,BCE
  (see also note 1 below)
Uxbridge/Mx
  ʌksbridʒ   EPD,BBC,Schr.,Chis.
Uxbridge Rd/Ldn
  _ _ ́   MEG 157

1) "There are other less common variants" (BBC); " [ʌksitə] is the pron
used by those connected with Denstone College and by members of
county families in the neighbourhood. The common pron. in the town
is [juː'tɔksitə] or [ʌ'tɔksitə]. The former is more frequent, and i
the pron. of most outsiders " (EPD).

V

The Vache/Bk
  ðə vætʃ   BBC
Valangates/Ess (f.n.)
  vɔləngəts   EssDD 159
Vale/St
  veil   EPD,Schr.
Vange/Ess
  vændʒ   PNEss 174,EPD
  olim vɑːndʒ   PNEss 174
Varley (as in V.Point/Co)
  vɑːli   EPD
Vasterne/W
  væstə(r)n   PNW(i)167
Vatche's Fm/Bk
  vetʃiz, viːtʃiz,
  fiːtʃiz   PNBk 145
Vauxhall
  'vɔks(h)ɔːl   PNSr 24,EPD,BBC
  ′ ′, _ ′   EPD
  vɔkshɔːl   Schr.(for V.in Sr)
             Kruis.
  vɔːks'hɔːl   Chis.
  vɔksɔːl   Hope (for V. in Sr)
  vɔzɔːl   Schr. (for V. in Sr)
  vɔ-   DEPN (for V. in Sr)
Vayres/Wt
  vɛərz   PNWt 110
Venn/Co,D
  ven   EPD,Kruis.
Venners/Wt
  venərz   PNWt 24
Venniscombe Ho/Wt
  veniskəm   PNWt 172
Ventnor/Wt
  ven(t)nər   PNWt 231
  ventnə   EPD,Schr.,Kruis.,Chis.,
           Bchm.27o
  ventnɔː   Schr.,Bchm.27o
Ver/Hrt (r.n.)
  vəː   BBC
Verney (as in V. Junction)
  vəːni   EPD,Kruis.
  vɑːni   Kruis.
Vernon (as in V.Pk/Wo)
  vəːnən   EPD,Kruis.
Verulam/Hrt
  veruləm   EPD,Schr.,Kruis.
Verulamium/Hrt
  veruleimiəm   BBC,EPD
  veruleimjən   EPD
Verwood/Do
  vəːwud, vəːrud   PNDo(i)1o7
Veryan/Co
  veriən   BBC,BCE
Vesses/Wt
  visiz, vesiz   PNWt 24
Via Gellia/Db
  vaiə dʒeliə   BBC

Vic, short for ⟶ Victoria Theatre
Victoria/Ldn
  viktɔːiə   CPP 66
Victoria Pk/Ldn
  viktɔːriə pɑːk   CPhon 164
Victoria Station/Ldn
  short: Victoria, Vic   Bau.
Victoria Theatre/Ldn
  short: Vic   Bau.,s.n. Vic.
Victoria Tower/Ldn
  viktɔːrəɑː tauə   Bau.
Vigo Inn/K
  vaigou   BBC
Vigo Street/Ldn
  vaigou   EPD
The Villa/ERY
  vilə   EPD
Vincent/K
  vins(ə)nt   EPD
Viney Hill/Gl
  vaini hil   EPD,BBC
Virginia Rd/Ldn
  və'dʒiniə roud   CPhon 52
Virginia Water/Sr
  və'dʒiniə wɔːtə   BBC
Vittlefield Fm/Wt
  vitlvild   PNWt 86
Vogue Beloth/Co
  voug bi'lɔþ   BBC
Vulcan/La
  vʌlkən   EPD
Vyrnwy/Sa (r.n.)
  vəːnui   BBC

W

Waberthwaite/Cu
 wɔ:bərþwət   PNCu 439
Wackland/Wt
 wæ:klən(dz)   PNWt 172
Wacton/He,Nf
 wæktən   BBC
 woutən   Hope (for W. in Nf)
Waddesdon/Bk
 wɔdzdən   PNBk 137,BBC
Waddington/Li,WRY
 wɔdiņtən   EPD
Waddlestone/D
 wɑ:sən   PNCu III/lxix
Waddon
 wɔd(ə)n   BBC
Wadebridge/Co
 weidbridʒ   BBC
Wad(e)ford/So
 wɔdfəd   BBC,BCE
Wadenhoe/Np
 wɔdnou   DEPN,PNNp 222
Wadham College/O
 wɔdəm   EPD,BBC,Schr.
Wadhurst/Sx
 wɔd(h)əst   MEG 377
 wɔdhə:st   EPD
Wadsworth/WRY
 wɔdzwə:þ   EPD,Kruis.,Förster
Waghen/ERY ⟶ Wawne
Waightshale/Wt
 weits hil   DWt,s.n. rig out
Wainfleet/Li
 weinfli:t   BBC
Waitby/We
 we:tbi   PNWe II/24
Waitham Hill/La
 we:ðəm   PNLa 222
Wakefield/WRY
 weikfi:ld   EPD,Schr.,Chis.
Wakering/Ess
 weikəriŋ   BBC
Wakerley/Np
 weikəli   PNNp 172,DEPN
Wakes Colne/Ess
 weiks koun   BBC,BCE
 (see also s.n. Colne)
Walaway/Cu
 waləwə   PNE'side 75
Walberswick/Sf
 wɔlzəwig   DSf 311
 wɔ:lbəzwik   BBC,BCE
Walberton/Sx
 wɔ:bətən   PNSx 143,Hope
 wɔ:bətn   PNSx(i)164
 -ɔ:b-   DEPN
Walburn/NRY
 wɔ:bən   PNYN 27o

Walby/Cu
 wɔ:bi   PNCu 76
Walcot (no reference to a particu-
 wɔ:lkət,   lar county)
 loc. wɔ:kət, wɔ:kwud   Schr.
Walcot/Li
 wɔ:kət, wɔ:kwud   Hope
Walcote/Le
 wɔ:lkout   BBC
Walcott/Nf
 wɔ(:)lkət, -kɔt   EPD
Walden
 wɔ:ldən, wɔldən   Schr.
 -d(ə)n   EPD
Walden/NRY
 wɔ:dən   PNYN 265
Waldon/D (r.n.)
 wɔ:ldən   MEG 265
Waldringfield/Sf
 loc. wʌnəfəl   PNE&W
 wɔnəfəl   PNDVall 16
Waldron/Sx
 wɔ:ldən   PNSx 4o5
 wɔ:(l)drən   PNSx(i) 165
Walesby/Li,Nt
 weilzbi   BBC
Walford
 wɔ(:)lfəd   EPD
Walgherton/Chs
 wɔldʒərtən,
 older wɔ:kər-   PNChs III/73
Walham Gn/Mx
 wɔləm   PNMx 1o3,PNMx(i),EPD
Walham/Nt
 wɔləm   EPD
Walhampton/Ha
 'wɔ:l'hæm(p)tən   BBC
Walkden/La
 wɔgdən   PNLa(ii),Guardian 1/1/79
             letters, p.8 (N.Ratcliff
             of Buxton)
 wɔ:kdən   BBC
Walker (as in W.'s Gn/He)
 wɔ:kə   EPD
Walkeringham/Nt
 wɔ:kriŋəm   PNNt 41
Walkern/Hrt
 wɑ:kən, wɔ:kən   PNHrt 141
 wɔ:lkə:n, -kən   EPD
Walkham/D (r.n.)
 wɔ:lkəm   BBC
Walkhampton/D
 wækiņtən   PND 243,Hope ('Waking-
                                ton')
 wækətən   PND 243
Walkington/ERY
 wɔ:kitən   PNYE 2o3
Walkley/WRY
 wɔ:kli   BBC

Wall
  wɔ:l EPD
Wallace (as in W.Village/Du)
  wɔlis, -ləs EPD
Wallange Bridge/ W. Fm/Chs
  wɔləndʒ PNChs II/212
Wallasey/Chs
  wɔləsi PNChs IV/332,EPD,BBC
Wallerscote/Chs
  'wɔləskout PNChs III/2ol
Wallingford/Brk
  wɔliŋfəd EPD,Chis.
  wɔliŋfɔ:d Schr.
  wɔ- DEPN
Wallington
  wɔliŋtən BBC,BCE (for W. in Nb)
Wallis (as in W.Down/Ha)
  wɔlis EPD
Wallop/Ha
  wɔləp BBC,Kruis.
Wallow (as in W. Crag/Cu)
  walə PNE'side 64
Wallsend/Nb
  'wɔ:lz'end BBC,BCE
  ⸍ _ EPD,Schr.
  _ ⸍ Chis.
Wallthwaite/Cu (or Wal-)
  walhwɛ:t PNCu 222,PNE'side 7o
Walmer/K
  wɔ:lmə EPD,BBC,Schr.533, PNK,HL 1221,Chis.
  wɔlmə EPD,HL 1221
Walmersley/La
  wɔ:mzli BBC
Walmestone/K
  wɔ:mstən PNK
Walmire/NRY
  wɔ:ma PNYN 283
Walmsley/La
  wɔ:mzli EPD
Walney/La (an island)
  wɔlni EPD
  wɔ:lni EPD,Schr.,Chis.
  wɑ:ni PNLa(ii)
Walpen Fm/Wt
  wɔ:pn PNWt 117
Walpole/Nf,Sf
  wɔ(:)pl DSf 311
  wɔ:lpoul EPD,Kruis.,HL 278, HSM 45
  wɔlpoul EPD,Kruis.
Walreddon/D
  wɔ:ldərn PND 248
Walsall/St
  -s- DEPN
  wɔ:lsɔ:l EPD,BBC,Chis.
  wɔl-, -sl EPD

  wɔ:lsəl Schr.
  wɔ:lsl BBC
  wɔ:sl BBC,Schr.("vulgar"), Ellis 484
  wɔ:sə, wɔsəl Hope
  wɔlsəl BCE
Walsden/WRY
  wɔ:lzdən BBC
Walsham/Nf,Sf
  wɔ:lʃəm EPD,BBC,BCE,HL 122o, Kruis.,MEG 377
  loc. wɔ:lsəm EPD,HL 122o
  wɔlʃəm Schr.
Walsingham/Nf
  wɔ:lziŋəm EPD,BBC
  wɔlziŋəm EPD
  wɔ:lsiŋəm EPD,Schr.
  wɔlsiŋəm EPD,Schr.,Kruis.
  -s- DEPN
  -iŋəm, -inəm PNing 172
Walsoken/Nf
  wɔ:lsoukən BBC
Walsworth/Hrt
  olim wɔ:lsə: PNHrt lo
Waltham
  wɔ:lðəm Potter 35
  wɔlþəm EPD,Chis.
  wɔ:lþəm EPD
  wɔ:ltəm EPD,Schr.
  wɔltəm EPD,Schr.,Kruis.
Waltham (White W.)/Brk
  (h)wait wɔ:ltəm BBC
Waltham (Gt W.,Little W.)/Ess
  wɔ:ltəm BBC

Note.—The traditional local pronunciation at Great Waltham and Little Waltham in Essex is 'wɔ:ltəm, and this is the pronunciation used by those who have lived there for a long time. Some new residents pronounce -lθəm. In telephoning to these places from a distance it is advisable to pronounce -lθəm; otherwise the caller is liable to be given Walton(-on-the-Naze), which is in the same county. (EPD)

Waltham/Ha (Bishop's W. and North W.)
  biʃəps wɔ:lþəm, - wɔ:ltəm BBC,BCE
  wɔ:lþəm BBC (for North W.)
Waltham/K
  wæltəm PNK
Waltham/Le
  wɔ:ltəm BCE
Waltham/Li
  wɔ:lþəm BBC,BCE
Waltham (Up W.)/Sx
  wɔ:ltəm PNSx 77
Waltham Abbey/Ess
  wɔ:ltəm PNEss 27,BCE,Hope,Schr.
  wɔ:lþəm BBC,BCE

Waltham Cross/Hrt
  wɔːlþəm krɔs BBC,BCE
  wɔːltəm BCE
Waltham-on-the-Wolds/Le
  wɔːlþəm ɔn ðə wouldz BBC
Waltham St. Lawrence/Brk
  wɔːlþəm snt lɔrəns BBC
Walthamstow/Ess
  wɔːtəmstou PNEss loʒ,
             Mawer(2)93
  wɔːlþəmstou BBC,Mawer(2)93,
             BCE,EPD
  wɔlþəmstou EPD,Chis.
  wɔːltəmstou Schr.,EPD ("old-
             fashioned")
  wɔltəmstou Schr.,Kruis.,EPD
             ("old-fashioned")
Walthwaite/Cu ⟶ Wall-
Walton
  wɔːlt(ə)n, wɔlt(ə)n EPD
  wɔːltən Schr.,Chis.
  wɔːltn Kruis.
Walton/Sf
  wɔltn PNDVall 42
Walton/Wo
  loc. wɔːtən Amph.164
Walwick/Nb
  wɔlik PNNbDu 2o5,DEPN,BBC,
         BCE
  wɔːlwik BBC,BCE
Walworth/Du,Ldn
  wɔːlwəþ Chis.
  wɔ(ː)lwə(ː)þ EPD
Wamil Hall/Sf
  wɔmil BBC
Wanborough/Sr,W
  wɔnbərə PNSr 151,PNW(i)167
Wandle/Sr (r.n.)
  wɔndl EPD
Wandon End, Wandongreen/Hrt
  wɔndən PNHrt 24
Wandsworth/Sr
  wɔndzwəþ BBC
  wɔːndzwəþ Chis.
  wɔn(d)zwəþ EPD,Schr.,Bchm.14o
     -wəːþ EPD,Bchm.14o
     -w- MEG 213
  wɔnswəːþ Hope
Wan Fell/Cu
  wɑːnfl PNE'side 75
Wangford/Sf
  wænfə Hope
Wanlip/Le
  wɔnlip BBC
Wannock/Sx
  wɔnək PNSx 165
Wansbeck/Nb (r.n.)
  wɔnzbek BBC,Schr.

Wansdyke/W
  wɔnzdaik PNW 17,PNW(i)168
Wansford/Np,ERY
  wɔnzfəd BBC
  wɔnzfəd, wanzwəþ PNYE 95
  wɔnzfþ Hope (for W. in ERY)
Wanstead/Ess
  wɔnsted EPD,Schr.,Hope,Bchm.62
    -stid EPD,Bchm.62
Wantage/Brk
  wɔntidʒ EPD,BBC,Schr.,Kruis.,
             Chis.
  wɔnteidʒ Chis.
Wanthwaite/Cu
  wanþət PNCu 315,PNE'side 66
Wantisden/Sf
  wɔntsdən BBC
Wantsley Fm/Do
  wɔnsli PNDo(i)268
Wantsum Channel/K
  wænsəm PNK
Wapley Ho/NRY
  wɔːplə uːs PNYN 141
Wappenham/Np
  wɔpnəm PNNp 62
Wapping/Ldn,Wa,WRY
  wɔpiŋ EPD,BBC,Schr.(for W. in
        Ldn),Bau.(for W. in Ldn)
Wapsbourne Fm/Sx
  vulgo wɔpsiz buːən PNSx 298
Warbrightsleigh Barton/D
  warpsle, wasple PND 394
Warbstow/Co
  wɔːbstou BBC
Warburton/Chs,WRY
  wɑːrbərtən PNChs II/34
  wɔːrbətn PNChs II/ix,GlossChs
  wɔːbətən Schr.,Kruis.
  wɔːbətn, wɔːbəːtn EPD,Bchm.67
Warcop/We
  wɑːkəp PNWe II/82
  wɔːkəp BBC
Ward (as in W.Gn/Sf)
  wɔːd EPD
Warden/Bd,K,Nb
  wɔːdn EPD
Ward Hall/Cu
  wɔːdəl PNCu 3lo
Wardle/Chs,La
  wɔːrdl PNChs III/322
  wɔːdl EPD,Kruis.
  wɑːdl, wɔːdl PNLa 57
  wəːdl PNLa(ii)
Wardle Rigg/NRY
  wɔːdəlrig PNYN 88
Wardour/W
  wɔːrdər PNW 197
  wɔːdə Kruis.,EPD

Ware/Hrt,K
  wɛə   EPD,Schr.,Kruis.
Wareham/Do
  wɛ:rəm   PNDo(i)145
  wɔrəm   PNDo I/152
  wɛərəm   PNDo I/152,EPD,Schr.
Waren Burn/Nb → Warren B.
Warenford/Nb
  wɛərənfɔ:d   BBC
Waren Mills/Nb
  wɛərən milz   BBC
Warenton/Nb
  wɑ:ntən   PNNbDu 2o7
  wɛərəntən   BBC
Waresley/Hu
  weizli   PNBdHu 273
Wargrave/Brk,La
  wɔ:greiv   EPD,Schr.
Warham/He,Nf
  wɔ:rəm   EPD
Warhill/Chs
  loc. wɔrl   PNChs I/xxii
Wark-on-Tweed/Nb
  wɑ:k   PNNbDu 2o7
  wɔ:k   BBC
Wark-on-Tyne/Nb
  wɔ:k   BBC,BCE
Warkleigh/D
  wɔ:kli   BBC,BCE
Warkton/Np
  wɔ:ktən   PNNp 188
Warkworth/Np,Nb
  wɔ:kwəþ   BBC,Schr.,Chis.,
             PNNbDu 2o7
Warlaby/NRY
  wɔ:ləbi   PNYN 276
Warleggan/Co
  wɔ:'legən   BBC,BCE,DEPN
             (stress only)
Warley/Ess
  wɔ:li   PNEss 133
Warley/WRY
  wɛəli   Hope
Warmingham/Chs
  -iŋəm, older local
  -intʃəm   PNChs III/262
Warminghurst/Sx
  wɔ(:)miŋ(h)əst   PNSx(i)167
Warmington/Np,Wa
  wɔ:miŋtən   EPD
Warminster/W
  wɔ:minstə   EPD,Chis.
Warmsworth/WRY
  wɔ:nsəþ   Hope
  wɔ:mzwə:þ   BBC
Warmwell/Do
  wɔ:məl   PNDo I/17o,
             PNDo(i)147
  wɔ:mwel   BBC

Warnham/Sx
  wɔnəm   PNSx(i)167
Warninglid/Sx
  wɔ:niŋlid   PNSx(i)168
Warningore Fm/Sx
  wɔrin'gɔ:r   PNSx 298
Warren
  wɔrin   Schr.,EPD
  wɔrən   Schr.,Kruis.
  wɔr(ə)n   EPD
Warren Burn/Nb
  wɛ:rən   PNNbDu 2o7
Warrington/Chs,La
  warintən   GlossChs,DSChs 19
  weritn   GlossChs ("by a few old
             people, but nearly ob-
             solete")
  wɑ:ritən   DSLa
  wɔriŋtən   EPD,Schr.,Chis.
Warsash/Ha
  'wɔ:sæʃ, wɔ:zæʃ   BBC,BCE
Warsick Close/Db (f.n.)
  wɔ:sitʃ   FnSDb 76
Warsop/Nt
  wɑ:səp   PNNt 1ol
  wɔ:səp   EPD
Warter/ERY
  wɑ:þə   PNYE 168
  weiþr   Hope
Warthermarske/NRY
  wɑ:ðəmask   PNYN 235
Warthill/NRY
  wɑ:til   PNYN 11,Ekwall 1o2
Warthole/Cu
  wɔrdl   PNCuWe 121
  wɔ:dəl   GlossCu xviii
Wartling/Sx
  wɔ:tliŋ   BBC,PNSx(i)169
Warton
  wɑ:tn   PNLa(ii)
  wɔ:t n   PNWa(i)117,Schr.
  wɔ:tn   EPD
Warwick/Cu,Wa
  warik   PNE'side 75,PNCu 157
  wɔrik   DEPN (for W. in Wa),Hope
             (for W. in Wa),EPD,BBC,
             Schr.,Kruis.,MEG 213,ESpr.
             394,ONwick 381
  wɔ:rik   Chis.
Warwickshire
  wɔrikʃə   EPD,Schr.
  -ʃiə   EPD
Wasdale/Cu,We
  wɔsəl, occasionally
  wɔʃdəl   PNCu 39o
  wɔsdl   BBC
  wazdəl   PNWe II/172
Wasdale Head/Cu (also spelt Wastdale)
  wɔsdl hed   BBC

The Wash/Li and Nf
 ðə wɔʃ EPD,Schr.
Washburn/WRY (r.n.)
 wɔʃbən Schr.
Washford/D,So
 wɔʃfəd Schr.
Washington/Du,Sx
 wɔʃiŋtən PNSx(i)169,EPD,Schr.
 -tn Kruis.
Wass/NRY
 wæs PNYN 195
Wassell Wood/Wo
 wæsl EPD
Wast Hills/Wo
 wɑːstəl PNWo 335
Wastwater/Cu (a lake)
 'wɔstwɔːtə EPD,BBC
Watchingwell/Wt
 wɔtʃnwel PNWt 87
Watendlath/Cu
 wɔ'tendləþ BBC
Waterbeach/Ca
 wɔtəbiːtʃ ONCa 191
Waterden/Nf
 wɔːtədən BBC
Waterford/Ha,Hrt
 wɔːtəfɔːd Schr.
Watergate/Co,Sx,WRY
 wɔːtəgeit EPD
Watergate Fm/Wt
 wɔːdərgɛət PNWt 286
Waterhead
 wɔːtəhed Chis.
Waterhouse/Ess,La
 wɔːtəhaus EPD
Waterloo
 'wɔːtə 'luː EPD,BBC,Schr.
 _ _ ´ , ´ _ _ EPD,Kruis.
Waterloo Rd/Ldn
 ´ _ _ _ EPD
Waterloo/Do
 wadərlu DDo
Water Millock/Cu
 watər milik PNE'side 7o
Waterrow/So
 wɔːtərou BBC
Watershoot Bay/Wt
 wɔːtərʃɔt bei PNWt 184
Waterton/Gl
 wɔːtətən Schr.
Watervale/D
 -vɑːl PND 216
Water Yeat/La
 wɔːtəjet PNLa 215
Watford/Db,Hrt,Np
 wɔtfəd EPD,BBC
Wath/Cu,ERY,WRY,NRY
 wɔþ BBC

wæþ DEPN (for W.in NRY),PNYN 52
 (for W.in Ryedale Wapentake
waþ PNYN 219 (for W.in Halikeld
Wathall Fm/Chs Wapentake
 watɔːl PNChs II/lo2
Wath Cote/NRY
 waþkoːt PNYN 287
Wath-upon-Dearne/WRY
 wɔþ , wæþ əpɔn dəːn BBC
 - , - ɔn - BCE
Watling Street
 wɔtliŋ striːt EPD,BBC,Schr.
Watnall/Nt
 vulgo wɔtnəː PNNt 146
 wɔtnə PNNt(i)146 [sic]
Wattisfield/Sf
 wɔtisfiːld BBC
Wattisham/Sf
 wɔtiʃəm BBC
Watton
 wɔt(ə)n BBC
 wɔtn EPD,Förster (for W. in
 Hrt)
Watton/ERY
 watən, waʔn PNYE 158
 wɔtn Förster

Wauldby/ERY
 wɔːdbi PNYE 221
Wavendon/Bk
 wɔndən PNBk 39
 wɔːndən, wɑːndən PNBk 39,Hope
 wɔndn DEPN
 wæv(ə)ndən BBC
Waveney/Nf,Sf (r.n.)
 weiv(ə)ni BBC
 weivni Schr.
Waverley/Sr
 weivəli EPD,BBC,Schr.,Kruis.,
 Förster
Waverton/Chs
 weivərtən PNChs IV/lo3,Brushf.
 wɑːrtən PNChs IV/lo3 ("older
 local"),GlossChs
 wɔːtən Brushf.67
Waverton/Cu
 wɑːrtən PNCu 159
 wɔːtən, wɛətən GlossCu xviii
Waverton/Wa ⟶ Warton
Wavertree/La
 wɔːtriː PNE&W,PNSt 16o,Hope,
 Brushf.67,H.A.(2)45
 wɔːtri PNLa(ii)
 weivətriː BBC,Chis.,Brushf.67
 weivətri PNLa(ii)
Wawne/ERY (also spelt Waghen)
 wɔːn PNYE 44,GlossHol 17,BBC,BC
 Hope

Waybutt Lane/Chs
    weibət   PNChs III/59
Wayland Wood/Nf
    weilənd   EPD
Waytes Court/Wt
    wɛːts kuərt   PNWt 285
Weacombe/So
    wiːkəm   BBC,BCE
Weald
    wiːld   EPD
Weald/Bk
    wiːl   PNBk 18
The Weald/Sx,K
    wiːld   PNSx 2,Schr.,Chis.,DK
    wild   PNSx 2
    "The Weald of Sussex is always
    spoken of as The Wild by people
    who live in the Downs"   DSx
Wealdstone/Mx
    wiːldstoun   BBC
Wear/Du (r.n.)
    wiːə   RN 441,Kruis.,Förster
    wiə   DEPN,EPD,BBC
    wiːr   Chis.,Schr.
Weardale/Du
    wiədeil   BBC
    wɑːdl   Ellis 634
Wearde/Co
    wɛəd   BBC
Weardley/WRY
    wiədlə   PNYW IV/185
Weards Cottage/Wt
    wiərd   PNWt 184
Weare Gifford/D
    wiə dʒifəd   PND 111,DEPN,BBC,
                   BCE
Wearmouth/Du
    wiəməþ   EPD,Kruis.
    -mauþ   EPD
    wiːrməþ, -mauþ   Schr.
    (see also s.n. Bishop W. and
    Monk W.)
Wearne/So
    wɛən, wiən, wəːn   BBC,BCE
Weasenham/Nf
    wiːz(ə)nəm   BBC
Weaste/La
    wiːst   BBC
Weatherriggs/We
    wedəriks   PNE'side 69
Weaver/Chs (r.n. and p.n.)
    wiːvə   Schr. (for the r.n.),
    wiːvər   PNChs III/163 (for the
            p.n.)
Weaverham/Chs
    wiːvərəm   PNChs III/2o5,
                 GlossChs
    loc. wɛːrəm,
    wɔːrəm   PNChs III/2o5
    wɛərəm   GlossChs,Hope
    wiːvəhæm   BBC

Weaverthorpe/ERY
    wiːəþrəp   PNYE 122,PNERY,Goodall
                 51,Hope
Wedhampton/W
    wediŋtən   PNW 316
    wed'hæmptən   cf. PNW(i)169
Wedholme Flow/Cu
    wedəm flau   PNCu 3o8
Wedmore/So
    wedmɔː   Schr.
Wednesbury/St
    wedʒbəri   BBC,BCE,Schr.,Hope,
                 Zachr.(3)132,Ellis 484
    wedʒbri   DEPN,HL 811
    loc. wedʒb(ə)ri, wenzb(ə)ri   EPD
    wenzbəri   BBC,BCE,Chis.,HL 811,
                 Zachr.(3)132,Ellis 484
    wenzbri   DEPN,Schr.,Hope
    wednzbəri   Schr.
Wednesfield/St
    wedʒfiːld   DEPN,BBC,BCE,Schr.,
               Hope,HL 811
    wensfiːld   DEPN,BBC,BCE
    wenzfiːld   Schr.
Wedneshough Green/Chs
    wensuf   PNChs I/3o9
Weedon/Bk,Np
    wiːdən   Schr.,Chis.
    wiːdn   EPD
Weedon Lois/Np
    wiːdən lɔi, lɔi wiːdən   PNNp 45
Week Fm/Wt
    wiːk   PNWt 162
Weekley/Np
    wiːkli   EPD,Schr.
Weeks/Wt
    wiːks   EPD
Weighton/ERY
    wiːtn   EPD,Kruis.
    (see also s.n. Little W. and
    Market W.; Market W. is also
    called W. Market)
    weitən mɑːkət   Chis.
Weir
    wiə   EPD
    wiːə   Kruis.
The Weir/W
    wair   PNW 297
Welbeck/Nt,WRY
    welbek   EPD
Welby/Le,Li
    welbi   Schr.
Welch (as in W.Whittle/La)
    welʃ   EPD
Welcombe/D,Wa
    welkəm   EPD
Weldon/Nb,Np
    weld(ə)n   EPD
Welford/Brk,Np,Wa
    welfəd   EPD

Welholme/Cu
    wedəm [sic] GlossCu xvii (a
        misprint for [weləm] ?)
Welland/Wo; r.n. in Np
    welənd   EPD,Schr.,Chis.
Wellesbourne/Wa
    welzbɔːn   BBC
Wellesley/So
    welzli   EPD,Kruis.
Well Head/WRY
    wel ied   DDd 13
Wellingborough/Np
    weliŋbərə   BBC,Schr.,Chis.
    -b(ə)rə   EPD
Wellington
    weliŋtən   EPD,BBC,Schr.,Chis.
    weliŋtn   Kruis.
    welintən   DSChs 19,Horn(Bei-
        träge)32,GlossSa
        xxxvii
    welitən   PNSa,Ellis 483 (for
        W. in Sa)
    welitn   EDG §273,GlossSa
        xxxvii,Horn(Beiträge)
        32
    wʌlitn   DWSo 11
Wellow/Wt
    welə   PNWt 213
    welou   PNWt 213,DWt,s.n.
        withybed
Wells/Nf,So
    welz   EPD,Schr.,Chis.
Welnetham/Sf ⟶ Wh-
Welwick/ERY
    welik   PNYE 22,BBC
Welwyn/Hrt
    welin   PNHrt 144,EPD,BBC,BCE,
        DEPN
    welwin   MEG 213
Wem /Sa
    wem   BBC
Wembdon/So
    wendin   Hope
Wembley/Mx
    olim wemli   PNMx 55
    wembli   EPD,BBC
Wembworthy/D
    weməri   PND 372
Wendlebury/O
    windəlberi   PNO 241
    windlbəri   Hope
Wendover/Bk
    'wendouvə   EPD,Schr.
    'wendəvə   Schr.
Wendron/Co
    wendrən   BBC
Wendy/Ca
    wendi   ONCa 182
Wenham/Sf
    wenəm   EPD

Wenhaston/Sf
    wenəs(t)n   DSf 312
Wenlock/Sa
    wenlək   Schr.
    wenlɔk   EPD,Schr.
Wenning/La,Yorks. (r.n.)
    wenin   RN 448,PNLa 169
Wensley/Db,La,NRY
    wenzli   BBC,Schr.
    wensli   BCE (for W. in NRY)
Wensleydale/NRY
    wenslədil   PNYN 246
    wenzlideil   BBC
    wenslideil   BCE
Wensum/Nf (r.n.)
    wensəm   BBC,Schr.
Wentworth/Ca,Sr,WRY
    wentwəþ   ONCa 186
    wentəþ   Hope (for W. in WRY)
    wintwəːþ   GlossSh 285 (for W. in
    wentwəːþ   EPD,Bchm.67   WRY)
    wentwəþ   EPD,Schr.,Chis.,Bchm.67
Weobley/He (also spelt -ly)
    wuːbli   Schr.,Hope
    webli   DEPN,BBC,BCE,DHe 44 (dial
        and StE)
Weoley Castle/Wa
    wiːəli   BBC
Werneth Low/Chs
    wernəþ lou, olim
    werni lou   PNChs II/vii
    werni lɔː   GlossChs
    wəːnəþ   BBC
Wervin/Chs
    wəːvin   PNChs IV/137
Wesham/La
    wesəm   DEPN,BBC,BCE
Wesley (as in W.End/Ess)
    wezli, wesli   EPD
    -z-   Dobson 941
Wessex
    wesiks   EPD
Westbourne
    wes(t)bɔːn   EPD,Bchm.131
    wes(t)bən   EPD,Schr.,Bchm.131
    wes-   ESpr.400
    wes(t)-   HL 1132
Westbrook
    westbruk   EPD
Westbury
    westbəri   Schr.,Chis.
    wes-   Schr.
    westb(ə)ri   EPD
West Cliff/Wt
    wesklif   PNWt 184
Westcott
    weskət   EPD,Schr.,Bchm.132
    westkət   EPD,Bchm.132
    westkɔt   Schr.

West Dean/Sx
  wezdi:n PNSx 49
West England
  is also called
  zedlænd Bau.,s.n.Zedland
Westerham/K
  west(ə)rəm EPD
  westrəm PNK
Westfield
  westfi:ld EPD
  wesvul PNSx 5o5
Westgarth Hill/Cu (f.n.)
  westkət Thorn.65,67 and 8o,
          note 136
Westgate
  wes(t)git EPD,Schr.,HL 1132
          and 1177
  wes(t)geit EPD,Schr.
  wes(t)gət Schr.
  rarely -geit Bchm.78
Westhall/Sf
  westl DSf 312
Westham/Sx
  west'hæm PNSx 446
West Hartlepool/Du
  west ha:tlipu:l BBC
Westhorp/Np
  westrəp PNNp 33
Westhoughton/La
  west'hɔ:t(ə)n BBC
  westaut(ə)n PNLa(ii)
Westlake/D
  westleik EPD
Westleton/Sf
  wesltən BBC
Westley/Ca
  westli ONCa 184
Westmill/Hrt
  vulgo wesməl PNHrt 2o9
Westminster/Ldn
  'wes(t)minstə EPD,BBC,Schr.,
          Kruis.,MEG 225
  _ ´ _ EPD
  wes- ESpr.4oo
  west- Chis.
  wesminstə, sometimes
  wesministə CPP
  westministə CPhon 51
Westmorland
  wes(t)mələnd EPD,BBC,Schr.
  westmələnd Kruis.
  wes- ESpr.4oo
  wesmələnd MEG 257,DSDu
  wesmlənd EPD
  westmɔ:lænd Schr.
  westmɔ:lənd Chis.
  wespərlənd PNE'side 75
Westoe/Du
  westou Chis.

Weston
  westən EPD,Schr.
  wesn Schr.
  wesən Mawer(4)285
Weston/Ca
  westən ONCa 22
Weston/Chs (in Bucklow Hd)
  westən PNChs II/ix
  wesn PNChs II/ix ("olim"),
          GlossChs
Weston/Chs (in Nantwich Hd)
  westn PNChs III/75
  wesn PNChs III/75 ("older
          local"),GlossChs
Weston/Wa
  wesn Hope
Weston Bampfylde/So
  westən bæmfi:ld BBC,BCE
Weston Favell/Np
  wesən feivəl PNNp 136
  westən feivl BBC
  - feivəl BCE
Westoning/Bd
  westəniŋ BBC
Weston-super-Mare/So
  westən sju:pə mɛə,
  - - mɛəri BBC,Schr.
  westən siupəmɛə BCE
  westən sju:pə mɛəri: Chis.
  s(j)u:pə mɑ:ri Schr.
  sju:pə,su:pə,s(j)upə EPD
  mɛə, rarely mɛəri EPD
Weston-under-Penyard/He
  westən ʌndə penjɑ:d,
  dial. - - DHe 44
Weston Zoyland/So
  westən zɔilənd BBC
Westover/Wt
  'west(o)uvər PNWt 91
Westport/So,W
  westpɔ:t, wespət Schr.
Westridge Down/Wt
  westridʒ PNWt 11o
Westside/Wt
  wessaid PNWt 119
  westzaid DWt,s.n.garbed-up
Westward/Cu
  west'wɔ:d BBC,BCE
Westward Ho!/D
  westwəd hou EPD
Westwell/O
  westəl PNO 332,PNO(i)218
Westwick
  westwik BBC,ONCa 19o
  westik Schr.,ONwick 374 (for W.
          in Nf),Hope (for W.in Nf)
Westwood
  westwud Schr.

Westwoodside/Li
  'westwudsaid BBC
Wetham Gn/K
  wetəm PNK
Wetheral/Cu
  weðərəl, -rɔ:l Schr.
Wetherby/WRY
  weðəbi EPD,Chis.
Wetherley/Ca
  weðəli ONCa 184
Wethersfield/Ess
  wʌðəzfl PNEss 465
Wettenhall/Chs
  wetnɔ:l. PNChs III/166
  wetnə PNChs III/166 ("older
        local"),GlossChs
Wetwang/ERY
  wetwan, wetwaŋ PNYE 128
  wetwæŋ BBC
Wey/Do;Ha,Sr (r.n.)
  wei EPD,Schr.,Chis.,Förster
Weybourne/Nf
  webən BBC
Weybridge/Sr
  weibridʒ EPD,Schr.
Weymouth/Do
  weiməþ EPD,BBC,Schr.,Kruis.,
        Chis.
  never -mauþ Bchm.77
Whaddon/Bk,Ca
  wɔdən PNBk 74,ONCa 189
  wædən ONCa 189
Whaddon Hill/Bk
  wɔdən PNBk 166
Whale/We
  we:l PNWe II/183
  hwɛəl PNE'side 72
Whale Chine/Wt
  wiəl tʃain PNWt 223
Whale Gill/Cu
  hwɛəl gil PNE'side 72
Whaley/Chs
  weili PNChs II/176,EPD
  hw- EPD
Whaley Bridge/Db
  weili bridʒ BBC
Whalley/La
  (h)wɔ:li EPD,BBC
  hwɔ:li BCE
  hwɔli Schr.
  wɔ:li PNLa 76
  -ɔ:- DEPN
Whalley Range/La
  wɔli reindʒ BBC
Whalton/Nb
  wɑ:tn DEPN
  wɑ:tən PNNbDu 211

Whaplode/Li
  (h)wɔploud BBC
  hw- BCE
  -ɔ- DEPN
Wham/WRY
  wam DDd 15
Wharfe/WRY (r.n.)
  hwɔ:f Schr.,Chis.
Wharfe/WRY (p.n.)
  wɑ:f PNYW VI/23o
Wharles/La
  wɔ:ləz PNLa 152,DEPN
Wharncliffe/WRY
  wɔ:nklif Hope
Wharram/ERY
  wərəm BBC
Wharram Percy/ERY
  warəm piəsi PNYE 134
Wharton/Chs
  hw-,wɔ:r-,wɑ:rtən PNChs II/213
  hwɔ:tən Schr.
  wɔ:tn EPD,Kruis.
  hw- EPD
Whashton/NRY
  waʃtən PNYN 292
Whatcroft/Chs
  (h)wɔt- PNChs II/215
Whateley/Wa
  weitli EPD,Kruis.
  hw- EPD
Whatley/So
  (h)wɔtli EPD
Whatlington/Sx
  wɔtliŋtn Förster
Whatstandwell/Db
  hɔlstænəl Hope
  wɔt'stændwel PNDb(i) II/195,BBC
  hɔlstanəl PNDb(i) II/195
Whatton/Le,Nt
  wɔt(ə)n BBC
Wheal/Co
  see note s.n. Halvean
Wheal Vor/Co
  _ ́ Jenner(2)3o4
Wheatacre/Nf
  hwitəkə HL 715,BCE
  (h)w- BBC
Wheathampstead/Hrt
  wetəmstid PNHrt 54
  (h)wetəmsted, (h)wi:təm- BBC
  hw- , hw- BCE
  (h)wi:təm(p)sted, (h)wet- EPD
Wheatley
  hwi:tli EPD,Schr.
  w- EPD
Wheatley/WRY
  hwi:ətli Hope
  hwi:tl DEY 8

Wheatley Wood/Bk
  wi:tli   PNBk 212
Wheaton Aston/St
  (h)wi:tn EPD
Wheaton Bread/Wt
  wiətn bred   PNWt 92
Wheatstone Pk/St
  (h)wi:tstən, -stoun EPD
Wheeler (as in W.'s Street/K)
  (h)wi:lə EPD
Wheelock/Chs
  wilək   PNChs II/ix,GlossChs
  wi:lɔk   PNChs II/273
  hwi:lək, -lɔk Schr.
Wheelock/Chs (r.n.)
  wi:lok   PNChs I/39
  hwi:lək, -lɔk Schr.
Wheldrake/ERY
  weldrik   PNYE 269
Whelnetham/Sf
  weltəm   Hope,PNSf 63[1]
  wel'ni:þəm BBC
  'welnetəm BBC,BCE
Whelpo/Cu (or -a)
  hwelpə   PNCu 278,PNE'side 62
Whenby/NRY
  weŋbi   PNYN 3o
Whernside/WRY
  hwə:nsaid Schr.
Whernside/WRY (a mountain)
  wiənsət   DDd 17
  hwə:nsaid Schr.
Wherstead/Sf
  wə:sted BBC
Wherwell/Ha
  (h)wə:wel BBC
  hw- BCE
Whetstone/Le,Mx
  (h)wetstoun EPD
  hw- Schr.
  -stən   MEG 128,Schr.
Whickham/Du
  wikəm EPD
  hw-   EPD,Schr.
Whildon Gn/Db
  wi:ldən   GlossSh lxiv,note
Whiligh/Sx
  (h)wailai BBC
  hw- BCE
Whippance/Wt
  wipənts   PNWt 286
Whippingham/Wt
  wipnəm   PNWt 234
  (w)wipiŋəm EPD
Whipsnade/Bd
  (h)wipsneid EPD,BBC

Whissendine/Ru
  (h)wis(ə)ndain BBC
  hwisəndain BCE
Whistle Gray/Wt
  wisəlgrei   DWt,s.n.pudden headed
Whiston/Np
  wiʃtən   PNNp 152
Whitacre/Wa
  (h)witəkə BBC
Whitbarrow/We (a hill)
  hwitbərə   DKe 5
  hwitbərə   PNE'side 67
Whitbarrow Hall/Cu
  hwitbərə   PNCu 213
Whitby/Chs,NRY
  witbi   PNChs IV/198
  widbi   PNYN 126,DSto
  (h)witbi   EPD,BBC,Bau.
  hw- Schr.,Chis.
Whitby Steads/We
  hwipəsti:dz   PNE'side 75
Whitchurch
  wittʃə:tʃ, hw- EPD
  hwitʃə:tʃ Schr.
Whitchurch Canonicorum/Do
  (h)wittʃə:tʃ kənɔni'kɔ:rəm BBC
Whitcombe/Wt
  wikəm   PNWt 11o
Whitechaple/Ldn
  (h)waittʃæpl EPD,Bau.
  hwaitʃæpl Schr.
  waitʃæpl Kruis.
  w- MEG 123
Whitechurch
  hwaitʃə:tʃ Schr.
Whitecliff Bay/Wt
  waitklif   PNWt 4o
Whitecliff Fm/W
  witli   PNW 165
White Colne/Ess
  hwait koun BCE
Whitefield
  (h)wit-, (h)waitfi:ld EPD
  witfi:ld   Kruis.,MEG 123
Whitefield/D
  witivəl   PND 58
Whitefield/La
  (h)waitfi:ld BBC
Whitefield Fm/Wt
  waitfild   PNWt 62
Whitefriars/K
  'hwait'fraiəz EPD,Schr.
  _ ⁄ _ EPD
  waitfraiəz EPD,Kruis.,MEG 123
Whitehall/Ldn
  '(h)waithɔ:l EPD,BBC

1) "I am informed that, not long since, the pron. of [this] place was
Wheltham" (PNSf 63).

_́ _   EPD,BBC,MEG 123
'wait'hɔːl   Kruis.
Whitehaven/Cu
  hwitən   PNCu 45o ("olim"),
        Schr. ("loc."),Hope,
        GlossCu xviii
  hwitheivən   PNCu 45o
  'hwait'heivn   Schr.
  'waitheivn   EPD,Bchm.35
  'hw-   EPD
  '(h)waitheiv(ə)n   BBC
  hwaitheivən   BCE,Chis.
  -ai-   MEG 123
  hwaithebən   DCu 186
Whitehough/Db
  waitɔf   PNDb 64
Whitehouse/Nb
  (h)wait'haus   BBC
Whitehouse Fm/Wt
  waithæus   PNWt 193
Whiteley
  waitli   Kruis.
  (h)w-   EPD
Whiteley Bank/Wt
  waitli bæŋk   DWt,s.n.hatched-
        up,PNWt 162
  witli -   PNWt 162
Whitemoor/Co,Nt,St
  (h)waitmuə   BBC
Whiteslea Lodge/Nf
  (h)waitsliː   BBC
Whitestone/D
  witsən   PND 456
  (h)witstən   BBC
Whitestone/He
  (h)waitstoun   BBC
Whitfield
  (h)witfiːld   EPD,BBC
  hw-   Schr.
Whitgift/WRY
  wigif   Hope,Schr.
  hwitgift   Schr.
  (h)witgift   EPD
Whiting Bank/Sf
  (h)waitiŋ   EPD
Whitley
  hwitli   Schr.
  witli   Kruis.
  (h)witli   EPD
Whitmore/Sa
  witmə   GlossSa xxx
Whitmore/Db,St
  hwitmɔː   Schr.
Whitney/He
  hwitni   Schr.
  (h)w-   EPD
Whitstable/K
  hwitstəbl   Schr.,Chis.
  (h)w-   EPD

Whitstone/Co,D
  (h)witstoun   EPD
Whittaker (as in W.Flat/Ess)
  (h)witikə, -təkə   EPD
Whittingham/La
  hwitindʒəm   Hope,PNing 17o,PNE&W,
        s.n.Birmingham,
        Zachr.(1)348f.
  (h)witinhəm   BBC
Whittingham/Nb
  hwitindʒəm   PNNbDu 214,PNing 17o,
        Dodgson(2)392,BCE,
        PNE&W,s.n.Birmingham,
        Ellis 655
  -ndʒ-   DEPN
  (h)w-   BBC
Whittington
  (h)witiŋtən   EPD,Bau. (for W. in
  hw-   Schr.   Ldn)
  short: The Whit   Bau. (for the
        prison in New-
        gate/Ldn)
Whittington/Wo
  hwitəntən   PNWo 178
  witəntən   GlossSEWo 82
Whittle/La,Nb
  (h)witl   EPD
Whittle-le-Woods/La
  witli wudz   PNLa 133
  (h)witl lə wudz   BBC
Whittlesey/Ca (also spelt -ea)
  hwitəlsi   Chis.
  witlzi   ONCa 182
Whittlesford/Ca
  olim witsə   PNCa 98
  witlzfəd   ONCa 187
Whitwell/Ca,Wt
  witwəl   ONCa 19o
  witəl, witl   PNWt 251
Whitwell Fm/Ca
  witəl   PNCa 73
Whitwick/Le
  hwitik   BCE,ONwick 38o,Hope
  (h)witik   BBC
  -itik   DEPN
Whitworth/Du,La
  hwitəþ   GlossR&R (for W. in La),
        DSLa
  (h)witwəːþ   EPD
Whixley/WRY
  hwiːslə   DYorks 63
Whyke/Sx
  wik   BBC
Whyly/Sx
  wai'lai   PNSx 4ol
Whyr Fm/W
  wəːr   PNW 31o
Whyteleafe/Sr
  '(h)waitliːf   BBC

Wibsey/WRY
    wipsi   DEPN,BBC,BCE
    wibzi   BBC,BCE
-wich,-wych
    "not pron. short as 'witch',
    but long"   GlossChs(i),
               s.n. Wich
Wichling/K
    witʃliŋ   PNK
Wichnor/St
    witʃnɔ: BBC
Wick
    wik   EPD,BBC,Schr.
Wicken/Ca
    wikn   ONCa 19o
Wicken Hill Lane/Wt
    wiknil liən   PNWt 72
Wickham/Ca,K,Wo
    wikəm   EPD,Schr.,PNK,ONCa 179
    wi:kən   GlossSEWo 82 (for
               Child's W./Wo)
Wickhambreaux/K
    wikəmbru: DEPN,BBC,BCE,PNK
Wickham Market/Sf
    wikəm mɑːkət   DSf 313
Wickham Skeith/Sf
    wikəm ski:þ   BBC,BCE
Wickwar/Gl
    wikwɔ: BBC
Wicor/Ha
    wikə   BBC
Widdick Chine/Wt
    widik   PNWt 23o
Widecombe in the Moor/D
    widikəm   EPD,BBC,BCE
Wide Irons/Db (f.n.)
    "This form is ... locally in
    use today ... But the present
    owner ... informs me that she
    and her mother and grandmother
    ... always knew it as Wild
    Irons"   Fraser(2)8o,
               cf.FnSDb 62
Widemouth Bay/Co
    widməþ bei   EPD,BBC
Wideopen/Nb
    waidoup(ə)n   BBC
Widewath/We
    waidwəþ   PNE'side 66
Widey/D
    waidi   PND 228
Widhill/W
    olim widəl   PNW 44
Widmerpool/Nt
    loc. windəpul, otherwise
    widməpu:l   PNNt(i)149
Widnes/La
    widnis   EPD,BBC,Schr.
    widnez   BCE

    widnes   Schr.
Widow Croft/Cu (f.n.)
    wi:də   Thorn.7o and 81,note 174
Wigan/La
    wigən   DEPN,EPD,BBC,Schr.,Chis.,
               Hope,Lloyd 127
    wigin   Ellis 343
Wiganthorpe/NRY
    wigənþrəp   PNYN 35
Wiggaton/D
    wikətən   PND 6o7
Wiggenhall St.Mary Magdalen/Nf
    mɔ:dlin   Hope
Wiggins Hill/Wa
    -inz   Dodgson(2)393
Wiggonholt/Sx
    wigənəlt   PNSx(i)173
Wight (Isle of Wight)
    wait   EPD,Kruis.,Chis.
    ailəwait   GlossHa,DWt,s.n.
               withybed
    (see also s.n. Isle of W.)
Wightwick/St
    witik   BBC,BCE,MEG 213
Wigmore
    wigmɔ: EPD,Schr.
    -mɔə   EPD
Wigton/Cu,WRY
    wigtən   EPD,Schr.,Chis.
Wilbarston/Np
    wibəstən   PNNp 175
    wil'bɑ:stən   BBC,BCE
Wilberfoss/ERY
    wilbəfɔs   Schr.
Wilbraham/Ca
    wilbr(əh)əm   ONCa 179
    wilbriəm   EPD
    wilbrəm   EPD,BBC,Schr.
    wilbrəhəm   Schr.
    'wilbrəhæm   EPD,BBC
Wilbraham's Walk,Wilbrahams Alms-
               houses/Chs
    wilbrəm   PNChs III/39f. and 61
Wilburlea/WRY
    wilbərli: DHd 15o
Wilburton/Ca,D
    wilbərtən   ONCa 22
    wil'bə:t(ə)n   BBC
    wil'bə:tən   BCE
Wildboarclough/Chs
    wilbərtluf   PNChs II/vii ("olim")
               GlossChs
    olim wilbərklʌf   PNChs II/vii
    now wilb rkl f,
    waildbə:r'kluf,
    wil(d)bər'kluf   PNChs II/vii
    wilbəklʌf   Hope

Wildboar Fell/We
 wilbərt fel   PNE'side 73
Wild Boar Scar/Cu
 wili bouər skɑːr   PNE'side 74
Wildcatbank/Cu
 wulkət bæŋk   GlossCu xviii
Wilden/Bd
 wildən   PNBdHu 66,DEPN
Wilderhope/Sa
 wildəhoup   BBC
Wilderspool/Chs
 'wildəzpuːl   BBC
Wiley/W (r.n.) ⟶ Wyley
Wiley Bridge/NRY
 wiləbrig   PNYN 157
Wilkesley/Chs
 wilksli   PNChs III/93
Willans/WRY
 wilənz   DDd 15
Willapark Point/Co
 wiləpɑːk   BBC
Willard (as in W.'s Hill/Sx)
 wilɑːd, -əd   EPD
Willaston/Chs
 wiləstən   PNChs III/78 (for W.
             in Nantwich Hd),
             PNChs IV/232 (for
             W. in Wirral Hd)
Willenhall/St,Wa
 'wilənhɔːl   BBC
 winəl   PNWa 19o
Willesborough/K
 wilsbərə   PNK
Willesden/Mx
 wilzdən   PNMx 16o,PNMx(i),
            Kruis.
 wilzd(ə)n   EPD,BBC
 wiləzdən   Chis.
Willesley/D
 wilzli   PND 217
Willhays/D
 wiliz   PND 2o3
Williamscot/O (formerly in Np)
 wilzkɔt   PNO 427
 wilskət   BBC,BCE
Willingale/Ess
 winigl   PNEss 5oo,Reaney(1)
           253
 winigəl   EssDD 158,Hope
Willingdon/Sx
 wil(ə)ndən   PNSx 424
 wiliŋdən   EPD
Willingham/Ca
 wiliŋəm   ONCa 179
Willington
 wiltn, wi(ə)ntn   DSDu (for
                    W. in Du)
 wiliŋtən   EPD

Williton/So
 wulitn   DWSo 11
Willoughby/Li,Nt,Wa
 wiləbi   EPD,Schr.,Kruis.
Willoughton/Li
 wilətən   GlossM&C,s.n.Willerton
Willy/Np
 wili   EPD
Willybower Nook/Cu
 wilbə'niuk   PNE'side 74
Wilmcote/Wa
 wimkət   PNWa 198
 wilmkout   EPD,BBC
 wiŋkət   DEPN,Schr.
Wilmingham/Wt
 wilmidʒəm, wulmidʒəm   PNWt 131
 (for -dʒ- see also PNing 171 and
  Dodgson(2)394)
Wilmington
 wilmiŋtən   EPD,Schr.
Wilminstone/D
 wilmistən   PND 2oo
Wilmslow/Chs
 wimzlə   PNChs II/vii ("olim"),
           GlossChs
 wilmzlou   PNChs II/vii,EPD,BBC,
             Schr.
 wimzlou   PNChs II/vii,Hope,BBC,
            Schr.,EPD ("loc.")
 wim-   DEPN
Wilnecote/Wa
 winkət   PNWa 27,DEPN,BCE,Hope
 wiŋkət   BBC
 wilnikət   BBC,BCE
Wilpshire/La
 wilpʃə   BBC
Wilscot/O ⟶ Williamscot(e)
Wilsden/WRY
 wilzd(ə)n   EPD
Wilshampstead/Bd (also spelt Wil-
               stead or Wilshamstead)
 wilsted   DEPN,BBC,BCE,Hope
 wilʃəmstəd   BBC
Wilson/He,Le
 wilsn   EPD
Wilsthorpe/ERY
 wilsþrəp   PNYE 88
Wilton
 wiltən   HL 733 (for W. in W),
           Schr.
 wilt(ə)n   EPD
Wilts. (short for Wiltshire)
 wilts   EPD,Schr.
Wiltshire
 loc. wilʃər   PNW 1
 wilʃə   BBC
 wiltʃə   EPD,BBC,Schr.
 wiltʃiə   EPD

Wimbledon/Sr
    wimbld(ə)n   EPD,BBC
    wimbəldən   Chis.
    wimbldən   Schr.
Wimboldsby/Chs
    'wimbouzli,
      -bə:zli   PNChs II/257
Wimbolds Trafford/Chs
    'wimbɔ:lz,
    wimblz   PNChs III/26o
Wimborne/Do
    wimbɔ:n   EPD,Bchm.69
    -bɔən   EPD
    never [ə]   Bchm.69
    never [uə]   Bchm.51
Wimbotsham/Nf
    wimbətʃəm   BBC
Wimpole/Ca
    olim wimpl   PNCa 81
    wimpəl   ONCa 194
    wimpoul   EPD,Schr.
Wincanton/So
    win'kæntən   BBC,BCE,DEPN
             (stress only)
    'winkəntən   Chis.
Wincham/Chs
    winʃəm   PNChs II/136,Dodgson
        (2)394
Winchcomb(e)/Gl
    winʃkəm   BBC,Schr.,Chis.
Winchelsea/Sx
    wintʃlsi: BBC,Schr.
    win(t)ʃlsi   EPD
    winʃlsi: Schr.
    wintʃlsi   Kruis.
    wintʃəlsi: Chis.
Winchenden/Bk
    witʃəndən   PNBk 111,DEPN
Winchester/Ha
    wintʃistə   BBC,Kruis.
    win(t)ʃistə   EPD,Kruis.
    wintʃəstə   Chis.
    "[ntʃ] seems more usual than
    [nʃ]"   MEG 224
Winchfield/Ha
    win(t)ʃfi:ld   EPD
Winchmore/Bk.Mx
    win(t)ʃmɔ:, -ɛcə   EPD
Wincle/Chs
    olim winkə   PNChs II/vii,
             GlossChs
    winkəl   PNChs II/vii
Winder/Cu,We
    wində   EPD
Windermere/We and La
    windəmiə   PNWe I/192,EPD,BBC
    -mi:r   Schr.,Chis.
    -mi:ə   Kruis.

Winderwath/We
    windənwaþ   PNE'side 73
Windfallwood Common/Sx
    waindfəl   PNSx 113
Windgate Copse/Wt
    wingeit kaps   PNWt 92
Windgates/Cu (f.n.)
    winjəts   Thorn.8o,note 133
Windhill/WRY
    windhil   Schr.
Windlesham/Sr
    olim winsəm   PNSr 152,DEPN
    windlʃəm   BBC
Windley/Db
    waindli   PNDb 617
    windli   EPD
Windmill Edge Field/W
    loc. waimil   Grigson 72
Windmoor End/We
    winmər   PNE'side 73
Windover Hill/Sx
    windɔ:r   PNSx 41o
Windrush/Gl,O (r.n.)
    windrʌʃ   BBC,Schr.,Bchm.ɔ8
Windsor/Brk
    winzə   EPD,DEPN,BBC,Schr.,Kruis.,
        MEG 223
    windzə   Schr.,Chis.
    winds'ɔ: HL 64o (see note s.n.
Wineham/K   Woolwich)
    wain'hæm   BBC,BCE
Winestead/ERY
    'wainsted   BBC
Winewall/La
    wainwɔ:l   PNLa 88
Winford/Wt
    wimfərd   PNWt 173
    winvərd   PNWt 286
Winfrith Newburgh/Do
    winfriþ nju:bə:g   BBC
Wing/Ru
    weŋ   GlossRu vii
Wingerworth/Db
    wiŋəwə:þ   BBC
Wingfield
    wiŋfi:ld   EPD,Schr.
Wingham/K
    wiŋəm   Schr.,PNK
Wingrave/Bk
    wingruv   PNBk 88
Winkfield/Brk,W
    wiŋfi(:)ld   PNW(i)174
    wiŋkfi:ld   EPD
Winkleigh/D
    wiŋkli   BBC
Winlaton/Du
    win'leit(ə)n, 'winlet(ə)n   BBC
    win'leitən, 'winletən   BCE
    'winlətən   Chis.

Winmarleigh/La
  win'mɑːli   PNLa 164,DEPN
Winnall/Ha
  winl   BBC
Winnington/Chs
  winiŋtən   PNChs III/191
  winitn   PNChs III/191 ("older
    local"),GlossChs
  winiŋtn   Kruis.
Winsford/Chs
  winzfəd   PNChs III/173
  winsfət   DSChs 2o
Winsham/D,So
  winsəm   BBC,BCE (for W. in So)
Winshill/St
  'winzhil   BBC
Winskill/Cu
  winskil   PNE'side 68
  winskəl   PNE'side 68 ("more
    often"),PNCu 2o8
Winslow/Bk,He
  winzlou   PNBk 75,EPD
  winslou   Kruis.
Winstanley/La
  'winstənli   EPD,BBC,Schr.,
    Kruis.
  win'stænli   EPD,BBC
  'winstænli   Schr.
Winster/Db,We (r.n. and p.n.)
  winstə   Schr.
Winston/Du,Sf,Wt
  winst(ə)n   EPD
Winstone/Wt
  wins(t)n   PNWt 259
Winterborne Houghton/Do
  hautən   PNDo(i)61
Winterborne Whitechurch/Do
  wintəbɔːn (h)wi(t)tʃəːtʃ   BBC
Winterbourne
  wintəbɔːn, -bɔən, -buən   EPD
Wint(e)ringham/Li
  wintəriŋəm   Hope
Winterington/Li (also spelt Win-
           terton)
  wintətən   Hope
Winterton
  wintət(ə)n   EPD
  (for W./Li see preceding
    entry)
Wintney Ho/Ha
  wintni   Schr.
Winton
  wintən   EPD
Wintylow/NRY
  wintəlou   PNYN 243
Winwick/Hu,La,Np
  winik   BBC,BCE,DEPN,PNLa(ii),
    PNNp 77

Wirksworth/Db
  wəːsə   PNDb 413,Hope
  wusə   PNDb 413
  wəːsidy   Hope
  wəːkswəːþ   Chis.,BBC
Wirral/Chs
  wurəl   PNChs II/vii ("olim"),
    GlossChs
  now wirəl   PNChs II/vii,Schr.
  wir(ə)l   BBC
Wirral Hd/Chs
  wirəl, older local
  wʌrəl   PNChs IV/167
Wirswall/Chs
  'wəːzwɔːl, loc. -(w)əl
            PNChs III/112
  wɔzə   DSChs 2o
Wisbech/Ca
  wizbitʃ   PNCa 291,Schr.,Hope,
    Ellis 252
  wisbidʒ   PNCa 291
  wizbiːtʃ   ONCa 192,EPD,BBC,BCE,
    DEPN,Schr.,Chis.
Wisborough Gn/Sx (also spelt Wyseberg)
  waizbə   PNSx(i)18o
Wiseton/Nt (also spelt Wyseton)
  wistən   PNNt 43,RitterNt 45o
  wistn   PNNt(i)153,DEPN
  waistən   BBC
Wishaw/Wa
  wiʃɔː   BBC
Wishay/D
  wizi   PND 556
Wisley/Sr
  wizli   PNSr 155,DEPN,BBC
Wissington/Sf (also spelt Wiston)
  wistən   PNSf 11o,BBC,BCE
  wistn   DEPN
Wistaston/Chs
  wistastən   PNChs III/45
  wistisn   PNChs III/45 ("older
         local"),GlossChs
  wistəsən   Hope
  'wistəstən   BBC

Wisteston/He
  wistəsən   Hope
Wiston/Sf ⟶ Wissington
Wiston/Sx
  wisən   PNSx 243,BCE
  wisn   DEPN
  wis(ə)n   BBC
  wistən   BBC,BCE
Witcham/Ca
  witʃəm   ONCa 179
Witchampton/Do
  witʃ'æmptən   PNDo(i)1o8

Witchford/Ca
  witʃfəd   ONCa 187
Witham (p.n. and r.n.)
  wiðəm, loc. witən [sic] Schr.
  wiþəm   Chis. (for the r.n.)
Witham/Ess
  witən   PNEss 299,PNE&W,BBC,
          BCE,EPD,DEPN
Witham/Li
  witn, wiðən   Hope
Witham/Li,Ru (r.n.)
  wiðəm   RN 467,PNE&W,EPD,BBC
  wiðm   DEPN
Witham/Nt (r.n.)
  wiðəm   PNNt lo
Witham Friary/So
  witəm fraiəri,
  wiðəm   -   BBC,BCE
Withampton/Do
  _ ′ _   DEPN
Witherington/W
  wiðriŋtən   Schr.
Withern/Li
  wiðən   Schr.
Withernsea/ERY
  wiðrənsi   PNYE 26,GlossHol 17
  wiðənsi: BBC
Withernwick/ERY
  wiðrənwig   PNYE 69,GlossHol 17
Withington
  wiðiŋtən   BBC
Withington/Chs
  wiþitn   PNChs II/vii ("olim"),
          Hope (or -ð- ?)
  wiðintən   PNChs II/vii,BBC
  wiðitn   GlossChs
Withington/He
  witiŋtən   Hope
Withnell/La
  wiþnəl   BBC
Withycombe Raleigh/D
  wiðikəm rɔ:li   BBC,BCE
Withyham/Sx
  widi'hæm   PNSx 37o,DEPN
  wiðihæm   PNSx(i)375
  _ _ ′   BBC,BCE
  ′ _ _   BBC
Witley/Sr,Wo
  witli   EPD
Witney/Ess,O
  witni   EPD,Schr.
Wittersham/K
  witəʃəm   BBC
  witsəm, witəsəm   PNK
Wittingham/Chs
  witinəm   DSChs 19

Witton Gilbert/Du
  witən dʒilbət   PNNbDu 218,BCE
  wit(ə)n dʒilbət, - gilbət   BBC
  dʒ-   DEPN
Wiveliscombe/So
  wivəliskəm   EPD,BBC,BCE
  wilskəm   EPD ("loc."),BBC,BCE,
            Bchm.137 ("loc."),Chis.
            Hope
  wivləskəm   Hope
Wivelsfield/Sx
  wilsfəl, wulsfəl   PNSx 3o5
  wilsfi:ld   Mawer(2)93
  wivlzfi:ld   EPD,BBC
  wivəlzfi:ld   EPD,BCE
Wivenhoe/Ess (also spelt Wyven-)
  wivnou   PNEss 4o3
  wiv(ə)nhou   BBC
  wivənhou   BCE
  -i-   DEPN
Wiverton Hall/Nt
  wə:tən   PNNt 23o,BCE
  wə:tn   PNNt(i)154,Hope
  -ə:-   DEPN
  waivət(ə)n, wə:t(ə)n   BBC
  waivətən   BCE
Wiveton/Nf
  wivtən, wivitən   BBC
Woburn/Bd
  wu:bən   PNBdHu 143,Schr.
  woubən   Schr.,Chis.
  wu:bə:n   EPD,BBC,BCE,Bchm.4o
  oubə:n   Hope
  wu:-   DEPN
Woburn Abbey/Bd
  wu:bə:n   BBC
Woburn Place, W. Sq./Ldn
  woubən, -bə:n   EPD,HL 1222,Bchm.4o
Woburn Sands/Bk
  wu:bən sændz   BBC
Woking/Sr
  woukiŋ   EPD,BBC,Schr.,Chis.
  oukiŋ   RSp 133 ("within living
          memory")
Wokingham/Brk
  woukiŋəm   BBC,EPD,Schr.
  woukiŋhəm   Chis.
  loc. oukiŋəm   Schr.,PNBrk 61
                 RSp 133 ("within
                 living memory")
  formerly also called
  Oakingham or Ockingham
  (cf. PNBrk 61)
Wolborough/D
  wulbərə   BBC,BCE
  -u-   DEPN
  wɔlb(ə)rə   EPD
  wɔlbərə   Chis.

Wold/ERY
  wɔ:d   Morris 32
  (see also s.n. Cold Wold)
Wold Fell/WRY (a mountain)
  wɔ:fl   DDd 17
Woldingham/Sr
  wouldiŋəm   EPD,BBC
Wold Newton/ERY
  wɔ:d niutən   PNYE 114
The Wolds/Li
  woudz   GlossM&C,s.n.Wouds
Wolfa/Cu
  wufə   PNCu 238,PNE'side 62
Wolferlow/He (or Wolver-)
  u:fələ   Hope
Wolferton/Nf
  wulfətən   BBC
Wolfeton Ho/Do
  wulftən,
  wouvətən   PNDo I/341,
                PNDo(i)183
Wolfhampcote/Wa
  wʌfənkət   PNWa 150
  wulfəmkout   BBC
Wolfstones/WRY
  u:stuənz, u:fstuənz   DHd 140
  -stənz   DHd 122
Wollaston/Np,Sa,Wo
  wuləstən   Schr.,Kruis.
  -t(ə)n   EPD
Wollaton/Co,Nt
  wulətən   PNNt 153,BBC,BCE
          (for W. in Nt)
  wulətn   PNNt(i)155,EPD
  -u-   DEPN (for W. in Nt)
Wolseley/St
  wulzli   EPD,Kruis.,MEG 334
Wolsingham/Du
  wulziŋəm   BBC,BCE
  wɔlsiŋəm   EPD,Schr.
Wolstanton/St
  wu:lstæntn, uʃitn,
  usitən   Hope
  'wulstæntən, loc.
  wulstən   EPD,Bchm.242
  wul'stæntən   Chis.
  wulstəntən   Schr.
  -u-   DEPN
Wolstenholme/La
  wu:znəm   ROS 40
  u:sləm   DSLa,s.n.Ooslum,
             GlossR&R 64
  wulst(ə)nhoum   EPD
Wolsty/Cu
  wusti   PNCu 294,BBC,BCE
  wulsti   BBC,BCE
Wolvercot/O (or spelt -cote)
  wu:lvərkout   PNO 33
  wulvəkət   BBC,BCE

ouvəkout   Hope
  -u-   DEPN
Wolverhampton/St
  wɔlvətən   Hope,Schr.("loc.")
  hæmptən   Hope
  'wulvəhæm(p)tən   EPD,BBC
  _ _ _ _ ´ _ , _ ´ _ ´ _   EPD
  wulvə'hæmptən   Kruis.,Chis.
  wulvə'hæmtən   Schr.,MEG 334
Wolverley/Sa,Wo
  wulvəli   BBC,Chis.,MWG 334
Wolverlow/He ⟶ Wolfer-
Wolverton
  wulvətən   EPD,Schr.,Chis.
  -tn   EPD
  ulvərtn   PNWt 286
Wolviston/Du
  wustən   PNNbDu 218
  wustn   DEPN
  wulvistən   BBC,BCE
Woman's Land/WRY
  wiminz land   DDd 14
Wombourn/St
  wɔmbɔ:n   BBC
Wombridge/Sa
  wʌmbridʒ   BBC
Wombwell/WRY
  wumwel   PNYW I/102,EPD,BBC,BCE
  wu:mwel   Kruis.
  wumw(ə)l   EPD
  wumwəl   Schr.,Bch.,91
  wumbl, wuməl, wuml   Bchm.91
  wu:mbil   Schr.,Hope
  wu:mbəl   Chis.
  -u-   DEPN
Womenswold/K
  wiminzwould   BBC,BCE,Hope
  wi:mzwould   BBC,BCE,PNK
  wiminswould   PNK
  -i-   DEPN
Womersley/WRY
  wuməzlə   PNYW II/54
Wonersh/Sr
  wʌnəʃ   PNSr 253
  wɔnə:ʃ   BBC,BCE
  -ʌ-   DEPN
Wooburn/Bk
  u:bən   PNBk 196
  wu:bə:n   EPD
Woodbastwick/Nf
  wudbæstik   Hope,ONwick 375
Wood Bevington/Wa ⟶ Bevington
Woodborough/Nt
  wudbrə   PNNt 180
Woodbridge/Do,Sf
  wudbridʒ   DSf 314,PNDVall 18 (for
           W. in Sf),BBC,BCE (for
           W. in Sf),EPD,Schr.

Woodburn/Nb
  wudbə:n   BBC
Woodbury
  wudb(ə)ri   EPD
  wudbəri   Schr.
Woodchester/Gl
  wutʃistə   BBC
Wooden/Nb
  u:dən   PNNbDu 219
  u:dn   DEPN
Woodford
  wudfəd   EPD
Woodford/Chs
  olim witfərt   GlossChs,
                  PNChs II/vii
  wudfərd   PNChs II/vii
Woodford Halse/Np
  wudfəd hɔls   BBC
Woodhall/Wo
  wudəl   PNWo(i)181
Woodhay/Brk
  -di   DEPN
Woodhead/Chs
  wuded   PNChs II/viii
  olim wudjed   PNChs II/viii,
                 GlossChs
Woodhey Gn,W.Hall,W.Chapel/Chs
  wudei, wudi   PNChs III/143
Woodhill/Bd
  wʌdl   DEPN
  (see also s.n. Odell)
Woodhill Pk/W
  olim oudəl   PNW 267
Woodhouse
  wudhaus   EPD,Schr.
  udhous   DDo
  wudəs   Hope (for W. in Nt),
           DHd 27 (for W. in WRY)
Woodhouse Cottage/Wt
  wudhæus   PNWt 249
Woodhuish/D
  wudiʃ   PND 5o8
Woodhyde Cottages and Fm/Do
  'udiaid   PNDo I/66
Woodlands/Do
  wudlændz, udlənz   PNDo(i)93
Woodlesford/WRY
  wudlzfəd   BBC
Woodmancote/Gl
  wudmæket   PNGl I/148,PNGl
              II/95 and 222,Hope
  wɔmkət   GlossCots 22 ("still
            [so] pron. by the
            common people")
Woodnesborough/K
  winzbərə, wunz-   BBC,BCE
  winsbrə   Hope
  winzbrə   DEPN,PNK
  wudnizbərə   BBC

  wudnezbərə   BCE
Woodrow
  wudrou   EPD
Woodroyd/WRY
  (h)udrɔid   Smith(2)219
  udrɔid   DHd 14o
Woodruff/K
  wudrʌf   EPD
Woods (as in W. Bank/St)
  wudz   EPD
Woods/WRY
  wudziz   DDd 16
Woods House/WRY
  wudz aus   DDd 12
Woodside
  'wud'said, ⸌ _   EPD
Woodstock/K,O
  wudstɔk   EPD,BBC,Schr.,Chis.,
             Bchm.64
  ud-   GlossO 118
  (the seven villages in the corpo-
  ration of W. are called 'The
  seven Remains', cf.GlossO
  (suppl.)95)
Woodyates/Do
  wudiəts, udiəts   PNDo(i)97
Woodhyde Fm/Do
  udiaid   PNDo(i)129
Wookey/So
  wuki   EPD
  -u-   DEPN
Woolaston/Gl
  wuləstən   PNGl III/268,BBC
Woolavington/So
  wul'ævintən   BBC
Woolbeding/Sx
  wulbədiŋ   PNSx 31
  'wulbidiŋ   BBC
Wooldale/WRY
  u:dl   PNYW II/253,DEPN,Hope
  u:dle [sic]   DHd 14o
  wu:dl   Hope
Wooler/Nb
  u:lə   PNE&W
  wulə   Schr.,Chis.
  ulər   Ellis 655
Woolerton/Sa
  wulətən   PNSa
Woolfall/Chs
  wulfɔ: PNChs III/84
Woolfall Hall/Chs
  wulfə   PNChs III/84
Woolfardisworthy/D
  ulsəri   Hope
  u:zəri   H.A.(2)32
  wulfɑ:diswə:ði,
  loc. wulzwə:ði   Bchm.86
  (see also following entries)

Woolfardisworthy/D (in Hartland
                              Hd)
   ulsəri   PND 8o,PNND 31,DEPN,
           DHtl 8
   wulzəri   EPD,BBC,BCE
   wulsəri   PND 8o,DEPN
   wulfɑ:diswə:ði   EPD
Woolfardisworthy/D (in Witheridge
                              Hd)
   wulzəri   PND 399,PNND 125,
           DEPN
   wulfɑ:diswə:ði   EPD,BBC
Woolfly Fm/Sx
   wulf'lai   PNSx 219
Woolford's Water/Do
   ulvəz wɔ:tə   Mayo
Woolgarston/Do
   wulgəstən,
   wu(:)sən   PNDo I/2o,
           PNDo(i)121
Woolhampton/Brk
   wul'hæm(p)tən   BBC
Woolley
   wuli   EPD
Woolmer Fm/W
   u:mər   PNW 3o5
Woolsery/D ⟶ Woolfardisworthy
           in Hartland Hd
Woolsington/Nb
   wisiŋtən   PNNbDu 22o
   wulziŋtən   BBC,BCE
Woolstanwood/Chs
   wulstən-, wustən wud,
   older local
   u:stən-   PNChs III/44
Woolstaston/Sa
   usəsn   GlossSa 519
Woolsthorpe/Li
   wu:strəp   Hope
   wulzÞɔ:p   BBC
Woolstone/Bk
   wulsən   PNBk 27
Wool Street/Ca
   wustid stri:t   PNCa 32
Woolthwaite/WRY
   wulfit   PNYW I/54
Woolverton/Wt
   (w)u(l)vərtn   PNWt 223
Woolwich/Ess
   wulidʒ   EPD,BBC,BCE,Schr.,
           Kruis.,ONwick 39o,
           PNK,MEG 2o5,DEPN,
           ESpr.316,Hope,HL 64o
   wulitʃ   EPD,BBC,BCE,Schr.,
           Kruis.,ONwick 39o,
           Hope,Chis.
wu'litʃ, wə'litʃ   HL 64o (so
stressed by railway attendants
at W. station)

Wooperton/Nb
   wapətən   PNNbDu 22o
   wɔpətən   PNNbDu 22o,DEPN
Woore/Sa
   wu:ə   PNSa
   wɔ: BBC
Wootton
   wutn   EPD
   wutən   PNK
   utn   PNWt 249
Wootton Basset/W
   wu:tən bæsət   Chis.
   u:tən   GlossW 214
Wootton Pillinge/Bd
   pilidʒ   PNBdHu 87
Wootton Wawen/Wa
   wu:t(ə)n wɔ:ən   BBC
Worbarrow/Do
   'wə:bærou   BBC
   "W.[...]is probably the same as
   Warborough,Oxfordshire; the loc.
   pron. is identical"   Arkell 45
Worbarrow Bay/Do
   'wə:bærou'bei   BCE
Worcester/Wo
   wustə   EPD,DEPN,BBC,Schr.,Kruis.,
           MEG 228,ESpr.39o,DHe 44,
           Hope
   wu:stə   Chis.
   ustə   PNWo 19,GlossWWo,GlossSEWo
           82,DHe 44,Hope
Worcestershire
   wustəʃiə   EPD
   -ʃə   EPD,Schr.
Worcs. (short for Worcestershire)
   wə:ks   EPD
Worfield/Sa
   wə:fi:ld   BBC,Hope
   wə:vəl   Hope
   wə:vil   GlossSa 519
Worgret/Do
   wə:gət   PNDo I/74,PNDo(i)131
Workington/Cu
   wʌrkitən   PNCu 454
   wə:kitən   GlossCu xviii
   wə:kiŋtən   EPD,Schr.,Chis.
Worksop/Nt
   wə:səp   PNNt 1o5 ("olim"),Schr.
           ("loc."),Hope
   vulgo wusəp   PNNt 1o5
   wəsəp   Ellis 449
   wɔsəp   Hope,Schr.
   wɔ:səp   Hope
   wʌsəp   PNNt(i)156
Worlaby/Li
   wɔləbi   Hope
Worle/So
   wə:l   DEPN,BBC,BCE
   wə:rl, wə:rdl   Ellis 9o

Worleston/Chs
 wɔːrlstn PNChs III/151
 wɔːlsn PNDb(i) II/101
Worlington/Sf
 wəːlintən BBC
Wormegay/Nf
 rʌŋei Hope
 'wəːmigei BBC
Wormelow/He
 wəːmilou BBC,BCE
Wormingford/Ess
 wəːmiŋfəd BBC
Worminghall/Bk
 wəːnəl PNBk 129
Wormleighton/Wa
 wəːm'leitən PNWa 275
 'wəːm'leit(ə)n BBC
Wormley/Hrt,Sr
 wəːmli BBC
Wormstone/Bk
 wɔːmstən PNBk 140
Wormwood Scrubs/Ldn
 wəːmwud skrʌbz EPD,Bau.
 short: The Scrubs Bau.
Wornditch/Hu
 wəːnditʃ PNBdHu 245
Worplesdon/Sr
 wɔbzdən PNSr 161
 wɔːplzdən EPD,BBC
Worrall/WRY
 wʌr(ə)l, -ɔ- EPD
 -ʌ- DEPN
Worsall/NRY
 wɔrsəl PNYN 173
Worsborough/WRY
 wʌsli Hope [sic]
 wəːsbərə Chis.
 wəːzb(ə)rə EPD
Worsham/Sx
 see note s.n. Chilsham
Worsley/La
 wəːsli EPD,BBC,BCE,Schr.
 wʌsli DEPN,Schr.,PNLa(ii)
 wəːsliː Chis.
Worsley Mesnes/La
 wəːsli meinz BBC,BCE
Worsoms/Db (f.n.)
 wɔsəmz FnSDb 106
Worstead/Nf
 wustid BBC,HL 929,Schr.,EPD
 wustəd EPD
 wusted DEPN,BBC,BCE
 wuː(r)stid Schr.
 wuːstəd Hope
 wuəstid HL 929
Worsthorne/La
 wəːsthɔːn PNLa 84
 wəːstɔən PNLa(ii)

 wəːsthɔrn Ellis 350
Worswick/La
 waːsik GlossR&R
Worth
 wəːþ EPD
Worth/Chs
 wuþ PNChs II/vii ("olim"),
  GlossChs
 now wərþ PNChs II/vii
Worth/K
 wəːd, wəːþ PNK
Worth/Sx
 wəːþ PNSx(i)179
Wortham/Sf
 wəːðəm BBC
Worthing/Nf,Sx
 wəːðiŋ EPD,BBC,Schr.,Chis.,
  DEPN (for W. in Sx)
Worthington/La,Le
 wəːðiŋtən EPD
Worth Matravers/Do
 wəːþ mə'trævəz BBC
Worting/Ha
 wəːtiŋ DEPN,BBC,BCE
Wortley/Gl,WRY
 wəːtli EPD,BBC,Schr.,Kruis.,
  Chis.
Worton/O,W,NRY
 wəːt(ə)n BBC
 wəːrtən PNW 248
Worts Hill/WRY
 wɔrsil, wɔrtsil DHd 152
Wortwell/Nf
 wɔtəl Hope
 wəːtwəl BBC
Wothersome/WRY
 wuðəsəm PNYW IV/179
Wothorpe/Np
 wʌðəp PNNp 247,DEPN
Wotton
 wutn, now generally
 wɔtn MEG 334
 wɔtn, wutn EPD,Kruis.
 wɔtən, wuːtən Schr.
Wotton/Bk
 wutn EPD
Wotton/Sr
 wutən PNSr 278,DEPN
Wotton St. Mary/Gl
 wutn PNGl II/158
Wotton-under-Edge/Gl
 wutn undəredʒ PNGl II/255
 wut(ə)n ʌndridʒ
 - ʌndər edʒ BBC
 wutən ʌndredʒ,
 - ʌnʊredʒ BCE
 wuːtən ʌndridʒ Schr.
 -u- DEPN

Woufa/We
  woufə PNE'side 62
Woughton-on-the-Green/Bk
  wuːftən PNBk 28,DEPN
  wuftən BBC,BCE
Wouldham/K
  wuldəm DEPN,BBC,BCE
  wouldəm PNK
Woundale/We
  wuːndəl PNWe I/191
Wrafton/D
  ræftən BBC
Wragby/Li,NRY,WRY
  rɔːbi PNYN 118
  rægbi Schr.
Wragmire/Cu
  ragmə PNCu 164
Wragmire Moss/Cu
  rægmər PNE'side 73
Wrangaton/D
  ræŋətən BBC,BCE
Wrantage/So
  rɑːntidʒ BBC
Wratting/Ca
  rætiŋ ONCa 197
Wratworth/Ca
  rætwəþ ONCa 186
Wraxall/Do,So,W
  ræksəl PNDo(i)243,PNW(i)18o
  ræksɔːl EPD
Wray, High Wray/La
  reː PNLa 182 and 219,
      PNLa(ii)
  rei DEPN,EPD
Wraysbury/Bk ⟶ Wyrardisbury
Wrea Gn/La
  rei griːn DEPN,BBC,BCE
Wreake/Le (r.n.)(also spelt Wreak)
  riːk DEPN,BBC
Wreaks Lane in Dronfield/Db
  reiks GlossSh 288
Wreay/Cu
  riːe PNE'side 72
  riːə PNCu 167,BBC
  riə BCE,EPD ("loc."),Ellis
      562
  rei EPD
Wreigh Burn/Nb (r.n.)
  raiþ, reː born RN 473
Wreighill/Nb
  riːhil PNNbDu 22o
Wrekenton/Du
  rekintən BBC
The Wrekin/Sa (also spelt Wrecken)
  ðə riːkin DEPN,BBC,BCE,EPD,
      Schr.534
  ðə rekin EPD(1),Schr.,Chis.
Wrenbury/Chs
  renb(ə)ri PNChs III/119

Wreningham/Nf
  reniŋəm BBC
Wrentham/Sf
  renþəm BBC
Wressell/ERY
  ræzl PNYE 242
Wrestlingworth/Bd
  resliŋwərþ PNBdHu 111
Wretham/Nf
  retəm DEPN,BBC,BCE
Wrexham Bridge/Chs
  reksəm EPD,Schr.
  riksəm DSChs 27
Wringworthy/Co
  riŋvə Picken 196 ("the vernac-
      ular pron. ... is still
      used")
Wrockwardine/Sa
  rɔk'wɔːdain Chis.
Wrinehill/Chs
  rainil PNChs III/56
Wrinstead Ct/K (or -sted)
  rinstəd PNK
Writtle/Ess
  ritl Chis.
Wrose/WRY
  rouz EPD,BBC
  rous EPD
Wrotham/K
  ruːtəm EPD,BBC,BCE,Hope,PNK,
      Schr. ("loc.")
  ruːtm DEPN
  ruːðm Hope (or -þ- ?)
  ruːþəm, rɔðəm Schr.
Wrottesley/St
  rɔtsli DEPN,BBC,BCE,EPD,Schr.
      534,Kruis.
Wroughton/W
  rɔːtən PNW 278,BCE
  rɔːt(ə)n BBC
  rɔːtn Kruis.
  -ɔː- DEPN
Wroxall/Wt
  raksəl, rɔkəlsər PNWt 256
  rɔksəl DWt,s.n. sterrup ile
Wroxeter/Sa
  rɔksitə, rɔkstə Förster
Wroxham/Nf
  rɔksəm EPD
Wroxton/O
  rɔkstən, occasioanlly
  rɑːkstən PNO 4o9
Wrynose Fell, W. Pass/We
  reinəz PNWe I/2o5
The Wrythe/Sr
  raið EPD
Wuerdle/La
  wuːdl PNLa 57,DEPN
Wyaston/Db
  waiəstn PNDb(i)2o9

Wyatt/He
    waiət   EPD,Kruis.
Wybersley/Chs
    wibəzli   PNChs III/xiv
Wyberton/Li
    wibət(ə)n   BBC
    wibətən   BCE
    -i-   DEPN
Wyboston/Bd
    waibəsən   PNBdHu 59
    -ai-   DEPN
Wybunbury/Chs
    wibmbri, winbəri,
    wibənbəri   PNChs III/8o
    widnbəri   PNChs III/8o ("older
        local"),GlossChs,
        PNDb(i) I/2ol
    wimbəri   PNChs III/8o,Hope,
        PNChs(i)lo,GlossChs,
        DEPN
    wibənbri   BBC
Wyeburne/We
    waibərən   PNE'side 67
Wych
    waitʃ, witʃ   EPD
Wych/Chs
    witʃ   PNChs III/37 (for W.Ho,
        W.Bank),PNChs IV/51
        (for Hr and Lwr W.)
Wych/Hrt
    waitʃ   PNHrt 196,BBC
Wych Cross/Sx
    witʃ krɔs   BBC
Wyche/Wo
    witʃ   BBC,BCE
Wychough/Chs
    witʃʌf   PNChs IV/53
Wychwood/O
    witʃwud   BBC
Wycliffe/NRY
    wiklif   PNYN 3oo,DEPN,EPD
    waiklif   Schr.
Wycoller/La
    'waikɔlə   PNLa 88,BBC
Wycomb/Le
    wikəm   Schr.
Wycombe/Bk (High W.,West W.)
    wikəm   EPD,DEPN,BBC,BCE,Schr.
    hai waikəm   Schr.,Chis.
    (see also s.n. Chipping W.)
Wydale/NRY
    widil   PNYN 98
Wydcombe/Wt
    wi(d)kəm   PNWt 256
Wyddial/Hrt
    widjəl, widʒəl   PNHrt 188
Wye/Bk;Db (r.n.)
    wai   EPD,Schr.,Chis.,Förster

Wye/K
    wai   EPD,PNK
Wyke/Sa,Sr,WRY
    waik   BBC
Wykeham/Li,NRY
    waikəm   PNYN 45 and 99,BBC
    wikəm   EPD,Kruis.
Wyken/Sa,Wa
    waikən   BBC
Wyke Regis/Do
    waik ri:dʒis   PNDo I/267,BBC
Wykey/Sa
    waiki   BBC
Wylam/Nb
    wailəm   BBC
Wylde (as in W.Gn/Wa)
    waild   EPD,Kruis.
Wylye/W
    waili   PNW 231,PNW(i)181,BBC
Wylye/W (r.n.)
    waili   PNW 11,RN 457
    wail [sic]   HL 733
    wai-   DEPN
Wymering/Ha
    wiməriŋ   DEPN,BBC,BCE
Wymeswold/Le
    waimzwould   BBC
Wymington/Bd
    wimiŋtən   PNBdHu 49,DEPN,BBC
Wymondham (no ref.to a partic. co.)
    wiməndəm   Schr.534,Bchm.86,Chis.
    windəm   Chis.,EPN 86,Bchm.86
Wymondham/Le
    waiməndəm   EPD,BBC,BCE
    wuməndəm   Hope
Wymondham/Nf
    windəm   EPD ("loc."),BBC,BCE,
        PNNf,s.n.Wyndham,ROS 43,
        Mawer(4)285,DNf 42
    wiməndəm   BCE,EPD
Wymondley/Hrt
    wimli   PNHrt 148
    waiməndli   BBC
Wyndham/Sx
    wainəm   PNSx 213
    windəm   EPD
Wynfield/Wt
    winvil   PNWt 41
Wynn (as in W.'s Gn/Hrt)
    win   EPD
Wynyard/Du
    winjəd   EPD,BBC,BCE
Wyrardisbury/Bk (also spelt Wrays-)
    wreizbəri   PNBk 244
    reizbəri   BBC,BCE,Mawer(2)93
    reiz-   DEPN
Wyre/La (r.n.)
    waiə   Schr.
    wair   Chis.

Wyreside Hall/La
  waiəsaid   BBC
Wyrley/St
  wə:li   BBC,BCE
Wysall/Nt
  waisə   PNNt 259,RitterNt 461,
             PNNt(i) 157
    waisəl   BBC,BCE
    -ais-   DEPN
Wyseberg Gn/Sx ⟶ Wisborough
Wyseton/Nt ⟶ Wiseton
Wythall/He,Wo
  waiðɔ:l   BBC
Wytham/Brk
  waitəm   DEPN,EPD,BBC,BCE
Wythburn/Cu
  waibərən   PNCu 315,PNE'side
               67
    waibərn   GlossCu xviii
    waiðbə:n, wai-   BBC,BCE
    -aið-   DEPN
Wythemail Pk Fm/Np (or Withmale)
  wilmər   PNNp 129
Wythenshawe/Chs
  wiðənʃɔ: BBC
  wiðenʃɔ: BCE
Wythmoor/Cu
  waimə   GlossCu xviii
Wythop/Cu
  widʌp   PNCu 457
  wiðəp   BBC,BCE
  -ið-   DEPN
Wythwaite/Cu
  waiþət   PNCu 214
Wyton/Hu,ERY
  witən   PNBdHu 23o,BCE (for W.
             in Hu)
    wetən   PNYE 52
    waitn   GlossHol 17
    wit(ə)n   BBC
    -i-   DEPN (for W. in Hu)
Wyvenhoe/Ess ⟶ Wivenhoe

Y

Yaddlethorpe/Li
   jælþrəp   Hope
Yafford/Wt
   jæ(:)fərd   PNWt 224
   jæfəd   DWt,s.n.chock-dog
Yalding/K
   jɔːldiŋ   BBC,BCE,PNK
Yalding/Ldn
   jɔːldiŋ   EPD
Yanwath/We
   jænəþ   PNWe II/2o4
Yapham/ERY
   japəm   PNYE 182
Yar/Wt (r.n.) (also spelt Yarl)
   jɑː   EPD,BBC
Yarbridge/Wt
   jɑːrbridʒ   PNWt 62
Yarburgh/Li (or -borough)
   jɑːbərə   BBC
Yardley/Ess,Wa
   jɑːdli   EPD
Yardley Gobion/Np
   gʌbinz   PNNp 1o8
Yare/Nf (r.n.)
   jɛə   EPD,BBC,Schr.
Yarhampton/Wo
   jærən   PNWo 37
Yarkhill/He
   jɑːkhil, dial. jɑːkl   DHe 44
Yarlside/We
   jɑːrlsit   PNE'side 69
Yarm/NRY
   jɑːm   PNYN 172
Yarmouth/Nf,Wt
   jɑːməþ   DSf 314,EPD,BBC,Schr.,
         Kruis.,Chis.,DWt,s.n.
         clem
   jɑːrməþ   PNWt 26o
Yarnacombe/D
   -ə-   ESpr.349
Yarnwick/NRY
   jɑːnik   PNYN 221
Yarridge/Nb
   jariʃ   PNNbDu 221
Yarrow/La (r.n.); Nb,So
   jærou   EPD,Schr.,Kruis.
Yarwell/Np
   jærəl   PNNp 2o9
Yarwoodheath/Chs
   jarəd iːəþ   PNChs II/ix,
         GlossChs
Yate/Gl
   jæt   PNGl III/44
   jeit   EPD
Yatehouse Fm, Y. Gn/Chs
   jeitaus   PNChs II/233

Yatton Keynell/W
   jæt(ə)n kenl   BBC
Yaverland/Wt
   jævərlən   PNWt 262
Yeading/Mx
   jediŋ   PNMx 4o,PNMx(i),DEPN,EPD,
         BBC
Yeadon/WRY
   jeːdn, jiː(ə)dən   PNYW IV/155
               (for Y. in
               Skyrack Wapentake)
   jiədən   PNYW V/15o (for Y. in
              Lwr Claro Wapentake)
   jidn   Hope
   jiːdən   Chis.
   jiːd(ə)n   BBC
Yealand /La (Y. Conyers, Y.Redmayne)
   jelənd   PNLa 188,DEPN
   -   kɔnjəz   BBC,BCE
   -   kunjəz   PNLa(ii)
Yealm/D (r.n.)
   jæm   PND 17,BBC,DEPN
   jelm   EPD,BCE
Yealmbridge/D
   jæmbridʒ   PND 263
Yealmpstone/D
   jempsən   PND 254
Yealmpton/D
   jæmptən   PND 261,DEPN
   jæmtən   BBC,BCE,Hope
   jæm(p)tən   EPD
Yearby/NRY
   jiəbi   PNYN 156,DEPN
   jəːbi   BBC,BCE
Yeardsley/Chs
   jəːdzli   PNChs II/vii
   jurdzli   PNChs II/vii,GlossChs
Yearsley/NRY
   jɑːzlə   PNYN 193
   jiəslə   DYorks 63
Yeathouse/Cu
   jethaus   BBC,BCE
Yeavering/Nb
   jivrin   PNNbDu 221
   jevəriŋ   BBC,BCE
   -i-   DEPN
Yedmandale/NRY
   jedmədil   PNYN 1oo
Yelden/Bd (also spelt Yielden)
   jeldən   PNBdHu 21,DEPN
   jiːld(ə)n   BBC
   jiːldən   BCE
Yellowham Hill, Y. Wood/Do
   jæləm   PNDo I/32o,DDo
Yelverton/D,Nf
   jelvətən   BBC,Schr.
Yeo/D (r.n.)
   jou   RN 48o

Yeo Edge/Sa
   vju: edʒ   GlossSa 519
Yeolmbridge/Co,D
   joumbridʒ DEPN,BBC,BCE
Yeoveney Fm/Mx
   ji:vni   PNMx 19,PNMx(i)
   -i:-   DEPN
Yeovil/So
   jouvil DEPN,EPD,BBC,Schr.,
           Hope,Chis.
   jouvəl Schr.
Yerling/Ess
   jəːliŋ BBC,BCE
Yestor Beacon/D (or Yes Tor)
   jestə bi:kən Chis.
Yielden/Bd ⟶ Yelden
Yiewsley/Mx
   juːzli PNMx(i)
   juːz- DEPN
Yoad Pot/We
   jɔːdpɔt PNWe I/150
Yockleton/Sa
   jɔkitn GlossSa 519
Yokefleet/ERY
   jukflit, joːk- PNYE 255
Yokefleet Creek/Ess (r.n.)
   ðə jɔtlət PNEss 17
York/Yorks.
   jɔːk EPD,BBC,Schr.,Kruis.,
         Förster
   jɔrk DEY 21,GlossHol 17
   jɔrək Smith(1)295
   (iː)jɔrik Hope
   jɑːk Hope,Smith(1)295 ("in
         the south-east of the
         West Riding")
   jərk GlossMY,s.n.Mai'n,
         DEY 21 ("in the south-
         ern part of the North
         Riding")
   jəːk GlossMY,s.n. Mai'n,
         DSDu
   jerk Smith(1)296 ("the Modern
         Lincolnshire pron.")
Yorks. (short for Yorkshire)
   jɔːks EPD
Yorkshire
   jɔːkʃə EPD,Schr.,Bau.,
           GlossCuWeNLa,s.n.Tike
   jɔːkʃiə EPD,DSWY 47
   jɔːrkʃir DSEY 34
   jɔːrkʃər Lloyd 127
   jɔrkʃər DHd 142,s.n.Uthers-
           field,GlossHol 17
   jɔːʃə Brunner 167,GlossR&R
         (so pron. in Rossendale)
   jurkʃə DSto
   jəːkʃə DSDu
   jəːkʃiə GlossM&C,s.n.Yerksheer

jɑːkʃiə DSWY 43
jɑːkʃir DSEY 38
Youlgreave/Db (or -grave)
   jɔlgreiv PNDb 182
   joulgreiv PNDb(i) II/212
   juːlgreiv BBC
Youlthorpe/ERY
   jouþrəp PNYE 175
Youlton/NRY
   joultən PNYN 22
Young Ausway/Np
   ɔːzə PNNp 154
Youngwoods Fm/Wt
   jʌŋwudz farm PNWt 112
Ypres/Sx (a tower at Rye)
   iːpr, iːprei EPD ("The 'Ypres
        Castle', a public house nearby,
        is called loc. [waipəz]")

Z

Zealand/W
   ziːlənd EPD
Zeal Monachorum/D
   ziːl mɔnə'kɔːrəm BBC
Zelah/Co
   ziːlə BBC
Zennor/Co
   zenə BBC
Zine/So
   zain Turner(1)122
Zoar/D
   zouɑː, zouə EPD
Zouch Mills/Nt
   zuːʃ EPD